THE GRAHAM GREENE FILM READER

THE GRAHAM GREENE FILM READER:

Reviews, Essays, Interviews & Film Stories

Edited by David Parkinson

THEATRE BOOK PUBLISHERS
211 WEST 71 STREET • NEW YORK NY • 10023

THE GRAHAM GREENE FILM READER: Reviews, Essays, Scripts, & Letters
Edited by David Parkinson

Published in Great Britain by Carcanet Press Ltd.

A CIP catalogue record for this book is available from the British Library.

Library of Congress Cataloging-in-Publication Data

Greene, Graham, 1904-
The Graham Greene film reader : revviews, essays, scripts & letters / edited by David Parkinson.
p. cm.
Includes bibliographical references (p. -) and indexes
ISBN: 1-55783-188-2 : $35.00
I. Parkinson, David. II. Title.
PN1994.G76 1994 94-33547
791.43--dc20 CIP

APPLAUSE BOOKS
211 West 71st Street
New York, NY 10023
Phone: 212- 496-7511
Fax: 212- 721-2856

First Applause printing: 1995

OTHER TITLES IN THE FILM READER SERIES

THE C. A. LEJEUNE FILM READER
edited by Anthony Lejeune

THE DILYS POWELL FILM READER
edited by Christopher Cook

THE HUMPHREY JENNINGS FILM READER
edited by Kevin Jackson

OTHER FILM TITLES FROM

APPLAUSE BOOKS

WILLIAM GOLDMAN: FIVE SCREENPLAYS

THE COLLECTED WORKS OF PADDY CHAYEFSKY

John Willis' SCREEN WORLD

Michael Caine: ACTING IN FILM

A FISH CALLED WANDA

JFK: The Book of the Film

JACOB'S LADDER: The Book of the Film

TERMINATOR 2: The Book of the Film

THE FISHER KING: The Book of the Film

THE ADVENTURES OF BARON MUNCHAUSEN

LOSING THE LIGHT:
THE UNMAKING OF BARON MUNCHAUSEN

Contents

Contents

Introduction

1 Film Fan 1911–1935

> If I had known it, the whole future must have lain all the time along those Berkhamsted streets. The High Street was wide as many a market square, but its broad dignity was abused after the war by the New Cinema under a green Moorish dome, tiny enough but it seemed to us then the height of pretentious luxury and dubious taste. My father, who was by that time headmaster of Berkhamsted School, once allowed his senior boys to go there for a special performance of the first *Tarzan* movie, under the false impression that it was an educational film of anthropological interest, and ever after he regarded the cinema with a sense of disillusion and suspicion.[1]

It is apt that Graham Greene should begin the autobiographical fragment *A Sort of Life* with a reference to the cinema. Few novelists have taken the films as seriously. None has been as heavily involved with so many aspects of the industry – as critic, scenarist, co-producer, performer, adaptor and adaptee. No other modern writer has been more frequently translated to the screen. Although he followed in the footsteps of Faulkner, Fitzgerald and others in accepting movie largesse to fund his literary aspirations, Greene had a genuine interest in the medium and a considerable knowledge of camera technique that were apparent in much of his film work and, indeed, in the majority of his 'entertainments'. Many still consider his most significant contributions to film culture to have been the scripts of such British classics as *Brighton Rock, The Fallen Idol* and *The Third Man*. Yet he had been one of the finest film critics of the 1930s – indeed, simply one of the finest film critics – and, on a number of occasions, he had even tried his hand at producing.

When his first play, *The Potting Shed*, opened in 1953, Greene still considered himself to be a 'film man'.[2] Yet by the time he wrote those opening lines he had come to share his father's disillusion and suspicion, and in the course of the John Player Lecture at the National Film Theatre in 1970, he was forced to confess that he had seen less than a dozen films in the previous decade and that the cinema no longer played a significant part in his life.[3] His father could point an accusing finger at Tarzan. The reasons for Graham Greene's loss of faith in the films were more complex and primarily stemmed from their failure to attain the goals he set for them as a young man.

Basil Wright, a British documentary director and one of his predecessors as film critic on the *Spectator*, claimed that Greene had been born 'a child of the film age'.[4] His earliest film memory was of an adaptation of Anthony Hope's *Sophy of Kravonia*, the story of a kitchen maid who becomes a queen, which he saw as a twelve-year-old while recuperating in Brighton.[5] Outings to the Berkhamsted pleasure dome presumably followed, but it was during another spell away from home that Greene's interest intensified. While patients of psychiatrist Kenneth Richmond, Greene and his cousin, Ave, became regular patrons of London's museums, galleries, theatres and cinemas. Both retained largely positive recollections of these visits and, consequently, Zoe Richmond's verdict on the future film critic seems puzzling: 'Perhaps the treatment was not entirely successful. For one thing, he discovered afterwards that he could no longer take an aesthetic interest in any visual thing – staring at a sight that others assured him was beautiful, he would feel nothing.'[6]

Although still primarily a film fan, the teenage Greene was, in fact, developing an increasingly acute appreciation of the medium. Thanks to pictures like D. W. Griffith's *Broken Blossoms, The Student of Prague* and *Brumes d'Automne*, Greene had come to expect more of a film than engrossing stories and realistic acting. He was particularly fortunate that his growing enthusiasm coincided with one of the silent screen's more inspired periods – that of Lang's *Nibelungen* and Robison's *Warning Shadows*, of

Clair at the peak of his powers and of Eisenstein, Pudovkin and Dovzhenko. Sadly, the British cinema offered little to quicken the pulse, at a time when Hollywood could boast such masterpieces as Von Stroheim's *Greed*, Chaplin's *A Woman of Paris* and his incomparable comedies amidst the usual plethora of dismal melodramas.

By the time he went up to Oxford in 1922, Greene was also an avid reader of *Close Up*. Despite regular articles by Marc Allégret and Vsevolod I. Pudovkin, this Swiss-based journal was rather leaden and technical, yet Greene remained fond of it, even keeping a bound volume of back-numbers at his flat in Antibes.[7] From its pages, Eisenstein's writings on montage and the films shown at the Super-Cinema and the Electra Palace, he acquired the discerning appreciation of narrative structure, camera angle and cutting for effect that was to inform his earliest writings for *The Oxford Outlook* and *The Times*.

'We are most of us considerably over-sexed.'[8] Thus began 'The Average Film' and Graham Greene's career as a film critic, with an essay in the February 1925 number of *The Oxford Outlook*. Many of the themes and preoccupations that were to recur until the last reviews he wrote for the BBC Spanish Service in 1941 were evident in this first article: the comparison of the moving picture and the Elizabethan stage, the appeal for a cinema of the people, and the uninhibited attitude to screen sex that was to long outlive the notorious Shirley Temple libel case. In his first notice, 'At the Super-Cinema', which appeared in the June issue, he alighted on the theory of the 'poetic cinema' – the duty of films to depict life as it is and life as it should be – that was to remain central to his critical credo.[9]

'The Average Film' was to prove important for another reason. Greene had assumed the editorship of *The Oxford Outlook* in Michaelmas Term 1924.[10] It was published by Basil Blackwell, who had already accepted Greene's volume of poetry, *Babbling April*. During that manuscript's preparation for press, Greene had scarcely noticed Vivien Dayrell-Browning. She was now to make a more lasting impression. In the article's second line, the then atheistic Greene had written 'we either go to Church to worship the Virgin Mary or to a public house and snigger over stories and limericks'.[11] This prompted Vivien to send a note informing him that one 'venerated' rather than 'worshipped' the Virgin. In a letter to his mother, Greene wrote peevishly about the pettiness of 'some ardent Catholic in Blackwell's',[12] but his reply to Vivien was couched somewhat differently:

> I most sincerely apologise. I'm afraid any excuses will seem very lame. But I wrote the article in a frightful hurry, and without preconceiving it, as the paper was already in press. At the same time I was feeling intensely fed up with things, and wanted to be as offensive all round as I could . . . I really am very sorry. Will you forgive me, and come and have tea with me as a sign of forgiveness?[13]

The apology and the invitation were accepted, and the word 'worship' remained in the article.

Greene was fortunate that 'going to the pictures' was a well-established part of the courtship ritual. He was thus able to indulge his twin passions simultaneously, indeed on one of his first dates with Vivien they went to the Super-Cinema to see a Garbo film (almost certainly *Joyless Street*).[14] Vivien did not share his conviction in their compatability, however, and when Greene was faced with the prospect of three years in China as an employee of the British American Tobacco Company, he expressed his fear that she would write irregularly in picture-going terms: 'If you write to me, it'll be only a very long conversation in a very darkened cinema, and the lights will go up again, and we shall both be still . . . '.[15] In the end he remained in London, working for BAT during office hours and on his second novel, *The Episode*, in the evenings when he did not visit the cinema.

After a brief spell tutoring, Greene became a sub-editor on the *Nottingham Journal*, although Vivien remained in Oxford. The cinema became an essential way of escape. Pretending Vivien was sitting beside him, he wallowed in such forgotten silents as *Smouldering Fires*,[16] starring Pauline Fredericks (whose moral of 'marry someone of your own age' he tried to impress on the still-reluctant Vivien), *Satan's Sister* with Betty Balfour,[17] *The Wages of Virtue*, and *Spanish Love*.[18] He walked out of the latter and even during his reviewing stint felt no compulsion to endure worthless movies to their inevitable conclusion. As Norman Sherry records, he preferred the manly swashbuckling of Douglas Fairbanks to the Latin loving of Valentino and Ricardo Cortez: 'One can imagine Novello as a matinee idol, because he is extra-ordinarily good-looking, but Valentino and this man Cortez are simply gross fleshy animals, behaving like animals. But all the shop girls and stout matrons of England and America go and are thrilled'. 'I really begin to like Doug. He's such a refreshing change from the Cortez-Valentino lot. It [*The Black Pirate*] was a really satisfactory film. Pirates & buried treasure & lots of fighting & ships & a princess held for ransom – altogether pleasant. It was a rather interesting experiment, too, as it was all in colour, & much the most successful effect I've seen. It certainly emphasised the "gory" bits! It's really worth seeing.'[19] Letters to Vivien were obviously one thing, professional criticism another. Greene scarcely had a good word for any colour process from that day on, even lamenting the fact that the 1966 adaptation of *The Comedians* had not been filmed in monochrome.[20]

The cinema was as much an inspiration as a consolation. Greene left films he had enjoyed convinced that he was destined to produce worthwhile literature. In a letter to Vivien of 12 February 1926, he explained that such confidence derived from the communal response to the ultimate popular art-form: 'It is the concentrated emotion of lots of people. Because it doesn't work if one is not alone, for then one's withdrawn from the general audience and can scoff at the ridiculousness of the picture. It's all very curious.' Nearly half a century later, at the Cannes Film Festival, Greene divulged that cinema-going still excited him, even if the pictures no longer could: 'There is the secrecy of sneaking into a cinema in the dark, perhaps with a girlfriend: no one need know.'[21]

On 10 March 1926, Greene became a sub-editor on *The Times*. By the end of the year, he had played his part in the General Strike, become a Catholic, had his appendix removed, been treated for suspected epilepsy, begun reviewing for a variety of newspapers and worked intermittently on *The Episode*, a 'shocker' called *Queen's Pawn*, the outline of a novel called *The Gaudy Ship*, based on a poem by Yeats, and innumerable short stories. He also began keeping a diary of books read. Would that he had done likewise for films watched!

With health and spirits restored, in 1927 Greene was back in pursuit of his twin passions: 'There are two films I very much want to see in town – "The Lodger" at the Marble Arch & "Hotel Imperial" at the Plaza. Apart from marrying you, I think the most wonderful thing in the world would be to write and produce a really first class film – something as good as Manon Lescaut. Ooo!'[22] What is perhaps most remarkable about this confidence to Vivien is the enthusiasm Greene shows for *The Lodger*, a film by Alfred Hitchcock, for whom in later years he would have nothing but regretful animosity. Shortly afterwards, he was in contact with John Maxwell of British National Pictures about the possibility of doing a script and excited at the prospect of attending the London opening of Lang's *Metropolis*.[23]

The following year, the Greenes were West End regulars. They saw such films as *Shooting Stars*, directed by Anthony Asquith and A. V. Bramble,[24] Arthur Robison's primitive sound version of *The Informer*, and Pudovkin's *The Last Days of St Petersburg*: 'a terribly good film . . . It has been put on for a run without any particular advertisement at the obscure Scala up behind Goodge Street. We arrived a quarter of an hour before the time of showing to find a tremendous queue. None of Pudovkin's films has been shown before publicly, & one never knew that his fame had spread so widely',[25] *The Fugitive Lover*,[26] *Thou Shalt Not* (an adaptation of Zola's *Thérèse Raquin*, which Greene considered 'the best film I've ever seen') and *The Patriot*, Lubitsch's fantasy on the assassination of Tsar Paul of Russia.[27]

Although a sub on the Court page, Greene's reputation as a film buff spread and he was soon contributing (albeit anonymously) to the Entertainments section. His first piece – 'The Province of the Film: Past Mistakes and Future Hopes' – appeared on 9 April 1928. Having castigated wasteful production techniques, he took up where he had left off in his 'Super-Cinema' review by lamenting the growing gulf between American and German methods of translating thought into imagery: 'If the best that America has done be compared – though not necessarily likened – to the English novel at the stage of Defoe, *Warning Shadows*, with its strange removal of action to the second hand, its shades of thought, represents the novels of Henry James and Conrad.' He concluded with an appeal for the general adoption of another strand of 'poetic cinema' – the use of contrasting images to convey a message, an effect – and cited *Greed* and *A Woman of Paris* as prime examples. However, few film-makers had a genuine talent for pure montage, and Greene came to despise the journeymen whose indescriminate use reduced it to a convenient, showy trick.

He attended the Film Society's Sunday afternoon shows and was tempted to join the Amateur Film Society: 'It gives one an opportunity I believe of taking part in the production of films.'[28] Three more articles appeared on the Entertainments page, each betraying the rather earnest pomposity of a disciple of *Close Up*. In 'Film Aesthetic' and 'A Film Principle', he lamented the coming of Talkies: 'If they succeed commercially the infant art of the screen may as well be abandoned, unless, separating itself from their uproar, it starts life again in independence and poverty; if they fail commercially, then, the industry dying, the art – of epic, fantasy and mental process – may be born again. But it is a hard and distant hope.' 'A Film Technique' prescribed how the film ('still the limping Pegasus of the arts') should achieve rhythms of time and space: 'If the top line of the space-graph be 100 and the bottom zero, then rapid action should not be allowed to take place before 25 or after 75. Fifty is most suitable for the quickest action which will gradually slow down as it moves from the centre line.'

The Man Within was published while Greene was still on *The Times*, and his star seemed in the ascendant. By 1931, however, *The Name of Action* and *Rumour at Nightfall* had failed critically and commercially, and his biography of John Wilmot, Earl of Rochester, had been rejected by his publishers. Now living at Chipping Campden, Greene was far from the consolations of the West End picture palaces and even further from fulfilling the ambition he revealed to the *Evening News* that he one day hoped to have his own private cinema.[29] But, as the first president of the Oxford University Film Society, his brother Hugh could provide the next best thing.

Greene was already at work on a new novel in 1932 when he attended an OUFS showing of Feodor Ozep's *The Crime of Dmitri Karamazov*.[30] Such was the impact of the film's star, Anna Sten, that he remodelled his heroine on her and resolved several problems of plot during the course of a lively Oxford weekend. *Stamboul Train* was a watershed for Greene as both novelist and cinéaste. The book had an undoubtedly filmic quality about it, and British and American studios were soon rising to the bait: 'Basil Dean is reading S.T. on the way to New York, another company RKO are interested, and now I hear that there are hopes in New York of the richest company of them all, except perhaps Paramount, Metro-Goldwyn-Mayer. There really seems a chance of big money from this book.'[31] Eventually the big money turned out to be £1,738 3*s.* 8*d.*, and the purchasers, rather ironically in the light of future events, were Twentieth-Century Fox.

Greene had nothing to do with the making of *Orient Express*, and fell victim for the first time to the anxieties that he recalled in 'The Novelist and the Cinema – A Personal Experience': 'Now when you sell a book to Hollywood you sell it outright. The long Hollywood contracts – sheet after closely printed sheet as long as the first treatment of the novel which is for sale – ensure that you have no "author's rights". The film producer can alter anything. He can turn your tragedy of East End Jewry into a musical comedy at Palm Springs if he wishes. He need not even retain your title, though that is usually almost the only thing he wishes to retain.' En route to Liberia with his cousin Barbara in 1935, he saw the film advertised in Tenerife. Writing in *Journey without Maps*, he admitted to a great sense of betrayal and no little shame: 'The direction was incompetent, the photography undistinguished, the story sentimental . . . By what was unchanged I could judge and condemn my own novel: I could see clearly what was cheap and banal enough to fit the cheap banal film.'

Nevertheless, *It's a Battlefield* (1934) was to be even more consciously cinematic, and it was ever a source of amusement to Greene that it was one of the few novels that was never adapted for a screen of any size.[32] His next book, *England Made Me* (1935), would not be filmed for another four decades, but in the months after his return from Africa Greene started *A Gun for Sale* (1936), which Paramount would translate to a war-time setting in 1942 under the title *This Gun for Hire*, and completed a short story, 'The Basement Room' (also 1936), which was to be the source for his first adaptation of his own work, *The Fallen Idol*.

He was by now also regularly reviewing books for the *Spectator*. Then, at a drinks party in June 1935, he was prompted by 'a sense of fun' and that 'dangerous third Martini',[33] to suggest to Derek Verschoyle, the magazine's Literary Editor, that he was given the post of film critic. Envisaging it as little more than the start of an amusing summer job, Greene produced his first column on 5 July.

II Film Critic 1935–1941

I well remember when I was beginning as a film critic reading with the most passionate envy the writings of Graham Greene in the *Spectator* and various other periodicals; it struck me that this was the kind of thing that film criticism should be. He liked the silent films, he liked the old popular films, but he also had an instinctive reaction to what was new or what was not so traditional. One was terribly grateful that

> somebody of his literary genius should care so much and with such deep and original feeling about a medium that was not literary, which is partly visual and partly literary.[34]

The 'care' to which Dilys Powell refers is the key to understanding Graham Greene the Film Critic and his subsequent attitude to the cinema. Notwithstanding the 'sense of fun', Greene was 'a film man', a cinéaste with considerable knowledge of screen techniques and pronounced ideas on what constituted both good entertainment and successful art. There seems little doubt that this four-and-a-half-year stint as a critic contributed to his later indifference to the medium. As early as June 1936, he was writing: 'I cannot help wondering whether from this great moneyed industry anything of value to the human spirit can ever emerge.'[35] As an enthusiastic picture-goer, Greene could avoid the dross churned out by Hollywood, Denham and the Nazi and Soviet propaganda machines. As a critic he all-too-frequently had to confront them, thus confirming his conviction that the twentieth-century's most effective form of communication was largely in the hands of those who delighted more in its commercial rather than artistic possibilities. Ultimately, one suspects that he abandoned the cinema with the reluctance of a lover who has recognized that cherished memories are not enough to sustain an affair that is no longer rewarding.

If Greene took the films seriously, he also had distinct views on the duties of the critic. In his introduction to *Garbo and the Nightwatchman*, Alistair Cooke defined the critic as a 'tipster, narrator, propagandist, father-confessor, and when he is left alone – a fan'. Greene echoed these sentiments in the opening paragraphs of his 1937 *Sight and Sound* article, 'Is It Criticism?':

> Film criticism, more than any other form of criticism except perhaps that of the novel, is a compromise. The critic, as much as the film, is supposed to entertain, and the great public is not interested in technicalities. The reader expects a series of dogmatic statements: he is satisfied, like any member of the

> Book Society, with being told what is good and what is bad. If he finds himself often enough in agreement with the critic, he is content. It never occurs to him to ask why the critic thought this film good and that film bad, any more than it occurs to him to question his own taste . . . One need not deny to either books or films of popular middle-class entertainment a useful social service, as long as it is recognized that social service has nothing to do with the art of cinema or the art of fiction. What I object to is the idea that it is the *critic's* business to assist films to fulfil a social function. The critic's business should be confined to the art.

Faced with the scarcity of worthwhile material, 'what in the cinema is the critic to write about?' If each week he confined himself to the truth 'showing how the script-writer, the director and the camera man have failed, he will soon lose his readers and afterwards his job'. Greene decided therefore, that satire was the only available approach: 'make a flank attack upon the reader, to persuade him to laugh at personalities, stories, ideas, methods, he has previously taken for granted'. While sympathizing with reviewers under orders to produce 'fanzine' stories and those censored by the dictates of the advertising executives, Greene considered many of his fellow critics as much fair game as the films. He deplored their habit of writing 'big' or from sham 'common man' angles, and had nothing but contempt for those who simply paraphrased studio handouts. The simperings of Sidney Carroll and the snobbery of C.A. Lejeune incurred his especial wrath.

He had even less time for the kind of studio 'ballyhoo' that had been meted out to *Orient Express*, and often turned it back on a film in order to damn it. Reviewing *The Crusades*, he used the details of the cast's vital statistics given in the programme to qualify the standard of its acting. Discussing another de Mille film, *Union Pacific*, Greene mocked the cloying intensity of Hollywood's publicity departments: 'They have an inexhaustible fund of admiration, and when they encounter a big story – full of history and high-mindedness like the Crusades or the Ten Commandments or the construction of a railroad – their reverence falls with the adhesive effect of a tin of treacle.' While never going so far as to state that some of his colleagues could be bought, Greene took much pleasure in lampooning the way in which they at least played the game in 'Film Lunch'.

If notices had to entertain *and* serve a critical purpose, so did the films themselves. Ford Madox Ford had categorized fiction into 'novels' and 'nuvvels', and Greene similarly divided films into 'cinema' and 'movies'.[36] The 'movie' was the idea of popular entertainment foisted on to picture-goers worldwide by the moguls – 'a mild self-pity, something soothing, something gently amusing'[37] – the middlebrow balm of a largely bourgeois audience, 'of the tired business man and the feminine reader'.[38] Greene lamented the fact that the films had been tainted with this respectability rather than immersed in the healthy vulgarity of the Blackfriars Ring, the Wembley final, the pin saloons, and the bear-pit. Patrons did not ask to be soothed, he argued, they craved excitement. 'The commonplace, that is the point . . . The cinema has got to appeal to millions; we have got to accept its popularity as a virtue, not turn away from it as a vice.'[39] The Elizabethan stage had produced action capable of arousing as communal a response as blood sports, and cinema, with its unrivalled potential for reaching the widest possible audience, offered the public a chance to sample the truly poetic for the first time since Cromwell closed the theatres. People wanted to be taken out of themselves, as they were at the F.A. Cup Final. Greene was doubtful if Bing Crosby's mournful crooning did as much. Echoing sentiments he first expressed to Vivien in that letter from Nottingham, he implored film-makers to seek inspiration in their own experiences as individuals in darkened cinemas, being caught up by the intimacy of a picture until they were an integral part of an involved, excited mass. 'An excited audience is never depressed; if you excite your audience first, you can put over what you will of horror, suffering, truth.'[40] There were few examples of what Greene meant by 'the proper use of the film': *Duck Soup*, the early Chaplins, a few Laurel and Hardy two-reelers. Serious contenders could be numbered on the fingers of one hand: 'perhaps *Fury, The Birth of a Nation, Men and Jobs*', and at a pinch 'such refined, elegant, dead pieces as *Louis Pasteur*: the Galsworthy entertainments of the screen: or intelligently adapted plays like *These Three*'.[41]

Noteworthy examples of 'poetic cinema' were even more scarce. When applying it to the cinema, Greene used the word 'poetic' in its widest sense, just as Ford had employed it in relation to the works of James, Conrad, Turgenev and Chekhov – 'not the power melodiously to arrange words but the power to suggest human values'.[42] Linking this to Chekhov's maxim that novelists should captivate their readers with portraits of life not only as it is, but also as it ought to be, Greene exhorted directors to construct their films from poetic images chosen for their contrasting value. As Judy Adamson has said, Greene did not ask 'film to present a slice of life. Rather, he asked of it an honest and poetic representation of reality',[43] in which realism was redundant unless the film also explored its obverse. For all its acute observations on life as it appeared to an American millionaire, its fine ear for dialogue, and its natural acting, *Dodsworth* was adjudged a failure primarily because it ignored life as it ought to be. The Soviet film, *We from Kronstadt*, however, satisfied all Greene's criteria. At one level this was a magnificent picture of schoolboy heroics, 'full of last charges and fights to the death, heroic sacrifices and narrow escapes, all superbly directed.' But what made the film so remarkable was 'less the heroics than the lyrical, the poetic, the critical sense. This is what the poetic cinema should mean: not plays by Shakespeare adapted to a medium even less suitable than the modern stage; but poetry expressed in images, which let in a little more of common life than is in the story.'[44]

Similarly, stunning photography and impeccable cutting did not make poetic cinema. They made 'arty', and occasionally dishonest, cinema, as in the case of Flaherty's *Man of Aran*, which Greene compared unfavourably to George Hoellering's *Hortobagy*, Armand Denis's *Dark Rapture* and Basil Wright's *Song of Ceylon.* Indeed, from his very first *Spectator* column, when he found more to praise in Walter Mittelholtzer's *Abyssinia* than Universal's *Bride of Frankenstein,* Greene often used the humble documentary to expose the excesses of the prestige product. The simplicity of these films was their key, because poetic cinema was founded on a few very simple ideas, which, while not requiring a great mind to conceive them, did 'require an imaginative mind to feel them with sufficient passion'. For Greene, successful cinema had to be 'simple, sensuous and passionate'.[45]

This latter remark somewhat bears out John Atkins's conclusion that 'Greene's power as a critic of both books and of films, derived almost entirely from his faculty of apprehending the significant symbols. His mind is not an analytical one, and his attempts at intellectual process are never impressive. But he can *feel* his subject more intimately than anyone else writing in England today. His criticism is that of the creative writer.'[46] Judy Adamson considered Greene 'a witty and creative journalist'[47] rather than a theoretician, with ideas about common and poetic cinema that, while not original in themselves, were unusual in combination. Certainly he had a happy talent for the brilliantly funny line. He ridiculed the performance in *Anthony Adverse* of Pedro de Cordoba, 'who dies on his back in the mud, his flippers feebly waving, his odd receding mouth opening and shutting, a masterly interpretation of Miss Potter's Ptolemy Tortoise', while he latched onto a detail from Louise Campbell's recent past to decry Wellman's *Men with Wings*: 'The new star, Miss Louise Campbell, was formerly a dental assistant, but none of the painful scences at which she then assisted ever lasted two hours.'

John Grierson labelled him 'the best critic we had'. Philip French pronounced his criticism 'the most ferocious I've ever come across'.[48] Neville Braybrooke proclaimed that 'whatever he elects to write upon . . . there is always at least one good original point . . . Greene has something of a Websterian quality about his work; his fiction is shot through with it – and so is his criticism. In both there are excesses: in his fiction, melodrama and Grand Guignol; in his criticism, slickness and cruelty'.[49]

Certainly Greene could be quite merciless when he chose. It is ironic that he should consider film criticism to be a compromise, because his is some of the most uncompromising ever written. John Atkins has detected 'a growing tendency to be irritated by films in general, shortcomings that might be almost invisible – in fact, to nag',[50] but such expressions of disappointment and frustration on Greene's behalf were quite understandable when one considers that each weekly batch of contrived melodramas and formulaic musicals took the cinema another giant step away from the path he had hoped it would follow.

Whenever he could applaud he did – sometimes enthusiastically. The documentaries of Grierson, Rotha and Wright, and the features of Robison, Chaplin, Griffith, Lang, Hawks and Capra were usually singled out for praise, while he greatly admired the realism of Duvivier and Feyder, Renoir and Pagnol, and Carol Reed's attention to authenticity and atmosphere ('Mr Reed, when he gets the script right, will prove far more than efficient').[51] The natural acting of Garbo, Paul Muni, the younger Bette Davis, Henry Fonda and Ingrid Bergman appealed to him, as did the pugnacity of Cagney and the clowning of W.C. Fields, the Marx Brothers, Sydney Howard and Will Hay. Perhaps because he was 'the nearest approach we are ever likely to have to a human Mickey Mouse',[52] Greene had a sneaking regard for Fred Astaire and always retained his enthusiasm for the Soviet cinema, particularly Pudovkin's *Mother*, Alexandrov's *Jazz Comedy* and, of course, Dzigan's *We from Kronstadt*. He also championed the 'bit' player: Albert Bassermann, J. Carroll Naish, Gene Lockhart, Lynne Overman, Edward Ellis, Hay Petrie and Harry Baur were all regularly accorded honourable mentions. Providing films adhered to his specifications, Greene was as willing to affix seals of approval to 'entertainments' such as *Königsmark, My Man Godfrey, Fra Diavolo, Knight without Armour, True Confession, Bonne Chance* and *The Arsenal Stadium Mystery*, as he was to the more prestigious *Barbary Coast, The General Died at Dawn, The Plainsman, The Texas Rangers* or *Dead End*. Even heartfelt praise, however, was invariably couched in terms which managed to decry the staple Hollywood offering: 'Occasionally a film of truth and tragic value gets somehow out of Hollywood on to the screen. Nobody can explain it – perhaps a stage needs using, all the big executives are in conference over the latest Mamoulian "masterpiece" – Jehovah is asleep, and when he wakes he finds he's got a *Fury* on his hands, worse still *They Won't Forget*.'[53]

Whether the Shirley Temple libel suit was the culmination of a studio vendetta against Greene, there is little doubt that his increasingly acerbic attacks on America and its film industry were deeply resented. Louis B. Mayer undoubtedly had been nettled by his portrayal in 'Film Lunch', and each of his fellow moguls had seen at least one picture of their own savaged by Greene's pen. They could permit him (reluctantly) to snipe at the adolescence, sentimentality and sexual hypocrisy of their films, but rubbishing the entire nation, as he did in the review of *The Road Back*, proved too much: 'What use in pretending that with these allies it was ever possible to fight for civilization? For Mother's Day, yes, for antivivisection and humanitarianism, the pet dog and the home fire, for the co-ed college and the campus. Civilization would shock them: eyes on the guide-book for safety, they pass it quickly as if it were a nude in a national collection.'[54] These words, as much as anything Greene had to say about Shirley Temple and the nature of her audience, were to cost him the £500 he was personally ordered to pay of the £3,500 awarded to Twentieth-Century Fox and its star. The defamation of a curly-haired moppet was always more likely to stand up in court than a slur on the world's largest democracy. Greene himself tells the full story of the *Wee Willie Winkie* case and its implications at various points throughout this book. Undaunted by its judgement and punishment, he continued to review in much the same vein until he left the *Spectator* in 1940. His feud with the United States of America, however, was to rumble on for a further five decades.

There is no doubt that Greene's opinions on the sexual precocity of the nine-year-old Miss Temple were daring and provocative – indeed, as early as August 1936, he had asserted that her popularity rested 'on a coquetry quite as mature as Miss Colbert's and on an oddly precocious body as voluptuous in grey flannel trousers as Miss Dietrich's'.[55] She was not the only American actress to attract his fire. Greene's very first published piece on cinema, 'The Average Film', had focused on the proliferation of sex on the screen. Otto Preminger believed that Greene was obsessed with sex, and John Atkins described him as 'a highly-sexed young man'[56] in attributing the animosity that gradually replaced his admiration for Hollywood's most glamorous stars to their inaccessibility and their complicity in the perpetuation of the Dream Factory myth. If earlier reviews had contained somewhat lustful references, such as those to Anna Neagle in riding breeches, to Mae West as a 'big-busted carnivorous creature in tight white sequins'[57] or to Dietrich's 'too beautiful body',[58] as his own editor on *Night and Day*, he allowed himself full rein. He doubted whether the lately dead Jean Harlow would 'ever have progressed beyond the scope of the restless shoulders and the protuberant breasts' as 'her technique was the gangster's technique – she toted her breast like a man totes a gun'.[59] In a notice that ironically also included a film called *Action for Slander*, he remarked on the lascivious close-ups of Linden Travers in *Brief Ecstasy* – 'a leg in the library, buttocks over the billiard table' and later her sobbing from 'the ugly drive of undifferentiated desire'. Finally, in an astonishing outburst, he berated the 'Dodie dream of a world' in Archie Mayo's *Call It a Day*, 'where all the heavy labour and the missed cues of infidelity are eliminated and the two-backed beast is trotted out quaintly, gaily and whimsically like a character in *Winnie-the-Pooh*'.

He also frequently resorted to plain bitchiness. Grace Moore was reduced to a genteel school ma'am – 'If you want to escape from a cinema where Miss Moore is playing – I always do – before the end, you feel impelled to raise a hand and wait for permission to leave the room.'[60] Irene Dunne, while singing to a farm horse in *High, Wide and Handsome* was distinguishable only as 'the one without the white patch on her forehead'. He was unsure whether the horses were more beautiful than Loretta

Young in *Kentucky*, while mention of Isa Miranda only conjoured up visions of an old donkey called Miranda, which his family had once used to ferry laundry. Even compliments occasionally drew on equine imagery – Garbo once being compared to a beautiful Arab mare, and in the review of *Marie Walewska*, she is referred to as 'the finest filly of them all'. Peter Lorre, Fernandel, Charles Boyer and Spencer Tracy apart, actors fared little better. Charles Laughton always left an aroma of cooked ham and the talents of Pat O'Brien, Freddie Bartholomew, George Arliss, Harold Lloyd and Eddie Cantor left Greene cold. Herbert Marshall was rendered 'in terms of a dog, something large, sentimental and moulting, something which confirms one's preference for cats'[61] and Emil Jannings possessed 'the meaningless gaze of a sea-lion with huge sloping shoulders and watery whiskers, to whose emotions we apply, for want of anything better, such human terms as pity, anger, terror, though we cannot tell, on the evidence of those small marine eyes, whether he is really registering anything more than a dim expectation of fish'.[62]

While he could applaud the comic realism of Will Hay and Alastair Sim, the restraint of Robert Donat (as opposed to the histrionics of Olivier) and the promise of Thorold Dickinson, Carol Reed and Edmond Greville, Greene was nearly always at a loss to find a good word for the British film industry. He detested its servile replication of Hollywood's worst traits and the timidity of its attempts to find a truly national voice. Of the films Greene loathed most, a revealing number were British: *Tudor Rose, Last Train from Madrid. The Tunnel, Me and Marlborough, The Man Who Could Work Miracles, Poison Pen, Ourselves Alone* . . . A fair proportion of the performers he found most resistible were also British, notably Jack Hulbert, Cicely Courtneidge, Ralph Lynn and Penelope Dudley-Ward, and his remarks on the efforts of directors such as Walter Forde, Brian Desmond Hurst, Anthony Asquith and Herbert Wilcox were invariably scathing.

Even Hitchcock failed to impress. He was 'a silly harmless clown', 'tricky, not imaginative',[63] the producer of nothing more than 'polished fairy-tales'.[64] Greene's main complaint against him was 'that he amuses but he doesn't excite. I should like to see him take over Ben Travers's excellent farces. He hasn't enough imagination to excite; he doesn't convince'.[65] Greene considered him careless and too willing to subjugate character for the surprise situation. Nothing had changed by the time he came to compose the introduction to *The Pleasure Dome*: 'Hitchcock's "inadequate sense of reality" irritated me and still does – how inexcusably he spoilt *The Thirty-Nine Steps*. I still believe I was right (whatever Monsieur Truffaut may say) when I wrote [of *The Secret Agent*]: "His films consist of a series of small 'amusing' melodramatic situations: the murderer's button dropped on the baccarat board; the strangled organist's hands prolonging the notes in the empty church . . . very perfunctorily he builds up these tricky situations (paying no attention on the way to inconsistencies, loose ends, psychological absurdities) and then drops them: they mean nothing; they lead to nothing."'[66] Grahame Smith has mischievously intimated that Greene's antipathy for Hitchock was rooted in a recognition of his own penchant for the shock of the unexpected that arose from the banality of the setting, 'the eruption of pain and terror in the everyday'.[67] In 1958, Hitchcock was as keen to film *Our Man in Havana* as Greene was to prevent him: a pity, as Hitchcock was about to hit the rich vein of form that yielded *Vertigo, North by Northwest* and *Psycho*.

Also high on his list of the guilty was the British Board of Film Censors (a curious body 'rumoured to consist of retired Army officers and elderly ladies of no occupation'[68] and 'at least one judge of over eighty years') under the control of Lord Tyrell and Edward Shortt. Greene could not forgive the Board's refusal to allow the portrayal of any controversial subject on the screen, thus virtually depriving film-makers the chance to excite their audiences, while the decision to deny Universal certificates to such films as *Boys Will Be Boys, She, The Peace Film*, and most astonishingly, *The Wizard of Oz*, rendered it something of a standing joke: 'Surely it is time that this absurd committee of elderly men and spinsters, who feared, too, that *Snow White* was unsuitable for those under sixteen, was laughed out of existence?

As it is, in many places, parents will be forbidden by the by-laws to take their own children to *The Wizard of Oz*.'

Studio executives were also culpable for the incompetence that either alienated or stifled home-grown talent. 'What is an English film?' Greene began his review of *The Marriage of Corbal* in June 1936. 'There are times when one cannot help brooding with acute distress on the cheap international pictures exported under that title . . . England, of course, has always been the home of the exiled; but one may at least wish that *émigrés* would set up trades in which their ignorance of our language and culture was less of a handicap.' He laid the brunt of the blame firmly on Korda's Denham Studios: 'In what can with technical accuracy be termed an English company you may have a Hungarian producer assisted by a Hungarian art director and a Hungarian scenario editor. Among its directors there may be Frenchmen, Hungarians, Germans and Americans. The language is strange to them, the ideas are strange: little wonder that the characters are slowly smoothed out of existence, the English corners rubbed away. The public – you may say – has been reached by something, and they'll be reached again next week and the week after by so many thousand feet of celluloid; they haven't been reached by an idea: that has died on the way, somewhere in the central-heated office, at a conference, among the foreign accents.'[69] In Greene's opinion, 'the Quota act had played into foreign hands, and as far as I know, there is nothing to prevent an English film unit being completely staffed by technicians of foreign blood. We have saved the English film industry from competition only to surrender it to a far more alien control.'[70] While he could mourn the loss of Clair, Duvivier, Lang and others to Hollywood, convinced that the system would subordinate their very individual talents, he was equally reluctant that they should come to Ealing, Gainsborough, or Denham.

'Abandon life all ye who enter here,' Greene suggested would make the perfect motto for Korda's studios.[71] The Hungarian-born producer was the subject of some of Greene's most personal attacks. He resented his importation of foreigners, the slowness, vulgarity and over-emphasis of his films, and his apeing of the mogul's lifestyle. 'He's a great publicist, of course, the Victor Gollancz of the screen. Only a great publicist could have put over so many undistinguished and positively bad films as if they were a succession of great masterpieces . . . No, I can't believe that Alexander Korda's talent is for the films.'[72] Greene admitted elsewhere that 'it would not grieve me to see Mr Alexander Korda seated before a cottage loom in an Eastern county following an older and a better tradition.'[73] The onslaught continued long after Greene actually began to write scripts for Korda in 1936. Twenty years later, however, Greene could write of his now 'great friend', the man who had produced his most acclaimed screen adaptations and been the inspiration for the character of Dreuther in *Loser Takes All*: 'with the death of Korda, fun has gone out of the film industry – yes, one begins to think of it again as just an industry'. Yet even here, Greene refused to allow nostalgia to cloud his judgement: 'He has no successor, no one with whom it is possible *not* to talk about films, the matter in hand, but about painting, poetry, music, anything in the world rather than that "industry" which always seemed to be on the point of quietly, out of neglect, becoming an "art" while he was away reading Baudelaire somewhere among the islands of Greece.'[74]

'Four and a half years of watching films several times a week . . . I can hardly believe in that life of the distant thirties now . . . More than four hundred films – and I suppose there would have been many more if I had not suffered during the same period from other obsessions . . . How, I find myself wondering, could I possibly have written all those reviews?' When Greene started at the *Spectator* 'these films were an escape – escape from that hellish problem of construction in Chapter Six, from the secondary character who obstinately refused to come alive, escape for an hour and a half from the melancholy which falls inexorably round the novelist when he has lived for too many months on end in his private world.' Wiser for his first-hand experience of the film industry, he was to emerge into 'a different world, a world at war',[75] where he was being vaunted as one of the best writers of his generation.

III Film Man? 1941–1991

Ever since *Stamboul Train*, film-makers have been seduced by the screen potential of Greene's work. The choice character parts, the lure of the locations, the doses of sex and religion all seemed to make them natural subjects for adaptation. Yet Greene was the first to admit that 'my books don't make good films. Film companies think they will, but they don't.'[76] He had little or nothing to do with the majority of these movies, and the fact that the filmography of his fiction contains more abject failures than it does unqualified successes seems to bear out his contention. Ford's *The Fugitive* and Mankiewicz's *The Quiet American* were deliberately adulterated, yet though Morton Dauwen Zabel could identify in *The Ministry of Fear* (1943) a world that was as much of Lang, Murnau, Renoir and Hitchcock as it was of 'putsches, pogroms, marches and mobilizations',[77] Lang himself was unable to recreate it on the screen. Yet for all this, Greene's fictional style was undeniably filmic.[78]

> When I describe a scene, I capture it with the moving eye of the cine-camera rather than with the photographer's eye – which leaves it frozen. In this precise domain I think the cinema has influenced me. Authors like Walter Scott or the Victorians were influenced by paintings and constructed their backgrounds as though they were static and came from the hands of a Constable. I work with a camera, following my characters and their movements.[79]

In *Felix Culpe?*, a review of *The Heart of the Matter*, which appeared in *The Tablet* in 1948, Evelyn Waugh wrote: 'It is the cinema which has taught a new habit of narrative.' It was a habit which had not touched all modern styles but for Graham Greene it had made possible a relation between author and action that was both special and effective. In novels like Greene's 'it is as though, out of the indefinite length of film, sequences have been cut which, assembled, compromise an experience which is the reader's alone, without any correspondence to the experience of the protagonists. The writer has become director and producer', in other words 'he controls the action, and moves freely about it, but he is not part of it. His camera eye is like the eye of God, seeing all, but withholding judgement'.

During BBC Radio Three's 75th birthday tribute, V.S. Pritchett said: 'I don't know whether he would agree with this but I would say he has been greatly influenced by the cinema. He was a cinema critic for a long time and he really studied the matter, and I therefore think that his technique as a writer – in presenting action – is really quite exceptional. It suddenly becomes very good, which it wasn't particularly in those earlier novels.'[80] Greene would not have agreed. 'The impact of the cinema on my way of writing comes from the films themselves rather than from my reviewing.' Furthermore, he considered that *It's a Battlefield* contained 'many descriptions which are supposed to be cinematic',[81] while Norman Sherry can point to sections of *Stamboul Train* and Samuel Hynes to the opening paragraph of *The Power and the Glory*, which read like shooting scripts. Greene was quick to notice this 'filmic' quality in the writing of others. In reviewing Eric Ambler's *Judgement on Deltchev* for *The Month* in 1951, he noted how 'the cinema has taught him speed and clarity, the revealing gesture. When he generalizes it is as though a camera were taking a panning shot and drawing evidence from face after face'.[82]

Not every critic has seen the screen as a positive influence on Greene's fiction. According to John Atkins, 'it is his worst work which invites the film comparison. Novels like *A Gun for Sale* could easily be filmed (and were) and remain secondrate literature. Later Greene was to learn that excellence in one particular art depends on an adherence to the rules of that art. It cannot be approached through another.'[83] Surely Atkins is wrong to assert that only the 'entertainments' were filmic and that Greene's talents as a novelist were debased by the influence of the cinema. Scott turned to art as a source of inspiration, yet none considered its effect deleterious to his fiction. James sought fame in the theatre (a considerable influence on his narrative style), while Conrad and Ford attempted historical potboilers, yet their failure in these ventures is not brought to bear in assessing their achievements as novelists. Equally, Greene 'the entertainer' should not be maligned because he was successful in discovering the secret of popular appeal. Nor should his work be deemed less worthy of serious consideration because it has cinematic qualities. Grahame Smith has claimed that 'one reason why even Greene's best work has reached a large public is his avoidance of the experiments in fiction associated with the names of Joyce, Faulkner and Virginia Woolf'.[84] Another is undoubtedly 'his involvement with the major popular art of the twentieth century'.[85]

If today it seems that Greene's route from film fan to popular novelist ran across a critical minefield, in 1936 he was confident that 'from film-reviewing it was only a small step to script-writing'.[86] By then, Greene had already had one novel adapted for the screen and sold the rights to another. Since toying with the idea of joining the Film Society, he had sought an active involvement in the making of pictures. He excitedly told his brother Hugh: 'I'm getting deep into films, so deep that Grierson sounded me the other day on whether I should be interested in a producing job . . . I hope he is picturing me as the head of the proposed BBC Film Unit. I'm on a kind of advisory committee on television as it is. Altogether I seem to have cut into the racket at the right angle.'[87] Later in 1936 he dined with Basil Wright and by May was acting as producer of a GPO Film Unit short, *Calendar of the Year*, a journey through the seasons which demonstrated how the Post Office enhanced the enjoyment of traditional British pastimes and festivities. At about the same time, negotiations opened with Basil Dean for an adaptation of a Galsworthy play, that was eventually to be released in 1939 as *Twenty-One Days*. He also mentioned to Hugh that Alberto

Cavalcanti had suggested a collaboration. Norman Sherry has identified this proposed film as *Went the Day Well?*, but as the letter is dated late May 1936, this is unlikely.

In November that year, he was introduced to Alexander Korda ('perhaps he was curious to meet his enemy'[88]). When they were alone, Greene was asked if he had any film story in mind. Having none, he began to improvise – 'early morning on Platform 1 at Paddington, the platform empty, except for one man who is waiting for the last train from Wales. From below his raincoat a trickle of blood forms a pool on the platform'.[89] As Greene wrote to his mother, Korda was hooked:

> The first day I'd invented a shocker idea for them which they liked immensely and they want if possible to have a character who will run through a whole series. Anyway in three weeks I have to elaborate the idea and turn it in. For this they pay £175 whether they use it or not. If they use it, they employ me on the film for four weeks at £125 a week. At the end of that time they can call on my services for six months at £125 a week. They insisted on tying me up over a further period, so the following year they could then call on my services for six months at £175 a week, and the next year for six months at £225 a week. They can sell me to Hollywood or elsewhere during that time, splitting the gain in salary 50–50. These figures sound astronomical, and of course, only £175 is certain, but these further arrangements were their own idea. It's all very exciting.[90]

Had Korda exercised that option, Greene's immediate future would have followed a very different path from the one which led to *Night and Day* and the Shirley Temple case.

By the end of 1936, Greene was 'thick in scenario. Medium Shots and Insert Shots and Flash Backs and the rest of the racket. Korda, I'm glad to say, has given up the Robey idea and seems to be leaving us alone. Casting is proving very difficult. Menzies finds lovely people with appallingly tough faces, but when they open their mouths they all have Oxford accents'.[91] With a script by Edward O. Berkman and Arthur 'Naughty' Wimperis, the film, *The Green Cockatoo*, went on release in 1937, the same year Greene scripted *The Future's in the Air* for Paul Rotha's Strand Films. In 1941, he produced the commentary for a Ministry of Information flagwaver, *The New Britain*. If Greene did turn his hand to other documentary or propaganda scripts, as seems likely, they would now appear either to be lost or perpetually anonymous. Another six years were to pass before he wrote for the screen again, *Brighton Rock* being his first adaptation of one of his own novels. 'I was really into my stride by the time *The Fallen Idol* and *The Third Man* came along',[92] but, in spite of their critical acclaim and box-office success, seven more years were to elapse before Greene produced another screenplay, *Loser Takes All*, in 1956. The next year he broke the promise he had made to himself after *Twenty-One Days* (never again to adapt the work of another writer) when he undertook a version of Shaw's *St Joan* for Otto Preminger. He concluded his screenwriting career with two further adaptations of his own novels, *Our Man in Havana* (1960) and *The Comedians* in 1967. Greene's recollections of his working relationships with producers and directors, his experiences as a producer and actor, and his views on the various adaptations of his fiction – by Fritz Lang, George Cukor, Joseph Mankiewicz, and others – are recorded elsewhere in this book.

If reviewing tarnished Greene's vision of the films as the bright hope of twentieth-century culture, writing for them caused him to avert his eyes almost completely. 'This is the side of my association with films that I most regret . . . Write down your own script and you will observe what can happen on the floor to your words, your continuity, your idea, the extra dialogue inserted during production (for which you bear the critics' blame), the influence of an actor who is only concerned with the appearance he wants to create before his fans.'[93]

The assumption of a co-producer's duties did little to rectify the situation. It was no job for a writer. 'One becomes involved with the producer's monetary troubles: one has to accept actors who are miscast because another man's money is involved. As a writer one hasn't the blind optimism of the film-maker who believes against all evidence that somehow the wrong actors, the wrong director, the wrong cameraman, the wrong art-director, the wrong colour-process, will all come together and produce a lucky accident.' Books were not made like that. Novelists had to learn their craft more painfully, more meticulously than these film folk, who were handsomely paid whatever the result. 'They can always put the blame for a disaster elsewhere which no novelist can. So the author – turned co-producer – shrugs his shoulders and gives up while the game is only half-through.'[94]

It is perhaps significant that as early as 1953, Greene had qualified his epithet 'a film man' with the words 'to date'. In time, he was to scarcely notice their absence from his life. As he told Marie-Françoise Allain:

> I've made films in the forties, fifties and sixties. But the time comes when one's enthusiasm begins to slacken. One's left with only enough enthusiasm for one's own work, which is writing novels . . . I was a very keen cinema-goer, but now I've lost interest, I don't know why. Perhaps it's because one has a better grasp of an art form which coincides with a given period of one's life. Thus I don't often read poets of two or three generations after mine. I think, too, that we grow less adaptable. We become fossilized.[95]

In 1958 it had obviously distressed him that the films, which had hitherto guaranteed a way of escape, were now something to be escaped from. Fourteen years later, on the publication of *The Pleasure Dome*, he found that the pain had eased somewhat and that he occasionally longed for those 'dead thirties, for Cecil B. de Mille and his Crusaders, for the days when almost anything was likely to happen'.[96]

David Parkinson
January 1993

1

Reviews

At the Super-Cinema

No one, I think, not its greatest admirer, would claim for *Warning Shadows* that it was an achieved success; its success is marked in the process of technical development, and, in a year or two's time, though still sensible to its individual charms, I can imagine thinking it poorly constructed and tawdry. Still, its individual beauties are not to be regretted; it would take a perception unusually coarse to ignore, for instance, that splendour and force which the German actor and producer have managed to give to the figure of the husband; again, what sublety and care made up the part of the younger footman; so that if the detached treatment of the theme erred in any way it was in aesthetic solicitousness and in a superabundance of delicacy.

Then to turn to its employment of technical device: the use made of shadow and reflection to get its effect of illusion and terror was obviously impressive; indeed, the whole production served to point out once again what unbounded power a film can exercise, how wide is its scope, what unnumbered possibilities lie hidden in its technique – all this could some creative intelligence be found to direct it; and none has yet appeared.

The new art may, of course, divide into several branches; but I hope – and this hope seemed to receive encouragement from *Warning Shadows* – that the gulf between naturalism and impressionism, between America and Germany, will not become wider, but much narrower, that, far from German producers becoming 'corrupted' to American commercial standards, a synthesis may be effected of the two manners; for we cannot do without the clarity and agreeable definiteness that American studios have brought to perfection.

Shortly after *Warning Shadows*, a Metro-Goldwyn film was to be seen that exemplified some of these peculiarly American virtues; it dealt – as the cinema should do, still a popular and primitive form of art – with an extremely simple theme; called *The Snob*. It dealt rather carefully with the ascent through American academic society of a young man: besides its admirable neatness of construction, it was shod with a certain veracity, and by comparison with life I seemed to recognize in its portraiture the exquisite insensitiveness and absolute blindness that characterizes a real snob. The story in itself was not very fortunate, but given as much probability and vigour as it would bear by the distinguished acting of Norma Shearer and John Gilbert.

But while American film production is one thing and German another, French films lag behind either. Whatever pleasure was to be gained from *Königsmark* came fortuitously; for instance, the tutor, author of *Les Roses de la Vie*, was a ludicrously charming figure; on the whole, it is a piece of work too elaborate yet badly contrived to be exciting, certainly doing nothing to satisfy whatever other demands we may make upon the cinema.

The Oxford Outlook (June 1925)

The Film Society: Rien que les heures

To sum up the life of man in the small segment of a day has always attracted these novelists whose talents are more poetic than dramatic. Mr James Joyce is the supreme example. Such a treatment, with its microscopic detail, is inclined always to dwarf man before his surroundings: make him petty, at the best pathetic.

Film producers have made some attempt with a difference – Mr Cavalcanti in *Rien que les heures*, Mr Ruttmann in *Berlin*, try to portray one day in the life of a city. Mr Cavalcanti's film of Paris is the more confined. It is an offering of pity for 'all things worn out and old'. These elderly, dirty men, thieves, harlots, tramps are dwarfed by the narrow streets in which they are seen living from one dawn to another, but their surroundings have no more dignity than themselves, and conquer by size alone. In *Berlin* human beings were puppets, but in their place machinery was given swiftness and beauty, even exultation. There is no swiftness in Mr Cavalcanti's film. The pictures drop one by one with a slow and sometimes impressive finality. An almost exaggerated use is made of still life, where the only movement that distinguishes the film from a magic lantern slide is, perhaps, the slow steam rising from a bowl of broth. There is, too, less artistic integrity in *Berlin*, an inclination at times to pause and lick lips over some sordid particular. Yet the film impresses because every 'shot' has evidently been composed with the care of an artist.

The programme included also an interesting 'impressionist' film, *The Love of Zero*, made by Mr Robert Florey at a cost of $200. It is a trivial and sometimes pretentious production, but is of interest as a text-book, as it were, of camera tricks.

The Times (14 January 1929)

The Bride of Frankenstein · The Glass Key · No More Ladies · Abyssinia · Wings in the Dark · Car 99

Poor harmless Mary Shelley, when she dreamed that she was watched by pale, yellow, speculative eyes between the curtains of her bed, set in motion a vast machinery of actors, of sound systems and trick shots and yes-men. It rolls on indefinitely, the first dream and the first elaboration of it in her novel *Frankenstein*, gathering silliness and solemnity as it goes; presently, I have no doubt, it will be colour-shot and televised; later in the Brave New World to become a smelly. But the one genuine moment of horror, when Mrs Shelley saw the yellow eyes, vanished long ago; and there is nothing in *The Bride of Frankenstein* at the Tivoli to scare a child.

This is not Mrs Shelley's dream, but the dream of a committee of film executives who wanted to go one better than Mrs Shelley and let Frankenstein create a second monster from the churchyard refuse, a woman this time, forgetting that the horror of the first creation is quite lost when it is repeated, and that the breeding of monsters can become no more exciting than the breeding of poultry. In a prologue to the film Mrs Shelley tells Byron and her husband, who has been writing poetry rapidly by the fireside, that she has imagined a sequel to her novel. 'To think,' says Byron, 'that this little head contains such horrors.'

But it is unfair to Mrs Shelley to include the old school tie among the horrors in her little head. Baron Frankenstein wears it with his Harris tweeds, and his school crest is embroidered on his dressing-gown. Mr Colin Clive acts the part with a sturdy old Rugbeian flavour ('This heart won't do,' he says to a rather scrubby fag, 'fetch me another'), which was more suitable to *Journey's End* than a Gothic romance. This is a pompous, badly acted film, full of absurd anachronisms and inconsistencies. It owes its one moment of excitement less to its director than to the strange electric beauty of Miss Elsa Lanchester as Frankenstein's second monster. Her scared vivid face, like the salamander of Mr De La Mare's poem, her bush of hardly human hair, might really have been created by means of the storm-swept kites and the lightning flash.

It has been a week, as far as fiction is concerned, of the second-rate and the transient. *The Glass Key*, at the Plaza, unimaginatively gangster, and *No More Ladies*, at the Empire, slickly 'problem' though brightened by the acting of Mr Charles Ruggles, have come and gone and call for no comment. The best film in London is *Abyssinia* at the Rialto, the finest travel film I have seen, made by a Swiss expedition and explained in an admirably plain commentary. Here is the last medieval State in all its squalor (the flies swarming round the eyes and nostrils as though they were so much exposed meat in a butcher's shop), its dignity (the white-robed noblemen flowing into the capital followed by their armed retainers, the caged symbolic lions, and the Lion of Judah himself, his dark crimped dignity, his air of a thousand years of breeding), its democratic justice (the little courts by the roadside, on the railway track; the debtor and creditor chained together; the murderers led off to execution by the relatives of the murdered). This film, alas, may prove the last record of independent Abyssinia. It leaves you with a vivid sense of something very old, very dusty, very cruel, but something dignified in its dirt and popular in its tyranny and perhaps more worth preserving than the bright slick streamlined civilization which threatens it. I don't refer particularly to Italy, but to the whole tone of a time whose popular art is on the level of *The Bride of Frankenstein*.

In the Suburbs and Country

Wings in the Dark may be sentimental and improbable, but it is as exciting as it is naive. Miss Myrna Loy is well worth seeing as a ballyhoo airwoman: she is one of the few actresses who can act tenderness. Here she is saved at the end of a disastrous Atlantic flight by the blind inventor of a mechanical pilot.

Car 99 is more competent and more conventional. A quick exciting crime film, it misses the level of the classical Paul Muni film or even of *G-Men*. These were social criticism, as well as entertainment.

The Spectator (5 July 1935)

The Bride of Frankenstein (USA, Universal, 1935) Dir.: James Whale. Cast: Boris Karloff, Colin Clive, Valerie Hobson, Elsa Lanchester, Ernest Thesiger, Una O'Connor.

The Glass Key (USA, Paramount, 1935) Based on the novel by Dashiel Hammett. Dir.: Frank Tuttle. Cast: Edward Arnold, George Raft, Claire Dodd, Ray Milland.

No More Ladies (USA, MGM, 1935) Dir.: Edward H. Griffith. Cast: Joan Crawford, Robert Montgomery, Charles Ruggles, Franchot Tone, Edna May Oliver.

Abyssinia (Switzerland, Praesens Films, 1935) Dir.: Walter Mittelholtzer.

Wings in the Dark (USA, Paramount, 1935) Dir.: James Flood. Cast: Cary Grant, Myrna Loy, Roscoe Karns, Dean Jagger, Samuel S. Hinds.

Car 99 (USA, Paramount, 1935) Dir.: Charles Barton. Cast: Fred MacMurray, Ann Sheridan, Sir Guy Standing.

St Petersburg · Paris Love Song · The Phantom Light

A new Russian film. How exciting it seemed in the days when questions were asked in Parliament, when *The Times* refused to review the Film Society, when pictures banned by the censors were passed by Labour councils and bright, knowing people went to Whitechapel to see the best films. But the old tricks are beginning to pall: the romantic use of scenery, the long whiskers of depraved aristocrats shot from one angle, the short whiskers of simple peasants shot from another. Here again are the satirical photographs of heavy statues, though the Communist cameraman is finding it increasingly difficult to get a new slant on the horses and the emperors. The moral of *St Petersburg*, of course, is just as impeccable as the moral of *Mother*: the poor musician who can't get a hearing in the capital is Good, and the rich insensitive patrons of music are Bad. You can tell how bad they are by their jewels, their busts, the cherubs and the chandeliers and the pictures of naked women. For a Communist is nothing if he is not a Puritan. At the end of the film the poor musician hears his song sung by convicts on their way to Siberia, and knows that he has done something for Russia.

It is a jerky, sentimental film, sometimes genuinely moving, sometimes absurdly inept. Like most Russian films it is best when it is most savagely satirical, and the scenes in which the rich old patron listens with a scared, covetous appreciation to the new revolutionary tune, and in which the Duke of Baden's violinist catches the dowagers in the boxes and stalls with his mannerisms and little tricky melodies, are admirable. It is the serious Socialist idealism that is embarrassing, the sentimental simplification of human nature, the Dickensian plot. O, we feel inclined to protest, we know that you are on the right side, that your ideals are above reproach, but because you are virtuous, must there be no more cakes and ale?

Paris Love Song is all cakes and ale. You wouldn't think that Mr Milestone, the director, was a Russian, so deftly has he caught the gay, the shameless Lubitsch manner. It is a silly, charming tale of an Italian count who goes up the Eiffel Tower to pretend to commit suicide, and finds at the top a young woman who intends to commit suicide. They agree, of course, to make their lovers jealous, and their lovers come together in the same conspiracy.

Mr Milestone has made out of this nonsense something light, enchanting, genuinely fantastic. Miss Mary Ellis's is the best light acting I have seen since Miss Francis appeared in *Trouble in Paradise*. She is lovely to watch and listen to; she has a beautiful humorous ease. It is a pity that a film a thousand miles away from any human moral standards should have had tagged to its end a dismal sermon on love and marriage to satisfy the new purity code. Only the cinema is able in its most fantastic moments to give a sense of absurd unreasoning happiness, a kind of poignant release: you can't catch it in prose: it belongs to Walt Disney, to Clair's voices from the air, and there is one moment in this film when you have it, as the Count scrambles singing across the roofs to his mistress's room; happiness and freedom, nothing really serious, nothing really lasting, a touching of hands, a tuneful miniature love.

A Georgian poet once wrote some dramatic lines about a lighthouse, where, if I remember right, three men died and six had gone mad. 'Three men alive', it went on, 'on Flannen Isle, Who thought on three men dead.' There was something too about 'A door ajar and an untouched meal And an overtoppled chair.' That roughly is the plot of the English melodrama *The Phantom Light*. It is an exciting, simple story of wreckers on the Welsh coast. Mr Gordon Harker gives his sure-fire Cockney performance as the new keeper unscared by ghost-stories or by the fate of his predecessors, and there is some lovely use of Welsh scenery. That fine actor, Mr Donald Calthrop, is fobbed off in a small part. Mr Calthrop has seldom been lucky in his parts. There is a concentrated venom in his acting, a soured malicious spirituality, a pitiful damned dog air which puts him in the same rank as Mr Laughton.

The Spectator (12 July 1935)

St Petersburg (USSR, Soyuzfilm, 1934) Directors: Grigori Roshal, Vera Stroyeva, B. Dobronrauov, K. Fariassoua. (US title: *Petersburg Night*)

Paris Love Song (USA, Paramount, 1935) Dir.: Lewis Milestone. Cast: Mary Ellis, Tullio Carminati, Ida Lupino, Lynne Overman. (US title: *Paris in Spring*)

The Phantom Light (GB, Gaumont British, 1935) Dir.: Michael Powell. Cast: Gordon Harker, Binnie Hale, Ian Hunter.

Becky Sharp · Public Hero No. 1 · Barcarole

Becky Sharp, the American film version of *Vanity Fair*, is a triumph for colour, for the scarlet cloaks of the officers galloping off under the lamps from the Duchess of Richmond's ball, for the black Napoleonic shadows passing across the white-washed farm, the desolate rush of the dancers streaming away in panic when the guns sound below the horizon. It is absurd, this panic; it isn't true; it isn't as dramatic as the truth, but the winking out of the yellow candle flames, the surge of blue and grey across the dark hall, the windy encroachment of nocturnal colour, give so much delight to the eye that it would be ungrateful to complain of the silly climax in Bath, the indecisive acting of Miss Miriam Hopkins as Becky. The colour is everything here; the process has at last got well away from the blurred mauve wind-flowers and Killarney lakes, and admits some lovely gradations, from the bright dresses to the delicately suggested landscapes on the walls. The only complaint I have against Technicolor is that it plays havoc with the women's faces; they all, young and old, have the same healthy weather-beaten skins.

But one must remember that colour has been tried out on the easiest kind of subject; the fancy dress. It would have been harder to produce *Barcarole* in colour, infinitely harder to produce a realistic film like *Public Hero No.1*. If colour is to be of permanent importance a way must be found to use it realistically, not only as a beautiful decoration. It must be made to contribute to our sense of truth. The machine-gun, the cheap striped tie, the battered Buick and the shabby bar will need a subtler colour sense than the Duchess of Richmond's ball, the girls of Miss Pinkerton's Academy, the Marquess of Styne's dinner for two. I can't help remembering how bright and new were all the dresses in *Becky Sharp*. Can Technicolor reproduce with the necessary accuracy the suit that has been worn too long, the oily hat?

Public Hero No.1 is a conventional but exciting film of a police spy's war against gangsters, in which Mr Chester Morris makes a welcome reappearance in a tough melancholy part punctuated with machine-gun bullets. Just as in *G-Men*, the realistic subject of 'men on the job' is spoilt by a romantic situation (the spy falls for the gangster's innocent sister). Mr Lionel Barrymore gives one of the best performances of his career as a drunken crook doctor, a pathetic, farcical figure, who bled gin when the police shot him down.

But I prefer the high tragedy mood of *Barcarole*. This film is made all of one piece. It doesn't mix the romantic and the realistic, but is all romance in the Elizabethan, or perhaps only the Rostand, manner. The story doesn't concern you too closely, so that you can leave the theatre feeling fine and sad, as if your human nature had been paid a very pretty compliment. You have had a taste, between the *News of the Week* and the *Silly Symphony*, of the Soul, Love, the Point of Honour, before the lights go on and the second house streams up the aisle, of Jealousy, Sacrifice, great abstract eternal issues, or perhaps only of ingenious artificial situations. A young reckless womanizer is trapped one night at his club into a bet with a Mexican that he will win his wife before morning. There will be a duel in any case: if he loses his bet the Mexican will fire first. The young man falls in love and rather than cheapen the woman pretends that he has lost the bet. The unity of a few hours of the Venetian night is beautifully preserved: the tenderness and the despair grow under your eyes in the dance-hall, in the horrible little wine-shop by the canal, as time ticks by. But the film owes most to the acting of Pierre Richard Willm as the lover, with his sharp, handsome, young-old face (he makes death real, as he sweats there in the wine-shop in fear of what he's recklessly pledged himself to suffer), of Edwige Feuillère as the gentle cat-like girl, and Roger Karl as Zubaran, the tortured husband with the psychic sense which has enabled him to read a violent end on the young man's features.

The Spectator (19 July 1935)

Becky Sharp (USA, RKO, 1935) Dir.: Rouben Mamoulian. Cast: Miriam Hopkins, Cedric Hardwicke, Nigel Bruce, Frances Dee, Alan Mowbray, Alison Skipworth, Billie Burke.

Public Hero No.1 (USA, MGM, 1934) Dir.: J. Walter Ruben. Cast: Lionel Barrymore, Jean Arthur, Chester Morris, Joseph Calleia, Lewis Stone, Paul Kelly.

Barcarole (Germany, Ufa, 1934) Dir.: Gerhard Lamprecht. Cast: Pierre Richard Willm, Edwige Feuillère, Roger Karl.

Private Worlds · Living on Velvet · Rome Express

Mr Ford Madox Ford once coined the word 'nuvvels' to describe the stories he couldn't treat seriously as art. So one might speak of 'pictures' as distinct from films. *Private Worlds* and *Living on Velvet* are both 'pictures': one might call them 'flickers' if that word didn't do less than justice to the slickness of their mediocrity. But because Miss Claudette Colbert appears in the one and Miss Kay Francis in the other, they do supply a kind of entertainment; they'll kill time, if you favour that kind of murder, as effectively as a 'nuvel'. You can find plenty of parallels between the flat, easy photography and the prose style of popular writers: a sense of loose unbuttoned ease which doesn't mind wasting a few thousand feet or a few hundred pages, which never picks out of the mass the sharp detail that puts the characters in *our* world. These are just 'pictures', one picture after another.

Miss Colbert is always pleasant to look at, and in the right part she is an able actress: it will be a long while before I forget her performance in *It Happened One Night*. But in *Private Worlds* she is as badly miscast as she was in *Cleopatra*. She plays the part of a medical psychologist, Dr Everest, in charge of the men's ward in a lunatic asylum: a woman whose sexual life has been arrested when her fiancé was shot for cowardice in the War. To the asylum comes a new Superintendant, a Frenchman with conservative ideas about the value of women doctors; his development too has been checked by tragedy (his sister murdered her husband and only his evidence saved her from the chair). So these two frozen people are meant to drift towards each other, half absorbed in the darkness of their private fantasies. Mr Charles Boyer's performances are always admirable; you can believe, listening to his deep nervous voice, in the icy country behind the eyes. But nothing could be less frozen than Miss Colbert; she is not an actress who can suggest abnormality, the austerity of the doctor any more than the sensuality of the Egyptian. It is her chief charm that she is so normal, she can be nothing but the pleasantest of light company. As for the direction, it shies away altogether from the subject of insanity: the lunatic asylum is not really 'used' at all; and the theme of 'private worlds', which should have made us disturbingly aware of the small difference between the fantasies of doctor and patient, is lost in a conventional love story.

Living on Velvet, too, pretends to treat an abnormal psychological case. An airman kills his father, mother and sister in a crash; obsessed with the idea that he ought not to have survived, he lives recklessly, tempting fate to kill him. At a party he and a girl fall in love at sight, and this fantastic rapturous evening of sudden love is made charmingly convincing by the acting of Miss Kay Francis. They marry, but the girl leaves him when she can't rid him of his obsession, and the psychological knot is cut quite arbitrarily by a motor accident which brings him to his senses. The picture would be nothing without Miss Francis and it doesn't amount to much with her.

I doubt if anyone will remember either of these pictures two years hence. It is more than two years since the production of *Rome Express*, but the sinister poker game in the Pullman between the murderer and his victim, the little double-crossing petty thief, sticks in the mind. The film came to an abrupt untidy end, but Mr Conrad Veidt and Mr Donald Calthrop brought to the screen a devilish ruthlessness and a mean cowardice which even the trivial plot about a stolen picture couldn't cramp.

The Spectator (26 July 1935)

Private Worlds (USA, Paramount, 1935) Dir.: Gregory La Cava. Cast: Claudette Colbert, Charles Boyer, Joel McCrea, Joan Bennett, Helen Vinson, Samuel S. Hinds.

Living on Velvet (USA, Warner, 1935) Dir.: Frank Borzage. Cast: George Brent,

Kay Francis, Warren William, Helen Rowell, Henry O'Neill, Samuel S. Hinds.

Rome Express (GB, Gaumont British, 1932) Dir.: Walter Forde. Cast: Conrad Veidt, Gordon Harker, Esther Ralston, Cedric Hardwicke, Donald Calthrop, Hugh Williams, Finlay Currie, Frank Vosper.

The Voice of Britain · Mimi

The superb complacency of the BBC was never more delightfully parodied than in the title of the official film made by Mr John Grierson and the GPO Film Unit: *The Voice of Britain*. It is certainly the film of the month if not the year; but I doubt if the BBC realize the devastating nature of Mr Grierson's amusing and sometimes beautiful film, the satirical background to these acres of dynamos, the tall steel towers, the conferences and contracts, the enormous staff and the rigid technique of a Kremlin which should be sufficient to govern a nation and all is directed to this end: Miss Nina Mae McKinney singing 'Dinah', Henry Hall's Dance Orchestra playing 'Piccadilly Riot', a spot of dubious education, and a spot, just a spot, of culture when Mr Adrian Boult conducts the Fifth Symphony.

This was the most cynical moment of a witty film: Mr Adrian Boult agonizing above his baton, and then his audience – a man turning the pages of his book beside the loud-speaker, a man eating his dinner, nobody giving more than his unconscious mind to Beethoven's music. The picture too of the cramped suburban parlour, the man with his paper, the woman with her sewing, the child at his homework, while 'Piccadilly Riot' reverberates noisily back and forth across the potted plant between flowered wallpaper and flowered wallpaper is even more memorable than the lovely shots of sea and sky and such lyric passages as Mr Chesterton driving gently like a sea-lion through the little tank-like studios. For this is the BBC's chief contribution to man's life: noise while he eats and reads and talks. I wish Mr Grierson had included a few shots from the damper tropics where the noise of the Empire programmes is not disguised at all as entertainment or education, but is just plain wails and windy blasts from instruments hopelessly beaten by atmospherics. At enormous expense from its steel pylon at Daventry the BBC supplies din with the drinks at sundown.

James once wrote of *La Dame aux Camélias*: 'The play has been blown about the world at a fearful rate, but it has never lost its happy juvenility, a charm that nothing can vulgarize. It is all champagne and tears – fresh perversity, fresh credulity, fresh passion, fresh pain.' Something of the same quality belongs to *La Vie de Bohème*. It too has been blown about the world and the studios at a fearful rate, and there still seems to me to linger in this slow decorative English version a little of the happy juvenility. *Mimi* owes much to Miss Doris Zinkeisen's dresses and to the acting of Mr Douglas Fairbanks Junior, more perhaps than to Miss Gertrude Lawrence's pinched out-of-place charm, but even without them I would have enjoyed the sense of a period when you had to load your dice to win your tears, when the heroine must die quite fortuitously of consumption on the night of her lover's success. What safety, prosperity, happiness must have been theirs, one exclaims, for them to have taken such an innocent delight in turning the screw of human misery.

The Spectator (2 August 1935)

The Voice of Britain (GB, GPO Film Unit for BBC, 1935) Dir.: John Grierson.
Mimi (GB, British International, 1935) Dir.: Paul L. Stein. Cast: Douglas Fairbanks Jr, Gertrude Lawrence, Richard Bird, Diana Napier.

The Trunk Mystery · Hands of Orlac · Look Up and Laugh · The Memory Expert · Devil Dogs of the Air

Every now and then Hollywood produces without any blast of publicity a comedy of astonishing intelligence and finish. *The Trunk Mystery* is one of these: it ought to take its place immediately with the classics. A young Wyoming farmer (Mr Franchot Tone), who has come to New York in the hope of finding a brunette to marry, happens to look through the connecting door of his hotel room and sees a dead body on the floor. By the time the manager has been found, the body has disappeared and no one will admit that he can have seen it. With the help of a telephone girl, played in her best silly boy-crazy way by Miss Una Merkel, he sets out to solve the mystery. There *is* a body, death is somewhere in the background, but what matters is the witty dialogue, the quick intelligent acting of Mr Tone and Miss Merkel, who juggle death so expertly and amusingly between them. One is used to death as a horror, one is used to it as a cypher (the body found stabbed in the library in Chapter One): death as a joke is less familiar; it bathes the film in an atmosphere fantastic, daring and pleasantly heartless.

Hands of Orlac is one of those horror films that Mr Shortt, the head of that curious body of film censors rumoured to consist of retired Army officers and elderly ladies of no occupation, has declared his intention of banning. I don't quite know why. If a horror film is bad, as *The Bride of Frankenstein* was bad, it isn't horrible at all and may be quite a good joke; if it is a good film, why should Mr Shortt narrow so puritanically the scope of an art? Can we no longer enjoy with clear consciences the stories of Dr M. R. James? It may be sexual perversity which leads us to sneak *The Turn of the Screw* out of a locked drawer, when all the house is abed, but must our pet vice be denied all satisfaction? Guilty, I admit to liking *Hands of Orlac* because it *did* make me shudder a little when Dr Gogol grafted the hands of a guillotined murderer on to the smashed stumps of Orlac, the great pianist whose hands had been destroyed in a railway accident, and because Herr Karl Freund's romantic direction did 'put across' the agreeable little tale of how the dead man's fingers retained a life of their own, the gift of knife-throwing, an inclination to murder. It would have been a thousand pities, too, if Mr Shortt's rigid good taste had prevented us enjoying the performance of Mr Peter Lorre as Dr Gogol. Mr Lorre, with every physical handicap, can convince you of the goodness, the starved tenderness, of his vice-entangled souls. Those marbly pupils in the pasty spherical face are like the eye-pieces of a microscope through which you can see laid flat on the slide the entangled mind of a man: love and lust, nobility and perversity, hatred of itself and despair jumping out at you from the jelly.

Mr J. B. Priestley is an admirable writer of light films. The Lancashire farces he constructs for Miss Gracie Fields have a pleasant local flavour, their plots are genuinely provincial. In *Look Up and Laugh*, Miss Fields, an actress on holiday, leads the stallholders of an old market in a lively battle against the local council and the owner of a big store who threatens to close the market down. One doesn't demand a high standard of realism in a farce, but *Look Up and Laugh* is distinguished from *The Memory Expert*, a slow worthy comedy in the same programme with Mr W. C. Fields, by the sense that a man's observation and experience, as well as his invention, has gone into its making.

As for the new James Cagney film at the Regal, it is all very boyish and boisterous. Military propaganda in America seems to have got into the hands of the rotarians. Here they are 'selling' the aerial arm of the American navy in just the same way as they will sell a Kleen-Eezy brush: the film has the striped tie air, the breathless flow of wisecracks, the toe insinuated across the doorway. But luckily there is no obligation on an Englishman to purchase.

The Spectator (9 August 1935)

The Trunk Mystery (USA, MGM, 1935) Dir.: Jack Conway. Cast: Franchot Tone, Una Merkel, Conrad Nagel. (US title: *One New York Night*)

Hands of Orlac (USA, MGM, 1935) Dir.: Karl Freund. Cast: Peter Lorre, Frances Drake, Colin Clive. (US title: *Mad Love*)

Look Up and Laugh (GB, Associated Talking Pictures, 1935) Dir.: Basil Dean. Cast: Gracie Fields, Douglas Wakefield, Harry Tate, Vivien Leigh, Robb Wilton.

The Memory Expert (USA, Paramount, 1935) Dir.: Clyde Bruckman. Cast: W. C. Fields, Mary Brian, Kathleen Howard, Walter Brennan. (US title: *The Man on the Flying Trapeze*)

Devil Dogs of the Air (USA, Warner, 1935) Dir.: Lloyd Bacon. Cast: James Cagney, Pat O'Brien, Margaret Lindsay, Frank McHugh, Helen Lowell.

Der Schimmelreiter · Star of Midnight · False Faces · All the King's Horses

Der Schimmelreiter is a film which can be confidently recommended to the middle-aged; its dignified progress demands no quickness of the cinematic sense. Solidly constructed and excellently photographed, it reminded me of the ponderous, talented novels of Sigrid Undset. It cannot meet such a film as *Star of Midnight* on equal terms because it represents a quite different conception of art, sailing majestically like an Armada galleon through the bright, agile, intelligent films, sniped at and harassed and unable to reply.

The story is of Friesland peasant-farmers some time during the last century, and the continual threat of the sea. You watch them at their feasts, their weddings and their funerals; they have the grossness and dignity of their animals; they are more genuine and less self-conscious than the characters of *Man of Aran*, which exploited the same kind of primitive life at the edge of land. Hauke, a farm-hand, who had gained the richest farm by marriage, was elected to the honour and responsibility of keeping the dikes in order. The farmers had become slack, and Hauke was determined to show that he deserved his position. When he planned a new dike to reclaim the foreshore, they opposed him with their inertia and their superstition. The moral is not clear, for to build a new dike Hauke neglected the old; in the autumn storms the waves set in and he saved the village only by cutting his own seawall and drowning himself and his farm. There was something about floods which appealed to the Victorian temperament (only Herr Freud could explain why), not the gigantic floods of China or the Mississippi, but little domestic floods which gave opportunities for sacrifice and the ringing of church bells and drenched golden hair. There is something of this atmosphere about *Der Schimmelreiter*; it takes one back to *The Mill on the Floss*, to *High Tide on the Coast of Lincolnshire*, and *The Sands of Dee*; the wind that blows so sombrely, banking the clouds over these drab Friesian fields, has shaken the windows of many Victorian parsonages. The moral, as I say, is confused, as confused as the religious beliefs of Charles Kingsley, but that only adds to the period flavour: you get a vague impression behind the poverty, the rigour of life and the greedy feasting, of nobility and profundity.

But of a film one expects something more agile: a speed which cannot be attained on the stage or in a novel. *Star of Midnight*, a light, quick sophisticated comedy, in which Miss Ginger Rogers takes Miss Myrna Loy's place as Mr William Powell's partner, has no content which one would trouble to read in a novel or to praise in a play. It is all suavity and amusement, pistol-shots and cocktails; but I am uncertain whether the Victorian profundity of the German film has any more to offer, that there is really more behind the whiskers than behind the polish. And this genre of humorous detective films, *Star of Midnight, The Trunk Mystery, The Thin Man*, has no superiors in streamlined craftsmanship.

Gangster films are a more simple-minded affair: their public the public of the old 'westerns'. All that they demand are a few grim wisecracks, a bumping-off, a federal agent and a fellow's sister and romantic love. They don't mind, I suppose, that the whole opening sequence of *False Faces* has already been used (whether in *G-Men, Public Hero No.1*, or *Men Without a Name* I cannot remember now): the newspaper powering off the presses, the scare headlines, the keep-calm air of the bald-headed Capitol dome, the Department of Justice, the eagle-badge in close-ups. *False Faces* is distinguished only by a grim little incident in a surgery, when a doctor, told at the revolver-point to change a gangster's face, carves the wanted man's initials on his cheeks.

All the King's Horses may appeal to those who care for Mr Carl Brisson's smug, boyish charm and the uniforms, the chancellors, the whiskers and impersonations, the junk of Ruritania. It is sad to see Miss Mary Ellis's sensuous appeal, her Bacchanalian gleam, wasted on sentiment so sweet and daring, so embarrassingly domestic.

The Spectator (16 August 1935)

Der Schimmelreiter (Germany, R. Fritsch-Tonfilm, 1934) Dir.: Curt Oertel. Cast: Mathias Wieman, Marianne Hoppe, Eduard von Winterstein.

Star of Midnight (USA, RKO, 1935) Dir.: Stephen Roberts. Cast: William Powell, Ginger Rogers, Paul Kelly, Gene Lockhart.

False Faces (USA, Edward Small, 1935) Dir.: Sam Wood. Cast: Richard Arlen, Virginia Bruce, Alice Brady, Bruce Cabot. (US title: *Let 'Em Have It*)

All the King's Horses (USA, Paramount, 1935) Dir.: Frank Tuttle. Cast: Carl Brisson, Mary Ellis, Edward Everett Horton, Eugene Pallette, Katherine de Mille.

Where's George? · The Great God Gold · Boys Will Be Boys · The Murder Man

This week's Grim Subject is Fun: that boisterous national form of humour which can be traced up from the bear-pit by way of the Shakespearian clowns, Fielding, Hood, Dickens, until its sentimental culmination in popular rough-diamond prose, a clatter of beer-mugs on a bar, a refined belch of two (fun has grown progressively more refined since Fielding's day), the sense of good companionship.

This is the class to which *Where's George?* naturally belongs: the story of a hen-pecked husband in a Yorkshire town whose only friend was a dumb animal until all the good fellows who formed the local Rugger team persuaded him to break from home, play in the great match and win for the team. But a curious thing has happened: into this badly acted and carelessly directed film a real actor has been introduced, Mr Sydney Howard, and comic actor though he is, he bursts like a realist through unrealities. He can do very little with the stale gags they have given him; even the Rugger game, which might have been thought foolproof, was made as tame as table tennis; what emerges is a character of devastating pathos: Mr Howard, faintly episcopal, in endless difficulties with his feet and hands, minding the kettle in the little cramped kitchen. We are whipped back, past the beer-drinkers and the punsters and the picaresque, to the bear-ring itself which began it all, to see the awkward beast driven in circles. But is isn't easy any longer to laugh at the bears and cheer the dogs on.

In the same programme is an excellent American melodrama of the depression, *The Great God Gold*, a story of the shady business racketeers who make money out of receiverships as the big firms fall. There are no stars, but a team of very able actors reproduce with delightful vividness the *bonhomie*, the plate-glass manner, the annihilating lack of trust. Even the hats have been carefully chosen: the crookeder the deal, the more flowing the brim.

Boys Will Be Boys, an adaptation of Beachcomber's chronicles of Narkover, is very amusing. Mr Shortt has found this realistic study of our public schools too subversive for a Universal Certificate. Mr Will Hay as Dr Alec Smart, appointed Headmaster on the strength of a forged testimonial, is competent, but the finest performance is that of Mr Claude Dampier as the half-witted Second Master whose uncle, the Chairman of the Governors, stops at nothing, not even at a false accusation of theft, to make room for his nephew's advancement. Realistic may perhaps seem not quite the right word to describe a film which ends magnificently in a struggle between the Rugger teams of past and present Narkovians for the possession of a ball containing Lady Dorking's diamond necklace. But Beachcomber in his fantasy of a school of crooks run by crooks has only removed the peculiar morality of the public schools just a little further from the standards accepted outside. It bears the same relation to truth as *Candide*. A free fantastic mind has been given just so many facts to play with; nothing is added or subtracted; but the bricks have been rearranged. The school cloisters particularly appealed to me with their tablets to old Narkovians who had passed successfully into gaol. The criminal features of the boys were excellently chosen, and the only jarring element in the quite Gallic consistency of the film was the slight element of good nature of the boys' gang warfare.

The Murder Man shows the life of the finished Narkovian. A business crook is murdered and the guilt of the crime is fastened on his equally dishonest partner. The man is innocent; and the interest of the film lies in the character of the crime reporter whose evidence is sending him to the chair. There is no more reliable actor on the screen today than Mr Spencer Tracy. His acting of these hard-drinking, saddened, humorous parts is as certain as a mathematical formula, but this film gives him the chance, in a grimly moral scene with the innocent man he has hunted down, of showing the reserve of power behind the ease.

The Spectator (23 August 1935)

Where's George? (GB, British & Dominions, 1935) Dir.: Jack Raymond. Cast: Sydney Howard.

The Great God Gold (USA, Monogram, 1935) Dir.: Arthur Lubin. Cast: Stanley Blackmer, Martha Sleeper.

Boys Will Be Boys (GB, Gaumont-British, 1935) Dir.: William Beaudine. Cast: Will Hay, Claude Dampier, Gordon Harker, Jimmy Hanley.

The Murder Man (USA, MGM, 1935) Dir.: Tim Whelan. Cast: Spencer Tracy, Virginia Bruce, Lionel Atwill, James Stewart.

The Crusades

Mr Cecil de Mille's evangelical films are the nearest equivalent today to the glossy German colour prints which sometimes decorated mid-Victorian Bibles. There is the same complete lack of a period sense, the same stuffy horsehair atmosphere of beards and whiskers, and, their best quality, a childlike eye for details which enabled one to spend so many happy minutes spying a new lamb among the rocks, an unobtrusive dove or a mislaid shepherd. As the great drawbridge falls from the besieger's tower on to the walls of Acre, you cannot help counting the little cluster of spent arrows quivering under the falling block; when Richard of England takes the Cross from the hairy hermit, the camera, moving its eye down the castle walls, stays on a couple of pigeons nesting in a coign of masonry. But one chiefly enjoys in Mr de Mille's films their great set-pieces; he handles, as no other director can, an army of extras. It is not a mere matter of spending money. The cavalry charge outside Jerusalem, the storming of Acre: these are scenes of real executive genius. No clanking of tin swords here, but a quite horrifying sense of reality, as the huge vats tip the burning oil down on to the agonized faces of the men on the storming-ladders, or when the riders meet at full gallop in the plain with a shock which jars you in the stalls.

But these moments occupy perhaps twenty minutes of a very long film. For the rest of the time we must be content with a little quiet fun at the expense of Clio, not always clean fun, although Mr Shortt has given this film the Universal Certificate he denied to *Boys Will Be Boys*. Richard Coeur-de-Lion, in Mr de Mille's pious and Protestant eyes, closely resembled those honest simple young rowing-men who feel that there's something wrong about sex. Richard took the Cross rather than marry Alice of France, and when the King of Navarre forced him at Marseilles to marry his daughter (the alternative was to let his army starve), he merely sent his sword to the wedding ceremony, which was oddly enough carried out in English by an Anglican – or possibly American Episcopalian – clergyman in the words of the Book of Common Prayer. There is, indeed, in spite of the subject, nothing Romish about this film, which has the air of having been written by the Oxford Group. Only when his wife has been captured by Saladin did Richard allow himself to pray, but he found prayer as effective as did the author of *For Sinners Only*, and his wife, whom he had learnt to love, was restored to him. Richard shyly confessed, 'Last night . . . last night . . .', and Berengaria encouraged him with bright tenderness, 'You prayed?' But Richard wouldn't go quite as far as that. 'I begged,' he said, 'I begged . . .', as the great Buchman heart melted at last and Berengaria slid to dry-dock in his arms.

Neither of the two principal players, Miss Loretta Young and Mr Henry Wilcoxon, really gets a chance in this film. The programme says all there is to be said about them. Mr Wilcoxon is 'six feet two inches tall, weighs 190 pounds. He was nicknamed "Biff" as a child.' Miss Young 'is five feet three and weighs 105 pounds.' The information is not as irrelevant as it sounds, for the acting can roughly be judged in terms of weight. Mr Wilcoxon leads over the hairy hermit, played by Mr C. Aubrey Smith, by six pounds, and Miss Katherine de Mille, who has an agreeably medieval face, as Alice of France beats Miss Young by ten pounds. (To quote the programme again. 'She avoids starches, sugars and fats; eats all greens and only enough meat to get the necessary proteins.')

As for the other Groupers, there was a delicious moment when I thought the Earl of Leicester said 'Aye, Colonel', when he was told to attack, but I think the din before Acre may have confused my ears. The Earl was made up distractingly to resemble Mr George Moore. He had one of the few English names in a finely orchestrated cast which included Sven-Hugo Borg, Fred Malatesta, Vallejo Gantner, Paul Sotoff, Hans von Twardowski, and the name I liked best, Pedro de Cordoba. One had to judge these actors by their names as their weights were not given.

The Spectator (30 August 1935)

The Crusades (USA, Paramount, 1935) Dir.: Cecil B. de Mille. Cast: Henry Wilcoxon, Loretta Young, Katherine de Mille, C. Aubrey Smith, Ian Keith, Joseph Schildkraut, Alan Hale.

Dood Wasser · Me and Marlborough · The Barretts of Wimpole Street

Mr Alexander Korda's company, London Film Productions, has lately started a 'national investigation' in the course of which the naive question is asked, 'Do you prefer films that are purely entertainment, or films with a serious message?' In the childlike eyes of the great film executives *Dood Wasser*, I suppose, would be classed with the serious messages (though what this one is it might be hard to say), while *Me and Marlborough*, one of the silliest films yet produced in this country, would be regarded as 'purely entertainment' (though in what the entertainment consists it would be harder still to discover). It may be thought very unlikely that many film magnates would be able to think of 'a serious message', but, if it may prevent more films of the *Me and Marlborough* type being produced, let us vote against entertainment and bear with fortitude the triangles, the divorce cases, the Great Marriage Problems of our celluloid Bjornstjerne Bjornsons. If by some happy accident they produce one film as exciting and genuinely entertaining as *Dood Wasser*, we shall be amply justified.

Dood Wasser is a story of the reclamation of the Zuyderzee and the opposition of the Vollendam fishermen, who see their catches getting yearly smaller. Its opening, a documentary prologue which presents the reclamation without the human factor, is an exciting piece of pure cinema. The geometrical instruments, the blueprints, maps and diagrams, the dance of numerals, the sad triumphant voice singing behind the figures, behind the diagrams of cranes and dredges: this is something neither the stage nor prose can present. It reminded me, in its dramatization of statistics, of Mr Eliot's 'Triumphal March' with its catalogue of armaments:

28,000 trench mortars,
53,000 field and heavy guns,
I cannot tell how many projectile, mines and fuses . . .

It is very seldom that the cinema has made this lyrical use of a human voice divorced from the singer's image. Certainly it has never been used more effectively even by M. Clair or in the lovely opening to *F. P. 1*, where the aeroplanes dived and turned against a background of chorus and cloud.

The story which followed, exhibiting the human stupidities and the tragic fidelities behind the bare Blue Book report, is produced rather slowly, but it has some of the magnificent drive one felt behind the classic Russian films, behind *Earth* and *The General Line*: no tiresome 'message', but a belief in the importance of a human activity truthfully reported. The old fisherman with the horny tortoise face, who was ready to blow up the new dike rather than become a farmer, is given the importance of a general creed; he represents all the fatal courage, honesty and loyalty that may exist in a stupid brain. The photography is uneven: at moments it is painfully 'arty', deliberately out of focus, but it will be a long while before I forget the boisterous fair, the balloons and masks and buffoonery, the low roofs of the merry-go-rounds under the low cloudy sky when the deep animal stupidity of the Vollendam fishermen reached its climax.

The title of this Dutch film, of course, is not encouraging, and it may seem a little kill-joy to find more pure entertainment in its slow serious march than in the bright coy antics of Miss

Cicely Courtneidge as a woman who disguises herself in men's clothes in order to follow her husband to the wars. She is not an actress who can suggest pathos or romantic love, and though Mr Victor Saville's direction has a smooth well-groomed air, while Mr Tom Walls plays Marlborough with dignity, I found myself too embarrassed by Miss Courtneidge's facial contortions to appreciate their share. Miss Courtneidge is used to throwing her effects to the back row of the theatre gallery, and the camera is not kind to her exaggerations.

The Royal Court continues its admirable series of revivals with *The Barretts of Wimpole Street*. This is well worth seeing for the sake of Mr Charles Laughton as Mr Barrett, a more macabre and openly sensual Mr Barrett than Sir Cedric Hardwicke's.

The Spectator (6 September 1935)

Dood Wasser (Holland, Nederlandsche Filmgemeenschap, 1934) Dir.: Gerard Rutten. Cast: Jan Musch, Teo de Maal, Betsy Ranucci-Beckman, Arnold Marle.

Me and Marlborough (GB, Gaumont British, 1935) Dir.: Victor Saville. Cast: Cicely Courtneidge, Tom Walls, Barry McKay, Alfred Drayton.

The Barretts of Wimpole Street (USA, MGM, 1934) Dir.: Sidney Franklin. Cast: Norma Shearer, Fredric March, Charles Laughton, Maureen O'Sullivan, Katherine Alexander, Una O'Connor.

On Wings of Song · Peg of Old Drury · Break of Hearts

I'm afraid we are in for a run of films presenting the Loves of the Artists. This week we have a singer's love-story, an actress's love-story, a musician's love-story. The great film executives have decided that Art is trumps (alas! that the final 'e' which so neatly distinguishes the artiste from the artist cannot be tacked on to that word Art). We have in one film extracts from *La Bohème*, in another speeches from Shakespeare, in the third a few minutes of *Tristan*. Personally, I preferred to any of these snippets the sight of Miss Anna Neagle in breeches and a three-cornered hat.

There is something rather pompous about the appearance of Miss Grace Moore on the screen: the profound silence of an audience that has never found it necessary to cease its chatter before the fine direction or fine acting; the immense queues of elderly ladies in peasant blouses and little jackets who have slipped away from their art pottery to see something they really can enjoy; the stuffy reverence like that of a pit before a Bernard Shaw play. Miss Moore, of course, has a lovely voice and a figure unlike the usual *prima donna*'s, but her acting is quite undistinguished. The success of her films as films and not as potted operatic extracts has so far been the success of her leading men. Mr Tullio Carminati gave that dull and worthy film *One Night of Love* the little sparkle it possessed, and now Mr Leo Carillo takes all the honours in *On Wings of Song* as the cheap, vulgar, pathetic little Italian racketeer who ruins himself for love of music and love of the singer and nearly throws his life away before a gunman's automatic rather than miss her appearance at the Metropolitan. I seem to remember Mr Carillo before in small gangster parts; here he gives one of the finest performances of the year: to my mind one of the three finest performances, to be remembered with Mr Charles Laughton as Ruggles of Red Gap and Mr Richard Barthelmess in *Four Hours to Kill*.

Neither Sir Cedric Hardwicke's smooth, well-bred playing of Garrick, nor Miss Anna Neagle's lively Peg Woffington is of that high standard, though I never tired of Miss Neagle's physical appearance, which was as pretty as a Chelsea figure. The whole film indeed is very pretty, with the sentiment neatly handled. But prettiness is a quality one wants, if at all, in small quantities. One wonders why the names Peg Woffington and Garrick have been attached to these characters; there is, of course, no historical truth to be found anywhere in the deft, neat tale. Peg Woffington lived before the days when 'the mummer' (to quote George Moore) 'grew ashamed of his hose and longed for a silk hat, a villa, and above all a visit from the parson'. She shares with Mrs Barry the distinction of having been one of our most sexually promiscuous actresses; *she* didn't die gracefully as the curtain fell on *As You Like It*; *she* didn't dream of domestic love with Garrick somewhere in Surrey. She had more life, more pleasing commonness one suspects, than this too sweet, too roguish figurine. But I am ungrateful: I have seen few things more attractive than Miss Neagle in breeches.

And so to the loves of the great orchestral conductor (Mr Charles Boyer) and the budding, dewy composer (Miss Katharine Hepburn). These are both actors of very great talent, Mr Boyer condemned by some grim Dante of a film executive to suffer and be redeened by love and suffer again in endless circles, Miss Hepburn to be so young, unsophisticated, idealistic, so very, very Barrie. Mr Boyer in *Break of Hearts* is an artistic philanderer, a character one doesn't associate with great conductors so readily as with crooners, who falls in love and marries and is faithless, loses his wife and loves her and takes to drink and is saved by her love. These two actors are talented enough to keep some of our interest even in a story of this kind: indeed Miss Hepburn always makes her young women quite horrifyingly lifelike with their girlish intuitions, their intensity, their ideals which destroy the edge of human pleasure.

The Spectator (13 September 1935)

On Wings of Song (USA, Columbia, 1935) Dir.: Victor Schertzinger. Cast: Grace Moore, Leo Carillo, Michael Bartlett. (US title: *Love Me Forever*)
Peg of Old Drury (GB, British & Dominions, 1935) Dir.: Herbert Wilcox. Cast: Anna Neagle, Cedric Hardwicke, Jack Hawkins, Margaretta Scott, Hay Petrie.
Break of Hearts (USA, RKO, 1935) Dir.: Phillip Moeller. Cast: Katharine Hepburn, Charles Boyer, John Beal, Jean Hersholt.

The Black Room · Gentlemen of the Navy

Mr Boris Karloff has been allowed to act at last. Like the late Lon Chaney, he reached stardom with the sole assistance of the make-up man. Any face would have done as well on a big body, and any actor could have produced the short barks and guttural rumbles, the stiff, stuffed sawdust gestures, which was all his parts required of him. A Karloff scenario must have made curious reading. Were those grunts phonetically expressed? One pictures the Karloff arriving in his luxurious car for a hard day's grunting at the studio, the hasty study of the part in the dressing-room while one eye is blacked out and all his teeth disappear, the dreadful moment when the distinguished actor forgets his part, whether this time he has to bark or rumble, at last the stately gollywog entrance under the lights . . . But in *The Raven* Mr Karloff was allowed a few minutes of ordinary speech before his face was mutilated and his tongue paralysed and we discovered that he had an expressive voice and a sense of pathos. In *The Black Room* he is given a long speaking part at last.

I liked this wildly artificial film, in which Karloff acts both a wicked central European count and his virtuous, cultured twin of the Byronic period. A curse rests on the family to the effect that the younger twin will kill the elder in 'the black room' of the castle. The room is bricked up by their father, but there is a secret entrance known to the elder brother, the wicked Count, who lives in the traditional atmosphere of boarhounds and wenches (when he finishes with a girl he flings her body down a kind of *oubliette* in the black room). At last, to escape the wrath of the peasants and the curse as well, he murders his younger brother, who is distinguished from him physically by a paralysed arm, and takes his place. The story follows a natural Gothic course, the deception is discovered at the altar when he is about to marry the young, pale, 'proper' heroine, he is pursued to the castle by the enraged peasants, takes refuge in the black room and is knocked into the pit by the brother's dog, falling on the dagger which sticks up through the rotting corpse. Karloff is not quite at ease with virtue, suavity and good looks, but he gives a very spirited performance as the wicked Count and carries the whole film, so far as acting is concerned, on his own shoulders.

The direction is good: it has caught, as Mr James Whale never did with *Frankenstein*, the genuine Gothic note. Mrs Radcliffe would not have been ashamed of this absurd and exciting film, of the bones in the *oubliette*, the scene at the altar when the dog leaps and the paralysed arm comes to life in self-defence, of the Count's wild drive back to the castle, the lashing whip, the rearing horses, the rocketing coach, the strange valley of rocks with its leaning cross and neglected Christ, the graveyard with its owls and ivy. There is much more historical sense in this film than in any of what Miss Lejeune calls, with curious lack of humour, the 'scholarly' works of Mr Korda. A whole literary period comes to life: Wyatt might be raising the huge tower of Fonthill, Monk Lewis writing of the false, fair Imogine and her ghostly betrothed (another part for Karloff):

His vizor was closed, and gigantic his height;
  His armour was sable to view;
All pleasure and laughter were hush'd at his sight;
The dogs, as they eyed him, drew back in affright;
  The lights in the chamber burnt blue!

Gentlemen of the Navy is another boyish clean-limbed piece of propaganda for America's armed forces. It is all about Rags and Rotters. It will be enjoyed by those who liked *Devil Dogs of the Air.* The only redeeming quality of a deeply sentimental film is to be found in the acting of Sir Guy Standing as an old retired commodore who had fought at Manila Bay and bored generations of midshipmen at the Academy with his reminiscences. In a climax of quite startling improbability he gets on board his old ship and goes down with her when she is used for target practice. Handkerchiefs pushed up through the dark all round me like mushrooms in a cellar. It was a tribute to Sir Guy Standing, not to the quality of the easy, false, comfortable emotion.

The Spectator (20 September 1935)

The Black Room (USA, Columbia, 1935) Dir.: Roy William Neill. Cast: Boris Karloff, Katherine de Mille, Marian Marsh, Alan Mowbray, Thurston Hall.
Gentlemen of the Navy (USA, Paramount, 1935) Dir.: Alexander Hall. Cast: Guy Standing, Rosalind Keith, Tom Brown, Richard Cromwell, John Howard. (aka *Annapolis Farewell*)

Jazz Comedy · Two for Tonight

Jazz Comedy is the best thing that has happened to the cinema since René Clair made *The Italian Straw Hat*. Alexandrov, who has been awarded a Soviet Order for his direction, has produced, just as Clair did then, out of the smallest resources and apparently with poor-quality film, a picture of almost ecstatic happiness. It is a freer happiness than Clair's, rougher, less sophisticated: behind Clair's film is always a sharp, smooth, satirical Gallic air, the faintest odour of the most expensive hair-oil; you never get further away from Paris than the dry herbage outside the gramophone factory where the ex-convict listened to the song from the horn of a convolvulus.

But Alexandrov's story of a shepherd who was mistaken by a rich snobbish woman for a famous conductor and who later, after a series of wild accidents and coincidences, became the head of a jazz orchestra in Moscow, has a simple irrelevance quite unlike Clair's tight expert tales. The opening sequence, when the shepherd leads his flocks and herds, of sheep and goats and cows and pigs, to graze by the seashore, is the most lovely a moving camera has yet achieved, as it follows him with the quickness of his long stride over hills and rocks, streams and veranda, while he sings, knocking the tune out on the slats of a bridge or the bars of a paling. And if something of the kind has been done before, in *Congress Dances* and Walt Disney cartoons, to convey a sense of lyrical happiness, this at any rate is completely original: Alexandrov's use of a moving camera to convey the grotesque in his long panorama of a crowded bathing beach. The wealthy woman in pyjamas swaying her munificent hips along the shore in pursuit of the famous conductor is followed by the camera behind a close-up frieze of enlarged feet stuck out towards the lens, of fat thighs, enormous backs, a caricature of ugly humanity exposing pieces of itself like butcher's joints in the sun.

I have no wish to criticize this film, but simply to rejoice in its wildness, its grotesqueness, its light, taking tunes, a sense of good living that owes nothing to champagne or women's clothes. If Alexandrov sometimes seems to dwell too long on an incident, at least no one has shown a richer comic invention, for, like Clair and Chaplin, this director has worked to his own scenario; it is to Alexandrov we owe the conception as well as the execution of the magnificent sequences when the shepherd pipes to the rich woman's guests and the notes bring all his animals trampling out of their enclosure, up the steps of the hotel, in at the windows, to eat and drink the feast laid out in honour of the conductor. The tottering tipsy bull, with the dignity and lack of humour of a King's Bench judge, who is laid to sleep in the woman's bed, and the pig who lies down in a dish and the drunken guest who tries to carve it belong to a fantasy more robust than Clair's.

This is genuine cinema: few English titles are needed: there is action all the time, a minimum of speech. *Two for Tonight* depends on dialogue. It is a very amusing and well-written entertainment; Mr Bing Crosby is attractively commonplace among the stars; Miss Mary Boland and Mr Lynne Overman are two of the most reliable players . . . So this picture forces one to write, in terms of actors and authorship. The camera has played a very small part in the entertainment. Even a spirited battle in a restaurant with soda-water siphons could have been transferred at a cost to the stage; and the studies of a theatrical magnate, of an Austrian producer turned manservant, of a madman with a passion for noughts and crosses would have been even more amusing behind footlights.

Sometimes one is inclined to believe that characters can all be left to the stage; the cinema generalizes. It is not one man called Kostia who sings his way through *Jazz Comedy*, but all brave, coarse and awkward simplicity.

The Spectator (27 September 1935)

Jazz Comedy (USSR, Mosfilm, 1934) Dir.: Grigori Alexandrov. Cast: Leonid Utyosov, Lubov Orlova, Maria Strelka, Yelena Tyapkina.
Two for Tonight (USA, Paramount, 1935) Dir.: Frank Tuttle. Cast: Bing Crosby, Mary Boland, Lynne Overman, Thelma Todd.

Song of Ceylon · Musik im Blut · The Dark Angel

Dog, I suppose, ought not to eat dog, otherwise I should be

inclined to cast a malicious eye towards my fellow film-reviewers who have gone into such curious Gothic attitudes of reverence before what must be one of the worst films of the year, *The Dark Angel*, writing of 'classical tragedy' and the 'great' acting of Miss Merle Oberon. It is the ballyhoo, of course, which has done it: the advance gossip and the advertisements, the crowds outside the cinema on the opening night, the carefully drilled curiosity as to what Mr Sam Goldwyn had done to Miss Oberon's eyebrows . . .

Song of Ceylon, on the other hand, made by the GPO Film Unit and directed by Mr Basil Wright, is introduced as a second feature into the Curzon programme with little notice from the ecstatic connoisseurs of classic tragedy, although it is an example to all directors of perfect construction and the perfect application of montage. Perfection is not a word one cares to use, but from the opening sequence of the Ceylon forest, the great revolving fans of palm which fill the screen, this film moves with the air of absolute certainty in its object and assurance in its method.

It is divided into four parts. In the first, *The Buddha*, we watch a long file of pilgrims climb the mountain-side to the huge stone effigies of the god. Here, as a priest strikes a bell, Mr Wright uses one of the loveliest visual metaphors I have ever seen on any screen. The sounding of the bell startles a small bird from its branch, and the camera follows the bird's flight and notes of the bell across the island, down from the mountain-side, over forest and plain and sea, the vibration of the tiny wings, the fading sound.

The second part, *The Virgin Island*, is transitional, leading us away from the religious theme by way of the ordinary routine of living to industry. In *The Voices of Commerce* the commentary, which has been ingeniously drawn from a seventeenth-century traveller's account of the island, gives place to scraps of business talk. As the natives follow the old ways of farming, climbing the palm trees with a fibre loop, guiding their elephants' foreheads against the trees they have to fell, voices dictate bills of lading, close deals over the telephone, announce through loud-speakers the latest market prices. The last reel, *The Apparel of a God*, returns by way of the gaudy gilded dancers in their devil masks to the huge images on the mountain, to a solitary peasant laying his offering at Buddha's feet, and closes again with the huge revolving leaves, so that all we have seen of devotion and dance and the bird's flight and the gentle communal life of harvest seems something sealed away from us between the fans of foliage. We are left outside with the bills of lading and the loud-speakers.

Musik im Blut, also at the Curzon, is a quiet agreeable film of a music academy. It lets one down more gently than most commercial films would do after *Song of Ceylon*, because in its own more conventional way it too is a film of integrity and truth. We believe in the music academy, the freshness and unsophistication of the students' love, the sad awkward mingling of art and adolescence. A story of which the climax is the performance of a prize-winning concerto seems closer to one's experience than the silly sentimental war story of *The Dark Angel*: the girl who is loved by her two cousins from childhood, who sleeps with one of them during his short leave from the front and who, when she believes that he is dead, is about to marry the other, when she finds him again, blinded and hiding from her. Although everyone wore the clothes and coiffures of 1935 (I particularly liked Miss Oberon's hat in her opening sequences), this film belongs to the Lyceum melodramas of the War years, *Seven Days' Leave* and flowery cardboard sets and old retainers. A very manorial, very feudal film, in which the young squires go off to fight after family prayers, while the butler and the chauffeur show becoming emotion and a few aristocratic women keep stiff lips before the upper servants, it is one you should go a very long way to avoid.

The Spectator (4 October 1935)

Song of Ceylon (GB, Ceylon Tea Propaganda Board, 1935) Dir.: Basil Wright.
Musik im Blut (Germany, 1934) Dir.: Erich Waschneck.

The Dark Angel (USA, Samuel Goldwyn, 1935) Dir.: Sidney Franklin. Cast: Merle Oberon, Fredric March, Herbert Marshall, Janet Beecher.

Anna Karenina · The Informer

A new film with Greta Garbo: the event is exciting, of course, but it has very little to do with the art of the cinema. The film does not need great actresses so much as great directors, and it is no reflection on Hollywood to say that no one there knows what to do with Garbo, with her awkward ungainly body, her hollow face strong and rough as an Epstein cast. *Mata Hari, Grand Hotel, The Painted Veil*: these are typical of the slick commercial products to which she has been expected to adapt her powerful personality. The result has generally been unfortunate. Power misapplied is apt to be a little absurd. Garbo's great talent might appear less confined on the stage.

In *Anna Karenina* she has been better served than in most of her films. Guilt and misery and passion, these suit the melancholy grandeur of her voice. Very nearly all her acting is in her voice: watch her among a crowd of other actresses in the mazurka, she is stiff, awkward, bony, rather grotesque among the graceful bodies, the lovely shoulders; but listen to her as she bends over her croquet-ball playing a game with her lover before all the gossips in St Petersburg and you are in the presence of deep authentic pain. The word 'doom' is frequently in the mouths of these characters, but there is no other actress on the screen who would have not made the idea of doom false and preposterous, who would have convinced us, as she does from her first appearance on the Moscow platform, her face emerging from the engine's steam, to the last scene when we watch her brain stagger with the thudding wheels, that she has been driven to her fate.

What can the cinema do with an actress of her quality and kind? The film, if it is to be true to itself, must depend first on picture and movement and only secondarily on dialogue; it is a director's art, neither an author's nor an actor's. The stage technique is forced on the other players in *Anna Karenina* by the personality of Greta Garbo, the slowing of the film to allow time for the incredibly lovely voice, the harsh suffering face, to make their points, calls for a standard of acting they cannot meet, with the exception of Mr Basil Rathbone, who as Anna's husband draws an intense bitter portrait of a man living for appearances alone. Mr Fredric March, so satisfactory in ninety-nine films out of a hundred because he is arranged in the right patterns by his directors, left to his own resources is unconvincing.

It is Greta Garbo's personality which 'makes' this film, which fills the mould of the neat respectful adaptation with some sense of the greatness in the novel. No other film actress can convey physical passion that you believe in its dignity and importance, and yet there is no actress who depends so little on her own sexual charm. Sitting in the corner of a freezing railway carriage, with the ugly shadows of the single globe deepening the crevices of her face, she is more like a man than a woman. What beauty she has is harsh and austere as an Arab's; and I was reminded of Mr Yeats's lines on Dante's mask:

An image that might have been a stony face,
Staring upon a bedouin's horse-hair roof
From doored and windowed cliff, or half upturned
Among the coarse grass and the camel dung.

Mr Liam O'Flaherty's novel of the Irish Rebellion has been filmed a second time. It is superb material for the screen; very few words are needed for this drama; terror is not a subtle sensation; it can be conveyed very much easier by images alone than scruples, guilt, tenderness. You need only the Black and Tan patrols through the Liffey fogs, the watching secretive figures outside the saloons as the drunken informer drifts deeper and deeper with his cronies into the seedy night life of Dublin. Mr Victor McLaglen has never given an abler performance, and the film, even if it sometimes underlines its points rather crudely, is a memorable picture of a pitiless war waged without honour on either side in doorways and cellars and gin-shops.

The Spectator (11 October 1935)

Anna Karenina (USA, MGM, 1935) Dir.: Clarence Brown. Cast: Greta Garbo, Fredric March, Basil Rathbone, Freddie Bartholemew, Maureen O'Sullivan, May Robson, Reginald Owen, Reginald Denny.

The Informer (USA, RKO, 1935) Dir.: John Ford. Cast: Victor McLaglen, Heather Angel, Margot Grahame, Una O'Connor, Wallace Ford, Preston Foster.

A Midsummer Night's Dream

I sometimes wonder whether film reviewers are taken quite seriously enough. Criticism, of course, may not be quite in our line, but the production of *A Midsummer Night's Dream* has demonstrated beyond doubt that no one can shake a better tambourine or turn a better table. We are superb mediums, or is it an intuitive sympathy with the poet which enables Mr Luscombe Whyte (to be remembered for his appreciation of Sam Goldwyn's 'classic tragedy', *The Dark Angel*, and to be distinguished from Mr Pedro de Cordoba who was a Crusader) to tell us that Shakespeare 'had he lived now' would have approved of Herr Reinhardt's film version of his play? 'He had a mind which must have chafed at the limitations of candle-lit, small stages and curtains. He would have conjured up mad woods with twisted trees, peopled with fantasies clothed in visibility.' A pregnant sentence, that, straight from the ouija-board.

Unfortunately, the mediums differ. Mr Sidney Carroll tells us with an even greater air of authority that Shakespeare would *not* have liked the film. It is his obligation, he says, 'as a man of English descent on both sides for generations to try to protect our national poet dramatist from either idolatry or desecration'. As I have said, apart from criticism, there is little we film-critics cannot do.

Alas! I have failed to get in touch with Shakespeare (my English descent is less pure than Mr Carroll's), but I feel quite sure that Anne Hathaway, 'had she lived now', would have thought this a very nice film (I am uncertain of the Dark Lady of the Sonnets). She would have liked the chorus of budding Shirley Temples drifting gauzily up the solid Teutonic moonbeams, and I am sure she would have liked the Bear. For Herr Reinhardt is nothing if not literal, and when Helena declares, 'No, no, I am as ugly as a bear; For beasts that meet me run away for fear', we see a big black bear beating a hasty retreat into the blackberry bushes. All the same, I enjoyed this film, perhaps because I have little affection for the play, which seems to me to have been written with a grim determination on Shakespeare's part to earn for once a Universal Certificate.

But Herr Reinhardt, lavish and fanciful rather than imaginative, is uncertain of his new medium. Although in his treatment of the Athenian woodland, the silves birches, thick moss, deep mists and pools, there are sequences of great beauty, there are others of almost incredible banality. After an impressive scene when Oberon's winged slaves herd Titania's fairies under his black billowing cloak, we watch a last fairy carried off over a slave's shoulder into the night sky. It is very effective as the slave sinks knee deep into the dark, but when the camera with real Teutonic thoroughness follows his gradual disappearance until only a pair of white hands are left twining in the middle of the Milky Way, the audience showed its good sense by laughing.

Much of the production is poised like this on the edge of absurdity because Herr Reinhardt cannot visualize how his ideas will work out on the screen. We are never allowed to forget the stage producer, a stage producer, though, of unlimited resources with an almost limitless stage. At every passage of dialogue we are back before footlights and the camera is focused relentlessly on the character who speaks. The freer, more cinematic fairy sequences are set to Mendelssohn's music, and this is the way Shakespeare's poetry ought surely to be used if it is not to delay the action. It must be treated as music, not as stage dialogue tied to the image of the speaker like words issuing from the mouth of characters in a cartoon.

The acting is fresh and vivid for the very reason that it lacks what Mr Carroll calls 'proper Shakespearian diction and bearing'.

I do not want to be ungrateful, the film is never dull, and the last sequences, when the human characters stream up the stairs to bed, and the fairies flood in and fill the palace in their wake, was a lovely and effective visualization of 'the sweet peace', 'the glimmering light', 'the dead and drowsy fire'.

The Spectator (18 October 1935)

A Midsummer Night's Dream (USA, Warner, 1935) Directors: Max Reinhardt, William Dieterle. Cast: James Cagney, Joe E. Brown, Mickey Rooney, Victor Jory, Anita Louise, Dick Powell, Olivia de Havilland, Jean Muir, Ross Alexander, Arthur Treacher.

Joan of Arc · Turn of the Tide · Top Hat · She

The German film, *Joan of Arc*, is of greater interest to students of Nazi psychology than to film-goers. One would have thought it almost impossible to produce so dull a film on so dramatic a subject (a subject which defeated even Mr Shaw's talent for triviality). It is very noisy, rather like the Zoo at feeding-time, which gives an odd impression in bright, dapper Curzon Street, and it is quite as inaccurate as any Hollywood spectacle of *The Crusades* order but not so funny. The author, Herr Gerhard Menzel, we are told, has 'made intensive studies in France, with the result that new light has been shed on some of the most famous figures in history'. But I hardly think that any research can have helped him to reject Joan's meeting with Charles VII at Chillon in favour of Joan appearing to Charles VII, in beleagured Orleans of all places, and saving him from an infuriated rabble.

Other inventions are less ingenious. But the pure Nordic mind, whether in its politics or its poetry, is doomed to be a little absurd, and Herr Menzel's new light on a Charles who lets Joan die 'for the sake of France', a Charles intended to be a noble, lonely, rather Machiavellian Führer is as ridiculous in effect as Schiller's conception (he was too sensitive to let her burn) of a Joan who died on the battlefield. Perhaps one should not condemn Fraulein Angela Salloker for her quite nerveless playing, for it is one of the purposes of this Nazi film to belittle a rival national saviour. The real hero is Charles with his Nazi mentality, his belief in the nobility of treachery for the sake of the nation. The purge of 30 June and the liquidation of Tremouille, the burning Reichstag and the pyre in Rouen market-place – these political parallels are heavily underlined. The direction is terribly sincere, conveying a kind of blond and shaven admiration for lonely dictators who have been forced to eliminate their allies.

Turn of the Tide, an unpretentious and truthful film of a Yorkshire fishing village, of rivalry over the crabpots, is one of the best English films I have yet seen, apart from the 'documentaries' in which this country has long led the world. It has been compared to *Man of Aran*, but it is on a quite different plane from Mr Flaherty's bogus and sentimental picture. Mr Flaherty's direction is hopelessly 'literary', he lays 'beauty' on inches thick, he contributes just about as little to the film as the author of *The Fountain* to the novel. But Mr Norman Walker is concerned with truth; he doesn't trouble about silhouettes on skylines, and the beauty his picture catches is that of exact statement. The ordinary life of a fishing village, the competition between lifeboat and salvage tug, the changing market prices, satisfy him: he does not have to *invent* drama as Mr Flaherty does, who painfully reconstructed a type of fishing which the Aran islanders had not practised in living memory.

Top Hat is a vehicle, a little better than *Roberta*, for Mr Fred Astaire's genius. It doesn't really matter much that the music and lyrics are bad. Mr Astaire is the nearest approach we are ever likely to have to a human Mickey Mouse; he might have been drawn by Mr Walt Disney, with his quick physical wit, his incredible agility. He belongs to a fantasy world almost as free as Mickey's from the law of gravity, but unfortunately he has to act with human beings and not even Miss Ginger Rogers can match his freedom, lightness and happiness.

The Wag of the Week is Mr Shortt, of our Board of Censors, who has granted to this quite pleasantly bawdy film the Universal Certificate he has refused to the earnest manly Boy Scout virtues of Rider Haggard's *She*. I cannot write reasonably about this film, for few books at one time excited me more than *King Solomon's Mines* and *Allan Quartermain*. *She* always bore its symbolism a little heavily: at that age one was not so interested in the lovely immortal woman and the flame of life as in the great ice-barrier, the avalanche, the cannibals in the caves, but to an unrepentant Haggard fan it does sometimes seem to catch the thrill as well as the childishness of his invention.

The Spectator (25 October 1935)

Joan of Arc (Das Mädchen Johanna) (Germany, Ufa, 1934) Dir.: Gustav Ucicky. Cast: Angela Salloker, Gustav Gründgens, Heinrich George.

Turn of the Tide (GB, British National, 1935) Dir.: Norman Walker. Cast: Geraldine Fitzgerald, Wilfred Lawson, John Garrick, Niall MacGinnis, Moore Marriott.

Top Hat (USA, RKO, 1935) Dir.: Mark Sandrich. Cast: Fred Astaire, Ginger Rogers, Edward Everett Horton, Eric Blore, Helen Broderick.

She (USA, RKO, 1935) Dir.: Irving Pichel. Cast: L. C. Holden, Helen Gallacher, Helen Mack, Nigel Bruce, Randolph Scott.

Barbary Coast · Episode · The Passing of the Third Floor Back

Barbary Coast is melodrama of the neatest, most expert kind, well directed, well acted and well written. The wit, vigour and *panache* of Mr Ben Hecht and Mr MacArthur have raised nearly to international halma form (in Mr Aldous Huxley's phrase) a conventional film story of a girl who comes to San Francisco one fog-bound night in the 1840s to marry a gold-prospector and finds that he has been murdered. She stays to become the mistress of his killer, the Big Shot, and falls in love with a young prospector who reads Shelley and wants to write poetry. The Big Shot, himself pursued by Vigilantes, follows his mistress with the intention of killing her lover, but, taking pity on them both, goes to meet his lynchers. The story, it will be seen, belongs to the 'far, far better' school, but the character of the Big Shot has a sourness, of the girl an unscrupulousness, which is fresh and interesting. The conventionality of the plot has provided a challenge to the director and the authors to make something real out of the hocus-pocus.

They have succeeded triumphantly. There are moments as dramatically exciting as anything I have seen on the fictional screen. *Sous les Toits de Paris* contained a sequence in which Préjean was surrounded by a gang with drawn razors in the darkness of a railway viaduct; the smoke blew continually across, and the dialogue was drowned in the din of shunting trucks. The steamy obscurity, the whispers, the uproar overhead combined to make the scene vividly sinister. There is a moment in *Barbary Coast* that takes its place with Clair's, when the Big Shot's gunman, on his way to commit another murder in the San Francisco of which he has long been one of the undisputed rulers, feels the pistols of the Vigilantes against his ribs. They walk him out to the edge of the acetylene-lighted town along streets ankle-deep in mud, holding a mock trial with counsel and witnesses as they go; the low voices, the slosh of mud round their boots, the rhythmic stride are terrifying because they have been exactly imagined, with the ear as well as the eye.

The Austrian film *Episode* has nothing comparable to offer, nothing even to equal the acting of Mr Edward G. Robinson and Miss Miriam Hopkins and half a dozen less-known players in their small vivid parts in *Barbary Coast.* I cannot understand the enthusiasm for Fraulein Paula Wessely, star of the slow decorative *Maskerade.* This stocky, rather graceless actress may be said, I suppose, to act naturally, rather in the same way that a Rodean girl may be said to play hockey naturally, but if one wants art to *imitate* the natural, to be conscious and precise in its effects, one will surely prefer Miss Lynn Fontanne or half a dozen other naturalistic actresses to Fraulein Wessely, whose air of healthy prudery I always find peculiarly odious. The background to this rather silly comedy about a rich old philanderer, his sons' tutor and an art student who wishes to keep from her widowed mother the fact that they have been ruined is supposed to be the Vienna of 1922, the Vienna of the inflation: but so tragic a breakdown of the framework of life deserves a less perfunctory, a less humorous and sentimental treatment.

To my surprise I enjoyed *The Passing of the Third Floor Back*. The pious note has been toned down, the milk of human kindness in the original play has been agreeably watered, and the types in the small London 'private hotel' are observed with malicious realism. Unfortunately, sweetness and light do break in, and the director cannot convey these qualities with the same truth as the cans of cooling water, the interminable uncarpeted stairs, the jangle of bells and nerves. The excursion steamer, on which the Stranger takes everyone for a trip to Margate, is as chromium-plated as a millionaire's yacht and carries a chorus of Goldwyn girls in bathing-costumes. This is to be a little too cynical. The right sense of sudden and happy release can surely sometimes be caught among the winkles and blare and sweat of an August holiday.

The Spectator (1 November 1935)

Barbary Coast (USA, Samuel Goldwyn, 1935) Dir.: Howard Hawks. Cast: Miriam Hopkins, Edward G. Robinson, Joel McCrea, Walter Brennan, Brian Donlevy, Donald Meek, Frank Craven.

Episode (Austria, Viktoria-Film, 1935) Dir.: Walter Reisch. Cast: Paula Wessely, Georg Tressler, Karl Ludwig Diehl.

The Passing of the Third Floor Back (GB, Gaumont British, 1935) Dir.: Berthold Viertel. Cast: Conrad Veidt, Anna Lee, Rene Ray, Sara Allgood.

The March of Time

The March of Time is the title of an American news series, and this first instalment ought to shock the complacency of British news directors. No attempt has ever been made over here really to edit news films; a football-match, minor royalty opening a housing estate, the launching of a ship, a wharfside fire; scraps of unimportant material are flung without arrangement on to the screen. A tremendous organization has been built up to bring the exposed film to the laboratory in the shortest possible time. A British heavy-weight takes the count somewhere in the Middle West, and a fleet of aeroplanes, acting in conjunction with Atlantic liners, bring the film to London at enormous expense in record time. But this is not news by any journalistic standard: the story is at least six days old and as dead as last season's tunes. Of course, if Sir Josiah Stamp were to break a bottle of wine over a new railway engine at Euston, it would be possible to exhibit the completed film in every cinema in London before the locomotive was dry, but that event might well be considered insufficiently important to upset the weekly programmes already showing, and we should have to wait for Sir Josiah Stamp quite as long as we have to wait for the boxer. So in spite of the aeroplanes most of the items in a news programme have ceased to be news by the time they are shown, however hastily and perfunctorily exhibited.

The producers of *The March of Time* have realized this. They have realized too that some forms of news do not grow cold in twenty-four hours. Their fortnightly programmes can be compared with an authoritative article by a special correspondent rather than with a haphazard page of photographs from the *Daily Mirror.* Their method is to connect newsreel shots with studio reconstructions, to make a vivid, and often politically partisan, story. The law of libel is not so dreaded in America as in England, or the bitter exciting film, which I saw privately, of the activities of the armaments ring could not have been made. But no less exciting and now publicly shown at three London cinemas is the account of the Croix de Feu, the French Fascist organization. The film opens with the riots of February 1934, and gives some idea of the extent of the bloodshed and the ferocity of the fighting. It was from these riots that the Croix de Feu gathered strength, and in *The March of Time* we can watch the recruiting, the processions of private cars driving out from Paris at night to secret meetings in the countryside, we can listen to Colonel de la Rocque's torch-lit violence.

But there is great danger that news films may not be allowed the same political freedom as the Press; the British Board of Film Censors have been known in the past to impose a political censorship over fictional films, and they have tried their hands with curious results on *The March of Time.* The sequences of the Paris riots have been severely cut, and the film has been made

Fascist in tone by the removal of the telling final shot which gave the source from which the Croix de Feu derives its funds.

It should not be forgotten, therefore, that the Board are merely the employees of the film industry, and that their decisions have no legal sanction except where it has been granted them by local authorities. They could if necessary be dismissed by the industry acting as a whole, or news films could be taken altogether out of their hands. The law of libel will always safeguard individuals better than the Board. Unfortunately, film companies have never shown a talent for co-operation or they would not have imposed on themselves so curious a form of censorship, a censorship working by a set of rules so absurd that it has imposed on *The Thirty-Nine Steps* a certificate for adults only and granted to the domestic indecencies of *The Crusades* a Universal Certificate. This means that in many districts a parent is not allowed to give his own child permission to see Mr Hitchcock's blameless film of Lord Tweedsmuir's patriotic 'thriller'.

The Spectator (8 November 1935)

The March of Time (USA, 1934 on) Produced by Louis de Rochement with *Time* Magazine.

Last Love · Moscow Nights · Oil for the Lamps of China

Last Love has a pleasant unpretentious air of truth about it, which is very rare in films about singers or composers. One knows what treatment they generally receive on the screen, how nobly and dolefully the Schuberts and Chopins sacrifice themselves for former room-mates. Even the story of *Last Love*, of the middle-aged 'finished' composer who returns to his home in Vienna after ten years in America, who falls in love with a Japanese student, writes his last opera for her to play in and watches at rehearsal her growing love for the young conductor, might have been made for Herr Tauber. But once accept the romantic plot and the rest is genuine: a creative career from a professional angle. Herr Albert Bassermann as the elderly composer gives one of the best performances I have seen this year. This is not a man romantically 'inspired', but a man with a profession, a man who works; watch the pleasure and cunning in his face as he recognizes a good trick, a technical dexterity. His acting in the wintry scene of the small country inn, where his tenderness comes to a head and he drinks with the village musicians, conducting over the beer-mugs, and the girl breaks into a spontaneous tipsy song and he feels the fun of life return because he has ideas again after ten years of sterility, is very moving. Miss Michiko Meini, who plays the Japanese student, has a charming voice. To a European the Oriental face doesn't, thank God, register emotions in the way we are used to, and the faint flicker across the broad rice-white surface of love, pain, tenderness helps the film to maintain, even at its less plausible moments, a pleasant muted quality.

Moscow Nights, Mr Anthony Asquith's new film, is completely bogus. Momentarily forgetting *The Dark Angel*, I wondered, as I came out from the assembly of peeresses and minor royalty and the high shriek of friend recognizing friend into the blue glare of searchlights, whether this was the worst, as well as the most ballyhooed, film of the year. Mr Asquith was once a promising director, though he was always more tricky than imaginative. Now his bag of tricks seems empty. This absurd romantic spy-drama of wartime Russia opens with Volga boatmen and carried on with every worn-out property of a Hollywood Russia, even to the gipsy orchestras. The direction is puerile, no one can drop a tray or a glass without Mr Asquith cutting to a shell-burst. But he has been well-served by his players, by M. Harry Baur as an awkward pathetic war-profiteer, by Miss Athene Seyler as an old genteel spy who haunts the hospitals, and Mr Laurence Olivier as an embittered front-line officer who loves a young society nurse engaged to the profiteer. The acting of Penelope Dudley-Ward, who plays the girl's part, belongs to another class altogether, to country-house charades. It is an error of taste to star this player above such brilliant professionals as Miss Seyler and Mr Hay Petrie, who makes a more vivid impression in the few feet of film allowed him and with his two words of dialogue than Miss Ward in all her reels.

The subject of *Oil for the Lamps of China* is excellent: the ballyhoo of sham idealism with which the young recruits of an American oil company are inoculated before they are dispatched to China, the appeals to their loyalty, the assurances that 'the company always takes care of its men'; and then the truth, the sacrifices they are expected to make without return, the appointments filled by intrigue in New York, the inventions stolen by their superiors, and finally, when they grow old, the studied attempts to rob them of their pensions by forcing them to resign. It is a pity that so interesting a theme should have been passed first through the mind of a good, sincere and sentimental woman and then through the mind of a perhaps less sincere but certainly not less sentimental Hollywood scenario-writer.

DIALOGUE OF THE WEEK
'Together. That's a nice word.'
'Yes, and it rhymes well with For Ever too.'
(*Oil for the Lamps of China*)

The Spectator (15 November 1935)

Last Love (Letzte Liebe) (Austria, Morawsky-Film, 1934) Dir.: Rudi Loewenthal. Cast: Fritz Schultz, Albert Basserman, Michiko Meini, Hans Jaray.
Moscow Nights (GB, Denham Productions, 1935) Dir.: Anthony Asquith. Cast: Laurence Olivier, Penelope Dudley-Ward, Harry Baur, Athene Seyler, Hay Petrie. (US title: *I Stand Condemned*)
Oil for the Lamps of China (USA, First National, 1935) Dir.: Mervyn Le Roy. Cast: Pat O'Brien, Josephine Hutchinson, Jean Muir, Lyle Talbot, Henry O'Neill, Donald Crisp.

Arms and the Girl · Accent on Youth · The Tunnel · New Babylon

Arms and the Girl may have set out, in the simple rather adolescent American manner which seems insolubly linked with high cheekbones, fraternities and curious shoes, to argue that a soldier's uniform has more sex-appeal than a pacifist's red tie, but it has developed *en route* into one of the best comedies of the screen since *It Happened One Night*. These two films have a very respectable ancestry, the Restoration duel of sex, Dryden's quarrelling lovers, the philosophy of love so beautifully stated in *The Mock Astrologer*:

Celimena, of my Heart
None shall e'er bereave you:
If with your good Leave I may
Quarrel with you once a Day,
I will never leave you.

A general's daughter in love with a college pacifist is kidnapped by her father and dumped safely out of the way, without the money to return, in Mexico. There she gets drunk with an American private soldier, they haven't the money to pay for the drinks, and by the time the soldier has come to his sober senses, he has deserted, smashed a Government car, rushed the boundary, stolen a motor caravan and finds himself driving towards California with a girl whose politics he can't stand, who loathes the sight of a uniform and who wants to go west to her pacifist at Washington and not east. Miss Barbara Stanwyck as the malicious-tongued aristocratic Red and Mr Robert Young as the reckless irritated private soldier give admirable performances. The tradition of sparring lovers usually survives in the form of facetiousness, a dreadful intellectual slap and tickle, but the dialogue of *Arms and the Girl* does belong, however great the difference of quality, to the same unsentimental genre as Wildblood's and Jacintha's ''Twas a meer Trick of Fate to catch us thus at unawares: To draw us in, with a what do you lack, as we pass'd by: Had we once separated tonight, we should have had more Wit, than ever to have met again tomorrow.' But for painful contrast: 'You are the type of girl a man can imagine in his own home – married I mean.' This lover's speech from *Accent on Youth* belongs to another world, and so do the direction and the acting of this dreary comedy. There is one good scene at the end of the picture, but I wouldn't advise any but dog-lovers to wait so long. *They*, of course, will enjoy Mr Herbert Marshall's usual canine performance of dumb suffering.

The worst films of the year succeed each other rapidly: *The*

Dark Angel, Moscow Nights and now *The Tunnel*, one of those lavish films about the future, with television, skyscrapers, gas masks, incomprehensible machines. This film is about an Atlantic tunnel and its inventor, whose family life was ruined because he was too busy joining England to America to come home for his small son's birthday. I was quite unable to sit this film through, though by leaving I missed the 'courtesy appearance' of Mr George Arliss as the Prime Minister of Great Britain, an actor from whose Athenaeum manner I sometimes derive a rather humble pleasure.

The Forum this week are reviving Trauberg's silent film of the Paris Commune, *New Babylon*, a slow decorative romantic picture which should be well worth seeing again. I remember a sense of dignity and desolation, mud and drenching rain which ought to suit the Forum admirably. I cannot too much admire the policy of Miss Wakeling who chooses her films to fit her theatre, its curious shape and situation. There could be no better impressionist setting for the Soviet films than the long dark tunnel, intermittent grinding of railway engines, the pervading atmosphere drifting in from Charing Cross of steam and slot machines.

The Spectator (22 November 1935)

Arms and the Girl (USA, Reliance, 1935) Dir.: Sidney Lanfield. Cast: Barbara Stanwyck, Robert Young, Hardie Albright, Cliff Edwards, Ruth Donnelly. (US title: *Red Salute*; aka *Runaway Daughter*)

Accent on Youth (USA, Paramount, 1935) Dir.: Wesley Ruggles. Cast: Sylvia Sidney, Herbert Marshall, Philip Reed.

The Tunnel (GB, British Gaumont, 1935) Dir.: Maurice Elvey. Cast: Richard Dix, Leslie Banks, Madge Evans, Helen Vinson, C. Aubrey Smith, George Arliss, Walter Huston, Basil Sydney, Jimmy Hanley.

The New Babylon (USSR, Sovkino, 1929) Directors: Leonid Trauberg, Grigori Kozintsev. Cast: Yelena Kuzmina, Pyotr Sobelevsky, Sophie Magarill.

The Last Outpost · The Irish in Us

The Last Outpost, which will be shown shortly at the Plaza, is a curious mixture. Half of it is remarkably good and half of it quite abysmally bad. One can even put one's finger on the joins, and it will be well worth a visit if only because it indicates what might be made of the short-story form on the screen. It consists of two stories unrelated except for the coincidence of characters. The first, which lasts for about half an hour, is a very well-directed and well-acted war-story of a British Secret Service agent and his success in warning a defenceless tribe against a Kurd attack and inducing them to move with their flocks over a flooded river and across a snow-bound range of mountains to safe pastures. It is one of those stories of dogged physical endeavour that the film does so well. It belongs to the order of *Grass* and *The Covered Wagon*. Mr Claude Rains as the Secret Service agent in Turkish uniform and Mr Cary Grant as the incurably light-minded and rather stupid British officer whom he rescues from the Kurds both act extremely well. Mr Rains's low husky voice, his power of investing even commonplace dialogue with smouldering conviction, is remarkable. He never rants, but one is always aware of what a superb ranter he could be in a part which did not call for modern restraint but only for superb diction. I should like to see him as Almanzor or Aurengzebe, for he could catch, as no one else could, the bitter distrust of the world, religious in its intensity, which lies behind the heroic drama.

The Last Outpost, if it had stopped on the mountain pass above the pastures with the officer on the way down to hospital and the comforts of Cairo and the secret agent turning back towards the enemy, would have been a memorable short-film. Mr Charles Barton, the director, has obviously used old documentaries: the crossing of the flooded river is not a Californian reconstruction, and all through this first section the camera is used with fine vigour to present a subject which could not have been presented on the stage.

I cannot see why we should not have serious films of this length as well as farces, short stories as well as novels on the screen. The essential speed and concision would be an admirable discipline for most directors, who are still, after seven years of talkies, tied to stage methods, and we might be saved from seeing such a good film as this padded out to full length by the addition of a more than usually stupid triangular melodrama of jealousy and last-minute rescue in the Sahara, where needless to say Mr Rains sacrifices his life at the end for his wife's lover, so that all may end in the fixed, almost Oriental, shorthand of military melodrama, 'It is better so', clasped fingers and topees off and fading bugle-calls.

Mr James Cagney is one of the most reliable actors on the screen; his vigour, speed and humour are just as apparent in *The Irish in Us*, a film to discourage a less hard-working and conscientious actor, as in *A Midsummer Night's Dream*. It is a film of exactly the complacent domestic sentimentality which one would expect from the title, of an old mother and her adoring sons. Mr Cagney is the youngest and the favourite son; his brothers, a cop and a fireman, disapprove of him because he won't take a proper job but tries unsuccessfully to become a boxing manager. His latest unfortunate discovery, Carbon Hammerschlog, who, when he is told can use the bath replies, 'Every time I wash in one of them things I get embarrassed,' is luckily played by Mr Allen Jenkins, so Mr Cagney has some support in a film which I admit has a few amusing moments and an excellent boxing match. The part of the cop, who loses his girl to his kid brother, is taken by Mr Pat O'Brien, who is one of those actors I should like to see perform once a year only in an all-star cast including Mr George Arliss, Mr Herbert Marshall, Mr Jack Hulbert, Miss Cicely Courtneidge, Mr Carl Brisson, and Miss Penelope Dudley-Ward. A nightmare, do you say? But I like to rationalize my nightmares.

The Spectator (29 November 1935)

The Last Outpost (USA, Paramount, 1935) Directors: Louis Gasnier, Charles Barton. Cast: Cary Grant, Claude Rains, Gertrude Michael, Kathleen Burke, Akim Tamiroff, Billy Bevan.

The Irish in Us (USA, Warner, 1935) Dir.: Lloyd Bacon. Cast: James Cagney, Pat O'Brien, Olivia de Havilland, Mary Jenkins, Frank McHugh, Allen Jenkins.

La Bandéra · Woman Tamer · Come Out of the Pantry

The camera swings down from the night sky above the Paris roofs to a narrow ill-lit street where a drunken girl is dancing with her lover. A man slips out of a doorway and she clutches him. Only after he has pushed her aside and disappeared into the warren of dance-halls and one-night hotels does she see the blood he has left smeared across her blouse.

This is the effective opening of *La Bandéra*, a French film of the Spanish Foreign Legion into whose anonymous ranks the murderer escapes after he has been robbed of all his money in a shabby Spanish port. It is an excellent illustration of the main advantage the film possesses over the ordinary stage play; the means it has to place the drama in its general setting. We have almost given up hope of hearing *words* with a vivid enough imagery to convey the climate of the drama. *La Bandéra* on the stage would be only one more melodrama saved from triteness by the character of the police spy, admirable and despicable, with his strung nerves and body of childish delicacy, who pursues the murderer even into the hard dangerous exile of the Legion. But the camera, because it can note with more exactitude and vividness than the prose of most living playwrights the atmosphere of mean streets and cheap lodgings, gives the story background and authenticity. We recognize the truth of the general scene and are more prepared to accept the truth of the individual drama.

But it is astonishing how seldom in English films a director uses the camera in this way to establish a scene, a way of life, with which he and his audience are familiar. Miss Lejeune's remark, quoted at the end of this article, is an example of the social snobbery which hampers the English cinema. The material of English films, unlike French or American, is nearly always drawn from the leisured class, a class of which the director and his audience know really very little. Mr Hitchcock sometimes indulges in crime or 'low life', but it is with the 'amused' collector's air of a specialist in sensation. An English film as a rule means evening gowns by Hartnell, suitcases by Asprey. An excursion steamer to Margate (*vide The Passing of the Third Floor Back*) becomes a luxury liner full of blondes in model bathing-dresses. Even in the worst French films one is not conscious of this class division, the cafés and dance-halls are of the kind familiar to the majority of the audience. The snobbery of such a film as *Come Out of the Pantry*, in which a duke's son plays the part of a footman and shows himself so 'amusingly' sociable in the pantry, would be quite meaningless to any but an English audience.

It is not that one wants English directors to 'go' proletarian (I remember with discomfort how Mr Anthony Asquith, of all people, was set to direct a film about workers on the Underground); one must accept this English class division which prevents the scenario-writer or director from treating naturally and truthfully more than a very limited material, but let that material at any rate be drawn from his own experience, which is probably neither that of the very rich nor of the very poor.

Woman Tamer is pure fantasy, a fast funny exciting story of how a rich banker pleads guilty to making false income tax returns in order to get a few years' peace from his publicity-hating family. It is the second best film to be seen in London this week, though a death-bed scene and a murder do not quite strike the right note of care-free farce.

> BON MOT OF THE WEEK
> By sheer diligence and enthusiasm the cinema, which 25 years ago was producing such morsels as 'What Drink Did', has now arrived at the point when the Queen, the Prince of Wales and the President of the United States are all prepared to patronize its shows within a fortnight.
> (C. A. Lejeune)

The Spectator (6 December 1935)

La Bandéra (France, Société Nouvelle de Cinématographie, 1935) Dir.: Julien Duvivier. Cast: Jean Gabin, Annabella, Pierre Renoir, Viviane Romance.

Come Out of the Pantry (GB, British & Dominions, 1935) Dir.: Jack Raymond. Cast: Jack Buchanan, Ethel Stewart, Fay Wray, Ronald Squire, Fred Emney.

Woman Tamer (USA, Columbia, 1935) Dir.: Tay Garnett. Cast: George Raft, Joan Bennett. (aka *She Couldn't Take It*)

Page Miss Glory · A Fire Has Been Arranged · Here's to Romance · The Port of Five Seas

There's not really much to write about in the Gossip Column this week. *Page Miss Glory* is meant to be funny and is quite funny, except that Mr Pat O'Brien pops up again: I couldn't hear what he said most of the time, his voice gets louder and faster with every film, and anyway something about him makes my flesh creep. The story is of two down-and-out promoters who win an advertising competition with a composite photograph of an imaginary girl they call Dawn Glory; the plot becomes agreeably crazy when radio firms, reporters, picture companies, kidnappers, all begin to bribe and blackmail for the use of her services. Miss Marion Davies acts the part of a plain chambermaid who is transformed by a beauty treatment. I liked her eyelashes and her Dawn Glory hair-wave and there was one particular coat with kind of square epaulettes . . . but I don't know how to describe it.

A Fire Has Been Arranged is meant to be funny and is very, very dreary. Flanagan and Allen seem to be famous comedians, some people laughed, but, like most English farces, it made me embarrassed. I wanted to stop everyone and tell them they oughtn't to play the fool in public; a private joke should not be repeated noisily before strangers. I felt rather sad and outcast, as I do on the rare occasions when I look at English comic weeklies. Perhaps it was that association which made me feel at the end that I had been waiting a long, long while for a haircut and had come away without one.

Here's to Romance is not meant to be funny, but it is very funny indeed. Unconsciously epicene, with delicate little controversial love-makings, like wisps of lingerie, with such tendernesses, such male oglings and male trippings and little bursts of happy song, only the late Ronald Firbank could have done justice to its pansy graces. It is the tale of a young Italian singer and his rich American patroness, who sends him to Paris to study, and how he doesn't understand her intentions until his eyes are opened by the girl he whimsically loves (Miss Anita Louise). The scene when Nino comes trilling up the stairs to have breakfast with his love in her 'cute' apartment, bearing two tall arum lilies in a pot, is perhaps the most deliciously characteristic in the film.

The Port of Five Seas is a Russian documentary describing the cutting of the White Sea canal through fifty miles of rock by gangs of prisoners. It is high-minded, absurd and rather sad; it can hardly be accused of propaganda; it is only too grimly veracious, one feels certain as one reads in the caption how 'In the forefront of the leaders' attention stood recreation and cultural training' and watches a committee woman, with spots and long straggling hair, teach another ungainly girl, in a tiny wooden room plastered with newspaper cuttings and photographs of eminent Ogpu leaders, to play a game of draughts.

One can't call these pictures cinema; they are all, with the possible exception of the last, just flickers; but I don't want it to sound too unhappy a week. *Page Miss Glory* is a good film to see after a good meal, and Miss Anita Louise is the kind of perfect, groomed blonde, who, however silly her part, gives the same satisfaction on the screen as a good advertising design in an American magazine. And then, of course, there's always a lot of quiet fun for the anthologist in film journalism.

> PORTRAIT OF THE WEEK
>
> 'I've always been a terrific film fan. It used to be a bit of a pose once, but now it's genuine. In the days when no respectable people went to pictures we used to go regularly to that little cinema off Shaftesbury Avenue, in Windmill Street, and see all the German and Russian silents. We thought it terribly clever then to boost them. It's not quite so much fun now, when everybody goes to pictures. The excitement of defending them is over, but I always enjoy them. I suppose I'm a bit of a highbrow still. I prefer pictures like *Maskerade* and the Chopin film; they're so soothing.'
>
> (Mr John Gielgud)

The Spectator (13 December 1935)

Page Miss Glory (USA, Warner, 1935) Dir.: Mervyn Le Roy. Cast: Dick Powell, Marion Davies, Pat O'Brien, Mary Astor, Lyle Talbot, Allen Jenkins.
A Fire Has Been Arranged (GB, Twickenham, 1935) Dir.: Leslie Hiscott. Cast: Bud Flanagan, Chesney Allen, Alastair Sim, Robb Wilton.
Here's to Romance (USA, Lasky/Twentieth-Century Fox, 1935) Dir.: Alfred E. Green. Cast: Nino Martini, Genevieve Tobin, Reginald Denny, Anita Louise.
The Port of Seven Seas (USSR, 1935)

Riders to the Sea · Thanks a Million

The cinema, as much as poetry in the eighteenth century, needs patrons. Little good work can come from commercial companies under the pressure of popular taste. The early Russian films showed the immense superiority of the State-aided over the popularly supported, and to see again such an old silent film as *The New Babylon*, which the Forum recently revived, is to be painfully aware that the modern commercial picture has not merely learned nothing in the last six years, it has even forgotten what it once seemed to be learning from the Russian cinema. Nor need one go as far as Russia to see the effect of State patronage. Mr Alexander Korda's publicity cannot blind us to the fact that the only important films being made in England today come from Mr Grierson's system of film units. Of course, the commercial cinema has had its fine moments: *The Front Page*, *City Streets*, *En Natt*, one could name a dozen films, but they seem to have crept into the cinema accidentally, while the big executives were dozing. Their makers have received so little encouragement that it was necessary for Mr Hecht and Mr MacArthur, the authors of *The Front Page*, to break away from Hollywood to produce *Crime without Passion*. So one has nothing but praise for the courage and generosity of Miss Gracie Fields who has financed an independent film version of *Riders to the Sea*, played by the Abbey Theatre players and produced for the most part in Connemara. The intention is admirable, but the result shows one danger of private patronage. I doubt if the best work has ever been produced in complete independence of a public. Even Mr Grierson has his public, a public of several millions, though his films may sometimes not be distributed at all in the ordinary way through cinema circuits. Popular *taste* makes a thoroughly bad dictator, but the awareness of an audience is an essential discipline for the artist.

There is something altogether too private about this Synge film, a touch of mutual admiration about the continual close-ups of the individual players, a self-conscious simplicity. The camera is always delayed for Synge's words, when in a true film words are less important than the camera. I confess I am not an admirer of Synge's plays, of the idea that style is a decoration, something you can apply to your subject, instead of being an economy and an exactitude. The attempt to express exactly an emotion or a half-conscious state, of course, may take the writer into queer places, but in Surrealist prose or in the pages of *Anna Livia Plurabelle* one can recognize the attempt as one cannot in Synge's incantatory style. But I do not think that even Synge's admirers will enjoy *Riders to the Sea*. Something has gone badly wrong with the continuity; the loss of act divisions has upset the sense of time. Though the movements of actors, between the set speeches which are nearly always delivered in close-up, are intolerably slow, so that most of the film seems to have been spent in getting from door to fire and back again, the events outside the fishing cottage follow quite another order of time, without interval or preparation. No sooner has one lost son been keened for than the dreary band of mourners enter to announce another death. What the film might have done, and the stage could not do so well, was to show us the manner of those deaths; it might have given us with its larger scope in space and time the sense of the poor hard lives before and after; a reason for their deaths. As it is the deaths do not matter, they are merely an excuse for dirges as resonant, and as hollow, as a church bell's.

With real reluctance I must admit that a commercial film this week offers better cinema. The one misses being art and the other succeeds deftly in being entertainment. *Thanks a Million* is a very amusing musical skit on American State elections. It is very well acted, even by Mr Dick Powell, and from the first sequences of a bankrupt musical troupe stranded in drenching rain in the most provincial of main streets, while an aged candidate drones to an empty hall of his birth in a log cabin and his thirty years of service, one is aware of a direction unusually vivid, amusing and inventive.

The Spectator (20 December 1935)

Riders to the Sea (GB, Flanagan-Hurst, 1935) Dir.: Brian Desmond Hurst. Cast: The Abbey Players.

Thanks a Million (USA, Twentieth-Century Fox, 1935) Dir.: Roy del Ruth. Cast: Dick Powell, Fred Allen, Ann Dvorak, Patsy Kelly, Phil Baker, Paul Whiteman and his band.

The Ghost Goes West · Foreign Affaires

M. René Clair made his name by a very individual form of fantasy. He was a realist, with a social conscience, dealing satirically with French types and scenes which he knew intimately. He was not a humorist in the modern English sense of a man who shares the popular taste and who satirizes only those with whom the majority are already displeased. His satire was so far from being safe and acceptable that his early film, *The Italian Straw Hat*, roused enough opposition to keep him out of the cinema for some years. I use the past tense. It is typical of the British film industry, whose leading showman if not producer is Mr Alexander Korda, that M. Clair should be brought to this country to direct a Scottish film full of what must be to him rather incomprehensible jokes about whisky and bagpipes, a humorous fantasy without any social significance, realistic observation, or genuine satire; it appeared first as a short story in *Punch*.

The story is of the Glowrie ghost, who is condemned to haunt an impoverished castle in the Highlands until, by forcing a Maclaglan to admit that one Glowrie is worth seven of his clan, he has recovered the honour he lost two hundred years ago on the battlefield. The ghost is the double of the present Glowrie, who sells the castle to an American millionaire in order to pay his bills and falls in love with the daughter. The girl, of course, confuses the free amorous eighteenth-century ghost with his rather shy descendant, the millionaire decides to build the castle up stone by stone in Florida, a rival manufacturer turns out to be of Maclaglan blood, and the complications are gently and traditionally obvious as coloured Christmas illustrations. The only opportunities for satire are at the expense of rich and tasteless Americans, as safe a form of weekly family fun as were war-profiteers a few years ago and as Cubists still seem to be today.

And yet I have never believed more firmly in Clair's genius than I did during this film. The silly story, the gross misuse of Clair's peculiar qualities, were forgotten in my admiration for his camera sense. In no other film this year has there been the same feeling of mobility, of visual freedom. And the actors responded with unforced lightheartedness. Mr Eugene Pallette as the American millionaire gives the finest performance of his career, and Mr Robert Donat as the ghost and his descendant acted with invincible naturalness.

It is only in memory that the silly tale begins to outweigh Clair's direction, for it is so much easier to carry a subject in the mind than a treatment. But even in the cinema there were moments when one realized the conflict between the scenario and Clair's poetic talent; these were the moments of which *this* ghost was unworthy, when we were much closer to Elsinore than pasteboard Glowrie, to Purgatory than the brandy flames of the seasonal pudding. One remembers the long drift of white cumulus while the voices of the dead father condemned the cowardly ghost; the moment on the ramparts at midnight when the great lace sleeve fell in close-up across the corner of the screen and with all the sudden shock of a striking clock one knew the ghost was there, just beyond the dark edge of one's vision; the seconds when the camera slowly climbed the long worm-eaten cobwebbed stairs and paced beside the cracked panelling.

So, curiously enough, the silly tale gave one a chance to see a more deeply imaginative Clair than had its own scenarios. The Scottish holiday may well prove valuable for his future. Surely no artist can continue indefinitely to write as well as direct, to double the creative demand on his nerves. One has seen the effect on Mr

Chaplin, and Clair's films since *A Nous La Liberté* have become rather tired and repetitive.

One cannot confidently recommend any funny film to another person. People still complain to me that *Jazz Comedy* was not funny at all. So it is with great caution that I recommend *Foreign Affaires*, a well-*written* film in which Mr Tom Walls gives a really lovely performance as an ancient and aristocratic rake who finds himself in Queer Street because 'a misguided jockey jerked the wrong horse'.

The Spectator (27 December 1935)

The Ghost Goes West (GB, London Films, 1935) Dir.: René Clair. Cast: Robert Donat, Jean Parker, Eugene Pallette, Elsa Lanchester, Everly Gregg.
Foreign Affaires (GB, Gainsborough, 1935) Dir.: Tom Walls. Cast: Tom Walls, Ralph Lynn, Robertson Hare, Norma Varden, Marie Lohr, Diana Churchill, Cecil Parker.

The Guv'nor · Midshipman Easy · Treasure Island

Mr George Arliss, who has dressed up as Disraeli, Voltaire, Richelieu, Wellington, Rothschild, now dresses up as a French tramp, and I suppose those who like Mr Arliss will like his latest film. They may not be disturbed by the thought of how little this tramp has in common with the broken-shoed stragglers they may meet making a daily monotonous march back and forth between the workhouses of Oxford and Chipping Norton, with no more freedom than the length of a chain. He belongs, of course, to the 'bird-song at morning, star-shine at night' school, and his admirers need not fear that he has lost any of his usual refinement or sentiment, his cultured English accent, the Universal Certificate. I do not know why he has to be a French tramp unless for this reason: that his accent need not be coarsened; unless too it is felt that the general Yuletide air of sweetness and light might have been broken if the wicked capitalists had been English.

I am not an admirer of Mr Arliss, but I found this film

rather more tolerable than his recent appearances as the family Wellington, the family Voltaire. The story, if it had been more consistently worked out, would have had quite a Clair ring to it. The tramp's name is Rothschild, and there is at least a hint of satire when the unscrupulous banker appoints him to the board of his bankrupt firm to restore public confidence for long enough to enable him to withdraw his own interests after enriching himself with a shady financial *coup*. The effect of the name is immediate; the old tramp has only to telephone for a little corn with which to feed the city pigeons and the Stock Exchange responds. Clair, one feels, would have made more of such incidents, nor would he have allowed the gross inconsistency which robs the film even of a fantastic reality. For the firm of Rothschild, who are so careful of the family name that when the tramp is arrested for poaching they secure his release and give him money to keep him out of the courts, apparently make no attempt to interfere with his activities as director of a great bank.

The film soon proceeds on more conventional Arliss lines. The banker's plot is so elementary that the tramp easily tumbles to it, and Mr Arliss defeats the wicked capitalist in favour of – not the honest worker, or even the honest Green Shirt or the honest collectivist, but of a pair of good women capitalists whose ignorance of the business in which they are the main shareholders is regarded as a rather disarming innocence (so far have we gone from any genuine social criticism). Mr Arliss, of course, goes back to the road where 'all days are good days when the sun is shining'.

Midshipman Easy can be unreservedly recommended to children. It is the first film of a new English director, Mr Carol Reed, who has more sense of the cinema than most veteran British directors, certainly more than Mr Wilcox or Mr Basil Dean. It is simply and dramatically cut, it contains the best fight I can remember on the screen, and I can imagine no child too sophisticated to be excited and amused. Hughie Green gives an excellent performance as the courageous, argumentative and rather absurd Easy whose father has brought him up, on the principles of Godwin, to believe in human equality, and Mr Harry Tate's boatswain is deliciously mellow.

If this film is not quite on the same level as *Treasure Island*, which the Royal Court Cinema has very sensibly revived for Christmas, the fault does not lie with either the director or the actors. The story of *Treasure Island* has a deeper, a more poetic value: the capture of the Spanish merchantman, the fight with the Italian convicts, these are exciting inventions: but the buried treasure, the desert island, the horrifying murder of the faithful sailor, the persons of Long John and blind Pew, all these have symbolic value. *Treasure Island* contains, as *Midshipman Easy* does not, a sense of good and evil. Even a child can recognize the greater dignity and depth of this Scottish Presbyterian's *Mansoul* written in terms of an adventure-story for a boys' magazine.

The Spectator (3 January 1936)

The Guv'nor (GB, Gaumont British 1935) Dir.: Milton Rosmer. Cast: George Arliss, Gene Gerrard, Frank Cellier, Patric Knowles, Viola Keats. (US title: *Mr Hobo*)

Midshipman Easy (GB, Associated Talking Pictures, 1935) Dir.: Carol Reed. Cast: Hughie Green, Harry Tate, Margaret Lockwood, Roger Livesey.

Treasure Island (USA, MGM, 1934) Dir.: Victor Fleming. Cast: Wallace Beery, Jackie Cooper, Lionel Barrymore, Lewis Stone, Otto Kruger, Douglas Dumbrille, Nigel Bruce.

Reifende Jugend · The Bride Comes Home · King of the Damned

There is a delightful moment in *Reifende Jugend*, a film which is described as 'a psychological study of three girls who enter a boys' school to prepare for their final examination', when the Headmaster tells the Science Master, who confesses to him that he has fallen in love with one of the girls: 'Be patient. Remember that after the examination she is no longer a pupil.' In another scene one of the senior class discloses a plot to steal the examination papers. 'Tonight the Head's room will be searched.' 'Suppose he finds nothing?' the other boy says. 'Then he will study the blotters with a mirror.' These two pieces of dialogue give a rough idea of the spirit of this entertaining film: the charmingly, realistic attitude of the Headmaster towards the sexual problem, the serious, absurd, emotional, Teutonically thorough schoolboys. It is an odd film because the situations seem fantastic to English eyes, and the bare summary which the management of the Forum supplies does justice only to this oddity:

> One of the girls is loved by both the Science Master and a pupil. Intense rivalry exists between them, and the boy threatens to expose the master unless he helps him through his exam. The master ignores this threat, consequently the boy fails. The Headmaster, touched by the boy's strength of character, persuades the Board of Examiners to pass him, asserting that strength of character and personal worth are more effective than examination papers.

It certainly doesn't do justice to the light lyrical treatment of some of the scenes, the truthful, unsentimental but not unkindly picture of emotional awkwardness.

Compare this film with that embarrassing play, *Young Woodley*. Mr Van Druten put an exaggerated value on adolescent emotion; it was a play about adolescence written by an adolescent, and he tried to make the boy's passion dignified and tragic. But the truth is seldom tragic, for human beings are not made in that grand way. The truth may be sad, but it is nearly always grotesque as well, and the value of this film is that it catches the absurdity just as effectively as it catches the freshness. Herr Heinrich George gives a charming performance as the realistic, coarse, kindly Headmaster and the acting of Fraulein Hertha Thiele, as unemphatic as her pale ashen hair, needs no recommendation to those who remember her in *Mädchen in Uniform*.

Miss Claudette Colbert has been three times lucky – in *It Happened One Night*, her best film, which has been revived this week at the Royal Court Cinema, in *She Married Her Boss*, and now in *The Bride Comes Home*, a comedy of fiery-tempered, and incompatible lovers who fight their way into marriage. For it is exceptionally lucky in the cinema to be given a chance to develop your proper talent, and the fact that Miss Colbert is the most charming light-comedy actress on the screen did not prevent Hollywood from starring her as Cleopatra, so that she might have complained with Nell Gwynn:

> . . . I walk because I die
> Out of my Calling, in a Tragedy.
> O Poet, damn'd dull Poet, who could prove
> So senseless! to make Nelly die for love.

None of the earlier films has a more memorable sequence than that of the nocturnal marriage by a small-town judge, the American equivalent of the Gretna Green blacksmith. The whole scene, the little hideous parlour, the cracked harmonium, the flowery mechnical service composed by the judge himself, is satirical comedy of a very high order.

Mr Walter Forde, who was responsible for one of the worst of last year's films, *The Tunnel*, has directed *King of the Damned*, with Mr Conrad Veidt, Mr Noah Beery and Miss Helen Vinson in the chief parts. One notices the same lavish expenditure, the same inability to cast the small parts realistically (one doesn't expect a convict in a tropical penal settlement to speak with an OUDS accent), but the dialogue is little better. The story of a wicked commandant and a mutiny led by a convict with ideas of social reform is unconvincing.

The Spectator (10 January 1936)

Reifende Jugend (Germany, Carl Froelich Film, 1933) Dir.: Carl Froelich. Cast: Albert Florath, Heinrich George, Paul Henkels, Albert Lieven, Hertha Thiele.

The Bride Comes Home (USA, Paramount, 1935) Dir.: Wesley Ruggles. Cast: Claudette Colbert, Fred MacMurray, Robert Young, Donald Meek.

King of the Damned (GB, Gaumont British, 1935) Dir.: Walter Forde. Cast: Conrad Veidt, Helen Vinson Noah Beery, Cecil Ramage.

Second Bureau · Sans Famille

One is inclined to exaggerate the value of another country's films, just as much as of its fiction, for only the selected few reach us. Those who think of the French cinema in terms of Clair and a few super-realists may learn a salutory lesson this week.

Second Bureau is a rather dull film, a long packed melodrama of the French and German Secret Services. It begins brilliantly enough with shots of blossoming trees and pastoral landscape, a trench in a field filled with yapping, snapping dogs of every breed (one dachshund sits aloof with an air of melancholy poetic foresight), four men in lounge suits wearing gas-masks and carrying small attaché-cases. One of them takes a bomb out of his case and throws it, the gas fumes spread, the field flowers wither, a pigeon falls dead from the sky, the yapping rises agonizingly and subsides, a single bark, and three grotesque masked men gather round the fourth with congratulations. The film, alas, does not maintain this sinister and satiric level. Two secrets stolen from the Germans, a double-crossing agent, a motor chase, a beautiful woman spy who falls in love with the Secret Service officer she has been sent to trap, two murders and an attempted suicide: the film is too thick with drama. The clever atmosphere of routine destruction in the opening sequence is quite lost.

It is a great pity, for what an amusing film of the Secret Service could be made if the intention was satiric and not romantic, the treatment realistic and not violent. One remembers Mr Maugham's Ashenden bored at Geneva, his official existence 'as orderly and monotonous as a city clerk's', and Mr Compton Mackenzie's office in Athens. There is a moment in *Second Bureau* when the French officer watching the German woman in the hotel lounge thinks of her with a handkerchief over her eyes bound to a post. This is an example of the film's unnecessary melodrama. After all it is peacetime. There is no reason why anybody should suffer more than a few years imprisonment and isn't there material enough in that. In the man who sketches near a dockyard and is arrested in a suburban teashop and put away for a couple of years? The true drama is the lack of drama, the pettiness of the actual climax against the background of arming nations, the meagreness of the information to be stolen, the smallness of the money earned, the unimportance of the agent. *Second Bureau* gains nothing by its violence because there is no room to make the violence convincing. One enjoys parts of the film for their touches of truth, not the acting of the stars but of M. Pierre Larquey as the silly pathetic under-officer Colleret, who is ruined by the spy, with his spray of cheap scent, his childish boasts and humble love; of M. Jean-Max as the double-crossing agent, an exiled Russian, a bored womanizer full of self-pity for the past, a self-pity as mechanical as the gallantry.

Sans Famille, directed with deadly seriousness, is very funny indeed. It is the story of how Lady Milligan's baby is kidnapped at the instigation of her wicked brother-in-law so that he may inherit her property, her husband having just died. It is a bad bargain because immediately after the child has disappeared she tells him that she is expecting *un autre enfant*. He means the child to be murdered, but the kidnapper instead takes it across the Channel and leaves it on the steps of Notre-Dame. The boy is adopted by peasants and then by a strolling singer, once a famous operatic star, who dies in a snowstorm, of which the constituent feathers are only too visible. The child makes his way to an appallingly foggy London and the arms of his mother. The chief fun is provided by the London police. They chase juvenile offenders with drawn truncheons, but even when they are inactive there is something subtly wrong with them. They are small men with sloping shoulders and enormous helmets which fall low over their eyes, and they have a dumb beaten-dog air as they creep through the thick fog past public houses where the London burglars dance apache dances with their women.

The Spectator (17 January 1936)

Second Bureau (Deuxième Bureau) (France, Compagnie Française Cinématographique, 1935) Dir.: Pierre Billon. Cast: Jean Murat, Véra Korne, Jeanine Crispin, Pierre Larquey, Jean-Max.

Sans Famille (France, Societé Agatos, 1935) Dir.: Marc Allégret. Cast: Robert Lynen, Dorville. (US title: *No Relations*)

KOENIGSMARK · THE THREE MUSKETEERS · I GIVE MY HEART

It hasn't been a good week for films and none of these three has any real value, but I enjoyed the first, because it is well acted and well directed; there are moments in the second of rather exhilirating freedom of movement, curiously rare on the screen, when the musketeers gallop through the woodlands on their dangerous mission, and the third is about the vulgarest film which has ever come out of Elstree. There is really nothing to be said at all of this film version of *The Dubarry*, a musical play written and made with smug hypocrisy.

There is only one possible 'subject' in the Dubarry's life, the same subject that produced the angry satire of our own Restoration poets against 'the royal Cully':

> The Misses take place, and advance to be Duchess,
> With pomp great as Queens in their Coach and six Horses;
> Their bastards made Dukes, Earls, Viscounts and Lords . . .

It is a subject which can only be treated morally, for its only interest is a moral one. The film has a skittish, coy vulgarity of a book like *Nymph Errant*. You know quite well why the subject has been chosen: the milliner's love affair with a poor poet, her promotion to a house of ill fame (of course, she doesn't realize where she is and thinks she is at a gay party), her marriage with Dubarry, who sells her to the King: the sexual subject is meant to attract, but the makers have not the courage of their pornography, the titillation is whimsically, prettily, sentimentally disguised. And so we have the climax of the film, when the Dubarry comes to the poet, who is rousing the rabble against her, and tells him that she truly *loves* the King. Then all is sweetness and tenderness and triumph . . .

The Three Musketeers is not much more truthful, I suppose but the film is more honest. It is a long time since I read the book and so I found the odd romantic politics, which all turn on a piece of jewellery the Queen of France has given to the Duke of Buckingham, rather difficult to follow. Even the tortuous mind of Richelieu could have conceived no intrigue quite so complex as Dumas'. But the film when it leaves Constance, D'Artagnan's rather tame Victorian betrothed, behind in Paris, is agreeably exciting in quite the manner of the old Westerns: galloping horses, last-minute rescues and a most seductive villainess acted by Miss Margot Grahame. It left me wondering how it was that Dumas, with the help of an American director, had caught so deftly the English public school atmosphere – or rather the English public school as it is reflected by a sympathetic and sentimental writer. When the film wasn't Western, it was authentic Stalky.

But *Koenigsmark* I did enjoy, a Ruritanian film made by a French director. A royal tutor in a small German estate, investigating the story of Koenigsmark's death, discovers the lime-stripped skeleton of the Grand Duke, who had been put out of the way some years before by his brother and who was supposed to have died in Africa. The tutor and the Grand Duchess, under the eyes of spies, work together to bring the brother to justice. The director has enjoyed the pomp of royal processions and has transmitted his innocent enjoyment, and Miss Elissa Landi has never before quite acted up to her beauty and obvious intelligence, but here she has shared the director's enjoyment of the exciting bogus decorative film. There is one excellent moment, when the Grand Duchess and the tutor are resting in a hunting lodge and the woman hears a spy rustle in the bushes alongside. She takes a gun from the tutor's hands, and on the pretext that it will look well if they take some dead animals back with them, ruthlessly shoots down her maid-in-waiting; then she quotes Hamlet with grim satisfaction: 'I took thee for thy better.' It is melodrama, of course, but at any rate it is melodrama of a less conventional kind than we are used to: one natural human strand of cruelty has been twisted into the usually immaculate character of a heroine.

The Spectator (24 January 1936)

Koenigsmark (France, Roger Richebé, 1935) Dir.: Maurice Tourneur. Cast: Elissa Landi, Pierre Fresnay, John Lodge.
The Three Musketeers (USA, RKO, 1935) Dir.: Rowland V. Lee. Cast: Walter Abel, Paul Lukas, Moroni Olson, Onslow Stevens, Margot Grahame, Heather Angel, Ian Keith, Miles Mander, Nigel de Brulier.
I Give My Heart (GB, Wardour Films, 1935) Dir.: Marcel Varnel. Cast: Gitta Alper, Patrick Waddington.

The Case of the Lucky Legs · Charlie Chan in Shanghai · The Amateur Gentleman

It is curious how little the cinema has done for the detective public; perhaps that public is not large enough to tempt the film magnates, consisting, as it chiefly does, of crossword-puzzlers and tired intellectuals. There have been a few unsuccessful attempts to transfer Sherlock Holmes to the screen, there was even a rather deplorable effort by an English company to film an adventure of Lord Peter Whimsey, but the only sustained detective characters on the screen are Mr Warren William's Perry Mason, Mr Warner Oland's Charlie Chan and Mr William Powell's suave suede impersonations in such agile and amusing films as *The Thin Man*, revived this week at the Royal Court Cinema, and *Star of Midnight*. Of course, the cinema cannot go in for the really dry, donnish game; the type of detection which depends on a Bradshaw's timetable has to be excluded, for a cinema audience cannot be expected to carry a series of mathematical clues in mind. Detection is almost necessarily the weakest part of a detective film; what we do get in the Perry Mason films is a more vivid sense of life than in most detective stories, the quality we get in some of Mr David Frome's novels, in all Mr Dashiell Hammett's, and in a few of the early works of Miss Sayers.

Perry Mason is my favourite film detective; he is curiously little known, perhaps because his films, as 'second features', are usually not shown in the Press. *The Case of the Lucky Legs* is an admirable film, but it is thrown in as makeweight at the Regal to the appalling film, *I Give You My Heart*. Perry Mason is a hard-drinking and not very scrupulous lawyer. He owes something to the character established by Mr William Powell:

there is some rather facetious badinage with a woman assistant, but he is, I think, a more genuine creation. Mr Powell is a little too immaculate, his wit is too well turned just as his clothes are too well made, he drinks hard but only at the best bars; he is rather like an advertisment of a man-about-town in *Esquire*, he shares some of the irritating day-dream quality of Lord Peter Whimsey. I find the cadaverous, not very well-dressed Perry Mason more real in his seedy straw hat with his straggly moustache; one does not find him only in the best bars; he is by no means irresistible to women; his background is the hiss of soda rather than the clink of ice. He is far more likely on the face of it to be a successful detective than Mr Powell's character because he belongs to the same class as his criminals. Often, indeed, as in his latest case, they are his clients. For I can never really believe that a good detective will be found in the Social Register or that Lord Peter Whimsey would be capable of detecting anything more criminal than a theft by a kleptomaniac duchess. To those who do not yet know Perry Mason I recommend *The Case of the Lucky Legs* as good Mason if not good detection, better, I think, than *The Case of the Curious Bride*.

Charlie Chan does a good deal more honest detection with finger-prints than Mason, and his break-up of a big dope-smuggling gang in Shanghai is a well-made, if conventional piece of genuine Chan. A much more desirable person, of course, this slow, astute Chinaman with his rather lovable turns of broken English than the shady lawyer. But the lawyer is better fun.

The Amateur Gentleman too is a kind of detective story set in Regency days. An innkeeper's son (Mr Douglas Fairbanks, Jun.) dresses up as a gentleman and mixes in Society in order to find the aristocratic thief for whose crime his innocent father is condemned to hang. There is a superbly unconvincing boxing match with bare fists before the Regent, and the film is very prettily dressed. Miss Clemence Dane has done a very workmanlike job with the dialogue which is never disagreeably mannered, but nobody can do much with Mr Jeffery Fasnol's romantic vision. I prefer myself Perry Mason's amusing chase in and out of bars and aeroplanes and the bridal suit of a seedy and immoral little country hotel.

The Spectator (31 January 1936)

The Case of the Lucky Legs (USA, Warner, 1936) Dir.: Archie Mayo. Cast: Warren William, Patricia Ellis, Genevieve Tobin, Allen Jenkins, Lyle Talbot, Baron Maclane.

Charlie Chan in Shanghai (USA, Twentieth-Century Fox, 1935) Dir.: James Tinling. Cast: Warner Oland, Irene Harvey.

The Amateur Gentleman (GB, Criterion, 1936) Dir.: Thornton Freeland. Cast: Douglas Fairbanks, Jr, Elissa Landi, Gordon Harker, Basil Sydney, Hugh Williams, Irene Browne, Margaret Lockwood, Coral Browne.

Dr Socrates · The Man Who Broke the Bank at Monte Carlo · The Imperfect Lady

There are occasions when I envy dramatic critics; Mr Agate after a bad week can fill up a column with what somebody else once said about Rachel. But Garbo, the screen's only classic, is alive, and frankly there is no film this week worth writing more than a few lines on. *Dr Socrates* is a third-rate gangster film, *The Man Who Broke the Bank at Monte Carlo* is a mildly agreeable comedy marred by the intrusion of White Russians into the plot (I can never appreciate the pathos of princes who have become taxi-drivers and drink coffee essence instead of champagne; unlike other taxi-drivers they have *had* their champagne), and *The Imperfect Lady*, Miss Cicely Courtneidge's first American film, is to be avoided at any cost.

Miss Courtneidge's performances in revue I remember enjoying with some reluctance fifteen years ago: it was in the theatre that she learnt to fling her odd facial contortions to the back of the gallery, and no film director has proved himself capable of softening the exaggerations she learnt then. Her last English film, the deplorable *Me and Marlborough*, revealed that Miss Courtneidge, like so many comedians, was going the Pagliacci way; the smile in future would not, alas, hide the tear. Pathos has nearly ruined Mr Chaplin, who is an artist of genius; what it has done for Miss Courtneidge is rather horrible to watch. Needless to say, too, that before the end of *The Imperfect Lady*

Miss Courtneidge is given an opportunity to dress up as a young soldier and sing a patriotic song. Gallantry is out of place in a review, but I will content myself with suggesting that Miss Courtneidge's career has been a longer one than Miss Jessie Matthews's and that male impersonation is really only permissible to the young.

Mr Ronald Colman, who breaks the bank on behalf of his fellow White Russians and whom the directors of the casino feel it necessary to lure back to the tables by any means and at any cost for the sake of the advertisment, is an actor of the opposite type. He is an excellent director's dummy. He has no personality of his own, only an appearance, and for that reason he is an almost perfect actor for the fictional screen. There was a time when Russian directors made a great point of using non-professional material and Mr Colman may be said to have all the merit of the moujik and this advantage as well: that he can obey with a rather more lively intelligence.

I say the almost perfect actor because there is still room in the cinema for the actor of genius, for the great personality, for Garbo as well as for Joan Crawford. I sometimes think that Mr Paul Muni, the 'star' of *Dr Socrates*, is of this rank. As with Garbo, you get an impression of immense force in reserve, an unexpressed passion of life. It is a quality of character rather than of acting. Miss Courtneidge acts, acts all the time; it is as tiring to watch her as to watch the defeated boat-race crew strain raggedly after Cambridge up the Thames. Neither Garbo nor Muni acts in this sense; they exist vividly and without apparent effort. This is the romantic style of genius, one feels, not the infinite capacity for taking pains, but a luck, a gift, a passion they were born with. *Dr Socrates* is not one of Muni's successful films; it is not another *I am a Fugitive* (that performance of agonizing power he has never quite repeated), nor even a *Black Fury*, but a trivial themeless film about a small-town doctor who, by persuading them that their leader has typhoid, puts a band of gangsters out of action, but there were too many beds, too many doped gangsters, it was only funny. But even in this poor film Muni establishes a background:

the accident and death which shook his nerve and ruined his career. That is what a director's dummy cannot do: he exists in the action and not outside it; though the chief problem for the film-writer, just as much as for the novelist, must always be to represent 'the dark backward and abysm of time'.

The Spectator (7 February 1936)

Dr Socrates (USA, Warner, 1935) Dir.: William Dieterle. Cast: Paul Muni, Ann Dvorak, Barton Maclane, John Eldridge, Henry O'Neill, Mayo Methot, Samuel S. Hinds.

The Man Who Broke the Bank at Monte Carlo (USA, Twentieth-Century Fox, 1935) Dir.: Stephen Roberts. Cast: Ronald Colman, Joan Bennett, Colin Clive, Nigel Bruce.

The Imperfect Lady (USA, MGM, 1935) Dir.: Tim Whelan. Cast: Cicely Courtneidge, Frank Morgan, Heather Angel, Henry Stephenson. (US title: *The Perfect Gentleman*)

Modern Times

I am too much an admirer of Mr Chaplin to believe that the most important thing about his new film is that for a few minutes we are allowed to hear his agreeable and rather husky voice in a song. The little man has at last definitely entered the contemporary scene; there has always before been a hint of 'period' about his courage and misfortunes; he carried about with him more than the mere custard-pie of Karno's days, its manners, its curious clothes, its sense of pathos and its dated poverty. There were occasions, in his encounters with blind flower-girls or his adventures in mean streets or in the odd little pitch-pine mission halls where he carried round the bag or preached in pantomime on a subject so near to his own experience as the tale of David and Goliath, when he seemed to go back almost as far as Dickens. The change is evident in his choice of heroine: fair and featureless with the smudged effect of an amateur water-colour which has run, they never appeared again in leading parts, for they were quite characterless. But Miss Paulette Goddard, dark, grimy, with her amusing urban and plebeian face, is a promise that the little man will no longer linger at the edge of mawkish situation, the unfair pathos of the blind girl and the orphan child. One feels about her as Hyacinth felt about Millicent in *The Princess Casamassima*: 'she laughed with her laugh of the people, and if you hit her hard enough would cry with their tears'. For the first time the little man does not go off alone, flaunting his cane and battered bowler along the endless road out of the screen. He goes in company looking for what may turn up.

What *had* turned up was first a job in a huge factory twisting screws tighter as little pieces of nameless machinery passed him on a moving belt, under the televised eye of the manager, an eye that followed him even into the lavatory where he snatched an illicit smoke. The experiment of an automatic feeding machine, which will enable a man to be fed while he works, drives him crazy (the running amok of this machine, with its hygenic mouth-wiper, at the moment when it has reached the Indian corn course, is horrifyingly funny; it is the best scene, I think, that Mr Chaplin has ever invented). When he leaves hospital he is arrested as a Communist leader (he has picked up a red street flag which has fallen off a lorry) and released again after foiling a prison hold-up. Unemployment and prison punctuate his life, starvation and lucky breaks, and somewhere in its course he attaches to himself the other piece of human refuse.

The Marxists, I suppose, will claim this as *their* film, but it is a good deal less and a good deal more than Socialist in intention. No real political passion has gone to it: the police batter the little man at one moment and feed him with buns the next: and there is no warm maternal optimism, in the Mitchison manner, about the character of the workers: when the police are brutes, the men are cowards; the little man is always left in the lurch. Nor do we find him wondering 'what a Socialist man should do', but dreaming of a steady job and the most bourgeois home. Mr Chaplin, whatever his political convictions may be, is an artist and not a propagandist. He doesn't try to explain, but presents with vivid fantasy what seem to him a crazy comic tragic world without a plan, but his sketch of the inhuman factory does not lead us to suppose that his little man would be more at home at Dneipostroi. He presents, he doesn't offer political solutions.

The little man politely giving up his seat to the girl in the crowded Black Maria: the little man when the dinner-bell sounds tenderly sticking a spray of celery into the mouth of the old mechanic whose head has been caught between the cog-wheels; the little man littering the path of the pursuing detectives with overturned chairs to save his girl; Mr Chaplin has, like Conrad, 'a few simple ideas'; they could be expressed in much the same phrases: courage, loyalty, labour: against the same nihilistic background of purposeless suffering. 'Mistah Kurtz – he dead.' These ideas are not enough for a reformer, but they have proved amply sufficient for an artist.

The Spectator (14 February 1936)

Modern Times (USA, Charles Chaplin, 1935) Dir.: Charles Chaplin. Cast: Charles Chaplin, Paulette Goddard, Henry Bergman, Chester Conklin, Tiny Sandford.

I Dream Too Much · Anything Goes · Faust · Hohe Schule · Captain Blood

Here are a pack of films to choose from; but I confess that though one or two of them offer a few moments of meagre entertainment, there is not one I would pay money to see.

I Dream Too Much irritated me the most because it disappointed me the most. About fifteen years ago the composer, Mr Jerome Kern, enjoyed the same popularity as Mr Cole Porter does today. Were the tunes of *The Cabaret Girl*, which once seemed so richly, sensually sentimental, as pompous and middle-aged as these numbers? There is a tiresome pseudo-serious air of domestic drama (a great singer's love-life) about this film that always seems to surround Metropolitan Opera singers when they go to Hollywood. *I Dream Too Much* might really have been written for Miss Grace Moore – a pity, because Miss Lily Pons has a less ponderous personality. As it is, a performing seal supplies the only light, I was about to say the only human, touches in this worthy picture of gay (oh, tiresomely, trillingly gay) abandon in

Montparnasse attics followed by marital squabbles in luxurious reception-rooms. Nor have American directors yet learnt how ugly the close-up of a woman singing must invariably be; we are treated to many dreadful shots of a cavernous mouth projecting high notes like shells from a trench mortar.

Anything Goes was very nearly as disappointing, for I had enjoyed the London stage version and Mr Cole Porter's music. Mr Charlie Ruggles's performance as Public Enemy No. 13 who escapes in an Atlantic liner from America, disguised as a clergyman, is a very faded affair after Mr Sydney Howard's. Mr Bing Crosby's moony methods, too, slow up a picture which should rattle quite as fast as a sub-machine gun. There are several new and undistinguished songs, the lovely lush sentimentality of 'All Through the Night' is missing, and a really dreadful woman singer murders the Audenesque charm of 'You're the Top'.

Then there's *Faust* at the Academy. I think this is the worst colour film I have ever seen. The characters, with their faces out of focus, move with slow primeval gestures through a thick brown fog – the scarlet cap of Mephistopheles occasionally gleaming out of the obscurity with the effect of a traffic-signal. They weave their arms in a curious shorthand which I suppose opera-goers understand, beating their breasts, dragging their feet (this at any rate is understandable) through the Spectra-colour gloom.

In the same programme is *Hohe Schule*, a silly Austrian film about a count who does High School riding on the variety stage wearing a little black mask: he has been cashiered from the Army during the war for duelling (his secret motive was quite unbearably high-minded) and he falls in love with the sister of the man he has killed. I have a fondness for Herr Rudolf Forster's middle-aged and unresilient charm, his heavy period moustaches, his well-bred voice, but breeding in this film has gone beserk, and there is something indescribably absurd about the Count's riding act, his shiny boots, his immense moustaches and rigid back and overpowering air of disguised nobility, as his horse dances delicately on hoof-tip round and round and round the stage.

That seems to leave *Captain Blood* unnaccounted for, and really I enjoyed *Captain Blood* the most. After three film versions everyone must know Mr Sabatini's romantic tale of Protestant slaves and chaste pirates, wicked West India governors, bad King James and good King William. Here is a fine spirited mix-up with clothes and wigs which sometimes hark back to the sixteenth century and sometimes forward to the period of Wolfe. One is hardly surprised, therefore, by the magnificently wrong characterization of dull grim virtuous James as a wicked witty debonair eighteenth-century aristocrat, and one is quite prepared for the culminating moment when the Union Jack breaks proudly, anachronously, forth at Peter Blood's masthead.

The Spectator (21 February 1936)

I Dream Too Much (USA, RKO, 1935) Dir.: John Cromwell. Cast: Lily Pons, Henry Fonda, Eric Blore, Osgood Perkins, Lucille Ball, Mischa Auer.

Anything Goes (USA, Paramount, 1935) Dir.: Lewis Milestone. Cast: Bing Crosby, Ethel Merman, Ida Lupino, Charles Ruggles, Chill Wills, Arthur Treacher.

Faust (GB, 1935) Dir.: A. E. C. Hopkins. Cast: Anne Ziegler, Webster Booth, Dennis Hoey.

Hohe Schule (Austria/Germany, ABC-Film/Tobis Sascha, 1934) Dir.: Erich Engel. Cast: Rudolf Forster, Angela Salloker.

Captain Blood (USA, Warner, 1935) Dir.: Michael Curtiz. Cast: Errol Flynn, Olivia de Havilland, Basil Rathbone, Lionel Atwill, Guy Kibbee, Henry Stephenson, Donald Meek.

Things to Come · Bonne Chance

'I've been timid, O'Man. I've been holding myself in. I haven't done myself justice. I've kept down the simmering, seething, teeming ideas . . .' The voice of Mr Polly's friend Parsons came irresistibly to my mind as the vast expensive Korda-Wells film of the future ground noisily on its way, as I watched the giant aeroplanes, the streamlined tanks, the bright complex, meaningless machinery of Mr Wells's riotous fancy. The reformed clothes, the odd rather Grecian dresses with square shoulders, and pouter-pigeon breasts, this whole vision of a world peopled by beautiful idealistic scientists would certainly have appealed to the rapturous literary provincial Parsons, the inventor of the

Port Burdock school of window-dressing. Parsons too was an idealist.

Nevertheless, a third of this film is magnificent. No one but the author of *War in the Air* could have created so vividly, with such horribly convincing detail, the surprise air raid with which the great war of 1940 opens: the lorry with loudspeakers in Piccadilly Circus urging the crowd to go quietly home and close all windows and block all apertures against gas, the emergency distribution of a few inadequate masks, the cohort of black planes driving over the white southern cliffs, the crowd milling in subways, the dreadful death cries from the London bus, the faceless man in evening dress dead in the taxi. But from this point the film steadily deteriorates, though the world's reversion to barabarism, the plague, the small parochial dictator who carries on twenty years later the same war with the same slogans against his parish neighbour, like a medieval Della Scala, has the acuteness and authenticity of a lesson properly drawn from history. It is with the intrusion of Mr Wells's 'Great Conspiracy', an organization of airmen working together from a base in Basra to clean up the world, that the film begins to lose all its interest in the clouds of Mr Wells's uncontrolled fancies, vague, optimistic, childlike. 'I am Wings over the World,' the strange airman persistently and irritatingly replies to the robber leader's question, 'Who are you?' As Mr Polly remarked when he saw Parsons's window-dressing, 'The High Egrugious is fairly On.'

The unreligious mind when it sets about designing a heaven for itself is apt to be trivial, portentous, sentimental. Out of the simmering, seething, teeming ideas of Mr Wells there emerges, after the reformed dresses, the underground city, the new machinery, the classless society, the television, the tiny wireless sets worn on the wrist, the endless little mechanical toys, the realization that something after all is still missing. It never ceases to come as a shock to a mind like Mr Wells's that a man can still be unhappy when he has leisure, food, comfort, and the best modern dynamos. But it comes as even more of a shock to his audience that Mr Wells can think of no less old-fashioned a way of appeasing this sense of dissatisfaction than by shooting two of his characters at the moon

('The best of life' – nobody in this film speaks less bookishly than that – 'lies nearest to the edge of death'), and the film closes with a sky of stars and some hollow optimistic phrase about the infinite spaces and the endlessness of man's future progress. It is in such smug and sentimental terms that the characters in this film always speak. Only Mr Polly, I think, could find the right words to describe their embarrassing eloquence. 'Sesquippledan,' one can almost hear him saying, 'sesquippledan verboojuice. Eloquent rapsodooce.'

When the noise and the shouting has subsided it may be possible to suggest that M. Sacha Guitry's *Bonne Chance* is worth a dozen *Things to Come*, whether you consider it as cinema, as entertainment or even as social criticism. It is a charming silly film in the Clair genre, a lyrical absurdity. It reminds one again that only the cinema and music among the arts have been able to convey this sense of poignant happiness, the quickness and lightness and transience of a sensation you cannot call by any name so heavy as joy: 'the phoenix hour': the nearest to a Utopia poor mankind is ever likely to get.

The Spectator (28 February 1936)

Things to Come (GB, London Films, 1936) Dir.: William Cameron Menzies. Cast: Raymond Massey, Ralph Richardson, Cedric Hardwicke, Sophie Stewart, Ann Todd.

Bonne Chance (France, Maurice Lehmann/Fernand Rivers, 1935) Dir.: Sacha Guitry. Cast: Sacha Guitry, Jacqueline Delubac, Robert Darthez.

Rose of the Rancho · Jack of All Trades · The 'Frisco Kid · Public Nuisance Number One

Miss Gladys Swarthout is the latest singer from the Metropolitan Opera House to 'go movie' and to my mind, which cares little for music, the most agreeable. *Rose of the Rancho* is a very long way indeed from being a good film, but at least it is without the bogus seriousness, the artiness, the pomposity of Miss Grace Moore's *prima donna*, no blithe Dôme or wistful Rotonde, no first appearance in New York threatened by unhappy Romance. It is just a commonplace Western (the scene is actually New Mexico) with galloping horses and last-minute rescues and masked riders and a secret Federal agent who falls in love with the bandit. One could do very happily without the music altogether, for Miss Swarthout is quite as attractive as any other star dummy, whether she is wearing a mantilla as Queen of Santa Something *festa*, or, as the mysterious leader of the patriotic brigands, black riding-breeches. And one could do very happily, too, without Mr John Boles. I find Mr Boles, his air of confident carnality, the lick of black shiny hair across the plump white waste of face, peculiarly unsympathetic; and never more so than in this film as he directs his lick, his large assured eyes, towards Miss Swarthout and croons:

I call you a gift from the angels,
For I feel in my heart you're divine.

That is about the standard of the lush last-century melodies which interrupt rather oddly the gunshots, the beating hoofs, the traditional American dialogue that one begins after a while to welcome rather wearily like very old friends whose conversations one has exhausted – 'Siddown won't you – Thenks.' 'A wise guy, huh?'

Mr Hulbert is another actor for whom I feel a perhaps unfair repugnance. The beginning of *Jack of All Trades*, however, shows him at his best, as he gate-crashes into a job with a big financial house by inventing on the spur of the moment a *plan*, the magic contemporary word. No banker dares to confess that he has heard of the Plan for the first time, and the scene at the board meeting, when Mr Hulbert, asked to explain it in connection with Rationalization (another magic word he doesn't know the meaning of), carries the directors with him by reciting Henry V's speech before Agincourt, is excellent and pointed fooling. Afterwards the film degenerates into nothing but the jutting jaw and the permanent grin, the same memory that one takes away from all Mr Hulbert's films, a nightmare memory, for what could be more horrifying than a jaw and a grin moving through restaurants and along streets, in and out of offices, down subways, an awful eternal disembodied Cheeriness?

I wish there existed an organization with the means to anthologize the excellent sequences that can often be found in the worst films and save them from oblivion. Mr Hulbert's scene at the board meeting might find a place, and the fight in *'Frisco Kid*, shown last week at the Regal, would certainly deserve to be included. *'Frisco Kid* was a stale sentimental worthless film with the same kind of tough, period subject, without the style, as *Barbary Coast*, but the fight between Mr James Cagney and a one-armed sailor with a hook was the most brutal and convincing I can remember seeing on the screen. Another sequence well worth saving occurred in a silly English musical farce shown last week at the Plaza, *Public Nuisance Number One*: the singing by Miss Frances Day of a delightful skit on a Victorian ballad: 'I had a dog. It got lost in a fog' (it thoroughly puzzled an audience which took the canine sentiment quite seriously). Admirably directed, admirably acted, this sequence was worth sitting through all the long weary film to see. It was even worth bearing with patience Mr Riscoe's contorted music-hall face which thrust every joke down one's gullet with the relentless energy of the machine that corks the bottles in a lemonade factory. Miss Frances Day, with her ashen hair, her humorous elongated face, her lovely witty and malicious eyes, given a Capra to direct her or a Guitry to write for her, would rival in one's affections Miss Claudette Colbert or Mlle Jacqueline Delubac.

The Spectator (6 March 1936)

Rose of the Rancho (USA, Paramount, 1936) Dir.: Marion Gering. Cast: Gladys Swarthout, John Boles, Charles Bickford, H. B. Warner.

Jack of All Trades (GB, Gainsborough, 1936) Dir.: Robert Stevenson. Cast: Jack Hulbert; Betty Astell, Robertson Hare, Gina Malo. (US title: *The Two of Us*)

The 'Frisco Kid (USA, Warner, 1935) Dir.: Lloyd Bacon. Cast: James Cagney, Margaret Lindsay, Ricardo Cortez, Lili Damita, Donald Woods, Barton Maclane.

Public Nuisance Number One (GB, Cecil Films, 1936) Dir.: Marcel Varnel. Cast: Frances Day, Arthur Riscoe.

Crime et Châtiment · Veille d'armes

I suppose it may be considered a laudable ambition to try to translate Dostoievsky's novels into film terms, but *Crime et Châtiment*, just as much as *The Brothers Karamazov* a year or two ago, suggests that such an attempt is almost bound to fail. It is the superficial violence of these novels which attracts the film director. 'Here,' one can imagine him arguing, 'are tales of murder. The cinema has always been successful at conveying violence, and what a remarkable film will be the result when our murderer is a really classic one.' I have long suspected that a high-class murder is the simple artistic ideal of most film directors, from Mr Hitchcock upwards.

And the murder, of course, *is* admirable: the director and the cameraman and the scenario-writer do their usual work to admiration. They are remarkably faithful, too, to the original murder, even to the tinny sound of the old money-lender's bell, to Raskolnikov's decayed, absurd and mournful 'topper'. For this is a more than usually intelligent film (once granted the initial mistake), and what of the novel's theme *can* be converted into visual terms has been converted. Raskolnikov's unbalanced pride is well suggested: in the mockery of a hat, in his crazy isolation as he makes his way through the friendly evening crowds to the scene of his crime; and of his sensitive conscience you can have no doubt watching M. Pierre Blanchar's hollow handsome haunted features.

But after all there is more to Dostoievsky's story than a case of conscience; Raskolnikov is a more subtle figure than Eugene Aram and a more general one. The director has not met his first difficulty: the fact that the book is written from inside Raskolnikov's brain. M. Chenal's camera takes its stand on the outside, the world's side. It would have been far better to have dropped the realistic approach altogether, to have battered the real theme into us with soliloquies, with aerial voices, with dream imagery, with every kind of superrealist trick. There would be no place in such a film, of course, for anything but the barest bones of the objective plot, though he has left a few untidy and bewildering pieces behind. And what is more unsatisfactory still, he has treated the character of Sonia with such curtness and false delicacy that an audience unacquainted with the book will find it very hard to understand her presence at all.

'Do not despise life', and again 'I look upon you as one of those men who, with a smile, would permit their executioners to tear their bowels out, provided they had found their fetish.' The magistrate Porphyrius thus stated the theme of the book, when he suggested to Raskolnikov that by confessing he would renounce his crazy egoistic Napoleonic fetish, which had proved in the act of murder so bestial, and discover 'the ordinary current of life'. Raskolnikov's worship of the prostitute, Sonia, his patient endurance of the Siberian prison, were not meant to be a spectacular atonement for his crime but a private means of one day attaining the ordinary, the humble, the communal happiness. He had no chance of freedom: proofs of his guilt were in Porphyrius's possession, but in the film the magistrate has no proofs; he presents him with a melodramatic choice between confession and liberty. M. Harry Baur's Porphyrius is a lovely performance, the finest I have seen in the cinema this year, with his tortoise movements, his streak of cruelty, his terrible good humour; it is a pity that the drama should have been narrowed down to one murderer's guilty conscience.

This narrowing, of course, is the usual commercial process. When you have narrowed your theme sufficiently you have obtained a fiction which has no disturbing features, the pure commercial article like that ably served at Studio One. A French naval captain's wife, hidden in her lover's cabin during a battle, is the sole surviving witness of the enemy signals, the only witness who can clear her husband from the charge of losing his ship by negligence. A rather less usual case of conscience this, and the theme narrowed to the safe absurd commercial limit.

The Spectator (13 March 1936)

Crime et Châtiment (France, Compagnie Générale de Production Cinématographique, 1936) Dir.: Pierre Chenal. Cast: Pierre Blanchar, Harry Baur, Marcelle Geniat, Madeleine Ozeray.

Veille d'Armes (France, SEDIF, 1935) Dir.: Marcel L'Herbier. Cast: Annabella, Victor Francen.

THE MILKY WAY · STRIKE ME PINK · NIGHT MAIL · CRIME AND PUNISHMENT

The gag-makers have been very well employed on the latest Harold Lloyd film. The great Lloyd factory has never constructed a better picture, and one is more amazed than ever at the good fortune of this youngish man whose chief talent is not to act at all, to do nothing, to serve as a blank wall for other people to scrawl their ideas on. He is a very amiable blank, he doesn't mind others acting, and Mr Adolphe Menjou in *The Milky Way* acts with the toughness and energy he showed in *The Front Page*. Mr Menjou in this kind of part is unbeatable, the part of a crooked boxing manager who nurses, by means of phoney fights, the publicity value of Lloyd – 'the fighting milkman' – in order to collect the big money when he matches him against his other protégé, the world champion. It is odd, as one watches Mr Menjou stride noisily and victoriously through this picture, ranting, raving, wheedling, double-crossing, to remember his first 'break' when Mr Chaplin starred him as a suave elegant vicious 'man of the world' in *Woman of Paris* and condemned him to years of miscasting. Mr Menjou runs away with the film: he doesn't need gags: he doesn't need to smuggle a foal into a taxi and disguise its neighs with his own: he doesn't need to boomerang bowler-hats. These gags are for the star, and so with the gag-makers at the top of their form and Mr Menjou at the top of his, we have the best 'Harold Lloyd' to date.

Mr Eddie Cantor is another matter altogether. He too has a fine team of gag-men behind him (one pictures these anonymous creatures as belonging to the same intellectual genre as the inventors of practical jokes which fill the windows of the Holborn shops at Christmas-time: the buns that squeak, the flies sculptured with Oriental nicety on real lumps of sugar, the rubber plate-lifters). But Mr Cantor does not depend entirely on his gags; he is an actor of distinction with his dim plaintive voice, his revolving eyes, his reckless gleam. He tries hard to raise himself to the Chaplin level, to represent a whole class, a philosophy, but he will never be quite good enough for that, his idea of the *victorious* little man is too patently optimistic and untrue. Nevertheless, one will have to wait a very long time for any film funnier than this one. Mr Cantor is appointed, after taking a correspondence course in character development ('Are you a Man or a Mouse?'), to the management of an amusement park. His predecessors have been put on the spot by gangsters who wish to install crooked betting-machines, and the scene between Mr Cantor and the gunman who has taken the same correspondence course but has stopped at an earlier chapter is superb.

Night Mail, directed by Mr Basil Wright and Mr Harry Watt for the GPO Film Unit, is one of the best films to be seen in London. It isn't a complete success; the opening sequences seem to lack design – and clarity (the pictures taken from the air are of poor quality and the eye doesn't immediately recognize them for what they are). But the final sequences as the train drives at dawn through the northern moors, the sheep-dog racing the train and the rabbits scurrying to cover, set to the simple visual verse of Mr Auden, are extraordinarily exciting. This use of verse has been rather obtusely criticized, notably by Miss Lejeune, whose comments show an amazing lack of cinema *ear*. To criticize Mr Auden's words (timed selective commentary made to match the images on the screen) as if they were lyric poetry is absurd.

The American *Crime and Punishment*, in spite of the fine acting of Mr Peter Lorre, is a dreadful contrast to the French. In the dark intense French picture there was at least something of Dostoievsky's religious and unhappy mind. This gleaming lunch-bar-chromium version – which opens at the University with Raskolnikov receiving his degree and listening to the Vice-Chancellor's earnest American abstractions about Youth and Alma Mater and the Future – is vulgar as only the great New

World can be vulgar, with the vulgarity of the completely unreligious, of sentimental idealism, of pitch-pine ethics, with the hollow optimism about human nature, of a salesman who has never failed to sell his canned beans.

The Spectator (20 March 1936)

The Milky Way (USA, Paramount, 1936) Dir.: Leo McCarey. Cast: Harold Lloyd, Adolphe Menjou, Verree Teasdale, Helen Mack, Dorothy Wilson, William Gargan, Lionel Stander.

Strike Me Pink (USA, Samuel Goldwyn, 1935) Dir.: Norman Taurog. Cast: Eddie Cantor, Ethel Merman, Sally Eilers, William Frawley, Parkyakarkus.

Night Mail (GB, GPO Film Unit, 1936) Directors: Basil Wright, Harry Watt.

Crime and Punishment (USA, Columbia, 1936) Dir.: Josef Von Sternberg. Cast: Peter Lorre, Edward Arnold, Marian Marsh, Mrs Patrick Campbell, Tala Birell.

Rhodes of Africa · October

Sober, worthy, humourless, *Rhodes of Africa* unrolls its eleven well-bred reels with all the technical advantages of 1936. It is a good film, judged by the ordinary standard. well photographed, well directed, well acted, particularly by Mr Oscar Homolka as Kruger, with some fine shots of African scenery. It is the kind of respectable picture (there was another some years ago of Livingstone) which reminds one a little of a biography by a modern Liberal: someone kindlier, more trustworthy, infinitely more charitable but not less dull than Lord Morely, with the anarchistic point of view of a man who never makes a moral condemnation. *October*, another historical picture made as long ago as 1928 by Eisenstein, is a curious contrast, restless, excited, crackling with venom: this is certainly not fair, certainly not Liberal (the sub-titles spit out 'Mensheviks' as one might exclaim 'Rabbits!' whenever these toothy well-meaning politicians in pince-nez pass across the screen).

Nobody concerned with the English film, neither its German director, Mr Berthold Viertel, nor its American star, Mr Walter Huston, has any passionate conviction whether for or against Rhodes and his work in Africa. Miss Peggy Ashcroft as a most unlikely woman novelist – one imagines she is intended for Olive Schreiner – rebukes Rhodes for his treatment of the Matabele in her usual gentle, carefully enunciated Shakespearian tones, flickering her young romantic Juliet lashes at stated intervals with the effect of too much punctuation; but the emphasis otherwise is all on the good side of human nature; Barney Barnato, Kruger, Jameson, Rhodes himself, the King of the Matabele – there is something to be said, that is the impression, for all of them; the kindly optimistic Liberal temperament does not recognize the Fall of Man. After ten days I can remember very little of this film but a sense of gentle titillation, of being scratched agreeably in the right spot.

But the talkies have come, and stereoscopy and colour no doubt will come, without destroying the vivid memories of *October*: Kerensky hounded from the capital by a camera which never fails to record with merciless caricature the gleam of gaiters, the Napoleonic gesture, the neurotic hands, the thin frightened defiant egotistical face, the braces hanging over the chandelier in the Tsar's bedroom; the macabre and comic Battalion of Death, large ungainly women in uniforms as shapeless as policewomen's, adjusting their stockings and brassires as they sprawl across the billiard-tables in the Palace, or wandering hand in hand, like affectionate hippopotami, through the great tank-like rooms; the huge crowds fleeing, in the July days, before Kerensky's machine-guns; the women in lace petticoats and picture hats stabbing out the eyes of the young agitator with their parasols; the scene, which recalls the Odessa steps sequence in *The Cruiser Potemkin*, when the bridges are raised between the workers' quarters and the city, and the ancient unhorsed cab is balanced for a while high above the river before it rushes down the long perpendicular slide.

To me the most vivid impression of revolution (and one which only a participant would have thought of presenting) was the committee-room door swinging continually open, the people pushing in and out, the telephone bells ringing, the crowded secretarial rooms, the shouting to make yourself heard, the little rabbitty scared people getting up and proposing resolutions. Compared with *Mother, October* is almost comedy; Kerensky inspecting the Tsar's footmen, weeping among the sofa cushions, playing with the royal decanters, is a figure for laughter; the film has something of that air of happiness Trotsky described in his history: 'the colossal task, the pride in success, the joyful failing of the heart at the thought of the morrow which is to be still more beautiful than today'. I suppose somebody once felt that about Rhodes too, about his Cape to Cairo ambition, the amalgamation of diamond-mines; a good film might have been made about it all in those days; now as an Empire we are too old, the pride isn't there, the heart seems to have failed once too often.

The Spectator (27 March 1936)

Rhodes of Africa (GB, Gaumont British, 1936) Dir.: Berthold Viertel. Cast: Walter Huston, Peggy Ashcroft, Oscar Homolka, Basil Sydney, Bernard Lee, Lewis Casson. (US title: *Rhodes*)

October (USSR, Sovkino, 1928) Dir.: Sergei Eisenstein. Cast: Nikandrov, Vladimir Popov, Boris Livanov, soldiers of the Red Army, sailors of the Red Navy, citizens of Leningrad. (aka: *Ten Days that Shook the World*)

Merlusse · The Day of the Great Adventure · Desire

French schoolboys supervised in their small asphalt yard, in their cold stone dining-hall, in their dormitory where a master sleeps in a square muslin tent: Nordic schoolboys (strictly speaking Polish, but their blond hair, their simple handsome brutish faces are exactly those of German boys) washing their shoulders in the snow, pillow-fighting in a mountain hut, skiing alone across the wastes. The contrast is extreme, and I cannot help preferring the French.

Merlusse, directed by Marcel Pagnol, with a cast of which only the principal player has appeared on the screen before, is a slight sentimental tale of a one-eyed master feared by the boys and distrusted by his colleagues, who on Christmas-night finds a way to the affections of the twenty boys left by their parents at the school. We are told that it is a true story of the Marseille Lycée where Pagnol was once a master and where the scenes are taken. But that matters less than the fine acting of Henri Poupon as Merlusse ('Codfish'), with his terrible dead twisted eye, his scrubby beard, his starved paternity, and his secret terror of the boys he has to control. Pagnol's direction has a simpleness, a directness that are admirable.

As for the children, how much more agreeable and varied they are, how much less aggressively healthy and priggish and normal than the Boy Scouts who in the Polish film hunt down a gang of cocaine-smugglers in the Tatra Mountains. These scrubby, rather miserable, and not too clean children, smoking illicitly round the corner of the asphalt yard, boastful over first love-letters, not above getting somebody else to leave a drawing-pin on the master's chair, overgrown louts and curly Fauntleroys, a nigger, an Asiatic, a Jew, these might well include in their number a Rimbaud, a Cézanne; but for the Boy Scouts with their communal song, their unnaturally developed sense of honour, their portrait of Lord Baden-Powell, their parade at evening to salute with raised arms the Flag, the best that any of these can become, one feels is a Hitler – or not even a Hitler, but a Hitler's lieutenant to be purged on some thirtieth of June. This film has been awarded medals at Venice and Moscow. Stalin's youth and Mussolini's youth both found it, I suppose, inspiring, but in this country, happy thought, it is still possible to find their well-drilled morality a little absurd. Particularly delightful to the comic sense is the moment when three Scouts, who for the most honourable and civic reasons have found it necessary to violate their Scout oaths, surrender their whistles to the Scout Captain. Their whistles are accepted, but a telegram from Warsaw at the last moment directs the Captain to return them. Yes, it is possible for us to laugh, but not with too great an assurance; it is these and not the French, who are nearer to the English public-school spirit, and it is an Englishman's portrait, not Pilsudski's or Hitler's, which hangs on the wall.

Desire – ridiculous and misleading title – is the best film in which Miss Marlene Dietrich has appeared since she left Germany, and the most amusing new film to be seen in London this week. Produced, though not directed, by Lubitsch, this comedy of an international jewel thief who smuggles her stolen pearls across the French frontier in the pocket of an American 'hick' on a holiday (one of Mr Gary Cooper's best performances), and who while she tries to retrieve them falls in love with the hick, has all the absurd delicious trimmings one expects in a Lubitsch film. Best of all is the sinister old female crook who remarks, 'If I *were* your grandmother, you'd offer me some brandy.' Miss Dietrich is allowed to act in this film, even to sing, and what memories of the cheap alluring cabaret figure, the tilted top hat, that husky voice recalls. But since those days Miss Dietrich has been so tidied, groomed, perfected that one simply cannot believe that she exists at all – though there are moments in *this* film when Absolute Beauty very nearly wavers into the relative, the human, the desirable.

The Spectator (3 April 1936)

Merlusse (France, Films Marcel Pagnol, 1935) Dir.: Marcel Pagnol. Cast: Henri Poupon.
The Day of the Great Adventure (Poland, Panta-Film, 1935) Dir.: Josef Lejtes.
Desire (USA, Paramount, 1936) Dir.: Frank Borzage. Cast: Marlene Dietrich, Gary Cooper, John Halliday, William Frawley, Akim Tamiroff, Alan Mowbray.

Liebesmelodie · Pot Luck · If You Could Only Cook · One Way Ticket

It has been a dead week so far as new films are concerned: after so many successes one must expect a few rather empty weeks, for there are not enough cinemas free with Charlie Chaplin, Harold Lloyd and Eddie Cantor still holding out at the Tivoli and London Pavilion, not to speak of the dull and depressing Cassandra in Leicester Square. All but the last of the new films are comedies; they are not bad comedies judged by the depth to which the cinema can fall, but they look rather small in company with Chaplin and Cantor. Each contains a player whom I find peculiarly antipathetic, however well directed: Fraulein Marta Eggerth in the first, Mr Ralph Lynn in the second, and most of all, Mr Herbert Marshall in the third.

Liebesmelodie is one of those devastatingly gay films of Austrian life: one's spirit withers as the glasses fill. Only too soon, one feels certain, they will be splintered on the floor in gallant and noisy toasts; the director will begin to cut his picture rapidly at fancy angles; the gipsy violinist will reach the table of the revue star who will then (improbable generosity!) burst into unpaid song. Then for contrast comes, of course, the trip into the Hungarian countryside (the revue star has long dreamed of an old farmhouse) and we begin to recognize the grim inevitability of that kiss on a haycock, the quaint national costumes of the peasants going by to a wedding. But there are consolations (though perhaps I ought not to count among them the odd use of incestuous love as a comic idea): the admirable performances of Herr Leo Slezak, who may be remembered as the old composer in *Musik im Blut*, now an old Hungarian landowner threatened by a relic of his immoral youth, and of Herr Hans Moser as his badgered and despairing moral bodyguard.

There are consolations too in *Pot Luck*: Mr Tom Walls as a retired detective-inspector of Scotland Yard acts with his usual ease, and Mr Robertson Hare is admirably true to form as the diffident owner of an old abbey in which a gang of art thieves have their secret hide-out. This is the best *directed* film that Mr Walls has made, but one misses the slightly salacious humour of the earlier pictures: there is too much melodrama, too little Hare, and, of course, as always to my mind, too much Lynn, too much of the scaly tortoise face and hollow imbecility.

The Regal programme will have changed by the time this review appears, and I do not think anyone need await the release of *If You Could Only Cook* with any impatience. It is produced by Mr Frank Capra, who made *It Happened One Night*, and it bears a few agreeable Capra touches, a few situations which might have had wit if the main performance had been less earnest, less conceited, less humourless than that of Mr Marshall, who plays the part of a millionaire on holiday posing as a butler. Not a bright situation, though Mr Capra, with the help of such players as Mr Leo Carillo, Miss Jean Arthur and Mr Lionel Stander, might have made something of it. But fantasy droops before Mr Marshall, so intractably British in the American scene. He does, I suppose, represent some genuine national characteristics, if not those one wishes to see exported: characteristics which it is necessary to describe in terms of inanimate objects: a kind of tobacco, a kind of tweed, a kind of pipe: or in terms of dog, something large, sentimental and moulting, something which confirms one's preference for cats.

One Way Ticket is a rather sentimental melodrama about a prison officer's daughter who helps a convict to escape. It is well acted and has one excellent sequence: the prison break when the captain of the guard (played by Mr Walter Connolly) mows down with a machine-gun two of his own men who are held as hostages in the floodlit yard. This picture will pass an hour at a local cinema better than many more pretentious pictures. The most conventional American melodramas usually have a bite about them: they criticize as well as thrill, and that even makes *One Way Ticket* more convincing and entertaining than the polished fairy-tales of Mr Hitchcock.

The Spectator (10 April 1936)

Liebesmelodie (Austria, Standard-Film, 1935) Dir.: Viktor Tourjansky. Cast: Marta Eggerth, Leo Slezak, Hans Moser.
Pot Luck (GB, Gainsborough, 1936) Dir.: Tom Walls. Cast: Tom Walls, Ralph Lynn, Robertson Hare, Diana Churchill, Gordon James, Martita Hunt.
If You Could Only Cook (USA, Columbia, 1935) Dir.: William Seiter. Cast: Herbert Marshall, Jean Arthur, Leo Carillo, Lionel Stander, Frieda Inescourt.
One Way Ticket (USA, Columbia, 1935) Dir.: Herbert Biberman. Cast: Lloyd Nolan, Peggy Conklin, Walter Connolly, Thurston Hall.

Kliou the Tiger

'Into her unfinished basket Dhi – the daughter of the Quan – was weaving dreams of her beloved one.' That is the kind of film the Marquis de la Falaise has brought back with him from Indo-China. Oh, the appalling conceit, one longs to exclaim, as the horrid Technicolor browns and greens stain the screen, of these travellers with movie cameras who, not content to photograph what they see, presume, on a few months' acquaintance, to write a tale of native life, to say *what* dreams . . .

This to my mind is the worst type of travel film. Better the travelogue, the 'views of old Japan', the cherry tree blossoming to point the wisecrack. Far better, of course, the plain statement of fact, such as Mr Smythe's *Kamet*. Best of all – there has been only one of this kind – *Song of Ceylon*, where the plain statement has the intensity of poetic experience. Mr Basil Wright was content to accept the limitations of ignorance, of a European mind, to be 'on the outside, looking in'; the film is a visual record of the effect on a sensitive Western brain of old, communal, religious appearances, not of a life which Mr Wright pretends to *know*.

'Thrice five suns had risen over Klien-hara, since the last forest had swallowed them up.' The Marquise de la Falaise is speaking again, and, of course, the caption is followed promptly by the sixteenth sun, an improbable ochre dawn . . .

But perhaps what annoys one most in this cheap vulgar film is the waste of good material – not such good material as Mr Zoltan Korda brought back from Nigeria to waste in *Sanders of the River*, for the Marquis has no eye whatever for the significant (an elephant or a tiger is always more important to his melodramatic mind than the men and women of the Moi tribe, though equally good shots of tigers could have been made in Hollywood; indeed . . . but to that later), still fairly good material: the house on stilts, the poor patches of cultivation at the hill foot, gentle lovely youth, ugly diseased age and a little of the ordinary life that goes between. The Marquis has preferred to dramatize, to use what – for want of a more accurate word – we must call 'imagination'. Into her unfinished basket . . .' and the strange faces can hardly restrain their smiles at the curious awkward emotional Western thoughts they are made to express. But first the prologue: the lonely French outpost on what we are told is the edge of 'tiger-infested' jungle, 'fever-ridden' swamps where live 'the mysterious' Moi, 'a very savage and dangerous tribe': the Marquis emerging in shorts and topee from a shubbery and recounting to the lonely officer over a sundowner his traveller's yarn, which consists of the love-story of Dhi, the daughter of the Quan, and Bhat, the hunter. The Quan is mauled by Kliou the tiger, and a medicine-man tells the tribe that unless the tiger is killed, the Quan will die. So Bhat goes out with his spear to hunt the man-eater and win his bride.

And now to the Problem of the Tiger so admirably photographed (the other wild animals, even the elephants, the pythons, the water-buffalo, 'most treacherous of horned beasts', presents no such difficult dilemma). We are told that for filming in Technicolor 'long-focus lenses cannot be used, so the pictures showing close-ups of tigers were genuine close-ups – not pictures taken hundreds of yards away. The Marquis vouches for the authenticity of every shot, the entire picture having been filmed in the jungle without any studio or specially staged scenes being added. The tigers are real tigers (certainly one had not thought of them as stuffed), photographed in their natural surroundings.' So definite a statement leaves us with a painful dilemma: we see the tiger leap upon the Quan, we seem to see the man mauled. None of the scenes, we have been told, were staged; the Marquis with eighteenth-century imperturbability must have continued to shoot his film within a few feet of the struggle. How are we to help doubting either his accuracy or his humanity? And the little well-shaven gentleman in shorts and topee emerging from that fever-ridden swamp has all the appearance of a kindly man.

The Spectator (17 April 1936)

Kliou the Tiger (USA, Barret, 1936) Dir.: Marquis de la Falaise. (aka *Kliou the Killer*)

Follow the Fleet · The Peace Film

It needs an effort of the mind to remember that Mr Fred Astaire was not invented by a film director and drawn by a film draughtsman. He is the nearest we are ever likely to get to a human Mickey, near enough for many critics to have noted the resemblance. If one needs to assign human qualities to this light, quick, humorous cartoon, they are the same as the early Mickey's: a touch of pathos, the sense of a courageous and impromptu intelligence, a capacity for getting into awkward situations. Something has to be done, and Mickey without a moment's hesitation will fling his own tail across an abyss and tread the furry unattached tightrope with superb insouciance. Something has to be done, and Mr Astaire bursts into a dance which in its speed and unselfconsciousness seems equally to break the laws of nature. They are both defending Minnie, though Ginger Rogers will never quite attain Minnie's significance (she is too brazen and self-sufficing for the part), and there is no villain type, no huge black Pasha cat continually to threaten her with ravishment: the plots of Mr Astaire's films are more everyday; one might almost say more decent, more 'family'.

That is a pity, for he doesn't belong to this unfantastic world: he ought not double his story with the sentimental romance of a Paris dressmaker, formerly of the tedious Russian nobility, and an American hick (*Roberta*), or of the nice homing girl and the untrustworthy sailor in the present film. He has never again been quite so good as in the *Gay Divorce*, not merely because he had Mr Cole Porter's music to dance to and the enchanting 'Night and Day' to sing, but because then the tale – of the professional co-respondent – had the right fantastic note. Our divorce laws do belong to Mickey's gravitationless world (no wonder that our national humorists should feel that they are inconsistent with this – the sensible, the middle-class, the *Punch* – globe).

But his new film, I think, is the best since *Gay Divorce*. Not that there is any merit to the story of this hoofer enlisted in the United States Navy who meets his former dancing partner when on shore leave. Not does Mr Randolph Scott as a Juanesque sailor provide less heavy entertainment than he did in *Roberta*, though his new partner, Miss Harriet Hilliard, with her Sylvia Sidney eyes and her husky voice, is infinitely to be preferred to Miss Irene Dunne. I think one reason why one so enjoys this film is that the human Mickey is more suitably clothed in the simple impersonal sailor blue and white than in 'top hat, white tie and tails'. There is something curiously ill at ease about the cinema's – and the music-hall's – attitude to evening dress, something horrifyingly doggish. (One remembers Mr Jack Hulbert and Miss Cicely Courtneidge twirling canes and raking unnaturally glossy hats.) Nothing is less graceful for a Mickey to dance in: the tails twirl round the performer in Laocoön coils. Mr Astaire dressed in a seaman's inhuman uniform does drop one more terrestrial envelope, comes nearer to soaring in those regions where once Mickey soared. Alas! where he soars no longer. Mickey in his Technicolor days has been refined out of all knowledge; no longer does Minnie struggle on the edge of the great cat's couch, and the very capable Fleischer cartoon *The Little Stranger*, in the same programme as *Follow the Fleet*, should be a warning to Mr Disney that if he relies only on agreeable colour, on pictorial prettiness, there will soon be others to equal him.

The British Board of Film Censors have once more supplied the best joke of the week by carefully preserving the devil from disrespect. This funny but really rather deplorable Board have substituted a sharp metallic click for Satan's name when Miss Hilliard sings the refrain of a charming sentimental song. 'Get thee behind me -'. Nor is it really to the credit of the Board that they have rendered a service to the cause of collective security by the publicity their absurd Fabian tactics have given to the 'Peace' film, an admirable little three-minute picture, which for its point and economy, its clever simultaneous use of image, caption and voice, deserves to be reckoned the best film of the week.

The Spectator (24 April 1936)

Follow the Fleet (USA, RKO, 1936) Dir.: Mark Sandrich. Cast: Fred Astaire, Ginger Rogers, Randolph Scott, Harriet Hilliard, Lucille Ball, Tony Martin, Betty Grable.

These Three · The Student of Prague

I have seldom been so moved by any fictional film as by *These*

Three. After ten minutes or so of the usual screen sentiment, quaintness and exaggeration, one began to watch with incredulous pleasure nothing less than life: a genuine situation, a moral realism that allows one of two school-mistresses, whose lives and careers have been ruined by the malicious lie of a child, to murmur before the rigid self-righteousness of the wealthy grandparent: 'It is the very young and the very old who are wicked.'

The credit, of course, rests primarily with the American theatre, with *The Children's Hour*, but the forbidden subject of the play has been adapted with very little loss of truth: only the beginning and the ending have been blurred and softened for the film public. Miss Merle Oberon and Miss Miriam Hopkins as the two school-teachers act admirably from the moment when the playwright really takes control, from the moment of entanglement in their horrible situation, and Mr Joel McCrea gives one of his amiable, if slightly monotonous, performances. These three represent innocence in an evil world – the world of childhood, the world of moral chaos, lies, brutality, complete inhumanity. Never before has childhood been represented so convincingly on the screen, with an authenticity guaranteed by one's own memories. The more than human evil of the lying sadistic child is suggested with quite shocking mastery by Bonita Granville. This character raises the film from the merely anecdotal, however ingenious and moving the anecdote; it has enough truth and intensity to stand for the whole of the dark side of childhood, in which the ignorance and weakness of the many allows complete mastery to the few. The eleven-year-old actress Marcia Mae Jones gives an almost equally fine performance as one of the weak, whose theft of another girl's bracelet puts her in the power of the blackmailer. The audience laughed when the smudged feeble child repeated to her school-fellow and torturer under threat of betrayal a solemn 'knightly' oath of vassalage, but it was a terrifying and admirably chosen example of the taboos which exist at that age in that egoistic world, compared with which the adult appears almost kindly and honest. 'It is the very young and the very old who are wicked': there is nothing incredible in the grandparent's support of the lying child, for human sympathies have to die as well as be born.

Of *The Student of Prague*, Dr Robison's last film, one can say that at any rate that it is on the right side. It may be dull, but this allegory of the divided personality, of the student who, by the enchantment of an evil and jealous doctor, leaves his dreaming good-natured self behind in the mirror and steps out of his room, undivided, acquisitive and cruel, is on the side of the imagination in an unimaginative industry. Dr Robison from his first film, *Warning Shadows*, was one of the few directors who could mark a picture with his own personality (Lubitsch, Lang, Pudovkin, Clair . . . the list soon peters out). There is no mistaking his slow decorative methods, the curious ballet-like quality he procured by the constant smooth panning of his camera. But dull the film undoubtedly is: a curiosity, a relic of the classical German film of silent days. The doctor 'out of hell', this Faust driven to suicide by remorse, this fair angel, the innkeeper's virtuous daughter with the horseface of awful Teutonic integrity: one admits their right in such a legend to feel, not as human beings do feel, but as they ought to feel, granted the faith behind the symbol. But one cannot believe that this neo-Gothic fantasy really represents any faith; the allegory doesn't satisfy, the sense of evil, one suspects, is there for merely decorative purposes. Nor does the acting help. *The Student of Prague* of silent days was more memorable; the magnificent fox-hunt when the hounds wheeled across the fields as the enchanter turned his hand; the moment when Conrad Veidt as the damned student went down through the woods to the duel he had no intention of fighting, and met his other self mounting the hill with the damp blade that showed he had been more punctual at the appointed place.

The Spectator (1 May 1936)

These Three (USA, Samuel Goldwyn, 1936) Dir.: William Wyler. Cast: Miriam Hopkins, Merle Oberon, Joel McCrea, Bonita Granville.

The Student of Prague (Der Student von Prag) (Germany, Cine-Allianz, 1935) Dir.: Arthur Robison. Cast: Adolf Wohlbrück [Anton Walbrook], Dorothea Wieck, Theodor Loos.

Anne-Marie · La Belle au Bois Dormant · Tudor Rose

Anne-Marie is a quite amazingly silly film about a girl (Annabella) in an aeroplane firm and the five aces who instruct her in flying: silly but with some amiable qualities. The five aces, in order to keep the girl's mind off an inventor with whom she is falling in love, arrange that one of them shall write her anonymous and passionate letters: the girl, without that ration of sexual interest, cannot be trusted to take her pilot's certificate successfully and afterwards win one of the innumerable records which it is the main livelihood of these pilots to accumulate.

But the film, as I have said, has redeeming qualities. The scenario, written by M. Antoine de Saint-Exupéry, the author of *Vol de Nuit*, has a pleasantly technical atmosphere: the dialogue jingles agreeably with gadgets. But it is chiefly worth seeing for an exciting and beautifully directed melodramatic climax, when the girl, attempting a night record, becomes lost in the neighbourhood of Angoulême with a failing petrol-supply in the path of a fleet of military planes: the shots of this dark formation passing overhead between the massing night clouds are finely dramatic. The fleet, of course, is averted just in time from Angoulême, and in an amusing and exhilarating final scene the inventor and the five aces storm the municipal electricity works and signal in morse with the lights of the whole city to the lost plane.

A very lively Gasparcolor cartoon, *La Belle au Bois Dormant*, is shown in the same programme. One of the directors is Alexeieff, who made the superb *Night on Bare Mountain*, and though the new picture, a little precious and pansyish, is not on that level, taken with Mr Len Lye's Shell-Mex cartoon, *The Birth of a Robot*, it is convincing proof of the immense superiority of Gasparcolor to Technicolor, at any rate for unrealistic purposes.

Tudor Rose is one of the more distressing products of the British screen: the fault is not in the director, who has made a smooth, competent, if rather banal, picture, but in the vulgarity of the scenario. The story of Lady Jane Grey is surely dramatic enough to be converted truthfully into film material, but this sentimental pageant in fancy-dress could have displayed no more ignorance of the period if it had been made in Hollywood. There is not a character, not an incident in which history has not been altered for the cheapest reasons. Edward VI is shown as a preparatory schoolboy who wants to get out and play with a gun: the weakling Lord Guildford Dudley becomes a tender and romantic 'boy husband': Lady Jane Grey herself, perhaps the nearest approach to a saint the Anglican Church has produced and a scholar of the finest promise, is transformed into an immature child construing – incorrectly – Caesar's *Gallic War* and glad to be released from tiresome lessons. This, I suppose, is the Dark Age of scholarship and civilization, and one ought not to expect anything better from celluloid artists than this sneering attitude to the learning of the Renaissance. The dialogue in English films is notoriously bad, from Mr Wells downwards, but I have seldom listened to more inchoate rubbish than in *Tudor Rose*. The style chops and changes; sometimes, when the Earl of Warwick (so the Duke of Northumberland remains throughout this film) or the Protector Somerset is speaking, the dialogue is written in unconscious blank verse; at other times it consists of the kind of flat simplified colloquialisms that Mrs Naomi Mitchison has made popular in historical novels.

The Spectator (8 May 1936)

Anne-Marie (France, Majestic, 1935) Dir.: Raymond Bernard. Cast: Annabella, Pierre Willm, Jean Murat.

La Belle au Bois Dormant (France, 1935) Directors: Alexandre Alexieff, Claire Parker.

Tudor Rose (GB, Gainsborough, 1936) Dir.: Robert Stevenson. Cast: Nova Pilbeam, Cedric Hardwicke, John Mills, Felix Aylmer, Gwen Francgon Davies, Sybil Thorndike, Martita Hunt, Miles Malleson, John Laurie. (US title: *Nine Days a Queen*)

A History of the Film, 1896–1936 [The Birth of a Nation] · The Trail of the Lonesome Pine · Secret Agent

The only film I have seen with any real excitement during the last fortnight was made in 1915. D. W. Griffith's *The Birth of a Nation*, shown in the first half of the Everyman Theatre's admirable historical programmes, has hardly dated at all; it is still in advance of the popular film as it exists today. Some of his technical devices, of course, have been adopted, though not the most striking, his way of escaping the ugly artificiality of the screen by fogging part of his film, so that the characters do not move up and down within a fixed rectangular frame but appear, as it were, out of the unfocused corners of the eyes with an effect of startling realism. A superb sense of reality dictates all his devices and is Griffith's main characteristic. Compare the dresses in this film wth those of any modern 'period' picture – *The Barretts of Wimpole Street* or *Little Women*: those are 'fancy-dress' in their newness, their archness, their exaggeration, but it needs an effort of the mind to realize that Griffith's film, with its dowdy convincing costumes, its daguerrotype air, was not made in the 1860s. Note too the realistic sense of place: how deeply we get to know the Southern house in Piedmont, seeing it first in its spruce pre-war days and then through all the stages of its decay, and note the careful documentation of Griffith's history, how continually we are told that such and such a scene is a historical facsimile – the circumstances of Lincoln's assassination, for example, which we follow minute by minute, so that even the shifting of a chair has its historical guarantee. And then remember the contemporary film: *Tudor Rose* and *Henry VIII*.

Realism, of course, is not everything, but for a long while the popular film director must expect to be judged by his ability to give an illusion of reality.

On the unrealistic screen colour is already acceptable, but *The Trail of the Lonesome Pine* shows no appreciable advance in realistic colour. It is just bad bright picture-postcard stuff, and if one sometimes forgets its picture-postcard quality, it is only because the images move, change, distract, the story (quite a good one of Kentucky hill feuds) interests, and the actors (Miss Sylvia Sidney in particular) charm. But picture-postcard the colour is, and a still would disclose how crude. The film has one merit: the director by trying to use the ordinary dissolve and obtaining only a distressing blur has demonstrated how many technical devices making for speed we must be prepared to sacrifice for the yet doubtful benefit of Technicolor.

There were those at the Everyman who found the occasional jerkiness of movement and Griffith's pre-war sentiment comic, and one wished them as sharp to detect the cruder absurdities of the contemporary film, for then Mr Hitchcock's latest picture might have been punctuated, and its dullness enlivened, by laughter: laughter at the secret agent who loudly discusses his instructions in front of the hall porter of a Swiss hotel and who brandishes his only clue to a murder in a crowded casino, laughter at the representation of a Secret Sevice which so arranges things that its agent's photograph appears in every paper, laughter in fact at Mr Hitchcock's inadequate sense of reality. It is all a great pity; a pity because of the immense wasted talent of Mr Peter Lorre, and because Mr Hitchcock too has talent. How unfortunate it is that Mr Hitchcock, a clever director, is allowed to produce and even to write his own films, though as a producer he has no sense of continuity and as a writer he has no sense of life. His films consist of a series of small 'amusing' melodramatic situations: the murderer's buttons dropped on the baccarat board; the strangled organist's hands prolonging the notes in the empty church; the fugitives hiding in the the bell-tower when the bell begins to swing. Very perfunctorily he builds up to these tricky situations (paying no attention on the way to inconsistencies, loose ends, psychological absurdities) and then drops them; they mean nothing: they lead to nothing. As for Mr Maugham's *Ashenden*, on which this film is said to be based, nothing is left of that witty and realistic fiction.

The Spectator (15 May 1936)

The Birth of a Nation (USA, Epoch, 1915) Dir.: D. W. Griffith. Cast: Henry B. Walthall, Mae Marsh, Miriam Cooper, Lillian Gish. Wallace Reid, Donald Crisp, Raoul Walsh, Eugene Pallette.

The Trail of the Lonesome Pine (USA, Paramount, 1936) Dir.: Henry Hathaway. Cast: Sylvia Sidney, Henry Fonda, Fred MacMurray, Nigel Bruce, Belulah Bondi.

Secret Agent (GB, Gaumont British, 1936) Dir.: Alfred Hitchcock. Cast: Madeleine Carroll, John Gielgud, Peter Lorre, Robert Young, Lilli Palmer.

Klondyke Annie · Professional Soldier · A History of the Film Part Two

'Ah'm an Occidental wooman. In an Awriental mood.' The big-busted carnivorous creature in tight white sequins sits as firmly and inscrutably as the fat tattooed women in the pleasure arcades. The husky voice drones, the plump jewelled fingers pluck, the eyes slant, and immediately we are in the familiar atmosphere – not the atmosphere of San Francisco's China Town where the beautiful white lily is in danger of mutilation at the hands of her Oriental lover, behind the bead curtains, among the burning censers – but the friendly, smoky, alcoholic atmosphere of a Private Bar, hung with advertisements for Guinness and Black and White, where for some years now it has always been possible to observe a small group of middle-aged, bowler-hatted businessmen knotted at the far corner away from the youngest barmaid: 'Have you heard this one? Why is Mae West like – '

One cannot but pay tribute to a personality so outrageously suggestive to the middle-aged. I am completely uncritical of Mae West: I enjoy every one of her films, aware all the time, whether the scene be the Bowery, the Klondyke, Texas or a New York drawing-room, of that bowler-hatted brigade gathered invisibly like seraphs about her stout matronly figure. It is with sorrow, therefore, that I have read the unfavourable notices of her latest picture, in which, escaping from the police (she has stabbed her Chinese lover), she puts on the dress of a dead Salvationist and brings prosperity to a Klondyke settlement house by instilling some vigour into the services. I should be sorry if anyone wasted money owing to my minority opinion; but I did not, as some did, find the satire on religious revivalists in bad taste; I thought the whole film fun, more fun than any other of Miss West's since the superb period piece, *She Done Him Wrong*, but then it never occurred to me that Miss West's conversion was intended to be taken seriously. I liked, too, Mr McLaglen's performance as the dumb dog of a coasting skipper who saves her from the Canadian police ('You're what makes me tick,' he declares with genuine eloquence), and I liked the whole parody of a Salvationist settlement: the unattractive soapy virtues. It is always necessary to review a Mae West film in terms of personalities. The director's job is confined to winning a particularly hazardous kind of obstacle race, to guessing correctly how much the censors will stand, to knowing when to fade out.

Professional Soldier should be carefully avoided. It is a silly and sentimental story of an American mercenary soldier who is hired by virtuous revolutionaries to kidnap the child king of a Ruritanian State and hold him out of harm's way until the revolution has been successful. The child, of course, wins the mercenary's heart, and, when he falls into the wrong hands and is facing a firing-squad, the American successfully breaks gaol, seizes a machine-gun and rescues him single-handed from a regiment of regulars. Mr McLaglen does his best, but Master Freddie Bartholomew never begins to act. He has never begun as far as I know. He recites his words by rote in whatever part he plays, and his directors help him to exercise a lustrous and repulsive charm. The setting and costumes in these Ruritanian stories have a character of their own: plumes and barley-sugar pillars, unbecoming trousers and ornate mantelpieces.

At the Everyman, *A History of the Film* continues. This week-end it is possible to see examples of Russian, English and French documentaries; early news-reels and sequences from the first talkie, *The Singing Fool*, as well as the whole *King of Jazz*. Apart from the documentaries, this is a programme which appeals chiefly to the historical imagination, but next week's, devoted to the *avant garde*, is of the finest interest. London is unlikely to offer any other film as interesting as Jean Vigo's *Zéro de Conduite*, and the programme is likely to contain as well Alexeieff's *Night on Bare Mountain*, a grim fantasia which has given at least one spectator the purest aesthetic pleasure he has received from the screen.

The Spectator (22 May 1936)

Klondyke Annie (USA, Paramount, 1936) Dir.: Raoul Walsh. Cast: Mae West, Victor McLaglen, Philip Reed, Harold Huber.
Professional Soldier (USA, Twentieth-Century Fox, 1935) Dir.: Tay Garnett. Cast: Victor McLaglen, Freddie Bartholomew, Constance Collier, Gloria Stuart.

The Robber Symphony · The Littlest Rebel · The Emperor's Candlesticks

Herr Friedrich Feher's *The Robber Symphony* is certainly the most interesting film of the last twelve months, heretical though it is, a picture cut to synchronize with the music. Containing moments of really sensitive direction, it goes on for nearly two hours, restless, scatterbrained, amusing, boring, cheap, lyrical, facrical. The story is derived rather obviously from *Emil and the Detectives*, but with a super-realist atmosphere foreign to the agreeable common sense of that fantasy.

I think one might be more ready to surrender to its charm if one did not detect a certain complacency, a conscious withdrawal from the corruption of the commercial film, in its painstaking irresponsibility. Virtue can afford to be charitable, and all those who have occasionally enjoyed the corrupt pleasures, the bright facile excitements of popular entertainment will feel as if an old friend (vicious, of course, but not always unamusing) has been too priggishly reprimanded. There is a didactic note, that is the trouble, in a film which promises to be peculiarly carefree and irrational from the moment when a symphony orchestra of a hundred musicians in curiously shaped bowler-hats begin to play the overture. The story is excellent, leading improbably up to the superb sequence of four player-pianos dragged across the Alps behind a monstrous wine-barrel containing a gang of robbers in pursuit of a fifth player-piano, in the mechanism of which, unknown to the boy in charge of it, lies a stocking filled with gold pieces. The gold pieces have been stolen by the Robber with the Straw Hat (an admirable piece of grotesque miming by Mr Michael Martin-Harvey) and deposited in the piano, which belongs to a family of strolling musicians. The robbers pursue it to a mountain village where the Man with the Straw Hat holds the attention of the people with a rope-walking act, while the others produce four identical pianos drawn by four identical donkeys with the complex idea of confusing the boy and stealing his piano. This whole sequence is delightful: one of the best pieces of direction and invention I have seen, genuinely irresponsible, but even here it is the music which dictates the pace, and as a result the mind moves quicker than the camera. To the credit of the music, though, it may be said that one is seldom conscious of the silence of the actors.

Herr Feher calls his picture the first 'composed' film, but in so far as his experiment is original, it is barren. In order to synchronize pictures with music in this way he found it necessary to shoot 600,000 feet of film; the synchronization is perfect but the cost is enormous, and the object – I do not quite know what the object is. Herr Feher composed the music, wrote the story, directed the film, but the music (of which I am no proper judge) surely does not require illustration. There seems to be a confusion of thought which prevents the picture – or the music – being quite the masterpiece which had been intended – intended, for there is no doubt about the bardic self-confidence of the director.

To return to our corrupt friend – never more so than at the New Gallery where Miss Shirley Temple appears in a very sweet and very simple tale of the American Civil War which culminates, as these dramas always do, with an appeal to Abraham Limcoln to save somebody – in this case a father, in Mr Drinkwater's play a son, in *The Birth of a Nation* a lover – from being shot. I had not seen Miss Temple before: as I expected there was the usual sentimental exploitation of childhood, but I had not expected the tremendous energy which her rivals certainly lack. A film like this makes one sympathize with Herr Feher's Puritanism: it is a little too enervating. If one must have disreputable enjoyments, let them have the glitter of *The Emperor's Candlesticks*, an absurd Edwardian tale of Polish plotters and secret documents hidden in stolen candlesticks, of a beautiful police agent and an idealistic revolutionary, acted in his usual sad, worried and endearing way by Herr Karl Ludwig Diehl. Good direction, fair acting and the attractively Baker Street dresses make this a pleasant film to doze at.

The Spectator (29 May 1936)

The Robber Symphony (GB, Concordia, 1936) Dir.: Friedrich Feher. Cast: Hans Feher, Magda Sinja, Webster Booth, George Graves, Michael Martin-Harvey.
The Littlest Rebel (USA, Twentieth-Century Fox, 1935) Dir.: David Butler. Cast: Shirley Temple, John Boles, Jack Holt, Bill Robinson.
The Emperor's Candlesticks (Die Leuchter des Kaisers) (Austria, Gloria-Film, 1935) Dir.: Karl Hartl. Cast: Sybille Schmitz, Karl Ludwig Diehl.

The Marriage of Corbal

What is an English film? There are times when one cannot help brooding with acute distress on the cheap silly international pictures exported under that label. *The Marriage of Corbal* is a fairly harmless example. It is incredibly silly and incredibly badly written but there is a kind of wide-eyed innocence about this story of the French Revolution which is almost endearing. But an English film? Is that a fair description of a picture derived from a novel by Rafael Sabatini, directed by Karl Grune and F. Brunn, photographed by Otto Kanturek, and edited by E. Stokvis, with a cast which includes Nils Asther, Ernst Deutsch and the American Noah Beery? The result is appalling: the dialogue is the worst I have heard these twelve months, the scenario the silliest, and as for the acting – let me be charitable to Hugh Sinclair and the young 'dumb' newcomer, Miss Hazel Terry, and put some of their faults down to Herr Grune and his international assistants.

England, of course, has always been the home of the exiled; but one may at least expect a wish that *émigrés* would set up trades in which ignorance of our language and culture was less of a handicap: it would not grieve me to see Mr Alexander Korda seated before a cottage loom in an Eastern county, following an older and better tradition. The Quota Act has played into foreign hands, and as far as I know, there is nothing to prevent an English film unit being completely staffed by technicians of foreign blood. We have saved the English film industry from American competition only to surrender it to a far more alien control.

It is not that there are no English technicians capable of producing films of a high enough standard to take their place in the international markets (an absurd idea when we think of *Song of Ceylon, The Voice of Britain, The Turn of the Tide, Night Mail, Midshipman Easy*). Aesthetics have nothing to do with the matter. In the last eleven months I have reviewed 124 films, of which only 13 conveyed any kind of aesthetic experience and another 48 were reasonably entertaining: the other 63 films were trash. The reason why English technicians are seldom employed is more likely to be financial: it is not English money that calls the tune, and it is only natural that compatriots should find jobs for each other. And so the big film families are founded, a system of nepotism which recalls the less savoury days of the Papacy, and as for 'the art of the cinema' it remains almost as unrealized as in the days of *The Great Train Robbery*. The peepshow, the fun-fair, the historical waxworks are triumphant.

And there is something unusually sinister about *this* collection of waxworks: it does in some moods appear to be a chamber of horrors. The wax corpse with the painted wound is often grotesque, and the anonymous letters one receives – I remember a particularly ill-scented specimen from High Wycombe – are amusing, if one ignores the animality and the ignorance of their source. But the chamber contains darker shadows: what is one to think of a Board of Film Censors (with at least one judge of over eighty years) which allows a far greater latitude to the big American companies than to its own less wealthy countrymen? And there is only too obviously a sinister side to many newspaper criticisms. Even the hardened Press audience at *The Marriage of Corbal* gave way to impatient laughter at the inflated dialogue, the grotesque situations, and yet when I examined the notices later, I found the film had made the contrary impression to what I had supposed. 'Second thoughts are best' – that, of course, is one proverb, but 'money speaks' is another.

Watching the dark alien executive tipping his cigar ash behind the glass partition in Wardour Street, the Hungarian producer adapting Mr Wells's ideas tactfully at Denham, the German director letting himself down into his canvas chair at Elstree, and the London film critics (I speak with humility: I am one of them) exchanging smutty stories over the hock and the iced pudding and the brandy at the Carlton, I cannot help wondering whether from this great moneyed industry anything of value to the human spirit can ever emerge.

The Spectator (5 June 1936)

The Marriage of Corbal (GB, Capitol, 1936) Directors: Karl Grune, F. Brunn. Cast: Nils Asther, Hazel Terry, Hugh Sinclair, Noah Beery, Davy Burnaby, Ernst Deutsch.

The Country Doctor · The Ex-Mrs Bradford · Thirteen Hours by Air

The Country Doctor is an honest film. The picture of the small Canadian timber station, shut off from the outside world, and the elderly G.P. who has practised there for thirty years, paid more often in kind than in cash, and who has never troubled, or had the necessary ready money, to take out his licence to practice, is admirably genuine: the camera – rare occasion in the cinema – doesn't lie, and Mr Jean Hersholt gives one of the most sympathetic performances I have seen this year as the patient courageous doctor, out of date through no fault of his own, with a core of obstinacy, a determination to make the rich corporation which owns the land build him a proper hospital. After an epidemic of diptheria, in which many of the workers' children have died for want of proper equipment, the doctor goes to Montreal to interview the Managing Director. He is told, as usual, to fill up form 48 and his request will be considered in due course; but with patient determination he follows the Director to a public dinner given by the medical association, the rich city specialists, and makes his protest. He has done no good. The corporation takes its revenge; the lawyers discover he has no licence, he is forbidden to practise and is about to leave the settlement altogether when a wretched father, whose wife spawns by calendar every fall, implores his help. The successful birth of quintuplets makes the doctor a national hero; for their sake he gets the hospital for the lack of which children have died every year for thirty years, and the Managing Director (a fine satirical portrait, this, of brutal complacency) receives the compliments of the Governor-General.

The theme is serious, the treatment has unusual edge, no one, after seeing this picture will complain again that the Dionne quintuplets and Dr Dafoe have received more than their due of attention. And perhaps it would be too austere to criticize the picture because it does not quite maintain its seriousness and realism. The scene of the birth, with the policeman protesting to the unlicensed doctor with every fresh arrival that he is only 'piling on the evidence', is not in the best of taste, perhaps, and the human values are quite forgotten, but it is undeniably comic. It would be harsh too to expect the director to cut his admirable sequence of the quintuplets playing with Mr Hersholt on the floor of the new hospital. From the point of view of a balanced film there is too much of them, but this again is to judge from the austerest angle, for the sequence is extraordinarily funny, and the professional actor sprawling on the floor with these reckless carnival characters can only suggest in his expression a bewildered admiration at their virtuosity, their impromptu and perfectly timed performance: a performance which reminded me of Buster Keaton's solemn slapstick, as a quintuplet with an air of methodical pedantry upset each chair in the room in turn.

The other two films are 'thrillers': *The Ex-Mrs Bradford*, like most in which Mr William Powell appears, an unusually entertaining one. The actual crimes, two murders carried ingeniously if unconvincingly with the help of poisonous spiders enclosed in gelatic capsules which melt with the heat of the human body, are unimportant. So is the detection by the successful surgeon, helped and hindered by his divorced and devoted wife. What gives these detective films, from *The Thin Man* onwards, their entertaining quality is a strong sense of reality. The detection may be faulty, but the characters behave realistically. I prefer this to the English school of scholarly detection and Whimsey psychology.

Thirteen Hours by Air belongs to a rather tiresome *genre*, of which the formula is too familiar to excite and too unrealistic to entertain, now that the novelty of a thriller worked out in the cramped surroundings of a train, hotel or 'plane has worn off. But I am ready to see any film with one of Mr Alan Baxter's gunmen in it. Young, good-looking, with a harsh, inhibited voice, he gives the same vivid impression as in *Mary Burns – Fugitive* of the completely callous brain and the hopelessly lost soul.

The Spectator (12 June 1936)

The Country Doctor (USA, Twentieth-Century Fox, 1936) Dir.: Henry King. Cast: Jean Hersholt, The Dionne Quins, June Lane, Dorothy Petersen.

The Ex-Mrs Bradford (USA, MGM, 1936) Dir.: Stephen Roberts. Cast: William Powell, Jean Arthur, James Gleason, Eric Blore, Robert Armstrong, Lila Lee.

Thirteen Hours by Air (USA, Paramount, 1936) Dir.: Mitchell Leisen. Cast: Fred MacMurray, Joan Bennett, Zasu Pitts, Brian Donlevy, Ruth Donnelly, Dean Jagger.

DANGEROUS · BIG BROWN EYES · LETZTE ROSE

Miss Bette Davis won some kind of a gold medal for her acting in *Dangerous*: the cinema is a shady business and one would like to know more about that medal, who gave it, how many carats, who the judges were: but at least it indicates that the publicity hounds recognized her disturbing talent. Her performance in *Of Human Bondage* was wickedly good – up to a point, the point when passion got a little tattered, and even the most inconsiderable film – *Border Town* and others of which I have even forgotten the names – seemed temporarily better than they were because of that precise nervy voice, the pale ash-blonde hair, the popping neurotic eyes, a kind of corrupt and phosphorescent prettiness. *Dangerous*, like the others, is a picture to see for her sake, although the story is poor, the ending atrociously sentimental (*Dangerous* and *Show Boat* tie for the worst endings of the week), and although alas! Miss Margaret Lindsay is also in the cast, as if to reassure people that, whatever the censor may say, this film is U.

Hollywood has never forgotten its startling discovery that raffishness – the wild parties, the drugs and bathing belles and suicides and Fatty Arbuckle – was bad business. There is nothing now it takes to heart so firmly as gentility: so that Miss Kay Francis is advertised as a woman who can wear the best clothes; Mr C. Aubrey Smith, that amiable and bush Wellington, is made to remind us, even in *The Crusades*, of the straight bat of his cricketing past, and Miss Lindsay is starred less as an actress than as a nice eligible girl, comradely and refined, who can pour out tea as if she really belonged to a tea-drinking nation. Miss Lindsay as the deserted but understanding fiancée provides the antidote to Miss Davis as the great actress who has become a drunken and friendless failure because of her intense selfishness which ruins every play she acts in or any man she likes. A highly coloured situation, this, which does little justice to Miss Davis's talent for vivid realism: we are aware all the time that she is acting, acting for the highest honours, for the questionable carats, acting with immense virtuosity, from the moment when the successful young architect (Mr Franchot Tone) spots her in the speak-easy. For Hollywood has a way of refining even Miss Davis: another performance so horrifyingly natural as her mean greedy little waitress in *Of Human Bondage* and her film career would have been ruined: and so with great ingenuity Hollywood adopts the homeopathic method, doubles the gin, multiplies the drink stains, intensifies the squalor, until you can safely cease to believe, until Miss Davis's latest picture becomes as curious, absurd and period as 'Sell No More Drink to My Father'.

Dangerous, then, is unusual, but only because of Miss Davis: a far more competent picture (though I would rather watch Miss Davis than any number of competent pictures) is *Big Brown Eyes*, a misleading title for a fast well-directed and quite unsentimental gangster film, pleasantly free from emotion – for emotion on the screen is nearly always false emotion. The chief players are Miss Joan Bennett and Mr Cary Grant, but they don't matter much: it is a director's picture.

One cannot complain of the absurd English settings of *Letzte Rose*, adapted from Friedrich von Flotow's comic opera, *Marta*, they are not more false than the Vienna of innumerable English pictures, but the tra-la-la melodies, the hearty Teutonic merry-making, and the determined prettiness of the photography are tedious, not the less tedious for being German. The Continental racket has become rather tiresome, and the films of Studio One have not been noticeably above the Hollywood level. Nor has the Academy's record lately been much better; neither cinema has taken the opportunity of showing the Russian comedy, *Men and Jobs*, which was given two special performances in London some weeks ago, a picture with an original subject, excitingly directed, quite free from political propaganda, with a quality of humanity, simplicity and good-humour rare on the screen. To ignore this film was either an astonishing oversight or a confession that the ordinary commercial standards are quite as binding in these cinemas as in any under American control.

The Spectator (19 June 1936)

Dangerous (USA, Warner, 1936) Dir.: Alfred E. Green. Cast: Bette Davis, Franchot Tone, Margaret Lindsay, Alison Skipworth, John Eldridge, Dick Foran.
Big Brown Eyes (USA, Paramount, 1936) Dir.: Raoul Walsh. Cast: Joan Bennett, Cary Grant, Walter Pidgeon, Lloyd Nolan, Alan Baxter.
Letzte Rose (Germany, Lloyd Film Productions, 1936) Dir.: Karl Anton. Cast: Carla Spletter, Heige Roswalage.

Show Boat · The Moon's Our Home

The latest version of *Show Boat* is very lavish. It runs for two hours, contains more than a dozen of Mr Jerome Kern's melodious songs, and is directed by Mr James Whale with a fine moneyed smoothness. Merely to illustrate one song, 'Ole Man River', he uses half a dozen sets and fifty people, and because there are times, particularly after several drinks, when one can watch money being squandered without a pang, *Show Boat* for three-quarters of its length proves good entertainment, sentimental, literary, but oddly appealing.

The story, by this time, is about as well known as that of *King Lear*: of the troupe of actors in Victorian days (the period is obscure, for the Zinkeisen dresses seem to span more than a human life-time) who tour the Mississippi in their own paddle-steamer; of the young girl, daughter of the old manager, who runs away with the handsome graceless gambler. He has played the hero's parts for a season on the river, and he abandons her with her young child in the great city; abandons her, of course, for the noblest reasons, because he feels himself unworthy of her love and does not wish to involve her in his ruin. She gets an engagement at a Chicago music-hall, becomes a world-famous singer, retires in time to watch from a box her daughter make a triumphant début on the New York stage, and since her husband, no older in appearance except for a few graceful grey hairs and a studiously shabby coat, turns out to be a doorkeeper in the same theatre, the family are reunited at curtain call. Veterans complain that the ending has been altered by Mr Whale, and certainly the extreme sentimentality and improbability of that reunion jars a little with the quite restrained and agreeable sentimentality of the rest. For there are moods of generosity towards life when the sentiment, the idealism, the earnest rather throaty melodies of *Show Boat* have charm; everything is for the best in the best of all possible worlds; everyone is a little blurred with nobility, partings are 'such sweet sorrow', tears rainbowed, and life – don't so much whisper the ugly word. For the first night was Gala: the three little pigs again defeated the big bad wolf in the latest silly symphony: the *Queen Mary* was the finest ship ever built, and we watched the ticker-tape falling for her in Broadway and heard the sirens blasting her towards the quay; and at the end of it all (the management's little surprise) we squealed with delight when first Mr James Whale, and then Miss Irene Dunne (the highest squeals), and last Mr Paul Robeson (the longest squeals) stepped in person before the screen. They had arrived in the *Queen Mary* just in time for Gala Night, and for two hours we too had lived on the *Queen Mary*, the Show Boat, level, in an atmosphere of immense expenditure, of boat-deck sentiment, of decorations lavish if not in the best of taste, of a huge machine grinding efficiently on, 'sweet sorrow' at last at Ellis Island.

In reality, though, I cannot help preferring *The Moon's Our Home*, a trivial charming comedy about people young and too famous, about a popular film star and a traveller who writes books (a character very delicately and sympathetically caricatured with his too vocal contempt for convention and his inappropriate memories, which wreck the wedding-night). They meet and marry in a holiday mood, but marry nevertheless for ever – under their real, not their invented public names, so that she does not know he writes (she hates his books) and he does not know she acts (he hates film stars). Miss Dorothy Parker has helped with the dialogue, the best recommendation of any comedy, but it is to Miss Margaret Sullavan and Mr Henry Fonda, as much as to anyone, that we owe the sense of something fresh and absurd and civilized, like a sixteenth-century epithalamium for a pair who will always be young and extravagant and at odds together in a Penshurst world. It isn't, of course, as good as all that; nothing is as good as all that in the cinema, but the great commercial wheel don't grind here quite so effortlessly; a little satire, a little imagination, a little feeling for human inconsistency, has got into the works.

The Spectator (26 June 1936)

Show Boat (USA, Universal, 1936) Dir.: James Whale. Cast: Irene Dunne, Allan Jones, Charles Winninger, Paul Robeson, Helen Morgan, Hattie McDaniel.

The Moon's Our Home (USA, Paramount, 1936) Dir.: William A. Seiter. Cast: Margaret Sullavan, Henry Fonda, Charles Butterworth, Beluah Bondi, Margaret Hamilton.

Fury · The Story of Louis Pasteur

Fury is Herr Fritz Lang's first American picture. The importation of continental directors is always a nervous business, Hollywood offers so much in the way of technical resources (so that a witty playboy like Lubitsch gains by the translation), so little help, among the yes-men and the entertainment racketeers, to the imagination. *M*, until *Fury* Herr Lang's best film, the study of a child-murderer, could hardly have passed the Hollywood executives; *Metropolis, The Spy, Dr Mabuse*, these melodramatic pictures of Herr Lang's apprenticeship, on the other hand, might possibly have been made with even more chromiumed efficiency in America; and I visited *Fury* in some trepidation lest Herr Lang had been driven back to melodrama (melodrama, of course, infinitely more expert than, say, Mr Hitchcock's). But *Fury*, the story of how a mob in a small Southern town lynches an innocent man who has been arrested under suspicion of kidnapping, is astonishing, the only film I know to which I have wanted to attach the epithet of 'great'. There have been other films – *Kameradschaft* comes to mind – where a generous theme, a sense of spiritual integrity, has somehow got conveyed *in spite of* the limitations of the screen, but no other picture which has allowed no value to slip, which has conveyed completely by sound and image better than by any other medium the pity and terror of the story. (The last third of the picture leading up to a neatly contrived happy ending is not on the same level, though the picture never falls below finely directed melodrama.)

Mr Spencer Tracy as the victim, a garage-keeper, a simple honest kindly creature saving up to be married; Miss Sylvia Sydney as his girl, a teacher in the Southern town; Mr Edward Ellis as the Sheriff, harsh, upright, ready to defend his prisoner to the last tear-gas bomb, with his own life if necessary, but belonging nevertheless to the same township as the mob, knowing it as individuals, each in his home, his office, the barber's chair, refusing at the trial which follows the lynching to identify a single culprit; all these give their finest performances. Miss Sydney in particular. She has never more deeply conveyed the pain and inarticulacy of tenderness. No film passion here, no exaggeration of the ordinary human feeling, as the two lovers shelter under the elevated from the drenching rain, say good-bye at the railway station with faces and hands pressed to wet fogging windows: it is the ordinary recognizable agony, life as one knows it is lived. And the same power to catch vividly the truthful detail makes the lynching of almost unbearable horror. I am trying not to exaggerate, but the brain does flinch at each recurring flick of truth in much the same way as at the grind-grind of an electric road-drill: the horrible laughter and inflated nobility of the good citizens, the youth leaping on a bar and shouting 'Let's have some fun', the regiment of men and women marching down the road into the face of the camera, arm in arm, laughing and excited like recruits on the first day of a war, the boy singing out at the Sheriff, 'I'm Popeye the Sailor-man', at last the first stone, until the building is ablaze, the innocent man is suffocating behind the bars, and a woman holds her baby up to see the fire.

Any other film this year is likely to be dwarfed by Herr Lang's extraordinary achievement: no other director has got so completely the measure of his medium, is so consistently awake to the counterpoint of sound and image. Even *Louis Pasteur*, an honest, interesting and well-made picture, suffers by comparison, and seems half-way to the stage. It would suffer more disastrously if it were not for the acting of Mr Paul Muni. Lucky the film-goer who has been able to see in one week the work of the greatest director and the greatest living actor. The range of his Protean figure (for unlike Mr Laughton he seems to lose voice and appearance in his part) is amazing: the convict in *I am a Fugitive*, the Polish miner in *Black Fury*, the half-caste racketeer in *Border Town*, Louis Pasteur. With his whole body he establishes not only the bourgeois, the elderly, the stubborn and bitter and noble little chemist, but his nationality and even his period.

The Spectator (3 July 1936)

Fury (USA, MGM, 1936) Dir.: Fritz Lang. Cast: Spencer Tracy, Sylvia Sydney, Edward Ellis, Walter Abel, Bruce Cabot, Walter Brennan.

The Story of Louis Pasteur (USA, Warner, 1936) Dir.: William Dieterle. Cast: Paul Muni, Josephine Hutchinson, Anita Louise, Donald Woods, Henry O'Neill, Akim Tamiroff.

ONE RAINY AFTERNOON · JANOSIK · THE PHANTOM GONDOLA

One Rainy Afternoon might so easily have been a good film, something light and absurd and happy in the early Clair tradition. Perhaps it *was* a good film once, somewhere far back, before the director, Mr Rowland Lee, knew that it existed, before Mr Francis Lederer, who has never plugged his Dodie charm, his Autumn Crocus accent, more strenuously, had so much as read his part, before the scenario-writers had begun to insert the gags; very far back indeed, before the author knew that his tale would be bought by Pickford-Lasky Productions, there surely existed in his mind a good film: a film about an unsuccessful actor in Paris who was trying his best to carry on an intrigue with a Cabinet Minister's wife, an intrigue which involved endless taxi-drives, round and round cinema blocks, until the films had begun and the foyers were empty: so that it was always the middle of films he saw, never, as he complained, the happy endings. One day in the dark auditorium there was a muddle, he kissed the girl next to him and it wasn't the Minister's wife. The girl screamed, the Purity League representive insisted on a prosecution, and the absurd irresponsible tale took wings.

But, alas, the wings didn't work. Too many people had to join in the fun, and by the time the executives of Pickford-Lasky (twelve are mentioned in the programme beside the director) had really set to work, the light silly charming tale of a wet afternoon, a too careful mistress, a dark cinema and a kiss had become as seriously gamesome as tip and run played by fathers on holiday at the sea. Mr Lee has given a useful demonstration of how not to direct this kind of story: he has been remorsefully logical when he should have been crazy; his only idea of humour is speed and noise, not speed of thought or situation, but just literal speed of walking and talking. Mr Lederer's mechanic charm I find embarrassing, like the boast of a womanizer in a public bar, but in the grim hurly-burly Miss Ida Lupino's fair sulky features, the impression she can give of something Cockney and cheap and endearing, is as refreshing as a natural voice at a stage party. Miss Lupino as yet is a dummy, but she is one of the more agreeable screen dummies to whom things are made to happen, and I feel some remorse when I think of the shootings and strangulations she will have to endure next year in a story of my own.

At least *One Rainy Afternoon* was a good film until they began to make it: so much cannot be said of the Czechoslovakian film at the Academy or the French film at the Curzon. The Czech film is historical: a tyrannical landowner, a serf who takes to the mountains and robs the rich so that he may give to the poor: this theme should retain its appeal until the Millennium, but it is treated in such a romantic rollicking tuneful way that we are reminded of *The Maid of the Mountains*, until the effective final sequence of Janosik's capture and his cruel death, hung like butcher's meat with a spike in his ribs. Romance and robber tunes and lyrical shots of a long-legged Fairbanks hero don't go with a spike.

The Phantom Gondola has exactly the opposite fault. A cheap, trivial and pretentious story by a popular writer of rather low reputation (M. Maurice Dekobra, author of *His Chinese Concubine* and *The Madonna of the Sleeping Cars*) has been directed with enormous gravity and the kind of Art which goes with Venice, sunsets and huge expensive palazzos. It is one of the only two films this year I have found myself unable to endure to the end (the other was *The Tunnel*), and so I cannot say how this tale of a mysterious and very aristocractic Englishwoman who steals a telegram from the study of the Turkish Ambassador, in order to prove her love for a still more mysterious Italian Count, ends. I couldn't wait long enough to learn his object, or to discover the name of the mournful Asiatic female with a good deal of sensual charm who followed him around and peered through windows. For never has a melodrama proceeded so slowly, with such a saga-like tread.

The Spectator (10 July 1936)

One Rainy Afternoon (USA, Pickford-Lasky, 1936) Dir.: Rowland V. Lee. Cast: Francis Lederer, Ida Lupino.
Janosik (Czechoslovakia, Lloyd-Film, 1935) Dir.: Mac Fric. Cast: Palo Bielik, Zlata Hajdukova.
The Phantom Gondola (La Gondole aux Chimres) (France, Film Expert, 1936). Dir.: Augusto Genina. Cast: Marcelle Chantal, Roger Karl, Henri Rollan.

Poppy · Living Dangerously · Charlie Chan at the Circus

It is the loud check trousers we first see, a pair of shoes which have known their best days, and as the camera travels up to the extraordinary swollen nose, the little cunning heartless eyes, the period top hat, we become aware of the W. C. Fields voice, that low rich grumble rather like the noise of a distant train, which will presently swell, we know from experience, into loud rotund periods, the words a little misapplied – 'Forgive my redundancy, my dear madam, forgive my redundancy.' Mr Fields's latest incarnation is Professor Eustace McGargle, a travelling quack, a three-card man (he uses one of his cards to stuff a hole in his daughter's shoe), temporarily down on his luck. The story is an old and sentimental one: how the Professor, with the help of a forged marriage certificate and the services of a crooked country solicitor, Mr Whiffen, claims for his innocent young daughter the local Pakenham fortune, how he is double-crossed by Whiffen, escapes with difficulty from the Sheriff, and how his daughter, who is not really his daughter at all, turns out to be the genuine heiress. Professor McGargle, of course, in the accepted Chaplin tradition, moves on – in the Mayor's best hat, with one of the Mayor's cigars in his mouth and the Mayor's best silver-knobbed cane in his hand.

But the story doesn't really matter, for Mr Fields has never acted better. There is no touch of sentimentality in *his* performance. When he says good-bye for the last time to his adopted daughter with spurious tears in the old boar eyes, his final word of advice is, 'Never give a sucker an even break.' The scenarist has had the good sense to leave Mr Fields's villainy undimmed by any genuine affection. He wins our hearts not by a display of Chaplin sentiment, not by class solidarity (he robs the poor as promptly as the rich), but simply by the completeness of his dishonesty. To watch Mr Fields, as Dickensian as anything Dickens ever wrote, is a form of escape for poor human creatures: we who are haunted by pity, by fear, by our sense of right and wrong, who are tongue-tied by conscience, watch with envious love this free spirit robbing the gardener of ten dollars, cheating the country yokels by his own variant of the three-card trick, faking a marriage certificate, and keeping up all the time, in the least worthy and the most embarrassing circumstances, his amazing flow of inflated sentiments. There is something in Mr Fields's appearance which has always reminded me of Mr Baldwin (or at any rate of Low's cartoon of Mr Baldwin), but it is Mr Fields's most delightful characteristic that his lips are never, for one moment, sealed, for he fills up even the blanks in the script with his rumble of unintelligible rotundities.

The other two films on my list will have left the Regal by the time this notice appears, but it is quite worth watching for them at local cinemas. *Living Dangerously* is an English melodrama with an American star, Mr Otto Kruger, the story of a doctor 'framed' by his partner, who accuses him of sexual relations with his wife while treating her professionally. He is struck off the register by the General Medical Council and goes to America with the woman. The husband follows them and tries to blackmail him, and the film begins with the murder of the blackmailer and ends with the District Attorney helping the doctor to make his 'self-defence' plea convincing. It is not a very satisfying film, but it is above the usual standard of English pictures, and the scene of the trial before the General Medical Council, where no witnesses are sworn and any lies can be told in the box without fear of perjury, is excellent. We are used to America criticizing her institutions on the screen, but it is unusual in this country for a picture with some bite and bitterness to get past the censor.

As for Charlie Chan he needs no recommendation. The films in which he appears are all genuine detective films as distinct from thrillers, they are always well made and well acted. The new picture is particularly agreeable, for we see Mr Chan for the first time in a domestic setting and meet not only his amorous eldest son but his complete family of fourteen.

The Spectator (17 July 1936)

Poppy (USA, Paramount, 1936) Dir.: A. Edward Sutherland. Cast: W. C. Fields, Rochelle Hudson, Richard Cromwell, Lynne Overman.
Living Dangerously (GB, British International, 1936) Dir.: Herbert Brenon. Cast: Otto Kruger.
Charlie Chan at the Circus (USA, Twentieth-Century Fox, 1936) Dir.: Harry Lachman. Cast: Warner Oland, Keye Luke, George and Olive Brasno.

The Petrified Forest

'Dramatize, dramatize.' Those were the words which used to ring in James's ear whenever some anecdote at a dinner-table touched his creative brain, but how seldom are they heard by even the most distinguished contemporary dramatists. Mr Sherwood, for instance . . . I seldom go to the theatre, but even I heard of Mr Sherwood as a playwright of uncommon ability, and it was with great hope that I visited *The Petrified Forest*. The opening movement of his drama is very promising: the lonely filling-station on the edge of the Arizona Desert; the old garrulous owner had once been shot at for fun by Billy the Kid and had kept a soft place in his heart for killers ever since; his grand-daughter with her taste for poetry who feels her life drying up in the dust-storms; her father, an officer in the Vigilantes, trying to get excitement from his fake uniform and bogus drills; the huge dumb hired hand with his eyes on the girl; and then the arrival of the educated down-and-out, the girl's outbreak of sudden starved love, his departure with his food unpaid for and a dollar the girl had given him from the till, and finally disaster breaking in with a killer and his gang on the run from Oklahoma, and the down-and-out's deliberate return.

There is good dramatic material here, but Mr Sherwood doesn't see his plays as certain things happening but as ideas being expressed, 'significant' cosmic ideas. As for the plot, the drama, these are rather low-class necessities, like the adulteries in Mr Charles Morgan's novels. The down-and-out, so that he may express the ideas, must be an unsuccessful author, for whose Art he sacrifices his life (Mr Sherwood is nothing if not literary). The hero leaves the girl his life-assurance money and then forces the killer to shoot him, though why, if he hadn't a cent in his pocket, was the life-assurance for five thousand dollars fully paid up, or if that be explainable, why had this homeless and friendless tramp not cashed it for its face value? But first all through a long evening, with the sad simian killer (the best character in the play) sitting above with his beer and his pistol, the self-pitying post-war ideas have to be bandied about. 'Dramatize, dramatize,' one longs to remind Mr Sherwood, as more and more the concrete fact – the gun, the desert, the killer – gives place to Life, Love, Nature, all the great stale abstractions. It is as if Othello had met the armed men outside his door not with 'Put up your bright swords or the dew will rust them', but with some such sentence as: 'Nature, men, is having her revenge. You can't defeat Nature with your latest type of swords and daggers. She comes back every time in the shape of neuroses, jealousies . . .' and had let Desdemona and the affairs of Venice, Iago and the one particular handkerchief vanish before Women, Life, Sex . . .

So this drama slackens under the weight of Mr Sherwood's rather half-baked philosophy. The moral is stated frequently, with the tombstone clarity of a leading article, when it ought to be implicit in every action, every natural spoken word, in the camera angles even (but this is not a film but a canned play). There remain in this picture a few things to enjoy: the killer himself, with his conventional morality, his brooding hopelessness, his curious kindness, is memorable, but not so memorable nor so significant (the word which I am sure means most to Mr Sherwood) as the murderer in *Four Hours to Kill*. That killer was a profound and legendary figure, this one the ingenious invention of a clever writer. Miss Bette Davis gives a sound performance, Mr Leslie Howard faithfully underlines the self-pity and the bogus culture of a character embarrassing to us but obviously admired by his creator, and everyone works hard to try to give the illusion that the Whole of Life is symbolized in the Arizona filling-station. But life itself, which crept in during the opening scene, embarrassed perhaps at hearing itself so explicitly discussed, crept out again, leaving us only with the symbols, the too pasteboard desert, the stunted cardboard studio trees.

The Spectator (24 July 1936)

The Petrified Forest (USA, Warner, 1936) Dir.: Archie Mayo. Cast: Leslie Howard, Bette Davis, Humphrey Bogart, Genevieve Tobin, Dick Foran.

Laburnum Grove · Ourselves Alone

Here at last is an English film one can unreservedly praise. How pleasant for that stubborn grain of national feeling which would, I suppose, endure for centuries, like the embryo tail, even in a bright Genevan international day. I refer to Mr Carol Reed's *Laburnum Grove*, not to Mr Brian Desmond Hurst's *Ourselves Alone*, one of the silliest pictures which even an English studio has yet managed to turn out. This latter picture has been extravagantly praised, even compared favourably with *The Informer*, and yet I defy any normal person (among whom one has long ceased to number the boisterous good fellows of the London Press) to find more than one effective sequence, more than one good sentence, in this sentimental and melodramatic story of the Irish Rebellion. The dialogue and the script are not the fault of Mr Desmond Hurst, who has indeed directed one good scene, when the Black and Tans search a public house and the Irish women hide the Sinn Fein revolvers under their skirts and a sentimental ballad-singer sings plaintively on, while the camera makes a complete circle of the room, from the singer's face back to the singer's face, picking out the right authentic details on its way. This scene has unmistakable quality and promise; otherwise *Ourselves Alone*, following Mr Desmond Hurst's previous picture, *Riders to the Sea*, might make one despair of this director, who cannot yet manage his actors (Mr John Lodge and Mr John Loder have never acted less convincingly) and who shows little idea of timing.

Mr Carol Reed is a director of very different quality. *Laburnum Grove* maintains the promise of his first picture, *Midshipman*

Easy. Both films are thoroughly workmanlike and unpretentious, with just the hint of a personal manner which makes one believe that Mr Reed, when he gets the right script, will prove far more than efficient. *Laburnum Grove* set him and Mr Anthony Kimmins, the author of the screenplay, a difficult problem, for it is much harder to adapt a play to the screen than a novel. Mr Priestley's suburban fairy-tale of the respectable amateur gardener of Ferndale, who confessed cheerfully over the supper-table to his family that he was really a successful counterfeiter wanted by the Yard, was admirably suited to the three acts of the stage. Nine directors out of ten would simply have canned the play for mass consumption: Mr Reed has made a film of it. One remembered the opening sequence of *Midshipman Easy*, the camera sailing with the motion of a frigate before the wind down the hedge and the country lane to Easy's home, when the camera in Mr Reed's new film led us remorselessly down Laburnum Grove up to the threshold of the tall grim granite church at the bottom. Mr Priestley has been allowed to tell his agreeable and amusing story in much the same order and the same words as on the stage; but Mr Reed's camera has gone behind the dialogue, has picked out far more of the suburban background than Mr Priestley could convey in dialogue or the stage illustrate between its three walls: the hideous variegated Grove itself, the bottled beer and the cold suppers, the crowded ferny glass-house, the little stuffy bedrooms with thin walls, and the stale cigarette smoke and Bertie's half-consumed bananas. Suburbia, one of the newest suburbias, where the gravel lies slightly over what was grass and clover, insinuates itself into every shot. There isn't a wasted foot, and Mr Desmond Hurst could take a lesson from Mr Reed in something as elementary as moving his characters from one room to another. Mr Desmond Hurst's camera wanders after the story, some way behind, so that when a character is being politely ushered through a door, the spectator is already in the passage waiting for the next action and chafing at the delay. Mr Reed's camera acts with a kind of quick shrewd independence of the dialogue, and presents its own equally dramatic commentary, so that the picture of suburbia seems to be drawn simultaneously from two angles – which is as near as the screen can come as yet to steroscopy.

The Spectator (31 July 1936)

Laburnum Grove (GB, Associated Talking Pictures, 1936) Dir.: Carol Reed. Cast: Cedric Hardwicke, Victoria Hopper, Edmund Gwen, Katie Johnson.
Ourselves Alone (GB British International, 1936) Dir.: Brian Desmond Hurst. Cast: Walter Summers, John Lodge, John Loder.

Under Two Flags · Captain January

How Ouida would have loved the abandon of this picture, the thirty-two thousand rounds of ammunition shot off in the Arizona Desert, the cast of more than ten thousand (we are told that twenty thousand salary cheques were paid out, which seems a bit on the mean side), the five thousand pounds which insured Miss Claudette Colbert, Mr Ronald Colman, Mr Victor McLaglen and Miss Rosalind Russell against the camel bites – a curious item this, for none of these players, as far as I could see, came within half a mile of a camel – and, in the words of the programme: 'a fort 200 feet square, an Arabian oasis with eight fair-sized buildings, and a forest of transplanted date palms, two Arabian cities and a horse market and a smaller fort'. The absurdities are for once not Hollywood's: the picture does momentarily lift one into the odd dream-world of a passionate and inexperienced lady novelist resident in Italy. When Lady Venetia meets Sergeant Victor of the Foreign Legion (formerly a Guards officer and, as the newspapers put it, a West End Clubman) at the oasis at midnight and remarks, while the vox humana moans resonantly on, 'What perfect silence. One can hear the leaves move', Ouida, I am sure, would not have complained, for the vox humana must have been her perpetual background too: whether she was writing of boat-races ('no one rowed faster than . . .') or penning fiery letters to *The Times* on the subject of cruelty to animals, she must have lived at an emotional pressure to which only a Wurlitzer organ could do credit.

It was many years since I had seen the play, acted by half-starved barnstormers in a Welsh village, and I had forgotten the superb climax. Victor's company, down to their last rounds, are beseiged by ten thousand Arabs in their desert fort. Help may reach them by the next noon, but they cannot withstand another attack: the Arabs' onslaught must somehow be delayed, and Victor, dressed in Arabs robes, sidles across the sand-dunes to the enemy. He asks to be led to Sidi-Ben-Youssiff, and in the Arab leader's presence flings off his burnous. 'Don't you recognize me? I was at Magdalen when you were up at Balliol', and the Arab chief, taking a longer look, begins to recall those forgotten Oxford days. 'Of course. We met first, didn't we, at one of Professor Lake's breakfast-parties . . .' But I couldn't help being a little shocked when next morning Sidi-Ben-Youssiff, whom Victor had deceived into delaying the attack with a trumped-up story of British troops in his rear (one was loth to distrust the word of a man one had met at Professor Lake's breakfast-table), announced the Legionary's fate. 'You remember those soccer games we used to play. Well, this time my men are going to play on horseback and you will be the ball.' This surely is the Brasenose, not the Balliol, manner.

My admiration for Miss Claudette Colbert is unbounded, even when she has to play Cleopatra or the Empress Poppaea or Cigarette, the mascot of the Legion. In this part she is as convincingly the passionate but pure cocotte who dies of her wounds, after a mad gallop with windblown fringe and in enchanting trousers to save the company, as Mr Colman is an Oxford graduate in reduced circumstances. It is evident that Ouida's reputation for daring has reached her contemporaries on the British Board of Censors, for they have given the film an Adult Certificate, or perhaps it is the result of six chaste, sandy kisses exchanged in the desert between the mascot and the Magdalen man.

Captain January, the latest Shirley Temple picture, is sentimental, a little depraved, with an appeal interestingly decadent. An orphan salvaged from the sea is brought up by an old lighthouse-keeper. A wicked school-inspector wants to remove the child to an institution, and the exciting climax of the film is the competetive examination, on which the child's fate depends, between Miss Temple and the Inspector's spotty nephew. Shirley Temple acts and dances with immense vigour and assurance, but some of her popularity seems to rest on a coquetry quite as mature as Miss Colbert's and on an oddly precocious body as voluptuous in grey flannel trousers as Miss Dietrich's.

The Spectator (7 August 1936)

Under Two Flags (USA, Twentieth-Century Fox, 1936) Dir.: Frank Lloyd. Cast: Ronald Colman, Claudette Colbert, Rosalind Russell, Victor McLaglen.
Captain January (USA, Twentieth-Century Fox, 1936) Dir.: David Butler. Cast: Shirley Temple, Guy Kibbee, Buddy Ebsen, Slim Summerville, June Lang, Sara Haden, Jane Darwell.

Rhythm on the Range

Bing Crosby as a cowboy: Bing Crosby crooning a prize bull to sleep on a freight car: Bing Crosby more than ever like Walt Disney's Cock Robin: it needs some stamina to be a film reviewer. Only the conviction that a public art should be as popular and unsubtle as a dance tune enables one to sit with patient hope through pictures certainly unsubtle but not, in any real sense, popular. What a chance for the creative artist, one persists in believing, to produce for an audience incomparably greater than that of all the 'popular' novelists combined, from Mr Walpole to Mr Brett Young, a genuinely vulgar art. Any other is impossible. The novelist may write for a few thousand readers, but the film artist *must* work for millions. It should be his distinction and pride that he has a public whose needs have never been met since the closing of the theatres by Cromwell. But where is the vulgarity of this art? Alas! the refinement of the 'popular' novel has touched the films; it is the twopenny libraries they reflect rather than the Blackfriars Ring, the Wembley Final, the pin saloons, the coursing.

> I'm not the type that I seem to be,
> Happy-go-lucky and gay,

Bing Crosby mournfully croons. That is the common idea of popular entertainment, a mild self-pity, something soothing, something gently amusing. The film executive still thinks in terms of the 'popular' play and the 'popular' novel, of a limited middle-class audience, of the tired businessman and the feminine reader. The public which rattles down from the North to Wembley with curious hats and favours, tipsy in charabancs, doesn't, apparently, ask to be soothed: it asks to be excited. It was for these that the Elizabethan stage provided action which could arouse as communal a response as bear-baiting. For a popular response is not the sum of private excitements, but mass feeling, mass excitement, the Wembley roar, as the Art Photos a businessman may turn over in the secrecy of his study; the weakness of Bing Crosby's sentiment, the romantic nostalgia of 'Empty saddles in the old corral', that is by its nature a private emotion.

There are very few examples of what I mean by the proper popular use of the film, and most of those are farces: *Duck Soup*, the early Chaplins, a few 'shorts' by Laurel and Hardy. These do convey the sense that the picture has been made by its spectators and not merely shown to them, that it has sprung, as much as their sports, from *their* level. Serious films of the kind are even rarer: perhaps *Fury, Le Million, Men and Jobs*, they could be numbered on the fingers of one hand. Because they are so rare one is ready to accept, with exaggerated gratitude, such refined, elegant, dead pieces as *Louis Pasteur*: the Galsworthy entertainments of the screen: or intelligently adapted plays like *These Three*.

'People want to be taken out of themselves,' the film executive retorts under the mistaken impression that the critic is demanding a kind of Zolaesque realism – as if Webster's plays were realistic.

But I very much doubt if Bing Crosby does so much. 'They don't want to be depressed', but an excited audience is never depressed: if you excite your audience first, you can put over what you will of horror, suffering, truth. But there is one question to which there is no answer. How dare we excite an audience, a producer may well ask, when Lord Tyrell, the President of the British Board of Film Censors, forbids us to show any controversial subject on the screen?

Perhaps I ought to add that *Rhythm on the Range* is quite a tolerable picture with a few scenes which do deserve to be called popular cinema and an excellent new comedian, Mr Bob Burns. I think one might even find a place, in one's ideal popular cinema, for Mr Crosby: he represents permanent, if disagreeable, human characteristics of nostalgia and self-pity: I would have him bobbing about at the back of the scrimmage like a worried referee – or like an Elizabethan clown crooning his lugubrious reminders.

The Spectator (14 August 1936)

Rhythm on the Range (USA, Paramount, 1936) Dir.: Norman Taurog. Cast: Bing Crosby, Frances Farmer, Bob Burns, Martha Raye, Lucile Watson, Samuel S. Hinds.

Everything is Thunder · Die Kribbebijter

A Canadian officer escapes from a German prison camp, after killing a sentry who has double-crossed him, is sheltered by a prostitute in Berlin, and finally escapes with her across the frontier with the help of bootleggers who smuggle butter from Holland to Germany. This English film is good entertainment, very ably directed and admirably acted by two of its three international stars. Mr Douglass Montgomery as Captain McGrath, the escaper, gives a nervous, hunted, goose-fleshed performance, and Mr Oscar Homolka as the police detective, who is also one of the prostitute's lovers, breathes into a film that grows at times dangerously lyrical a pleasing coarseness, an earthiness, a sense that in spite of such flummery as a marriage 'in the sight of God' and a heroic sacrifice, we are in touch with human beings. His sacrifice at the end, so that the lovers may escape, arises, of course, from that curious fixed managerial idea that the public, which has always, from *East Lynne* to *The Constant Nymph*, enjoyed its good cry, demands a happy ending. As for Miss Constance Bennett it would be unfair to say much. I suspect that her blurred blonde performance can be laid to the account of our maleficent Board of Censors, who have imposed on Miss Bennett the complicated task of acting a prostitute without ever mentioning her profession. Innuendos, hints, little embarrassed flights from the truth, clients who may after all be just friends: the central situation is heavily obscured. The descriptive letter A – 'for adults' – can never under the present dispensation be taken literally.

But the film is very good entertainment of a kind, the kind that deals with disguises and pursuits and incredible resourcefulness, with policemen on the stairs and hunted men in bathrooms. Captain Hardy's book, from which the film is drawn, was better than that. In a novel he was able vividly to represent the mental background of his professional escaper, a man who was regarded by the other officers with a mixture of disapproval and contempt, someone who couldn't settle down with prisoners of his own age and play the right recognized games. It was Captain Hardy's interesting achievement to show that the wartime escaper is born, not made, that a man who breaks prison three times and tries again is a mental case. But this kind of psychological theme film directors seem unwilling to tackle. There is an admirably exciting sequence at a Berlin railway station when the police close the exit and examine every male passenger: no novel could represent the danger and terror of the trap more vividly, but to authenticate McGrath's sudden love for the Berlin prostitute who takes him home, something less purely visual is needed, it is necessary to go further into the escapist mind than the film takes us. The book was not sentimental: the film is. Here was an occasion for soliloquy, for the voices from the air Clair used in comedy, for all the resources too of wild-track sound, to get the escapist mind upon the screen.

The dismal continental cavalcade goes on. 'The first Dutch comedy' – so the Academy advertise their film – is very badly photographed and very badly directed. The story proceeds with dreadful inevitability. A rich man's son marries a typist and is disowned by his father, a household tyrant. The typist introduces herself into the castle as a housekeeper and wins the heart of this male shrew. That is really the whole story, though there was one very funny scene – at the end of an hour. It was a long time to wait, when all the time you could see the conclusion ahead, like a church spire visible for ten miles to the tired walker across the Flemish flats. The direction was of that grim slow kind which never shows you a car without following it to the horizon or lets a character leave one room for another without a prolonged study of opening and closing, and then reopening and reclosing doors, with a glimpse of the passage perhaps as well, lest the imagination should bear too heavy a burden.

The Spectator (14 August 1936)

Everything is Thunder (GB, Gaumont British, 1936) Dir.: Milton Rosmer. Cast: Constance Bennett, Douglass Montgomery, Oscar Homolka, Roy Emerton,

Die Kribbebijter (Holland, 1935) Dir.: Herman Kosterlitz, Ernst Winer. Cast: Cor Ruys, Louis de Bree, Louis Borel.

Mr Deeds Goes to Town

Mr Deeds is Capra's finest film (it is on quite a different intellectual level from the spirited and delightful *It Happened One Night*), and that means it is a comedy quite unmatched on the screen. For Capra has what Lubitsch, the witty playboy, has not: a sense of responsibility, and what Clair, whimsical, poetic, a little precious and *à la mode*, has not, a kinship with his audience, a sense of common life, a morality: he has what even Chaplin has not, complete mastery of his medium, and that medium the sound-film, not the film with sound attached to it. Like Lang, he hears all the time just as clearly as he sees and just as selectively. I do not think anyone can watch *Mr Deeds* for long without being aware of a technician as great as Lang employed on a theme which profoundly moves him: the theme of goodness and simplicity manhandled in a deeply selfish and brutal world. That was the theme of *Fury*, too, but Capra is more fortunate than Lang. Lang expresses the theme in terms of terror, and terror on the screen has always, alas! to be tempered to the shorn lamb; Capra expresses it in terms of pity and ironic tenderness, and no magnate feels the need to cramp his style or alter his conclusion.

Mr Deeds is a young provincial who inherits twenty million dollars from an uncle he has never seen. An ardent tuba-player in the local band, he makes his living by writing verses which are printed on postcards on such occasions as Mothers' Day. The uncle's solicitors, who have absorbed, with the help of a Power of Attorney, half a million dollars of his money, hope to continue the process with his unsophisticated nephew who is quite unexcited by his fortune and only wants to do good with it. They bring Deeds up to town. Wealth educates Deeds, he learns the shabby side not only of business but of art, with the help of the opera directors and the fashionable poets; he learns, too, the deceit which may exist in ordinary human affection (the girl he loves, and who loves him, is all the time writing newspaper articles which make front-page fun of the activities of the Cinderella Man). A revolver and a would-be assassin's nerveless hand educate him socially, and he is arranging to use the whole of his fortune in providing ruined farmers with free land and free seed when society – controlled by racketeers – strikes its last blow at the elements it cannot absorb, goodness, simplicity, disinterestedness. Claimants are found to dispute his sanity and to try to remove the management of the estate from his hands.

It sounds as grim a theme as *Fury*; innocence lynched as effectively at a judicial inquiry as in a burning courthouse, but there is this difference between Lang and Capra: Lang's happy ending was imposed on him, we did not believe in it; Capra's is natural and unforced. He *believes* in the possibility of happiness; he believes, in spite of the controlling racketeers, in human nature. Goodness, simplicity, disinterestedness: these in his hands become fighting qualities. Deeds sees through opera directors, fashionable intellectuals, solicitors, psychologists who prove that he is insane merely because he likes playing the tuba and isn't greedy for money. Only for a few minutes in the courtroom does he lose heart and refuse to defend himself: he is never a helpless victim, like the garage-man behind the bars watching the woman lift her baby up to see the fun, and he comes back into the ring with folk humour and folk shrewdness to rout his enemies for the sake of the men they have ruined. The picture glows with that humour and shrewdness, just as Lang's curdles with his horror and disgust; it is funny, most of the time, as *Fury* was terrifying. It is not a question of truth or falsehood: two directors of genius have made pictures with curiously similar themes which present a conviction, a settled attitude towards life as it is lived. The pessimist makes a tragedy, the optimist makes a comedy. And Capra, as well as Lang, is supported by a perfect cast. Every minor part, however few the lines, is completely rendered, and Mr Gary Cooper's subtle and pliable performance must be something of which other directors have only dreamed.

The Spectator (28 August 1936)

Mr Deed Goes to Town (USA, Columbia, 1936) Dir.: Frank Capra. Cast: Gary Cooper, Jean Arthur, George Bancroft, Lionel Stander, Douglas Dumbrille, Raymond Walburn, H. B. Warner.

The Man Who Could Work Miracles

A dark handsome colossus broods obscurely through a starry sky, broods, rather like Mr Wells himself, histrionically. From the remark of two equally enormous, even more handsome, but this time indubitably Aryan giants, we learn in the authentic late-Wells dialogue his name. 'Our Brother, the Giver of Power, is yonder.' We remember the Dictator and the Airman in Mr Wells's previous film: 'Who are you?' 'I am Wings over the World', and arm ourselves against a sea of abstractions, couched in Mr Wells's embarrassing poetic diction. But, fortunately, after an interchange of rather wilting remarks about this obscure planet, we come to earth, to a Kentish inn and Mr Fotheringay, floor-walker in the local drapery, whom the Giver of Power has decided to endow with miraculous gifts, so that he may learn what really lies in the heart of a small mortal creature. The late Wells, we realize, has decided that the early Wells, the author of some of the finest comedies in English fiction, was not significant enough. A few immortals and great conspiracies are tacked, like news-cuttings in a Surrealist picture, to the early short story. The result is pretentious and mildly entertaining, with no moments as good as the war sequences in *Things to Come*, nor as bad as what followed them.

The direction and the production are shocking. That is not Mr Wells's fault. And it may not be altogether the fault of Mr Lothar Mendes, the director, for the slowness, vulgarity, over-emphasis are typical of Mr Korda's productions. Take for example an early sequence. The Giver of Power leans through the sky with outstretched finger. 'I will choose anyone,' he says, 'this little man for instance', and the film cuts to the stagy pasteboard (why not use a proper exterior?) country inn and Mr Fotheringay hesitating at the door. You would think an audience could be trusted to catch the idea, you would think the spotlight which then shines down on the little man was the very limit of emphasis, but no! an enormous hand and wrist, a celestial signpost, is projected from the sky to point Mr Fotheringay out to dullards. For all this, and for the deplorable miscasting, Mr Wells is not responsible. Mr Korda, a publicity man of genius, who has not yet revealed a talent for the films, casts his pictures with little regard for anything but gossip paragraphs. Mr Roland Young is quite the wrong type for Fotheringay, with his intermittent accent and his eyes which twinkle merrily with lack of conviction: Mr Ralph Richardson's Tory colonel might have been entertaining in a stage farce, but there is no room on the screen for 'wigs by Clarkson' and false whiskers. The only performance of real character is Mr Lawrence Hanray's as the scared bird-like bank manager. As for trick photography, of which this film is naturally an orgy, and like orgies of another kind grimly repetitive, it is always to my mind dull and unconvincing and destroys illusion.

There remains Mr Wells's ideas. What *does* the Giver of Power find at the heart of his ordinary mortal? The answer is muddle, a rather too Wellsian muddle. The little man, badgered by business, by conservatism, by religion to make *their* world, rebels, and, announcing that he will make his own, summons before him all the great men, soldiers, politicians and lawyers, and gives them till day to form a plan for a peaceful society. Yet when the Reverend Mr Maydig protests that the time is too short, that the sun is already setting, Mr Fotheringay, for no reason at all, chooses to abolish his time-limit and stop the sun. The result is chaos, and Mr Fotheringay wheeled round by the ferocious elements puts everything back as it was before. Add to this Mr Wells's childish love of fancy-dress (the little man as dictator of the world goes, most improbably, Tudor) and a touch of sexual vulgarity (a beauty chorus of Kentish concubines suspiciously reminiscent of Mr Korda's idea of Henry VIII's wives) and you have the whole entertainment, sometimes fake poetry, sometimes unsuccessful comedy, sometimes farce, sometimes sociological discussion, without a spark of creative talent or a trace of film ability.

The Spectator (4 September 1936)

The Man Who Could Work Miracles (GB, London Films, 1936) Dir.: Lothar Mendes. Cast: Roland Young, Ralph Richardson, George Sanders, Ernest Thesiger, Edward Chapman, George Zucco, Lawrence Hanray.

As You Like It · Cover to Cover

As You Like It is a respectful film: that is to say there is far more Shakespeare in it than there was in Reinhardt's *Dream*, and I dare say it is a better production than you will often see on the stage. In Miss Bergner's Rosalind freedom may have become elvishness and poetry sometimes whimsicality, her tear-smudged, bewildered features may be more easily associated with a constant nymph than with the reckless-tongued Rosalind, but certainly in her private version she is, like white witches, 'mischievously good';

while Mr Laurence Olivier's Orlando, sullen, brooding, a little oafish, is even more satisfying. The only jarring notes in the acting were Mr Henry Ainley's Duke and Mr Leon Quartermaine's Jacques. Mr Ainley's false fruity enunciation carries us back to the Edwardian stage, when every Shakespearean actor ranted like a little Irving, and as for Jacques, his sting has been quite drawn. The great public may well wonder why this hearty good fellow was known to his companions as 'melancholy'. Horns and cuckolds have been heavily censored, the streak of poison which runs through the comedy has been squeezed carefully out between hygenic finger-tips, and what is left, apart from Arden and absurd delightful artificial love, is Shakespeare at his falsest, Adam and church bells and good men's feasts and sermons in stone, all the dull didactic unconvincing images. That, I think, is the chief objection to Shakespeare on the screen: the British Board of Film Censors will see to it that only the school versions of his plays are produced.

Regarded as a film, *As You Like It* is less satisfactory. There are far too many dull middle-length shots from a fixed camera, so that we might just as well be seated in the circle above the deep wide stage at Drury Lane. The special possibilities soliloquy gives are ignored: the 'Seven Ages of Man' is as falsely italicized as it usually is on the stage: we watch Jacques taking deep breath for the too famous passage, we watch his audience intently and unaccountably absorbed in the rather banal recital. How much more effectively this speech could have been expressed on the screen: say, through the ears and eyes of a *bored* listener who wanders off from the prosy cynic out of earshot but turns suddenly back to hear the better when a finer, more truthful line happens to reach his ear: 'even in the cannon's mouth', 'sans teeth, sans eyes, sans taste, sans everything.' Dr Czinner has been too respectful towards stage tradition. He seems to have concluded that all the cinema can offer is more space: more elaborate palace sets and a real wood with room for real animals. How the ubiquitous livestock (sheep and cows and hens and rabbits) weary us before the end, and how disastrously the genuine English woodland is spoilt by too much fancy, for when did English trees, in what is apparently late-autumn, bear clusters of white flowers? Freedom of movement, too, is often misused, and why should poetry be cut merely to leave time for girlish games of touch-wood through the trees? On only one occasion is the camera a definite gain. The lyrical repetitions between Sylvius and Phebe, Orlando and Rosalind: 'It is to be made of sighs and tears: And so am I for Phebe.' 'And I for Ganymede.' 'And I for Rosalind.' 'And I for no woman,' with the help of the rhythmically panning camera move beautifully into the memory.

Cover to Cover, Mr Paul Rotha's short film made for the National Book Council, is a far more interesting picture, for this director uses the counterpoint of sound and image with sublety. Among the distinguished authors who take part, Miss Rebecca West has the best lines, and Mr T. S. Eliot, I was grieved to notice, has not so good a screen face or manner as Sapper. Verse is skilfully used in the commentary, though it has less simplicity, is less 'seeable' than Mr Auden's in *Night Mail*, and all the stages of a book from MS. to library and counter are dramatized with real imagination. From the documentary point of view I have one serious criticism. Did there ever exist such a heaven-born publisher as this who consults an author in the choice of his type and paper.

SAYING OF THE WEEK
'The whole of *As You Like It* is really an intimate memoir of a girl's first love-affair.' (C. A. Lejeune)

The Spectator (11 September 1936)

As You Like It (GB, Inter Allied, 1936) Dir.: Paul Czinner. Cast: Laurence Olivier, Elisabeth Bergner, Leon Quartermaine, Henry Ainley, Sophie Stewart, Felix Aylmer, John Laurie.
Cover to Cover (GB, National Book Council, 1936) Dir.: Paul Rotha.

The Great Ziegfeld · It's Love Again · Marchand d'Amour · East Meets West

The Great Ziegfeld is another of those films which belong to the history of publicity rather than to the history of the cinema. This huge inflated gas-blown object bobs into the critical view as irrelevantly as an airship advertising someone's toothpaste over a South Coast 'resort'. It lasts three hours: that is its only claim to special attention. Like a man sitting hour after hour on top of a pole, it does excite a kind of wonder; wonder at how it manages to go on. It justifies its length as little as do the *Faraways*, the *Anthony Adverses*, the Severn novels which wind their dim protracted course through the realm of fiction. The padding is only too obvious. Instead of one love-affair, we have two; instead of one big musical set-piece, we have half a dozen. There is really no reason, except the patience of the public, why such a picture should ever stop. 'Long enough to bore, but not yet big enough to boost', I can imagine one of the great executives remarking, when the picture has not yet passed far beyond the second hour, 'throw in another grand passion and three more super-spectacles, and draw out for another thousand feet that death scene.' So Ziegfeld, for a quite unconscionable time, passes out to dim music, while the sky-signs of his latest show flicker beyond the window-panes. This New World hero, who has 'glorified the American girl', in other words the dumber carnalities, the great glittering bogus blondes, is heard questioning for a moment the eternal values of his career, but his valet reassures him, 'You have done the most beautiful things that have ever been done on any stage.' Alas! we have watched them for the last three hours, and now for several minutes more they crowd back to their dying creator's memory. The glorified girls push him up towards Paradise, like the cherubs which throng round the topboots of William of Orange in Rubens's apotheosis. Mr William Powell does his best. Miss Myrna Loy rather less than her best, and Miss Luise Rainer brings a few moments of real distinction and of human feeling to this, the longest and, if superlatives have got to be used, the silliest, vulgarest, dullest novelty of the season.

For once it is possible to praise an English 'musical' above an American. Mr Victor Saville has directed *It's Love Again* with speed, efficiency, and a real sense of the absurd. Nor has the long tubular form of Miss Jessie Matthews, the curious charm of her ungainly adolescent carriage, ever been better exploited. The story is agreeably silly, a long way from the grand, the showman's, passions, the huge misplaced seriousness of the American film which weighs on the spirits like a visit to the Royal Academy. It is the story of a talented young singer and dancer who cannot get an audition until she has gate-crashed into the gossip columns with a bogus career of Eastern exploration and tiger-shooting behind her. Her encounter in a shower of superb double meanings and enormous gallantries, at an Oriental party given in her honour, with a genuine old tiger-shooting colonel, whom she believes to be her friend, a former gossip-writer, in disguise, is memorable indeed.

Apart from this picture and Mr Edmond Greville's *Marchand d'Amour*, a melodramatic and rather silly tale of another showman's great, but frankly more carnal love, directed with immense *panache* and a secret sense of amusement, the most enjoyable film I have seen this week has been *The Gift of the Gab*, an item in Gaumont-British News which I hope will not disappear altogether when the week is over. A carefully arranged anthology of modern oratory, it ranges maliciously from Mr Lloyd George's mechanic passion to the mumbled, almost inaudible, 'Awfully nice', of the too British winner of a King's Cup Air Race. And finally a warning – to avoid like the plague *East Meets West*, in which Mr George Arliss appears in one of his most kindly parts to date. This time he is an Eastern Rajah, but who can change the sly soft episcopal speech, the long upper-lip, like that of a well-bred horse, the general tone of a good club?

The Spectator (18 September 1936)

The Great Ziegfeld (USA, MGM, 1936) Dir.: Robert Z. Leonard. Cast: William Powell, Myrna Loy, Luise Rainer, Frank Morgan, Virginia Bruce, Fanny Brice, Harriet Hector.

It's Love Again (GB, Gaumont British, 1936) Dir.: Victor Saville. Cast: Jessie Matthews, Robert Young, Sonnie Hale, Robb Wilton, Sara Allgood, Athene Seyler, Ernest Milton.

Marchand d'Amour (France, S. H. O. Films, 1936) Dir.: Edmond Greville. Cast: Jean Galland, Rosine Deréan.

East Meets West (GB, Gaumont British, 1936) Dir.: Herbert Mason. Cast: George Arliss, Lucie Mannheim, Godfrey Tearle, Romney Brent.

The Song of Freedom · Anthony Adverse

The Song of Freedom is the story of Zinga, a black London dockhand, who, unknown to himself, is the descendant of a seventeenth-century 'Queen' of Cassanga, an island off the West Coast. All he has inherited is a crude medallion and a few bars of a song, handed down from father to son. Born in London he remains an exile at heart, passionately longing for some knowledge of his home. A distinguished musical impresario hears him singing in a public house, trains him and makes him a famous singer, but on the first night of an opera founded on *The Emperor Jones*, he meets an anthropologist who recognizes 'the king's song' of Cassanga and the medallion. Cassanga, he tells Zinga, is a poor impoverished place. White men have not been allowed to land, and the island is ruled by witch-doctors. Zinga and his wife set out immediately with the idea of helping the people and – alas! for the inconsistencies of the tale – bringing them the blessings of white civilization. At first the witch-doctor's influence is too strong. Zinga's wife, who has watched a forbidden rite – the shadow of Hollywood has fallen across the screen – is condemned to death, and only at the last moment does Zinga remember 'the king's song' and establish his authority, for luckily these curious islanders seem to have as strong an instinct for hereditary rule as members of the White Rose League. Apart from the profound beauty of Miss Elizabeth Welch and Mr Robeson's magnificent singing of inferior songs, I find it hard to say in what the charm of this imperfect picture lies. The direction is distinguished but not above reproach, the story is sentimental and absurd, and yet a sense stays in the memory of an unsophisticated mind fumbling on the edge of simple and popular poetry. The best scenes are the dockland scenes, the men returning from work, black and white in an easy companionship free from any colour bar, the public house interiors, the dark faces pausing at tenement windows to listen to Zinga's songs, a sentimentality, a touch of 'quaintness' and patronage, but one is made aware all the time of what Mann calls 'the gnawing surreptitiousness hankering for the bliss of the commonplace', the general exile of our class as well as the particular exile of the African.

But everything goes badly wrong when Zinga reaches Africa, the fabulous island where the witch-doctors speak Biblical English ('The heart of Mandingo is heavy because you come'). That is not an authentic situation, for the part of Africa untouched by white influence is minute. If we were to take the film seriously, it should have been to a white colony that Zinga returned, a colony of the half-educated like Sierra Leone where the teaching must be stopped at a point not goverened by the pupil's capacity but by the Government's policy. There, rather than in a fairy-tale primitive island, lies the real dramatic situation, but I doubt whether it could have been resolved as happily and easily. A few bars of a 'king's song' would not abolish the bounce and the subservience, the contempt and the laughter.

Anthony Adverse goes on too long, otherwise it might have been the funniest film since *The Crusades*, with its lyrical captions taken over from silent days: 'Thus an unwanted child was given a name, and for ten years heard it spoken only by the good sisters and his kindly teacher, Father Xavier.' The sexual chronology is curious. I am still puzzled by the dreadful child in an Eton jacket who was waiting unexpectedly to call Anthony 'father' at the end of his wanderings, for Anthony, who married his wife secretly one morning, mislaid her before noon and only saw her again after seven years: a fishy situation which perhaps our film censors have unduly obscured. But most I welcomed our old friend Pedro de Cordoba, with his weaving tortoise head, who crops up in odd unexplained ways in Havana and West Africa wearing a cowl, and who dies at last on his back in the mud, his flippers feebly waving, his odd receding mouth opening and shutting, a masterly interpretation of Miss Potter's Ptolemy Tortoise.

The Spectator (25 September 1936)

The Song of Freedom (GB, Hammer, 1936) Dir.: J. Elder Wills. Cast: Paul Robeson, Elizabeth Welch, George Mozart, Esmé Percy.
Anthony Adverse (USA, Warner, 1936) Dir.: Mervyn Le Roy. Cast: Fredric March, Olivia de Havilland, Claude Rains, Gale Sondergaard, Edmund Gwenn, Anita Louise, Louis Heyward, Donald Woods, Akim Tamiroff, Ralph Morgan, Henry O'Neill.

Maria Bashkirtseff · My Man Godfrey

It is a little more than fifty years since Maria Bashkirtseff died; if her lungs had not failed, she might have been alive today, but already the film magnates are rearranging her life in what they consider a better film pattern. No historical novelist would dare to take such liberties, to invent for the eighteen-year-old Maria Bashkirtseff, who as far as anyone can tell from her journal had no experience of sexual passion (the nearest she came to it was for the sick Bastien-Lepage), a reciprocated love for Maupassant. This melancholy, introspective and ambitious girl with the broad shoulders, big breasts and Spanish hips, becomes a blithe and bony girl of mature years, who holds hands with Maupassant in moonlight and dreams of country cottages. The same evening she overhears her family doctor telling Maupassant's rival that she has only a few weeks to live, and so she dismisses Maupassant, feigning that she cares less for him than for the gold medal of the forthcoming exhibition. But the film imagination rises even higher into the great inane, the rival lover himself wins the medal, takes it to Maupassant and asks that he, as one of the judges, shall present it to Maria, so that she may die happy. And to Maupassant at her bedside, Maria reveals that she cares nothing for the medal and had dismissed him only because she loved him. Who, after all this, could believe that there is not a single mention of Maupassant in Maria Bashkirtseff's journal? 'A free adaptation of historical facts', the programme calls it, and one wonders that the adapters lost such an opportunity for Oriental passion, Disraeli and desert sands as Maria's meeting with De Lesseps at an Embassy reception gave them, where he told her 'a long story of nurses and babies and Suez canal shares', a story on which much might have been founded to convince the great public that real lives are as banal and melodramatic as those of the screen. It is difficult, repelled by the dishonesty and vulgarity of this 'free adaptation', to be quite fair to the merits of the picture: the careful and discreet period setting and Herr Hans Jaray's performance as Maupassant, which gives the right impression of dapper despair, of spiritual nihilism in a well-cut coat, against the plush, the Baroque mirrors, the ornate decorations of private rooms.

My Man Godfrey, for three-quarters of its way, is acutely funny. The adventure of the sane man among the witless wealthy, the story opens with a 'scavenging party' at the Waldorf-Ritz to which competitors are expected to bring, besides such assorted objects as bowls of goldfish, goats and mangles, 'a forgotten man'. Mr William Powell, unshaven and for once more bitter than bright, is secured by a lovely nitwit from a rubbish-dump under Brooklyn Bridge. The chaotic scene of the shrieking alcoholic rich, leading goats and waving mangles through the great chromium halls, is perhaps the wittiest, as well as the noisiest, sequence of the year, but the film does not maintain quite so high a standard. Mr William Powell, adopted in place of a dead Pomeranian by the lovely brainless competitor, Miss Carole Lombard, whose voice unwinds in an endless enchanting ribbon of inanities, becomes the family butler, but alas! before the end he proves to be of even better blood, and Boston blood at that, than his employers, nor does 'the social conscience' remain agreeably implicit. Mr Powell is made to preach a sermon to the assembled family on social reform after saving them from bankruptcy by his knowledge of the stock markets and – curious moral – a huge luxury club rises on the site of the old rubbish-dump in which his old down-and-out friends are given employment in elegant uniforms. But though 'the social conscience' is a little confused, the film, in the earlier sequences, well conveys the atmosphere of an American Cherry Orchard, of a class with little of the grace and all the futility and some of the innocence of its Russian counterpart. Unfortunately, to these Americans prosperity returns, there is no dignified exit while the axes thud in the orchard, only the great glossy club rising over the wilderness of empty tins, and, last muddle and bewilderment, the marriage of the reformer and the brainless 'lovely'.

The Spectator (2 October 1936)

Maria Bashkirtseff (Austria, Tobis-Sascha, 1935) Dir.: Hermann Kosterlitz. Cast: Olga Tschechowa, Leo Slezak, Paul Heidemann, Hans Jaray.
My Man Godfrey (USA, Universal, 1936) Dir.: Gregory La Cava. Cast: William Powell, Carole Lombard, Mischa Auer, Alice Brady, Eugene Pallette, Gail Patrick, Alan Mowbray.

The Texas Rangers · Savoy Hotel 217 · The King Steps Out

The Big Parade, The Crowd, Hallelujah; these are some of Mr King Vidor's previous films, and *The Texas Rangers* is in the same tradition. Mr Vidor is one of the best of popular directors; D. W. Griffith, a much finer artist, is his master. No one who had not learnt a great deal from Griffith could have directed the battle between the Indians and a handful of Rangers with so sure a sense of old-time suspense; will help come in time? And the Indians swarm up the rocks, revolvers jam, the rescuers come galloping between the hills. A more sophisticated age has dealt in this case kindly with Vidor, for in a Griffith film it was unthinkable that help should ever *not* arrive, while now we are allowed to doubt.

In another way, too, Vidor is Griffith's successor: he does his best to give his pictures epic value. At the beginning of this film a voice describes the circumstances, the Indian wars and the bushranging, which brought the Texas Rangers into existence, and in the last sequence, the commanding officer, played by that fine actor, Mr Edward Ellis, with his thin, twisted farmer's face, speaks over a Ranger's grave an oration, pompous and political in its resounding abstractions, yet curiously moving in Mr Ellis's plain, honest enunciation, on the 'guardians of the frontier, makers of the peace'.

But in Vidor's epics, just as in Cruze's somewhat overpraised picture, *The Covered Wagon*, the story gets in the way: they bear about as much relation to epic drama as do the huge, artless, historical novels which have been so popular recently in the United States. The story of *The Texas Rangers*, I should add, is a great deal better than that of *The Covered Wagon*. It is the story of two bandits, acted by Mr Fred MacMurray and Mr Jack Oakie, who join the Rangers in order to send useful tips to a bushranging friend. They are converted to law and order, and when one has been murdered in an attempt to trap his former friend, the other goes out and gets his man. The morality of their actions is all the more convincing for its curiously twisted nature: one does, at moments, feel a little way lowered into the unplumbed complex caverns of the simple soul.

Savoy Hotel 217, directed by Gustav Ucicky (who made that excellent melodrama of the submarine war, *Morgenrot*), and photographed by Fritz Lang's old cameraman, takes us agreeably back to the classical old Ufa days of *Dr Mabuse* and *The Spy*. A philandering waiter (Hans Albers), an old-fashioned vamp who has one husband put out of the way and ruined and divorced another and who meets a violent and expected end, a lover from Siberia, a little chambermaid and a jealous housekeeper: the fates of all these are agreeably crossed in a slow, good-humoured murder-story set in pre-war St Petersburg. The most vivid character is that of the murderer, the vamp's husband, a little bankrupt merchant with popping eyes and tiny moustache and breaking voice, who gives the impression of a small, soft, tormented animal, of a mouse-like tragedy. Love on the servants' twisting iron stairway, jealousy round the linen-cupboard; the melodramatic passions are given a pleasantly realistic setting by a very competent director and a first-class cameraman.

Miss Grace Moore as a Bavarian princess who pretends to be a dressmaker and wins the heart of a young Austrian Emperor to save her sister from a loveless marriage: a plot like that can hardly fail to have its painful moments. Miss Moore acts with the exaggerated vivacity of a games-mistress letting herself noisily go on the last night of term, but unexpectedly the film has some light and amusing sequences, a Lubitsch touch, while Mr Herman Bing's innkeeper holds the stage. Mr Bing's rolling eyeballs, his enormous splutter, his huge lack of understanding, have never before been given such generous room. He bears the whole film on his wildly expressive shoulders.

The Spectator (9 October 1936)

The Texas Rangers (USA, Paramount, 1936) Dir.: King Vidor. Cast: Fred MacMurray, Jack Oakie, Jean Parker, Lloyd Nolan, Edward Ellis.
Savoy Hotel 217 (Germany, Ufa, 1936) Dir.: Gustav Ucicky. Cast: Hans Albers, Käthe Dorsch, Brigitte Horney.
The King Steps Out (USA, Columbia, 1936) Dir.: Josef von Sternberg. Cast: Grace Moore, Franchot Tone, Herman Bing, Walter Connolly, Raymond Walburn, Victor Jory, Frieda Inescort.

Nutrition

We are apt to forget, among the gangsters and the grand passions, that the cinema has other uses than fiction, and yet it is the Gas Light and Coke Company which is responsible for the most interesting film I have seen for a long time. This Company deserves the highest praise. For the second time it has undertaken a work which should have been the responsibility of the Ministry of Health. There is no gas propaganda in *Nutrition*, any more than there was in *Housing Problems*. Both pictures are the work of Mr Edgar Anstey, who is contributing something new to the documentary film. The documentary film has sometimes hovered too uneasily on the edge of art and story-telling. The GPO Film Unit in *Song of Ceylon* produced the most aesthetically satisfying film ever made in this country, but there have been times – *Night Mail*, for example – when the demands of instruction and the instinct to create a work of art have conflicted. The final sequences in *Night Mail* were aesthetically satisfying, but earlier in the film one was aware of hesitation: we were shown too many technicalities for atmospheric purposes, we were shown too few for understanding.

In *Housing Problems* Mr Anstey was superbly untroubled by the aesthetic craving: he used the camera as a first-class reporter, and a reporter too truthful, too vivid, to find a place on any modern newspaper. He produced a poignant and convincing document simply by taking his camera and his microphone into the slums, the terrible tiny peeling rooms, up the broken stairways, into the airless courts and letting the women talk in their own way about the dirt and rats and bugs. The method was simple, certainly, but it cannot have been easy; it must have needed human qualities more common among Russian than English directors. (Compare the characters in *Housing Problems* with the frightened ironed-out personalities with censored scripts whom the BBC present as 'documentary'.)

Nutrition has everything which *Housing Problems* had (the same human interest, handled with the finest, self-effacing sympathy) and a great deal more besides. It goes deeper and speaks with more authority. It takes the statistics, the categories of food (energy, body-building, protective), and presents the problem at different dramatic levels: the chemist in his laboratory examining his rats (the small, under-sized piebald creature, who scrambles in a scared way beneath his plump capitalist companion, has been fed on a typical working-class diet), Sir John Orr on his experimental farm, the Medical Officers of Bethnal Green and Stockton-on-Tees in conference, the street markets, the Bluecoat boys on their playing-fields, the working-class boys in their back streets. Professor Julian Huxley speaks the admirable, quite unpolitical commentary, which is interrupted occasionally for Mr Herbert Morrison to describe what London County Council is doing for elementary schoolchildren, for medical officers to discuss the proper balancing of diets, for working women themselves to speak with a sad courage of their house-keeping, of cabbages at sixpence a pound, of the inevitable hungry Thursdays. It is the foods which build and the foods which protect that are the most expensive: the energy foods, which the children need least, are the cheapest, and who can blame the parents if they choose to give their children the foods which will at least prevent them *feeling* their starvation? And a long parade goes past the camera of cheerful child faces above under-developed bodies.

Mr Anstey has had no aesthetic end in view: he has wanted to explain the problem clearly and to make the fight for better diets personal by means of showing the actual sufferers, the actual investigators, but there is always an aesthetic delight in complete competence. Conrad once wrote an essay in praise of the literary merits of the official Notes to Mariners, and as the film reaches its end, the summing-up of the commentator coinciding with a quick repetition of images, one is aware of having attended not only a vivid and authoritative lecture but a contribution to Cinema.

The Spectator (16 October 1936)

Nutrition (GB, Gas Light & Coke Company, 1936) Dir.: Edgar Anstey.

Romeo and Juliet

'Boy Meets Girl 1436' – so the programme heads the story of *Romeo and Juliet*, which it tells with some inaccuracy; but this fourth attempt to screen Shakespeare is not as bad as that. Unimaginative, certainly, coarse-grained, a little banal, it is frequently saved – by Shakespeare – from being a bad film. The late Irving Thalberg, the producer, has had a funeral success second only to Rudolph Valentino's, but there is nothing in this film to show that he was a producer of uncommon talent. He has made a big film, as Hollywood recognizes that adjective: all is on the characteristic Metro-Goldwyn scale: a Friar Laurence's cell with the appearance, as another critic has put it, of a modern luxury flat, with a laboratory of retorts and test-tubes worthy of a Wells superman (no 'osier cage' of a few flowers and weeds); a balcony so high that Juliet should really have conversed with Romeo in shouts like a sailor from the crow's-nest sighting land; a spectacular beginning with the Montagues and Capulets parading through pasteboard streets to the same church, rather late, it appears from the vague Popish singing off, for Benediction; Verona seen from the air, too palpably a childish model; an audible lark proclaiming in sparrow accents that it is not the nightingale; night skies sparkling with improbable tinsel stars; and lighting so oddly timed that when Juliet remarks that the mask of night is on her face, 'else would a maiden blush bepaint my cheek', not Verona's high moon could have lit her more plainly.

But on the credit side are more of Shakespeare's words than we have grown to expect, a few more indeed than he ever wrote, if little of the subtlety of his dramatic sense which let the storm begin slowly with the muttering of a few servants, rather than with the full-dress riot. The picture has been given a Universal Certificate, and one was pleasantly surprised to find how safely our film censors had slumbered through many a doubtful passage: even 'the bawdy hand of the dial' had not disturbed the merry gentlemen's rest. The nurse's part has suffered, but more from Miss Edna May Oliver's clowning than from a censor. This part and Mercutio's suffer most from overacting. Mr John Barrymore's middle-aged Mercutio is haggard with the grease-paint of a thousand Broadway nights. Mr Basil Rathbone is a fine vicious Tybalt, and Mr Leslie Howard and Miss Norma Shearer spoke verse as verse should be spoken and were very satisfying in the conventional and romantic and dreamy mode (one still waits to see lovers hot with lust and youth and Verona fevers, as reckless as their duelling families, 'like fire and powder which as they kiss consume').

It is the duel and violence which come off well, Mercutio's death and Tybalt's, and, more convincing than on the stage, the final fight with Paris in the tomb, but I am less than ever convinced that there is aesthetic justification for filming Shakespeare at all. The effect of even the best scenes is to distract, much in the same way as the old Tree productions distracted: we cannot look and listen simultaneously with equal vigilance. But that there may be a social justification I do not dispute; by all means let Shakespeare, even robbed of half his drama and three-quarters of his poetry, be mass-produced. One found oneself surrounded in the theatre by prosperous middle-aged ladies anxiously learning the story in the programme for the first time; urgent whispers came from the knowing ones, as Romeo went down into the Capulet tomb, preparing their timorous companions for an unexpected and unhappy ending. It may well be a social duty to teach the great middle class a little about Shakespeare's plays. But the poetry – shall we ever get the poetry upon the screen except in fits and starts (the small scene between Romeo and the ruined apothecary he bribes to sell him poison was exquisitely played and finely directed), unless we abjure all the liberties the huge sets and the extras condemn us to? Something like Dreyer's *Passion of Jeanne d'Arc*, the white-washed wall and the slow stream of faces, might preserve a little more of the poetry than this commercial splendour.

The Spectator (23 October 1936)

Romeo and Juliet (USA, MGM, 1936) Dir.: George Cukor Cast: Leslie Howard, Norma Shearer, John Barrymore, Basil Rathbone, Edna May Oliver, C. Aubrey Smith, Reginald Denny.

La Kermesse Héroïque · The General Died at Dawn

La Kermesse Héroïque is the rarest thing in the cinema, a really adult film. M. Jacques Feyder, who made one of the most memorable of all silent films, *Thérèse Raquin*, has produced a comedy which should appeal to the public which is now discovering *The Country Wife*. Like Restoration prose, his photography moves with a fine strut to the music of horns. The period is the sixteenth century, the place the town of Boom in Flanders during the rising against the Spanish domination. But virility in Boom is low, though male conceit is as blown as the breeches. The Burgomaster, the butcher, the baker, the fishmonger, in their black balloon trousers and ribbons and chains of local office, are being painted at the council table for the municipal gallery when two dusty professional soldiers spur in to announce the Spaniards' approach. Action is quick and prudent: the volunteers disband: their arms are hidden in the bowels of fish, and the Burgomaster poses upon his bed, a stout and pompous corpse lit by candles and guarded by councillors with halberds. He will sacrifice himself, he announces through the town-crier, for the safety of the town: the Spaniards will respect the dead.

But his wife is of another mettle. She summons the women to a mass meeting: she lays her ambush, and when the weary Spanish troops arrive, ready for another night of street fights, flames, and the exaggerated pleasures of rapine, they find the women, dressed in mouring for their dead Burgomaster, waiting with refreshments and offers of hospitality. The husbands cannot resist: their weapons, even if they had the courage to use them, are in the bellies of tomorrow's fish course; nor can the Burgomaster protest at the courtesy of the Spanish Duke towards his wife, for officially he is dead. The Spaniards leave the next day, their halberds wreathed in flowers, while his wife fingers her new pearl necklace. Boom is saved, the Burgomaster takes the credit, and the little town has as many horns as a hunting-lodge.

It is an admirable film, a little obscene like most good comedies, and beautifully acted. I admired particularly the Dominican chaplain with his mannered austerity and his concealed humour, the unctuousness which slips aside to disclose a pleasing natural frailty: the screen seldom allows one the pleasure of seeing more than a single layer of the human mind. M. Feyder's camera picks out with vividness and invention absurdities in costume and character and almost as skilfully as a Restoration dramatist he lightly works into his ribald story a touch of the genuine, the simple emotion. Even Mrs Pinchwife has her moments, and, so has this war-weary Duke and this woman of character married to a Flemish clod, and a touch of lyrical poetry breaks charmingly and unexpectedly through the close of the bawdy comedy: the first grey watery Lowland light behind the shuttered houses and the solitary drummer strutting out into the small deserted square.

The first few silent sequences of Mr Lewis Milestone's *The General Died at Dawn* are as good as anything to be seen on the screen in London: the dead Chinese village with kites circling down towards the corpses, the long pale grasses shivering aside as the troops trample through, the General with the scarred satisfied face riding away along the rough road in the slick American car. After that it becomes a melodrama, though a melodrama of more than usual skill, about an American with a social conscience (Mr Clifford Odets has written the dialogue) who tries to run a beltful of gold through to Shanghai with which arms may be bought to overthrow the local war-lord. He gets mixed up with a girl, of course, who's on the wrong side and shoots her father, and is pursued, even into the chromium Shanghai suite, by the sinister General. Mr Akim Tamiroff as the war-lord and Mr Porter Hall as his 'poor white' agent give vivid support to Mr Gary Cooper's tough laconic friend-of-the-underdog. If it were not for a rather ludicrous ending, this would be one of the best 'thrillers' for some years.

The Spectator (30 October 1936)

La Kermesse Héroïque (France, Film Sonores Tobis, 1935) Dir.: Jacques Feyder. Cast: Françoise Rosay, Louis Jouvet, Jean Murat, Alfred Adam, André Alerme. (US title: *Carnival in Flanders*)

The General Died at Dawn (USA, Paramount, 1936) Dir.: Lewis Milestone. Cast: Gary Cooper, Akim Tamiroff, Madeleine Carroll, Porter Hall, Dudley Digges, William Frawley.

Dodsworth · Mayerling · Fox Hunt

Dodsworth is a very well-made and well-acted film, with an essentially trivial subject. Dodsworth, a retired American magnate, urged by his wife, takes his first trip to Europe in the *Queen Mary* (the film has a breathless topicality about its inessentials). Mrs Dodsworth is a priggish, conceited woman, her thin mundane shell is stretched above a deep abyss of unsophistication. She feels the approach of old age and grand-maternity, and is determined to get in her fling first irrespective of her husband's feelings. She begins in the ship disastrously and ignominiously with a young Englishman of half her age and ten times her experience, but she graduates slowly at the various European capitals towards a degree of well-mannered adultery. Mr Walter Huston is admirable as the devoted and uncultured husband who is ready to stand almost anything once, even adultery, and who cannot rid himself of the deep sense of responsibility he has accumulated in twenty years of marriage, and Miss Ruth Chatterton presents grimly the fake worldliness, embittered egotism, meanness intense enough to verge on real evil, as his wife. Like *These Three*, another realistic film produced by Mr Goldwyn, *Dodsworth* is a little marred by almost incessant music, a relic of the small orchestras who used to accompany silent films. Music may be occasionally justified in a fictional film, but certainly not in *Dodsworth* or *These Three*, where the music sentimentally underlines emotional situations which have been carefully played down by actors and the dialogue-writers.

No one, I think, will fail to enjoy *Dodsworth*, in spite of its too limited and personal plot, the sense it leaves behind of a very expensive, very contemporary, Bond Street vacuum flask. Naturalness is so rare on the screen that it is difficult not to overpraise any picture which possesses it, but more than naturalness is needed for deep enjoyment. 'The best of them', Chekhov wrote of a few of his fellow novelists, 'are realistic and paint life as it is, but because every line is permeated, as with a juice, by its awareness of a purpose, you feel, besides life as it is, also life as it ought to be, and this captivates you.' Life as it ought to be – the nearest *Dodsworth* comes to that is a quaint Italian villa on the Bay of Naples and the company of a too gentle, too flower-like widow. The subject of *Mayerling*, the love-story of the Archduke Rudolph and Marie Vetsera which ended with the discovery of their two bodies in a hunting-lodge, is equally purposeless – in the romantic manner this time, a too romantic manner for my taste. The shot which ends Marie's life leaves her in a lovely waxen pose upon her bed, with one becoming streak of blood and the eyes tactfully closed. Duncan's body may be 'laced with its golden blood', because we are not concerned with Duncan's death so much as with Macbeth's crime, but if we romanticize the horrible end of the Archduke and his mistress, we lose all sense of tragedy. The smashed cartilage, the face so disfigured that it was unrecognizable, the fear of mortal sin and damnation which must have accompanied the two shots, all this makes the tragedy, the contrast with what was young and happy. We are left with a Vienna 'musical' without the music: a pathetic ending. Granted the romantic manner of the film is well made, M. Charles Boyer acts with distinction, and Mlle Danielle Darrieux is lovely and lost and childlike.

Undoubtedly the best film of many weeks is the coloured cartoon, *Fox Hunt*. The artists, Mr Hector Hoppin and Mr Antony Gross use Technicolor with a freedom and beauty quite outside Mr Disney's picture-book range. A hunt which turns into a mechanized chase, a motor bus playing an agile part; swollen narcissine, decadent horses preening before gilt mirrors: both theme and drawings have unusual wit, but what remains in the memory is the lyrical use of colour: the white ringletted horse ballooning over the dark box hedges of the little enclosed garden with its classical statue, the rich autumn ruin under hoof, the by-pass road lined with gay sublimated posters.

The Spectator (6 November 1936)

Dodsworth (USA, Samuel Goldwyn, 1936) Dir.: William Wyler. Cast: Walter Huston, Ruth Chatterton, Mary Astor, David Niven, Paul Lukas, Marie Ouspenskaya.
Mayerling (France, Nero Film, 1935) Dir.: Anatole Litvak. Cast: Charles Boyer, Danielle Darrieux, Marthe Regnier, Suzy Prin, Yolande Laffon.
Fox Hunt (GB, London Films, 1936) Directors: Hector Hoppin, Antony Gross.

Fredlös · The Gay Desperado

There are moods when one almost believes, remembering the great Westerns, from *The Virginian* to *The Texas Rangers*, and the classical Russian films, *October* to *Storm over Asia*, that the cinema is only about its proper business if it is in the open air, in natural surroundings, whether the open air be that of the American or Siberian plains or a stony Petrograd square. These scenes, at any rate, the theatre cannot reproduce. *Fredlös* gives us long sledge-rides across plains of snow, herds of reindeer moving north, Lapp encampments among frozen thorn trees: it is a Finnish Western, with a fine villain in the person of a despotic Russian Governor who, when he fails to rape the hero's Lapp wife, outlaws them both. The knife flung promptly across the snow at fifty paces takes the place of the quick shot from the hip; the pack of wolves breaking into the hut where the Lapp wife lies sick is a Nordic substitute for Red Indians and scalping-knives. There is even a moment of Griffith suspense when a Cossack soldier, under the orders of the wicked Governor, begins to saw through the piles supporting a bridge which the hero is about to cross as he journeys home.

A small wooden bridge, one reindeer, a single Cossack: there is something agreeably small scale about the familiar melodramatic formula: the elements of this Nordic film are closer to us than the crowded heroics on the Western plains, just as nature here seems more intimately part of our inheritance. The Redskins go back to Fenimore Cooper, but the wolves go back to Little Red Riding Hood and Grimm, and the reindeer to Hans Andersen. They are images from our racial memory, as the Texas plains will never be, and I found *Fredlös*, slower and more serious-minded though it is than a good Western, curiously moving. The melodramatic bones may have long lost their flesh, a threatened rape may no longer rouse our excited interest, but the lovely dark Lapp faces convey a nostalgia, as when we see a village or a house for the first time which somehow we seem to recognize.

The Gay Desperado, made by Mr Rouben Mamoulian, is one of the best light comedies of the year. Set in Mexico it opens with the performance of an American gangster film, *Give 'em the Works*, to which a notorious Mexican bandit (acted with immense high spirits by Mr Leo Carillo) has brought his band so that they may profit from a lesson in American methods. His joyous and noisy comments provoke a free fight in the cinema, just as on the screen the police and the gangsters meet in battle. The desperate manager sends Mr Nino Martini on to the stage to sing, while the tough picture is quickly removed and a travelogue substituted: *A Glimpse of Sunny Mexico*. The fight subsides, but the bandit has been so charmed by the singer's voice that he has him kidnapped after the performance. He offers him, casually punctuating his sentence with a bullet for another prisoner, any rank in his band from lieutenant to general, and when he understands that the singer's ambition is confined to radio, he holds up a station for his benefit and puts him on the air. The scene in which Mr Martini sings extracts from *Aïda* before the bristling guns and beards of the bandits, in the neat glass cage of the radio station, is beautifully directed. There are many such moments, and a certain edge is given to the comedy by the implicit satire on two literary conventions, that of the free romantic bandit, killing according to traditional rules, and that of the American racketeer, quick and cold and reptilian. When the Mexican joins the kidnapping racket and calls on Butch from across the border for help and advice, the contrast comes comically into the open. Mr Mamoulian's camera is very persuasive: Eisenstein's Mexico was no more sensuous than this. In a serious film the effect of the careful compositions might have seemed precious and unconvincing, but in artificial comedy these lovely shots of cacti like cathedral pillars, of galloping horses before old Spanish churches, of sombreros against skyscapes, are like a framework of fine and mannered prose.

The Spectator (13 November 1936)

Fredlös (Finland, Nordisk, 1935) Dir.: George Schneevoigt. Cast: John Ekman, Sten Lindgren, Gull-maj Norin.
The Gay Desperado (USA, Pickford-Lasky, 1936) Dir.: Rouben Mamoulian. Cast: Nino Martini, Ida Lupino, Leo Carillo, Mischa Auer, Harold Huber.

Rembrandt

Reverance and a good cameraman are not enough. Mr Alexander Korda in his latest film has chosen the most difficult of all subjects, the life of an artist, and though he is undubitably on the side of Art with a capital A against the *bourgeoisie*, represented by the steeple-hatted Dutchmen who somehow always seem to remain film extras, literary and not realistic types, like the benevolent Doctor Mannasseh, that Jew with the long white beard we have seen on so many screens, he has not himself produced a film which one can treat as a work of art. There are some good scenes: I remember a small dark figure making his way across a waste of snow, and Rembrandt, who has returned ruined to his father's mill, sitting down with the words, 'Black bread, peasant's bread, I am home': there are other scenes of melodramatic sentiment in an agreeable tradition, the scene when Rembrandt paints the beloved mistress whom he knows is dying, the scene when he softens the heart of the beggar posing for him as the King of Israel by telling him the story of Saul and David: these may be false, but they are false in a pleasant familiar way, like robins on Christmas cards, and they give Mr Charles Laughton a chance to show his remarkable powers as a 'ham' actor – the very best 'ham' – and they will undoubtedly be popular.

But the film is ruined by lack of story and continuity: it has no drive. Like *The Private Life of Henry the Eighth*, it is a series of unrelated tableaux. Tableau One (a far too emotional beginning): wife of famous painter dies while he is being feasted by the burghers. Tableau Two: famous painter loses, by his artistic experiments, his bourgeois clients. Tableau Three: but already I begin to forget how these unrelated scenes follow one another. From the dramatic point of view the first might just as well be the last and the last first. Nothing is led up to, nothing is led away from. In one tableau the painter, sold up by his creditors, goes back to his father's mill, but in a tableau a little further on we see him back in an apparently well-furnished home, only to be sold up for a second time in a later scene. The death of his first wife is duplicated by the death of his mistress, but I doubt if the tear-ducts will work a second time for the same cause. Odd scraps of biography litter the film like shavings in a carpenter's shop. When Rembrandt wants to marry his mistress, we learn for the first time of an impediment in the shape of a son by the first wife, and his inheritance. At the end of the film we are casually informed that there is a child by his mistress.

I have called the film reverent, but pompous, I fear, would be nearer the mark. Emotions are too obviously forced on us, like a card in the hands of an inexpert sharper. When Rembrandt, in Mr Laughton's beautiful voice, expresses at the burghers' dinner-table his views on marital love, the camera takes us from one whiskered face to another, each one baring his emotions with the dreadful intimacy of a peeress recommending a cream for oily skins (incidentally these are the same insensitive burghers who mock his later pictures). When Rembrandt reads the Bible at his father's table, you would think, from their expressions of amazement and rapture, that these pious peasants had never heard the Bible read before. Their faces are like warnings to us that these are solemn words beautifully uttered and that though they may have nothing to do with the story, we, too, ought to be, nay, must be, moved. But our cynical hearts, I am afraid, react in wicked amusement.

'Scenes from the Life of . . .' – that is how this picture should be described, and, in spite of Mr Charles Laughton's amazing virtuosity and Miss Elsa Lanchester's attractive Flemish impersonation (her refined voice, alas! betrays the charming ungainliness of her appearance), it is chiefly remarkable for the lesson it teaches: that no amount of money spent on expensive sets, no careful photography, will atone for the lack of a story 'line', the continuity and drive of a well-constructed plot.

The Spectator (20 November 1936)

Rembrandt (GB, London Films, 1936) Dir.: Alexander Korda. Cast: Charles Laughton, Gertrude Lawrence, Elsa Lanchester, John Clements, Roger Livesey, Edward Chapman, Walter Hudd, Raymond Huntley.

The New Gulliver · Bullets or Ballots · The White Angel

The new, the Soviet Gulliver is a long way after Swift. The inventor of the Yahoos would have been amused by the blithe Bolshevik optimism of Mr Roshal and Mr Ptushko, the inevitable victory of the Lilliputian proletariat, the Victorian sense of Progress. But even if the theme seems to us a little dusty, like the sermons of Charles Kingsley, the execution and invention awake our admiration.

The New Gulliver begins like *Alice in Wonderland*, as an idyll of a summer's day. The best workers in a corps of Soviet children have the honour of being the first to sail the little yacht they have built. They land on a small island off the shore, and the boy leader reads Gulliver aloud, a bowdlerized Gulliver, I feel sure, in this brave new world where virtue is always victorious. With the sound of the waves in his ears the boy falls asleep and dreams . . . Only in dreams (but I doubt if the authors intended to point this moral) can he escape – unhappy Gulliver – from triumphant virtue to a world where evil can still put up a sporting fight. After a battle and a shipwreck ('Save my box. It has all my schoolwork in it'), he is cast ashore on Lilliput. Lilliput is oppressed by a King, a Parliament and at least one priest, and there are numerous police spies and armaments manufacturers. An exciting old world, but one already on the point of learning dialectical materialism. The workers plan the Revolution in a cave on the sea-shore, and there they find Gulliver's exercise-book washed up by the sea and on the first page a Soviet slogan. The rest of the film shows the triumph of the workers assisted by Gulliver. There are moments of delightful satire: the Chancellor putting a small gramophone under the robe of the King who cannot make a speech ('my people are muddled, are muddled, are muddled . . .' creaks the record as the needle sticks in a crack); the tiny Queen hastily packing her hats at the news of the workers' seizure of the arsenal.

The invention is often delightful (one wonders how such humour in detail can exist with so humourless a philosophy), and the marvellous ingenuity of the puppets is beyond praise. One soon begins to regard them as real people and to give critical applause to the performers who amuse Gulliver at dinner: the ballad-singer (an exquisite parody), the elderly mezzo-soprano, and the troupe of ballet-girls with their black gloves and transparent fans. This doll world is pure pleasure, a child's dream with its inconsequence: the tiny tanks manoeuvring on the shore with frigates attacking from the sea, the periwigged ladies listening to the radio, the cameraman in check plus-fours filming the royal procession; sometimes a child's nightmare: the gross idiot faces, the evil King with his loopy laugh, the arsenal with its white-hot furnaces and pounding machines in the caves underground. But Gulliver wakes, that is the profound difference, wakes into the bright, happy, virtuous Soviet day; he has not to live on, like his poor ancestor, among his native Yahoos.

Bullets or Ballots is a good gangster film of the second class. Mr Edward G. Robinson (his mouth more than ever like a long flat slit in a pillar-box) gives a reliable performance as a tough detective who stages a dismissal from the police in order to work from inside a racket. Third degree is curiously idealized, and the detective dies on the field of honour with a bullet in the guts. All the old chivalrous situations of *Chums* and the *B. O. P.* are agreeably translated into sub-machine-gun terms.

The White Angel is not another Pasteur. Miss Kay Francis, handicapped by her beauty, does her best to sober down this sentimental version of Florence Nightingale's character, but she is defeated by the scenario-writers. There is one dreadful sequence when Miss Nightingale is made to visit a Crimean cemetery at night in order to read above a soldier's grave a letter from his mother, and another, less agreeable to English than American ears, when she patrols the wards, lamp in hand, to the accompaniment of voices repeating Longfellow's too famous poem.

The Spectator (27 November 1936)

The New Gulliver (USSR, Mosfilm, 1935) Directors: Grigori Roshal, Alexander Ptushko. Cast: V. Konstantinov.

Bullets or Ballots (USA, Warners, 1936) Dir.: William Keighley. Cast: Edward G. Robinson, Joan Blondell, Humphrey Bogart, Barton Maclane, Frank McHugh, Dick Purcell, George E. Stone.

The White Angel (USA, Warner, 1936) Dir.: William Dieterle. Cast: Kay Francis, Ian Hunter, Donald Woods, Nigel Bruce, Donald Crisp, Henry O'Neill, Halliwell Hobbes.

The Green Pastures

Mr Marc Connelly's black Biblical pageant has come to us with the best possible advertisement: the Lord Chamberlain's ban. It has lost nothing by being transferred to the screen, not so much as a line of dialogue, and the rather jerky succession of short stage scenes is given smoothness and continuity in the cinema. The author, too, in this version is able to emphasize the point of his narrative by bringing us back again and again to the Sunday school, where the black minister, Mr Deshee, is explaining the Old Testament to the children, telling how the Lord (a black minister with a string tie) created man at a fish-fry in heaven; how the Lord banished Cain and preserved Noah;

how He brought a chosen people out of Egypt; how He saw his prophet murdered in Babylon. Hollywood must be praised for the simplicity of the settings. Pharaoh's throne-room, the King of Babylon's Court must have offered enormous temptations which have been admirably resisted. Moses performs his miracles under the dusty guild flags of a small church hall, and the Prophet in Babylon is shot down by a smirking waiter at a scene of dingy revelry, based, in the mind of the preacher, on a long-ago visit to a cheap cabaret.

Most people, I think, will find the film continously entertaining, if only intermittently moving. But it is a little absurd to class it, as some critics have done, with the medieval mystery plays. It is not only that pathos has taken the place of poetry, that the anonymous and popular playwrights had better words at their command than Mr Connelly's, and that 'the five cent seegar, Lawd?' humour cannot take the place of 'Wode and wynde and watters wane', but that those plays, like the cathedrals, were spontaneous expressions of popular belief. Mr Connelly is a sophisticated writer trying to see through the eyes of a negro preacher. He is on the outside looking in. The result is occasionally patronising, too often quaint, and at the close of the film definitely false. For at the end Mr Connelly deserts the Bible story and indulges in a little personal Protestant mysticism, and I do not think the author of *Dulcy, To the Ladies* and *Helen of Troy, N. Y.* is naturally a mystic. He invents a character, Hezdrel, a soldier fighting to preserve Jerusalem from the Romans, whose prayers penetrate disturbingly to the ears of God after He has long given up the world in despair. God comes down among the smashed artillery and the dead and dying, and in the light of a camp-fire encounters Hezdrel. 'He looks like the first man I made, but he ain't in no garden now.' It is an excellent melodramatic scene, but Mr Connelly has quite forgotten the negro preacher and the Sunday-school class. Hezdrel begins to teach God the quality of mercy and to proceed to the sentimental end when Gabriel, peering over Heaven's wall, reports to the Lord a man's weary progress under a cross to Golgotha and God with His arms outstretched shares the suffering. The author of *Dulcy* has neatly, smartly and unsatisfactorily by-passed Christianity.

But Mr Connelly deserves praise for his ingenious pathos (though the theme of pity poor God might, perhaps, have a sentimental ring even to a black preacher) and his great technical dexterity. The Noah sequence is admirably dramatic when it is not too easily comic; the dingy sexual drama played out beside the Ark under the rain-clouds, the jealous gangster with his razor-blade and his cheap girl, the sudden heartless, passionless knifing, occupies only a very few feet of film, but it conveys the right snake-like air of incurable corruption. One may feel uneasy at Mr Connelly's humour and wonder whether the negro mind is quite so material, but he is extraordinarily successful with the two extremes of good and evil. Mr Rex Ingram's performance as De Lawd (he also plays Adam and Hezdrel) is very moving, whether he is presiding at a Paradisiacal fish-fry or walking disillusioned through the evil world. Indeed this is as a good religious play as one is likely to get in this age from a practised New York writer.

The Spectator (4 December 1936)

The Green Pastures (USA, Warners, 1936) Directors: Marc Connelly, William Keighley. Cast: Rex Ingram, Eddie 'Rochester' Anderson, Oscar Polk, Frank Wilson, George Reed.

Sabotage · The Tenth Man

I have sometimes doubted Mr Hitchcock's talent. As a director he has always known exactly the right place to put his camera (and there is only one right place in any scene), he has been pleasantly inventive with his sound, but as a producer and as a writer of his own scripts he has been appallingly careless: he has cared more for an ingenious melodramatic situation than for the construction and continuity of his story. In *Sabotage* for the first time he has really 'come off'.

Sabotage is not, of course, Conrad's *Secret Agent*. That dark drab passionate tale of Edwardian London could never find a place in the popular cinema, and only M. Jacques Feyder, I think, the director of *Thérèse Raquin*, could transfer its peculiar qualities – of madness and despair and four-wheelers and backstreets – to the screen. But Mr Hitchcock's 'variations on a theme' are on a different level from his deplorable adaptation of Mr Maugham's *Ashenden*. This melodrama is convincingly realistic, perhaps because Mr Hitchcock has left the screenplay to other hands.

The story retains some of the ruthlessness of the original. Mr Verloc, no longer an *agent provocateur* but a straightforward destructive agent of a foreign Power, keeps a tiny independent cinema in the East End, and the film opens with his secret return home during a sudden black-out. (Mr Hitchcock has not overcome in these sequences the difficulty of lighting a black-out. How far a little candle throws its beams!) Mr Verloc has succeeded in getting sand into the Battersea generators, but his employers are dissatisfied: he is told to lay a bomb in the cloakroom at Piccadilly Circus on Lord Mayor's Day. Mr Verloc's friends fail him, he is himself closely watched by the police, and he has to entrust the bomb to his wife's small brother, who, delayed by the procession, is blown to fragments with a busload of people. Mrs Verloc, after hearing the news, passes through the little cinema to her living-room. A children's matinée is in progress and Walt Disney's *Cock Robin* is on the screen. She is pursued by the children's laughter and the diminishing repetitions of the song, 'Who killed Cock Robin? Who killed Cock Robin?' This ingenious and pathetic twist is stamped as Mr Hitchcock's own, but unlike so many of his ideas in the past it is an integral part of the story: it leads on to the admirably directed scene when Mrs Verloc, serving dinner to her husband, finds herself against her own will continually picking up the carving-knife – to serve the potatoes, to scoop up the cabbage, to kill Mr Verloc. The happy ending of course, has to be contrived: Mr Verloc's body is plausibly disposed of: a young detective is there to marry her: but this is all managed with the minimum of offence.

Mr Hitchcock has been helped by admirable dialogue, written by Mr Ian Hay and Miss Helen Simpson, and a fine cast, a cast with only two weak members. Mr John Loder as the detective is unconvincing, and as for Master Desmond Tester's prep. school accent I feel an invincible distaste (it glares out at you, like a first fifteen muffler, from every disguise). Mr Oscar Homolka, a slow, kindly, desperate Mr Verloc, and Miss Sylvia Sidney, as his innocent wife, raise the melodrama at times to the tragic level, and Mr William Dewhurst gives a superb performance as the Professor, a soapy old scoundrel who supports his shrewish daughter and her bastard child with a bird business, concocting his explosives in the one living-room, among the child's dolls and the mother's washing.

Another English director, Mr Brian Desmond Hurst, has upset prophecies this week with a well-directed film: *The Tenth Man*, the story of an English Kreuger written by Mr Maugham. There was nothing in Mr Hurst's two previous films, *Riders to the Sea* and *Ourselves Alone*, to show him capable of these humorous and satirical political sequences, and the very fine melodramatic close. The credit is all Mr Hurst's, for the dialogue is stagy, and the principal actor, Mr John Lodge, continues to suffer from a kind of lockjaw, an inability to move the tight muscles of his mouth, to do anything but glare with the dumbness and glossiness of an injured seal.

The Spectator (11 December 1936)

Sabotage (GB, Gaumont British, 1936) Dir.: Alfred Hitchcock. Cast: Oscar Homolka, Sylvia Sidney, John Loder, William Dewhurst, Desmond Tester. (US title: *The Woman Alive*)

The Tenth Man (GB, British International, 1936) Dir.: Brian Desmond Hurst. Cast: John Lodge, Antoinette Cellier, Athole Stewart, Clifford Evans, Aileen Marson.

Girls' Dormitory · Go West, Young Man · Hortobagy

This week we have run the gamut of sex, from the incredible virginities of *Girls' Dormitory* by way of Mae West to the leaping stallions in *Hortobagy*. For dignity and decency the horses have it. Was there ever quite so virginal a finishing school as that in the Tyrolean Alps presided over by Dr Stefan Dominik, acted by Mr Herbert Marshall in his Old English sheep-dog manner? This film of adolescence is the more curious coming as it does from America. We are accustomed to the difficulties of adolescence in Teutons; Americans, one has always understood, have solved their problems characteristically. There has never been any hint of shy pent passions on the campus among the co-eds.

Mr Marshall is loved by one of his pupils, Marie Claudel, acted with staggering conviction and charm by Mlle Simone Simon. He is also loved by Professor Anna Mathe (Miss Ruth Chatterton), who has been assisting him in compiling an Ancient History for Advanced Classes. 'I wish you to share in any glory there may be,' he tells her, but he does not realize the worm that feeds on her cheek. Nor does he realize Miss Claudel's love even when a compromising letter in her writing is found in a waste-paper basket. Marie is nearly expelled for a quite imaginary meeting with her dream-lover, but when she runs away in a nocturnal thunderstorm pursued by her headmaster (it is difficult not to recall the less virginal chase through the rain in *Lady Chatterley's Lover*), he learns the truth. Complications, of course, have still to be devised before the happy ending, for Mr Marshall must be allowed to put on his characteristic act: dumb suffering. This picture, dewy as it is, has merit even apart from Mlle Simon (it is well directed and the performance of Mr Edward Bromberg as a cruel, warped pedagogic type is admirable), but I am afraid its concentrated atmosphere of young innocence (even the bathing-costumes are white like the nightdresses) defeats its own purpose. Mr Marshall, of course, has the damp muzzle of a healthy British dog, but the film itself is undoubtedly sexy.

Not quite in the manner of Miss West: the Edwardian bust, the piled peroxided hair, the seductive and reeling motions reminiscent of an overfed python. Miss West, for once, has not written her own script, and this story of a film star, forbidden by contract to marry for five years and closely watched for that reason by her agent, is quite incredibly tedious, as slow and wobbling in its pace as Miss West's famous walk. The wisecracks lack the old impudence, and seldom have so many feet of film been expended on a mere dirty look.

Undoubtedly the horses have it. *Hortobagy*, a film of the Hungarian plains, acted by peasants and shepherds, is one of the most satisfying films I have seen: it belongs to the order of Dovzhenko's *Earth* without the taint of propaganda. The photography is extraordinarily beautiful, the cutting superb. The thin thread of story, of a shepherd's young son drawn away from horse-breeding to agriculture, is unimportant: we need no story to enjoy the sight of these wild herds tossing across the enormous plain, against the flat sky, the shepherds in their traditional cloaks, with the heavy buckles and the embroidery, galloping like Tartar cavalry between the whitewashed cabins. The leaping of the stallions, the foaling of the mares are shown with a frankness devoid of offence and add to the impression that here we are seeing, as far as is humanly possible, the whole of a way of life. But we are not asked to admire one way more than another, the horse more than the tractor. We see the mounted shepherd deliberately smash his small son's bicycle with the hooves of his horse, and the act is as ugly and as natural as the mare's foaling. Alas, one has little hope that this film will be passed by the British Board of Film Censors, who are not quick to distinguish between a Yahoo and a Houyhnhnm. In their eyes, I am afraid, it is Miss Mae West who wins.

The Spectator (18 December 1936)

Girls' Dormitory (USA, Twentieth-Century Fox, 1936) Dir.: Irving Cummings. Cast: Herbert Marshall, Simone Simon, Ruth Chatterton, Constance Collier, J. Edward Bromberg, Tyrone Power.

Go West, Young Man (USA, Paramount, 1936) Dir.: Henry Hathaway. Cast: Mae West, Warren William, Randolph Scott, Alice Brady, Lyle Talbot.

Hortobagy (Hungary, Hoellering Film, 1935) Dir.: George Hoellering. Cast: Istvan Kamyasi, Janos Cinege.

The Garden of Allah · Confetti · Walt Disney Season

Mr Charles Boyer, a renegade monk from a Trappist monastery in North Africa, Miss Marlene Dietrich, a lovely orphan heiress suffering from world weariness ('Go to the desert', she is told at the convent school to which she returns for advice and prayer. 'In the face of the infinite your grief will lessen') meet in a Moroccan dance-hall. A desert soothsayer does his best to warn the woman against her doom ('I see a camel by a church door, and then a tent in the far desert', as he describes it with Surrealist fervour), and so does the local Catholic priest, who distrusts this man who is apt to stagger uneasily back at the sight of a crucifix. 'This is the land of fire,' he says, 'and you are a woman of fire.' Nobody talks less apocalyptically than that: the great abstractions come whistling hoarsely out in Miss Dietrich's stylized, weary, and monotonous whisper, among the hideous Technicolor flowers, the yellow cratered desert like Gruyère cheese, the beige faces. Startling sunsets bloom behind silhouetted camels very much as in the gaudy little pictures which used to be on sale on the pavements of Trafalgar Square. Needless to say – but many thousand feet of film are expended in saying it – the pair are married by the Catholic priest (according to the Church of England service), and there, waiting for them outside the church door, is The Camel, the foredoomed camel, ready to carry them, with an escort of twenty-five thousand armed Arabs, on their honeymoon – to that Tent in the Far Desert. There Fate has a coincidence in store for them in the person of a French officer lost in the Sahara with his men. 'We are a lost patrol', he succinctly explains to the lady in a low-backed evening dress who is waving a lighted torch from the top of a ruined tower (the Surrealism of this film is really magnificent). He recognizes the former monk (he had been a guest in the monastery), and sitting together on the Gruyère cheese, silhouetted like camels, the lovers make the great decision to renounce all. The Catholic priest (Mr Aubrey Smith, who has kept a straight county bat to the bodyline bowling) shakes hands all round at the railway station, the monk slowly wends his way up an avenue of cypresses, a grey glove flaps from the window of a four-wheeler. Alas! my poor Church, so picturesque, so noble, so superhumanly pious, so intensely dramatic. I really prefer the *New Statesman* view, shabby priests counting pesetas in their fingers in dingy cafés before blessing tanks. Even the liqueur made at this

Trappist monastery is Mysterious. Only one monk at a time knows the secret of its making, and when Mr Charles Boyer disappears from the monastery the secret is irrecoverably lost. The thought that this sweet and potent drink will be once again obtainable during licensed hours mitigates for us the agony of the parting.

Confetti, after a bad opening, is not quite so devastatingly cheery as most Austrian films. It is true there are a good many balloons and paper streamers at the Carnival ball (when will producers realise there is no more dismal sight for the outsider than that of others riotously and incomprehensibly enjoying themselves?), but the course of events which follow the presence there of a priggish and miserly professor, the proprietor of a big store, who should have been elsewhere on business, and a girl from the dress department who has borrowed an exclusive model, becomes quite agreeably entangled. No film with Hans Moser and Leo Slezak could fail to have human as well as humorous moments.

The Tatler Theatre, it should be noted by unfortunate parents confused by the 'A' certificates and the incomprehensible moral distinctions of our censors, has begun its Christmas Disney season. Next week's selection contains three of the best of the late Disneys: *Moving Day, Mickey's Grand Opera*, with Donald Duck as Romeo and Pluto pitiably badgered by a conjuror's top hat, and the charming *Three Orphan Kittens*. Walt Disney, after a very bad period (*Mickey's Polo Match* was perhaps his nadir) has recovered some of his old freshness, and I would highly recommend *The Country Cousin*, which supports with some difficulty *The Garden of Allah* at the Leicester Square Theatre.

The Spectator (25 December 1936)

The Garden of Allah (USA, Selznick International, 1936) Dir.: Richard Boleslawski. Cast: Marlene Dietrich, Charles Boyer, C. Aubrey Smith, Basil Rathbone, Tilly Losch.

Confetti (Austria, Luxor Films, 1936) Dir.: Hubert Marischka. Cast: Hans Moser, Leo Slezak, Friedl Czepa.

The Jungle Princess · Windbag the Sailor

A laughing tiger puts fear into the hearts of the Malayan natives; but we, of course, who have borne the white man's burden of sunny Southsea and the picture page, as soon as we hear that silvery and self-conscious tinkle, recognize its source. This particular holiday girl is the daughter of a dead American, and has been brought up by an old Malayan until a stampede of elephants wrecks the village and a tiger kills her foster-father. Aged about six, and accompanied by a tiger cub, she goes alone into the jungle; and from that time on she is seen by no human being until an American expedition arrives in the island: a retired Colonel and his daughter, her fiancé (a travel-writer), and poor Mr Lynne Overman, who is expected to lend humorous relief to a film already richly comic. The Colonel and his daughter go to Shanghai for the rains, but the other two stay to investigate the native superstitions.

Needless to say, the hero is attacked in the jungle by the pet tiger, now as mature as his mistress, and Lemo (its name is Lemo) is called off only just in time. The girl assists the wounded travel-writer to her lair (a scurry in the tree-tops overhead, and we recognize the simian features of one of Hollywood's most famous comedians), and the rains opportunely catch him there with Bogo, the baboon, and Lemo and the girl. Mysterious white women whom explorers discover in the world's jungles always have an embarrassing directness towards the male. The horror of triumphant possessiveness, the snaking of well-covered limbs along the floor, the animal flash of strong female teeth in a confined space, is vividly conveyed:

When you hold me tight
In a jungle night,
My sweet,

as an old Malay ballad, translated by our hero, puts it. But the possessiveness is not immediately triumphant: he remembers his betrothed in Shanghai firmly all through the rainy season, and at its close we see him manfully resisting the temptation to kiss his companion. Her directness while sun-bathing scares him, and he departs ('You won't mind really. You have Bogo and Lemo') to rejoin his companions who have given him up as dead. 'It's time for you to shave, dear, and change for dinner,' his fiancée remarks (she has returned with the Colonel from Shanghai) to her lover resurrected a bare half-hour. The girl has followed him, and the Colonel's daughter cannot, petty-minded creature, believe in a chastity maintained all through the rainy season in a cave. She plans to make her rival ridiculous and we have one of those scenes, so common in pictures from the great democracy, of exaggerated social consciousness. Will this jungle-bred girl use a spoon with her grape-fruit? Heavens, she has taken a fork: her rival will conquer. But no! Mr Lynne Overman in the nick of time has conveyed with a wink and a whisper the correct information; the hero hasn't noticed.

The climax is magnificent. The natives, who think the girl is a witch, trap the party, tie them to trees and begin to bury the girl alive. Who is to save her? Lemo, you think, but you are wrong. He charges and they kill him. The overseer frees himself – but he, too, dies heroically (the girl by this time is buried up to the neck). The hero gets free – but what is one travel-writer among a horde of natives without a rook-rifle? No, it is Bogo who saves them all, who spies their plight from the tree-tops and summons every baboon in the jungle to a magnificent charge.

The censors have given this lively picture an 'A' Certificate in spite of the hero's heroic chastity. To those under sixteen debarred from these adult delights by Lord Tyrrell, I recommend *Windbag the Sailor*, a farce with Mr Will Hay admirably directed by Mr William Beaudine. Mr Hay, since his Narkover days, has progressively improved, and he has never had a better part than that of Captain Ben Cutlett, the skipper of a canal barge given to boasting of experiences on the seas he has never sailed, who finds himself in command of a cargo steamer, with a villainous crew under secret orders to scuttle the ship.

The Spectator (1 January 1937)

The Jungle Princess (USA, Paramount, 1936) Dir.: William Thiele. Cast: Dorothy Lamour, Ray Milland, Lynne Overman, Akim Tamiroff.
Windbag the Sailor (GB, Gainsborough, 1936) Dir.: William Beaudine. Cast: Will Hay, Moore Marriott, Graham Moffatt, Norma Varden.

Sensation · Mazurka

A curious air of unreality pervades *Sensation*, the story of a murder in a country village and the mob of crime reporters from Fleet Street who settle down at the local pub and unscrupulously manufacture good copy. Nothing, a novice might think, could be easier than to catch reality with a camera, and yet this shy bird evades almost every English director. There is a moment in *Mazurka* when an experienced womanizer kisses an awkward adolescent girl. The director cuts up from her bewildered eyes as the mouth presses home, to the electric globes hanging from the ceiling: they mist, disappear, come back to view again, and the uneven mixture of passion and practice has been vividly conveyed. Mr Desmond Hurst's *Sensation* never comes so close to life, and as its failure is typical of English films, perhaps I may be forgiven for discussing its unrealities in some detail.

It is never easy for a film critic, who has no sight of the script, to appoint responsibility between actors, writers and director. Mr Desmond Hurst has obviously been handicapped by his cast. Mr John Lodge, who plays the crime reporter, remains dumbly dependent on a stony and protuberant jaw, and there is a persistent Oxford and BBC undertone to the synthetic accents in the local bar. The only players who help illusion are Mr Anthony Holles as a reporter, Miss Athene Seyler as a fortune-teller, and Miss Joan Marion as the murderer's wife.

Now for the screenplay. A cowardly 'commercial' murders one of his many girl-friends, a reporter robs a bedroom, finds a clue to the crime and bullies the murderer's wife into supplying his paper with her love-letters, the details of her private life, her small son's picture, in return for money to defend her husband who stands no chance of acquittal. A promising plot, which could be handled with pity and anger, but the genuine situation is lost in false trails, in an absurd love-story, in humour based on American films, and in the complete unreality of the 'murder gang'.

There remains the director, and I am afraid he has contributed little to illusion. The lovers drive down Fleet Street before one of the worst false backgrounds I have ever seen. The Yard detective picks up a hammer, which he believes the murderer used, with his bare fingers and carries it with him into a crowded café. Worst weakness of all, two independent situations which depend for their effect on accumulating excitement – the fortune-teller in a fake trance describing the wife – are run concurrently, the director cutting from one to another, so that the excitement of each scene drops like a stone at every cut. Bad casting, bad story construction, uncertain ending: these are the three main faults of English films.

Mazurka leaves a rather sinister impression. The first twenty minutes – the scared duel between the adolescent girl (beautifully acted by Ingeborg Theek) and the middle-aged expert in sexuality – are admirable. With the appearance of Miss Pola Negri Herr Willi Forst seems deliberately to guy not only the melodramatic tale of an unknown mother and a good woman's ruin, but the star herself. Miss Negri's technique belongs to the war years and the silent film. Forst makes her run across rooms, bound along streets, a crazy corsetted Cassandra in 1917 draperies. In a scene of drunken seduction which is like an ancient still from Mr Rotha's album, the villain (with long Svengali hair and the manner of a lion-tamer) props tipsy Miss Negri against the doorpost while he takes down his top hat. Miss Negri may be unwise to return to the films, but it is a cruel idea of fun to guy this stout, glossy, gesticulating woman for the pleasure of audiences who have forgotten the star of Lubitsch's *Forbidden Paradise*.

> SECOND OPINION
>
> 'Every pert little miss who fancies herself an embryo star should, in a spirit of awed humility, takes this opportunity of studying the methods of an artiste whose passions come from the heart, whose voice is vibrant with feeling and

whose emotions are expressed with every fibre of her being.' Sydney Carroll on Miss Negri.

The Spectator (5 February 1937)

Sensation (GB, British International, 1937) Dir.: Brian Desmond Hurst. Cast: John Lodge, Athene Seyler, Anthony Holles, Diana Churchill, Francis Lister, Joan Marion.

Mazurka (Germany, Cine-Allianz, 1935) Dir.: Willi Forst. Cast: Pola Negri, Ingeborg Theek, Paul Hartmann.

The Plainsman · The Great Barrier

Mr Cecil B. de Mille: there has always been a touch of genius as well as absurdity in this warm-hearted sentimental salvationist. *The Crusades, The Ten Commandments* were comic and naïve, but no director since Griffith has handled crowds so convincingly. Now – startlingly – Mr de Mille seems to have grown. *The Plainsman* is certainly the finest Western since *The Virginian*: perhaps it is the finest Western in the history of the film.

The story is of the Indian rising after the Civil War when General Custer's forces were annihilated, with Mr Gary Cooper as a famous Scout, Wild Bill Hickok, the lover of Calamity Jane. Mr de Mille has never before handled stars of Mr Cooper's and Miss Jean Arthur's quality, and another unexpected trace of sophistication, the music is by George Antheil. Indeed, one might wonder whether Mr de Mille's name has been taken in vain if it were not for the magnificent handling of the extras in the big sets: the brilliant detail, depth and solidity of the dockside scenes at St Louis, the charge of the Indian cavalry. A few great spectacular moments in the history of the film remain as a permanent encouragement to those who believe that an art may yet emerge from a popular industry: the long shots of the Battle of Bull Run in *The Birth of a Nation*, the French attack in *All Quiet*. Some of the scenes in *The Plainsman* belong to that order.

That might have been expected, and the excellent dialogue may be a fortunate accident; what takes one by surprise in a de Mille film is the firm handling of the individual drama: the silent moments in the cleared street of the shabby frontier town when Hickok crosses the road to meet his would-be murderers: the final poker-game he plays in the barred saloon with the white prisoners he is keeping for the military to hang, the air of doom while we wait for the inevitable shot in the back from the little treacherous bowler-hatted comic behind the bar: and most surprising of all the brilliant satirical sequence when the armament directors, whose new repeating rifle has been put on the market too late for the Civil War, discuss how to dispose of their unwanted stocks and the cynical old Pickwickian chairman persuades them to sell to the Indians 'for hunting purposes'. This actor's performance, when the news of Lincoln's murder comes roaring down the street, is superb: the conventional shocked regrets, the roaming, faintly speculative eye. It is a pleasure to see Mr Charles Bickford back in one of his rough scoundrelly parts as the trader who smuggles the rifles to the Indians. Only in the character and treatment of Buffalo Bill Cody does the dreaded softness of the traditional de Mille intrude.

The Plainsman takes the wind out of Gaumont British sails. *The Great Barrier* is a sporting and fairly successful attempt to make a film of *The Iron Horse* type with the smaller resources of an English company. It deals with the building of the Canadian Pacific Railway at the moment when the work was held up by the mus-keg, the swamps deep enough to swallow whole trains. The men are in revolt for want of pay, no more money will be invested in the company unless a new way to the coast is discovered past the great barrier of the Rockies, and an expedition sets out . . .It is one of those films which are sometimes called 'epic', though their intellectual and poetic quality is hardly higher than that of the interminable historical novels which reach us from America. It should appeal enormously to CPR shareholders, it is a thoroughly worthy picture, with an excellent saloon shindy, an exciting race on horseback to save the Montreal express, and an attractive new English star, Miss Lilli Palmer. Well acted, well produced (a little less than well written: 'Hell's bells, boys, we are in luck. We've struck the Old Trail'; 'Is that all you've got to say?') it shrinks into insignificance, with its conventional love-story and the impression it leaves that the building of a railway depends on the heroic efforts of two or three men and a girl, beside *Turksib* or the dash and drama of *The Plainsman*.

The Spectator (12 February 1937)

The Plainsman (USA, Paramount, 1936) Dir.: Cecil B. de Mille. Cast: Gary Cooper, Jean Arthur, Charles Bickford, James Ellison, Helen Burgess, Porter Hall.
The Great Barrier (GB, Gaumont British, 1937) Dir.: Milton Rosmer. Cast: Lilli Palmer, Richard Arlen, Antoinette Cellier, Roy Emerton. (US title: *Silent Barriers*)

The Deserter · Dreaming Lips

The Deserter is Pudovkin's first talkie, the story of a Hamburg strike put down by machine-guns, of the German strike delegate to the USSR who settles down as an engineer in the country where the revolution is already won, until his conscience tells him that he is a deserter and should go back. Though the picture is only three years old it would be unfair to forget that, as far as Pudovkin himself is concerned, it belongs to the stage of *The Singing Fool*.

It is a bad film with some superb moments. Technically it cannot be compared with the older Soviet film *Men and Jobs*, which the Forum will soon be showing. We are aware all the time of the theorist who has written many articles on the new medium of sound, who has produced on paper in the *avant-garde* Press a number of ideas for its unrealistic use, faced by the picture itself, by the so many weeks of production, by a job which has got to be done. And to a great extent the ideas have vanished: they are left as isolated tricks, like the suicide in slow motion, outside the context of the picture. A curious feature of the studio world is the number of old *avant-garde* directors who spend their energies in avoiding production. Pudovkin at any rate comes into the open, with his stale caricatures (how much better Lang can work on our feelings with his sense of real evil), his shocking continuity, his Boy Scout idealism, his misuse of fast cutting, and a few sequences which remind us that after all this is the director who eleven years ago shot *Mother*.

The opening is admirable. Pudovkin establishes at once the documentary scene for the fictional story, which few directors trouble to do: the ships and tugs in Hamburg harbour, the great docks and tunnels, the unemployed sleeping on benches, the crowded proletarian trams; he works inwards towards the centre of the city, to the uniformed street-sweepers in the flowery boulevards and the smart cars and the gross and obsequious police on point duty. But there he throws away his hand, throws away all the value of the documentary approach for the sake of caricature, very good caricature sometimes as in the restaurant ritual with tiny bottles over the salad. There may be ideological value in the contrast between the capitalist automatons and the real, the suffering, thinking workers, but there isn't dramatic value. The awful Victorian shadow of inevitable Progress falls across the screen.

But the film should be seen: there are moments magnificent as well as naïve, and again one notices the curious fact that Pudovkin is never a better movie director than in his still-lifes, never worse than in his fast movements. One will go on remembering these static scenes: the body of the dying picket, shot diagonally from far above, sprawled and motionless on the grey cobbles, the whimper of pain that carries on, a mournful chorus, through the following scenes: the view-point of the pickets down the empty industrial road to the huge grit-blackened tunnel, the silence, waiting and emptiness, and then the first hardly detectable movements of the strike-breakers coming out at the edge of the tunnel.

Unsatisfactory picture it may be, but it takes the heart out of any praise one might have given to *Dreaming Lips*, a sumptuous glossy rendering of *Der Traumende Mund*, which at least avoided the falsity of these luxurious English sets. Anyway it doesn't need a critic's praise, although one critic has been so moved by its discreet sentimentality that she has bared her heart embarrassingly to her large newspaper public. The theatre is packed with just such ecstatic women who squeal with admiration as Miss Bergner's mechanical sure-fire performance proceeds: the bemused and avaricious eyes, the swinging arms, prehensile cooing lips: an elfin charm maybe, but how sex-conscious an elf. And how the handkerchiefs flutter at the close, when the policeman reads aloud the last letter of the drowned wife unable to choose between the lover-genius and the boy-husband. The story, of course, is neat and plausible, the acting refined, the photography expensive, it is a shapely piece of sentiment. But there is nothing to remember when the night's over: it is not the Constant Nymph but the constant corpse on the cobbles which has imaginative truth.

The Spectator (19 February 1937)

The Deserter (USSR, Mezhrabpomfilm, 1933) Dir.: V. I. Pudovkin. Cast: Boris Livanov, Tamara Makarova, Vasili Kovrigin, Judith Glizer.

Dreaming Lips (GB, Trafalgar Film Productions, 1937) Dir.: Paul Czinner. Cast: Elisabeth Bergner, Raymond Massey, Romney Brett, Felix Aylmer, Donald Calthrop, Joyce Bland.

We from Kronstadt

From the moment when the elderly Commissar with a sad and unprofessional face, dressed in a shabby macintosh and a soft hat which has known better days, takes his seat in the naval motor-boat which chugs softly out in the last evening light, under the bridges of Petrograd towards the lamps of the naval port, *We from Kronstadt* takes a firm hold on the imagination, and it will be a thousand pities if the British Board of Film Censors prevents this unusual mixture of poetry and heroics from enjoying a success in London equal to that which it has met in Paris and New York.

The story of 1919, the year of foreign intervention, up to the last shot of Balashov, the marine, standing on the cliff where his companions have been flung to death, shaking his fist towards the sea – 'And now does anybody else want Petrograd?' – this very simple story of rivalry between the marines and the workers' battalions is in the tradition of boys' stories, full of last charges and fights to the death, heroic sacrifices and narrow escapes, all superbly directed: the single soldier crawling, grenade in hand, towards the monstrous tank which has terrified the marines; the ragged band in the last trench between the enemy and the capital striking up the cheerful rallying tune which calls the wounded from the dressing-station to stagger back into a last desperate action; the voice whispering 'Kronstadt, Kronstadt, Kronstadt' into the dumb phone as the camera tracks along the wire, the birds peacefully preening, to the ragged ends, the fallen post, and silence.

But magnificently as all this is done, what makes the picture remarkable is less the heroics than the lyrical, the poetic, the critical sense. This is what the poetic cinema should mean: not plays by Shakespeare adapted to a medium even less suitable than the modern stage; but poetry expressed in images, which let in a little more of common life than is in the story. This the stage can only crudely do (it has its words), but the cinema is closer to the novel, and *We from Kronstadt* was written and directed by the countrymen of Chekhov and Turgenev. In Pudovkin's early pictures of course we had our glimpses of nature, but nature strictly harnessed to the revolutionary idea; the hurrying clouds, dust-storms over the Asiatic plains, the Baltic ice breaking in the spring, had small lyrical value, they were used metaphorically to reinforce the one-sided plot. *We from Kronstadt*, on the other hand, from the first shot to the last, is as impregnated with the poetic sense (poetic as defined by Mr Ford Madox Ford: 'not the power melodiously to arrange words but the power to suggest human values') as *A Nest of Gentlefolk*, and, curiously enough, among the gunshots, the flag-waving, the last stands, it is of the same gentle and reflective and melancholy kind. There is a scene here of humorous and pathetic irony which might have been drawn directly from one of the great classic novelists. The hall and stairs of a one-time palace on the Baltic shore is packed nearly to suffocation with soldiers and marines; they lie massed together like swine: at dawn a door opens at the stair-head and a little knot of children, lodged for safety in the palace, emerges, climbs softly down again among the sleepers persistently, to finger a butt, a holster, the barrel of a Lewis gun.

There are many other examples of the poetic use of imagery and incident: the gulls sweeping and coursing above the cliffs where the Red prisoners are lined up for their death by drowning, the camera moving from the heavy rocks around their necks to the movement of the light white wings: one sooty tree drooping in the huge rocky Kronstadt walls above a bench where a sailor and a woman embrace, against the dark tide, the riding lights of the battleships, the shape of the great guns, the singing of a band of sailors going home in the dark to their iron home. Life as it is: life as it ought to be: Chekhov's definition for a novelist's purpose comes to mind. Every poetic image is chosen for its contrasting value, to represent peace and normal human values under the heroics and the wartime patriotism.

The Spectator (26 February 1937)

We from Kronstadt (USSR, Mosfilm, 1936) Dir.: Yefim Dzigan. Cast: Vasili Zaichikov, Grigori Bushuyev, Oleg Zhakov, Raisa Yesipova.

Fire Over England · Maid of Salem · Theodora Goes Wild

Herr Pommer, the German producer, and Mr William K. Howard, the American director, of Mr Korda's great national Coronation-year picture of Elizabethan England, have done one remarkable thing: they have caught the very spirit of an English public-schoolmistress's vision of history. *Fire Over England* should be enormously popular at Roedean and Cheltenham, and Miss Robson catches the very accent and manner of an adored headmistress, that blend of refined authority (alas! for great Harry's daughter), of familiar crotchets to set common-rooms buzzing, and a hidden histrionic tenderness towards the younger worshippers. I know I find myself in a tiresome minority (there are always a few sour disloyal spirits in every common-room). It is not, I am sure, Miss Robson's fault: she has only too faithfully carried out the suggestions of the script, and it must be remembered that the screenplay is by the author of *Will Shakespeare* and the novel by the author of *The Four Feathers*.

From neither of these authors do we expect a very penetrating or realistic study of the Queen, but at least they might have avoided a few of the absurdities which mar this well-directed and lavish picture. No headmistress, leave alone Elizabeth Tudor, would have allowed quite so much cuddling and kissing in her presence, and a study of Court etiquette might have assisted the actors in deciding when they had to kneel and on what occasions they could sprawl negligently at Her Majesty's feet. The occasional suggestions that all is not quite straightforward in the Queen's character are only embarrassing; they don't belong, they have strayed out of history; one doesn't want this sex stuff in the common-room. As for the story of a young spy sent to Madrid to discover the names of English plotters, it belongs to the good old horsehair tradition of Charles Kingsley and the Low Church romancers: the distinction is between Papists who burn their prisoners in the name of religion and the honest Protestants who sail round the world and singe Philip's beard, sportsmen all. No stench from Campion's quarters offends the nostrils here.

Nevertheless, this is the best production to come from Denham yet. The sets are magnificent (in the case of the English Court too magnificent, if we are to accept the dramatic theme, presented in the opening lines by Burleigh, of a small poor island rashly threatening the wealth and power of a great empire), the direction, until the closing scenes which are spoilt by the absurdity of the story, spirited, and the acting is far better than we are accustomed to in English films. Mr Laurence Olivier can do the hysterical type of young romantic hero with ease, Mr Leslie Banks is a Leicester who might have been on the board of governors of any school, and Mr Raymond Massey presents a fine and plausible portrait of King Philip. Mr Massey is the only memorable thing about the film.

Maid of Salem is historical romance in the American manner, a story of witch-hunts in New England. *Fire Over England* has the easier dialogue (*Maid of Salem* is pompously period) and is more pleasing to the eye, but as a story the American picture derives from Hawthorne not Kingsley, and a little authentic horror is allowed to creep in. Miss Bonita Granville, as the child who pretends for her own mean motives that she has been bewitched, gives a performance equal to her earlier study of evil adolescence in *These Three*. Miss Claudette Colbert and Mr Fred MacMurray as the Puritan girl and her rebel lover are a little out of place: but not so that magnificent actor Mr Edward Ellis, a fierce and austere player who strides through this picture with a terrifying conviction.

I have it on my conscience that I have not yet recommended *Theodora Goes Wild*. Miss Irene Dunne will be remembered for many patient, womanly and rather smug performances (*Roberta* and *Magnificent Obsession* are the worst cases on record); now she has been regroomed and appears as one of the best comedians on the screen in the best light comedy since *Mr Deeds*.

The Spectator (5 March 1937)

Fire Over England (GB, London Films, 1937) Dir.: William K. Howard. Cast: Flora Robson, Laurence Olivier, Leslie Banks, Raymond Massey, Vivien Leigh, James Mason, Tamara Desni, Morton Selten, Lyn Harding.

Maid of Salem (USA, Paramount, 1936) Dir.: Frank Lloyd. Cast: Claudette Colbert, Fred MacMurray, Harvey Stephens, Gale Sondergaard, Edward Ellis, Louise Dresser, Beulah Bondi, Bonita Granville.

Theodora Goes Wild (USA, Columbia, 1937) Dir.: Richard Boleslawski. Cast: Irene Dunne, Melvyn Douglas, Thomas Mitchell, Thurston Hall, Spring Byington.

Pluck of the Irish · The Sequel to Second Bureau · Thunder in the City · Head Over Heels

Weighing machines which can be made to record any weight at the touch of a finger; chickens filled with lead sausages which fall quietly into a drawer of sawdust after the chicken has been weighed: the racket which cheats housewives of a few cents every time they make a purchase is the subject of Mr James Cagney's new film. *The Sequel to Second Bureau* deals with the theft of a new French cartridge by German agents and the successful attempt of two French spies, posing as an art critic and his sister, to recover the cartridge before it has been analysed by the head of the German Secret Service. The issue, compared with that of the American picture, seems oddly theoretical. The imagination, however Francophil, refuses to to really stirred. 'You carry the best wishes of four million Frenchmen,' an officer remarks loudly outside the Paris-Berlin wagon lit (after reading Mr Compton Mackenzie's reminiscences we can swallow any amount of military indiscretions), but the imagination refuses to forget entirely the bad wishes of the four million Germans. The cartridge is treated with immense pomposity by the heads of the rival Secret Services, but one knows quite well that very soon someone else will invent a better one. It is all an amusing game to keep the Army Estimates up. It hasn't the immediate importance of the weighing-machines in the grocery stores. But as a military variation on the Tale of the Three Bears – 'Who's been eating up my porridge?' – this French melodrama has charm. The story is told with a great deal of malicious humour, especially in the Haus Vaterland scenes – the bogus Tyrolean singers, the huge tankards, the absurd painted mountains under an artificial storm, the Horst Wessel song booming from the loud-speaker, the outstretched arms and the heartfelt *Heils*.

Mr Cagney as the Deputy Chief of the Weights and Measures Department of a big American city: one knows what to expect and Mr Cagney seldom disappoints: the lightweight hands held a little away from the body ready for someone else's punch: the quick nervous step of a man whose footwork is good: the extreme virtuosity of the muted sentiment. In his latest picture it is all there, with perhaps a more sophisticated humour than usual: the scenes with the ward politicians, the Mayor, the philanthropist, crooks all, are pleasantly phosphorescent with corruption and so is the admirable climax at an evening party (given by a retiring boxer) where all is tuxedos and gentility, but a little uppercut in a corner passes unnoticed among pals.

Thunder in the City, with the American star Mr Edward G. Robinson, and *Head Over Heels*, with Miss Jessie Matthews, compete for the position of worst English film of the quarter. I think the former has it, with its tricky self-conscious continuity, its horde of Hollywood stars on holiday. Mr Ned Mann's worst 'special effect' to date, and its complete ignorance – in spite of its national studio – of English life and behaviour. It is a fantasy (an American publicity man dismissed from his New York firm because they want English dignity comes over to England and puts over a big business flotation by what are supposed to be American methods), a fantasy by an elephantine disciple of M. Clair (astonishingly his name is Robert E. Sherwood) but even a fantasy needs some relation to life. Perhaps the only really English thing about this picture is its humour: an awful vista of old bound *Punch*'s dwindling down the shelves of a country-house library.

As for Miss Jessie Matthews, she has been ill served in her latest film, a moribund tale of poor young people with ambitions in Parisian garrets. The dialogue has a moral earnestness for which it would be hard to find a parallel even in the Victorian Age. 'You do – trust me?' the hero asks the heroine after she has accepted an invitation to lunch in his garret. Only one song:

> Why must I weep on
> The pillow I sleep on?

possesses a kind of awful charm.

The Spectator (19 March 1937)

Pluck of the Irish (USA, Grand National, 1936) Dir.: John Blystone. Cast: James Cagney, Mae Clarke, James Burke, Edward Brophy, Henry Kolker. (US title: *Great Guy*)

The Sequel to Second Bureau (Les Loups entre eux) (France, Compagnie Française Cinématographique, 1936) Dir.: Léon Mathot. Cast: Renée Saint-Cyr, Jules Berry.

Thunder in the City (USA, Columbia, 1937) Dir.: Marion Gering. Cast: Edward G. Robinson, Ralph Richardson, Lulu Deste, Nigel Bruce, Constance Collier, Arthur Wontner.

Head Over Heels (GB, Gaumont British, 1937) Dir.: Sonnie Hale. Cast: Jessie Matthews, Robert Flemyng, Louis Borell, Sonnie Hale, Romney Brent. (US title: *Head Over Heels in Love*)

Three Smart Girls · For Valour

Since Henry James wrote *What Maisie Knew* a good many writers have been attracted to the subject of divorce as it affects the child –

one remembers Mrs Wharton's *The Children* and the novel and film *Little Friend*. It is a real subject as James described it, and as these other writers to the best of their ability dealt with it: 'To live with all intensity and perplexity and felicity in its terribly mixed little world would thus be the part of my interesting small mortal; . . . really keeping the torch of virtue alive in an air tending infinitely to smother it; really, in short, making confusion worse confounded by drawing some stray fragrance of an ideal across the scent of selfishness by sowing on barren strands, through the mere fact of presence, the seed of the moral life.' It has needed Hollywood to make of this subject, which of its nature contains all the possible darkness of corruption, a story almost as dewy as *Girls' Dormitory*, when it is not relieved by passages of quite amusing farce. As for the fragrance of an ideal – one's nose detects at once the vapid and virginal and inexpensive odour of lavender water.

That scent lies most heavily over the first half-hour: the new young star, Deanna Durbin, singing sentimental and precocious lyrics while her sisters manoeuvre a boat on a Swiss lake surrounded by over-romantic woods; squeals and tussles, a chalet in a garden full of smudged and bogus blossoms, the old family servant, a mother's tears, and as much as possible of that unnaturally mature soprano voice. (As usual we become acquainted only too intimately with the hideous cavern of the human mouth.) The three children – so consciously girlish that they might all be budding Bergners – learn from their mother's tears that their father, ten years divorced, is about to marry a blonde gold-digger, and with an old servant they sail for New York to stop the marriage at all costs and reconcile their parents. Only then with the tardy entrance of 'Precious' (Miss Binnie Barnes), her scheming mother (Miss Alice Brady), a bogus Hungarian Count (Mr Mischa Auer) and a real English nobleman (Mr Ray Milland) does some welcome humour of an adult kind creep tardily into the sentimental film. It is these actors who make the picture, rather than the much-advertised Miss Durbin (Mr Mischa Auer confirms the fine impression left by *The Gay Desperado* and *My Man Godfrey*).

It may seem unfair to complain that this picture does not do something more serious and more worth while: I would be the last to complain if the note had been set in the farcical passages: it is hopeless to expect an American to remain unmoved by mother love, and the tears with which the picture begins fall again with happiness at the close. Father and mother clasp hands, while Miss Durbin's face appears between them in place of the traditional horse.

For Valour is a very pleasant antidote to the Coronation, though it is a little marred by an inability to remain wholly flippant. Mr Tom Walls as an old convict and also as his son, a crooked financier: Mr Ralph Lynn as an ancient Boer War veteran and also as his thieving and incompetent grandson, play most of the parts themselves. The burlesque on wartime patriotism – recruiting meetings in the Victorian and in the Georgian manner with the appropriate songs strummed out in church halls under the painted stare of Roberts and Kitchener – may prove puzzling to audiences properly conditioned by the patriotic Press, and our more earnest visitors from the Dominions may be a trifle put out by the elaborate and almost universal roguery (even the Boer War veteran becomes a kleptomaniac at the close). But those of us who are tired of the sturdy, sober and imperial virtues of the new reign will welcome this return to the tradition of *The English Rogue* and *Moll Flanders*. It is not, of course, quite as good as all that; Mr Tom Walls is better as an actor than he is as a director, and the shadow of schoolmaster *Punch* – 'so much cause for mirth and so little for harm' – has to be placated with an honest character and a few good resolutions.

The Spectator (26 March 1937)

Three Smart Girls (USA, Universal, 1937) Dir.: Henry Koster. Cast: Deanna Durbin, Barbara Read, Nan Grey, Charles Winninger, Binnie Barnes, Ray Milland, Alice Brady, Mischa Auer.

For Valour (GB, Capitol, 1937) Dir.: Tom Walls. Cast: Tom Walls, Ralph Lynn, Robertson Hare, Veronica Rose, Joan Marion, Hubert Harben.

The Good Earth · Dark Journey

The way is less long from China to Stockholm than is the

imaginative distance between these two pictures. One is about life and the other is about – what? I find it hard to say, but certainly not life. One is simple and direct and true: it catches successfully that legendary quality Mr Flaherty failed to put into *Man of Aran*: the characters are shown in incidents common to their class and race, a marriage, a famine, a revolution; the other is composed (unwise policy even for a thriller) of incidents which never happened to anybody yet: a kind of collage of old Lyceum dramas and Drury Lane dialogue.

The Good Earth is the story of a Chinese peasant-farmer, how he marries a wife, who is a slave in the Great House, has children, adds field to field; how drought comes and kills his crops and cattle, how he refuses to sell his land, though his family starves, how they trek south to the city. A revolution quite meaningless to them sweeps through the town, his wife is caught up in a mob and flung through a looted palace, luck saves her incomprehensibly from a firing-squad, luck leaves in her hands a bag of jewels. Understanding nothing of what it is all about they can go back to their land, and Miss Luise Rainer's beautiful performance, the stupid stuck-out lips, the scared, uncalculating and humble gaze, convey all the peasant's fear of hope, of the envious gods, the Oriental equivalent of the touched wood, the salt over the shoulder. 'My daughter is of no account' (and a hand shields the *son's* face from the dangerous heavens) 'and ugly with smallpox.' Mr Muni's performance is not of the same quality, he exaggerates his Chinoiserie, it is Miss Rainer and the character she presents who carries the film: the awful pathos of the wedding walk from the Great House at the heels of the bridegroom she has never seen, the scrabbling in the ditch for the peach stone he has spat out (from it a tree may grow); toiling heavy with child in the fields to save the harvest from the hurricane; her proud and ceremonial return to the Great House to show her son to the Ancient One; in the long drought taking the knife to the ox her husband fears to kill ('Infirm of purpose, give me the dagger', in acting like Miss Rainer's we become aware of the greatness of all echoes). The drought marks the highest point of the film. Like clear exact epithets the images stab home: the plough jammed in the rocky soil, the vultures on the kid's carcase, the dark sullen stare of the starved child.

Afterwards the picture becomes a little less than life. Something goes wrong with the story and direction when the farmer has returned to his land with the loot and bought the Great House: too much plot-making, too many cinematic themes (father against son, love against lust): not even the big set-piece of the locust plague saves the last hour from banality and ennui. The peasant is no longer legendary: he is no longer any peasant who marries and suffers and endures: he is a character called so-and-so who becomes astoundingly rich and loves a dancing-girl, who loves his son whom he turns out of his home, and so on and so on, plot running away with subject, life left behind in those magnificent earlier reels.

'Abandon life all ye who enter here': the pedestrian unreality of most Denham pictures lies over this spy drama directed by Mr Victor Saville, about a fashionable dressmaker in Stockholm who works for the German Secret Service when all the time she is in French pay. Mr Saville directed *The W. Plan*, a good thriller, but he is defeated by the incredible naïvety of this script. 'Fig leaves were good enough for Eve and she was the first lady in the land.' So runs the wicked cosmopolitan dialogue. 'You love me – why are you trying to resist? I want to take you away from here,' and the Count's monocle glitters. There is one superb moment of anti-climax when the Germans accuse the heroine of bringing false information about French movements at Verdun. She pleads nervously: 'But wasn't there an attack?' to receive the stern reply, 'Yes, but our troops stopped the wrong one.' The heroine is rescued by a Q-ship in the nick of time from a German submarine, and the final shot is of two small and dubious ships on a waste of water. One of them hoots derisively, and to that maritime 'raspberry' the film fittingly fades out.

The Spectator (2 April 1937)

The Good Earth (USA, MGM, 1937) Dir.: Sidney Franklin. Cast: Paul Muni, Luise Rainer, Walter Connolly, Tilly Losch, Jesse Ralph, Keye Luke,

Harold Huber.

Dark Journey (GB, London Films, 1937) Dir.: Victor Saville. Cast: Vivien Leigh, Conrad Veidt, Joan Gardner, Anthony Bushell, Ursula Jeans, Austen Trevor, Edmund Willard, Eliot Makeham.

Winterset · After the Thin Man

Winterset belongs to the same kind as *The Petrified Forest.* Adapted from a romantic play, in which poetry and gangmen are curiously linked, it still bears about it on the screen some of the unreality of the stage; almost as desperate a pursuit of the unities as you will find in Corneille lands all the characters, during the course of a few night hours, on one bleak rain-drenched square under the arches of Brooklyn Bridge. The hero, too, has some likeness to Mr Sherwood's Sparkenbrokish tramp, and there are occasions when Art is rather embarrassingly wooed, but the resemblances end there: this play (in the original it was in blank verse) has far more solid merits.

The film begins with a prologue, a rather obvious echo of the Sacco-Vanzetti case. Romagna, a Radical, is electrocuted for a murder of which he is innocent, committed by gangsters in his car. Sixteen years later he is not forgotten: a Professor of Jurisprudence throws doubt on the whole case: why was Garth Esdras, an important witness connected with the gang that did the killing, not called? The Judge who tried the case has gone out of his mind, he is wandering from State to State trying to prove to everyone he meets that Romagna was really guilty (even acted by Mr Edward Ellis he remains the stock mad figure of Georgian poetic drama and is more unconvincing than ever upon the screen). Esdras is hiding away with his father and sister in a basement under Brooklyn Bridge, Romagna's son Mio is on the hunt to prove his father innocent, and Trock, the man who did the killing, is on parole from the gaol where he has served a sentence for dope traffic, carrying the prison doctor's verdict in his brain that he has less than six months to live. We have had plenty of Scarfaces, of men whose trigger-fingers act like the conditioned reflexes of dogs who dribble when a bell sounds: Trock has more interest: the sick man who hates the healthy, who kills from envy because he has to die himself. In this character, acted with evil magnificence by Eduardo Ciannelli, there is some of the poetry of a Renaissance tyrant, with basilisks in the eyes and the everlasting cold pinching the heart.

And there are situations, too, which have more intensity than mere 'thriller' stuff: Mio's dance with Esdras's sister to the barrel-organ in the square: the return of Shadow, Trock's chief gunman, from the East River into which he has been pitched with two bullets in his body: the whole wintry scene in the drenching sleet under the sooty arches of people 'passionately met in this sad world'. It would be almost as easy to burlesque this film (love at first sight, the scraps of not quite good enough poetry, the mad Ophelian judge) as *The Petrified Forest*, but the latter film depended, almost entirely for its effect on philosophic ideas of more than Emersonian solemnity and emptiness. Here, as in all good plays, it is in the acts themselves, as much as in the dialogue, that the poetic idea is expressed. And in the cinema it is only right that the symbols should be popular ones: a disappearing body, a sentimental barrel-organ tune, silencers and sub-machine guns. We may have our doubts about the literary dialogue; the physical images at any rate convey a general and poetic idea. Watching Trock dragging others to the grave along with him, one remembers Webster's line: 'Security some men call the suburbs of hell, Only a dead wall between', for it is the merit of *Winterset* that when we are not reminded of Mr Masefield at his vaguest we are reminded of the Jacobeans at their most bloody and exact.

The stars, director and the author of *The Thin Man* have together manufactured a new film of light-hearted murder and marital badinage, if anything rather superior to the first. Between them they attain a rather awful efficiency: not thirty seconds is left unfilled by an expert and amusing gag. In a flat-footed world one is grateful for pictures like this, where entertainment is reduced to a well-tested formula, where every laugh is timed and counted and no effect is unforeseen, where no author builds better than he knows. Perhaps in five years it will all seem as dull and ugly as tubular steel chairs, but at the moment it is – amusingly and excitingly – 1937.

The Spectator (9 April 1937)

Winterset (USA, RKO, 1936) Dir.: Alfred Santell. Cast: Burgess Meredith, Eduardo Ciannelli, Margo, Paul Guilfoyle, John Carradine, Edward Ellis, Stanley Ridges, Mischa Auer.

After the Thin Man (USA, MGM, 1936) Dir.: W. S. Van Dyke. Cast: William Powell, Myrna Loy, James Stewart, Elissa Landi, Joseph Calleia, Jessie Ralph, Alan Marshal, Sam Levene.

Elephant Boy

Mr Robert Flaherty is said to have spent more than a year in India gathering material for this picture: a scene of elephants washed in a river, a few shots of markets and idols and forest, that is all. It cannot be compared in quantity or quality with what Mr Basil Wright brought back from Ceylon after a stay of a few weeks. *Elephant Boy* has gone the same way as *Man of Aran*: enormous advance publicity, director out of touch with the Press for months, rumours of great epics sealed in tins, and then the disappointing diminutive achievement. In *Man of Aran*, a so-called 'documentary', Mr Flaherty had the islanders taught to hunt sharks for the sake of an exciting climax: there is nothing quite so flagrantly bogus in the new picture, but in all other respects it is inferior, even in the inevitable Flaherty skylines, against which the elephants in single file tactlessly take up the graduated positions of those little ebony and ivory toys Indian administrators bring back to their female relatives at Cheltenham. With this exception, Mr Flaherty's faults are negative: the more positive crimes, the bad cutting, the dreadful studio work, the pedestrian adaptation so unfair to Kipling's story, must be laid at Denham's door.

The climax of Kipling's story of an elephant-drive is the dance of the wild elephants which little Toomai, the Mahout's son, watched from the back of Kala Nag. The story is quite legitimately padded out up to this point with incident: Toomai's father is killed by a tiger, Toomai is ordered home by the great white hunter, Petersen,

Kala Nag infuriated by the brutality of his new mahout runs amok, and Toomai returns only just in time to quieten the elephant as the hunter prepares to shoot it down. Kala Nag has broken the mahout's leg and the man claims that its life is forfeit; Toomai, not knowing that Petersen has made the man forgo his claim, slips out with the elephant at night from the camp and is carried at dawn by Kala Nag to the secret dance. This is all reasonable and necessary emboidery on Kipling's story, but Mr Zoltan Korda, who is associated as director with Mr Flaherty, has made nothing of these incidents. The episodes are not led up to, they just happen and are over before you have time to feel excitement or even interest.

Kala Nag's attack on the camp should have been the first great climax of the picture, but through lack of preparation and rhythm in the cutting, the scene is thrown away. As for the elephant dance – I suppose the fault rests with the Indian elephants who will not dance as Kipling describes them, stamping steady as trip-hammers, rocking the ground, though a little could have been done with music and we might have been spared the models. But what has no excuse at this point is the story construction. To use the gathering of the wild elephants on their jungle dance-floor merely to resolve the problem of Petersen Sahib who has got to trap a certain number of elephants for labour if he is to retain his job – this is to throw away the whole poetic value of the original.

Anyone who has had experience of British studios will know how they are governed by one word – suspense – and here is a case where the most childish form of suspense is preferred to any other value, human or poetic. No attempt has been made to interest us in Petersen (Mr Walter Hudd acts with a tiring over-emphasis), and yet the whole story is made to turn on whether or not his hunt will be successful, and we are expected to feel satisfaction at the thought of the wild dancers driven into the stockade to be tamed. Kipling's mind, heaven knows, had its chasms; he was capable of crudities and cruelties, but not of that, and it is noticeable in this faltering and repetitive picture that it is only when Kipling speaks – in his own dialogue when Machua Appa apostrophizes Toomai –

that the ear is caught and the attention held. 'He shall take no harm in the Keddah when he runs under their bellies to rope the wild tuskers; and if he slips before the feet of the charging bull-elephant, that bull-elephant shall know who he is and shall not crush him.' Unwise, unwise to let those weighted and authoritative syllables fall among the cheap china values, the 'Presents from Mysore'.

The Spectator (16 April 1937)

Elephant Boy (GB, London Films, 1937) Directors: Robert Flaherty, Zoltan Korda. Cast: Sabu, Walter Hudd, Allan Jeayes, Wilfrid Hyde White, W. E. Holloway.

Pépé le Moko · The Golem

A thief wanted by the French police who has found a safe, but terribly constricted, asylum in the Casbah, the native quarter of Algiers, from which he cannot move without arrest: a native Police Inspector, allowed, in return for a certain licence, the contemptuous liberty of the quarter: the mistress of a millionaire, drawn by curiosity to the Casbah and used without her knowledge by the inspector to lure Pépé into the European town: on these three simple and well-realized characters, the first generous, natty and common, his pockets chock-a-block with fags and revolvers, the second sly, patient, obsequious, the third, the woman, acquisitive, prehensile, risen from the ranks, and groomed for chromium concubinage, on these three is based one of the most exciting and moving films I can remember seeing.

It is rarely, very rarely, that a picture is produced so unhampered as this by plot-making, where theme dominates incident in so masterly a manner. In this film we do not forget the real subject in a mass of detail: the freedom-loving human spirit trapped and pulled at the chain. A simple subject, but fiction does not demand complex themes, and the story of a man at liberty to move only in one shabby, alien quarter when his heart is in another place widens out of touch the experience of exile common to everyone. One of the subtlest and most moving scenes is that in which the thief and the mistress count over their memories of Paris, starting a world and class apart, her Bois de Boulogne capped by his Porte d'Orleans, until they meet on common ground with the Place Blanche on both their lips at once. In the love scenes we are a whole continent away from the usual studio banalities, and when some gesture of the beloved woman calls up the fish-and-chip shops on the boulevards, her scent the Métro, we are aware (rare and unexpected delight) of a film which is really trying to translate into dramatic terms the irrelevances, the grotesque wit, the absurd, passionate tangle of associations which make up the mind.

Perhaps there have been pictures as exciting on the 'thriller' level as this before (though it would be hard to equal the shooting of Regis, the informer, with its comic horror: the little fat eunuch sweating and squealing in the corner between the aspidistra and the mechanical piano, the clash and clatter of the potted music as his dying victim is helped across the room to finish him at point-blank range, friends steadying the revolver on its mark), but I cannot remember one which has succeeded so admirably in raising the thriller to the poetic level. *Winterset* seems a little jejeune and obvious and literary beside it. *Fury*, perhaps, is its equal, but in *Fury* Fritz Lang was not allowed to follow his subject to the right, grim conclusion. *His* hero couldn't burn; but Pépé cuts his throat with the penknife in his handcuffed hands outside the dock gates as the steamer leaves for France. The theme of no freedom anywhere is not lost in a happy ending.

Acting and direction are both superb. No tricky montage here, but a beautiful smooth flow of images which results in the frank use of panning and trucking shots. It is as if the camera were handled like a brush in broad sweeps as distinct from the restless *pointilliste* effect given by many cuts. Particularly successful is Pépé's last walk in his glossy shoes and his best muffler down the steep steps to the European town where the Inspector awaits him, the camera trucking down ahead of him registering the happy, crazy stride, the rash, nostalgic impulse.

The Golem is very Jewish, very traditional: if it were not for sound and dialogue, it might belong to the classic Ufa days:

synagogues and sacred music, pale, dark Rebeccas, a monarch who wines and wenches in the *Jew Süss* manner. There is a curious, almost Surrealist, acceptance of the most fantastic situations, so that no one seems in the least surprised by the presence in an enormous, raftered attic above the synogogue of a human statue which may at any moment come alive at the right incantation and rescue the downtrodden and chosen race. M. Harry Baur as the Emperor gives one of his most brilliant performances, and the film, I suppose, is quite worth seeing as a kind of survival – a Semitic survival – of the old, romantic Caligari cinema.

The Spectator (23 April 1937)

Pépé le Moko (France, Paris Film, 1936) Dir.: Julien Duvivier. Cast: Jean Gabin, Mireille Balin, Line Noro, Lucas Gridoux, Gabriel Gabrio, Gilbert-Gil, Saturnin Fabre.

The Golem (Le Golem) (France, AB-Film, 1936) Dir.: Julien Duvivier. Cast: Harry Baur, Roger Karl, Germaine Aussey, Jany Holt, Ferdinand Hart, Charles Dorat. (aka: *The Legend of Prague*)

Lost Horizon

Nothing reveals men's characters more than their Utopias: the scientific sentimentality of Mr Wells, the art-and-craftiness of William Morris, Mr Shaw's eternal sewing-machine, Samuel Butler's dusty alpaca. Shangri-La must be counted among the less fortunate flights of the imagination, the lamaserai in Thibet ruled by a Grand Llama, a Belgian priest who discovered the rich valley among the mountains in the eighteenth century and who was still alive when Robert Conway, explorer, diplomat and – rather improbably – Foreign Secretary elect was kidnapped from a Chinese town and brought there by aeroplane. This Utopia closely resembles a film star's luxurious estate on Beverly Hills: flirtatious pursuits through grape arbours, splashings and divings in blossomy pools under improbable waterfalls, and rich and enormous meals. 'Every man carries in his heart a Shangri-La': but I prefer myself the harps and golden crowns and glassy seas of an older mythology. Shangri-La is intended to represent a haven of moderation, beauty and peace in the middle of an uncompromising and greedy world, but what Conway finds there, what he loses in a weak moment of disbelief, and struggles across the Himalayas to find again, is something incurably American: a kind of aerated idealism ('We have one simple rule, Kindness') and, of course, a girl (Miss Jane Wyatt, one of the dumber stars), who had read all the best books (his own included) and has the coy comradely manner of a not too advanced schoolmistress.

It is a very long picture, this disappointing successor to *Mr Deeds*, and a very dull one as soon as the opening scenes are over. These are brilliantly written and directed, and show Conway (Mr Ronald Colman) organizing the aerial evacuation of the white inhabitants from a Chinese town in the middle of a revolution before he takes the last plane himself in company with a crooked financier wanted by the police, a prostitute (sentimental variety), a scientist (comic), and a younger brother. Here the Capra-Riskin partnership is at its best, and we are unprepared for the disappointments which follow: the flavourless uplifting dialogue, the crude humour, the pedestrian direction, and the slack makeshift construction. 'You shouldn't look at the bottom of the mountains. Try looking at the top.' So Chang, the suave philosophical second-in-command of Shangri-La, addresses the prostitute who believes that she is dying of consumption (one of the virtues of this mysterious valley is health, the body beautiful, and a life which goes on and on and on). It might be Wilhelmina Stich translated into American prose, and one can hardly believe that this script is from the same hands as *Mr Deeds*, though perhaps Mr James Hilton, the author of the novel and of *Goodbye, Mr Chips*, may be responsible for the sentimentality of these sequences.

Of course, the picture isn't quite as bad as that. It does attempt, however clumsily and sentimentally, more than the average film; a social conscience is obscurely at work, but at work far less effectively than in *Mr Deeds*, and as for the humour – it consists only of Mr Edward Everett Horton wearing Eastern clothes. The conscious humour that is to say, for the glimpses of English political life give a much needed relief. 'The Far Eastern

Conference must be postponed. We cannot meet these nations without Conway': the Prime Minister's measured utterances to his Cabinet gathered Gladstonianly round him fall with an odd sound on ears accustomed to more dispensable Foreign Secretaries. But it is in the last sequence that the Capra-Riskin collaboration fails most disastrously. Conway, persuaded by his younger brother that the Grand Llama has lied to him, that there is misery and injustice in this seeming Utopia, makes his way back to China across the mountains. A few newspaper headlines tell us that Conway has reached safety, and it is only at second-hand in a long uncinematic scene in a London club that we learn what we should have seen with our own eyes: Conway's reaction to 'civilization'. If the long dull ethical sequences had been cut to the bone there would have been plenty of room for the real story: the shock of Western crudity and injustice on a man returned from a more gentle and beautiful way of life.

The Spectator (30 April 1937)

Lost Horizon (USA, Columbia, 1937) Dir.: Frank Capra. Cast: Ronald Colman, Jane Wyatt, H. B. Warner, Thomas Mitchell, Margo, Edward Everett Horton, Sam Jaffe.

Generation of Conquerors · Lloyds of London · The Gap · Glamorous Night

The pictures I have had to see this week have been terribly voluble: voluble about patriotism, voluble about romance, most voluble of all about the class war. Oh, how that Generation of Conquerors seems to have talked: little wonder that the Revolution was drawn out from 1905 to 1917. I fell asleep on the hot Sunday Film Society afternoon and when I woke five minutes later everything was just the same, the same Siberian hut, the same serious faces arguing in Russian the same point: whether the Bolsheviks and Menshiviks were right to split the Party Congress in 1903. For it was a period film, the women wore wildfowl in their hats and high celluloid collars and sometimes smoked a cigarette with an awkward emphasis, and everyone talked and talked, earnest, fanatical, oddly domestic revolutionaries. One remembered how Lenin in his Siberian exile presented his wife with a little ornamental brooch made in the shape of a book labelled *Das Kapital*.

Generation of Conquerors is hardly likely to be seen in London again: the poor entertainment-loving flesh is weak, and for those who do not understand Russian there is little to recommend it. Its presentation was chiefly interesting for the new method the Film Society used to translate the picture. Between the sequences, between the fade-out and the fade-in of images, a voice, dubiously BBC in accent, gave a short synopsis of how the plot was going to progress (this synopsis did not quite agree with that in the programme; perhaps the film was too much even for the Society's Council, and we were left in doubt whether the gentleman in black waxed moustaches and a bowler who dogged Sophia – celluloid collar, feather hat – through the park was really a secret police officer or, as the programme states, a *roué*).

Lloyds of London is a fairly astute piece of sentimentality which occasionally overreaches itself when the stage becomes a little too packed with historical figures rather oddly juxtaposed like the waxworks at Madame Tussaud's, so that it is almost a miracle that Lord Nelson doesn't actually meet Benjamin Franklin or Dr Johnson the Prince Regent. The name of England is so frequently on the characters' lips that we recognize at once an American picture. These people live, make love, bear children from the most patriotic motives: and it is all rather like London in Coronation Week. Like a colonial visitor, Miss Madeleine Carroll falls heavily about the screen, large and lost and oddly dressed.

The Gap at the same cinema is more worth seeing, an appeal for Territorial recruits to fill the gap in London's air defences. The actors who play the parts of staff officers behave with unmilitary enthusiasm, but the imaginary air raid on London is very ably directed and the special effects, not by Mr Ned Mann, are finely managed. War without a declaration, a fleet of bombers from the East zooming out of the evening mist over a British trawler in the North Sea, civilian observers grouped round their metal tripods as they report the strange planes crossing the coast in the late evening light, the bomb-proof control-room where wireless-operators sit round an enormous map moving model aeroplanes while lights flash on as the patrolling squadrons take off over Kent and Sussex and the Eastern counties: zero hour modern style is impressively conveyed.

Glamorous Night is about a Ruritanian King who loves a gipsy, and a scheming Prime Minister, who exiles the royal mistress, makes himself dictator and is about to murder the King when the gipsy enters the capital at the head of her people. The plot belongs to the age of *The Bing Boys* and *The Maid of the Mountains*; one waits for jokes about Blighty, although Mr Novello has tried to bring it up to date with arch references to coloured shirts. It is about as bogus as a film could be, but it is well photographed by Wagner, Lang's ace cameraman in the old Ufa days, and quite well directed by Mr Brian Desmond Hurst. It has the advantage of Miss Mary Ellis's daemonic good looks, and Mr Hurst deserves some credit for never once taking Miss Ellis's mouth in a close-up as she sings Mr Novello's peculiarly flat songs.

The Spectator (7 May 1937)

Generations of Conquerors (USSR, Mosfilm, 1936) Dir.: Vera Stroyeva. Cast: Boris Shchukin, Nikolai Khmelyov, Xenia Tarasova, Vera Maretskaya.

Lloyds of London (USA, Twentieth-Century Fox, 1936) Dir.: Henry King. Cast: Tyrone Power, Madeleine Carroll, Freddie Bartholomew, George Sanders, C. Aubrey Smith, Guy Standing, Virginia Field, Montagu Love, Miles Mander, Una O'Connor, E. E. Clive.

The Gap (GB, GB Instructional, 1937) Dir.: Donald Carter.

Glamorous Night (GB, British International, 1937) Dir.: Brian Desmond Hurst. Cast: Mary Ellis, Otto Kruger, Victor Jory, Trefor Jones, Barry Mackay.

Lenin and Lavender

We from Kronstadt · The Frog · Make Way for Tomorrow · Der Herrscher

No need to stop and think about which is the best film to be seen in London. It's undoubtedly *We from Kronstadt*. Russian, full of absurd heroics, noble deaths, last-minute rescues, wounded men played up to the trenches by a scarecrow band, it is no more propagandist than Henty. In a sense all writing for schoolboys is propaganda for the established order, and in this film, just as much as in *Tom Brown's Schooldays*, the people who don't stick to the old school code end by having a thin time. What makes the film immeasurably superior to its rivals is the strain of adult poetry, the sense of human beings longing for peace, grasping moments out of the turmoil for ordinary human relations, and the most cynical Conservative will cheer at the defiant closing line: 'Who else wants Petrograd?'

The best line to cheer on in *The Frog*, an English thriller, is 'I must get John Bennett's gramophone record if I am to save his son's life.' The dialogue otherwise goes rather like this: 'My name is Bennett. Stella Bennett.' 'No, not really? Stella Bennett? What a charming name! I very much hope we shall meet again one day soon.' 'Must you really go? Good-bye then.' 'What Stella! Are these gentlemen still here?' 'We were on the point of leaving, Sir.' 'This is my father, Inspector. May I introduce Inspector Elk of Scotland Yard?' 'Good-bye, Miss Bennett. Please don't trouble to see us out. Good-bye, Sir. Haven't we met somewhere before?' 'No. Good-bye.' While the well-mannered dialogue drones on, a bomb is touched off in Scotland Yard, the voice of the master criminal is trapped on a gramophone disc by a bird-watcher, the factory containing the matrix is burnt to the ground, an innocent man is sentenced to death, and the public executioner entering the condemned cell finds his own son there. Badly directed, badly acted, it is like one of those plays produced in country towns by stranded actors: it has an old-world charm: Scotland Yard is laid up in lavender.

Make Way for Tomorrow is a depressing picture about an old couple driven by hard times to live on their children. No one wants them, no one can put them both up at the same time. After months of separation they meet for a few hours in New York before the old man goes off to a daughter in California and the old woman into a home, with no hope of seeing each other again. The Pullman slides out, the aged tortoise in fact runs away, the tight thin bun of hair drearily fades out, and a sense of misery and inhumanity is left vibrating in the nerves. Anyhow that was how the story appeared to me, though Paramount describe in in these terms. 'One of the Three Smart Girls goes a lot faster. She wants to taste the Thrills of Life itself. *What Happens*?'

Der Herrscher, except for a pleasantly savage opening, a funeral frieze of dripping umbrellas and heartless faces, is a wordy picture about an elderly ironmaster who wants to marry his secretary and is almost driven insane by his children's opposition. Herr Jannings has the meaningless gaze of a sea-lion with huge sloping shoulders and watery whiskers to whose emotions we apply for want of anything better, such human terms as pity, anger, terror, though we cannot tell, on the evidence of those small marine eyes, whether he is really registering anything more than a dim expectation of fish.

Night and Day (1 July 1937)

We from Kronstadt (USSR, Mosfilm, 1936) Dir.: Yefim Dzigan. Cast: Vasili Zaichikov, Grigori Bushuyev, Oleg Zhakov, Raisa Yesipova.

The Frog (GB, Herbert Wilcox Productions, 1937) Dir.: Jack Raymond. Cast: Gordon Harker, Jack Hawkins, Noah Beery, Felix Aylmer, Esmé Percy.

Make Way for Tomorrow (USA, Paramount, 1937) Dir.: Leo McCarey. Cast: Victor Moore, Beulah Bondi, Thomas Mitchell, Fay Bainter, Porter Hall, Barbara Read, Maurice Moscovitch, Elizabeth Risdon, Gene Lockhart.

Der Herrscher (Germany, Tobis-Magna-Film, 1937) Dir.: Veit Harlan. Cast: Emil Jannings, Marianne Hoppe, Käthe Haack, Rudolf Klein-Rogge, Hilde Körber.

Horror for Adults

Black Legion · Night Must Fall · Top of the Town · The Last Train from Madrid

Black Legion, an intelligent and exciting, if rather earnest film, is intended to expose the secret society of that name and the financial racket behind it. The Black Legion, with its policy of America for Americans, its melodramatic black hoods, must have had an appeal as wide as humanity: to the natural bully, to the envious and the unsuccessful, the man with a grievance, the romantic. Frank Taylor (admirably acted by Humphrey Bogart), a factory-hand who finds himself passed over for the post of foreman in favour of a Pole, attends a meeting at the local chemist's, a little rabbity man with defective eyesight who resents the cut-price drugstore further down the street. We hear the long pompous literary oath full of words too difficult for Taylor to pronounce; then the playboy hoods are raised to disclose the familiar faces, the chemist's, the bully's from the works, the organizer's, who informs the new recruit that he can now get 'a regular thirty-dollar revolver for fourteen dollars fifty cents', and afterwards the drinks all round, the hearty good fellowship.

It is an intelligent film because the director and script-writer know where the real horror lies: the real horror is not in the black robes and skull emblems, but in the knowledge that these hide the weak and commonplace faces you have met over the counter and minding the next machine. The horror is not in the climax when Taylor shoots his friend dead, but in the earlier moment before the glass when he poses romantically with his first gun; not in the floggings and burnings but in the immature question at the inaugural meeting, 'If we join up don't we get a uniform or something?', in the secret accounts read to the Managing Director, so much from the sale of uniforms and regalia, so much from officers' commissions, so much from revolvers at wholesale rates: total profits for the month, $221,049, 15 cents.

Comparisons can obviously be made with *Fury*, and at least

one to the advantage of *Black Legion*: no factitious happy ending is tacked on (though the producer probably has one up his sleeve in case of need). But *Fury* with all its faults was the work of a very great director, *Black Legion* only of an intelligent one. The immediate impact of the horror has seeped away somewhere – perhaps in the camera positions – between the script and the 'take'.

There never was any genuine horror in *Night Must Fall*, and Emlyn Williams's pretentious little murder play has made a long dim film. Like an early talkie, it is no more than a photographed stage play and its psychological absurdities are mercilessly exposed. But there are worse pictures in town than this. *Top of the Town* may appeal to readers of *London Life* (the heroine wears very high heels, a kind of long Cossack coat and carries a little cane), but it is one of those distressingly carefree musicals (elderly people in evening dress romping up and down a restaurant for ten whole minutes at a stretch) when the only ungay faces are among the audience.

As for *The Last Train from Madrid*, it is probably the worst film of the decade and should have been the funniest. Emotional and uplifting dialogue ('I don't want to die, Señorita. I'm young, I want to live. My father kept a farm . . .') Mr Lionel Atwill ('a grand old trouper', as Miss Lejeune would say) playing the Madrid Commandant, full of sternness and duty and tenderness ('You will be tried by court martial tomorrow', and his warm encouraging paw falls like a headmaster's on the prisoner's shoulder): all we still need for a really good laugh are the presence of the Dean of Canterbury and the absence of actual war. For there is something a little shocking about these noble self-sacrifices and heroic deaths – the eyes close always of their own accord – in front of a back projection of ruined Madrid itself, about the facetiousness of the screen journalist in a screen air raid mingled with news-shots of the genuine terror.

Night and Day (8 July 1937)

Black Legion (USA, Warners, 1936) Dir.: Archie Mayo. Cast: Humphrey Bogart, Ann Sheridan, Dick Foran, Erin O'Brien Moore, John Litel.

Night Must Fall (USA, MGM, 1936) Dir.: Richard Thorpe. Cast: Robert Montgomery, Rosalind Russell, Dame May Whitty, Alan Marshall, Kathleen Harrison, E. E. Clive, Merle Tottenham.

Top of the Town (USA, Universal, 1937) Dir.: Ralph Murphy. Cast: Doris Nolan, George Murphy, Hugh Herbert, Gregory Ratoff, Ella Nogan, Mischa Auer, Samuel S. Hinds, Peggy Ryan.

The Last Train from Madrid (USA, Paramount, 1937) Dir.: James Hogan. Cast: Lew Ayres, Dorothy Lamour, Lionel Atwill, Anthony Quinn, Gilbert Roland, Helen Mack, Robert Cummings, Lee Bowman.

What Man Has Made of Man

God's Country and the Woman · Michael Strogoff

The Technicolor expert, like Wordsworth, is most at home with Nature. In *God's Country and the Woman*, a tale of the timber forests, we see some pretty shots of tress cutting huge arcs against the sky as they fall, but no technical advance since *The Trail of the Lonesome Pine*. In the city sequences the lounge suits don't come out too badly, but there's an appalling orange taxi and the headlights of cars are curiously ugly. An attempt at fast cutting and quick dissolves confirms our belief that colour will put the film back technically twelve years.

The plot may roughly be described as a combination of *Romeo and Juliet* and *The Taming of the Shrew*. Katharina has become a Capulet, the Montagues and Capulets run rival timber companies, and Romeo has to do some taming as well as loving. But it is his loving which fascinated me. A wealthy young man fresh from Paris and the Riviera, he has earned a reputation as a wonderful quick worker with women, a breaker of hearts, an American Juan. His technique is interesting and perhaps national. We see a few flashes of it in a Paris lift and on the quayside at Cherbourg: he treads hard on a woman's foot and then apologizes or else he takes a crack at her ankle and catches her as she falls. The method never fails. When he meets Juliet-Katharina for the first time he remarks 'O boy, what a fuselage!' with his eye on her bust, and when he kisses her he says 'That went right down to the soles of my goloshes.' Irresistible in strong-toed shoes, he hacks his way to happiness.

It isn't a very good film, and Mr George Brent is hardly improved by blue-black Technicolor hair and a little Parisian moustache (next to the orange taxi he's the worst bit of colour in the picture). Far more interesting is the effect it has had on a veteran film critic. 'The thought of so much beauty of forest and mountain being ruthlessly destroyed,' Mr Sydney Carroll writes, 'almost broke my heart. These trees were treated so savagely. Their sufferings made me feel the need for a Society for the Prevention of Cruelty to Trees.' And Mr Carroll concludes his outburst, written on woodpulp which ought to account for a fair-sized sapling: 'I could not see this picture again. It would for this reason alone give me a heartache.'

'Captain Strogoff, the fate of Siberia is in your hands. Go for God, for Russia and the Tsar.' The words echo down the years from the caption of the early Mosjoukine film. Mosjoukine will be remembered as the player Pudovkin cites as an example to prove that acting was a matter of montage. Intercut Mosjoukine's face with a child's coffin and you got tragic acting. Intercut the same white turnip of countenance with charging cavalry and you had the heroic. Mr Anton Walbrook does a lot better than Mosjoukine in this new *Michael Strogoff.* As dashing and open-air as a good Western, this Jules Verne tale of a Tartar rising is motivated in the grand manner. A Grand Mission to save the Russian Empire; a Grand Sacrifice when the hero denies his mother; a Grand Courtesan who repents and dies grandly for love ('Do you not want to be a Quin?' the renegade Colonel – Mr Akim Tamiroff – whispers into her jewelled ear); even the Sensualities are Grand in a torture scene which begins with dancing-girls and ends with a white-hot sword. Simple, passionate and certainly sensuous, the whole thing is like a poem for boys, and not a bad poem either. If we cannot treat it quite seriously, it's because Russia, whether under Tsar or Stalin, remains uncurably comic even in tragedy. 'To Omsk!' the renegade leader cries to his Tartars; 'I must get to Omsk,' the heroine piteously murmurs, and the hero, wounded and feverish in a peasant's hut, can find no better syllables to murmur than 'Irkutsk, Irkutsk.' How wise the Soviet policy of renaming their cities – and how pathetically useless when 'Gorki' is the only substitute.

Night and Day (15 July 1937)

God's Country and the Woman (USA, Warners, 1936) Dir.: William Keighley. Cast: George Brent, Beverley Roberts, Alan Hale, Barton MacLane, Robert Barrat, Billy Bevan.
Michael Strogoff (USA, RKO, 1937) Dir.: George Nicholls Jr. Cast: Anton Walbrook, Akim Tamiroff, Elizabeth Allen, Margot Grahame.

Without Beard or Bed

PARNELL · CALL IT A DAY

The fictional screen has never really got beyond wish-fulfilment dreams, and the only interest this week is in seeing the kind of wish-fulfilment the big film executives enjoy. In that light *Parnell* becomes almost interesting. At any rate it isn't shocking like *Call It a Day*, the close adaptation of Miss Dodie Smith's popular play, the day-dream of a good woman.

Of course the first thing one notices about the Metro-Goldwyn-Mayer dream of how history should have happened is the absence of Parnell's beard. Pigott is allowed a beard (a magnificent spade-shaped affair in which there is ample room for two owls and a wren, five larks and a hen), but he's a villain. How exactly this beard-neurosis has arisen one cannot say. I think it may have something to do with the astrakhan coats film financiers wear: a kind of whisker-weariness.

Then, too, anything secretive, anything middle-aged, anything a little bit lecherous in the story has been eliminated. No illegitimate children, no assignations in seaside hotels under assumed names, no furtive vigils at Waterloo Station. In the divorce suit O'Shea hasn't a leg to stand on (it's just his dirty mind): the suit is followed immediately by Parnell's political overthrow and his death the same night. Far from any adulterous meetings the lovers are not even allowed to marry, and never in this film hangs the engraving of Lord Leighton's *Wedding* above the legalized bed. But poor though the picture may be, it is pleasing to think how clean a film magnate's wish-fulfilments are, how virginal and high-minded the tawdry pathetic human past becomes when the Mayers and Goldwyns turn the magic ring.

I'm a lot less happy about *Call it a Day*. A picture of one spring day in the life of an ordinary prosperous English family, full of characteristic touches about bathrooms and the cat kittening and how women can't be trusted to read *The Times* tidily, crowded with dreadfully recognizable details ('My dear, that's just how Henry behaves'), it might have been compiled from the sly diaries of members of the PEN Club. Good aunts or wives all, we know, whatever we may think at literary parties of their long incisors and prominent shoulderblades, but who would imagine, before seeing this film, of what *their* wish-fulfilments consist?

In this picture the middle-aged husband, a chartered accountant, is 'tempted' by an actress with whose income-tax he is dealing. She is the sort of vicious woman only a really unsullied female could invent, and sets to work on the traditional pair of steps as soon as she is alone with her man. Then it's no time at all before she's playing hot music to him after a little dinner in her flat. Follows the dirty look, the well-known phrase, 'Do you mind if I slip into something more comfortable?', the strategic retirement. But at this point the authoress's imagination wavered, or perhaps fear of being blackballed from the PEN checked her exuberant fancy, for to our astonishment the temptress reappeared in just another evening dress. Meanwhile, the wife, middle-aged but handsome in an aunt-like way, understanding and healthy minded, is ardently beseiged at home by a man she only met at tea-time. Nobody, of course, gives way: but what agreeable titillations and temptations, what a Dodie dream of a world where all the heavy labour and the missed cues of infidelity are eliminated and the two-backed beast is trotted out quaintly, gaily and whimsically like a character in *Winnie the Pooh*.

Night and Day (22 July 1937)

Parnell (USA, MGM, 1936) Dir.: John M. Stahl. Cast: Clark Gable, Myrna Loy, Edmund Gwenn, Edna May Oliver, Alan Marshal, Donald Crisp, Billie Burke, Berton Churchill, Donald Meek, Montagu Love, George Zucco.

Call it a Day (USA, Warners, 1937) Dir.: Archie Mayo. Cast: Olivia de Havilland, Ian Hunter, Bonita Granville, Anita Louise, Alice Brady, Roland Young, Frieda Inescourt, Una O'Connor.

On the West Coast . . .

The High Command · On the Avenue · Yiddle with his Fiddle

It isn't often that the English cinema throws up a new director of promise – Mr Edmond Greville, whose *Secret Living* is being shown this week at the Paramount, had to go to France for his opportunity – and when a new face does appear among the old gang, it is often greeted with rotten vegetables. That the critic of so distinguished a paper as the *Sunday Times* should dismiss Mr Thorold Dickinson's *The High Command* in two glib sentences is rather shocking. 'As for *The High Command*, this is a picture made by Fanfare, a new British film company. Its avoidance of reality and its slowness make it a first-class soporific in this sultry weather.'

No one will deny that *The High Command* is full of faults. The story is wildly improbable: of an English officer who murders a man for chivalrous reasons in an Irish ambush, of how years later, as a Major-General in command of a West African fort, he finds his crime discovered and allows himself to be murdered in his turn so as to save his daughter from the disgrace. The first half of the film suffers from a slow, jerky and obscure script, and there is one unfortunate scene of unconscious humour when a villainous trader about to placate his wife with a pearl necklace is interrupted by an unexplained woman in a similar pearl necklace who pops silently through a window, gives a dirty smile and pops out again, like the horse in Mr James Thurber's story which was always putting its head through the drawing-room curtains. Then the sets sometimes reveal too obviously the strict economy with which the film was made (£30,000, including the cost of sending a unit to West Africa, is a remarkable bill to put beside the enormous expenditures of Denham). The devil's advocate indeed has plenty to play with in this picture, but a film critic should be capable of distinguishing, from the faults due to a poor story, an uncertain script and mere poverty, the very high promise of the direction.

Taking a tip perhaps from Duvivier and *Pépé le Moko*, Mr Dickinson establishes the West African scene at the start in a series of beautifully cut documentary shots, though I would have preferred a rather different choice of image from the picturesque market and the native hospital to represent the white civilization of the Coast. Tin roofs, maybe, and broken windows, long dreary bars and ants on the floor, vultures pecking like turkeys in arid back gardens.

What will remain longest in my memory is the little scene in the Club when the band breaks into 'God Save the King' for the Governor, just as the evening wind begins to blow: the black servants start towards the flapping shutters and banging doors and then, seeing the rigidity of their masters, leap to attention while the tune penetrates fitfully through the din of the Hammatan.: 'happy and glorious', the potted palms bend towards the floor, the great green lights swing above the billiard-table, 'long to reign over us', and the wind smashes through the clubroom and British West Africa comes alive as it never did in Mr Korda's lavish and unimaginative *Sanders of the River*.

There are other moments of direction one might expect a critic, however irritated by a stumbling script, to notice. The human crisis worked out in whispers as the native village dance reaches its climax, flames on the bystanders' faces, shaken spears, the polite accusation, and then the General's harsh order as he learns his secret is known. 'Put out those fires', the slow withdrawal of the two Africans behind the rising smoke after they have drenched the flames; the whole scene has a touch of lyric imagination one seeks in vain in most English films.

No musicals could be less alike than *On the Avenue* and *Yiddle with his Fiddle*. *On the Avenue* is a magnificently efficient, very entertaining piece of American routine work, only a little marred by Miss Madeleine Carroll's performance as the heroine. She has what must be, to all but the most blindly devoted keepers, the less endearing traits of a young elephant. We expect to see the sets rock a little beneath her stupendous coquetry, and we cannot help wondering whether Mr Dick Powell, with his little moustache and his laving hands, has the stamina to withstand her more-than-lifesize embrace. Handsome in a big way, given to intense proboscine whispers, she lends an impression of weight to every action, of awful fidelities to the lightest love ('an elephant never forgets'), but we don't want weight or fidelity in a musical comedy.

Nevertheless, it is a good film with some charming songs – 'I saw the girl I can never forget, on the cover of the Police Gazette', 'I can't remember a worse December', and a delightfully dreary and nostalgic piece about last year's kisses which the director, Roy del Ruth, astutely and with excellent effect throws away on a routine rehearsal, with men chewing gum and the hero busy revising a scene and no one paying the least attention to the deep belly-ache of the torch-song.

There are no torch songs in *Yiddle with his Fiddle*, a Polish film made in Yiddish, a story as old as the hills about vagrant musicians and a girl who is dressed as a boy, with all the ancient situations – the bathe in the river, the bed in the barn – guyed with a lightness, a charm, a sense of poetry, a story in which even the music seems to have the dignity and patina of age and race. An odd feeling of freedom pervades the film full of ugly people in bowler-hats strumming in courtyards, walking through cornfields, dancing at weddings, freedom even from the closer tyranny of a well-made script, as if the whole picture were an impromptu performance, like the stories in the *Decameron*, people of incredible accomplishment happy for a while among themselves on a hill-top while the world dies.

Night and Day (29 July 1937)

The High Command (GB, Fanfare, 1937) Dir.: Thorold Dickinson. Cast: James Mason, Lionel Atwill, Lucie Mannheim, Steve Geray.
On the Avenue (USA, Twentieth-Century Fox, 1937) Dir.: Roy del Ruth. Cast: Dick Powell, Alice Faye, Madeleine Carroll, The Ritz Brothers, Joan Davis, E. E. Clive, George Barbier.
Yiddle with his Fiddle (Poland, 1936) Directors: Joseph Green, Jan Nowina Przybylski. Cast: Mollie Picon, S. Fostel, M. Bozyk.

Tribute to Harpo

A Day at the Races · King Solomon's Mines

Of course the long vulpine stride of Groucho is still there, *ventre terre* with a suitcase and an umbrella, Chico's piano-playing and Harpo's dumb pagan beauty – but there is so much else these days as well. The money is fairly splashed about; the capitalists have recognized the Marx Brothers; ballet sequences, sentimental songs ('Your eyes will tell me secrets your lips cannot say'), amber fountains, young lovers. *A Day at the Races* is a lot better than *A Night at the Opera*, it is easily the best film to be seen in London, but all the same I feel a nostalgia for the old cheap rickety sets, those titles as meaningless and undifferentiated as Kipling's, *Duck Soup* and *Horse Feathers*. I confess to a kind of perverse passion for Miss Maureen O'Sullivan (she satisfies a primeval instinct for a really nice girl), but what business has she in a wild Lear world where a veterinary doctor is in charge of a sanatorium, with Chico as handyman and Harpo – no room to tell why – as a jockey? Miss O'Sullivan is a *real* person – at least I have a dim idea that one met girls like her when one was adolescent; she is the archetype of 'a friend's sister'; but real people do more than retard, they smash the Marx fantasy. When Groucho lopes into the inane, they smile at him incredulously (being real people they cannot take him for granted), and there was one dreadful moment when Miss O'Sullivan murmured the word 'Silly'. Silly – good God, we cannot help exclaiming since we are real people too, have we been deceived all along? Are Groucho and Chico just silly people and not poets of Edward Lear stature?

> 'Sun-Up's the worst horse on the course.'
> 'I've noticed he wins every race.'
> 'That's only because he comes in first.'

Silly? How horribly possible it sounds when we watch Miss O'Sullivan, and how thankful I felt that I was not in her company at the Surrealist Exhibition. Those charming, dewy and hygienic eyes would have taken all amusement out of an exhibit like the *'Virginal Slipper'* – the white dance-shoe, the piece of fungus and the contraceptive.

No, these revellers of the higher idiocy should not mingle with real people nor play before lavish scenery and an arty camera. Like the Elizabethans, they need only a chair, a painted tree. There *are* moments in this picture as good as there have ever been, and it is Harpo who shines the brightest, with his carved curls, his lunatic goodness, his air of having strayed out of Greek woods in his battered topper. I shall remember the short miming scene at night in the hedged garden where Harpo tries to convey to Chico that Groucho (Dr Hackenbush) has fallen for a woman and is about to be framed (it takes Chico a long time to understand the ritual of whistle and gesture – 'Dr Hackenbush has got an apple-dumpling?'), a scene oddly young and Shakespearian in its lunacy. And in the scene when Harpo takes his pipe and leads a rabble of negro children from hut to hut, interrupting this black man tying his best tie, that black woman at her cooking, to the musical refrain, as the faun face peers in, 'Who dat man?', he has an emotional effect he has never previously secured.

King Solomon's Mines must be a disappointment to anyone who like myself values Haggard's book a good deal higher than *Treasure Island.* Many of the famous characters are sadly translated. It remains a period tale, but where is Sir Henry Curtis's great golden beard (into which, it will be remembered, he muttered mysteriously 'fortunate' when he first met Allan Quartermain)? Mr Loder's desert stubble is a poor substitute. Umbopa has become a stout professional singer (Mr Robeson in fact) with a repertoire of sentimental lyrics, as un-African as his figure, written by Mr Eric Maschwitz. Worst crime of all to those who remember Quartermain's boast – 'I can safely say there is not a petticoat in the whole history' – is the introduction of an Irish blonde who has somehow become the cause of the whole expedition and will finish as Lady Curtis (poor Ayesha). Miss Anna Lee's performance is rather like one of Miss Carroll's seen through the wrong end of a telescope, with the large tortuous mouth, the intense whispers and the weighty coquetry.

Yet it is a 'seeable' picture. Sir Cedric Hardwicke gives us the genuine Quartermain, and Mr Roland Young, as far as the monocle and the white legs are concerned, is Captain Good to the life, though I missed the false teeth, 'of which he had two beautiful sets that, my own being none of the best, have often caused me to break the tenth commandment' (what a good writer Haggard was). The one-eyed black king Twala is admirable, the direction of Robert Stevenson well above the English average, the dovetailing of Mr Barkas's African exteriors with the studio sets better than usual, but I look back with regret to the old silent picture which was faithful to Haggard's story: I even seem to remember the golden beard.

Night and Day (12 August 1937)

A Day at the Races (USA, MGM, 1937) Dir.: Sam Wood. Cast: The Marx Brothers, Margaret Dumont, Allan Jones, Maureen O'Sullivan, Douglas Dumbrille, Esther Muir, Sig Rumann.

King Solomon's Mines (GB Gaumont British, 1937) Dir.: Robert Stevenson. Cast: John Loder, Cedric Hardwicke, Anna Lee, Roland Young, Paul Robeson, Sydney Fairbrother, Robert Adams.

Pawn's Moves and Knight's Moves

Slave-Ship · Stradivarius · Woman Chases Man

This is the season of slow-motion emotions: Warner Baxter in

Slave-Ship staring from his boat at back-cloth Africa (we still read in little books on cinema: 'The film as compared with the play has the advantage of real backgrounds') registers his conscience coming on, and come on it does, reel after reel of it, as he flaps his heavy insomniac eyelids at Elizabeth Allen, saying, 'I tried to tell you, but I couldn't . . . Will you ever find it possible to forgive?'; at the cabin-boy, remembering he slapped his face; at his friend and first officer whom he has just shot in the stomach: 'I didn't want to do it, Thomson . . .'; flapping them stubbornly at the English court martial.

It isn't a bad film, it has excellent moments – seamen flinging knives from top-gallants and Wallace Beery as the soapy and mutinous mate, less soft-hearted than he has been for years, giving his finest performances since *Treasure Island*. The film story is by William Faulkner, the direction by Tay Garnett, the course seems set for distinction, but it remains a hot-weather picture: human relationships converge with the slowness and inevitability of pawns, though a film should consist of knight's moves only: the oblique jump, the unexpected counter.

In *Stradivarius*, the worst film to be seen in London, we are so much ahead of the picture that we can come out, thank God, half-way through. A violin, which brings bad luck to all who own it, is left to a young Austrian army officer who takes it for valuation to a Professor. In his house he meets an Italian pupil-teacher (the year, of course, is 1914), and we watch an infinitely slow-motion love registering on Pierre Willm's foxy features. The violin is an unsigned Stradivarius (dreadful hark-back to seventeenth-century Cremona and Stradivarius, in a little white sailor's cap, lifting a pointed nose and remarking pansily 'What does the reward matter? My dream is to liberate the voice that dwells within'). Then the Great War breaks out, and the rest of the picture is just hearsay to me. *Stradivarius* is full of sublimated sexuality and artistic abandon. 'I adore it', the heroine says, stroking the violin. 'It has such a tender note . . .' People are always hearing violins played on the other side of doors and going into rapt attitudes in passages. It is packed with the awful gusto of the balletomane: the sweet Haskell-trained tooth, nourished on nougat and Nijinski, moistening at the sound of music.

Woman Chases Man is a blessed relief. Sex isn't sublimated, and the knights do move, jumping obliquely, landing the rich man and the out-of-work female architect drunk in a tree at midnight, and instead of gipsy orchestras, classical music, back projections of Budapest, Miriam Hopkins's sad volubility and her predatory and rewarding eyes. This picture is what *Easy Living* sets out to be, though *Easy Living* has the better subject: the huge importance in a moneyed world of the rich man's eccentric act. But *Easy Living* is too strenuously gay: people drop plates and fall cheerily downstairs on every foot of film. And it is the cheeriness which is wrong. As Chaplin learnt long ago, the man who falls downstairs must suffer if we are to laugh; the waiter who breaks a plate must be in danger of dismissal. Human nature demands humiliation, the ignoble pain and the grotesque tear: the madhouse for Malvolio.

Night and Day (19 August 1937)

Slave-Ship (USA, Twentieth-Century Fox, 1937) Dir.: Tay Garnett. Cast: Warner Baxter, Elizabeth Allen, Wallace Beery, Mickey Rooney, George Sanders, Jane Darwell, Joseph Schildkraut, Billy Bevan, Arthur Hohl.

Stradivarius (Stradivari) (Germany, Boston-Film, 1935) Dir.: Geza von Bolvary. Cast: Pierre Willm, Edwige Feuillère (French version); Gustav Frölich, Sybille Schmitz (German version).

Woman Chases Man (USA, Samuel Goldwyn, 1937) Dir.: John Blystone. Cast: Miriam Hopkins, Joel McCrea, Charles Winninger, Erik Rhodes, Broderick Crawford, Leona Maricle, Ella Logan, Charles Halton.

What's Left is Celluloid . . .

Saratoga · High, Wide and Handsome · His Affair

There is more than curiosity in *Saratoga*, Miss Jean Harlow's last film which she didn't even live to finish. A comedy of the race-tracks with Mr Clark Gable as a bookie, it has points of odd documentary interest: a yearling sale attended by Miss Harlow in a silver lamé evening dress, an amusement car in the Racing Special noisy with the innocent songs of men who in this country would be busy in the third-class carriages with packs of cards. At first one may be a little repelled by the unlikelihood of such enormous good-fellowship. The broad poster smile of 'The Old Firm' on a racing-card doesn't seem quite plausible in private life. But wait awhile and you'll find it's only the Rotarian smile after all. The bookie at the start may refuse payment of a fifty thousand dollar debt because it means foreclosing on a stud-farm which is the sole joy of somebody else's 'grandpop' (Mr Lionel Barrymore makes his usual blot on a not so virgin film), but his morality isn't as strict as that for long; he's quite crooked enough before the film's through to satisfy our passion for probability, wringing the dollars out of Miss Harlow's rich and unoffending fiancé, helped by Miss Harlow who double-crosses her fiancé by tipping the wrong horses. Later she has a quarrel with the bookie and double-crosses him, but that cross doesn't come off, the millionaire retires baffled by these bewildering moralities, and Mr Gable and Miss Harlow are left together in the happy expectation of a lifetime of false tips and bought jockeys. Tough and conscienceless, containing one admirable scene of carnal comedy with a nerve specialist, *Saratoga* is one of Miss Harlow's better films, though there is no sign that her acting would ever have progressed beyond the scope of the restless shoulders and the protuberant breasts: her technique was the gangster's technique – she toted a breast like a man totes a gun. The film has been skilfully sewn-up, and the missing scenes and shots lend it an air of originality which the correctly canned product mightn't have had: the story proceeds faster, less obviously: the heroine is less unduly plugged. The psychological transitions have a surface obscurity similar to those of living people, and not the steady movie progression from love to jealousy to reconciliation.

The old Irene Dunne, not the new groomed Dunne of *Theodora Goes Wild*, appears in *High, Wide and Handsome*. She plays a showgirl, oh so generous and unspoilt, in the 1850s who loves and marries a Pennsylvanian farmer. He discovers oil, gets too busy fighting the wicked railroad trusts, neglects her; so she goes back to the road and returns only in the nick of time with the elephants and trick-riders of the circus to defeat the hired toughs who are breaking up his pipe-lines. There are two hours of this long, dumb and dreary picture ('so good that it might have been inspired' – Mr Carroll); the story doesn't really get under way for an hour; and one is left with a few dim distressing memories: Miss Dunne splashing and kerning away in her bathtub while Mr Mamoulian's camera pans coyly round the kitchen, carefully avoiding her till it fetches up for climax on the glossy face and the shiny knees and the discreet soapsuds: Miss Dunne singing beside the farm horse (Miss Dunne is the one without the white patch on her forehead): a song by Mr Kern about 'Darby and Joan who used to be Jack and Jill', and masses of irrelevant Mamoulian blooms flowering at the right, the sentimental, time: nature panting to keep abreast with studio passions, flowering for first love and falling for separation.

His Affair, on the other hand, is exactly what a melodrama should be: the best American melodrama of the year, a tough story of bank-robbers set in Edwardian times to give it a light and spurious romance. The boater and belted waist take the too-sweetness off the love, and we don't mind suspending the disbelief we should normally feel when the President of the United States personally sets a young naval officer to track down men his whole Secret Service has failed to catch, because we get so much in return: admirable acting by Mr Robert Taylor and Mr Victor McLaglen and quick and cunning direction which gives us from the first shot an expectation of the worst, so that this shocker does – however fallaciously – carry about it a sense of doom, of almost classic suspense in the skittle-alley and the music-hall.

Night and Day (26 August 1937)

Saratoga (USA, MGM, 1937) Dir.: Jack Conway. Cast: Jean Harlow, Clark Gable, Lionel Barrymore, Frank Morgan, Walter Pidgeon, Una Merkel, Cliff Edwards, George Zucco.

High, Wide and Handsome (USA, Paramount, 1937) Dir.: Rouben Mamoulian. Cast: Irene Dunne, Randolph Scott, Dorothy Lamour, Alan Hale, Raymond

Walburn, Charles Bickford, William Frawley, Akim Tamiroff, Irving Pichel.
His Affair (USA, Twentieth-Century Fox, 1937) Dir.: William A. Seiter. Cast: Robert Taylor, Victor McLaglen, Barbara Stanwyck, Brian Donlevy, Sidney Blackmer, John Carradine, Sig Rumann, Douglas Fowley. (US title: *This is My Affair*)

More Song than Dance

A Castle in Flanders · For You Alone

English films often enough have their senses laid abroad, but the compliment is infrequently returned. At the moment I can recall only that delightful picture *Sans Famille*, in which a troop of London police, small men with sloping shoulders wearing curious helmets which fell low over their eyes, drew their truncheons to pursue juvenile offenders through the London fog. The German director of *A Castle in Flanders* has really returned good for evil. For all the ruthless militarists in monocles, the sentimental inn-keepers, the student princes and Schuberts in lilac time, he offers us a romantic and aristocratic England where a man falls in love (a love of Nordic depth and fidelity) with a singer called Gloria Delamarre merely from hearing her voice on a gramophone record; an England where a gentleman must take the blame – and go to Australia – for a forgery he hasn't committed, to save a woman's name. It isn't *our* England, and yet we are haunted by an odd sense that somehow we know this fairy-tale place, that we've been here before. It isn't only that the officers in the prologue, listening to the gramophone while the shells burst over Ypres, smoke pipes to the English manner born (the sturdy word while the thumb prods the bowl, the pat-pat on the pocket feeling for the pouch); nor can we be misled by the oddly wrong taxis with huge luggage-racks like howdahs, nor by the sight of Tower Bridge through the window of an aristocratic study. This *is* a place we know, and at last when the hero is vindicated, when Gloria Delamarre has got her man, we realize this is the England of the early tattered Tauchnitzes on continental bookstalls (2271. Rita: *Introduced to Society*; 3243. Alexander, Mrs: *Barbara, Lady's Maid and Peeress*; 3617. Norris, W. E.: *Lord Leonard the Luckless*). Writers have often been called their country's ambassadors abroad; but from what a curious diplomatic service they are usually recruited.

Yet this picture has merits: there are excellent scenes in dark wet post-war Ypres: the little stuffy hotel where every room is booked when Gloria Delamarre arrives; the leering porter who directs her to a neighbouring castle; and by the fireplace, where the pipes were prodded years ago and the gramophone ground, what we believe to be the ghost of the English officer last seen at zero hour. The ambiguous atmosphere is admirably maintained; it is when the hero turns out not to be a ghost at all that we lose interest and the film reality. There remain some songs of the Ho-ho-ho-Ha type only too adequately sung by Miss Marta Eggerth, who has been well groomed this time – a very necessary grooming to prevent confusion, for Miss Eggerth used to look a ghost herself, her pale blonde features shading off into her background so that you could never be quite certain where her face ended and the tallboy began.

I prefer her to Miss Grace Moore. Miss Moore, even in trousers singing 'Minnie the Moocher', can make the craziest comedy sensible and hygienic. In *For You Alone*, the story of an Australian singer who buys an American husband in Mexico so that she may re-enter the States where her permit has expired, Mr Riskin, the author of *Mr Deeds* and (let's forget it) *Lost Horizon*, has tried his best to write crazily, but he comes up all the time against Miss Moore. That friendly, genteel and frolicsome personality would be more at home among blackboards and the smell of chalk and dusters and the dear children. If you want to escape from a cinema where Miss Moore is playing – I always do – before the end, you feel impelled to raise a hand and wait for permission to leave the room.

Night and Day (2 September 1937)

A Castle in Flanders (Das Schloss in Flandern) (Germany, Tobis-Magna-Film, 1936) Dir.: Geza von Bolvary. Cast: Marta Eggerth, Paul Hartmann, Georg Alexander, Otto Wernicke.

For You Alone (USA, Columbia, 1937) Dir.: Robert Riskin. Cast: Grace Moore, Cary Grant, Aline MacMahon, Henry Stephenson, Thomas Mitchell, Catherine Doucet. (US title: *When You're in Love*)

A Flicker from the Flames

Marked Woman

'It's feudal,' a character remarks with resignation in *Marked Woman*, and there are moments of creative imagination (vivid enough to have suffered British censorship) in this picture of the night-club racket and the night-club baron which do convey some of the horror and pathos the Anglo-Saxon chronicler recorded of Stephen's reign: the exactions, the beatings and murders, and above all the hopelessness. We remember Faustus' questions and Mephistopheles' replies.

'Where are you damned?'
'In Hell.'
'How comes it then that thou art out of Hell?'
'Why, this is Hell, nor am I out of it.'

The time is 3.30 in the morning and the cars drawn up outside the Club Intime; the new boss with the lined scorched face of Eduardo Ciannelli taking a look round while his henchman gives his pekinese an airing (the air's too stale inside for a dog), issuing orders to the dancing partners (he owns every club in town: there's no escape); the trailing of the long evening gowns down the pavement to the shabby digs as the milkman goes his rounds; the routine murder of a young man who has paid with a phoney cheque; the impregnability of the baron in his tenth-floor flat with his seedy lawyers. It's been done before, of course, this picture of the feudal hell, but it has never been done better than in some of these scenes: the awful contrast between the Rotarians' liquored cheerfulness in the early hours with the bad champagne and the sentimental songs, and the next morning, when one of them has been found dead in the river, and the little sober shamefaced group drifts into the police-station to identify their dance companions; the spirituous poetics of the middle-aged lecher in the roof-garden – 'Those stars . . . they remind me . . . that moon, you've only to ask me for that . . .' between the nuzzlings of the big grey moustache. Ciannelli lends distinction to any film: he can convey not only corruption but the sadness of corruption: the mind in – unpolitical – chains. But it is unfortunate so many of us said once that Miss Bette Davis was potentially a great actress, for now she plugs the emotions with dreadful abandonment. Only once does she really get across: in the horrifying scene of her beating up by the pervert henchman Charlie (her sister has been murdered and the worm tries to turn).[1]

Night and Day (9 September 1937)

Marked Woman (USA, Warners, 1937) Dir.: Lloyd Bacon. Cast: Bette Davis, Humphrey Bogart, Eduardo Ciannelli, Isabel Jewell, Allen Jenkins, Mayo Methot, Henry O'Neill.

Two English Pictures

Action for Slander · Brief Ecstasy

Mr Victor Saville is one of the few directors who bring something of value out of Denham, and *Action for Slander* is a picture of which we needn't feel ashamed if it reaches the United States, even though the story is novelettish in the extreme. Mr Clive Brook, falsely accused of cheating at cards by a brother officer whose wife he has pursued, suffers as only Mr Brook can suffer: the routine of suffering, suffering in *Cavalcade*, suffering in *Shanghai Express*, suffering in a hundred feature films, has indelibly lined his not very expressive face. In *Action for Slander* he suffers all the time with immense virtuosity, smelling a little of tweeds and pipe-smoke. His wife leaves him, he is slandered at a house-party, the rumour gets about and he suffers in the club, in the mess, in a four-shilling bed-and-breakfast hotel (last degradation for an officer and a gentleman and quite sufficient to bring his wife hurrying back); he brings an action and suffers in the law-courts (the legal procedure here is very odd, and Mr Morton Selton is badly miscast as the Judge – why not Billy Bennett while they are about it?); then the film snaps quickly to a close before he can be asked to do anything else but suffer. Yet Mr Saville has made something out of this unpromising material: people on the whole behave naturally – and shabbily – in rather Galsworthian circumstances: the wife leaves her husband without fuss: the tactical moves in adultery are played between shots at pheasants. The Denham love scene for once is not written in.

We need not feel ashamed of *Action for Slander*, but we can feel proud of *Brief Ecstasy*, directed by Mr Edmond Greville for a small English company, Phoenix Films. It must have cost only about a third as much as *Action for Slander*, but the producer Mr Hugh Perceval, has learnt to wring twenty shillings' worth out of every pound. The subject is sexual passion, a rarer subject than you would think on the screen, and the threatment is adult: there isn't, thank God, any love in it. In *Action for Slander*, of course, there's a hint of adultery, but the characters have really little more sex-life than amoebas. They haven't time, poor things, mixed up all the while in elaborate plots: card-games, false accusations, law-courts. Mr Greville's story is the simplest possible – a young man picks up a girl, sleeps with her, goes to India: she marries a middle-aged scientist and four years later the young man turns up; the story is of the struggle between tenderness and sexual desire. With so bare a plot Mr Greville has time to dwell on everything other directors cut: the 'still-lifes': the husband's trousers laid pedantically in the press, while the wife beautifies herself in the bathroom for nothing at all. Other directors have to 'get on with the story'. Mr Greville knows that the story doesn't matter; it's the atmosphere which counts, and the atmosphere – of starved sexuality – is wantonly and vividly conveyed. Mr Greville learnt in France how to photograph a woman's body – uncompromisingly: every close-up of Miss Linden Travers drives the sexuality home: a leg in the library, buttocks over the billiard-table. We can leave 'characters' to the stage (the jealous housekeeper in this picture would be more at home there): the film at its finest – in the acting of Garbo and Chaplin or in the direction of Pudovkin – generalizes, and Miss Linden Travers sprawling across the bed behind her locked door, sobbing with passion while the man she wants hammers to come in, represents any human being under the ugly drive of undifferentiated desire.

Night and Day (16 September 1937)

Action for Slander (GB, London Films, 1937) Dir.: Victor Saville. Cast: Clive Brook, Ann Todd, Margaretta Scott, Arthur Margetson, Percy Marmont, Morton Selton, Athole Stewart, Frank Cellier.
Brief Ecstasy (GB, IFP, 1937) Dir.: Edmond Greville. Cast: Linden Travers, Hugh Williams.

Knight without Armour · Café Metropole

One had thought it was good-bye to M. Feyder when he entered the gates of the Denham studios: one began to write the obituary of the director of *Thérèse Raquin* and *La Kermesse Héroïque*. The news that Mr ('Hungarian') Biro and Mr ('Naughty') Wimperis were responsible for the scenario and dialogue: the sight of Miss Dietrich floodlit before well-advertised crowds at first nights: a New York première – followed by months of silence: rumours of gigantic expenditure – some put it at over £300,000: all prepared us for the traditional Denham mouse.

But – astonishingly – a first-class thriller has emerged, beautifully directed, with spare and convincing dialogue and a nearly watertight scenario (only marred by a bath and a bathe in the Naughty Wimperis vein). The story, of course, is melodrama, but melodrama of the most engaging kind, the heroic wish-fulfilment dream of adolescence all the world over – rescues, escapes, discarnate embraces. A young Englishman, who translated novels for a Russian publisher in pre-war St Petersburg is ordered by the police to leave the country because of an indiscreet magazine-article. Instead he joins the British Secret Service, takes on with beard and passport a Revolutionary personality and is condemned to Siberia after a bomb outrage of which, naturally, he is innocent. From this point his second personality has complete control: as an Englishman he is dead. War is followed by Revolution and he becomes automatically and will-lessly a hero of the new Russia, a Commissar. He is entrusted with the job of taking an important prisoner, a Countess, to Petrograd. He lets her escape, she is recaptured, he saves her again: White prisoners fall to Red machine-guns and Red prisoners to White and White to Red again, a kaleidoscope of murder: we get the impression, so difficult to convey on the screen, of almost interminable time and almost illimitable distance, of an escape along the huge corridors of a prison an Asiatic empire wide. Mr Robert Donat as the stubbornly chivalrous Englishman deserves more than the passing tribute we accord to a director's dummy. Mr Donat is the best film actor – at any rate in star parts – we possess: he is convincing, his voice has a pleasant roughness, and his range is far greater than that of his chief rival for film honours, Mr Laurence Olivier. Mr Olivier's burnt-out features, his breaking voice requires the emotional situation all the time; he wants all Blackfriars to rant in: he must have his drowned Ophelia, his skull and sword-play. Mr Donat is sensible, authentic, slow; emotion when it comes has the effect of surprise, like plebian poetry.

There is one sequence in *Knight Without Armour* which should take its place among the classic moments of the screen – the student of Prague in the old silent days running down from the wood to the duelling-place and meeting his second self coming up with dripping sword between the tress; the perambulator bouncing down Odessa steps: the lovers in Von Stroheim's *Greed* walking down the long breakwater between the grey seas under the drenching rain. The English Commissar with his prisoner has reached a small wayside station: the station-master tells him a train is due, and presently his repeated call 'Train No. 671. All aboard for Petrograd' brings the Englishman from the waiting-room to an avenue of empty line and the station-master striding beside an imaginary express repeating his mad parrot cry, while the soundtrack grinds with his proud and gleeful dream. Beautifully shot, adeptly written and finely acted by Mr Hay Petrie as the station-master (Mr Petrie enriches every picture in which he appears) the scene owes a great deal of its authenticity to Mr Donat's quiet stocky personality. And how Mr Olivier would have torn into haunted neurotic tatters a later scene in the waiting-room when the Commissar recites to his prisoner a poem of Browning's ('Fear Death? To feel the fog in my throat . . .') and the Red soldiers pass across the window come to rape and murder. Mr Olivier's acting is of the nerves: it demands an audience and a partner: Mr Donat's acting is so calculated that no tape-measure from nose to lens, no studio rabble of make-up men and continuity girls, no fourth 'repeat' from the director affects it. And as to a partner – he has in this picture to do without, for Miss Dietrich never acts. She lends her too beautiful body: she consents to pose: she is the marble motive for heroisms and sacrifices: as for acting – that is merely the word for what goes on all round her: she leaves it to her servants.

But the measure of Feyder's achievement cannot really be judged from this film: one must take into account the failure of his predecessors at Denham after who knows what internecine conflicts with a producer who can pick men but who cannot delegate responsibility – M. Clair, Mr William K. Howard, the lost adventurers, his peers. No Denham stamp has obliterated his private signature – the very rare use of long shots – long shots used like close-ups to punch an effect home, not as by most directors to get through the duller parts of a narrative. To me the most aesthetically satisfying of all cinematic shots is – in rough script terms – the medium close shot, and this is the distance at which Feyder remains consistently from his characters: close enough for intimacy and far enough for art.

It is instructive, after Feyder's picture, to visit *Café Metropole*. Here is a very amusing script, admirable acting by Mr Menjou, Miss Loretta Young and Mr Tyrone Power, all thrown away by inferior direction: the wrong angle, the ugly shot, the cluttered set, so that the faces of the characters have to be distinguished from a fog by furnishing (a nose disentangled from a picture-frame, a dowager's hair from the window curtains), and the camera is planked down four-square before the characters like a plain, honest, inexpressibly dull guest at a light and loony party.

Night and Day (30 September 1937)

Knight Without Armour (GB, London Films, 1937) Dir.: Jacques Feyder. Cast: Robert Donat, Marlene Dietrich, John Clements, Austin Trevor, Irene Vanbrugh, Herbert Lomas.

Café Metropole (USA, Twentieth-Century Fox, 1937) Dir.: Edward H. Griffith. Cast: Loretta Young, Tyrone Power, Adolphe Menjou, Charles Winninger, Gregory Ratoff.

The Road Back · Gangway

The Road Back, adapted from a novel by Herr Remarque, is meant to be a grim picture of the kind of life to which the German soldier returned from the trenches in 1918: starvation, revolution and the family tragedies of infidelity. It opens in the trenches, with the one imaginative scene in the whole film when the wild geese pass over no-man's land and their drumming is taken for a gas warning and the old soldier (Slim Summerville, hopelessly miscast) remarks 'They'll be in Egypt for the week-end.' Apart from this minute in the hundred minutes, it's an awful film, one big Mother's Day, celebrated by American youth, plump, adolescent faces with breaking sissy voices. Voices which began to break in the trenches – remembering the kid sister or watching a companion die – are still breaking an hour and a quarter later and the film's not over yet. We've lived through a lot in that time, but not through war, revolution, starvation – but through 'Can you turn me a little so I can see you go down the road?' and the young fleshy face is turned away from the dying friend to hide the drip of tears; French girls dancing in a barn and crying 'O-la-la'; the sudden and puzzling inability of the whole cast of so-called Germans to speak their native American to a company of Yankee soldiers they meet on the road (even Slim Summerville is rendered speechless); love scenes in Teutonic beer-houses – 'You are just as I've been dreaming of you all these years.' Like Buchman boys starved of confession they break out on the moral front – 'There's one more battle to be fought. I must find myself.' And always all the time the breaking voices, the unformed unlined faces and the well-fed bodies of American youth, clean limbed prize-cattle mooing into the microphone. They call it an all-star cast and that always means there isn't a single player of any distinction to be picked out of the herd.

It might be funny if it wasn't horrifying. This is America seeing the world in its own image. There is a scene in which the returning soldiers all go back to their school. Sitting in uniform on the benches they are addressed by the Headmaster; they start their lessons again where they left off – it may be meant as irony (I'm not sure), but what it really emphasizes is the eternal adolescence of the American mind, to which literature means the poetry of Longfellow and morality means keeping Mother's Day and looking after the kid sister's purity. One came daunted out of the cinema and there, strolling up the Haymarket, dressed in blue uniforms with little forage-caps and medals clinking, were the American Legionaries, arm in arm with women dressed just the same – all guide-books, glasses, and military salutes: caps marked Santa Anna and Minnesota: hair – what there was of it – grey, but the same adolescent features, plump, smug, sentimental, ready for the easy tear and the hearty laugh and the fraternity yell. What use in pretending that with these allies it was ever possible to fight for civilization? For Mother's Day, yes, for anti-vivisection and humanitarianism, the pet dog and the home fire, for the co-ed college and the campus. Civilization would shock them: eyes on the guide-book for safety, they pass it quickly as if it were a nude in a national collection.

Miss Jessie Matthews has only once been properly directed – by Mr Victor Saville. Mr Sonnie Hale, whatever his qualities as a comedian, is a pitiably amateurish director and as a writer hardly distinguished. The best one can say of *Gangway* is that it is better than his previous picture. It is a comedy about a Scotland Yard detective (acted with repulsive boyishness by Mr Barry Mackay – he should have been in *The Road Back*) and a newspaper reporter (Miss Matthews) and it develops, about three-quarters of the way through, into a passable shocker when American gangsters mistake the reporter for one of the old school, an international jewel thief. It is Mr Alastair Sim, however, as an insurance detective who really saves the film. Horrifying passions pent in his twisting secretive body, Mr Sim always shatters illusion right and left. His acting, unctuous with Nonconformity, demands other characters too that are larger than life, or else ones like these so dim they don't disturb the dreadful and comic dream. As for Miss Matthews she isn't given a chance. Her figure like an exaggerated and Voguish advertisment is oddly asexual: coquetry – much less love – should never be demanded of her. When she dances – attractive and ungainly – it should be by herself; no dance of hers should end in the sentimental lyric and the labial embrace.

Night and Day (7 October 1937)

The Road Back (USA, Universal, 1937) Dir.: James Whale. Cast: John King, Slim Summerville, Andy Devine, Richard Cromwell, Noah Beery Jr., Lionel Atwill, Spring Byington.

Gangway (GB, Gaumont British, 1937) Dir.: Sonnie Hale. Cast: Jessie Matthews, Barry Mackay, Alastair Sim, Noel Madison, Nat Pendleton.

Big City · Tales from the Vienna Woods · Children at School

It has been a bad week in the commercial cinema – *Big City* and *Tales from the Vienna Woods*. I think it is just possible to sit through the first, thanks to Borzage, the sentimental but competent director who made *Seventh Heaven*. Spencer Tracy plays a taxi-driver, Luise

Rainer his foreign wife. In a war between a taxi combine and the independent owners a bomb is thrown, a man is killed, the woman framed. Though she is the wife of an American, by United States law the woman can be deported because she hasn't been in the country three years. If the drivers can hide her another six weeks from the police she'll be safe. Pathos accumulates. She is going to have a baby, she gives herself up when her friends are arrested for sheltering her, harrowing farewell in a steerage cabin, last-minute release. Domesticity and tenderness are heavily laid on: people in this film are *too* happy before disaster: no one is as happy as all that, no one so little prepared for what life is bound to do sooner or later. One remembers with how few shots Lang in *Fury* established the deep affection between his characters: the shop-window gazing in the rain, the torn macintosh sewn up on the platform. This good-bye while the detectives wait in the corridor and the drabs watch from the other bunks is moving, of course, but one resents being moved by so exorbitant an agony – the eight-berth metal cabin, the imminent labour, the permanence of the separation – the woman bound for some central European village, the husband without the money to follow her.

Tales from the Vienna Woods is an Austrian film and you know what that means: it means Magda Schneider's deep-sunk eyes and porcine coquetry; courtyards where everyone in turn picks up a song as they mend cars, clean windows, wash clothes; a festival in a beer-garden with old Viennese costumes, balloons, slides, laughter, and driving home at dawn in a fiacre; Magda Schneider's trim buttocks and battered girlishness; a musical tour of Vienna – no sign, of course, of the Karl Marx Hof, only palaces and big Baroque dictatorial buildings; Magda Schneider's mouth wide open – rather too much gum like a set of false teeth hung up outside a cheap dentist's. Leo Slezak with his magnificent buffoonery tries to save the film, but Austrian films are born dead: horrible bright fakes from a ruined country, libellous laughter.

The Gas Light and Coke Company – an uncompromising and gritty name – provide the only relief from these gay and gloomy fictions. They have followed up their excellent nutrition film of last year with an even better documentary, *Children at School*, directed by Mr Basil Wright with a commentary by the editor of *The Spectator*. It begins a little untidily with the Parthenon (only because the commentary refers to Plato), it reverts too often to Mr Wilson Harris's modulated and Liberal features, his discreet tie-pin, and Lady Astor tries to storm Hollywood with untimely histrionics, but these are the only serious criticisms to be made against a film with the exciting lyrical quality one admired in Mr Wright's *Song of Ceylon*. The picture starts with a comparison between State education in England and that of the Dictatorship countries ('Drill the children, school them into believing that the Dictator is always right'). It presents first the new type of Infant and Nursery Schools – romantically in terms of sunlight, of absorbed and brooding infant faces, of a child by a blackboard telling an obscure Surrealist tale to his class about a policeman, a man with a sword . . . The romantic movement reaches a lovely and nostalgic climax as the camera sweeps a huge grass plain, children exercising, playing games, a sense of freedom in the bright wide air, while high immature voices are overlaid in a traditional hymn, overlaid across open windows, gymnasium, changing-room. ('O les voix d'enfants chantant dans la coupole.') Then the realistic movement, the reminder that hell too lies about us in our infancy. A small child hurries down a dreary concrete passage, while from behind a door comes a voice reciting the rich false lines – 'And softly through the silence beat the bells along the Golden Road . . .' Cracks in the ceilings and the beams, damp on the walls, hideous Gothic exteriors of out-of-date schools, spiked railings, narrow windows, scarred cracked playgrounds of ancient concrete: AD 1875 in ecclesiastical numerals on a corner-stone: the wire dustbin, the chipped basin, the hideous lavatory-seat and the grinding of trains behind the school-yard. Teachers with drawn neurotic faces flinching at the din: two classes to a room: conferences of despairing masters – the thin-lipped face, the malformed intellectual night-school skull, the shrewish voice of the cornered idealist as he reports progress to his colleagues – a new set of desks.

For the second time this commercial company has done the Health Ministry's work. It is just as well: a politician is professionally an optimist: he has the cheery complacency of the salesman (listen to Mr Chamberlain in a week or two); and in spite of its romantic first movement this is not an optimistic or a complacent picture.

Night and Day (14 October 1937)

The Big City (USA, MGM, 1937) Dir.: Frank Borzage. Cast: Spencer Tracy, Luise Rainer, Charley Grapewin, Janet Beecher, Irving Bacon, William Demarest.

Tales from the Vienna Woods (G'schichten aus dem Wiener wald) (Austria, Mondial International, 1934) Dir.: Georg Jacoby. Cast: Magda Schneider, Leo Slezak, Georg Alexander.

Children at School (GB, Realist Film, 1937) Dir.: Basil Wright. Commentary: Wilson Harris.

Les Perles de la Couronne · Exclusive

It is not easy to review M. Guitry's films – so much depends on the effect of M. Guitry's personality. To me it is always, at the beginning of a picture, before the charm works, a little repulsive: the rather fleshy figure seems to have been ripened by so many Riviera suns; so many years of popular applause have contributed to the flat arrogance of the voice: he seems the image of that superb Gallic complacency which drove Henry James from Paris. There is more than a touch of astrakhan . . . Late in life he has taken light-heartedly to the cinema, breaking every rule, using – in *Bonne Chance* – the most outrageous wipes successfully. Successfully: there's the rub. There is some jealousy in our distaste. Everything seems to have come to him so easily. He behaves outrageously, accepting none of the dogmas we have chosen as guides through the awful un-Aristotelean waste of this Semitic and commercial craft. But he is no revolutionary. The rules remain rules for all of us but M. Guitry. The impertinence of it!

So I find myself driven back to the personal statement – that I was delighted by *Bonne Chance* (but how far as an aphrodisiac?); that *Le Roman d'un Tricheur*, with its silent miming and continuous Guitry, rather bored me; that *Les Perles de la Couronne*, callous, impudent, disregarding all continuity, entertained me even more than it irritated me. One can generalize about M. Guitry's personality, not about his films or his ideas. He is quite without integrity.

Perhaps the experiment in his latest film has more general value than usual: ingeniously he attempts to give a wider circulation to a French picture by working the story out in three languages – French, English and Italian according to the characters, with the essential clues to understanding expressed in every language (I suppose to a really accomplished linguist the tale would seem unbearably repetitive). Unfortunately, others have not taken the opportunity M. Guitry gives them for eliminating the tiresome sub-title. Even when M. Guitry has cunningly and quite naturally arranged that an English telephone-girl, listening at a switchboard, should translate to a friend a conversation which is being carried on in French, we are not spared sub-titles to make the conversation clearer still.

The story – a fantastic tale constructed round the four pearls in the English crown and three missing pearls, which once formed part of the same necklace – starts in the reign of Henry VIII, Clement VII and Francis I, and ends in the *Normandie* at Southampton, with the last of the missing pearls slipping from M. Guitry's grasp and falling through the water, nuzzled by curious fishes, until it sinks appropriately into the open shell of an oyster. M. Guitry plays Francis, Napoleon III, and a writer of our own day, and Mlle Delubac is consistently beautiful as Marie Stuart, Josephine Beauharnais and the writer's wife.

Exclusive is a routine film of American newspaper life. Charlie Ruggles – it has been looming on us for a long time – acts a tragic part, that of an old-style journalist whose daughter rats on him and joins a rival paper owned by a racketeer. It should be tough enough – an honest politician commits suicide in front of the girl after she has dug up his past record for her scandal sheet, a lift at a department store crashes with a load of women and children (a good scene this), and Ruggles bleeds to death across his typewriter after saving his daughter from the gangster – but curiously enough the general impression is one of slow old-fashioned sentiment.

In the tough race it falls behind – it can't make the 1937 speed in murder, and the result, like lavender, is not unagreeable. I liked the dying lines of the old journalist to his daughter: 'Just state the facts in the simplest words you can find. Make your paragraphs short.' But the smell of lavender became rather too overpowering at the curtain: 'There's a heaven somewhere for old used-up newspapermen, and Pop's up there looking down, thinking we've done a good job.'

In the same programme there was a little film in technihorror of a Schubert symphony: it revealed, so we were told, the pictures which must have passed through the composer's brain. They were odd pictures under the circumstances: an Alsatian dog, a mountain in the Rockies, a sunset, the sea, and, most puzzling of all, a blond American youth wearing an open-necked shirt and carrying his sports coat over his arm. He never dropped the coat, though most of the time he was singing to a girl in evening dress in a garden. It hung there, over the left arm, carefully folded while he kissed her. Then the mountain again, the sunset, the sea, but not the dog. There seems to have been some Freudian censorship in Schubert's mind over the dog: it only slipped through once.

Night and Day (21 October 1937)

Les Perles de la Couronne (France, Cinémas, 1937) Dir.: Sacha Guitry. Cast: Sacha Guitry, Jaqueline Delubac, Renée Saint-Cyr, Lyn Harding, Percy Marmont, Arletty, Raimu, Claude Dauphin, Jean-Louis Barrault, Marguerite Moreno. (US title: *Pearls of the Crown*)

Exclusive (USA, Paramount, 1937) Dir.: Alexander Hall. Cast: Charles Ruggles, Fred MacMurray, Frances Farmer, Lloyd Nolan.

Wee Willie Winkie · The Life of Emile Zola

The owners of a child star are like leaseholders – their property diminishes in value every year. Time's chariot is at their back; before them acres of anonymity. What is Jackie Coogan now but a matrimonial squabble? Miss Shirley Temple's case, though, has peculiar interest: infancy is her disguise, her appeal is more secret and more adult. Already two years ago she was a fancy little piece (real childhood, I think, went out after *The Littlest Rebel*). In

Captain January she wore trousers with the mature suggestiveness of a Dietrich: her neat and well-developed rump twisted in the tap-dance: her eyes had a sidelong searching coquetry. Now in *Wee Willie Winkie*, wearing short kilts, she is completely totsy. Watch her swaggering stride across the Indian barrack-square: hear the gasp of excited expectation from her antique audience when the sergeant's palm is raised: watch the way she measures a man with agile studio eyes, with dimpled depravity. Adult emotions of love and grief glissade across the mask of childhood, a childhood skin-deep.

It is clever, but it cannot last. Her admirers – middle-aged men and clergymen – respond to her dubious coquetry, to the sight of her well-shaped and desirable little body, packed with enormous vitality, only because the safety curtain of story and dialogue drops between their intelligence and their desire. 'Why are you making Mummy cry?' – what could be purer than that? And the scene when dressed in a white nightdress she begs grandpa to take Mummy to a dance – what could be more virginal? On those lines her new picture, made by John Ford, who directed *The Informer*, is horrifyingly competent. It isn't hard to stay to the last prattle and the last sob. The story – about an Afghan robber converted by Wee Willie Winkie to the British Raj – is a long way after Kipling. But we needn't be sour about that. Both stories are awful, but on the whole Hollywood's is the better.

It's better cinema anyway than *The Life of Emile Zola*. More pompous than *Pasteur* and far more false, this picture's theme is supposed to be the truth – but truth to the film mind is the word you see on news posters. We begin in 1862 with Zola starving in a garret with Cézanne who keeps on popping up irrelevantly from then on. Zola meets Nana, and soon she is giving him her diaries and letters, but not – what apparently Zola particularly wants – a baby's vest. ('Take all, all but this'). Then Cézanne pokes his head round the door, and Zola writes *Nana* which is an enormous success. (He had really, of course, been a successful writer for about eighteen years before he wrote *Nana*). Then suddenly – everything in this picture happens suddenly including Cézanne – comes war.

Soldiers in the street; a woman says 'Where are they all going?' and a man says 'Haven't you heard? War's been declared.' Zola says 'Never did I think I should live to see France grovelling in the dust under the German heel.' Cézanne pokes his head round the door – or doesn't he? Anyway the war's over. Zola's middle-aged at Meudon, though his wife's not changed at all. Cézanne looks round the door again. 'The old struggling carefree days.' He takes an ugly look at the majolica and starts away. 'Paul, will you write?' 'No, but I will remember.' Then the Dreyfus case, and on the night before Dreyfus's rehabilitation Zola – he's an old man now – dies (it's more than unstudio, it's un-American to live another two years). Paul Muni acts Zola quaintly, and lots of old friends turn up in fancy dress but quite themselves as the Governor of Paris, Clemenceau, Colonel Piquart, Count Esterhazy.

Night and Day (28 October 1937)

Wee Willie Winkie (USA, Twentieth-Century Fox, 1937) Dir.: John Ford. Cast: Shirley Temple, Victor McLaglen, C. Aubrey Smith, June Lang, Michael Whalen, Cesar Romero, Constance Collier, Gavin Muir.

The Life of Emile Zola (USA, Warners, 1937) Dir.: William Dieterle. Cast: Paul Muni, Joseph Schildkraut, Donald Crisp, Gale Sondergaard, Gloria Holden, John Litel, Henry O'Neill, Ralph Morgan, Louis Calhern, Vladimir Sokoloff.

They Won't Forget · Nitchevo

Occasionally a film of truth and tragic value gets somehow out of Hollywood on to the screen. Nobody can explain it – perhaps a stage needs using, all the big executives are in conference over the latest Mamoulian 'masterpiece' – Jehovah is asleep, and when he wakes he finds he's got a *Fury* on his hands, worse still *They Won't Forget*. Worse because Lang is a showman as well as a great director: he knows how to get his mixture down: he gives the melodramatic close, the happy ending, and the executives, after the first shock, discover a success. But I doubt whether *They Won't Forget* will have the same success – it hasn't in this country. It's a better less compromising story than *Fury* – taken as a whole a better picture, though Mervyn Le Roy isn't in Lang's class.

It is the story of a murder trial run by an ambitious District Attorney for political reasons (Mr Claude Rains gives his finest performance to date). It takes place in the South and the South has banned the picture. A girl in a business college is found murdered on Commemoration Day – again the picture is uncompromising, she isn't a lay figure, the audience see enough of her before her death, young, quiet and vital, to feel the shock of her murder. The police at first settle on the negro janitor of the building, but the District Attorney isn't satisfied. Beat a negro up enough and, innocent or guilty, he'll confess – it's all too easy, it's unspectacular. The Attorney's a stranger and he has the Governorship in mind, and so a young teacher in the school – who has come down with his wife from the North – is charged. He was in the building, there is a spot of blood on the jacket he sent to the cleaners, the girl was in love with him – but above all, of course, he's a Northerner. 'Sell prejudice angle,' the tape-machines of the newspapers tap out continually: the trial becomes a sensational sporting event: a detective is sent by a Northern newspaper and is beaten up by a Southern mob: a well-known New York counsel arrives and conducts the defence with cynical and heartless efficiency to get the spotlight on the prejudice and hang his client: the rival mothers are flung into the arena. The Attorney, tie off, sweating in braces down the ranks of the jury while electric fans hum and the Judge smokes a pipe and the audience applaud, wins all along the line; the man is – inevitably – found guilty; the Governor, an honest man, commutes the sentence to life imprisonment and ruins his career; a mob takes the young man from the train which is carrying him to the State prison and lynch him; the Attorney's well on his way to the Senate. In the last shot the Attorney and the newsman who has supported him watch the widow go down the street – 'I wonder if he was guilty?' The doubt is valuable – we are not sold the usual story of the innocent man. The evidence was heavy against the teacher, the Attorney was not completely unscrupulous – we are dealing with human beings. The direction of the picture is brilliant, the cameraman agilely snapping the wife as she falls in a faint at the news of her husband's arrest; the last scene of the lynching with the down-line express sweeping by and extinguishing the screams, snatching from the gallows-shaped erection by the line the small bundle of the mail-bag. If it makes a little less impression than Lang's more melodramatic story it is because Lang has a finer talent for expressing human relationships; we are never so close to the married pair as we were to the garage-man and his girl; relationships give the last twist to the agony – and we are spared that here.

Nitchevo has a bad story – and a very obscure one; it boils down in the end to the usual situation of French naval films – elderly officer with young wife; arrival of junior officer who once – platonically – served her in a sensational but not discreditable past; unreasonable mystifications; arrival of gunrunner and blackmail; 'Bring me the news of your husband's consent at the Pacha ball'; 'Your wife can at this moment be found at the house of Lieutenant . . .' But the picture is worth a visit for the final situation in a sunk submarine and for the acting of M. Harry Baur. Those features – of an old reptile which has learnt all the secrets the jungle can offer – can adapt themselves with perfect naturalness to any profession. A submarine commander, a police officer, a Kulak – M. Baur always seems about his proper unsensational business.

Night and Day (4 November 1937)

They Won't Forget (USA, Warners, 1937) Dir.: Mervyn Le Roy. Cast: Claude Rains, Allan Joslyn, Gloria Dickson, Edward Norris, Otto Kruger, Elisha Cook Jr., Lana Turner, Elizabeth Risdon.
Nitchevo (France, Méga Films, 1937) Dir.: Jacques de Baroncelli. Cast: Harry Baur, Marcelle Chantal, Georges Rignaud.

The Great and the Humble

Land Without Bread · Personality Parade

'First I will question with thee about Hell . . .' Two films shown last Sunday by the Film Society were enough to shake anyone's complacency or self-pity: they followed each other in the programme with horrifying force: *Land Without Bread*, a five-year-old documentary study of the Hurdanos, a Spanish people inbred, diseased, forgotten, the adjective 'poor' a mockery of their complete destitution, and *Personality Parade*, a deft little dramatization of one day in the life of Mr Godfrey Winn.

Land Without Bread is the picture of a pocket of misery in the mountains within a few miles of Burgos – life petering out in the stone crevices; images of awful inertia and more awful patience: a man shaking with fever: the goitered antique face of a woman of thirty-two: a child left in the road three days to die: the little edge of cultivation, a foot or two across, beside the river which will wash it out in the rains: the men trudging to Castile for work and returning without it, bony wrists and hollow chests, incredible rags: dwarf morons cackling at the camera, bobbing empty turnip faces above the rocks: the look of a mother whose baby has just died, shaken by human feeling into something you might take for the shadow of happiness after all those blank faces: the small body carried along stony tracks, up rocks from which we have seen even the goats tumble, pushed across a shallow river on its platter – like a tiny ferry-boat on an ignoble Lethe – until it reaches their only cemetery miles away – a few wood sticks stuck in long grass and weeds: at night between the stone cells, up a street like a crack in parched ground, an old woman walks clapping a death-bell. An honest and hideous picture, it is free from propaganda, except for a single shot of a church interior – a couple of cheap statues and a little cheap carving – with some glib sentence about clerical wealth . . . Wealth! one smiles at the word in face of that twopenny interior and wonders whether five years of Republican politics have done so much for these people that one can afford to stop up this one hole they have to creep to for cleanness and comfort.

It is a grotesque world: the morons touching each other with private incommunicable meanings among the rocks, the dying child showing her throat to the cameraman ('We couldn't do anything about it. A few days later we heard she was dead'), and Mr Winn waking prettily to order, kissing his dog upon the pillow – 'the famous Mr Sponge'. 'He really lives his page,' the commentator remarks, and we watch him, at his country cottage, get into his car ('some flowers and a kiss from his mother'), start for the office. Next he is at work with his secretary, opening letters from readers. A mother writes: will he come and see her new-born baby? 'Other things must wait. He will not disappoint her,' the commentator tells us, and Mr Winn kneels by the bed and the baby is introduced to 'Uncle Godfrey'. After that we are shown Mr Winn entering a neo-Gothic doorway ('He finds time from his engagements to pause at church'), and while the organ peals a voluntary we see in close-up Mr Winn's adoring face lifted in prayer, sun falling through stained glass on the soft, unformed, First-Communion features. Lunch at Quaglino's ('his genius for friendship'), a swim in the Serpentine, tea with a reader in Regent's Park, back to the office for his article, a game of tennis, behind the scenes at the ballet, and so home to mother – 'sometimes after twelve o'clock'. The commentator sums Mr Winn up: 'At ease with the great and happy with the humble.' We have seen him with the great – with M. Quaglino and Mr Nelson Keys – and we are tempted to imagine him for a moment with the humble. (After all his commentator describes him as a 'traveller' – mother waving over the horizon and Mr Sponge chaperoning him in his berth.) Suppose that among those rocks a correspondent should summon him to see her new-born, or new-dead, baby. 'He will not disappoint her', and we picture him among those goitred and moron and hunger-tortured faces – the set boyishness, fifth-form diffidence and thinning hair. What message for these from 'Uncle Godfrey'? and Mr Winn's own voice recalls us to the actual screen: 'Friendship is the one thing that matters in the end', and the eyes look out at us so innocently, so candidly, so doggily they might really be the eyes of 'the famous Mr Sponge'.

Night and Day (18 November 1937)

Land Without Bread (Las Hurdes) (Spain, Ramón Acín, 1932) Dir.: Luis Buñuel.
Personality Parade (GB, 1937) Produced by *The Daily Mirror*.

Dead End

The slum street comes to an end on the river-bank: luxury flats have gone up where the slum frontage has been cleared, so that two extremes of the social scale are within catcall: the Judge's brother's son has breakfast with his governess on a balcony in sight of the juvenile gang on the waterside. For some reason the front entrance of the flats cannot be used and – too conveniently – the tenants must take their way by the service door past the children's ribald gibes. In this coincidence alone do we get a whiff of the cramped stage. Several plots interwind – a housepainter (Joel McCrea) has a transitory affair with a rich man's mistress from the flats; a girl (Sylvia Sidney) hides her kid brother from the police – he is the leader of the children's gang who beat up the Judge's brother's son. And all the time, looking on at the game, is Baby-Face Martin (Humphrey Bogart), a gangster on the run with eight deaths to his credit. He is the future as far as these children are concerned – they carry his baton in their pockets. He was brought up in the same dead end and like a friendly Old Boy he gives them tips – how to catch another gang unawares, how to fling a knife. Only the housepainter recognizes him and warns him off. I'm doubtful whether this interweaving of plots, which end in the kid brother giving himself up, in the housepainter realizing he loves the sister, in the gangster's death from the housepainter's bullet, is wise. It gives too melodramatic a tone to the dead end: some emotion of grief, fear, passion happens to everybody, when surely the truth is nothing ever really happens at all. It remains one of the best pictures of the year – but what we remember is the gangster, the man who in a sentimental moment returns to the old home. He wants to see his mother and his girl: sentiment is mixed with pride – he's travelled places; he shows his shirtsleeve – 'Look – silk, twenty bucks.' And in two memorable scenes sentimentality turns savage on him. His mother slaps his face ('Just stay away and leave us alone and die'), his girl is diseased and on the streets.

This is the finest performance Bogart has ever given – the ruthless sentimentalist who has melodramatized himself from the start (the start is there before your eyes in the juvenile gangsters) up against the truth, and the fine flexible direction supplies a background of beetle-ridden staircases and mud and mist. He and the children drive virtue into a rather dim corner, and only Sylvia Sidney with her Brooklyn voice and her driven childish face is visible there.

Night and Day (25 November 1937)

Dead End (USA, Warners, 1937) Dir.: William Wyler. Cast: Humphrey Bogart, Joel McCrea, Sylvia Sidney, Claire Trevor, Wendy Barrie, Allen Jenkins, Marjorie Main, Ward Bond, James Burke, The Dead End Kids (Billy Halop, Leo Gorcey, Bernard Punsley, Huntz Hall, Bobby Jordan, Gabriel Dell).

Lo Squadrone Bianco

It is a change to hear Italian spoken on the screen – an ugly language which spits like a quick-firer, and though this story of passion, disappointed love and forgetting-a-woman-in-the-Libyan-desert may sound as conventional as *Beau Geste*, it has odd and refreshing differences – it isn't, for one thing, a bit tight-lipped ('What!' exclaims a Commander, showing a Subaltern orders to pursue maurauders, 'such news doesn't excite you at all?'), and the morality is totalitarianly changed. Mr Ronald Colman, of course, might quite well quarrel with a woman and join a Foreign Legion, but to romantic Nordics such an action is meritorious, like shooting lions. We cannot imagine his Commander – who would obviously be played, with heavy moustaches and a straight bat, by Mr C. Aubrey Smith – being anything but sympathetic – what else can a fellow do but join the Legion or a Buchman house-party? But Captain Santelia complains on meeting the new Subaltern, 'another of those who come here simply to forget', and the Subaltern himself, when his Commander has been killed and he has led the squadron back to safety, politely dismisses his mistress who has hunted him down with a tourist-party. He isn't a bit high-minded about it. He has simply learned to prefer the military kind of service. Indeed, there is something pleasantly reasonable and undignified about this superficially melodramatic film: the lover making a hellish din outside his mistress's door, wailing 'Why do you tease me so, Christiana?' – heroics are left to the set military orations over dead heroes which have the right tombstone serenity and are moving in their marble way. It is a very slow picture – but at the end we realize slowness is a value. The long desert chase of the marauding Arabs – first the delay at an oasis waiting for overdue spies, then the fever, the forced march over waterless sands, the guide losing the way, the storm, the nearly drained wells on the other side, the pause for rest, pursuit again, the protracted and confusing fight – we do get the impression of time passing, of immense privation which would be lost in the smartly cut Hollywood scramble. *This* squadron behaves with unheroic common sense: when they are too tired they stop. The photography is at the same time unsensational and memorable: the curious crosses on the camels' saddles coming up in a long line over the dunes like a pilgrimage of friars; the bounce and dip, the riders' bare soles kneading at the necks. The names of the players, all excellent, will convey nothing, but we cannot help noting Fulvia Lanzi who brings to the screen a thin Renaissance beauty, a Florentine arrogance.

Night and Day (2 December 1937)

Lo Squadrone Bianco (Italy, Roma, 1937) Dir.: Augusto Genina. Cast: Antonio Centa, Fulvia Lanzi, Fosco Giacetti. (US title: *White Squadrons*)

Un Carnet de Bal · Underworld

A rich widow looks back on her first ball with melancholy nostalgia, she wonders what fate has done to the men who said they loved her when she was sixteen. Their names are there on an old dance-programme . . . The mood is meant to be autumnal – memories dance through empty *salons*, woo her at her bedside. But Duvivier is not the director for so intangible a mood (we remember what Kirsanov did ten years ago in *Brumes d'Automne* with a few dripping boughs). A great director – *Pépé le Moko* his masterpiece – his mood is realistic, violent, belongs to the underside of the stone. This widow's nostalgia is too corseted; some other device than her prosaic ringing of doorbells and presenting of cards was needed to introduce the story of the men's lives – the provincial Mayor marrying his cook, the mad mother pretending her son had never killed himself, the night-club keeper and gang leader quoting Verlaine with deft sentiment as the detectives arrive at 4 a.m., the middle-aged monk teaching choirboys to sing. Each episode is beautifully acted and directed, whether comic, melodramatic, sentimental, but whenever the widow appears upon the scene illusion rocks like stage scenery under her heavy and soprano tread. Nevertheless, it is a film which must be seen – Harry Baur, Françoise Rosay, Raimu, Fernandel, it contains the finest French acting, and in one episode we have Duvivier's real greatness – the seedy doctor at Marseilles so used to furtive visitors and illegal operations that he doesn't wait for questions before he lights the spirit flame: the dreadful cataracted eye: the ingrained dirt upon his hands: the shrewish wife picked up in God knows what low music-hall railing behind bead curtains: the continuous shriek and grind of winch and crane. Nostalgia, sentiment, regret: the padded and opulent emotions wither before the evil detail: the camera shoots at a slant so that the dingy flat rears like a sinking ship. You have to struggle to the door, but you can run downhill to the medical couch and the bead curtains. There has been nothing to equal this episode on the screen since *Pépé*. It makes Renoir's *Underworld*, a slow agreeable undistinguished picture based on Gorki's novel, about a thief and a bankrupt Baron and a doss-house keeper and innocent love, oddly stagy and unconvincing. The doss-house squalor is laid Dickensianly on, but you never believe in its aspiring thief, its poetic madman, its old philosopher, its virginal affection. This isn't what poverty does – tatter the clothes and leave the mind unimpaired. The genuine poverty is in Duvivier's Marseille flat – the tin surgical basin, the antiseptic soap, the mechanical illegality and the complete degradation.

Night and Day (9 December 1937)

Un Carnet de Bal (France, Sigma Films, 1937) Dir.: Julien Duvivier. Cast: Marie Bell, Françoise Rosay, Louis Jouvet, Pierre Richard Willm, Harry Baur, Pierre Blanchar, Sylvie, Raimu, Fernandel. (US title: *Life Dances On*)

Underworld (Les Bas-Fonds) (France, Albatros, 1936) Dir.: Jean Renoir. Cast: Jean Gabin, Louis Jouvet, Vladimir Sokolov, Jany Holt, Suzy Prin. (aka *The Lower Depths*)

Monica and Martin · Mademoiselle Docteur · Eastern Valley

An artist who doesn't trouble about money, who isn't interested in selling his pictures, who lives in domestic bliss with his wife (she is his model too) – it's the old Bohemian fairy-tale which once, I suppose, represented a nostalgic dream of the successful bourgeois making money to satiety in the industrial age. But it was already a bit unconvincing by the time of du Maurier and *Monica and Martin* has the added disadvantage of being Teutonic – Germans are congenitally unfitted for irrational behaviour. We sigh with relief when the plot emerges from the garret (Monica sells Martin's pictures as her own and complications arise when she is commissioned to paint a mural in a new sports stadium and is awarded the Cranach Prize), away from the playful hunger and the humorous poverty which is like a cruel insult to genuine destitution. There *is* one point of interest: Colonel Brenckow, a stupid, self-important would-be patron, insulted, mocked, led up the garden. That absurd poster dignity and preposterous moustache: where have we seen them before? We are haunted by the memory of an upraised arm and a fast car and lines of Storm Troops facing inwards with hands on their revolvers towards a loyal populace.

Mr Ford Madox Ford has divided fiction into novels and nuvvels. So one may divide films into movie and cinema. *Monica and Martin* is movie: so, too, I'm afraid, is Mr Edmond Greville's spy film *Mademoiselle Docteur.* Mr Greville has an impeccable cinematic eye, but he has been badly served by a really shocking script, with childish continuity. Even a thriller cannot thrill unless the characters are established in our imaginations, and the packed plot of this film allows them no chance. Things are happening all the time: there's no opportunity to establish anything. Once the ghost of a theme did seem about to emerge when the medical student turned spy (played by Miss Dita Parlo with a charming spherical vacancy) protests to her employer 'My ambition was to save lives.' But the idea is never developed: it is swept away on a torrent of secret plans, villainous agents, dancing-girls, passwords. As for the dialogue, it ambles flatly along, like conversation between strangers at the beginning of a cocktail-party before anyone's had a drink. The general idea seems to be that people must talk all the time even if they've got nothing relevant to say. Erich von Stroheim makes his come-back in this film – one recognizes the uniform and the monocle. The uniform is as tight but a good deal less shapely than it used to be in the old silent days of *Foolish Wives*. 'The man you will love to hate' – so they used to advertise him (climbing a ladder in his skin-tight Prussian breeches towards an innocent bed). No one will hate him now. Inclined to stoutness, with a rough friendly American accent, he looks dressed up for a party. I shall prefer to remember him as the great realistic director of *Greed* (1923) – the dentist's chair, the hideous servant's bedroom, the lovers walking in the rain down the long grey breakwater.

Finally, one example of cinema. *Eastern Valley* has been made by the Strand Film Company to describe the activity of a society called the 'order of friends' in a distressed Welsh area. The older men have been given a chance to work on the land without losing their unemployment pay. The object is a pyschological one – they receive no pay; but the whole community of unemployed families benefit by the cheaper goods. The film has been directed by a newcomer, Donald Alexander. He has learnt from Anstey the value of direct reporting: the appalling cottages held up by struts from falling, dwarfed by the slagheaps; the trout stream turned into a drain, one empty fag packet floating down between the old tins; the direct interview with the wife of an unemployed man; but he has learnt too from Basil Wright how to express poetically a moral judgement. Life as it once was before industry scarred and mutilated the valley; life as it is; life as it should be.

EUPHEMISM

'*Price of Ignorance* – Herbert Marshall, Barbara Stanwyck, Eric Blore and Glenda Farrell, in an attempt to cash in on the vogue for crazy comedy. But I doubt if the public is as crazy as all that.' *Daily Telegraph*.

Night and Day (16 December 1937)

Monica and Martin (Versprich mir Nichts) (Germany, Meteor-Film, 1937) Dir.: Wolfgang Liebeneiner. Cast: Viktor de Kowa, Luise Ullrich, Heinrich George.

Mademoiselle Docteur (GB, Grafton, 1937) Dir.: Edmond Greville. Cast: Dita Parlo, Erich von Stroheim, John Loder, Claire Luce, Clifford Evans. (French Version: Dir.: G. W. Pabst. Cast: Pierre Blanchar, Pierre Fresnay, Dita Parlo.) (US title: *Street of Shadows*)

Eastern Valley (GB, Strand Films, 1937) Dir.: Donald Alexander.

Marie Walewska · True Confession

She is, of course, the finest filly of them all . . . And yet a dreadful inertia always falls on me before a new Garbo film. It is rather like reading *Sartor Resartus* – Carlyle's a great writer, but need one – now – this week . . . he's waited half a century: he can afford to wait a little longer: he'll still be on the public library shelves when one is old. And so too, I expect, will Garbo be: she will figure like Duse and Rachel in the reminiscences of bores; that magnificent mare's head of hers will puzzle our descendants, seeking a more obvious beauty, as it stares dumbly from the printed page, caught in a still in Napoleon's embrace, in Armand's embrace, in – the fictional names fail us – Fredric March's embrace, John Gilbert's embrace. A great actress – oh, undoubtedly, one wearily assents, but what dull pompous films they make for her, the slow consummation of her noble adulteries. She is a Houyhnhnm in a world of Yahoos, but, being Yahoos ourselves, we sometimes yearn for less exalted passions, for people who sin for recognizable reasons, because it's pleasurable. 'It's a bawdy planet.'

She has been badly served, of course, by writers and producers. They seem to feel uneasily that the films are unworthy of so superb an actress, and in compensation they treat her with deathly reverence: she is like a Tudor mansion, set up again brick by numbered brick near Philadelphia. *She Married Her Boss, True Confession,* films like these – contemporary, carefree – are good enough for Claudette Colbert, Carole Lombard, but for Garbo you've got to have Great Scenarios (supplied lavishly and rotundly to order by S. N. Behrman). So we are given *Queen Christina, Marie Walewska*: fake history, masquerades in fancy-dress, dialogue written in the conventional rhetoric of the middlebrow historical novelist. But there's no satisfactory half-way house between poetic and realist drama: if you can't give Garbo poetry to speak, you ought to give her prose. 'I kiss the hand which refused to sign away our country's independence' – that isn't prose.

Marie Walewska is one of the dullest films of the year. O, it has its moments when the Frenchman Boyer and the Swede Garbo are together alone, but the awful ocean of American vulgarity and good taste (they are the same thing) laps them round – soon Marie's brother will bounce in like a great Buchmanite Blue troubled about sex, or her husband (Henry Stephenson) will slip through the lath and plaster, honeyed and Harvard and humane, behaving as America thinks the Polish aristocracy behaved – with New World courtesy. There are moments too of unconscious comedy – when Prince Poniatowski (one of our old gangster friends, uneasy, speechless and pouter-breasted in his Hussar uniform) and one or two unidentifiable Polish leaders call on Marie Walewska and in her aged husband's presence suggest gently and avuncularly that she sleep with Napoleon for the sake of her country. An awkward situation for romantic drama, and one which attains a fine height of crazy comedy when they embrace Count Walewska – 'Good-bye, old friend' – and retire reverantly on tiptoe from the awkward domestic impasse they have created. There is another scene too which is dangerously close to laughter when Napoleon's bastard child prays by the bed in Elba – 'Bless my father whom I have never seen and help him to be good' – and Napoleon lurks and listens round the night-nursery door. There's 'Old Stephan', too, the faithful retainer; a Revolutionary whom you recognize at once by his tousled straw-coloured wig, who cries 'Liberty' in front of a firing-squad; and printed captions – 'Two Months Later. The Castle of Finkenstein.' And all the while the great fake emotions booming out – Love, Country, Ambition – like a *Times* leader-writer taking a serious view of the Abdication crisis.

You aren't like me – you don't *have* to see Garbo. Go to *True Confession* instead – this is that rare thing, cinema, and the best comedy of the year. Do not be put off by the stock phrase – 'crazy comedy': this picture is constructed firmly and satisfactorily on human nature. It is – more or less – about the murder of a lecherous businessman who goes in for private secretaries; the heroine – an inveterate and charming liar played by Carole Lombard – pleads guilty to a murder she didn't commit because it seems easier to get off that way, the trial scene is a magnificent parody of all American trail scenes, and the picture succeeds in being funny from beginning to end – never more funny than when the corpse is disclosed under the carpet, or the heroine is warned that she will 'fry'. If it appears crazy it is only because we are not accustomed on the screen to people behaving naturally and logically. An inexperienced young barrister defends his wife on the charge of murder; we expect heroics and we get comic incompetence: that isn't crazy – it's an old melodramatic situation presented for once in terms of how people really behave. This is one of those comedies – Capra made them before he read James Hilton – in which the small parts are perfectly cast and played. I advise a quick visit: the public, I think, found it oddly shocking, for the middlebrow screen is more and more dictating how people ought to behave – even at a deathbed. I remember lying in bed a few years ago in a public ward listening with fascinated horror to a mother crying over her child who had died suddenly and unexpectedly after a minor operation. You couldn't question the appalling grief, but the words she used . . . they were the cheapest, the most improbable, the most untrue . . . one had heard them on a dozen British screens. Even the father felt embarrassment standing there beside her in the open ward, avoiding every eye.

Night and Day (23 December 1937)

Marie Walewska (USA, MGM, 1937) Dir.: Clarence Brown. Cast: Greta Garbo, Charles Boyer, Reginald Owen, Alan Marshal, Henry Stephenson, Leif Erickson, Dame May Whitty. (US title *Conquest*)

True Confession (USA, Paramount, 1937) Dir.: Wesley Ruggles. Cast: Carole Lombard, Fred MacMurray, John Barrymore, Una Merkel, Porter Hall, Edgar Kennedy, Irving Bacon, Lynne Overman.

Orage

Robert Browning, you remember, wrote a poem called 'A Light Woman' – about 'my friend and the mistress of my friend with her wanton eyes and me'. An old story even in those days, it hasn't worn well with the years – but it is better in its latest French disguise than it has ever been in an Anglo-Saxon.

An engineer in a French naval dockyard (the dockyard doesn't matter; it's only an excuse for a good opening documentary shot) goes to Paris on business and promises to intercede for his young brother-in-law with a girl who has led him to the verge of suicide – or so he passionately protests as he runs beside the Paris express panting out his grief with Gallic irreticence. The engineer persuades the girl to come back with him, they miss the train, go for a ride in the country, and you know the rest, know it even to the tinkling sheep-bells which waken them, the secluded inn:

> . . . see – my friend goes shaking and white:
> He eyes me as the basilisk.

You would say it was a very Anglo-Saxon story in its muddled morality and irrational sentiment, with its Constant Nymph and Constant Wife confronting each other in the traditional great scene, before the Nymph, with poison in her tooth-mug, performs the traditional sacrifice; but admirably acted as it is by M. Charles Boyer and Mlle Michèle Morgan, and superbly directed by M. Marc Allégret, it does possess an odd and unexpected reality. All of us at one time or another must have found ourselves in some deplorable and banal situation haunted by literary parallels and discovered how actual life provides the untraditional twist: the untimely hiccups; the laugh in the wrong place. So in this film it is the twists (very Latin twists) which make the story look like truth.

The French, of course, in a tale of this kind have an immense advantage over us. An English or American director would regard this quadrilateral story as 'a love interest': it would be affixed, like part of a Surrealist collage, to some odd plot of Bengal Lancers on the North-West Frontier or gangsters in Chicago – a kiss stuck in a corner next a sub-machine gun, a night of love obscured by an overlapping Afghan attack. But to the French director passion is the whole plot – the camera is focused all the time upon the bed; and we can believe in this untidy desperate affair as we have no time to believe in a Lancer's love – because it is a whole-time job: the little hot bedroom in the country inn with the girl asking for the fly-swatter and the man too lazy to stir from his chair and the clothes flung untidily about, the sense that they haven't been downstairs for days and the bed hasn't been made: the listening at doors: the opening of other people's letters: the sudden appearance of the former lover with his scarecrow face, his hysterical impudence, his too short sleeves and bony wrists and immature jumper: all the ignobility of a besetting pleasure. Only compare that inn room with the one Garbo and Gilbert occupied in *Queen Christina* and you have the difference between literary and living passion – Garbo dangling the grapes and fumbling whimsically along the walls, and these two, lazy and hot and happy among the cigarette ash and the too many flies.

Admirable, too, are the backgrounds – the concierge's lodge, palms and hideous china and overcrowding; the small French restaurant with its '8 francs 50 table d'hôte' which ends with assorted cheese. 'What is the assorted cheese tonight?' 'Camembert.' 'Ah, he never recommends the Camembert.' And there are flashes of symbolism which take us back in memory to the old classic silent days when people thought about such things – the lover attempting to analyse the girl's character while the lights of a passing train break up the simple outline of her face. It is only when M. Berstein's story begins its noble sacrificial drift that reality seeps away – gondolas and evening dress and trying to forget Venice: the wife saying 'When you're tired of her, I shall still be there' – and then the train pounding back to Paris: scraps of sentimental morality: 'You're doing right as long as you don't cause suffering': and the girl saying 'It's you he really loves' as the wife and mistress both try with broken hearts to pass the male like a marked card.

The Spectator (10 June 1938)

Orage (France, Lauer Films, 1937) Dir.: Marc Allégret. Cast: Charles Boyer, Michèle Morgan, Jean-Louis Barrault. (US title: *The Storm*)

L'Alibi · A Slight Case of Murder

Murder, if you are going to take it seriously at all, is a religious subject; the interest of a detective-story is the pursuit of exact truth, and if we are at times impatient with the fingerprints, the time-tables and the butler's evasions, it is because the writer, like some early theologians, is getting bogged down in academic detail. How many angels can stand on the point of a needle?

L'Alibi begins very promisingly because very simply. A professional fortune-teller (Mr von Stroheim) shoots an old enemy and arranges an alibi with one of the dance-partners attached to the night-club at which he performs. She doesn't know he has committed a murder, she thinks he has something to do with the drug traffic. Then when the Detective-Inspector has got the hollow, deceiving-no-one statement from her, he lets her learn the truth – suddenly, and there is an admirable cinematic moment as she stands horror-struck and hesitating in the hygenic corridor: shot of M. Louis Jouvet's astute sad reptile face watching the handle of his door: shot of the handle beginning to turn: shot of M. Jouvet's face, hopeful and incredulous (he knows from long experience how seldom human nature gives way at the first attack): the handle ceases to turn. The whole plot now should be psychological: a female Raskolnikov resisting the urge to confession: a French Porphyrius waiting like a priest in the confessional-box: and life putting on its pressure – the *peine forte et dure*.

Alas, *L'Alibi* doesn't work out that way. It explodes, as it were, at the edges into thriller terms – Professor Winkler's absurd consulting-room where he sits, surrounded by plaster hands, dressed in monkish robes and cowl, like one of those waxwork figures you see in little dirty Mexican booths beating naked nuns; a sinister manservant, slavishly devoted, who will do anything for his master, and a Chinese girl who manicures Winkler in his bath. Mr Stroheim in a dinner-jacket and a boater acts very well, loosened from the constriction of those tight Prussian uniforms he used to wear: his slow uncertain French is effectively evil; but there is something about Mr Stroheim which apparently calls for dressing-up – like a wooden torso behind plate-glass he mutely demands a costume, and so we have the monkish robe, and an odd creation in tight white silk – court breeches and a rapier.

But the picture remains worth seeing if only for Mr Jouvet's acting. He represents all that Mr Conrad Veidt did in the old Ufa days: he had only to turn from a window and disclose that ugly, humorous and tragic face to exercise the charm of something real – as in *Un Carnet de Bal* he steps out of a bogus story into life. Listen to him soliloquizing in the morgue as he turns the sheet back over the murdered man's face: 'Ex-convict, ex-gangster and now ex-Gordon': the nutmeg-grater voice, a rasp capable of extraordinary expression, like those musical instruments made out of old metal which street performers play.

Murder is certainly not taken seriously at the Odeon. There was one corpse, you will remember, in *True Confession*, last year's funniest film: there are four corpses in *A Slight Case of Murder* and the picture is nearly four times funnier. Where will this mathematical progression end? Mr Edward G. Robinson, admirably supported by Mr Allen Jenkins and various Damon Runyon boys, plays an ex-gangster and unsuccessful brewer of post-Prohibition beer who drives out one evening with his wife and daughter to spend a week-end in the country and finds the bodies of Little Dutch and his three associates sitting dead and murdered round a table in the spare bedroom. Mr Robinson, a bit uneasy about the police but exhilarated by a breath of the old life, decides to leave the bodies on the neighbours: there are wild discussions – 'Old so-and-so, what about leaving one on *his* doorstep?' 'Say, boss, can't I keep one in the kitchen for later on?' Afterwards his henchmen read there's a reward offered for the gangsters dead or alive (ten grand apiece) and they fetch the bodies back in the middle of a party and stow them in a clothes-cupboard, on coat-hangers – the complications crazily mount, sentiment never raises its ugly head, a long nose is made at violence and death.

The Spectator (17 June 1938)

L'Alibi (France, Tellus, 1936) Dir.: Pierre Chenal. Cast: Erich von Stroheim, Louis Jouvet, Jany Holt.

A Slight Case of Murder (USA, Warners, 1938) Dir.: Lloyd Bacon. Cast: Edward G. Robinson, Ruth Donnelly, Allen Jenkins, Edward Brophy, Harold Huber, Jane Bryan, Willard Parker.

From the Manger to the Cross · Swing, Sister, Swing · Sally, Irene and Mary · Sinners in Paradise · The Devil's Party

From the Manger to the Cross was made in 1913, and shown at the Albert Hall. As it runs for an hour and a quarter, it must have been a 'super-production' in those days – it is a rousing picture even in these. The exteriors – and the film is very nearly all exterior – were taken in Palestine and Egypt, and the unobtrusive backgrounds give the film an authenticity no studio could get from technique alone. How often in the most lavish Hollywood spectacle, when the sets have cost half a million and the heroine weighs 128 pounds, the illusion of life is broken by the use of back projections or unconvincing models: in this old faded picture the Holy Family rest before the genuine Sphinx and Judas comes with torchbearers to the real Garden of Olives. You have only to accept certain period conventions of film acting and no further demand is made on your credulity.

The Rev. Brian Hession has inserted a few close-ups (in 1913 Griffith was only just introducing them to the screen): he has added a commentary from the Authorized Version: those are the only human changes, but time too has done its work well. Perhaps when the picture was first shown, all glossy in the Albert Hall, the audience was aware of 'art' doing its self-conscious and destructive work, but art has been successfully faded out – twenty-five years in film history is equal to five centuries of painting. This is a primitive: the producer has no cunning; he hasn't learned the modern tricks of angle and close-up, panning and trucking – he can't move his camera about, and we seldom come closer to the characters than what some scenarists call 'a medium close shot'. They stand in the middle distance, emotion stamped like a humour on the face, expressing themselves with the minimum of movement. That is Herod – you recognize him by the attitude, head sunk on arms, and by the expression of broody hate. He is like the Herod you sometimes see in cribs at Christmas-time, leaning down from his battlements towards the miniature Bethlehem – the plaster sheep and Wise Men and cows. The contrast with modern methods becomes vivid in one sentimental, melodramatic and symbolic shot of the empty tomb, inserted by Mr Hession – a white slab and the black shadow of a moving door, and in the final fancy cuts of skyscrapers and Chinese churches and Rome, culminating rather parochially with St Paul's and Canterbury and a flickery cross like an electric sign. The only false notes in fact are the modern notes.

Granted that *From the Manger to the Cross* is well made, was it worth making? The film critic of *The Times* who didn't like it at all – 'sincerity is not enough' – noted 'a tendency towards gross materialism', and certainly, as in Spanish churches, you are allowed no escape at all from physical suffering; Christ is a man beaten up, like a Nazi prisoner in the Brown House. The physical horror is never far away amd always well conveyed – whether it is the Massacre of the Innocents, dark passages and patches of brilliant sunlight and the sudden intrusion of spears in the old city, or the raising of Lazarus from the tomb – the awful wait after the stone has been rolled back until out of the cave the grub-like figure emerges, the tight cerements and the face all eyes. With all due respect to the *Times* critic, I find the value of the film in what he dislikes – the unsentimental reminder of the material horror, the link between the raising of Lazarus and *The Monkey's Paw*.

Of the other films this week – *Swing, Sister, Swing; Sally, Irene and Mary; Sinners in Paradise; The Devil's Party* – I retain a confused impression of carnality on the campus ('U' certificate), a night-club, a showboat, a coral island, a lot of people making good – a casino proprietor and ex-reformatory boy dying nobly, his pal in a clerical collar kneeling beside him, and a plaque unveiled at a boys' club in his memory; a manicurist becoming a star; a murderer giving himself up ('unless we face our responsibilities' – Madge Evans's sunken eyes and whimsy teacher's voice – 'we can't respect ourselves'); and Miss Gracie Allen passing an examination: the horrifying inanity of human entertainment.

The Spectator (24 June 1938)

From the Manger to the Cross (GB, Kalem, 1937) Dir.: Brian Hession.
Swing, Sister, Swing (USA, Universal, 1937) Dir.: Joseph Santley. Cast: Ken Murray, Johnny Downs, Kathryn Kane.
Sally, Irene and Mary (USA, Twentieth-Century Fox, 1938) Dir.: William A. Seiter. Cast: Alice Faye, Tony Martin, Fred Allen, Joan Davis, Jimmy Durante, Gypsy Rose Lee, Gregory Ratoff, Marjorie Weaver.
Sinners in Paradise (USA, Universal, 1938) Dir.: James Whale. Cast: John Boles, Madge Evans, Gene Lockhart, Bruce Cabot.
The Devil's Party (USA, Universal, 1938) Dir.: Ray McCarey. Cast: Victor McLaglen, Beatrice Roberts, William Gargan.

L'Homme du Jour · You and Me

Now that the great Russians have shot their bolt and belong to history – the age of early *Close Ups* and the old Windmill Theatre, of earnest lectures (which have come to so little) in tea-shops on how to use sound 'constructively' – one would name, I think Julien Duvivier and Fritz Lang as the two greatest fiction directors still at work. Duvivier has gone to Hollywood, where Lang has been now for some years – I hope Hollywood doesn't treat Duvivier as it has treated Lang.

For it is impossible not to believe that Lang – surrounded by the Virginia van Upps and the Paul Weatherwaxes, by the odd names of Hollywood credit titles – has been sabotaged. Given proper control over story and scenario, Lang couldn't have made so bad a film as *You and Me*: the whole picture is like an elegant and expensive gesture of despair. The advertised subject is '50,000 Girls Forbidden by Law to Marry', which merely refers to the reasonable regulation that convicts mustn't marry while they are still on parole. This surely is to go through the code-book with a fine-toothed comb in search of an injustice, a hard case, a little social significance. In fact, the inability of Sylvia Sidney to marry George Raft (I don't remember what they are called in the picture: it doesn't matter: they are only a couple of capable actors registering the regulation heartbreak) isn't an important part of the story at all. The real plot is concerned with an incredible philanthropist who makes a point of employing paroled convicts in his mammoth store as shop-assistants. Raft, who has worked off his parole, marries Sylvia Sidney, who hasn't finished hers – he tells her his past, but she's afraid to tell him hers. He learns the truth, takes a high moral line about deception, and joins with the other convicts in robbing the store. They are caught by the obstinate philanthropist and a couple of private guards, and as the price of their forgiveness have to sit through a talk by Miss Sidney, who demonstrates on a blackboard that crime doesn't pay. She then disappears into the night without telling Raft that she's going to have a baby, and has it – apparently next day. Physiological tact could hardly be carried further.

Everyone has heard of the Hollywood 'doghouse' – the practice of ruining a star by providing bad parts. No star has been treated worse than Lang is here by his scenario-writers. The continuity is quickie in its naïvety. 'How do we get to the information bureau?' Miss Sidney asks. 'By subway,' Raft says, and there, of course, they are – in the subway. A few experiments are made with verse and chanted speech (how unhappy Roscoe Karns looks about it all), but they are only the desperate contortions of a director caught in the Laocoön coils of an impossible script.

L'Homme du Jour – a charming comedy, with Maurice Chevalier, about an electrician who becomes famous for a day after he has given blood to save the life of a tragic actress, who is taken heavily up by the great interpreter of Racine and then, when he sleeps through a bedroom date, heavily dropped again – may not be vintage Duvivier, but it is admirable *vin ordinaire*. It is the kind of story Clair might have directed in the old days; the Pressmen cynical over the champagne, the enthusiastic straphangers in the Métro, are Clair characters, inhabitants of a whimsical fairyland where Providence strikes blindly and luck never lasts long and the lottery-ticket gets lost among the top-hats, yet no one really cares. But Duvivier's pictures have a stronger sense of human life – even in a comedy the shadow is there, and somehow in the shadow the abortionist throws a fit at Marseille and Pépé cuts his throat with an inadequate knife. Strangers in the Métro may be carried away by a wave of altruistic sentiment, but in the electrician's boarding-house – among his *friends* – there is only jealousy, the mean middle-aged passion to take him down a peg. And so we get, in this airy ridiculous comedy, one of Duvivier's saddest episodes – bogus letters that arrange an assignation between the electrician and a flower-girl who secretly and hopelessly loves him, while the hideous inhabitants of the boarding-house sit in the evening light sniggering over their cruel joke.

The Spectator (1 July 1938)

L'Homme du Jour (France, Films Maurice, 1936) Dir.: Julien Duvivier. Cast: Maurice Chevalier, Elvire Popesco, Josette Day, Alerme.

You and Me (USA, Paramount, 1938) Dir.: Fritz Lang. Cast: Sylvia Sidney, George Raft, Robert Cummings, Barton Maclane, Roscoe Karns.

Kidnapped · I Cover the Waterfront

They call it *Kidnapped*: that is what I resent most as Mr Warner Baxter, with a gleam of those too prominent and even teeth of his, waves a sword among the sepia-tinted Highlanders and shouts – in an American accent – 'On to Edinburgh', and Mr Freddie Bartholomew, with his Fauntleroy features and Never-Never-Land voice, makes winsome remarks – to Jennie

Macdonald. And who in Tusitala's name is she? She is the girl who loves Alan Breck (that is what they call Warner Baxter), and Breck is trying to restore her to her betrothed, James Stewart, whom he wants to ship out of the country because he has killed the Red Fox . . . Do you catch strange echoes of a story you once read? There *was* a Red Fox, and a James Stewart, though neither killed the other, and as for Alan trying to get anyone but himself out of the country or loving a girl . . .

I doubt if the summer will show a worse film than *Kidnapped*; the only fun you are likely to get from it is speculation, speculation on the astonishing ignorance of film-makers who claim to know what the public wants. The public will certainly not want this *Kidnapped*, where all the adventures which made them read the book have been omitted. Is it even honest to bring in Stevenson's name? (There should be a society for protecting authors who may be out of copyright.) Apart from the title and the circumstances of David Balfour's kidnapping, there is practically nothing of the original story here – you will find no trace of the magnificent battle in the round house or of the flight in the heather. Alan Breck's character, with its cunning and vanity, is not so much altered as lost – he is only an American voice shouting over and over again, 'To Edinburgh' or 'The Redcoats': he is only a set of teeth like those exhibited in the windows of cheap dentists. A little of David's priggishness is left (it comes easily to the actor), but none of that 'darkness of despair and a sort of anger against all the world' which when we were young dragged us with him through the heather. All that remains is an odd echo – familiar names misused, lines out of the book misplaced, trivial incidents, which any competent scenarist would have cut, dragged in to take the place of – everything. All the great filmic scenes of battle and flight are eliminated, and a tiny incident without bearing on the story, like that of the minister who asks David for snuff, is retained. As for the girl with her great dewy eyes, her dimples and her tartan and her kissing mouth, she represents, I suppose, the love interest – as if there wasn't love enough in the original story to wither these wistful caresses and misunderstandings and virginal pursuits, the love of an exile for a particular scene and of a sick man for a life of action he couldn't lead.

I Cover the Waterfront is a revival from a period before the Hays dictatorship – when it was still just possible that the films might have become an adult art. It dates a little with its hard-drinking newspapermen and its boisterous badinage, but it does achieve something of value and maturity in the character of Eli Kirk, played by the late Ernest Torrence, an illiterate sea-captain who smuggles Chinamen into a Pacific seaport and throws them overboard, tied to an anchor chain, when he's in danger from the Revenue officers. Watch the stubble face sweat as the Chink drops, the rudimentary conscience at work in the old starry eyes: listen to the rough, deep, melancholy voice like something heavy and phosphorescent dragged out of a well: see him scared and huddled in a corner while his Mate dies from a shark's bite, breaking out at his men. 'Don't you men know enough to take off your hats,' while he forgets his own: watch him drunk in a brothel – the awful paralytic happiness caged in the huge body. There are scenes in this film which Hays now would never pass – they are the scenes which give the picture veracity – the daughter (Miss Claudette Colbert) waiting in the cheap brothel to take her tipsy father home, quite naturally, exchanging friendly words with the big blonde madame; the Chinaman's body fished out of the water by the harbour scavenger, the death casually dated ('Not more'n a day. Crabs aint got 'im yet'). A bit raw and a bit sentimental and a bit routine, the film does let life in through the cracks.

The Spectator (5 August 1938)

Kidnapped (USA, Twentieth-Century Fox, 1938) Dir.: Alfred Werker. Cast: Warner Baxter, Freddie Bartholomew, Arleen Whelan, John Carradine, Nigel Bruce, C. Aubrey Smith, Reginald Owen.

I Cover the Waterfront (USA, Reliance, 1933) Dir.: James Cruze. Cast: Claudette Colbert, Ben Lyon, Ernest Torrence, Hobart Cavanaugh.

Little Tough Guy · Gold is Where You Find It · Liszt Rhapsody

Don't be put off by the absurd title. *Little Tough Guy* is one of the best melodramas in recent years – very nearly as good as *Dead End*, and with the same cast of boys. The theme too is roughly the same: the natural adolescent virtues decaying on the East Side under the iron ladder of the Elevated, courage becoming toughness, the love of justice a hatred of the whole possessing world. Billy Halop, in appearance a younger Robert Taylor but with twice the acting ability, takes the part of Johnny Boylan, whose father is sent unjustly to the chair. The whole family – the lower-middle, keeping-up-appearances class – have to move away from home into the slums: the daughter drops from shop-girl to burlesque-girl, the son from schoolboy to newsboy, the leader of a tough gang. It isn't a gang which usually would get further than an occasional petty theft for bravado's sake or a stone flung through a window – an impotent protest against Justice in a luxury car, Justice keeping a luncheon appointment – without the assistance of a leader with more imagination and more cruelty; and an original feature of this melodrama is the way it keeps an adolescent unity in the character of the Big Shot. The Big Shot (admirably acted by Jackie Searle) is a rich youth who wants excitement. We see him first under pious posters and ugly banners, the honoured guest of the Young America Onward and Upward League, listening to the Chairman's speech ('I've seen this movement grow – from the teeniest idea . . .') with well-bred patience: a long cynical eyelid and a nervous nihilist humour. He takes the gang up, organizes their petty thefts, and then, when the police pressure grows too great, betrays them. Boylan and his henchman Pig (a pale weedy bully with strangled loyalties cleverly hinted at) escape and are brought finally to bay in a small grocer's shop, with guns in their immature hands and an armed police cordon across the road. That scene in its psychological horror atones for much false sentiment, for naïve sociology and a truly appalling happy end – the tough gang with busbies and bugles at a State school, and Johnny Boylan twirling a baton on prize-day. Day-dream violence is confronted appallingly with actuality – the guns they had played with must be either used or surrendered. There is a long spell of inaction, while the old grocer prays to God under the counter, 'Let me get safe home . . . let me get safe home', the antique whisper eating at the boys' nerves, and then the squeal of the ambulance – 'I guess that's what they're waiting for' – the noise of the brakes going on, and all the cramped loneliness between the counter and the wall with the lights turned out and the police guns pointed and death really about to happen.

Gold is Where You Find It is good old-fashioned cinema: a war between brutal gold miners, assisted by unscrupulous money-bosses and slimy lawyers, and simple farmers whose land is being ruined by the mud from the mines. Miss Olivia de Havilland comes out rather beautifully in Technicolor, and Mr George Brent is the hero – it's that kind of film: a Montague-Capulet plot and decorative Victorian dresses and a waster's heroic death and a bar-room fight and a sermon from the bench and a fade-out at sunset. Technicolor is at its dubious best in a picture like this – though the painted backgrounds in the long shots are dreadful: it all adds to the delicious self-pity, the glowing adolescent agony. It's jam but good jam – with a few better moments you don't often find in films like this, and Mr Claude Rains, as the farmers' leader, is chiefly responsible for these. His precise, fine voice can give a chisel edge to the flattest sentiments.

As for *Liszt Rhapsody*, it is a routine German musical romance with more humour and less beer and balloons than usual. A lot of the picture is shot in Rome – very pleasantly, with broken pillars and wild flowers and period parasols, but with no purpose I can see, except to advertise the strength of the Rome-Berlin axis. The Teutons in their tight trousers strut amiably like cocks, lifting up their little claws, disdaining bird seed, setting all the hens in a bustle of love or hate, and Liszt himself – that doubtful dog – appears angelically to help the young people to pair off.

The Spectator (12 August 1938)

Little Tough Guy (USA, Universal, 1938) Dir.: Harold Young. Cast: Billy Halop, Jackie Searle, Robert Wilcox, Helen Parrish, Marjorie Main, Huntz Hall.
Gold Is Where You Find It (USA, Warners, 1938) Dir.: Michael Curtiz. Cast: Olivia de Havilland, George Brent, Claude Rains, Margaret Lindsay, John Litel, Barton Maclane, Tim Holt, Sidney Toler.
Liszt Rhapsody (*Wenn die Musik nicht Wär*) (Germany, 1938) Dir.: Carmine Gallone.

Son of Mongolia · Battle of Broadway

Trauberg, the director of *New Babylon*, that magnificent, ludicrous and savage version of the Paris of 1871, has made *Son of Mongolia*. This Trauberg has a genius for legend; one is sometimes still haunted on evenings of rain and despair by the midinette of *New Babylon* with her rain-soaked face and her gawky body, her expression of dumb simplicity and surprise, as she plods painfully in her own person through the stages of evolution and dies with the first glimmer of human intelligence. The son of Mongolia, too, is a simple and stupid creature whom we watch evolve an intelligence, but with his physical strength and his rich half-conscious humour he is the hero of a happier legend – though one we find more difficult to accept than goodness dying in the rain against a wall.

This son of Mongolia loves a shepherdess (the Trianon title could hardly be less applicable than to this girl astride her stocky pony – small, rough and almond-eyed). A rival bribes a fortune-teller in a caravanserai (full of bicycles and old priests telling beads, spittoons, and ancient melancholy traditional songs) to get rid of him, and the fortune-teller reads the Mongolian's palm: 'Many days journey to the East you find an enchanted garden. Taste one of its fruits and you will become a hero. If you encounter any obstacles simply call out "I am Tseven of Shorot".' And so poor simplicity starts out in the usual manner of a youngest son, slipping in a sandstorm past the border-posts into Manchuria, into a world of feudal injustice, of astute Japanese spies, of the casual execution, where human suffering goes on and on like breathing and sleeping. He befriends a shepherd who has been flogged for saying that Mongolia will one day be free; he listens to a Japanese officer plotting a secret assault with a wrestler in a circus, and when he denounces the spy, he finds himself shut in a cage in the enchanted garden of his imagination, condemned to death by the local Chinese Prince who is preparing to betray his country.

There is a rescue and a flight – little fairy-tale ponies pursued by a tank across the long Mongolian plain; there is last-minute salvation by means of a Biblical subterfuge; Tseven and the shepherd lie on the ground hidden by a friendly chewing unfrightened flock while the soldiers sweep the horizon in vain with their Leitz lenses. Let us forget the crude propaganda close, and remember the curious mixture of the very old and the very new, of melodrama and fairy-tale. Inside a Daimler decorated with flower-pots on the hood and quilted with satin the Chinese Prince makes desultory and lubricious love; the spy swings in a hammock dressed in long Oriental merchant's robes and discusses troop movements with a half-naked wrestler; a clown in a long white beard packs an army revolver; and while the executioner stands by with naked blade, the Prince's secretary, in a lounge suit and horn-rimmed glasses, reads the *Arabian Nights* sentence: 'Tseven of Shorot is to be made shorter by a head.' There is one magnificent panoramic shot when the camera sweeps down a whole long Chinese street: camels and bicycles: criminals squatting on a little platform with their heads stuck through great square wooden collars: butchers' stalls and tea-drinkers: soldiers on an unexplained hunt through the crowd: rows of sewing-machines: a garbled gateway through the ancient walls and the dusty plain outside.

Battle of Broadway is one of those boisterous pictures based on sexual rivalry – *What Price Glory?* set the fashion years ago. Mr Victor McLaglen and Mr Brian Donlevy wear American Legion uniforms with little forage caps and more war medals than you'd think possible and double-cross each other noisily for the possession of a woman. Sexual lust is neutralised in hearty good-fellowship. It is all loud greetings, community singing ('We are the Legionnaires'), chorus girls in steel helmets, nostalgic references to Armentires, comic Jews to be kicked about, and a former strip-tease artiste, Miss Gypsy Rose Lee, who makes her first film appearance under the name of Miss Louise Hovick – with excessive refinement: 'All reht, boys. Er'll give it a treh,' long drooping aristocratic eyelids, and a figure so elaborately balanced it might have come out of a ship-breaker's yard.

The Spectator (19 August 1938)

Son of Mongolia (USSR, Lenfilm, 1936) Dir.: Ilya Trauberg. Cast: Tseven, Itchin-Horlo.

Battle of Broadway (USA, Twentieth-Century Fox, 1938) Dir.: George Marshall. Cast: Victor McLaglen, Brian Donlevy, Gypsy Rose Lee, Raymond Walburn, Lynn Bari, Hattie McDaniel, Jane Darwell.

Fools for Scandal · Booloo · Five Faces

They say you cannot hear a bat squeak . . . and certainly Miss Carole Lombard's high enchanting fatuous voice has risen in this latest film of hers beyond the capacity of the microphone – or so it seemed at the Press show. It rises, breaks, is lost . . . and that's a pity for all of us. But it is more of a pity that her directors should have given her so humourless, so hopeless a story (perhaps that's why she has to scream so loud). Even Mr Allen Jenkins, sure-fire Jenkins, can make nothing of this picture. A penniless French Marquis (acted with plump repulsive confidence by Mr Fernand Gravet) pursues a film actress (Miss Carole Lombard of course) to London, and after dining at her house takes advantage of a joke to install himself there as her cook and butler, answers telephone calls – compromisingly, so that soon a pack of reporters are waiting at the door trying to glean a paragraph about the 'love chef', and the actress finally succumbs . . . Perhaps it is meant to be a crazy comedy, but the secret of the crazy comedy is that people do behave with the irrelevance of human beings and break out through the

Hollywood frame into life. Here they proceed with daunting high spirits and dreadful inevitability between the pasteboard walls towards – what an end! The only character for which the script-writer does deserve some praise is Miss Lombard's cavalier, an insurance agent, the parody of a familiar type: the big boyish lover with his sulks and his enormous optimism and his gawky abandonment to joy and grief. As for Miss Lombard . . . it is always a pleasure to watch those hollow Garbo features, those neurotic elbows and bewildered hands, and her voice has the same odd beauty a street musician discovers in old iron, scraping out heart-breaking and nostalgic melodies. But you will be well advised to wait another occasion of serving at her shrine.

Jungle pictures are always great fun, and the *Booloo* expedition led by Captain Rogers to discover in the Wilds of Malaya a white tiger and a maiden sacrifice deserves to rank with the epic exploits of the Marquis de la Falaise and the heroes of *The Jungle Princess.* Captain Rogers had produced a volume from the hunting reminiscences of his father, a famous explorer, and some of these, which concerned the tiger and the sacrifice, so shocked the Imperial Geographical Society that they removed the old man's portrait from their walls ceremoniously in the presence of the son. So Captain Rogers left his sweetheart in Aldershot and penetrated into the territory of 'the Sakai savages' to prove his father's tales were true. How familiar we are by now with that jungle: 'stir but a stone and start' – not a mere wing, but whole tribes of monkeys, tigers, herds of elephant. Laboriously, the expedition backs its way along a little path with machetes, studiously averting their faces from the wide easy clearing a foot away: faces peer out of the shrubbery; poisoned arrows flick into tree-trunks ('One scratch, you must know, means death. Do you still want to go on?' 'Yes, Sir.' 'Stout fellow' – it's that kind of dialogue), and a girl dressed like a South Sea islander from *Hurricane* waits in a trap for the tiger.

Those who will see Mr Alexander Shaw's picture, *Five Faces*, at the Academy in a few weeks will wonder – 'Why the Sakai of all people?' In *Five Faces*, a documentary study of Malaya, we have genuine pictures of these gentle persecuted people. We watch them use their poisoned arrows – against small rodents, the poison just strong enough to kill but not to taint the meat. And we see, too, the real Sakai women – decorative creatures, certainly, with sticks poked through the nostrils and uncovered breasts, but hardly to be compared for shampooed beauty with the maiden sacrifice of *Booloo*, the long combed raven hair, the Dorothy Lamour eyes, the elegant and refined sarong.

Five Faces is good workmanlike documentary, and it has more important values than the exposure of jungle absurdities. Most interesting is its treatment of history – the use of old prints to illustrate the commentary, the alternation on the screen of the seventeenth-century engraving and the ruins as they stand today. The effect is exciting and reassuring – to see how little Time can really do: to recognize the face so easily from the skull.

The Spectator (26 August 1938)

Fools for Scandal (USA, Warners, 1938) Dir.: Mervyn Le Roy. Cast: Carole Lombard, Allen Jenkins, Fernand Gravet, Ralph Bellamy, Isabel Jeans, Marie Wilson.

Boloo (USA, Paramount, 1938) Dir.: Clyde Elliott. Cast: Colin Tapley, Jayne Regan.

Five Faces (GB, Strand Films, 1938) Dir.: Alexander Shaw. (aka: *Five Faces of Malaya*)

KATIA · SIXTY GLORIOUS YEARS · OLD IRON

Perhaps it is as well that Mlle Darrieux has gone to Hollywood to be groomed for crazy comedy. Her type demands too much of the scenario-writer: the innocence she conveys has nothing to do with life: it must be poetry or nothing. The sense of extreme youth, death and eternity and love-for-ever glib upon the tongue – it doesn't signify whether it's fine acting or fine camerawork or just a trick of carriage, the head so precariously poised on the long slender immature neck. Whatever the cause, the effect she makes demands poetic tragedy: innocence like that has got to be legendary, doomed, a scapegoat.

She succeeded in *Mayerling* because her partner Charles Boyer could carry the right atmosphere of predestination. She was sentenced to death by the world as soon as she appeared in the pleasure-garden, lost in the boisterous darkness. In *Katia* the French have tried to repeat *Mayerling* – a meeting in a pleasure-garden, royalty incognito, the girl's secret visit to the palace interrupted by a wife this time instead of a mother. We can see now that if she had stayed she would have been used over and over again to play the child-mistress of nineteenth-century royalties, until the time came when she couldn't make-up quite so young and innocence would have been turned on like a tap. In *Katia* she is first the mistress and then the wife of the Tsar Alexander. The story is conventional, naïve, loosely constructed: the assassination of the Tsar is followed by an interminable deathbed – 'This is your little Katia. Speak to me.' A story could have been made out of the constant threat of the terrorists, private life broken all the time by the need of protection, and the end inevitable. But no such story is attempted. There is nothing doomed about this Tsar, played by Mr John Loder, who even on our shores is hardly known as a pliant actor and who, under the added handicap of the French language, becomes no more than a dummy for full-dress uniforms. The story too, is absurdly speeded up. 'Free the serfs,' the child implores Alexander on their first meeting, and freed the serfs are – in the next shot. There is one good scene, when the Tsar drives with Napoleon III through the Paris streets and the two Emperors salute the loyal people with bows and smiles, as they talk about boots and caviare, illicitly like chorus-girls.

And so to another royal romance, heavy this time with lavender and right feelings, Elgar and quotations from Kipling. Sweet Nell of Old Drury, Nell Gwyn, Queen Victoria – Miss Neagle seems to be attempting all our great national figures, and though it is sometimes a little difficult to distinguish between them, I think I prefer her in breeches as sweet Nell: her dimpled aseptic coquetry is a bit out of place under a crown, just as the straining naked naiads trailing golden bath-towels who leap towards the Odeon screen are not well suited to this rather absurd picture of royal domesticities, all loyalty, sentiment and Technicolor. The dialogue by Mr Miles Malleson and Sir Robert Vansittart is undistinguished, and the casting which begins grotesquely with Miss Neagle remains – to say the least of it – odd. What strange whim induced Mr Wilcox to cast one of our youngest actors in the part of Disraeli? If there is one thing as bad as age imitating youth, it is youth imitating age. And that, I fear, goes for Miss Neagle, too. Both the director and the star seem to labour under the impression that they are producing something important, and this gives what is really an inoffensive picture a kind of humourless pomp. Incidentally, the Indian Mutiny and the Boer War, not to mention other rather inglorious campaigns in Africa and Afghanistan, are omitted: the Crimea and the Sudan alone disturb this love-life of a queen.

Mr Tom Walls is a very competent actor, but in *Old Iron* he shows no improvement as a director: an embarrassing little stage comedy of parental affection, shot hurriedly from the front as you would shoot a charging lion. A bad week is completed by a Gaumont-British News reel which scores the lowest marks yet for editing – if it was edited at all. Beginning with a football match it ends with the Chinese war sandwiched between a performing ape and – I can't remember what. This is not only bad journalism: it is bad taste.

The Spectator (4 November 1938)

Katia (France, E. Alcazy, 1938) Dir.: Maurice Tourneur. Cast: Danielle Darrieux, John Loder.
Sixty Glorious Years (GB, Imperator, 1938) Dir.: Herbert Wilcox. Cast: Anna Neagle, Anton Walbrook, C. Aubrey Smith, Walter Rilla, Charles Carson, Felix Aylmer, Lewis Casson.
Old Iron (GB, British Lion, 1938) Dir.: Tom Walls. Cast: Tom Walls, Eva Moore, Cecil Parker, Richard Ainley, David Tree, Enid Stamp-Taylor.

You Can't Take It With You · There Goes My Heart

It is really what we should have expected from Frank Capra, whose portrait hangs outside the cinema: bushy eyebrows, big nose and the kind of battered face which looks barnacled with life, encrusted with ready sympathies and unexacting friendships, a good mixer. It is always dangerous, of course, to generalize about a director's subjects – he hasn't invented his own stories; but the Capra-Riskin combination is strong enough by now to dictate, and we can assume Capra is doing what he wants to do. What he wants is increasingly what the public wants. It will adore the new picture which contains what it treasures most – a good laugh and a good cry.

As for the reviewer, he can only raise his hands in a kind of despair. The new picture is the *Christmas Carol* over again – with its sentimentality and its gusto and its touches of genius: no techinical mistakes this time as there were in *Lost Horizon*. The director emerges as a rather muddled and sentimental idealist who feels – vaguely – that something is wrong with the social system. Mr Deeds started distributing his money, and the hero of *Lost Horizon* settled down in a Tibetan monastery – equipped with all the luxury devices of the best American hotels – and Grandpa Vanderhof persuades, in this new picture, the Wall Street magnate who has made the *coup* of his career and cornered the armaments industry to throw everything up and play the harmonica. This presumably means a crash in Wall Street and the ruin of thousands of small investors, but it is useless trying to analyse the idea behind the Capra films: there *is* no idea that you'd notice, only a sense of dissatisfaction, an urge to escape – on to the open road with the daughter of a millionaire, back to small-town simplicity on a safe income, away to remote, secure Shangri-La, into the basement where Mr Vanderhof's son-in-law makes fireworks with the iceman who came seven years ago with a delivery-van and stayed on. A belief, too, in bad rich men and good poor men – though Mr Vanderhof doesn't, when you come to think of it, seem to lack money. Like the British Empire, he has retired from competition with a full purse.

That is really all there is to the film – a contrast between life on Wall Street and life in the Vanderhof home, where everybody is supposed to lead the life he likes and like the life the others lead. A granddaughter practices ballet-dancing while she lays the table, a boy-friend plays on the marimba, a daughter writes novels which will never be published, just for fun – what an extraordinary idea of fun! It is very noisy with the fireworks going off, and good-hearted and Christian in the *Christmas Carol* tradition. The most embarrassing moments in a film which is frequently embarrassing occur at meal-times when Grandpa Vanderhof (Mr Lionel Barrymore) talks to God in a man-to-man way instead of saying Grace. 'Well, sir, here we are again. We been getting on pretty well for a long time now . . .' This whimsical household is meant, I think, to be symbolic of life as it should be lived (one prefers Wall Street), and mixed up in the whole thing is the routine love-story of Vanderhof's granddaughter and the magnate's son, played sensitively by Miss Jean Arthur and Mr James Stewart.

It sounds awful, but it isn't as awful as all that, for Capra has a touch of genius with a camera: his screen always seems twice as big as other people's, and he cuts as brilliantly as Eisenstein (the climax when the big bad magnate takes up his harmonica is so exhilarating in its movement that you forget its absurdity). Humour and not wit is his line, a humour which shades off into whimsicality, and a kind of popular poetry which is apt to turn wistful. We may groan and blush as he cuts his way remorselessly through all finer values to the fallible human heart, but infallibly he makes his appeal – to that great soft organ with its unreliable goodness and easy melancholy and baseless optimism. The cinema, a popular craft, can hardly be expected to do more.

There Goes My Heart – a reporter pursues and falls in love with a rich man's rebellious daughter. Everything here is machine-made except the blonde beauty of Miss Virginia Bruce and Miss Patsy Kelly's vital underdog humour.

The Spectator (11 November 1938)

You Can't Take It With You (USA, Columbia, 1938) Dir.: Frank Capra. Cast: James Stewart, Jean Arthur, Lionel Barrymore, Edward Arnold, Spring Byington, Mischa Auer, Ann Miller, Samuel S. Hinds, Donald Meek, H.B. Warner, Halliwell Hobbes, Eddie Anderson, Harry Davenport.

There Goes My Heart (USA, Hal Roach, 1938) Dir.: Norman Z. McLeod. Cast.:

Fredric March, Virginia Bruce, Patsy Kelly, Nancy Carroll, Eugene Pallette, Claude Gillingwater, Harry Langdon.

ALERTE EN MÉDITERRANÉE · MEN WITH WINGS

This latest French film is a routine melodrama of naval life in the Mediterranean. It enables us better than more unusual films to judge the quality of the French industry, for it is hard to remember that usually we are shown nothing but the best. In this picture there is no originality; its theme of international comradeship between men of the same trade recalls the far finer German picture *Kameradschaft* (how the world has altered! It was France in those days who had to be reminded that there were other values than that of war).

A tramp steamer puts into Tangier, where German, English and French men-of-war ride at anchor: there is said to be yellow fever on board, so the Customs officer neglects his duty. Then the ship's drunken doctor slips on shore with a tongue ready to blab and is murdered during a brawl. French, English and German sailors are arrested; they each blame the other nationalities, and their officers who have made friends over a child's toy destroyer quarrel now like their Governments over death-guilt. Then the Captain of the tramp escapes from his own ship (an exciting scene, handled very quietly); he brings news that the sailors are innocent; the murderer is the man who chartered the steamer – a mysterious Mr Martin who is smuggling a dye called 424 through the Mediterranean. The French torpedo-boat leaves in pursuit, bearing the English and German officers with her to keep liaison with their Admiralties. They must not sink the steamer, for if the dye mixes with salt water it throws off poison gas, capable of killing all life within two hundred miles. So they run alongside and bluff with blank charges. The crew surrender and Mr Martin scuttles the ship. The poisonous fog moves at 20 knots across the sea, and a liner from Tangier to Marseille lies with engine trouble helpless in its path – on board the French Commander's wife and son. Seaplanes are sent to rescue the children, but for the adult passengers and crew the only chance is for the torpedo-boat to break through the gas.

The attempt succeeds with ten minutes to spare, and the German officer – who had been gassed in the War – dies protractedly on the bridge with a message for the French child. There are moments when internationalism becomes as sentimental as some forms of patriotism, but on the whole the film succeeds – not as a peace tract but as a naval thriller.

It succeeds mainly in the accuracy of its details – which is where English films so often fail – in the dying seagull scrabbling against the glass: the top of the masts moving into obscurity through the black clouds of gas: the unnautical fountain-pen in Mr Martin's breastpocket and his sad drooping outcast mouth. It may be the function of the French cinema to teach us how to handle realism, as they taught it in the novel years ago – realism on a more imaginative level than our facile and whimsical use of national types. The Anglo-Saxon – whether English or American – always tempers the direct impact of life sooner or later with a laugh or a good cry.

Men With Wings is also routine melodrama – on the Anglo-Saxon level. One of those clean stories which call for Freudian analysis, it is about two men who have loved one woman from childhood. One marries her and is always leaving her; the other stays around, doglike. Eventually, the husband gets killed flying in China – and I suppose the dog has his day. This story is said to be about 'man's conquest of the air from the first flight of the Wright Brothers in 1903 to the making of super-speed bombers in 1938' (the last a family affair of the woman, the child, and the dog – Mr Ray Milland). But we saw no Wright Brothers, and what we heard ran on these lines: the heroine asking in the maternity ward, 'How can I be this happy?' frail under Technicolor sunburn, and the nurse saying, 'That's why there's so many mothers.' The director has dedicated his prize egg 'To all women who love and admire the fearless heroes of the air, and, who, with brave hearts, encourage them, hope, and pray for them.' The new star, Miss Louise Campbell, was formerly a dental assistant, but none of the painful scenes at which she then assisted ever lasted two hours.

The Spectator (18 November 1938)

Alerte en Méditerranée (France, Véga Films, 1937) Dir.: Léo Joannon. Cast: Pierre Fresnay, Rolf Wanka, Kim Peacock. (US title: *SOS Mediterranean*)
Men With Wings (USA, Paramount, 1938) Dir.: William A. Wellman. Cast: Fred MacMurray, Ray Milland, Louise Campbell, Andy Devine, Lynne Overman, Porter Hall, Walter Abel, Donald O'Connor, Virginia Wiedler.

Lenin in October · Stranded in Paris

Lenin in October is one of the best entertainments we have seen in a cinema for a long while, and I hope for everyone's sake that it will soon be shown publicly. Hardly less entertaining are the programme notes put out by the Film Society in that curious gritty hyphenated prose which seems to go with ideological convictions:

> By contrast with *October, Lenin in October*, covering the same ground, concentrates upon a particular figure and deals with the part he played therein. This concentration is obtained at the expense of what, in comparison with certain identical mass scenes in *October*, will be seen as a considerable relative neglect of the compositional qualities of the image. This falling-off is characteristic of Soviet films of the period, and apparently a concomitant of the effort at reorientation of interest around personality on the part of the creative group. In later films, those recently completed and still in production, it is apparent that already usage is affording sufficient facility to enable a high compositional level to be retained together with depiction of personality.

From this lumpy gruel of inexact and abstract words, you may or may not get the idea: that we have reached the end of the Communist film. It is to be all 'Heroes and Hero-Worship' now: the old films are to be remade for the new leaders: no more anonymous mothers will run in the van of the workers against the Winter Palace. The USSR is to produce Fascist films from now on.

History, of course, has to be rewritten in the process, and it would be absurd to expect from *Lenin* the old excitement of conviction (which used to drive the very bourgeois members of the Society to sing the 'Red Flag'). What is left is the excitement of melodrama handled with the right shabby realism, the interest of seeing an actor reconstruct the mannerisms of Lenin (his widow believes them to be over-emphasized), most agreeable of all the unconscious humour of the rearrangement – the elimination of Trotsky and the way in which Stalin slides into the all-important close-ups.

'Before anything else,' Lenin commands his bodyguard as soon as he has set foot in Petrograd (he has been smuggled in by train from Finland in the driver's cabin), 'before anything else arrange a meeting with Stalin.' And at that meeting he tells the Central Committee: 'Comrade Stalin is absolutely right. The proposals of Kamenev and Zinoviev and Trotsky are either complete idiocy or a betrayal' (more names, it is to be supposed, will be added to the soundtrack after every trial). Then we have the kind of shadowgraph upon a window once popular in love-stories – Stalin statuesque with his pipe and Lenin, little and nervous, gesticulating up at him. Throughout Lenin is played on humourous lines, a little Robin Goodfellow of a man, full of elfish tricks, who has to be controlled and looked after and lent macintoshes by Stalin and the Central Committee, while his big sound brother-in-arms is played on Worcestershire lines: you feel he reads Mary Webb. In the final close-up of Lenin addressing the first Soviet, he sidles up behind Lenin's shoulder, pipe in hand, wearing an approving and patronizing smile – a headmaster on founder's day glad to welcome an old boy who has made good. You expect a sly comment about canes.

There is the usual fine assortment of unreliable old liberal faces among the Mensheviks and of simple tow-haired workers who wear cartridge-belts, with the gawky charm of Bottom and his flowers. But everybody, even Lenin, is acted off the set by whichever Honoured Artist of the Republic it is who plays the police agent sent by the Mensheviks to trace Lenin. This is a magnificent portrait – in the Cruikshank manner – of seedy and unscrupulous gentility; the wet loose hand and the battered bowler, the mole and the lank lock and the stringy tie and the calculated impudence.

Stranded in Paris is a film of an unrelieved gaiety, set in the American Paris – all subservient waiters, long loaves, comic hotel keepers, sidelong looks and naïve carnality. It slides down fairly easily like an Alpine Glow or a Knickerbocker Glory, and you emerge a little cloyed perhaps, but without any distinct feeling of nausea – unless you happen to be French.

The Spectator (25 November 1938)

Lenin in October (USSR, Mosfilm, 1937) Dir.: Mikhail Romm. Cast: Boris Shchukin, Nikolai Olchlopkov, Vasili Vanin, Golshtab.

Stranded in Paris (USA, Paramount, 1938) Dir.: Mitchell Leisen. Cast: Jack Benny, Monty Woolley, Mary Boland, Charley Grapewin, Fritz Field, Joan Bennett. (US Title: *Artists and Models Abroad*)

The Dawn Patrol · Persons in Hiding · Kentucky · Never Say Die

There has been such a chorus of praise for *The Dawn Patrol* that to let the little worm of doubt creep in on this heroic occasion seems like a breech of taste. Never have the critics been so unanimous since those *Glorious Years* – and perhaps psychologically the two pictures have something in common. They both flatter our national pride by emphasizing what are known as the 'masculine virtues'. The theme of this flying picture is that of *The Light Brigade*: somebody at headquarters has blundered, and day after day the Light Brigade, as it were, rides forth against the guns – 'Their's not to make reply, Their's but to do and die.' The officers who in turn command the flight, condemned to a desk and a whisky bottle, unwillingly send out batch after batch of replacements – schoolboys with less than ten hours' solo flying – to be shot down by the German ace and his squadron, and their nerves rather histrionically collapse. As a protest against war, it is insincere: the emphasis is on the heroic and the patriotic – Von Richter, it will be noted, always wears an ugly sneer behind his machine-gun.

It *is* quite a good picture, well directed and in some cases well acted, but I don't believe it's true – a great deal of self-pity and romanticism have gone to the making of this excellent ham-sandwich. The critics have made great play with the fact that there isn't a woman in the cast, but personally I found myself regretting the old intruder in her abbreviated skirt and her WAAC hat – the film wouldn't have been any less like life, and in her stead we get an even more romantic love. The young blond officer with the Fröhlich face weeps over the dead school-friend, and the kid brother arrives full of morning glory to join his brother's squadron – the last war seems to have been littered with younger brothers. Mr Basil Rathbone adds to the general effect of melodrama: he can't – whatever his part – do much else with that dark knife-blade face and snapping mouth.

Persons in Hiding is a gangster picture, a little on the tame side, distinguished by the presence of a crooked and merciless heroine, acted by a newcomer, Miss Patricia Morison. Miss Morison is lovely to look at, but never persuades us she is more. She has small chance, since the story opens, as it were, in the middle, with her first theft as a hairdresser's assistant – and after that it's all speeding cars and montage: we are given no background, and there is nothing in her acting to suggest the past which launched her on this anarchic storm. That is exactly what Mr Lynne Overman as the G-man supplies: with every intonation and weary cock of the head we get the whole contented bourgeois home, the comradely wife and the furniture from a plain van, the melancholy crack over the breakfast-table, the law-abiding background to the dangerous life.

Kentucky is the first film I have seen which has been made by its colour. A banal story of an old Kentucky feud, dating from the Civil War, with Montague and Capulet owning rival race-studs, it wouldn't amount to much without colour – as it is, there is continuous pleasure in watching the horses and Miss Loretta Young – I am not sure which are the most beautiful; and there are one or two touches of direction – when the child, whose father has been shot by the Federal troops come to seize his horses, runs frantically beside the dusty blue breeches and the chestnut flanks babbling incoherently of brood mares, and again when a commentator reads out the names of old Kentucky winners – Diamond, Rocksand, Gallant Fox and Galahad the Second – while the mares stream across the wide pastures.

But the most enjoyable film for weeks has slipped by unnoticed among the heroic and romantic. *Never Say Die* is consistently absurd – it has no dignity, no passion, and a magnificent cast, headed by Mr Bob Hope as Kidley, a multi-millionaire who is supposed to be suffering from quite abnormal acidity (the chemist has mixed up his test with that of a dog called Kipper) and to be slowly digesting himself. 'Side by side', his physician proudly announces, 'we will live down eternity – Schmidt and his disease.'

The Spectator (3 March 1939)

The Dawn Patrol (USA, Warners, 1938) Dir.: Edmund Goulding. Cast: Errol Flynn, David Niven, Basil Rathbone, Melville Cooper, Donald Crisp, Barry Fitzgerald.

Persons in Hiding (USA, Paramount, 1938) Dir.: Louis King. Cast: Lynne Overman, Patricia Morison, J. Carrol Naish, William Henry, William Frawley, Helen Twelvetrees.

Kentucky (USA, Twentieth-Century Fox, 1938) Dir.: David Butler. Cast: Loretta Young, Richard Greene, Walter Brennan, Moroni Olsen, Douglass Dumbrille, Karen Morely.

Never Say Die (USA, Paramount, 1938) Dir.: Elliott Nugent. Cast: Bob Hope, Martha Raye, Andy Devine, Gale Sondergaard, Alan Mowbray, Sig Rumann, Monty Woolley.

Three Smart Girls Grow Up · Black Eyes · Inspector Hornleigh

Innocence is a tricky subject: its appeal is not always quite so clean as a whistle, and in *Black Eyes* the Edwardian dresses, the droshkies and chandeliers of pre-war Russia do not altogether disguise the brutality of the plot – which is simply will the roué get the innocent? Innocence is just the turn of the screw, to make the suspense more breathless.

Miss Deanna Durbin's film, needless to say, is not a bit like that. She is not the innocent centre of a sly story; everything is innocent all round her: youth is laid on with a trowel. The white feminine room which the three sisters share, the quilted beds, the little furry jackets over the pyjamas – the whole upholstery is so virginal that it awakes little twitters of nostalgia from the stalls. Pillow-fights and first love and being sent to bed without any dinner – the awkward age has never been so laundered and lavendered and laid away. And it is all charming, very charming. There is no doubt any longer of Miss Durbin's immense talents as an actress; any undertones that there are in this amusing, astute and sentimental tale are supplied by her. Singing 'The Last Rose of Summer' to her preoccupied Wall Street father, blundering into her sisters' love-affairs and rearranging them with crude, unscrupulous success, she swings the picture along in her gauche and graceful stride. The competence of the director, Mr Henry Koster, matches hers: a kind of national value emerges from the *schwarmerei* – it is all Fifth Avenue and girlish freedom – tea at the Waldorf and cold, clear New York spring.

Black Eyes is slower, dingier, really more sentimental. Hollywood has tampered with Mlle Simone Simon's acting, and even her appearance: she gives the impression of having been smudged. It is on M. Harry Baur that we depend – of course, not in vain – for our pleasure, on M. Baur and the odd, outmoded plot which takes us back in memory nearly twenty years. Seduction in the early cinema was always a serious and nearly always an unsuccessful business – a matter of galloping horses, lariats and pistol-shots, or else of gipsy singers and champagne. *Black Eyes* belongs to the champagne school. The climax is reached when the young girl, Mlle Simon, is shut in a restaurant's private room with a lustful banker and a buffet large enough for a battalion, while her father – he has kept from her all these years the knowledge that he is a head waiter – palpitates outside the door. First the gipsies emerge, jingling with spangles and tips, then one by one the waiters – has she taken wine? are they still safely at table? – at last the anxious parent can contain himself no longer and breaks in . . . I enjoyed this picture. The cinema has lost some of its charm since those naïve days, and I could not help feeling a little wistful watching the elaborate surgical preparations for a seduction – the practised movements of waiters like nurses round an operating-table, everybody and everything assigned an exact part from the insinuating musical harridans to the chosen vintage, until the climax – the dirty look and the turning of the key. M. Baur, too, is a great enough actor to lend what might otherwise seem a somewhat grotesque situation genuine suspense. No mockery can survive those heavy pouched eyes set in the antique turtle face: they convey an abysmal experience of human nature: and we are reminded as we watch that turtles are said to survive for many hundred years.

How the financial crisis has improved English films! They have lost their tasteless Semitic opulence and are becoming – English. *Inspector Hornleigh* is a routine picture, the first of a series, starring Mr Gordon Harker as the Inspector and Mr Alastair Sim as his incapable subordinate, and it nearly deserves to be classed with the Chans and the Motos. The opening shots – the murder in the squalid lodging and the stamp auction with the row of poker faces and the elaborately mute bids – are not only good cinema, they are good English cinema, as national as a shot, say from a Feyder, a de Mille or a Pommer. But the picture doesn't quite maintain that realistic level: there are too many bogus exteriors and menacing shadows, talk, and the murderer's motives remain hopelessly obscure at the end.

The Spectator (7 April 1939)

Three Smart Girls Grow Up (USA, Universal, 1938) Dir.: Henry Koster. Cast: Deanna Durbin, Nan Grey, Charles Winninger, Helen Parrish, Robert Cummings, William Lundigan.

Black Eyes (Les Yeux Noirs) (France, Milo Films, 1935) Dir.: Victor Tourjansky. Cast: Simone Simon, Harry Baur, Jean-Pierre Aumont. (US title: *Dark Eyes*)

Inspector Hornleigh (GB, Twentieth-Century Fox, 1939) Dir.: Eugene Ford. Cast: Gordon Harker, Alastair Sim, Hugh Williams, Steve Geray, Wally Patch, Edward Underdown, Gibb McLaughlin, Ronald Adam.

Hotel Imperial · The Three Musketeers

Perhaps it is because I associate the name Miranda with an old family donkey which used to take the washing to the laundry on Saturdays that I cannot enter wholeheartedly into Paramount's enthusiasm for their new imported star. 'The most glamorous woman in the world comes to the screen at last! Beautiful . . . exciting . . . Isa Miranda . . . Men drank to her loveliness and marched off to die! Her love sealed the fate of armies! . . . Generals moved armies to be near her!' We are told that D'Annunzio rushed home to write poems after he had seen her on the screen, and that Mascagni held up the rehearsal of an opera to lead the orchestra impromptu through a piece she loved: it seems horribly flat after all that to write for this sober and reliable journal one's little prosaic piece describing the long, gaunt face, the husky Marlene accent, and the slinky feathery dress. And the acting? Oh, well, I don't think it can have been the acting which sent D'Annunzio to his poetry. Miranda (forgive me if I smile, remembering that other long, awkward, friendly face) is not a Duse.

As for the picture, it is a very competent rehash by Robert Florey of the story Pommer directed so brilliantly in 1926 with Pola Negri: you may remember Sucha, the small Galician town, captured four times by the Russians, three times by the Austrians: the faded elegance of the hotel which caters alternately for the staff of two armies – the portrait of Franz Josef is quickly changed for the portrait of Nicholas, the order for cutlets is cancelled in favour of beef. An Austrian officer who has been on patrol returns to find the town fallen again; he is hidden in the hotel by the porter and the chambermaid and dressed as a waiter: a traitor from the Austrian Staff arrives with the plans for the counter-attack, is killed in his room by the fugitive, who escapes to the Austrian lines, and the girl is about to face a Russian firing-squad when – tanks go over the top, cavalry charge, bombing squadrons take off, and all the old hocus-pocus of the last-minute rescue is set going with a grotesque mechanized elaboration which must make Griffith turn in his retirement. I miss the old finale when the chambermaid was decorated before the troops and kissed on the cheek by the Commander-in-Chief – we have grown a little more wary in these days of heroics. And there are other alterations

– this chambermaid is not a real chambermaid, but an actress who is trying to discover an officer who betrayed her sister: have we grown more snobbish? And I seem to remember that the old film was full of charming central European humiliations, and there was no Don Cossack choir (the first time on any screen), and it was economical and shoddy and convincing, and Negri scrubbed the steps to the manner born instead of slinking around, like Miranda, singing huskily and drinking champagne.

All the same, the picture has merits – Mr Gene Lockhart, for instance, as the timid and heroic hall porter; Mr Ray Milland until he has to speak, looks just right, muddy and tired and desperate – it is the waiter's uniform and love which spoils all; Mr Carroll Naish is excellent as the vulgar, cynical, amusing spy, and the whole heroic picture warms into first-class comedy, with Mr Reginald Owen as the Russian General who paints. Even the dialogue comes to life as when he phones headquarters, after recapturing Sucha, 'How dare you bombard the civilian population, when it lives in such picturesque houses?' or rebukes the spy on his last spectacular entrance for 'an increasing tendency towards melodrama in your opening lines'. And for one glorious moment the hearts of all old lovers of the cinema are elated at the sight of Von Seyffertitz's narrow white photogenic features bobbing speechlessly up like memory out of a black cloak. Yes, for the unexacting the picture has its moments.

Of *The Three Musketeers* I was unable to endure more than half an hour. Somebody has had the idea of trying to give this old drab of stage and screen a new life with the help of the Ritz Brothers – but their hideous performance lends only a nervous monkey-gland twitching to the corpse. Everybody shouts to drown the music, and the old old story is got through rapidly and perfunctorily between the awful spells of buffoonery.

The Spectator (14 April 1939)

Hotel Imperial (USA, Paramount, 1939) Dir.: Robert Florey. Cast: Isa Miranda, Ray Milland, J. Carroll Naish, Reginald Owen, Gene Lockhart, Gustav Von Seyffertitz, Albert Dekker.

The Three Musketeers (USA, Twentieth-Century Fox, 1939) Dir.: Allan Dwan.

Cast: Don Ameche, The Ritz Brothers, Binnie Barnes, Joseph Schildkraut, Lionel Atwill, Miles Mander, Gloria Stuart, John Carradine. (GB title: *The Singing Musketeer*)

Idiot's Delight · Beach Picnic · They Drive By Night

It is possible that Mr Sherwood as a film-writer does small credit to Mr Sherwood as a dramatist; I have not seem his plays, but *Idiot's Delight* has exactly the same pseudo-qualities as *The Petrified Forest*, a moral pretentiousness, a kind of cellophaned intellectuality. They are all supposed to make one think, these windy abstractions, the literary quotations, the little scraps of popular philosophy. The introduction in one film of a realistic killer and in the other of a rather less realistic air raid does not alter the fact that we are in a Sparkenbroke world in which literature, passed through the filter of a naïve mind, is a substitute for character. Mr Eliot once remarked that the metaphysical poets experienced thought as directly as the scent of a rose, but Mr Sherwood and his kind seem to experience a rose as dimly and indirectly as a thought.

The plot of *Idiot's Delight* is by now well known. Padded out for the screen with a long, rambling, not unamusing prologue, it loses all grip at the very point where the play started, in the winter-sports hotel perched over a military aerodrome at the start of a European war. We have the usual set of representative characters, a munition-maker, a cancer expert, a sentimental lefty, a hoofer with his chorus-girls, young English honeymooners. 'Jimmy feels he must do his bit,' the child-wife remarks as they leave for England and the dialogue is all on that level – it either reads like a war poster or a peace poster ('Wings of Death' is what the feverish, all-for-love Communist calls a bomber), or else like a passage from Dr Hiram Q. Entwhistle's *World's Greatest Philosophers for Everyman*. In the end everybody escapes, except the Communist, whom we gather has been obscurely shot off-stage, the hoofer, and the girl he had met years ago in variety and who is now unconvincingly in back projection all around while they swing a tune. Why? Nobody knows: the play has no theme – except the widely held notion that war is unpleasant, and no character is given any personal life against the too important background – if one can refer to the bad models and worse back projections as important. Mr Clark Gable does his best, but Miss Norma Shearer adds to the heavy saturated ennui the weight of a far too powerful personality. Over-acting could hardly go further. The programme is saved by one of the best Disneys for years – the adventures of Pluto with a rubber sea-horse, coy, flippant and aerated.

The resurrection of the English film continues. In another twelve months we may find ourselves pursuing English films into obscure cinemas in the Edgware Road. *They Drive by Night* is a murder-story set against an authentic background of dance palaces, public houses, seedy Soho clubs, and the huge wet expanse of the Great North Road, with its bungaloid cafés, the grinding gears, and the monstrous six-wheeled lorries plunging through the rain. Well acted by Mr Emlyn Williams as a young gaol-bird wanted for a murder he hasn't committed, and superbly acted by Mr Ernest Thesiger as Mr Hoover, the sedate, pedantic sex-maniac with the sloping, humble walk, the grasshopper head, and the abominable pride, it gets the realistic twist out of every situation. One remembers Mr Hoover expatiating on the crime in the public house – the most authentic pub conversation I have heard on the screen: Mr Hoover saluting the stray cat, 'Ah, you pretty thing! Ah, my subtle one!': the absurd formalities of the dance palace. Dialogue, acting and direction put this picture on a level with the French cinema – the settings for the first time in an English low-life story are not romanticized, and for once we are not conscious of the brooding auntie-like presence in Carlisle House – perhaps they didn't know what some of the words meant. Set beside this picture, Mr Sherwood's picture can be seen for the sham it is. *Idiot's Delight* begins vaguely with an idea, an idea that it is treating an important subject – war and peace; but war is only important in the sense that an elephant or a dowager is important, by size. The author of the English film has taken characters in a simple melodramatic situation and given them a chance to show with some intensity their private battlefields.

The Spectator (21 April 1939)

Idiot's Delight (USA, MGM, 1938) Dir.: Clarence Brown. Cast: Norma Shearer, Clark Gable, Edward Arnold, Burgess Meredith, Joseph Schildkraut, Laura Hope, Skeets Gallagher.
Beach Picnic (USA, 1939) Disney cartoon.
They Drive by Night (GB, Warners, 1939) Dir.: Arthur Woods. Cast: Emlyn Williams, William Hartnoll, Ernest Thesiger, Anna Konstam, Allan Jeayes, Antony Holles, Ronald Shiner.

The Four Feathers · The Sisters · Thanks for Everything

The story of *The Four Feathers* must be known by this time to everyone – four films have now been made of this ham-heroic tale, which describes how Lieutenant Harry Faversham, the Coward who resigned his commission at the start of the Sudanese War, disguised himself as a dumb Sangali and forced his brother officers to take back the white feathers they had sent him. What is new is the drive – and in the Sudanese sequences the conviction – of this new version. Far better than the American, it cannot fail to be one of the best films of the year. Even the thickest of the ham – the old veterans discussing the Crimea in the Faversham home, among the portraits of military ancestors – goes smoothly down, savoured with humour and satire. For almost the first time the huge ambitious Denham studios have produced something better than a mouse.

On the screen a ham story doesn't matter. *The Sisters*, too, is ham and even more conventional – the girl who marries a hard-drinking journalist who loves her, but loves his freedom more. The pathos is very familiar – the husband returns drunk on the evening when his wife intends to tell him she is pregnant: they quarrel on Christmas Day beside the Christmas-tree. The San Francisco earthquake is thrown effectively in as makeweight, there is a tiny, timid sketch of a brothel which probably passed our universal aunts as a happy picture of family life, but the main situation is as old as the cinema

– you remember it in *Cimarron* – the husband who rides away and goes on loving all the time. But, as I say, ham doesn't matter: *The Sisters* is worth seeing for the sake of the adroit period direction and the fragile, pop-eyed acting of Miss Bette Davis.

So in *The Four Feathers* the plot hardly matters: what is important is the colour, which is almost invariably pleasant and sometimes gives a shock of pleasure such as we have not experienced since the moment in *Becky Sharp* when the scarlet-cloaked cavalry poured out by the dark Brussels street on the road to Waterloo. What is important is nocturnal London smoking up through Faversham's grey windows: the close-up of mulberry bodies straining at the ropes along the Nile: the cracked umber waste round the dried-up wells: the vultures with their grimy serrated Lisle-street wings dropping like weighted parachutes. It is impossible to divide the credit between Mr Zoltan Korda, the director, who has wiped out the disgrace of *Sanders of the River*, and Mr R.C. Sherriff, author of the film-play. They seem to have perfectly fulfilled each other's intentions – as Riskin and Capra did in the old days. We forget the silly plot when the voice repeats monotonously, 'Load, present, fire', behind the black smoke of the burning zariba: when the blinded man, the only survivor of his company, cries for his brother officer, and at every cry the vultures rise squawking from their meal and settle again. The picture is finely acted by Mr John Clements and Mr Ralph Richardson, and Miss June Duprez not only looks lovely, but also holds her own with these first-class actors.

This is, I fear, a week of monotonous praise. *Thanks for Everything* is the funniest film I can remember seeing for many months, with something of the old Kauffman touch. It is a great deal in these days to be made to laugh at the sight of a man in a gas-mask. An advertising agency through a competition discover a 100 per cent average American (whom they bilk of the prize so as to keep even his income average). By watching his reactions they are able to predict with uncanny accuracy movements of public taste. The representative of a European Power asks them to discover what would induce the American public to fight:

the wretched man is quarantined with an imaginary disease, supplied through specially printed papers with imaginary news, but remains unstirred by attacks on Embassies, tourists, trade. Only when an imaginary air raid is ingeniously staged for his benefit does he react – embarrassingly. Adolphe Menjou walks through this ingenious and witty film with a kind of brazen efficiency, followed dubiously and protestingly by Jack Oakie as his henchman.

The Spectator (28 April 1939)

The Four Feathers (GB, London Films, 1939) Dir.: Zoltan Korda. Cast: John Clements, Ralph Richardson, June Duprez, C. Aubrey Smith, Allan Jeayes, Jack Allen, John Lurie, Donald Gray, Henry Oscar.

The Sisters (USA, Warners, 1938) Dir.: Anatole Litvak. Cast: Bette Davis, Errol Flynn, Anita Louise, Ian Hunter, Donald Crisp, Beulah Bondi, Jane Bryan, Alan Hale, Dick Foran, Henry Travers, Patric Knowles, Lee Patrick, Harry Davenport.

Thanks for Everything (USA, Twentieth-Century Fox, 1939) Dir.: William A. Seiter. Cast: Jack Oakie, Adolphe Menjou, Arleen Whelan, Jack Haley, Tony Martin, Binnie Barnes, George Barbier.

Wuthering Heights · La Bête Humaine

How much better they would have made *Wuthering Heights* in France. They know there how to shoot sexual passion; but in this Californian-constructed Yorkshire, among the sensitive neurotic English voices, sex is cellophaned; there is no egotism, no obsession. This Heathcliff would never have married for revenge (Mr Olivier's nervous, breaking voice belongs to balconies and Verona and romantic love), and one cannot imagine the ghost of this Cathy weeping with balked passion outside the broken window: Miss Merle Oberon cannot help making her a very normal girl. The plot has been simplified (quite reasonably) to cover only one generation: the minor characters have been tidied up or away: and darkness, darkness most of the time, takes the place of the original's disquieting passion. Candle-flames flicker, windows blow in draughts, monstrous shadows lie across the indifferent faces of the actors, all to lend significance to a rather dim story which would not have taxed the talents of Mr Ben Hecht to have invented himself. Perhaps Mr Goldwyn, who has a bold mind, realized what was needed, for he chose the admirable director of *Dead End*, and the fault may not be altogether Wyler's. There is Hecht's script to be considered – and the cast of sensitive and distinguished Britons. So a lot of reverence has gone into a picture which should have been as coarse as a sewer. Some readers may remember *Orage*, a not very distinguished French film: the lovers in the stifling inn room beating off flies, lying about among the soiled clothes without the will or wish to go down for meals. Something of that carnality was needed here: the sentimental rendezvous under a crag where Heathcliff and Cathy used to play as children is not a substitute. The whole picture is *Keepsake* stuff.

La Bête Humaine is a very different matter: Zola's story of a sadistic maniac may not be much more plausible, but Renoir aided by a magnificent cast gets right underneath the plot – so that again and again we hear the ghost in the cellarage: as when Jean Gabin, as the maniac, questions Simone Simon about the murder to which she has been an unwilling accomplice (the murder of a former lover by her jealous husband), the very gentle twitching of the eyebrows as the stifled excitement begins to work, the uneasy movements of the mouth, the strained, too casual, voice seeking details: 'And how many times did he strike?' Gabin gives an impeccable performance. Watch him after the murder of the girl as he pauses by the mirror on the bourgeois sideboard – the relaxed muscles, the unobtrusive weakening of the mouth, the appalling sense of melancholy satiety. And Mlle Simon, too, acts with intensity the little, sensual, treacherous wife. Pitiably ineffective in *Les Yeux Noirs*, she is helped here by a cameraman who knows how to deal with the coarse black electric hair, the snub nose, the rather African features. But *La Bête Humaine* is more a director's than an actor's picture – a director who knows how to get the most out of the everyday life of his characters, the routine of their work – in this case the immediate surroundings of a great railway station: all the small incidents which English directors cut out of a script because they are not 'on the story line' and do not advance the plot. As if a plot mattered at all except as a dramatized illustration of a character and a way of life. The picture opens with Gabin and his taciturn, anxious fireman (a lovely piece of acting) on the footplate of the Paris-Havre express, and closes in the reverse direction – sidings flowing back into fields. That is easy: it has been done before, though not so well: what is most deft is the way in which Renoir works the depot and a man's job into every scene – conversations on platforms, in washrooms and canteens, views from the station master's window over the steaming metal waste: the short, sharp lust worked out in a wooden platelayer's shed among shunted trucks under the steaming rain.

The *Paris*, in which this picture is shown, is a new, charming and unpretentious theatre: but why have the architects chosen white walls and a white ceiling, which reflect all the light there is and destroys the stereoscopic effect of exteriors and the screen as completely as would a row of floodlights.

The Spectator (5 May 1939)

Wuthering Heights (USA, Samuel Goldwyn, 1939) Dir.: Wiliam Wyler. Cast: Laurence Olivier, Merle Oberon, Hugh Williams, David Niven, Flora Robson, Leo G. Carroll, Donald Crisp, Geraldine Fitzgerald, Cecil Kellaway, Miles Mander.

La Bête Humaine (France, Paris Films, 1938) Dir.: Jean Renoir. Cast: Jean Gabin, Simone Simon, Julien Carette, Fernand Ledoux, Jean Renoir. (US title: *The Human Beast*)

The Oklahoma Kid · The Lone Ranger (Episode One) · Tail Spin

I open the only Western I have at hand, and come immediately on one of those classic sentences (Hardy's phrase about the President of the Immortals is a familiar example) in which an author's whole way of writing and thinking is crystallized. '"There's certainly a pile of hell being raised about Cougar," Blaze commented thoughtfully.' That expresses about everything – the heavy decorative gun-holsters and the ten-gallon hats, the wooden sidewalks and the saloons, the double-crossing sheriff, the corrupt judge, the fine old man with white whiskers and the girl in gingham, and the final 'slug feast' – to borrow a Western phrase – among the toppling gas-lamps.

The Oklahoma Kid is a good specimen of new-style Western, more refined than the old silent ones with their rapes and hair-breadth escapes (it is typical of a certain intellectuality nowadays that the only rescuers here arrive too late): it hasn't the expensive finish of *The Virginian* or *The Plainsman,* and Mr James Cagney, the gunman with a social conscience, takes perhaps a little less kindly to the big hat and the tight breeches and the intense sexual purity than Mr Humphrey Bogart as the bad man in black. But Mr Cagney can do nothing which is not worth watching. On his light hoofer's feet, with his quick nervous hands and his magnificent unconsciousness of the camera, he can pluck distinction out of the least promising part – and this part has plenty of meat. A pile of hell is certainly being raised around Cougar – or, rather, the new Tulsa city, built by pioneers in the Cherokee strip of Oklahoma, where the bad man has established by trickery his monopoly of vice centres, and has corrupted the law with bought juries. There's a lot of gun-play around the sinister Mr Bogart before he frames the fine old man with white whiskers and has him lynched by saloon loungers. That's when the Oklahoma Kid begins to make good – the dead man's worthless son with a price on his head takes the law into his own hands and disposes of his father's murderers one after another. His brother is the new reforming Sheriff, who, at the end of the last magnificent slug feast with Mr Bogart, dies with a bullet in his stomach after telling the Kid that he has procured his pardon. So the Kid is free to marry his brother's girl, the dumb plain creature in gingham with little filly ways – you expect her to whinny whenever she opens her mouth. (In the old days it would have been the no-good who died nobly, ginghams then were more careful of the stock they raised.) Apart from one scene in which Mr Cagney sings 'Rock-a-bye-Baby' rather unconvincingly to an Indian papoose, this is a direct and competent picture.

The Lone Ranger is a serial which has swept the States. Before it finishes there will be a bigger pile of hell raised than in any known Western – there are big twenty-minute gobbets of riding and gunning every week. The first instalment, called *Hi-yo, Silver,* introduces the now-famous call of the masked ranger to his white steed – a cry uttered, often in the most unsuitable circumstances, in an odd and congested, rather Harvard voice. Who is the Lone Ranger, sworn to avenge his comrades, who are ambushed by the villain in the first instalment? We shall not know until the last. Meanwhile the first chapter lines up the characters of this immense saga: the chief villain, a snakey hound who is posing with false papers as the Federal Commissioner of a new territory; his henchman, small, treacherous and dirty, who betrays first the rangers and then the farmers who have risen against the tyranny of the false Commissioner; the hero, his horse, a few assorted Texans, and the girl in gingham – or so I suppose, for she has not yet had a word to say. There has been no time; events have moved with such rapidity. The hero has escaped a massacre and a firing-squad already, and we leave him with his guns empty, the farmers' stockade blown up by gunpowder, falling under the charging hooves of the villain's cavalry.

Tail Spin is an embarrassing story of female comradeship at an air carnival. As usual in these pictures, you can spot the mortality types from the start – pale, long-legged, uxorious creatures who stare moonily at each other in canteens. 'She just flies,' as one woman says of the doomed female ace, 'to be close to him.'

The Spectator (12 May 1939)

The Oklahoma Kid (USA, Warners, 1939) Dir.: Lloyd Bacon. Cast: James Cagney, Humphrey Bogart, Rosemary Lane, Donald Crisp, Ward Bond, Harvey Stephens, Edward Pawley, Charles Middleton.

The Lone Ranger (USA, Republic, 1939 – 15 episodes) Directors: William Witney, John English. Cast: Lee Powell, Chief Thundercloud, Herman Brix, Lynne Roberts, Stanley Andrews, William Farnum.

Tail Spin (USA, Twentieth-Century Fox, 1939) Dir.: Roy del Ruth. Cast: Alice Faye, Constance Bennett, Joan Davis, Nancy Kelly, Charles Farrell, Jane Wyman, Kane Richmond, Harry Davenport, Wally Vernon.

JAMAICA INN · J'ÉTAIS UNE AVENTURIÈRE · THE LONDONERS

This passionate, full-blooded yarn could only have been conceived by a young authoress of considerable refinement. The drinking, leching, blaspheming, Cornish wreckers are reminiscent of the noisier characters in Shakespeare acted at a girls' school – the well-cushioned Falstaff with the voice of beloved Miss Peridew, the games-mistress, and tight-laced Pistol from the sixth form. But, after all, we are not concerned with the story: a bad story is a small handicap to a good director or a good actor, and there must have been something in Miss Du Maurier's novel which caught the attention of Mr Laughton and Mr Hitchcock. Mr Laughton may have seen in one character the germ of his own magnificent and vinous portrait of a Regency buck, Sir Humphrey Pengallan, the secret leader of the wreckers. With his nose adeptly reconstructed into a little cocky beak and his too familiar mannerisms sternly checked, he gives a superb performance, though I am reminded uneasily when I write this of those too perceptive dramatic critics who are able to recognize genius even when it speaks Yiddish, for, owing presumably to the acoustics of the cinema, no one where I was seated was able to hear more than scattered words of the dialogue.

It is more difficult to know why Mr Hitchcock embarked on this bogus costume-piece and submitted himself to a producer. There is only one Hitchcock incident here in embryo, when the pseudo-wrecker, saved by the heroine from his comrades who are hanging him, takes refuge with her in the house of the nearest magistrate, and he, of course, is Pengallan, the wreckers' leader. This situation translated into contemporary terms might well have been the high-spot of a Hitchcock chase, with rather more care taken over the realistic details; but costume has so confused Mr Hitchcock that he allows the hero, wet through by a long swim, to borrow a tight-fitting officer's uniform from Pengallan which fits him like a glove. This is only one example of frequent failures in imagination which sometimes caused untimely laughter from the audience – laughter which swelled as the film dragged on to the absurd rape and the cavalry to the rescue, and stout booted Pengallan climbing backwards up the shrouds for his suicidal jump. Mr Hitchcock's talent has always been for the surprise situation, but here, perhaps because he had to stick closely to a conventional and sentimental tale, perhaps the presence of a producer cramped him, there are no surprises – and no suspense: we can see everything that will happen half an hour away.

The unsatisfactory picture has been lavishly produced, though the whole set of the sinister inn creaks like its own signboard. No expense has been spared, and I was irresistibly reminded of an all-star charity matinée. A face looks round a door – and it is Horace Hodges, or Stephen Haggard, Hey Petrie, Clare Greet, George Curzon, Jeanne de Casalis (so good of them, we feel, to give their services for the Fresh-Air Fund). Mr Emlyn Williams has a rather longer part as a wrecker, but that plump Celtic face lamentably failed to make my flesh creep; Mr Robert Newton is the hero, the naval officer who is playing spy, but I find this young actor with his gasps and glittering eyes peculiarly unsympathetic; and there is a brand-new heroine, Miss Maureen O'Hara, who leaves (it is really not her fault) a rather comic impression: she, too, finds a perfectly fitting costume in the Squire's house, and the smart Regency dress doesn't look well at midnight on the Cornish coast. Only Mr Leslie Banks matches Mr Laughton as an actor and introduces some sense of real evil into a girl's dream of violent manhood.

The new French film at the Academy, about jewel thieves and a girl (Mlle Edwige Feuillière) who turns over a new leaf and is blackmailed by her old friends, is lightweight, but competent and amusing, and *The Londoners*, which is shown with it, one of the best documentaries Realist Films have yet produced. It celebrates the jubilee of the L.C.C., and the opening sequence, with its Doré slides of Victorian London and its dramatised characters, the corpse-washer who is also a midwife, and the sewage men at work under the walls of the fever hospital, compares ironically as a period piece with Miss Du Maurier's feuilleton.

The Spectator (19 May 1939)

Jamaica Inn (GB, Mayflower, 1939) Dir.: Alfred Hitchcock. Cast: Charles Laughton, Maureen O'Hara, Robert Newton, Emlyn Williams, Leslie Banks, Wylie Watson, Marie Ney, Mortland Graham.
J'étais une Aventurière (France) Dir.: Raymond Bernard. Cast: Edwige Feuillière.
The Londoners (GB, Realist Film Unit, 1939) Dir.:John Taylor.

Men in Danger · Spare Time · Health of a Nation · An Elephant Never Forgets

I am getting a little tired of that word 'documentary'. It has a dry-as-dust sound: we think of incomprehensible machinery revolving before the camera-eye: earnest 'expert' faces mouthing abstractions behind very polished and very empty desks: it carries a false air of impartiality, as much as to say 'this is what is – not what we think or feel'. But the best documentaries have never been like that: as long ago as Rotha's *Shipyard* they took political sides, and to call *The River* – or Wright's *Children at School* – documentary is about as meaningless as to call a sonnet documentary: they document the creator's mind, that is all.

So the personal element – the lyrical and the ironic – is the important thing in the documentaries which the GPO are sending to the World Fair. Only one of them might easily have belonged to the dry-as-dust order – Cavalcanti's *Men in Danger*, which begins as a factual record of occupational diseases and the methods used to minimise the danger. It is, at the start, frankly dull: information is being painstakingly conveyed. Then the horror begins to grip – the director as well as the audience. What will America think of these children working barefooted at the looms, in danger of cancer-creating oils? 'It is hoped,' we hear, 'to find a safer oil', and the laboratory assistant holds up his tentative test-tube, and the child pads back and forth. It is the atmosphere – and, alas, the country – of 'The Song of the Shirt'. Perhaps more horrifying still are the shots of monotony – and of the means taken to alleviate it: interminable trays of potted-meat jars passing before stooping, spotty girls: the information that in a biscuit factory the girls can sing to relieve the boredom and 'are allowed to choose their own songs'. *Allowed* – a word to make the angels weep. We see psychological researchers at work – the unimaginative theoretical faces, that can judge a worker's nervousness so much better by watching him knot string than by any human contact. We hear the lectures to miners' children on the safety-lamp: they wear already the steel shock-helmets and the grime of the future.

Next *Spare Time* by Humphrey Jennings, a study of how the industrial worker spends his off-hours: greyhounds, pigeons, bicycles and bands: we see the Victoria Prize Band – Morris Troop – hoisting a gauche Britannia up among the twirling brass and batons in the withered, hemmed-in recreation-ground: zoos and toy boats, cinemas and wrestling: we watch the miner's leisure dying out with daylight: the casual, friendly choir gathering round the pianist, trying the first notes as they take off their overcoats, settling in to the oratorio – and the sad sedate singing is carried on over long sweeping shots of small confectioners and window-gazing lovers, the high tea, the darkening windows and the pubs closing, and the night-shift going on. Simply and without self-consciousness this film catches a mood of pity.

Cavalcanti's *Health of a Nation* is more ambitious and perhaps not quite so successful. The commentary, spoken by Mr Ralph Richardson, is far too reminiscent of *The River*. A pity, because the visual and sound effects are magnificent. The picture shows the industrialization of England, and the measures taken to clean up afterwards: a lyrical counterpart of *Men in Danger*, and a contradiction. In the latter we saw the latest mechanical safety devices, but here they seem oddly lacking. Where are the robot men in their heavy boots and gas-masks and protective spectacles? The most effective feature is the soundtrack: for the first time a director has allowed his sound really to rip: the roar of a furnace, the terrific crack of a pick underground, the blast of sparking steel – they explode in the ear.

An Elephant Never Forgets, with Oliver Hardy. Mr Hardy thought he could bring it off alone – he even tries to be dignified and pathetic, reading the Declaration of Independence – but it won't work. When his hat is flattened under an enormous hoof and he lifts it with the expression of patient stifled fury, we look sadly round for blinking twisting Laurel, and Zenobia, the elephant, is no substitute.

The Spectator (26 May 1939)

Men in Danger (GB, GPO Film Unit, 1939) Dir.: Pat Jackson. Producer: Alberto Cavalcanti.
Spare Time (GB, GPO Film Unit, 1939) Dir.: Humphrey Jennings.
Health of a Nation (GB, GPO Film Unit, 1939) Dir.: Alberto Cavalcanti.
An Elephant Never Forgets (USA, Hal Roach, 1939) Dir.: Gordon Douglas. Cast: Oliver Hardy, Harry Langdon, Billie Burke. (aka: *Zenobia*)

Union Pacific · The Lone Ranger (Episode Four)

'The guns which Gary Cooper carried as Wild Bill Hickok in *The Plainsman* bark again in *Union Pacific*. Owned by de Mille, they were taken down from the peg in his office, where they had been hanging for two years, and buckled on Joel McCrea.' So runs the publicity sheet, and the little reverent anecdote will be believed by anyone who has had any personal contact with film-makers. They have an inexhaustible fund of admiration, and when they encounter a big story – full of history and high-mindedness like the Crusades or the Ten Commandments or the construction of a railroad – their reverence falls with the adhesive effect of a tin of treacle. This latest de Mille epic contains all the Excelsior qualities we expect in his work – that sense of a Salvationist drum beating round the next corner – but it is never as funny as *The Crusades* and he has lost his touch with crowds, the stamp of a broad, popular genius who used to remind us a little of Frith.

Apparently the Union Pacific was constructed in a race against the Central Pacific. The motives are extraordinarily obscure, but a bad businessman apparently stood to gain by delaying the UP and helping the CP. As both railways were going, eventually, to join with the rival directors amicably knocking in a golden sleeper, it doesn't seem to the ordinary spectator to matter a great deal where they meet. This casts rather a damper over the suspense, over the murders and the Indian massacre and the wrecking of a train and the robbery of a pay-roll – all laboriously engineered by the bad man with the idea that the complimentary speeches shall be made at one obscure siding rather than another. Mr Joel McCrea plays a 'trouble-shooter' – a kind of Western G-man, whose job it is to see that law and order are kept all down the line. One of his old army friends is a gambler employed to delay the construction, and we can recognize him at once as a mortality type, one of the gay reckless kind who prepare for a far, far better thing all through a long film. This one can hardly fail to die, since he marries the railway girl Mr McCrea loves, who is acted – for want of a better word – by Miss Barbara Stanwyck. Paramount supply us with a sketch of this actress's career, which could hardly be bettered by the sourest critic. 'Beauty opened doors for her and talent got her jobs. By fifteen she was in the Ziegfeld Follies. In such vehicles as *A Night in Spain* and *A Night in Venice* she was seen hanging from chandeliers composed of herself and other beauties.' The trouble is that there are no chandeliers in *Union Pacific*, and Miss Stanwyck has no chance of displaying her curious talent or her beauty. She does display the most bogus brogue I have ever heard on the screen. Lines like 'You have turned the night to fear and the wind from warm to cold' sound a bit spiritual to a girl used to hanging upside-down. The cast is enormous, with a little real acting from Mr Akim Tamiroff as a Mexican bodyguard; Mr Lynne Overman peeps oddly out of a thicket of pioneering whiskers, and all sorts of funny elfish men with black beards and top hats, looking like Grumpy or Dopey, turn up inappositely at intervals and refer to each other as General Dodge or General Casement or General Grant.

I have missed three episodes of *The Lone Ranger*, and the synopsis at the beginning of the fourth doesn't help much. I last saw the Ranger, his guns empty, falling under the charging hooves of the villain's cavalry at the entrance to the fort set up by the oppressed Texan farmers – there don't seem to be any Texan farmers any more, the Ranger is galloping – 'Hi-yo, Silver!' – in pursuit of Joan (who is Joan?), who is riding into a trap set by Keston (who is Keston?). It doesn't really matter: that trap's evaded in the first two minutes and another one is ready. 'Fetch me Black Taggart', and even a little later 'Looks like they're torturing someone', one of the Ranger's troop comments behind a boulder; at the end of this episode the Ranger, knocked out by a stone and covered by guns, is unconscious at the feet of his enemies, and a hand is already stretched out to tear away the mask – 'Now we shall know who the Lone Ranger is.' I doubt it. This week: *The Steaming Cauldron*.

The Spectator (2 June 1939)

Union Pacific (USA, Paramount, 1939) Dir.: Cecil B. de Mille. Cast: Joel McCrea, Barbara Stanwyck, Robert Preston, Brian Donlevy, Akim Tamiroff, Lynne Overman, Anthony Quinn, Robert Barrat, Stanley Ridges, Henry Kolker, Evelyn Keyes, Regis Toomey.

The Story of Vernon and Irene Castle · La Femme du Boulanger

It's no use going to the new Astaire-Rogers film in a hard-boiled mood – it is all, as Henry James said of *La Dame aux Camélias*, champagne, young love and tears. The scene is pre-war America and war-time France, but you won't find those countries on any map, any more than you will find any stage history in this particular Vernon and Irene Castle. It must have been an odd experience for Mrs Castle herself, who acted as technical adviser, to watch her own life lifted out of reality altogether – her first meeting with Vernon Castle at New Rochelle becoming a period piece with funny bathing-costumes and grotesque blazers; failure in America, ruin in Paris, sudden overwhelming success when they danced for their dinner at the Café de Paris, becoming light, sad, humorous and agile like the long black spider legs of Fred Astaire; the War, Vernon Castle snatching leave in Paris from the RFC, the instructor's appointment in Texas, the crash due to a novice's silly mistake – all the horror and finality of loss becoming something sentimental, pathetic, tear-jerking, as the faithful retainer comforts Irene Castle: 'There's got to be something of him in every boy and girl who gets up to dance', and the dream figures move through the hotel garden in the Castle Walk. It must have been a bit creepy watching one's own life become so fictional.

This is not to say it's a poor film – it's an admirable film, perhaps the best the marvellous couple have made since *Gay Divorce*. We can accept the sentimental convention because it is never broken: no other world than the film world of eternal fidelity, picturesque starvation and meteoric success is ever held up to it for comparison. The whole affair takes wings, and what do we care if it is through the inane? The tiny black and white figures dance over an immense map of the States (thirty-five cities in twenty-eight days) sowing a crop of dancers everywhere, shot from a lunar angle: or they are whirled in diminishing persepctive down Broadway, or dance, with an effect of triviality and gaiety, against a background of spangles. Perhaps the picture is at its best when they are alone in this way, without people acting, an abstraction.

Nothing could be more different from the method of M. Pagnol, whose latest picture, *La Femme du Boulanger*, is the best entertainment to be seen at the moment in any cinema. He uses no pasteboard and as few professional actors as he can manage: he planks his camera down in a Provençal village and shoots in brick and stone. A new baker has come to the village, and the inhabitants gather for the first baking – even the silly old lecherous Marquis, with his plus-fours and his patronage. The oven-door creaks open and the baker takes a sniff – no, another two minutes. The suspense is terrific: again the heavy door creaks: perfect: the village has obtained a good baker at last. But the baker is an old man with a young and sensual wife, who already at that baking has marked down her man – the Marquis's shepherd. She elopes in the early morning while the baker sleeps and the loaves burn. There is no more bread for the village – the baker drinks to drown his sorrow, and the inhabitants, who have been split into warring groups by quarrels about politics, religion, untrimmed trees, unite to bring back the wife and save their bread. Even the Curé makes up his quarrel with the school-teacher, who has told the children that Joan of Arc *believed* she heard voices. It is a long film with a small subject, but the treatment is so authentic that it seems over far too soon, and the acting is superb – Raimu as the pathetic, good-hearted old cuckold: Ginette Leclerc as the young wife with the thirsty bivalve mouth, and Robert Vattier as the Curé – a man of thin, hard principles with a discreet respect for wealth. How often in a French country church has one heard the kind of sermon he gives us here, with the precise, melodramatic gestures and the too carefully modulated voice. But the human actors are only part of the general setting – the well and the olive trees and the crude, crowded church and the Cercle Republicain with the tin advertisements, and the hunter going out in the dawn with his dog and his gun while the baker sleeps in his trough beside the oven.

The Spectator (9 June 1939)

The Story of Vernon and Irene Castle (USA, RKO, 1939) Dir.: H. C. Potter. Cast: Fred Astaire, Ginger Rogers, Edna May Oliver, Walter Brennan, Lew Fields, Etienne Girardot, Donald MacBride.

La Femme du Boulanger (France, Charles Pons, 1938) Dir.: Marcel Pagnol. Cast: Raimu, Ginette Leclerc, Robert Vattier, Charpin, Maximilienne. (US title: *The Baker's Wife*)

Goodbye Mr Chips · Louise · You Can't Cheat an Honest Man · The Good Old Days

Some of us feel unsympathetic to Mr Chips and the rosy sentimental view of an English public school, but there can be no doubt at all of the skill of this production. The whole picture has an assurance, bears a glow of popularity like the face of a successful candidate on election day. And it is wrong to despise popularity in the cinema – popularity there is a *value*, as it isn't in a book; films have got to appeal to a large undiscriminating public: a film with a severely limited appeal must be – to that extent – a bad film.

Nor, even to those of us whose ideas of a public school can best be expressed in terms of discomfort, cracked bells, stone stairs, bad food and inadequate amenities, is *Mr Chips* often embarrassing. The picture, it is true, opens earnestly among the mouldering courts of Brookfield, where a new master is spelling reverently out the inscription beneath the statue of the founder; but, on the whole, sentimentality is ably balanced by humour, the direction and acting are almost everything to be desired, and the school-song by Mr Richard Addinsell has the right banality and the right grim swing. Miss Greer Garson as Mr Chips's short-lived wife lifts the whole picture temporarily into – we are tempted to call it reality: common sense and tenderness, a sense of happiness too good to last – this is an atmosphere more easily recognizable than the cleanness, the earnestness, the quaintness of Brookfield.

Mr Chips would have gained from quick reviewing – one enjoys it enough at the time to feel as ungrateful this creeping back of the critical faculty which asks whether there is really any continuity in the chief character – any common experience between the young Chips (Mr Donat mustn't overdo his popular wide-eyed stare) asserting his authority with difficulty, the stuffy middle-aged timid Chips who falls in love on a Tyrolean mountain, the quite normal and too rejuvenated married Chips, and the quaint old creature with the straggle of white hair and the senile voice who haunts the school precincts and is brought back during the War to act as temporary Headmaster. The portrait is half caricature, half-straight – this is not Mr Donat's fault, but the author's, and the make-up man's. And why should the charming episode of Mr Chips's foreign walking tour be spoilt by a silly scene at a Vienna ball? Apparently he had carried his tails in his rucksack, and Miss Garson an elaborate evening gown on her bicycle.

Louise is a French film of Charpentier's opera with Miss Grace Moore. I know nothing about the music or the quality of the singing – but visually and dramatically it is one of the funniest films to be seen in London. It is all bacchanalia among the blossoms and situations whose grotesqueness is deliciously enhanced by the personality of the distinguished singer. Oh, the tiptoeings of Miss Moore, the sedate coquetry, the little trills and carollings, and the great stony teeth. And M. Georges Thill, the great tenor (is it?), with his plumpness and roguery and tiny moustache. Memories crowd back disjointedly of these artistic abandoned 'doings' in old Montmartre – Miss Moore's aged puritanical father turning over the little socks she wore when she was young, the magic phrases of the English captions – 'All around I see but laughter and light and joy', the scene in the garden – like one of those mauve amorous French postcards – when M. Thill kneels at her feet, pressing her hand against his cheek, among the dubious paper blossoms, while Miss Moore sings 'Ever since the day when unto thee I gave me', then floats away among the bowers, leaving him, plump and ecstatic, kissing her picture hat. Undoubtedly a film to be seen.

That Mr W.C. Fields appears in *You Can't Cheat an Honest Man* is its only recommendation. This story of an impecunious circus proprietor is unworthy of the magnificent voice 'drawn from the wood'. I am inclined to avoid a Max Miller film, but *The Good Old Days* has one Regency sequence of a pie-eating contest in a public-house which almost makes it worth a visit. The sight of seconds massaging the huge stomachs of the contestants – the voice of the referee tolling out the score, 'The Champion is starting his ninth pie, leading by four pies from the Camberwell Cannibal' – has a pleasant period grossness.

The Spectator (16 June 1939)

Goodbye Mr Chips (USA, MGM, 1939) Dir.: Sam Wood. Cast: Robert Donat, Greer Garson, John Mills, Paul Henreid, Austin Trevor, Milton Rosmer, Judith Furse, Terry Kilburn.

Louise (France, Société Parisienne, 1939) Dir.: Abel Gance. Cast: Grace Moore, Georges Thill, André Pernet.

You Can't Cheat an Honest Man (USA, Universal, 1939) Dir.: George Marshall. Cast: W.C. Fields, Edgar Bergen, Constance Moore, Mary Forbes, Thurston Hall, Charles Coleman, Edward Brophy.

The Good Old Days (GB, Warners, 1939) Dir.: Roy William Neill. Cast: Max Miller, Hal Walters, Kathleen Gibson, Allan Jeayes, Roy Emerton, H.F. Maltby.

Confessions of a Nazi Spy · Hôtel du Nord

Confessions of a Nazi Spy is an impressive piece of propaganda. Based on the recent spy trials in the United States, it adopts the techniques of *The March of Time* – between the fictional scenes there are spoken commentaries, maps and extracts from newsreels to give the impression of a sober news record. The moral is drawn by the Judge, who sentences the four prisoners that remain after Gestapo agents have removed the others against their own will, to the country they served. 'You are fortunate,' he tells them. 'Here we spread no sawdust on the surface of our prison yards.' (Propaganda appeals to the emotions, not the reason – otherwise it would be hard for us to forget the overcrowding, the brutality, the tear-gas and machine-guns we have learnt to associate with

American prison-yards in such films as *The Big House.*) Well, the war of nerves is on, and the Censor who refused last autumn to pass a *March of Time* issue criticizing the Munich Settlement now allows an actor made up as Dr Goebbels to refer to 'our glorious victory at Munich': he even gives the 'U' Certificate, which he refuses to most Westerns, to this picture of methodical violence and treachery. Our children must be allowed to hate, and we can really feel, when the Board of British Film Censors abandons the policy of appeasement, that it is really dead at last. So – repressing a slight shudder – let us give as whole-hearted a welcome as we can to this magnificently constructed engine-of-war.

The picture opens in Scotland where a middle-aged spinster acts as a forwarding agent between certain leaders of the Nazi Bund in the United States and the Ministries in Berlin. We watch the activities of Gestapo agents on board German liners and in the Teutonic beer-houses of New York: we are present at Bund summer camps, where young American boys *heil* Hitler and young girls recite their maternal duties to the State. Nothing is too dramatic to be convincing: the kidnapping of unwanted German-Americans and their transfer to the Fatherland by way of Hoboken Pier is managed with little fuss. All is muted, and the more creepy for that. Mr Paul Lukas gives a fine performance as the fanatical doctor at the head of the Bund who breaks down under examination and is betrayed to the Gestapo by his wife, and Mr Francis Lederer bursts his bonds of central European charm to play the stupid egocentric failure who ruins the whole spy system by his absurd co-operation. This is a magnificent performance, edged one feels, by hatred, for Mr Lederer is a Czech. 'It is terrific, daring', so he describes his schemes – and in the end gives everything away to the Federal Investigator who plays on his vanity. There is one moment of the finest imaginative acting when this stupid man, who has been successful in a minor job of work, finds himself suddenly accepted – by an impatient and contemptuous agent – on a beggarly salary of fifty dollars a month and listens to a long list of dangerous demands rapped out to his trapped and shifty face.

The method of this does impose a kind of reality – the reality of 'news'. The trouble is – none of us believes very deeply in news, and news anyway is concerned only with the big events, the march of an army corps and the elimination of a people. French directors at their best have always known the trick of presenting a more intimate reality: the horrible or the comic situation – in the hands of Duvivier or Clair – is made convincing, by its careful background of ordinary life going on, just as Madame Bovary's furious passion was caught up in the dust and cries of the cattle auction. So in *Hôtel du Nord* we believe in the desperate lovers and the suicide pact on the brass bed in the shabby room, just because of the bicyclists on the quay, the pimp quarrelling with his woman in another room, and the First-Communion party on the ground floor with its irrelevant and unsuitable conversation. And the French novelist taught the French cinema too the immense importance of the careful accessory: the ugly iron bridge down which the lovers silently and sadly emerge into our lives: the tuft of cotton-wool in the young man's ears which seems to speak of a whole timid and untidy life.

The Spectator (23 June 1939)

Confessions of a Nazi Spy (USA, Warners, 1939) Dir.: Anatole Litvak. Cast: Edward G. Robinson, Paul Lukas, Francis Lederer, George Sanders, Lya Lys, Henry O'Neill, Sig Rumann, James Stephenson.

Hôtel du Nord (France, SEDIF, 1938) Dir.: Marcel Carné. Cast: Annabella, Arletty, Louis Jouvet, Jean-Pierre Aumont, Bernard Blier, Jeanne Marken.

Beethoven · Peter the Great · This Man in Paris

The echoes of laughter at *Louise* have hardly died away when M. Abel Gance pops up again with another musical film, based on the last years of Beethoven's life. Pops up? No words could be less suitable to describe M. Gance, a kind of Victor Hugo of the screen – terrific storms blow out of his characters' cloaks, enormous chords bellow from the microphone: the actors gesture and moan and wring their hands in Gargantuan griefs, and the banal symbols of blossom and thunder and dawn, all shot with a fine pictorial sense, magnify still further the human emotions. Only once, I think, has M. Gance 'brought it off' and that was in his huge *Napoleon* (terrific, enormous, huge – one cannot avoid these adjectives). A vulgar and popular mind like M. Gance's can express itself best in tales of violent action, and Griffith, with whom M. Gance has much in common, never made the mistake of directing the lives and loves of intellectuals. In spite of M. Harry Baur's acting – that roughly carved monumental face never fails to convey a great reserve of power and when it drops into the hands it is as if a statue were to weep – this film never rises above the level of a cheap novelette – Beethoven's passion for Juliette Guicciardi and the fidelity of Teresa of Brunswick become words, two-penny-library words so that it is impossible not to laugh at the ubiquitous devotion of the suffering woman who is always cropping up in thunderstorms, in old mills, with rain-drenched clothes. There is a hideous vulgarity, indeed, about all these pictures based on composers' lives (we have already had Chopin, Mozart, Liszt); the human melodrama belittles the music all the time like programme notes, so that Beethoven's music becomes only a sentimental illustration to sentimental dialogue. 'That piece you have been playing – what is it?' 'The Moonlight Sonata.' Only once does M. Gance make his effect, and that is when Beethoven becomes deaf – the hideous grinding of atmospherics in the ear-drum followed by complete silence: the panorama of the silent smithy, the silent washerwomen, the silent birds, and then the jumble of selected sounds recalled by the imagination – one ring of steel, an isolated bird note, the slap of a wet cloth, a single laugh played over in the brain.

Peter the Great is the kind of picture Gance should be engaged in making – a boisterous violent tale. There have been no better battle scenes since *The Birth of a Nation*, and the Marxist interpretation of history gives a kind of contemporary vividness to the costume-piece. The defence of foreign experts, the defence of violence for social ends, the contempt for religion – these have the interest of modern controversy: only the sentimentality of the last scene a little jars when Stalin-Peter fills his pipe and watches with paternal devotion the awkward movements of his naked baby feeding among the Boyars. What is most effective – apart from the admirable photography (how dusty and shabby and real the costumes look!) – is the dramatic contrast between the old and sad and the new and vigorous, between the grotesque Boyars, bearded and solemn and superstitious, and the pastry-cook aide-de-camp to the Tsar, with his cheerful eye for a woman, his irreverence, and his parvenu laugh which sweeps through the picture like the high wind in *Storm Over Asia*.

This Man in Paris is an extremely competent, and sometimes very exciting, sequel to *This Man is News*, with Mr Barry K. Barnes, of course, as the crime reporter. Miss Valerie Hobson as his rather too comradely wife, and Mr Alastair Sim again acting everybody else off the set as the Scottish news-editor. The picture ends with the hint of yet another sequel: I only wish that either Mr Barnes or Miss Hobson would this time stay at home. Five years have passed since *The Thin Man*, and this particularly uxorious relationship of loving insults, hygenic sex, and raillery from twin-beds is period enough for *Punch*. If only the boyishness of Mr Barnes had got a little lined, and the bright breezy intelligence of Miss Hobson had become a little tarnished by these later thirties, how much more we should have enjoyed this care-free record of forgery and murder.

The Spectator (30 June 1939)

Beethoven (*Un Grand Amour de Beethoven*) (France, Général Production, 1937) Dir.: Abel Gance. Cast: Harry Baur. (US title: *Beethoven's Great Love*)

Peter the Great (USSR, Lenfilm, 1937) Dir.: Vladimir Petrov. Cast: Nikolai Simonov, Alla Tarasova, Nikolai Cherkassov.

This Man in Paris (GB, Pinebrook, 1939) Dir.: David MacDonald. Cast: Barry K. Barnes, Valerie Hobson, Alastair Sim, Edward Lexy, Garry Marsh.

Boy Slaves · Captain Fury

The summer doldrums are here at last, and the reviewer is faced with such dubious high-spots of entertainment as the latest pictures of Mr Bing Crosby (crooning to a new screen baby), Mr George Formby (as a private detective with the inevitable ukulele), and

Mr Douglas Fairbanks, jun. (saving the British Empire in an odd mix-up on the West Coast). Any films of merit there are just run on and on, and perhaps for once the reviewer may be allowed to give a refresher course and recall to memory: *Stage Coach*, the best directed film to be seen in London, a model of simplicity, by the man who made *The Informer*; *La Femme du Boulanger*, Pagnol's Provençal picture with Raimu at his finest as the grotesque pathetic cuckold; *Confessions of a Nazi Spy*, documentary technique applied excitingly to fiction; *The Story of Vernon and Irene Castle* – dancing with tears in the eyes; *This Man in Paris*, with light-hearted murder and the incomparable Alastair Sim; *Education de Prince*, a revival worth seeing for the sake of M. Louis Jouvet; *Peter the Great*, the jovial noisy Kremlin view of history; and *Hôtel du Nord*, a fine example of French realism, even though the story doesn't add up. If you've seen all these, you'll have to go farther afield and hunt down *Fra Diavolo*, the magnificent Laurel and Hardy opera, at the Star, Fulham; *Mayerling* and Mae West's first picture, *Night After Night*, in one programme at Brixton Astoria, and *Mr Deeds* at the Royal Court in Sloane Square.

The only new picture of any merit at all is *Boy Slaves* (a silly and suggestive title), which has been given an 'H' certificate by the Censor. I don't know why, unless a child's death from a bullet is more horrifying than a man's. Some of the Dead End Kids appear in this, but they have been diluted with weaker companions, and the terrific impact of their team work is missing. It is a story which should have made a good film, and only just doesn't; a number of vagrant boys instead of being sent to prison, are accepted for work on a turpentine farm by the apparently charitable boss, Mr Albee (a fine piece of unexaggerated acting has gone to this thin, quiet, vicious character with his reasonable violence, his commercial acumen, and his passion for toy trains). Food, equipment, clothes – everything is supplied on credit by the farm store, and all credits have to be wiped out by work; no wages are paid only credit notes, and the farm is surrounded by barbed wire (it is the kind of free labour one can sometimes see practised in West Africa). There is an attempt to escape, a 'mutiny', the tyrannical foreman (played with a dead-pan intensity by Mr Alan Baxter) is burnt alive, a child is accidentally shot dead, and the escaping children are run to earth by Mr Albee and his men at a farmhouse. He is about to exterminate them quietly and legally, for they carry arms – when the police arrive, and the film ends with a sermon from the judge on the guilt of society, and a heavy sentence for peonage on Mr Albee. This is a picture which should have been given to Fritz Lang or to Mervyn LeRoy, who made the unforgettable *They Won't Forget*; they would have driven the horror home by never letting-up on details. As it is, most of the punches have been pulled – too much humour (comic characters are out of place on Mr Albee's farm), boyish heroisms, and a long-drawn-out sob of a death scene rob it of tension.

Captain Fury is written to the Robin Hood formula – a few wallabies are meant to convince us that this is Australia, and a dozen red-coats that this is history. There is a wicked land-owner with a taste for flowers and a dozen lashes, oppressed settlers who are being driven from their holdings, and a chivalrous Irish convict (Mr Brian Aherne), who escapes with some of his fellow-prisoners (including Mr Victor McLaglen), and protects the settlers. He is captured, and Richard Lion-Heart (wearing a top-hat and calling himself Governor of New South Wales) turns up in the nick of time, and saves him from hanging. It is all noisily, dismally boyish, with barn-dances and horseplay and incredible purities – the smell of prep, and day-dreams. Men who shoot on sight hesitate over a Christian name; robbery, arson, murder reach a climax with inarticulate scenes under the stars, and when a girl kisses Captain Fury, he tells her gently, 'I think we'd better be getting back to the dance now.'

The Spectator (7 July 1939)

East Side of Heaven (USA, Universal, 1939) Dir.: David Butler. Cast: Bing Crosby, Joan Blondell, Mischa Auer, C. Aubrey Smith, Irene Harvey.

Let George Do It (GB, Ealing, 1939) Dir.: Marcel Varnel. Cast: George Formby, Phyllis Calvert, Garry Marsh, Romney Brent, Bernard Lee, Coral Browne, Torin Thatcher, Hal Gordon.

The Sun Never Sets (USA, Universal, 1939) Dir.: Rowland V. Lee. Cast: Basil

Rathbone, Douglas Fairbanks, Jr., Virginia Field, Lionel Atwill, Barbara O'Neil, C. Aubrey Smith, Melville Cooper.

Boy Slaves (USA, RKO, 1938) Dir.: P.J. Wolfson. Cast: Anne Shirley, Roger Daniel, James McCallion, Alan Baxter.

Captain Fury (USA, Hal Roach, 1939) Dir.: Hal Roach. Cast: Brian Aherne, Victor McLaglen, Paul Lukas, June Lang, John Carradine.

The Hound of the Baskervilles · Man of Conquest

The cinema has never yet done justice to Sherlock Holmes. The latest attempt is by no means the worst – that palm must go to the early talkie with Mr Clive Brook, when the great detective shipped as passenger on the latest transatlantic liner in pursuit of Professor Moriarty who used electricity, sub-machine guns, the radio, in eliminating his enemies, instead of a two-horse van and a broken slate. For the most grotesque, the prize undoubtedly goes to Germany. I happened to see the Ufa *Sherlock Holmes* in Mexico, and I still wonder what they made of it, those dubious *mestizos* in the cheap seats, made of the two crooks who, posing in a German spa as Holmes and Watson, were always encountering an enigmatic man in a deerstalker and a cape given to fits of hearty Teutonic laughter in hotel lounges whenever he caught sight of them – he finally testified in court, to the astonishment of Judge and police, that there were no such people as Holmes and Watson and that his name was Conan Doyle. An erudite and rather Pirandelloish plot.

In this new film Holmes is undoubtedly Holmes, and he hasn't to compete desperately with telephones and high-speed cars and 1939. '"Your hat and boots, Watson, quick! Not a moment to lose!" He rushed into his room in his dressing-gown, and was back again in a few seconds in a frock-coat.' That atmosphere of unmechanized Edwardian flurry is well caught: the villain bowls recklessly along Baker Street in a hansom and our hero discusses plans of action in a four-wheeler. The genuine Holmes London, too, is neatly touched in through the cab windows – the long trailing skirts and the Sargent hats; and if Dartmoor is a rather

Gothick landscape, so it was in the original book. It is quite forgiveable, I think, to have transformed young Dr Mortimer into a formidable figure with thick glasses and a black beard and a terrified-terrifying wife with a little plump pastry face who dabbles in the occult: the film is better for an added suspect. Nor am I worried at all by the fact that the hound is no longer painted with phosphorus – such a monster sounds well in print, but he would be a little too bizarre upon the screen. Even the transformation of wronged revengeful Mrs Stapleton ('it is my mind and soul that he has tortured and defiled') into a Miss Stapleton, blonde and innocent and made for a baronet, may possibly pass. What is wrong, surely, is Mr Rathbone's reading of the great character: the good humour (Holmes very rarely laughed) and the general air of brisk good health (there is only one hushed reference to the depraved needle). And, of course, as always happens, the deductions are reduced to a minimum and the plot is swollen. So we have an absurd scene with Holmes following the Hound's bloody spoor by the light of an electric torch and getting shut into an empty tomb by Stapleton at the end of the hunt. Producers of detective films are getting obsessed with action: there is no dramatic value in that tomb: Holmes immediately begins to cut his way out with a scout knife, but something, they feel, is happening – nobody's standing around, just detecting. Yet what we really need in a Holmes picture is far more dialogue and much less action. Let us be presented in a series of close-ups, as poor Doctor Watson was, with all the materials for deduction, and let the toothmarks on a walking-stick, the mud on a pair of boots, the stained finger-nail be the chief characters in a Holmes film.

Man of Conquest is the story of Sam Houston, the political freebooter who seized Texas from Mexico. It is the kind of big idealistic middlebrow epic that America does very well. We feel how unbearable it would be in book form, but in visual terms the love scenes beside covered wagons, the drinking and horse-play and good fellowship have a kind of vulgar and honest appeal. My only doubt is whether Mr Richard Dix is really well cast. The blunt and fleshly figure, the massive growl, the soft inexpressive mastiff eyes may be political enough, but they introduce a rather operatic quality into the character of the hard rider and Indian fighter.

The Spectator (14 July 1939)

The Hound of the Baskervilles (USA, Twentieth-Century Fox, 1939) Dir.: Sidney Lanfield. Cast: Basil Rathbone, Nigel Bruce, Richard Greene, Wendy Barrie, Lionel Atwill, Morton Lowry, John Carradine, Barlowe Borland, E.E. Clive, Beryl Mercer, Ralph Forbes, Eily Malyon, Mary Gordon.

Man of Conquest (USA, Republic, 1939) Dir.: George Nicholls Jr. Cast: Richard Dix, Joan Fontaine, Gail Patrick, Edward Ellis, Victor Jory, Robert Barrat, George Hayes, Ralph Morgan, Robert Armstrong, Henry Gordon, Janet Beecher.

Hostages · Undercover Doctor · The Modern Miracle · Man About Town

Academic critics are apt to refer to the comedy of humours as an historical curiosity belonging to the time of Ben Jonson, as though it were not still the most common form of comedy – from Mr Coward upwards. *Hostages* is a very charming and intelligent example. This is not a realistic French village, the kind of village Pagnol cuts accurately in celluloid. The dispute between the Mayor and the landed aristocracy about a right of way – a dispute that survives war, foreign occupation and the danger of death – doesn't belong to human nature as we know it: it is human nature simplified and reconstructed and legendary. There is one big difference between these modern humours and Jonson's. Nowadays we want flattery, and these petty, quarrelsome, but, at the pinch, noble figures, make us feel that, after all, man is a fine creature: there's no harm in us really, and if we dispute one day over a parcel of land, we will die extravagantly the next for love of our village. It is a fairy-story, but it makes the most agreeable film to be seen in London.

It is the story of a village on the Marne, of the outbreak of war, and the sudden arrival of the German cavalry while the Mayor, the barber and the landowner quarrel about strategy in the café and stick little flags into a map – gloved fingers suddenly descend and alter their arrangement. A love-story goes dimly on in the background between the Mayor's daughter and the landowner's conscript son: a Uhlan is shot in a barn by the boy, who escapes to join his regiment, and the grotesque little Mayor drives the body out by night to bury it in the woods. But the Germans find it and threaten to destroy the village if the murderer is not found. The Mayor offers himself as a hostage instead, and is told there must be four others. In his astute provincial way he haggles over the number – but the German Commandant is not commercially minded. The Mayor and the landowner claim the privilege of being hostages, and the other villagers draw lots – the poacher gate-crashes by a ruse into the company of these respected men. The clerk, the policeman and the braggart draw the winning cards, and the braggart hangs himself: so the scared barber is invited with ceremony to take his place. Of course, at the last minute, the taxis of the Marne drive out of Paris, and the hostages are saved from the firing-squad. Then the quarrel begins again whimsically . . . I have said it was a fairy-story. All the same, finely acted and magnificently shot, the picture does again and again strike the right legendary note: the little lay figure under the lamplight at the door of the Marne raising his best bowler with depressed dignity to the German officer; the scene in the silent square at dawn when the hostages gather for their long walk to German Headquarters, and the walk itself, the finest piece of symphonic cutting on the screen since Pépé took *his* last walk – the early morning light over the flat French countryside, the Mayor in his sash of office and the landowner in his top hat, and human self-control failing – in the barber first – and the hasty embarrassed dodging behind the haystacks.

Undercover Doctor – like *Persons in Hiding*, another story out of Mr Hoover's casebook – is realistic and convincing: the story of a doctor who gets his first valuable patient outside the law and rockets up the financial ladder with the help of gun-wounds. It contains a brilliant piece of neurotic acting by Mr Broderick Crawford (a new name to me) as Public Enemy No. 1: it is acting, well worth seeing, and alongside *Hostages* nowhere at all.

The Modern Miracle is yet another awful example of good taste, another sober pompous film biography, this time of Bell, the inventor of the telephone. I find Don Ameche a very unsympathetic actor, with the large white face of an advertising hoarding, and his ecstatic gasps and mouthings at the prospect of becoming a father supply the most embarrassing moments in the cinema this week. As for *Man About Town*, it is just one of those doggish American films of sexual and social ambition which sadly recalls Davenant's definition: 'Humour is the drunkenness of a Nation which no sleep can cure.'

The Spectator (21 July 1939)

Hostages (*Les Otages*) (France, Helvetia Films, 1939) Dir.: Raymond Bernard. Cast: Charpin, Saturnin Fabre, Pierre Larquey. (US title: *The Mayor's Dilemma*)

Undercover Doctor (USA, 1939) Dir.: Louis King. Cast: Broderick Crawford.

The Modern Miracle (USA, Twentieth-Century Fox, 1939) Dir.: Irving Cummings. Cast: Don Ameche, Henry Fonda, Loretta Young, Charles Coburn, Gene Lockhart, Spring Byington, Bobs Watson. (US title: *The Story of Alexander Graham Bell*)

Man About Town (USA, Paramount, 1939) Dir.: Mark Sandrich. Cast: Jack Benny, Dorothy Lamour, Edward Arnold, Binnie Barnes, Phil Harris, Eddie Anderson, Monty Woolley, Isabel Jeans, Betty Grable, E.E. Clive.

Le Drame de Shanghai · The Rebellious Son

It would be funny, of course, if it wasn't Pabst: if we could forget *Kameradschaft*, *Jeanne Ney*, *Dreigroschenoper*, *Pandora's Box*, *The Joyless Street*, *Secrets of the Soul*, *Westfront* 1918, that long unsurpassed record of sombre German talent. The great Russians are nowhere beside the director who created Rasp in the hall of the shabby Parisian hotel-for-a-night, sent the rescuing miners tapping along the pipes, and showed Garbo to us in the shabby fur and the black stockings of her disreputable beat. It is possible to grasp the rise and fall of the post-war film by this man's work alone. Well, I suppose we must attribute this absurd Chinese thriller to the exigencies of exile and the stupidity of producers. Pabst isn't really here at all, except for a few seconds in a neat knifing, in a little squalid set in the studio corner with a forger of passports, and in the march of the workers at the climax, a beautifully cut movement, though one would have liked to be clear as to who they were and what exactly they were doing: the plot of this thriller is appallingly obscure.

I can't pretend to say what it's about and how all these people fit in. There's a young Chinese intellectual called Tcheng, whom the members of an organization called the Black Serpent want to liquidate. That's why – they couldn't get him any other way – war is arranged against Japan. That doesn't help, because then China is united and their men join Tcheng's men and Tcheng, who is a pacifist, puts on uniform, and after an orgy of news-shots of Japanese bombers, all the characters live happily ever afterwards – except Kay Murphy, who has been stabbed by a man in a sun-helmet and Ivan, whom Kay shot to save her little girl, who had arrived from an English High-School in Hong Kong (architecture Scotch Baronial) and didn't know her mother was a singer in a cabaret, where the tatty costumes – all spangles and ostrich feathers – and the debauchery – all champagne in ice-buckets – seem to date from 1925. 'Won't you kiss me?' Kay says, and the girl shrinks away. 'It's just the rouge, Mummie.'

Kay's name is not really Kay – they are all White Russians in the cabaret ('Hunger holds them prisoner'), and she has a photograph of Ivan in Guards uniform. He nearly repents before she shoots him to save her child from the Black Serpent, blowing out her bosom like a puff adder. With her big black eyes and her plump soulful features, she reminded me a little of Pola Negri caught in the coils. 'I am reborn!' she exclaims prematurely. 'O for pure air! wind!' – though she gets plenty of that. She toasts her lovers, presenting an immovable and melancholy profile: 'Here's to the night that passes'; and when she lures a man to death, she carries herself with sad self-pity. 'This hurts me more than it hurts you' is her daunting attitude towards a victim. O those pure maternal eyes peeking coyly above the ostrich fan, those slightly bandy legs in black silk, the rather prominent behind which swings in a thicket of plumage up towards the attic where the emissaries of the Black

Serpent wait. One must mournfully add that M. Louis Jouvet is wasted on this film: that slow soporific voice, the heavy eyes with their pessimistic amusement, and the nihilist gait, are butchered in a minor part.

The Rebel Son is hardly less incredible. A bad French film about Tarass Boomdeay, with M. Harry Baur as the old Cossack leader, seems to have been bought by an English firm with some of the shots remade with our most refined young men and women – including Miss Joan Gardiner ('I can fight like a man'). M. Baur's voice has been unsuitably dubbed, and the dialogue has the prattling innocence of a play written by a Women's Institute. I liked particularly the scene when the young Cossack (played by Mr Anthony Bushell with his keen young Oxford accent) bursts into the bedroom of the girl he loves, 'I know it's very late to call, but . . . O, I'm glad you are not angry.' After half an hour the joke had gone on long enough and I left. A man in the audience was remarking slowly, with some of Dr Johnson's weight, 'I am still wondering what the reason for the existence of this film can be.'

The Spectator (28 July 1939)

Le Drame de Shanghai (France, Gladiator Films, 1939) Dir.: G.W. Pabst. Cast: Louis Jouvet, Raymond Rouleau, Dorville, Elina Labourdette, Suzanne Desprée.

The Rebellious Son (France, Omnia Films, 1939) Dir.: Adrian Brunel. Cast: Harry Baur, Joan Gardiner, Anthony Bushell, Patricia Roc, Roger Livesey. (English version of *Tarass Boulba*, directed by Alexis Granowsky)

The Rich Bride

So they still dream in Russia of going to Moscow; Revolution hasn't altered that; again and again in this bouncing boisterous musical comedy of a collective farm we are reminded of Chekhov – perhaps the difference is that these people, unlike the three sisters, will really get there: the tractor-driver because he is a shock-worker, the girl Marina because she has put in more working days than anyone else on the farm; they'll get their tenement and their Parks of Culture. As for the others, they get the next best thing – a brass bedstead or a trumpet or a radio set – when the prizes are given out at Harvest Home: even the comic villain, the assistant book-keeper, gets the bicycle he has dreamed about; and they are all so noisy and delighted at their new toys that perhaps even Moscow may seem worth the bother to those who win it. The awful simplicity of these characters weighs on the spirits like a long summer afternoon at a school sports – the earnest competition, the unacceptable loyalties, and the odd-shaped cups of silver alloy handed out at the end.

It is an incredible and a pathetic picture. One begins to hope that it is just propaganda for internal use – to tell the Russian world of the happy time had by what the English caption-writer calls with coy, fairy-like, progressive joviality 'the lusty lads and bouncing lasses' – music and dancing, and even babies, if the prefects approve. One wouldn't like to feel that this Angela Brazil world really existed anywhere: the stout female shock brigadier giving a first-day-of-term speech to her girls (a chorus, to Western taste, of incomparable dumplings) – 'Save your strength to keep our banner': the stout male brigadier addressing his tractor-drivers – 'It's our task to attack along the whole front', warning them that the rival House is two hundred acres ahead and has economized six hundred gallons: the Ukrainian School Song. At midnight the old watchman stops the dancing – it is time for dormitory: 'Citizens, remember the harvest', and the girls break squealing through the underbrush before the heavy tread of their brigadier – 'Run girls, it's Pelaga.' The book-keeper wants to marry Marina for the sake of her working days (he'll go to Moscow as her husband, and even perhaps to the seaside), so he sows suspicion between her and a young tractor-driver who looks astonishingly like Laurence Olivier. The dreadful question which all lovers have to face is 'Is he – or she – a loafer? Or a real shock-worker?' There's a lot of dirty juggling with figures, but the two shock brigadiers put their heads together in the end for the sake of their favourite pupils, and two young Stakhanovites find happiness. If it's true, of course, it's awful – but as long as you can treat it as a fairy-story for simple laughter, the continuous sounds of animal satisfaction, which seems to be roused even by a simple shave, and by the sight of that awful acreage of stout female flesh in the Ukrainian sun, stirring sluggishly during the midday rest, scratching a little, satisfied under the team banner. Sometimes, as the film draws to an end, with the huge panorama of the rain-threatened harvest, an effect does get through – of air and sky and space and liberty: gets through, that is to say, to us, the tired inhabitants of a small industrial island: not to them who seek only smoky Moscow – or a prize bedstead and the honour of the side.

POSTSCRIPT

There is a disquieting account in the last *New Yorker* to reach this country of the films which are being shown at the British Pavilion at the World Fair – the inevitable newsreel of Mr Chamberlain's face: some view of Stratford-on-Avon ('a beautiful item' called not *Shakespeare's England* as one would expect, but *England's Shakespeare* – in this can one detect the style of one of the judges, Mr Philip Guedalla?): and – 'the most exciting offering' a little picture about penguins. Are these the best English documentaries that the Committee could show Americans familiar with *The River*? One might have expected *North Sea, Spare Time, Children at School* . . . but perhaps the Committee, like one of our censors, does not attend the cinema.

The Spectator (4 August 1939)

The Rich Bride (USSR, Ukrainfilm, 1938) Dir.: Ivan Pyriev. Cast: Maria Ladynina, Anna Dmokhovskaya, B. Bezgin, Ivan Lyubeznov.

Beau Geste · Un de la Légion

Thirteen years have passed since the first *Beau Geste* was produced with Ronald Colman, William Powell, Noah Beery, but not a set seems to have been altered. Of course, memory plays strange tricks, and Fort Zinderneuf, with the dead legionaries leaning from the baronial embrasures, can hardly have stood unchanged since 1926 in the Arizona deserts; yet I feel the old English mansion of Brandon Abbas has been tucked away all those years on some abandoned stage in the great rambling lots, dust collecting on the stained glass, and the panelling, and the suit of armour in the hall, and on Lady Patricia too, her aristocratic suffering only bleaching a little with the years, and the birds beginning to roost in the high rooky hair. For why trouble to destroy what is certain to be needed sooner or later? Alas! we have not yet reached the end of *Beau Geste*; Technicolor and stereoscopy wait another decade. There is something in the brazen tale which appeals to the worst in human nature – the cowardly will always find satisfaction in the impossible heroisms they will never have to imitate, and the weak in the disgusting and irrational brutalities of Sergeant Markoff, the Tom Brown bully who kicks over a water-bucket in the presence of the deserters dying of thirst.

A morbid picture, but I doubt whether any morality council will take action, the whole story being wrapped up in the school colours – in comradeship and loyalty and breeding, and the pure girl left behind; morbid because the brutality has no relation whatever to the real world; it is uncriticized day-dreaming. We do not criticize our dreams, or feel responsible for our Markoffs. Indeed, this particular product of the half-conscious mind is praised by one of the heroic characters as 'the best soldier we're ever likely to know', much as a bully is excused if he is a good centre-forward. Day-dreams, adolescence, the popular story go together, and out of the same nocturnal sub-region as the Sergeant emerges the little scene when the three Gestes as children play with toy boats and real gunpowder, and one gets hit in the leg, and another gouges out the bullet with a penknife – exquisite agonies! – and the third asks, 'Are you crying because you are proud or because you are wounded?' Only sentimentality? Then take the crucifixion of Rassilof on the mess-table. I am glad to note that our Censors, with a moral discrimination they do not always show, have given this unhealthy picture an 'A' Certificate.

What a relief to change from Beau's Legion to Fernandel's. This Legion, too, may not be the real thing (at least, we have correct uniforms, genuine exteriors, and a sense of routine – it isn't hell and heroism; it is medical inspections and routine-marches and meals and leaves); but if it's a little too good to be true, with the charming officers and the humorous companionships, and Miss Suzy Prim on a Sunday afternoon – a frankly recruiting picture – at any rate, there's nothing adolescent about it, and no apparent reason for its 'A' Certificate. Fernandel, the inspired hen-pecked husband, who is not allowed meat or wine because he suffers from aerophagie ('whenever I eat I swallow air I cannot digest'). He is robbed by a crook, stuck drunk on a boat with a recruit's papers in his pocket, and after a few indignant muddled days settles happily down in the Legion. When his wife traces him, he disowns her, goes south with his batallion, and wins the Legion of Honour with a good deal less fuss than the Geste family play boats.

Fernandel's laugh is the most memorable thing in any of his pictures; he can carry half a minute of film with a laugh alone, the camera fixed on the huge mouth and the great mulish teeth. Watch him in the café with the crook as he suddenly realizes that he doesn't love his wife; the sudden disconcerting bellow, then the splutter, the attempt to explain, the feeble flap-flap of one hand, the hopeless movements of the equine head, and laughter welling out, bursting between the big rocky teeth, unstemmable, like an oil-gusher running to waste over a whole countryside.

The Spectator (11 August 1939)

Beau Geste (USA, Paramount, 1939) Dir.: William A. Wellman. Cast: Gary Cooper, Ray Milland, Robert Preston, Brian Donlevy, J. Carrol Naish,

Susan Hayward, Heather Thatcher, James Stephenson, Donald O'Connor, Albert Dekker, Broderick Crawford.

Un de la Légion (France, Calamy, 1936) Dir.: Christian Jaque. Cast: Fernandel, Suzy Prim, Thérèse Dorny.

The March of Time · Shipyard Sally · Blind Alley · There Ain't No Justice

The new *March of Time* includes a quick survey of screen history which in fifteen minutes gives a better idea of cinema changes (one cannot with confidence talk of advances) than Cochran's rather ignorant and inefficient *Flashbacks*. True, the Continental cinema is excluded, but here we have selected shots from a range of American pictures beginning with *The Great Train Robbery* (1903), and ending with *All Quiet* (1930). We see William S. Hart in *The Fugitive* as he detects a cheat in a Mexican dive under the starry eyes of his bushy girl; Theda Bara offers her plump importunate lips to a nervous man with a little revolver in *A Fool There Was*; Chaplin and his dicky reel into fame in *Tilly's Punctured Romance*; here's Valentino in *The Four Horsemen*, his lustrous almond eyes and his legendary insolence; Mary Pickford, young, lovely, undated. How little has dated in many of these pictures, except the dresses and the jerky movements! The battle scenes in *The Birth of a Nation* have never been surpassed; Garbo in *Flesh and the Devil* is far lovelier and more expressive than the gaunt, inhibited great actress of today, and from *The Big Parade* (1926) we have the advance of the American troops through the French wood, the camera wheeling and retreating before the bayonets and the anxious faces – one of the finest moments of the screen.

We come heavily to earth in 1939 with Miss Gracie Fields's new film – about a variety singer with an improvident father who saves Clydebank from ruin by forcing her way into the house of an old peer and presenting a petition from the workers; at the end a large close-up of Miss Fields singing 'Land of Hope and Glory' is transposed over the launching of a new liner by the Queen – values are confused: the liner is the background to the face. All Miss Fields's pictures seem designed to show a sympathy for the working class and an ability to appeal to the best circles: unemployment can always be wiped out by a sentimental song, industrial unrest is calmed by a Victorian ballad and dividends are made safe for democracy. This picture has the embarrassment of a charade where you don't know the performers well. What is Mr Sydney Howard doing in this household?

Blind Alley has crept rather silently into the West End. Survive a sticky ten minutes and you have a thriller of quite unusual merit. A killer (Mr Chester Morris) escapes from gaol, eliminates the warden and arrives with his girl and bodyguard at the lakeside house of a university psychiatrist. He expects to be picked up by a motor-boat which doesn't come; he is jittery, shoots down a young student of the Professor's who shows fight, tries to sleep. Time passes – a gunman watches from the nursery window among the juvenile junk – the killer tosses in nightmare. One bad dream has haunted him since childhood – a dream of rain dripping through an umbrella, bars all around; two fingers of his gun hand are paralysed: he fears insanity. The Professor, with the intention of destroying his motive power, offers to rid him of the dream. We watch the neurotic damned-to-violence creature struggle against the analysis. Everything, of course, is simplified and speeded up, but that's legitimate. There's nothing false about the analysis itself, and the camera is magnificently used to express the selected distorted facts of memory as it returns; the lens is transformed to a child's eye, seeing the hated father sitting far off at the bar-room table, swinging round to the group of police following across the street to the scene of betrayal, the underside of a table, the legs of policemen closing round, while blood drips through a crack. This is the old Ufa touch. The analysis is completed, the police arrive, the killer hesitates, and is shot down. The end, like the beginning, falters, but that doesn't harm the central situation and the superb acting of Mr Chester Morris, sweating, badgered, disintegrating.

There Ain't No Justice is intended to be an English tough film, but somebody's nerve failed – and the rather winsome personality of Mr Jimmy Hanley. The etceteras – setting of bar rooms and coffee stalls – are admirable, but the whole picture breathes timidity and refinement.

The Spectator (18 August 1939)

Shipyard Sally (GB, Twentieth-Century Fox, 1939) Dir.: Monty Banks. Cast: Gracie Fields, Sydney Howard, Morten Selten, Norma Varden, Oliver Wakefield.
Blind Alley (USA, Columbia, 1939) Dir.: Charles Vidor. Cast: Chester Morris, Ralph Bellamy, Ann Dvorak, Melville Cooper, Rose Stradner, Marc Lawrence.
There Ain't No Justice (GB, Ealing, 1939) Dir.: Pen Tennyson. Cast: Jimmy Hanley, Edward Rigby, Mary Clare, Edward Chapman, Phyllis Stanley, Michael Wilding.

Les Disparus de St Agil · Young Man's Fancy · Golden Gloves

It would be possible, I suppose, to praise and dismiss the new French film at the Polytechnic as a skilful, exciting, rather absurd 'story for boys', similar to the innumerable tales which come out around Christmas – *The Boys of St Ethelburga's, For the Sake of the Side*, and their like. There is a Headmaster who commits murder, and is tracked down and denounced by one of his pupils; there is an art master who forges banknotes, a kidnapping, a secret passage behind a blackboard, but, strange though it may seem in such a plot, there is also a sense of reality; a child's dream of what Alain-Fournier called 'this wild life, full of risks, games and adventures', is expressed through an adult imagination. One is reminded again and again, in the elusive poetry of the story of escape, of Fournier's great novel *Le Grand Meaulnes*: the small curtained dormitory cells, the school play with its daggers and doublets, the master padding by at night on insomniac feet, the classroom after dark by candlelight with the white phosphorescent chalk marks on the board, these are like vivid inexplicable symbols in a Surrealist painting. One remembers Fournier's remark: 'If

I have been childish and weak and foolish, at least I have, at moments, had the strength in this infamous city to create my life like a marvellous fairy-tale.' One is apt to forget that the literature of escape is literature just because it is a real escape; it contains a recognition of life as much as the action of a deserter contains the recognition of an enemy; *For the Sake of the Side* is not an escape – it is hallucination. But the author and director of *Les Disparus* know all there is to know about 'the infamous city'. You can recognize escape by its unsuccess: the shadow is always there across the fantasy, just as it is in folk-tales, in the stories of Grimm. *Golden Gloves, Young Man's Fancy* – these do not belong to the literature of escape, they are the novelettes of hallucination. The characters are older in years than those in *The Boys of St Ethelburga's*, that's all.

Les Disparus has inevitably been compared with *Emil and the Detectives*: in both the criminals are brought to justice by a horde of children, and the infamous city casts much the same kind of shadow. We remember Rasp going to bed in his bowler in the horrible little hotel which belongs in a quarter nobody from St Ethelburga's has ever visited, and we shall remember a long while after the details of *Les Disparus* are forgotten M. Michel Simon as the forger and secret drinker, with his great loose squashy face and his unconvincing swagger, getting tiddly and malicious at the school play, furious with his class in an observation test because no one has noticed the engraver's signature on a banknote (they had all noticed the naked woman), a grotesque and dangerous figure of fun who ends with a scream and a thud. (There are times when Simon reminds us of Laughton, but he is a less histrionic actor: we never notice the mechanics of his elastic voice.) Perhaps it is as well to add in these jittery days that the story is more humorous than sombre – the kidnapped child writing an account of his adventures in the old mill, badgering his admiring captors who read out the last chapter every evening with pride and excitement; the little groups of quarrelling pedants; the pale porter who believes in the evil eye; the whole unfamiliar atmosphere of a French school where a drum takes the place of the cracked bell and the worst accusation you can bring against another master is harshness to his class. The acting of the children is magnificent.

Young Man's Fancy is directed by Mr Robert Stevenson, who made *Tudor Rose*. That picture seemed to me hopelessly false in atmosphere, but it was cleverly directed. We don't possess many good fiction directors in this country, and it is a pity Mr Stevenson was not given something better to make than his own refined and bitter-sweet story. This is a period piece in the worse – the Coward – sense. One can, however, get through it: *Golden Gloves* with Mr McLaglen as a retired and tearful champ (I nearly wrote chimp), who works as a doorkeeper so that his worthless son can be really 'class' in a top hat, beat me after twenty minutes.

The Spectator (25 August 1939)

Les Disparus de St Agil (France, Francinex, 1938) Dir.: Christian Jaque. Cast: Michel Simon, Erich von Stroheim, Armand Bernard, Marcel Mouloudji. (US title: *Boys' School*)

Young Man's Fancy (GB, Ealing, 1939) Dir.: Robert Stevenson. Cast: Griffith Jones, Anna Lee, Seymour Hicks, Billy Bennett, Edward Rigby, Francis L. Sullivan.

Golden Gloves (USA, Paramount, 1939) Dir.: Edward Dmytryk. Cast: Richard Denning, Jeanne Cagney, William Frawley, Robert Ryan.

Professor Mamlock · Dodge City · Five Came Back

Professor Mamlock is a Soviet film which attacks the brutality of the Nazi revolution. Played with sincerity by so many 'Honoured Artists of the Republic', breathing an honest indignation against the political racketeers who put Dimitrov in the dock, the picture would have seemed a fortnight ago rather more moving. History has travelled fast: we are reminded too often in the first half of the film that the ideological argument is made more of wind than stone. But I think in any case the first half-hour would have proved disappointing: like so many worthy middlebrow novels, it has about it the air of a Foyle Luncheon; the characters are all caught at their most abstract, talking like Left Book Club speakers. The theme of a story should never be expressed so plainly; argument is valueless in fiction unless it is dramatic and individualized. For a long time we feel little interest in Professor Mamlock, the Jewish head of a Berlin hospital, who disapproves of politics. To discover in the blood of a patient the right germ is the important thing, and he urges his son, who is also his assistant and an ardent Communist, to take as his models Koch and Pasteur. But he isn't alive; he is just a martyr type, until argument ceases, and we watch him paraded through the streets in his rubber gloves and his surgical dress marked with the word Jew, the victim of his assistant, a vicious, jealous little figure in pince-nez, who has been appointed Commissar of the hospital.

The dead wood in this picture is divided from the live by the night of the Reichstag fire: enormously impressive the noisy radio followed by shots of rain-wet silent streets: hardly anybody about, except a few little groups of scared people scurrying home, and at intervals the squads of Brown Shirts marching heavily on unknown errands. This is real cinema; and so are the last-minute attempts to hide the evidence, lorry-loads of Brown Shirts draw up to the kerb below. All that is more or less silent in this film is first class; it is only when the characters talk too glibly of their ideals that we lose touch with the truth, and there is very little talk after the Reichstag fire, except in the final shots when Dr Mamlock arraigns the armed Gestapo guards from the balcony of the clinic in the name of humanity (but not, we know now, in the name of Communism), and is shot down by a machine-gun.

Dodge City is a good example of the Western formula; pioneers build their city, racketeers build gambling halls; pioneers though outnumbering gunmen a hundred to one, are all old men with Bibles, old ladies sewing shirts for the little ones, the little ones themselves, poor widows, and a few mortality types: straight-shooting cowboy is asked to become sheriff, refuses, sees child killed, accepts, cleans up. There is always one moment of excellent drama when cowboy advances slowly towards gunmen along sidewalk or across square (see *The Virginian* and *Stagecoach*). Personally, I never tire of those pictures and *Dodge City* is well acted, well directed, and the Technicolor is excellent, except at sunset. My only complaint is that we see rather too much of the girl in gingham (Miss Olivia de Havilland) in comparison with the bad girl (Miss Ann Sheridan), who is entrancing in colour. One thing has never ceased to puzzle me in Western films; the racketeers always shoot the mortality types back, front, sideways, whether he carries a gun or not, without hesitation. You'd think anyone could get a man that way, and yet the hero never has to bother about people shooting him unawares. He's usually caught at least once unarmed, and then he's just warned off.

Five Came Back is a welter of mortality types; twelve people are travelling in an aeroplane which crashes in an Andean forest. One falls off first which leaves six to dispose of, and the only fun in an absurd picture is spotting who will be liquidated. I did make one mistake: the golden-hearted prostitute didn't die nobly, shielding the little boy; she made good in a more professional way.

The Spectator (1 September 1939)

Professor Mamlock (USSR, Lenfilm, 1938) Dir.: Adolf Minkin. Cast: Herbert Rappoport, Sergei Mezhinsky, Oleg Zhakov, Nina Shaternikova, Vasili Merkuriev.

Dodge City (USA, Warners, 1939) Dir.: Michael Curtiz. Cast: Errol Flynn, Olivia de Havilland, Ann Sheridan, Bruce Cabot, Alan Hale, Frank McHugh, John Litel, Victor Jory, William Lundigan, Henry Travers, Henry O'Neill, Gloria Holden, Guinn Williams.

Five Came Back (USA, RKO, 1939) Dir.: John Farrow. Cast: Chester Morris, Lucille Ball, C. Aubrey Smith, Elizabeth Risdon, Wendy Barrie, John Carradine, Joseph Calleia, Allen Jenkins, Kent Taylor, Patric Knowles.

Young Mr Lincoln · I Was a Captive of Nazi Germany

At the best of times *Young Mr Lincoln* would be impressive, and entitle Mr John Ford, who made *The Informer* and *Stagecoach*, to be regarded as one of the best directors of the day, but now there seems an added value in this attempt to draw in the simplest and least rhetorical terms a man who cared passionately for justice.

We see Lincoln first as a storekeeper exchanging goods for a cask full of old books which include Blackstone: his love for Ann Rutledge is touched in with unexpected restraint – an inarticulate duologue on a river-bank and a monologue over a grave. We watch him begin his career as a lawyer, take part in the small-town celebrations of Independence Day, win a log-splitting contest, defeat an opposing team in a tug-of-war by hitching the rope to a mule-cart, judge with extreme deliberation in a pie contest between the merits of apple and peach. Mr Henry Fonda gives a fine performance; the grotesque slow wisecracks seem to emerge from a whole background of country breeding, and Mr Ford and his cameraman never let us forget the odd leggy appearance – an interesting example of what camera angles can do with a young actor as well made as Mr Fonda. Mr Fonda's performance has been compared to Muni's as Pasteur – certainly we never feel that the acting falls below the legendary nature of the subject, and he has none of the mannerisms which grate on us a little with Muni. But it must be remembered that the direction is far finer, and much of the credit we give to Fonda belongs to Ford. That flash of fanatical hatred in the eyes when a man pays him in bad coin is less a matter of acting than of cutting, and much of Mr Fonda's expressiveness is montage. But all the same it is not every actor who allows himself to be so cut and mounted into his part by a great director.

The main part of the plot is, I imagine, fictitious. That doesn't really matter: this is intended to be legend, not history, and it may not have been impossible to discover in the events of the early life a single incident which could bear the weight of the whole future. So we have a story of two simple country boys who are suddenly on Independence Day caught up in the murder of a bully: they each for the other's sake admit guilt, and their mother, who thought she saw the stabbing, will not say which of her sons struck the blow – tortured by her appalling knowledge, she won't save one at the expense of the other. The scene of the fight, taken in the half-dark from a long way off, the little swaying group under the trees, the dull gunshot as the bully fires, then the bush of smoke standing still over the body, the two children (they are little more) running together to their mother's side, all obscurity and hurry and muffled sound, will remain in mind as a classic example of direction which does more than directly represent an action, direction which conveys a mood.

Lincoln saves them from lynching, undertakes their defence, and the opening stages of the trial are particularly well written: the direction of the little country judge, 'Now, you men, take off your hats and put down those jugs'; the choosing of the jury. The climax is the only weak point in the film. For Lincoln to discover that a witness for the prosecution is the real murderer (from a point in his evidence which would not have escaped any member of the audience) is banal. There have been so many court dramas and ingenious plots, and for a while the picture loses its legendary interest, and we find ourselves concerned with an exciting situation and not with a man who, loving justice and hating iniquity, was preparing himself for his last defeat at the hands of a violent world.

I Was a Captive of Nazi Germany is the story of Miss Isobel Steele, a young American who was imprisoned in 1934 on a charge of espionage. It was an odd shabby picture, with cheap sets and nameless players of indeterminate nationality, full of queer accents and queerer dinner jackets. Miss Steele plays Miss Steele as if she was sleep-walking, a lanky figure in a shapeless skirt protesting innocence to blond fanatics. As propaganda it is as complete a failure as Dr Goebbels's: the only emotion it arouses is hilarity.

The Spectator (22 September 1939)

Young Mr Lincoln (USA, Twentieth-Century Fox, 1939) Dir.: John Ford. Cast: Henry Fonda, Alice Brady, Marjorie Weaver, Richard Cromwell, Ward Bond, Arleen Whelan, Eddie Collins, Donald Meek.

I Was a Captive of Nazi Germany (USA, Malvin Film Productions, 1939) Dir.: Alfred T. Mannon. Cast: Isobel Steele.

News Reels

War always seems to surprise somebody; a year after Munich trenches which were begun that autumn are still being dug on the common outside; even the news-reel companies have been caught unprepared. They must have expected the temporary closing of the cinemas; they must have been prepared for censorship, and, yet, like the newspapers, they have to rely on Germany as their chief source of supply – an admirable picture of the siege of Westerplatte, and another of the war in Poland. What have they got ready for us from the home front, and how have their commentators risen to the great occasion? One remembers what Hemingway did for *Spanish Earth*, and one hopes . . . Even a war of nerves has its heroic angle.

As we fumble for our seats the too familiar voice, edgeless and French-polished, is announcing: 'The Queen has never looked prettier.' Royalty is inspecting something or other: 'Royal interest inspires them to redoubled efforts.' Women bus-conductors climb aboard: 'For men passengers it will make going to work almost a pleasure'; they wave holiday-girl hands. Mr and Mrs Chamberlain walk in the Park; complete strangers take off their hats – an odd custom. The Duchess of Kent, instead of going to Australia, makes splints: 'We never thought we would live to be grateful to Hitler.' Very slowly we approach the violent reality; the Expeditionary Force marches to the coast, whippet tanks move through the woodlands and the voice remarks something about 'shoulder to shoulder in this death struggle for liberty'. Surely by now we should realize that art has a place in propaganda; the flat and worthy sentiment will always sound hypocritical to neutral ears beside the sharp and vivid statement. There was much that Hemingway had to slur over in his commentary: his cause was far more dubious than ours, but the language was much more effective. Let us hope that Germany is not employing a commentator of his standard, for I cannot believe that neutral opinion – or home opinion if it comes to that – will be impressed by the kind of words we listen to – shoulder to shoulder, liberty, baby-killers . . .

The siege of the Westerplatte provides the best few minutes in any news cinema. It would have been interesting to hear the German commentary, for the picture seems to make the same odd psychological mistakes as the Italian film of the Abyssinian War. The emphasis is all on power directed towards an insignificant object – we cut from the belching guns of Schleswig-Holstein to the huge bombers taking off, from the calm complacent face on the Captain's bridge to the pilot's face at the wheel, sweating, shadowy, intent: it is all smoke, flame, blast, inevitability. Nobody, we feel, can stand against this for an hour, and the mind answers quickly back that two hundred men stood it for a week. It was an astute move to show this film in England.

From Poland come some pathetic scenes of mob enthusiasm. Colonel Beck and the British Ambassador bow from a balcony: the faces of the crowd are excited, enthusiastic, happy . . . The German film of the advance into Poland is beautifully shot and well staged – so well staged (the cavalry cantering in broken sunlight through the woods, the machine-guns rushed to the edge of the meadow grass) that one suspects old sequences of manoeuvres turned and mounted at leisure. Only the huge smashed bridges – like back-broken worms writhing in water – carry the stamps of real war. The same effect is given by the French films cleverly cut in with shots from pre-war German film of the Siegfried Line: the balloon falling in flames is too tidy.

None the less, fake or not, these pictures from the East and West are impressive, well directed, and edited with imagination, and there is no reason why pictures from the defence front should not be equally effective. A different conception of news is needed – shadows of gold keys and cut ribbons and beauty queens linger. But news no longer means leading figures; we want the technique Anstey used in *Housing Problems*; America is more likely to listen with sympathy to the rough unprepared words of a Mrs Jarvis of Penge, faced with evacuation, blackouts, a broken home, than to the smooth-handled phrases of personalities. Above all, we don't want the old commentators, with their timid patronizing jokes; this is a people's war.

The Spectator (29 September 1939)

An Englishman's Home · The Face at the Window · L'Homme du Jour

It has already become a war-time habit for reviewers to iron out their criticism. The poor old British film industry has had another knock: better not say anything to do it further harm. The result, one supposes, will be the survival of the worst. Art in England after three years of war may, if we are not careful, resemble art in Germany after three years of Nazi dictatorship. Far better to sharpen our pencils and stab the poor thing to death. No art is better than bad art, for somewhere in some ruined barn an ignorant peasant may begin to whittle at a stick.

An Englishman's Home, written before the last war, was brought up to date with radio, bombing fleets and ARP, just too late to anticipate this one. New dialogue has been written by Ian Hay, Edward Knoblock and Rodney Ackland – I don't know why, for Guy du Maurier's dialogue could hardly have been more absurd. Mr Edmund Gwenn acts the Brown father with his too well-trained pawkiness – the sob in the throat perfected by ten thousand performances; he is the only star. He lives in an awful house, all fake beams and leather-seated lounges, in a garden the size of a small park, and has the oddest friends – a retired sailor, a little piece, and the German owner of a radio-shop: his daughter is loved by a Territorial officer, who wears curious cad breeches, and loves the German – who is, of course, a spy. This is meant to be a typical English home. A radio-set in the attic guides the German air fleet, and their attack coincides with an old English custom, Mr Brown's birthday party – an enormous candled cake and a dance and a lot of aircraft officers and the Territorial who snoops around, reading inscriptions in his girl's books. The radio suddenly goes dead: all stations closed down – most improbable as we know now: the BBC would certainly have put on gramophone records. The Germans arrive by parachute, clanking up the garden-path, and Mr Brown is shot and the house is bombed and Betty loves the Territorial after all and England goes to war rather tardily in montage. There is nothing to be said for this film – though it might prove useful propaganda in enemy countries, purporting to illustrate the decadence of English architecture and taste.

The Face at the Window is a much older melodrama about Victorian Paris with a wicked Count who commits murders under the name of Le Loup, helped by the awful appearance at windows of his moron foster-brother whom he keeps between whiles in a cage in a cellar. He is hunted down by a bank clerk who loves his banker's daughter: the Count, of course, covets her and lures her to a disreputable tavern and a private room. It doesn't sound very promising, but it is one of the best English pictures I have seen and leaves the American horror films far behind. You go to laugh, but find yourself immediately – from the ingenious titling on – in the grip of the fine firm traditional dialogue, the magnificent casting, sets and camerawork which plank you surely back into that vague Victorian period, when anything might happen – when Jekyll was shrinking into Hyde and the ape committed its murders in the Rue Morgue. Mr Tod Slaughter is certainly one of our finest living actors; we see in this picture at whose feet Mr Laughton must have sat – that dancing sinister step, the raised shoulder and the flickering eyelid. What makes this kind of melodrama so much more convincing than the Du Maurier brand? Perhaps it is that the author really believes – however fantastic his illustrations – in good and evil, in a morality which has the tradition of a thousand years behind it; the characters are at least as distinguishable as black is from white, while the characters in *An Englishman's Home* are all of the same piece, just fine chaps doing their duty according to their lights and putting up a good show.

The Embassy is a new Continental cinema near Heal's which has bravely opened in war-time London. *L'Homme du Jour* has already been reviewed in *The Spectator*, but it deserves a second recommendation. A comedy with Maurice Chevalier about an electrician who becomes famous for a day by giving blood to save the life of a famous tragic actress, it is a charming conversation piece of Parisian characters, with the undertone of sadness and disappointment seldom absent from Duvivier's work.

The Spectator (6 October 1939)

An Englishman's Home (GB, Aldwych Productions, 1939) Dir.: George Dewhurst. Cast: Edmund Gwenn, Mary Maguire, Paul von Henreid, Geoffrey Toone. (US title: *Madmen of Europe*)

The Face at the Window (GB, Pennant/Alexander, 1939) Dir.: George King. Cast:

Tod Slaughter, Marjorie Taylor, John Warwick, Leonard Henry, Audrey Mallalieu.

Ignace · The Story of Vernon and Irene Castle · Dark Victory

There are people, I gather from other reviews, who do not like Fernandel. They must on no account go to this film, for there is very little else in the picture to please. It is certainly not a good picture: it begins as fair comedy and ends as fair farce, with a heavy slab in the middle of bad musical comedy: and it is oddly confusing in its details – why, for instance, should a troop of lovelies be rehearsing a charity performance in a colonel's house, the commander of the local barracks to which Fernandel has been sent as a conscript? And why should the superbly heavy and foolish Baron des Orfrais be drinking the waters there? And why should he send a bottle of champagne across to a fellow guest as if he were dining in a hotel? Is it, after all, a hotel? But, if so, why is all the service done by the Colonel's batman (Fernandel) and his very piquant maid? Why? . . . But let us leave it to the enemies of Fernandel to clean out all the holes in this sieve.

There remains Fernandel: Fernandel of the huge teeth, the heavy soprano eye-lids, the mulish face and the long ape-like arms: an animal that laughs – it sounds like somebody's definition of Man: Fernandel with the celluloid collar that always creaks and the long greasy lock of hair. Nobody has ever laughed so infectiously as Fernandel: it is like an epidemic, and yet a prim collegaue has found him in close-up disgusting. Fernandel in this film is a conscript and the most intractable material any army has to deal with – a human being. It is, with all its faults, a better picture than *Un de la Légion* because there is no propaganda: it doesn't pretend, as the other film did, that the military mind can deal with human beings – in no time at all Fernandel has been sentenced to thirty days – the good-humoured innocent creature impervious to discipline because it doesn't make sense. There comedy ends and farce begins, for the thirty days must be worked off as batman to the Colonel and slave to the Colonel's wife, a great brawny woman with hips like the horses she rides who is absurdly pursued by the shifty and romantic Baron. The Colonel himself (acted with his usual lovely suavity by Charpin) is as human as Fernandel: he doesn't like wearing uniform and he prefers a bicycle to a horse. This trait, when the bicycle breaks down on the day that the Inspector-General makes a surprise visit, provides the climax, for Fernandel rising hurriedly from the maid's bed puts on the Colonel's uniform she had been given to mend, and is mistaken . . . Before he knows where he is, he is presiding at luncheon and addressing the Colonel's wife by her Christian name (he has learnt too much of who loves whom in the household for anyone to betray him). A humanity which is not permitted to a private is charming in a Colonel, and he earns his commanding officer promotion.

Told like that the story seems to go quite smoothly: I cannot understand why the middle of the film should be filled with lovelies and a stage show and Fernandel dressed as a Mexican blundering on to the stage with a note for the wrong person and pursuits up and down stairs and a cast-off mistress of the Baron – only real lovers of Fernandel will put up with all that. There is one delightful piece of direction, the high-spirited pairing off of Fernandel and the maid – and then the silent scurry up the stairs against time (will the bugle blow from the barracks?), the breathless dash across the dark room, the clothes flung quickly from invisible hands upon the hooks, black-out – a curious sense of lightness and poetry and companionship is conveyed.

IN THE COUNTRY

Perhaps the best release of the week is *The Story of Vernon and Irene Castle*, with Fred Astaire and Ginger Rogers: the scene pre-1914 America and war-time France. Gay, sad and sentimental, full of old tunes, with picturesque starvation, sudden success, eternal fidelity, it isn't so much the story of two real dancers as a fairy tale stepped out by the marvellous couple with incomparable lightness.

Dark Victory can also be recommended at 'the local' to those who like the taste of tears, if only for the sake of Miss Bette Davis's streamlined histrionics as the girl doomed by her doctor to death.

The Spectator (13 October 1939)

Ignace (France, Gray Film, 1939) Dir.: Pierre Colombier. Cast: Fernandel, Charpin, Dany Loris, Raymond Cordy.

Stanley and Livingstone · Only Angels Have Wings

Stanley and Livingstone lost all chance of being a good film when the producers gave it that title. A pity, because it begins well: a tough newspaper reporter defeats the American military authorities in Indian territory during a rising, and is summoned back to New York by his live-wire proprietor, who snaps out a new assignment at the other end of the world. 'Ever heard of Livingstone?' 'Do you mean the new bar-tender at Joe's?' The fatal name has been spoken; this isn't the story of a missionary lost in Africa, and a hard-boiled reporter sent across the world to find him, and prove that a rival paper (the London *Globe*) is wrong when it declares him dead. This is history (though what a Miss Eve Kingsley, a dewy colleen, with whom Stanley falls in love in Zanzibar, can be doing in history I don't know).

History is responsible for the dreary travel sequences shot by Mrs Martin Johnson in Uganda – with the stock lions, giraffes, hippopotami. Most of the film, indeed, consists of long shots of stand-ins moving across undistinguished scenery, while Mr Spencer Tracy reads out extracts from Stanley's diary – into which thoughts of Miss Eve Kingsley oddly intrude (credit for the very remarkable 'historical research' is given to two gentlemen called Hal Long and Sam Hellman). Finally Mr Tracy finds Sir Cedric Hardwicke, and learns Christianity from him – Mr Tracy is always a human being, but Sir Cedric is an elocution lesson, a hand-clasp . . . The picture ends with a meeting of the Royal Geographical Society, which refuses to admit Stanley's claims until an opportune telegram arrives from Zanzibar, conveying Livingstone's last messages. Stanley's girl hadn't realized his love, she's married into the London *Globe*, and Stanley, ignoring cables from the New York *Herald*, returns to Africa to carry on Livingstone's work.

History, by which I no longer mean the researches of Hal and Sam, tells us how he carried on that work: the heavily armed ferocious forays, the massacre of natives who had learnt not to trust his Führer's temperament, the disastrous expedition to rescue Emin Pasha (who like Livingstone had no desires to be rescued), the unpleasant sexual rumours which drifted back to London clubs. Mr Tracy, learning not to strike a black, listening to Sir Cedric conducting 'Onward Christian Soliders', has little in common with the filibuster, poisoned by a childhood in a Welsh workhouse, who replied to the Aborigines Protection Society at a dinner-party: 'He would undertake to provide them with seven tons of Bibles, four tons of Prayer Books, any number of surplices, and a church organ into the bargain, and if they reached as far as longitude 23° without chucking some of those Bibles at some of the negroes' heads he would –'

Only Angels Have Wings has everything a good film needs except a good story. It is admirably acted by Mr Cary Grant, Miss Jean Arthur, Mr Thomas Mitchell and Mr Richard Barthelmess (who makes another sombre and impressive return to the screen: he did it before in *Four Hours to Kill*; what happens to him in between returns?), and it is quite magnificently directed by Mr Howard Hawks – who made *Scarface*. Unfortunately, Mr Hawks has written his own story, a sentimental tough tale of a third-rate air line trying to make both ends meet somewhere near the Andes, the girl who steps off a cruise and stays behind (Miss Arthur) and a pilot who once parachuted from his plane and left his mechanic to die (Mr Barthelmess). At the airport, where he arrives with his wife seeking a new job under a new name, he meets the mechanic's brother (Mr Mitchell), and of course the wife was once engaged to the boss (Mr Grant), who is now forcefully loved by Miss Arthur. It's a regulation muddle which needs the regulation devices to untangle it – storm, sacrifice, heroism, redemption. What does remain in the memory is the setting, drab, dusty, authentic, and a few brilliantly directed scenes, as when a young pilot is trying to land in a ground fog; those below can't see the plane, but they can hear his engine and talk to him by telephone, warn him as he overshoots and hear from the vulcanite the regular record of his doomed descent – 1,000 feet, 500, 200, a long-drawn-out waiting for the inevitable crash.

The Spectator (20 October 1939)

Stanley and Livingstone (USA, Twentieth-Century Fox, 1939). Dir.: Henry King. Cast: Spencer Tracy, Cedric Hardwicke, Richard Greene, Nancy Kelly, Walter Brennan, Charles Coburn, Henry Hull, Henry Travers, Miles Mander.

Only Angels Have Wings (USA, Columbia, 1939) Dir.: Howard Hawks. Cast: Cary Grant, Jean Arthur, Thomas Mitchell, Richard Barthelmess, Rita Hayworth, Sig Rumann, Victor Kilian, John Carroll.

Nurse Edith Cavell · French Without Tears · 'Arf a Mo' Hitler

Mr Herbert Wilcox proceeds on his applauded course. As slow and ponderous and well protected as a steam-roller, he irons out opposition. We get from his films almost everything except life, character, truth. Instead we have flags, anthems, leading articles, a tombstone reticence. It would be unfair to call his Way of a Neagle vulgar showmanship (though a certain lack of taste may be suspected in the portmanteau title of his company, Imperadio), for there is seldom anything vital enough to be called vulgar in the successive patriotic appearances of this rather inexpressive actress. Miss Neagle looked nice as Queen Victoria, she looks just as nice as Nurse Cavell: she moves rigidly on to the set, as if wheels were concealed under her stately skirt: she says her piece with flat dignity and trolleys out again – rather like a mechanical marvel from the World's Fair. This is not, I daresay, Miss Neagle's fault: I remember how attractive she was in tight breeches as Nell of Old Drury – then she was allowed a little vivacity, almost an allure: she had not in those days been crowned.

There is very little to say about her latest picture – it is all exactly as you would expect: Belgians sing Anglican carols in the Brussels streets: Germans, who are distinguished by a foreign accent, are all brutes in boots (except for the one regulation officer who is always inserted in such films to show the measure of our impartiality): there is a comic Cockney soldier and a sensitive sissy one: Miss Neagle recites 'Abide with Me': there is a ceremony in Westminster Abbey, all organ notes and flags and memory, and the ghost of Miss Neagle recites 'Patriotism is not enough . . .'; Mr Wilcox has undoubtedly given us the works. Who are we to complain that Miss Cavell was not young and lovely (Miss Neagle may consent to be an old Queen, but hardly to be a middle-aged commoner), or to protest that no film could have more contradicted her most famous utterance? Hatred and bitterness are certainly here in good measure; when the drums of propaganda begin to beat again we can hardly expect a popular film producer to stand aloof seeking the tragic values in Miss Cavell's story. Nevertheless, one regrets a little that the English creative spirit has never risen higher in her commemoration than a statue cut in soap and an emotional melodrama. Of the two, one prefers the statue: it seems a little truer to the staid heroism, the Anglican rectitude, the clinical love for patients and mankind.[2]

French Without Tears is a triumph for Mr Anthony Asquith. After the first ten minutes his witty direction and firm handling of the cast (Mr Ray Milland has never acted so well as this before) conquer the too British sexuality of Mr Rattigan's farce. There is always something a little shocking about English levity: the greedy exhilaration of these blithe young men when they learn that another fellow's girl is to join them at the establishment where they are learning French, the scramble over her luggage, the light-hearted badinage and the watery and libidinous eye – that national mixture of prudery and excitement – would be unbearable if it were not for Mr Asquith's civilized direction (unlike most adaptations from stage plays it is the padding that is memorable). The situation is saved, too, by the Navy; Mr Rattigan must be given credit for the sketch of a stiff, shy Commander who finds himself dumped down from his ship into this adolescent kindergarten, and Mr Roland Culver for a brilliant performance. One's enjoyment of the picture (rather reluctantly one admits that it is enjoyable) is a little impaired by the too punctual laughter of feminine addicts.

Let nobody be put off by the title, *'Arf a Mo' Hitler*. This short documentary picture is an interesting record of British army training dramatized against an international background. An admirable eye for satirical effect has set the Aldershot Tattoo with its fireworks and costumes against the grim mechanized advance into Prague. The odd period caps and blazers and bicycles of Sandhurst, the incredible little bristly Crimean moustaches of cadet officers – these belong to the same fantastic world as the shots of Van de Lubbe, hunched and beaten and imbecile between his warders.

The Spectator (27 October 1939)

Nurse Edith Cavell (USA, Imperadio Pictures, 1939) Dir.: Herbert Wilcox. Cast: Anna Neagle, George Sanders, Edna May Oliver, May Robson, Alan Marshall.

French Without Tears (GB, Two Cities/Paramount, 1939) Dir.: Anthony Asquith. Cast: Ray Milland, Ellen Drew, Janine Darcey, David Tree, Roland Culver, Guy Middleton.

'Arf a Mo' Hitler (GB, British Paramount News, 1939) Dir.: G.T. Cummins.

The Lion Has Wings

A lion with wings would be no odder an exhibit than this documentary picture of the Royal Air Force constructed by Mr Alexander Korda with the help of little fictional scenes acted by Mr Ralph Richardson, Miss Merle Oberon and others; of irrelevant shots from Mr Korda's unfortunate historical picture *Fire Over England*; and of sequences, showing the Central Control Room of the Air Defence, from the admirable recruiting picture of two years' back called *The Gap*. All the first half of the picture is excellent, from the opening words of the commentary, 'This is Britain where we believe in freedom', with the shots of oast houses and country churches and grazing cattle, on to the new workers' flats and the new hospitals and the new schools and the words: 'Is all this to stop because one man wants to dominate the world?' It is propaganda of an intelligent kind; England at peace is contrasted with Germany preparing for war; there are amusing cuts from beach donkeys to German cavalry; from the mathematical ranks of the Brown-shirts, the guardians of one life, to the King strolling unprotected down a Scottish country lane. One cut is magnificently dramatic and a fine example of reticence: from the small dapper Dollfuss with his pale puzzled waxen features, like those of a tailor's dummy, as he pronounces in broken English 'Good-baye' into the microphone, straight without explanation to the coffin and the bearers and the aftermath of murder. The management of sound, too, is excellent: over the shots of swimmers in a bathing-pool suddenly breaks the music of a military band before we cut to the goosestep and the grey lines; Hitler, in close-up, addressing a Nazi rally, is cut quickly in and out with bookies hurling their impassioned advice, hucksters wheedling. From England at peace we go to England arming: superb shots of the Air Force – shadows racing across tarmac, lifting on to the roofs of hangars and racing on; grey planes moving in formation over a whole watery countryside; planes diving and twisting among the cumulus, carrying smoke like carnival ribbons straight across the sky; the making of the guns; the balloon barrage; the war.

With the war the film loses force and authenticity: we soon begin to tire of the fake elocutionist voices of trained actors. The Germans, I believe, have remarked, that the Kiel battle was fought in the Denham film studios (rather tamely fought, it may be noted), and we become aware of some point in the jest as we watch imaginary battles between fighter squadrons and raiders (who for some reason are called 'bandits'), in which all the deaths are German and all the heroics English. It would be a serious error, I think, to exhibit this film in the United States until we have shown in the air as well as in the studio that we can save London from the raider: imaginary battles are all very well in a thriller –

they are unpleasantly out of place in a documentary, and smack of bravado. One curious effect of using an old propaganda film may be noted: the shots from *The Gap* contradict the whole theme. *The Gap* was made to show that unless recruiting improved the raiders must get through: so now we watch an actor frenziedly biting his nails in a control-room which has become part of a picture preaching invincibility. This dreary unconvincing fictional battle, however, is only the worst failure in tact and taste: almost as bad are scenes which introduce Mr Ralph Richardson as an Air Force officer, Miss Merle Oberon as a voluntary worker and Miss June Duprez as a nice boy's sweetheart. Americans are unlikely to laugh at the massed salute of the Nuremberg Rally – power and discipline are seldom humorous – but they will not, I imagine, restrain their laughter when Miss Oberon pulls Miss Duprez to attention in the drawing room beside the radio set as 'God Save the King' follows Mr Chamberlain's announcement of war or hide their smiles when Miss Oberon whispers to Mr Richardson, 'Darling, are we ready?' The film ends on a note as false as the opening was true. Miss Oberon in nurse's uniform is speaking for all the women of England, telling the world, through United Artists, that we are fighting for 'Truth, and beauty, and fair play, and –' with whimsical hesitation and a professional quaver, 'kindliness'. As a statement of war aims, one feels, this leaves the world beyond Roedean still expectant.

The Spectator (3 November 1939)

The Lion Has Wings (GB, Alexander Korda, 1939) Directors: Adrian Brunel, Michael Powell, Brian Desmond Hurst. Cast: Ralph Richardson, Merle Oberon, June Duprez, Anthony Bushell, Bernard Miles, Flora Robson.

Daughters Courageous · Poison Pen · The First Days

Daughters Courageous has three stars, and one of them is the cameraman, Mr James Wong Howe. Mr Howe is the best cameraman in the industry: he is an incomparable manufacturer of what the industry badly needs – the glittering cellophane packets which give a kind of desirability to the suppressed sobs and the cheeriness and the good hearts you find inside. One can say of Mr Howe's films that, in spite of directors and scenario-writers, they are always lovely to look at.

The other stars are Mr John Garfield and Mr Claude Rains. It is unnecessary to differentiate between the four daughters: they just belong – with their jollity and innocence – to the absurd tale: they add nothing to it. Their mother is a dress-designer; she has been forced to work because her husband walked out on her when the children were small; she is terribly understanding. Now she's taken up with a nice prosperous businessman, and as they celebrate (a contented family party) her engagement, and the husband-to-be sits at the head of the table carving the roast, the old husband walks in. He is Mr Claude Rains – so the story suddenly seems to contain genuine misery, disappointment, bitterness. He takes the stock Ishmael character – with the cynical wisdom and the traveller's tales – and transforms him into something you might really meet on a wet pavement with a gold nugget to sell, making two ends meet round his hopelessness. The scene after dinner when he sits apart by the radio, and the respectable youths drop in and the girls cluster round his successor lighting his pipe and filling his glass, and he silences every conversation by turning the dial and reminding them in a burst of music of his uncomfortable presence – this scene is finely acted. We know, of course, what his banal destiny is to be; how he will charm his daughters cunningly back into affection: and how he will be forced to walk out on them all again rather than ruin their settled futures (what do these Ishmaels use instead of money?): we know every stage of the routine tear-jerker; but Rains surprises us into belief, with that small triangular withered face which can suggest almost any emotion with a movement of the scaly and weather-beaten eyeball. Mr Garfield, too, acts with the venom of real conviction his parallel part of the anti-social youth with whom the youngest daughter falls in love and who finally accompanies Mr Rains into voluntary exile. The film should be very popular: it is so easy to watch, and perhaps the muddled morality is not nowadays noticeable. I confess it seemed a little odd to me, when we cut from the mother and the new husband swearing their vows binding 'till death us do part', to husband number one packing his bag and making his noble unobtrusive exit.

Poison Pen is a deplorable example of an English film which tries to create an English atmosphere. The story is about an anonymous letter-writer in a small town who causes a suicide and a murder and turns out to be the rector's sister. Miss Flora Robson acts the unconvincing part as it deserves, turning on a little routine passion at the close as you would a geyser. The dialogue is appalling, full of unnecessary words, like a charade: 'Do you want a porter?' 'Oh, no, I can manage, thank you.' 'We've got the car outside.' 'What a lovely morning'; and the background of the picture is as quaint and false as a Broadway tea-shop. Everybody – from the postman to the Squire – is a character: the villagers – who have oddly assorted accents – are such simple creatures that they crowd into the Post Office to listen to a private call from Australia: the ignorant patronage of men who have spent their lives among the sets of suburban studios is spread thickly over the English countryside.

Mr Cavalcanti's film of London at war is disappointing, with longeurs and silences which convey a feeling that nobody can think of anything to play or say. The commentary is full of highflown clichés, and though many of the shots will have historic interest, he has failed to dramatise the first days for those who lived them. I am not sure that anyone, who, like Mr Cavalcanti, has a concern for truth could have succeeded.

The Spectator (10 November 1939)

Daughters Courageous (USA, Warners, 1939) Dir.: Michael Curtiz. Cast: Claude Rains, John Garfield, Fay Bainter, Priscilla Lane, Rosemary Lane, Lola Lane, Jeffrey Lynn, Gale Page, Donald Crisp, May Robson, Frank McHugh, Dick Foran, Berton Churchill.

Poison Pen (GB, Associated British, 1939) Dir.: Paul S. Stein. Cast: Flora Robson, Robert Newton, Belle Chrystal, Ann Todd, Reginald Tate, Geoffrey Toone,

Edward Chapman, Edward Rigby.
The First Days (GB, 1939) Dir.: Alberto Cavalcanti.

The Frozen Limits

The Frozen Limits seems to this reviewer the funniest English picture yet produced; more than that, it can bear comparison with the Lloyds and Keatons of Hollywood, with *Safety Last* and *The General.* The credit is not all the Crazy Gang's: that rather repulsive troupe tumble through it – in furs, feathers, nightshirts – with appalling vigour; they seize the comic spirit and impose a kind of mob rule; you may easily be disgusted by the browsing and sluicing; the circus smell of sawdust and human skin. It is all noises and shouts and unintelligible wisecracks. They break through the scenery as if it were a paper hoop. Everything comes to pieces in their boisterous hands. But if you have no sympathy with that savage tribe you will still enjoy the direction of Mr Marcel Varnel and the script of Mr J.O.C. Orton.

The Crazy Gang, bankrupt performers on Hamsptead Heath, pick up a newspaper which tells them of a gold-rush to Red Gulch, Alaska. It must be a recent paper, because the Prime Minister, Mr Chamberlain, is saying that England must be prepared – 'he's only talked like that lately'. But when they arrive in Red Gulch on an old horse bus the place seems deserted. When they knock on the Sheriff's door the whole house collapses like a mummy exposed to air: *East Lynne* is advertised outside the theatre, a spider-web drapes the box-office, and the only human being they can disinter is Mr Moore Marriott, of the thin beard and the piping voice and the exultant eye. He is manager, box-office clerk, commissionaire rolled into one: a mad relic of the pioneering days who lives there with his niece, dreaming of the gold he thinks he once discovered and sleep-walking to find it. He admits them to the ruined theatre and makes them pick their way past the legs of an imaginary audience, and how well the Crazy Gang clown it: the sharp exclamation, the muttered apology, the twisting of the back, the little twitters of impatience and irritation in a dark theatre. The truth at last dawns on them – the Chamberlain they read about carried a monocle and not an umbrella: they are two wars too late.

Nevertheless, there is gold. When the pioneer walks in his sleep that night he brings back a lump of ore in his pail: the Crazy Gang take it in to the nearest town and, using it to pay for their drinks, unintentionally start a new gold-rush. Red Gulch swarms back to life again, but the Crazy Gang, who fear the boom won't last, are caught salting the diggings with the pioneer's lump. Bill McGrew – a cat among mice – threatens them with lynching unless gold is struck before next midday, so the old pioneer must walk again and lead them to his seam. Fill him up with cheese, but that's not enough. He needs a full moon, and a cardboard one is dangled outside the window while Flanagan rocks him to sleep with a lullaby:

> Got a full tum-tum.
> Got a full moon.

Meanwhile the Mounties are riding to the rescue – a delightful touch this, as they trot slowly through the mountains, singing a song in complacent tenor voices about 'always getting our man', straight out of a Nelson Eddy picture. Back in Red Gulch the pioneer walks, but the villains have heard of the ruse, and to outwit them six ancient pioneers in nightshirts must wander through the town with pails and candles. It would be wrong to tell more: of the forced wedding, with one of the gang impersonating the bride, of the wild chase up and down the curtains and beams of the ancient theatre, of how the Mounties do at last arrive and arrest the wrong man, and of how the gold is discovered. It isn't often that one dwells on the story of an English film, but just as there is always an undertone to the best clowning, the drumming of the rain every day, so this farcical tale of a temporary town abandoned to the beetle and the rat has an odd touch of poetry: the ancient melodrama, the bus which runs only in an old man's mind, the long-vanished better people who must be bowed to in their carriages. It is as if a troupe of clowns had suddenly with raspberries and rude gestures and the tang of the ring on their clothes irrupted into a tale of Mr De La Mare's, all silence, spider-web and vacancy.

The Spectator (17 November 1939)

The Frozen Limits (GB, Gainsborough, 1939) Dir.: Marcel Varnel. Cast: The Crazy Gang (Flanagan and Allen, Nervo and Knox, Naughton and Gold), Moore Marriott, Eileen Bell, Anthony Hulme, Bernard Lee, Eric Clavering.

Juarez · Rulers of the Sea

Juarez (pronounced, so the programme tells us, War-ezz) is what is known in the trade as a distinguished film: it follows *Pasteur* and *Zola* and might easily have died of distinction as *Zola* did. Listen to what happened in Warner's studios, if we are to believe the publicity-writers, when it was decided to make the picture. A Doctor Herman Lissauer assembled as complete a bibliography as he could, and within one month turned in to the unfortunate producers and director '372 books, documents, pieces of correspondence and albums of rare and authentic [*sic*] photographs.' Three writers – one of them with the picturesque name of Aeneas MacKenzie – got to work on this material, though, as the credit refers to a play of Werfel's and Miss Bertita Harding's *The Phantom Crown*, from which they could learn all they needed to know for this rather superficial picture, one imagines the 372 books, documents, etc., soon went into store. Meanwhile, the art director was drawing 3,643 sketches, the construction department was making 7,360 blueprints (they might surely have done less, since the same Mexican village set seems to have been used for Vera Cruz, Matamoros and Queretaro), the directors were making a tour of Mexico and Miss Bette Davis was cutting her hair three inches shorter. Presumably the directors looked in at Oaxaca on their trip, but the sight of the ruined convent there did not suggest any alteration in their portrait of Juarez as a Liberal democrat of the Abraham Lincoln school.

It must be admitted, however, that a quite impressive film has emerged from all the muddles – perhaps the muddle wasn't really as great as the publicity department makes out, and the two parts of Juarez and Maximilian are well written and admirably acted by Mr Paul Muni and Mr Brian Aherne (Mr Muni's make-up is extraordinarily impressive: he is an Indian to the very shape of his skull and the stony Aztec profile). I have not usually been an admirer of Mr Aherne's acting: his personality has always seemed to go with a pipe and Harris tweeds and a boundless complacency, but here he nearly acts Mr Muni off the set. With his forked and silky beard, the blond whiskers and curls, the gentle worried inflexibility, he is every inch a Hapsburg, and the film is his from that first puzzled inquiry at Vera Cruz – 'Why are the streets so empty?' – to his long, careful frock-coated stride up the rocky hill of the death-place. (Miss Bette Davis's Carlotta simply does not exist beside him.) Mr Muni as the whitewashed Juarez has a smaller and easier part: he has only to be simple, kindly, ruthless from the best ideological motives: he is preaching to the converted. He hasn't got to put over such an unfashionable doctrine as the divine right of kings to be the servant of their people, and when he defines democracy to General Porfirio Diaz every Left Book Club heart will beat a little faster (who cares or knows about the ruined schools and churches?). Many of my colleagues have objected to the dialogue, which they call stilted: it seemed to me to go admirably with the stiff dated Hapsburg court set down, like a millionaire's purchase from Europe, with its gold-leaf and scarlet hangings, its ushers and rules of precedence, in the dry savage countryside, where we watch a vulture peck at a child's body in a ruined village. The cameramen have for once resisted the temptation to make Mexico picturesque – there are hardly any cactuses and no sky-lined peons.

Rulers of the Sea is a not-so-historical film of the first Transatlantic steamboat: it tells how a humane first officer (Mr Douglas Fairbanks, jun.), tired of the brutality of sail, takes up with a pawky old Scots engineer (Mr Will Fyffe) who has invented an engine, which he believes will drive a ship across the Atlantic. He has a daughter, acted by Miss Margaret Lockwood – all sharp features, poke bonnet and refinement. There's a lot of discouragement, starvation and unscrupulous competition, but all ends well with cheering crowds in New York harbour, lovers united, the old engineer scalding to death at the right moment, and a shot of the 'Queen Mary'.

The Spectator (24 November 1939)

Juarez (USA, Warners, 1939) Dir.: William Dieterle. Cast: Paul Muni, Bette Davis, Brian Aherne, Claude Rains, John Garfield, Donald Crisp, Gale Sondergaard, Joseph Calleia, Gilbert Roland, Henry O'Neill, Pedro de Cordoba, Montagu Love, Harry Davenport.

Rulers of the Sea (USA, Paramount, 1939) Dir.: Frank Lloyd. Cast: Douglas Fairbanks Jr., Margaret Lockwood, Will Fyffe, Montagu Love, George Bancroft, Mary Gordon, Alan Ladd.

Golden Boy · On the Night of the Fire · Where's that Fire

Perhaps because the original play did not seem to me of great importance – a well-told sentimental story of a boxer who wanted to be a violinist, and broke his hand and killed himself in one of those convenient Green Hat car smashes – the film of *Golden Boy* pleased me. The crusty amusing Odets dialogue is still there – we have the fatal fight that the stage could not give us, and if the ending is now a happy one, with the boxer comforted by his girl, who assures him that his hands will one day get back all their musical skill, does it matter very much? Was the symbolism of the play so significant? Wasn't it really a bit of hooey? *Golden Boy* has been directed by Rouben Mamoulian, and apart from the foggy sepia tones which do justice only to Mr Menjou's lounge suits, it has all the vigorous hard-hitting close-up effect one expects from the director of *City Streets* (let's forget and forgive *Queen Christina* and the rest). Mr Menjou as the boxer's manager, with his desperate humour, his unfortunate sexual life, and his recurring disappointments ('Ah, sweet misery of life!') has one of the best parts he has played since *The Front Page*, and Mr William Holden almost persuades us to believe in the boxing violinist. But the real stars are Mr Mamoulian and Mr Joseph Calleia. You can tell the quality of a director by his close-ups, and I would put the final boxing-match, when the Golden Boy, with hate in his gloves for the sport and his exploiters, kills his black opponent in a cruel knock-out, among the finest sequences of the talking film. It is shot almost entirely in close-up, close up to the fighters and close to the audience, back and forth from the plugging gloves to the febrile blondies with their moistened lips, the stout complacent backers at the ringside, and screaming Harlem in the gallery; it is shot subjectively, with hate in the lens as well as in the gloves. And then there is Mr Calleia: Mr Calleia is being groomed these days for sympathetic stardom. The anarchist in *Five Came Back*, with his bloodshot canine suffering eyes, was meant to prepare us for his Father Damien. Here he is back in one of his old gangster parts – the rigid back, the graceful functional body carried like a gun, a haunting picture of a lonely crook who wants to own a champ.

On the Night of the Fire is about a barber who steals some money and then is driven by blackmail to murder. It has been extravagantly praised – an odd thing for those of us who heard the ribald laughter at the Press show. Based on Mr F.L. Green's unconvincing novel, it aims at more than thriller rank; it is meant to be all destiny and the furies in a grim depressed industrial town. The book has been very closely followed – far too closely, for Mr Green's romantic brain seemed to contain no knowledge of how men really act. Fantastic police methods; sudden reversals of character; mobs who are whipped up with the speed of Elizabethan drama – it seems even more unreal upon the screen. Nor is it helped by acting or direction. A lot of aitches carefully and symmetrically dropped never disguise the classy origins of Mr Ralph Richardson, Miss Diana Wynyard and Mr Romney Brent, while Mary Clare as a half-witted old ragpicker reminds us in her mummery of a hard-working hostess determined to make her dumb-crambo party go. The director has taken most of the dreary story in medium long shots, the camera firmly placed as it were in the front row of the stalls. Watching the dull distances, the ineffective angles and the bad lighting, I found myself wondering – as I have wondered before at Mr Brian Desmond Hurst's *Ourselves Alone* and *Riders to the Sea* – what constitutes promise in an English studio. Can it be that well-worn shot of a gramophone-needle scraping to a close as a man dies out of sight? The second-rate cinema mind has always been attracted to symbolism – the apple blossom falling in the rain, the broken glass, all the sham poetic ways of avoiding the direct statement, which demands some insight into the way men really act.

The next fire is a comic one, with Messrs Will Hay, Moore Marriott, Graham Moffat, an old horse-engine and lots of spiders webs. A superb sequence when they try to fix a pole in the station: otherwise not so funny.

The Spectator (1 December 1939)

Golden Boy (USA, Columbia, 1939) Dir.: Rouben Mamoulian. Cast: William Holden, Barbara Stanwyck, Adolphe Menjou, Joseph Calleia, Lee J. Cobb, Sam Levene, Edward Brophy, Don Beddoe.

On the Night of the Fire (GB, G & S, 1939) Dir.: Brian Desmond Hurst. Cast: Ralph Richardson, Diana Wynyard, Romney Brent, Mary Clare, Henry Oscar, Frederick Leister.

Where's the Fire (GB, Twentieth-Century Fox, 1939) Dir.: Marcel Varnel. Cast: Will Hay, Moore Marriott, Graham Moffat, Peter Gawthorne, Eric Clavering, Charles Hawtrey.

In Name Only

This is a well-made depressing little picture of unhappy marriage. It is often quite sentimental, but the general impression which remains is quite an authentic one – a glass photographic likeness of gloom: fruitless discussions about Reno, polite chicanery over the long-distance 'phone, hate in the sherry glass, the rattled nerve and the despair of any day being different from today. *Dodsworth* and *Craig's Wife* come to mind: these, too, were pictures of mental distress among the higher incomes, but *Dodsworth*, at any rate, had more saving humour. Humour here pops up only incidentally – with a drunk little clerk on Christmas Eve (surprisingly acted by that icy gangster, Mr Allen Baxter), with a scared fat youth in a restaurant-car listening to the forked war of women's tongues. I wonder sometimes where pictures like this find the money for production: the huge cinema masses surely have a shorter and sharper way of satisfying their loves and hates: are they not a little puzzled and bored by the well-groomed classy tragedy with a happy ending, the sense of sex isolated from any other kind of trouble, money or work, what Mr Aiken has described so well as 'the late night wrangles, the three-day silences, the weepings in dark rooms face downward on dishevelled beds . . . the livid eyes of hate over the morning grapefruit'?

The picture is made, quite credibly, by three people – Miss Carole Lombard, Mr Cary Grant and Miss Kay Francis. Both actresses break new ground. Miss Lombard's wavering and melancholy voice, her bewildered eyes, which have in the past faltered so well among the rapid confused events of crazy comedy, and Miss Francis, 'the best-dressed woman in Hollywood', who used to step unresilently, with a lisp, as the hard unscrupulous wife who is after something more valuable than alimony, her father-in-law's money. I liked this whole-heartedly unpleasant character, who presents a cunning picture of understanding and patience to the parents, driving a wedge between them and their son, and when at last her husband's open preference for another woman forces her to consent to a divorce, double-crosses relentlessly going to Paris with the parents on the secret understanding that there she will break the truth to them and get her decree, but all the time determined to hold on, inventing delay after delay to sap the girl's trust in her lover, until she at last returns without it. The main theme of the picture is the strain on the Paris home and listening to the time-saving lies: the atmosphere of triumphant war between a woman with complete mastery of her feelings and her tongue and an ordinary kindly man and a rather guiless girl.

But this is a classy, not a first-class picture. Shot with a refined taste for interior decoration, well-groomed, advertising only the best cars, it is oversweetened with the material for tears: Miss Lombard's young widow has a small child addicted to winsome wisecracks; the last hope of divorce crashes on Christmas Eve with the parcels stacked beside the tree and the candles ready for lighting; the hero lies traditionally drunk before the open window of a seedy hotel. Here the film comes to life again for a few minutes with the fine study of the hotel manager – the narrow prudish face, the sly suggestion, the cigarette-case always open in the palm, the sacred secretive lechery. But after that brief appearance the well-worn path of the tear-jerker has to be trodden to the bitter and the happy end. Pneumonia, the girl forbidden the bedside, the old specialist saying, 'There is only one person who can give him the will to live,' the white lie – 'everything is all right now,' and then the wife's arrival, the rash betrayal of what she's really after while the parents listen out of sight, everything cleared satisfactorily up in a few seconds, even the pneumonia – 'he's sleeping now,' just as though the slow dubious movements of the human intelligence could be shot by an ultra-rapid camera, happiness seeded and bedded and blossomed with the knowing speed of a *Secrets of Nature* flower.

The Spectator (8 December 1939)

In Name Only (USA, RKO, 1939) Dir.: John Cromwell. Cast: Cary Grant, Carole Lombard, Kay Francis, Charles Coburn, Helen Vinson.

The Marx Brothers at the Circus · Disputed Passage · Paramount News

The old crazy sets have gone now for good, that air of a world run up like a pioneer village overnight at the least expense. We must regretfully accept the fact that, thanks to the Metro millions, the Marx Brothers are finally imprisoned in the Hollywood world. I prefer the circus to the opera and the races – there is no Miss Maureen O'Sullivan here to bring our enjoyment crashing down with the whisper 'Silly' as Groucho lopes lecherously past. There *are* young lovers and a story that runs carefully from A to B – Mr Kenny Baker with his soprano speech and his plump eye-sockets plays a rich Newport young man who shocks his relatives by managing a circus and musically loving an equestrienne ('We've got it oh so bad, but isn't it good . . . Don't know fish from cake, Don't know if it's doughnut or a wedding-cake . . . two blind loves'), there's a villain who wants to own the circus and hires a strong man and a dwarf to rob the manager of the takings, and Groucho, the small-town lawyer with his old umbrella, his stained frock-coat, his wild gleam and erratic intelligence, is on the trail, *ventre à terre*. He may be cramped by the classy direction, by the fine circus sets and the exciting shots of freight-trains moving against a dark sky, the admirable Mervyn Le Roy dope, but he manages all the same to break away to the padded silken side of Madame Dumont (one of Newport's 400) stretched as usual on her Pompadour couch as though she had never moved an inch since the delectable days of *Horsefeathers* and *Duck Soup*.

This is Groucho's film: Chico and Harpo are a long way behind: Groucho singing about a woman tattooist – 'Lydia, oh Lydia, that encyclopaedia': Groucho putting on the dingy tails ('It would take a magician,' he complains, 'to get into this suit', and Chico replies, 'I got it from a magician'), unearthing the white rabbit, the flags of all nations (Harpo pulls out a toy rifle and a band plays), a pigeon ('It's all right. It's a homing pigeon.' 'Then I'll keep a light burning in my pocket.') Groucho stuck upside-down on the ceiling in suctional boots: Groucho undressing coyly behind the circus lady's screen, hanging up his combined black stockings and long pants: Groucho bearding Madame Dumont in her bedroom. Impossible to explain all the stages to the superb climax when Madame Dumont is shot protestingly out of a cannon, and Groucho, Harpo, the villain and a murderous ape cling to the flying trapeze while she hurtles towards them in her Newport robe and her bursting seams.

Is it, when you come to think of it, a much odder story than *Disputed Passage*, which is about a great surgeon and his great pupil, and how the pupil falls in love with a Chinese girl (but she's only Chinese by upbringing, so the tale is eugenically sound), and how the surgeon tries to break the romance in the cause of science (but really it's because his wife died two years ago of appendicitis), and his pupil in the last twenty minutes quarrels with him, pursues the girl to China and gets bombed by Japanese: his life's despaired of, the great surgeon arrives by plane and operates, 'science has done everything it can', the girl turns up too, all's well, and the surgeon admits – for dubious reasons – that there must be a soul. A prologue shows the author, Mr Lloyd Douglas – who wrote that other medical marvel, *Magnificent Obsession* – penning a few lines in his library to the producers: 'Dear Paramount, thank you for preserving the full flavour of my story . . .' I should describe the flavour as a rather nauseating blend of iodine and glucose.

Mr Douglas's heart-wounds look a bit shabby in this mined, torpedoed world. The Paramount News, with its remarkable record of the rescue by the *Independence Hall* of the survivors of the *Yorkshire* – the broken ship diving out of sight, the white drifting faces on the water – beat any so-called 'serious' film off the screen. No Hollywood tragedy can afford comparison with the beaten puzzled faces of the Lascar sailors (their heads are bandaged because their officers had to knock them out with life-preservers before pitching them overboard in lifebelts), the orphaned child who looks as if she's missed a party, the coffin pitched into the sea wrapped in another country's flag – there's got to be a flag.

The Spectator (15 December 1939)

The Marx Brothers at the Circus (USA, MGM, 1939) Dir.: Edward Buzzell. Cast: The Marx Brothers, Margaret Dumont, Florence Rice, Kenny Baker, Eve Arden, Nat Pendleton, Fritz Feld.

Disputed Passage (USA, Paramount, 1939) Dir.: Frank Borzage. Cast: Dorothy Lamour, Akim Tamiroff, John Howard, Judith Barrett, William Collier Snr., Victor Varconi, Keye Luke, Elizabeth Risdon.

First Love · Our Neighbours – The Carters · Espionage Agent · Ducks and Drakes

First Love is an honest fairy-tale, based even to the slipper and the midnight sanction on *Cinderella*: it doesn't for a moment pretend to be life, this story of the Deanna Durbin orphan with a golden voice who comes to live, when she leaves school, with her rich morose uncle, her hazy and eccentric aunt who dabbles in astrology, and their children – a spoilt society beauty and a backboneless youth who has been conserving energy all his life against an emergency that he is determined shall never turn up. Miss Durbin, of course, wins the hearts of the trampled domestics, even of her soured uncle (Mr Eugene Pallette looking very much like Mr Tod, the badger, with his bowed back and twitching nostril, as he disappears regularly to ground), and at the great ball of the season the local police force come to her aid, outwitting the wicked cousin who is determined, through jealousy, that she shall stay at home. Her relatives are all side-tracked into a magistrates' court while she arrives at the ball in the Commissioner's car, wins her coveted prince and leaves a slipper in her hurried midnight exit. The whole tale is carried off: even the butler might sprout pantomime wings at any moment; and as for Miss Durbin's first real affair, it is managed with infinite tact (the halting talk about auxiliary engines on the penthouse roof and the first kiss and the hurried conversational recovery – 'What is a Diesel?'). There is nothing at all to resent in the picture; it is admirably directed, amusingly written, and acted with immense virtuosity by a fine cast. It isn't true: the world is nobody's oyster – no young girl will ever in this way oust the *prima donna* at her first ball and snatch the season's prize, but that doesn't matter, because there is nothing shabby or hypocritical in the dream which Miss Durbin expresses with the drive of irresistible conviction.

The Carters belong to a fairy-tale of very different quality. This *does* pretend to be life – from the awful bluff note on the programme: 'Here's the Carters – the grandest family you've ever met', it tries with blasts of loyalty, cheeriness and good-fellowship to put across a fake idea of middle-class virtue. A genuine subject – the defeat of the small family druggist by the cut-price store – is lost in the appalling sentimentality – all the more appalling for the expert mechanized acting of Mr Frank Craven. No family like this has ever existed: it doesn't even represent, like *First Love*, a natural human hope, but directed with great competence, it makes its effect – the easy tears of middle-aged women all round.

Espionage Agent is a timid successor to *Confessions of a Nazi Spy*. A young Consul marries a stray girl who faints in his office, and hears from her afterwards that she has been in Nazi pay: he has to resign from the service, and the two of them go to Europe with the intention of amassing enough proof to convince the Congress that Nazi agents have prepared an elaborate scheme for sabotaging industry in the event of a European war. They get their proofs in Geneva on the eve of the Polish invasion: a burglary, a motor chase, an assault in an express train just before it crosses the German frontier, a waiting aeroplane, 'We'll make it: we've got to' – and then a comforting shot of the good old Queen Mary (stuck on like a seal at the end of so many films). The whole job seems to have been done very easily.

There is far more drama in the latest *Secrets of Life* picture: a (visually) admirable film called *Ducks and Drakes*. The secrets are now shot in Dufaycolour, which renders the dim nondescript tones of water and weed better than the greens and blues of trees and sky. Mr Emmett's too familiar potted voice turns out the usual hateful cracks – 'Our distinguished friend, Mrs Widgeon,' and the usual fake poetry – 'Our duckling gazes with wonder at the golden Kingcups,' that are thought necessary to put over even the most exciting instruction – the polecat torpedoing through the grass and the pale pike moving below the convoy of ducks.

The Spectator (22 December 1939)

First Love (USA, Universal, 1939) Dir.: Henry Koster. Cast: Deanna Durbin, Robert Stack, Helen Parrish, Eugene Pallette, Lewis Howard, Leatrice Joy.
Our Neighbours – The Carters (USA, Paramount, 1939) Dir.: Ralph Murphy. Cast: Fay Bainter, Frank Craven, Genevieve Tobin, Edmund Lowe.
Espionage Agent (USA, Warners, 1939) Dir.: Lloyd Bacon. Cast: Joel McCrea, Brenda Marshall, Jeffrey Lynn, George Bancroft, Stanley Ridge, James Stephenson, Nana Bryant.

Remontons les Champs-Elysées · The Rains Came

How unbearable these films of M. Sacha Guitry would be if they were not so successful. One remembers the superb impertinence with which a few years ago this elderly actor and playwright stalked into the studios, ignoring all rules, all unities, all the painstaking calculations of worthy directors who had been learning all their lives from experience, and began to make pictures which challenged by their very triviality (we had become so used to epics); like his plays, they were nothing at all except mediums for that sagacious hollow voice, that swinging monocle and the conqueror's gait.

Now with his latest picture we can see that he has learnt nothing humdrum and lost nothing valuable. He is the only director who can make films as personal as essays: he might be described as the Montaigne of the screen – we can almost watch him think as he shoots: a momentary pause as a new idea strikes him, and then away with plot, continuity, turn the cameras over here, switch on those lights, scrap that part and read this one. What we seem to see is not a finished product of the creative mind but the art of creation itself, as M. Guitry plays with the pageant of French history. Le Roi Soleil steps like a young conqueror into his coach and out again the other side, withered and monkeyish and old – it is as if M. Guitry had just at that moment thought of that. Foremen are urging on the lazy workmen who are building the Café des Ambassadeurs – 'in those days men were encouraged to work': an idea strikes M. Guitry: in a flash of the eyelid it is the other way about, the foremen sprout twentieth-century cloth caps as they try to make their men go slow: another flash and we are back in the days of Louis-Philippe. It has nothing to do with the story, with continuity, but M. Guitry can leave all that to others: his aim is to catch ideas on the wing.

The framework of his picture is a simple one: M. Guitry plays an elderly school-master (if he can ever be said to play anything but himself) who talks to his pupils with remarkable broad-mindedness about the history of the Champs-Elysées: a rare schoolmaster this, in whose veins, we soon begin to learn, flows the blood of Louis XV, of Marat and of Napoleon – a model Frenchman, royal, revolutionary, bourgeois, and perpetually amorous. (All his ancestors have fallen in love at fifty-four and died at sixty-four, and as this is his sixty-fourth birthday, he must rapidly unload his knowledge.) Most of the picture is in monologue with little acted scenes, and M. Guitry plays his ancestors at ardent fifty-four – with Napoleon III thrown in as good measure. Never was genuine patriotism expressed so lightly, wittily, scandalously, or with more real dignity; and the impudent direction touches poetry when the beaten Napoleon dimisses his carriage and walks alone for the last time up the Champs. 'I cannot believe,' M. Guitry says, 'that Napoleon and Bonaparte were the same man. How interesting if they had met there . . .', and there, as the idea strikes him, the meeting crystallizes between the misty trees, the young revolutionary and the tired old Emperor. 'We couldn't even love the same woman.'

Any other films this week must seem pedestrian. *The Rains Came* – made by Clarence Brown, a reliable old-timer – is a very 'seeable' picture about a native State in India, in spite of the stock characters who all 'find themselves' with the help of an earthquake, a flood, and a cholera epidemic, and in spite of dialogue on well-worn lines – 'He loves me.' 'That's why you must go.' 'You're asking me to give up the only chance of real happiness I've ever known.' The characters are either very explicit or very pent-up: sentences like 'May I have a cigarette?' convey all sorts of classy emotions (incidentally, I feel that 'the will to live' as a medical property is rather overworked: we have had it three times in a fortnight). I haven't read Mr Bromfield's book, but I think it would be safe to say that this is the sort of story which is unbearable in book form because of the dim characterization and the flat prose, but becomes likeable as a film because a vivid camera takes the place of the pen.

The Spectator (29 December 1939)

Remontons les Champs-Elysées (France, Cinéas, 1938) Dir.: Sacha Guitry. Cast: Sacha Guitry, Raymond Galle. (US title: *Champs-Elysées*)

The Rains Came (USA, Twentieth-Century Fox, 1939) Dir.: Clarence Brown. Cast: Myrna Loy, George Brent, Tyrone Power, Brenda Joyce, Maria Ouspenskaya, Joseph Schildkraut, H.B. Warner, Nigel Bruce, Mary Nash, Jane Darwell, Marjorie Rambeau, Henry Travers.

Mr Smith Goes to Washington · Each Dawn I Die

Here is Capra, without the help of Riskin, back to his finest form – the form of *Mr Deeds*. It has always been an interesting question, how much Capra owed to his faithful scenario-writer. Now it is difficult to believe that Riskin's part was ever very important, for all the familiar qualities are here – the exciting close-ups, the sudden irrelevant humour, the delight – equal to that of the great

Russians – in the ordinary human face. (Claude Rains has not got an ordinary human face, and for that reason he seems out of place and histrionic, great actor though he is, in a Capra film.)

The story is regulation Capra in praise of simplicity and virtue and acting naturally. As a fairy-tale it is a little Victorian: it is not that we are less moved by virtue in these days, but we are more aware of how the author cheats – virtue is not bound to win, and the easy moral of a Capra tale comes dangerously close to a Benthamite apothegm about honesty being the best policy. Young Jefferson Smith, acted with a kind of ideal awkwardness by James Stewart, is appointed a Senator to fill an unexpired term: he is a youth leader whose guilelessness is considered useful by the other State Senator, Joseph Payne, and his business boss, Jim Taylor. They are putting over a tricky piece of graft and they don't want a new Senator who can see his way. So Smith goes up to Washington with his naïve ideals and his patriotism (he knows Lincoln's speeches off by heart) and his sense of responsibility below the bony marble fingers of the Lincoln statue, and Paine entertains him and side-tracks him.

Then suddenly Smith's secretary, with all the harsh, don't-give-a-twopenny-curse charm of Miss Jean Arthur, opens his eyes to the real Washington, where you can't look round a monument without starting a grafter. He refuses to be a party to fraud and Jim Taylor (Edward Arnold) proceeds to break him – papers are forged, witnesses perjure themselves, he is declared by a Committee of the Senate unworthy to hold his seat. 'Beautiful,' says a reporter at the framed inquiry, 'that Taylor machine.' But Smith won't surrender: when the Senators refuse to listen to him, he takes advantage of the Constitution and holds the floor for twenty-three hours, hoping that his State will support him – in vain because the newspapers have been bought by Taylor. This constitutional battle of one man against the Senate is among the most exciting sequences the screen has given us. But it is a fairy-tale, so Smith wins: Joseph Paine, like a Dickensian Scrooge, is caught by conscience, and I imagine it is easier for us, than for an American who knows his country's politics, to suspend disbelief.

It is a great film, even though it is not a great story, acted by a magnificent cast, so that Capra can afford to fling away on tiny parts men like Eugene Pallette, Guy Kibbee, Thomas Mitchell and Harry Carey. A week later one remembers vividly the big body of Pallette stuck in a telephone-box, the family dinner of the weak crooked Governor (Kibbee) whom even his children pester over the nomination, the whole authentic atmosphere of big bland crookery between boss and politician – the 'Joes' and the 'Jims', the Christian names and comradeship, the wide unspoken references, and one remembers too the faces chosen and shot with Capra care – worried political faces, Grub Street faces, acquisitive social faces and faces that won't give themselves away.

Each Dawn I Die is like something left over that's been hotted up. This story of a reporter who gets wise to some political grafters and who is framed and stuck away in prison for manslaughter really belongs to the early 'thirties, but it hasn't quite the melodramatic vitality of *The Big House* or the sincerity of *I am a Fugitive*. It's just an exciting story we've heard before, made by the not quite good enough director of *G-Men* – worth seeing for the sake of James Cagney's alert and nervous acting and the good regulation performance of George Raft, his gangster friend, who stages a prison mutiny to wring a confession out of the right man. The picture goes out in a blast of bombs and bullets: odd that it leaves so little impression behind.

The Spectator (5 January 1940)

Mr Smith Goes to Washington (USA, Columbia, 1940) Dir.: Frank Capra. Cast: James Stewart, Jean Arthur, Edward Arnold, Eugene Pallette, Thomas Mitchell, Guy Kibbee, Beulah Bondi, Harry Carey, H.B. Warner, Ruth Donnelly, Porter Hall, Astrid Allwyn, Charles Lane.

Each Dawn I Die (USA, Warners, 1939) Dir.: William Keighley. Cast: James Cagney, George Raft, Jane Bryan, George Bancroft, Maxie Rosenbloom, Stanley Ridges, Alan Baxter, Victor Jory.

The Real Glory · Twenty-One Days

This, we are tempted to exclaim at *The Real Glory*, forgetting for a while men like Duvivier, who have brought a mature intelligence to the film, is what cinema should be: a simple story of adventure and sudden death, and will they arrive in time? Every value which exists in a boy's story has been put cunningly into this film – self-sacrifice, misunderstanding, heroism, and if it were not for the intrusion of a couple of females about a third of the way through, it could hardly be improved. It is directed by Henry Hathaway, who made *Bengal Lancer*, and the star is Gary Cooper, with David Niven and others sparkling in the background. I can't remember the women's names – one of them had a sweet and pallid charm which reminded me of Heather Angel: I, too, much resented their presence, dressed up in spotless Sargent dresses, in this dangerous outpost of the Philippines.

The American army has withdrawn, leaving a few white officers to train the native levies, and make them fit to fight for their own independence. 'In twenty-four hours,' the senior officer protests, 'we shall be screaming for help', because the Moros are up under their pirate leader, and are only waiting for the Americans to withdraw before they burn, kill, rape and enslave the frightened Philippinos. The last boats leave, watched by the despairing natives, and the Catholic priest greets the retiring Commander: 'We who are about to die salute you.' The isolation of the almost defenceless town of Mysang is admirably conveyed. The pirates' aim is to provoke the ill-trained troops into the jungle after them, and so they send assassins to cut down the American officers one after another. The most exciting action shots I have seen for a long while on the screen are of the first assassination: the huge half-naked shaven swordsman levering himself up on to the jetty, the townspeople fleeing at the sight of a Moro face, and then his controlled fanatic charge across the deserted quay right to his mark unstopped by bullets. It isn't necessary to give away any more of the story – the ambush and the cholera epidemic, the diverted river, and the last great scene of the assault against a weakened garrison, the pirates catapulted from trees into the fort, while help comes rushing down the dynamited river on rafts. Mr Cooper as the military doctor, who arrives with a present of orchids and a colonel's gallstone for his friends, has never acted better. Sometimes his lean photogenic face seems to leave everything to the lens, but there is no question here of his not acting. Watch him innoculate the girl against cholera – the casual jab of the needle, and the dressing slapped on while he talks, as though a thousand arms had taught him where to stab and he doesn't have to think any more.

Perhaps I may be forgiven for noticing a picture in which I had some hand, for I have no good word to say of it. The brilliant acting of Mr Hay Petrie as a decayed and outcast curate cannot conquer the overpowering flavour of cooked ham. Galsworthy's story *The First and the Last*, was peculiarly unsuited for film adaptation, as its whole point lay in a double suicide (forbidden by the censor), a burned confession, and an innocent man's conviction for murder (forbidden by the great public). For the rather dubious merits of the original the adaptors have substituted incredible coincidences and banal situations. Slow, wordy, unbearably sentimental, the picture reels awkwardly towards the only suicide the censorship allowed – and that, I find with some astonishment, has been cut out. I wish I could tell the extraordinary story that lies behind this shelved and resurrected picture, a story involving a theme-song, and a bottle of whisky, and camels in Wales . . . Meanwhile, let one guilty man, at any rate, stand in the dock, swearing never, never to do it again . . .

Readers of the late *World Film News* will be glad to hear of its successor, a *Documentary News Letter*, published monthly by the same editorial board for subscribers only. The rate is threepence a copy, and the address 34 Soho Square. If anything the paper has been improved, as the editors in this Roneographed edition need make no bid for the larger popularity. The reviews are admirable: I am glad to see in the January number that *The Lion has Wings* gets the treatment it deserves.

The Spectator (12 January 1940)

The Real Glory (USA, Samuel Goldwyn, 1939) Dir.: Henry Hathaway. Cast: Gary Cooper, David Niven, Andrea Leeds, Broderick Crawford, Reginald

Owen, Kay Johnson, Russell Hicks, Vladimir Sokoloff.

Twenty-One Days (GB, London Films, 1939) Dir.: Basil Dean. Cast: Laurence Olivier, Vivien Leigh, Leslie Banks, Robert Newton, Hay Petrie, Francis L. Sullivan, Esmé Percy, Victor Rietti. (US title: *Twenty-One Days Together*)

The Light that Failed · The Old Maid

These two pictures succeed admirably in what they attempt – to jerk the waiting tear out of its duct. Human nature is seldom more incomprehensible than in its sympathies; art which is supposed to enlarge them has left us, after all these centuries, reading with casual interest of the casualties in a wrecked train, or passing over a street accident altogether ('no news today'), though both are within range of our experience. But to tell a story about a great artist who receives a spear slash in the Sudan, and a long time later goes blind just after painting the picture of his career – a picture which he doesn't know has been spoiled with turpentine by his angry model, and who later, when he does learn the truth, goes out, blind as he is, to the Sudan, hits on his old newspaper friends and an English square at the moment of attack, and dies happily and quickly with a bullet in the right place – tell a somewhat unusual anecdote of that kind, an anecdote which can hardly appeal to the personal experience of anyone in the audience, and you will have every tenth man and woman weeping in the dark. Take, too, the subject of *The Old Maid* – churned out, it may be noted, by the late Edith Wharton at a time when she must have forgotten the lesson of the Master: you wouldn't say that story either was likely to happen twice on the same planet. A younger sister (Bette Davis) loves the man her sister (Miriam Hopkins) has jilted: he goes off to the Civil War and is killed, leaving her pregnant: so in order to hide her child she opens a home for war orphans. But she becomes engaged to her sister's brother-in-law (the whole story reads like the table of forbidden degrees), and her sister learns of the child: she stops the marriage on the wedding-day, pretending that sister Davis has consumption. Then her own husband dies, and for rather inadequate reasons sister Davis comes to share her home, and it isn't long before the child is calling sister Hopkins 'Mummie' and sister Davis 'Auntie'. Then we skip the years and find sister Davis is a typical old maid, disliked by her child, who finds her harsh and unsympathetic (this is to hide the awful truth from her), and it all ends with the daughter's marriage and a farewell kiss to poor auntie at the instigation of kind mummie. This story will undoubtedly prove a winner: in a world of bombed towns tears will fall with delirious ease over this rather improbable life of an old maid.

Kipling's novel has been reproduced with great fidelity, and the period is admirably caught, with Norfolk jackets and Sargent hats and gentlemen's rooms: even the pictures painted by Helder are period – big action canvases in the style of the *Illustrated London News*, and we can well imagine the masterpiece, *Melancholia*, as the Academy picture of the year. This is intelligent – it is easier to sympathize with a popular artist we can believe in than in any great unlikely genius. Ronald Colman's Helder is agreeable, but his voice has a way of breaking into insincerity, of giving up the ghost of acting altogether (perhaps the Kipling dialogue is too much for him, admirable coloured stuff though it is), and he is sometimes acted right off the set by Walter Huston as his friend Torpenhow and by Ida Lupino, with her lovely barmaid features, as the vicious little cockney model. Newspapermen will feel envious at this picture of correspondents who really went to Khartoum with Kitchener, or to Kandahar with Roberts, instead of watching endless football-matches and ENSA entertainment behind the lines.

Great actresses choose odd mediums, and perhaps Miss Davis is a great actress – she seemed so in her early pop-eyed appearances, all nerves and nastiness (you remember *Of Human Bondage*). Her performance in *The Old Maid* is of extraordinary virtuosity – as the young girl and the secret mother, and the harsh prim middle-aged woman with her tiny lines and her talcum. It is like a manual of acting for beginners in three lessons, but beside Miss Lupino's vivid outbreak it has the dryness of a textbook. The whole picture is very lavish and competent, with a New World moral outlook which is summed wonderfully up in a phrase addressed by sister Hopkins to sister Davis: 'If Tina is to be made happy her position must be made unassailable, financially and socially.'

The Spectator (19 January 1939)

The Light That Failed (USA, Paramount, 1939) Dir.: William Wellman. Cast: Ronald Colman, Walter Huston, Ida Lupino, Dudley Digges, Muriel Angelus, Fay Helm.

The Old Maid (USA, Warners, 1939) Dir.: Edmund Goulding. Cast: Bette Davis, Miriam Hopkins, George Brent, Donald Crisp, William Lundigan, Jane Bryan, Louise Fazenda, Henry Stephenson, Jerome Cowan, Rand Brooks.

The Stars Look Down · Escape to Happiness

Dr Cronin's mining novel has made a very good film – I doubt whether in England we have ever produced a better. Mr Carol Reed, who began some years ago so impressively with *Midshipman Easy* and then became involved in the cheap little second features that were regularly churned out by the smaller English studios, has at last had his chance and magnificently taken it. Since this is the story of a mine disaster his work will inevitably be compared with Pabst's in *Kameradschaft*: he can bear the comparison. When the miners who are on strike advance against the butcher who has refused meat to a sick woman, and when the siren blows for the accident and the children rush across the cement school playground to the rails, and when we listen to the condemned imprisoned men – the youth who was to have been played in a football trial on Saturday and who refuses to believe that Saturday has ever come and gone in their darkness: the old miner feeding the new young hand with cough lozenges: the man with religious mania and the boozer's muttered confession – we are aware of direction which is every bit as good as Pabst's. If the film – constructed authentically though it is of grit and slagheap, back-to-back cottages, and little scrubby railway stations – fails to remain in the memory as long as *Kameradschaft*, it will be because there is too much story drowning the theme: the particular is an uneasy ally in literature of the general. The theme is the dangers of private ownership: Michael Redgrave plays a miner who gets a scholarship and leaves the pits, and he expresses this theme in two speeches – at a college debating society and a meeting of union representatives: the theme is that there will always be owners ready to take a gamble sometimes, while the miner takes a gamble always. It isn't so dramatically effective a theme as Pabst's, and the punch is a little pulled. The owner responsible for the disaster has a stroke, repents and dies – this, I imagine, is pure Cronin. Once before Mr Reed tried his hand at a documentary story – *Bank Holiday*. It was highly praised and was full of 'characters', but it smelt of the studio. Here one forgets the casting altogether: he handles his players like a master, so that one remembers them only as people. Miss Lockwood alone as the studious miner's disaster of a wife remains an actress to the bitter end.

Escape to Happiness is one of those pictures of unhappy passion among the artistic and the successful, with smart white-wood sets, grand pianos, good beach clothes and Riviera fishing-villages in which it is natural to expect Miss Bergner to appear, turning somersaults and dying of a weak heart . . . . Only in that case the lovers, I suppose, would escape to the Tyrol. Mr Leslie Howard acts the part of a famous composer and violinist, happily married, with a small girl whom he adores: he falls in love with her music-teacher, a promising young pianist, there are clandestine meetings, she decides it's best to leave him for ever – and instead they are off, first on a professional tour and then on a passionate holiday. But, as you will expect, the pull of his family is too strong, so she leaves him again for his own good and he creeps back home to see his child and stays. There's nothing really wrong in the story: the only falsity is at the end, when the child is knocked down by a car as she runs to meet her father, and in the dialogue which treads in boots the beaten literary path: life, we must admit, often follows these lines, though perhaps less elegantly. It is in its way a good film: the awful sense in the man of a divided personality is sometimes well conveyed, and the first parting is directed with miserable truth. But the film is most worth seeing for the new star, Miss Ingrid Bergman, who is as natural as her name. What star before has made her first appearance on the international screen with a highlight gleaming on her nose-tip? That gleam is typical of a performance that doesn't give the effect of acting at all, but of living – without make-up. Mr Howard with his studied inflexions can't help seeming a little false beside the awkward truth of this young actress, and I am afraid we shall regretfully remember this picture after the grooming and the training have done to her what they did to Sten.

The Spectator (26 January 1940)

The Stars Look Down (GB, Grand National, 1939) Dir.: Carol Reed. Cast: Michael Redgrave, Margaret Lockwood, Emlyn Williams, Linden Travers, Edward Rigby, Nancy Price, Allan Jeayes, Cecil Parker.
Escape to Happiness (USA, Selznick International, 1940) Dir.: Gregory Ratoff. Cast: Leslie Howard, Ingrid Bergman, Edna Best, John Halliday, Cecil Kellaway. (US title: *Intermezzo*)

The Arsenal Stadium Mystery · Pièges

A detective-story must be one of the hardest jobs a director can be assigned, because there's got to be a lot of talk. He must be on his toes all the time to snatch out of the pages of dialogue any opportunity for visual wit. A thriller is comparatively easy: a gun is photogenic: bodies fall easily in good poses: the camera can move at the speed of a G-man's car, but in a detective-story it has to amble at the walking pace of the mind. Mr Thorold Dickinson, who will be remembered for his promising first film *The High Command*, has admirably succeeded in keeping his detection alive as well as obscure – this picture is as good to watch as either of the *Thin Man* films, and he gives us wit instead of facetiousness – wit of cutting and wit of angle. The action takes place mainly in the offices and changing-rooms at the Stadium: we listen to managers addressing their teams on strategy (one of them is Mr George Allison himself, who deserves a film contract for the vivid way in which he plays George Allison): we watch Mr Emmett of the canned Gaumont voice commentating on the match: we get to know what the jars in the treatment-room contain – the sterilized horsehair and the rest: we learn where to look for a phone-box and which passages lead to the ground. Then one of the Trojans – an amateur team – falls dead in the middle of a match with the Arsenal, and we move to Scotland Yard, but a Yard as undramatic and familiar as the Arsenal rooms. A police pantomime is in rehearsal, and Mr Leslie Banks as Inspector Slade is coaching the beauty chorus. The whole film is kept on that pleasant level of the unexpected. Cross-examinations are made leaning over putters in a practice-room: Inspector Slade borrows a Turkish fez from the pantomime box as he talks to the Home Office pathologist on the phone. The cutting is excellent – 'It's a desperate job', Slade says when the blonde friend of the murdered man is discovered dead on her bed with the poison bottle he has been seeking in her hand, 'two murders in two days', and immediately we cut to the bobbing heads of the Arsenal team at practice, as flippant as balloons in the park. The explanation of the murder depends on another death outside the story and a Coroner's report, and Mr Dickinson's skill is never more evident than his grim sad dramatization of the dull typewritten pages.

For a while it seemed as if in *Pièges* we were to have another *Carnet du Bal* – a series of episodes amusing, ghastly and sorrowful hung round a woman's neck. A dance-hostess disappears – she is one of eleven disappearances, but this time there is a clue, for she told a friend that she was answering one of those intimate suggestive little advertisements that mention 'companionship'. Her friend helps the police by answering in turn all the doubtful advertisments in the Paris Press – and when von Stroheim looms sadly and secretively up at the dark street-corner rendezvous we hopefully expect a whole series of studies of the lonely, the shy and the warped – the advertisers who are 'broad minded' or lovers of music, who offer 'artistic' employments. But after the von Stroheim episode – a beautifully acted sketch of a mad dress-designer – we plunge into a rather broken-backed *roman policier*, with white-slavers and a homicidal maniac and Maurice Chevalier confessing to murders he never committed for fear of a life sentence. Chevalier seems a little out of place as a rich impresario – he can't help looking like a waiter or a chauffeur of immoderate charm, but there's Jean Renoir [*sic*] and a lovely new actress, Marie Déa, and all sorts of admirable minor parts

– a sinister and pathetic manservant, a white-slaver from Athens with a barber's gentility and a sense of his rights, and a police detective who looks like Oscar Wilde. If it's not the film that the Stroheim episode seemed to promise, at least it goes easily, excitingly, amusingly down.

The Spectator (2 February 1940)

The Arsenal Stadium Mystery (GB, G & S Films, 1940) Dir.: Thorold Dickinson. Cast: Leslie Banks, Anthony Bushell, Greta Gynt, Esmond Knight, Brian Worth.

Pièges (France, Spéva Films, 1939) Dir.: Robert Siodmak. Cast: Maurice Chevalier, Marie Déa, Erich von Stroheim, Pierre Renoir. (US title: *Snares*)

The Wizard of Oz · Dust Be My Destiny · Fifth Avenue Girl · African Skyways

The Wizard of Oz is an American drummer's dream of escape. The book has been popular in the States for forty years, and has been compared there to *Alice in Wonderland*, but to us in our old tribal continent the morality seems a little crude and the fancy material: the whole apparatus of Fairy Queen and witches and dwarfs called Munchkins, the Emerald City, the Scarecrow Man without a brain, and the Tin Man without a heart, and the Lion man without courage, rattles like dry goods. Once a drummer always a drummer, and the author of this fantasy remained the agile salesman, offering his customers the best material dreams – nothing irrational: the Wizard of Oz who sends the dreaming child with her three grotesque friends to capture the witch's broomstick turns out to be a Kansas conjurer operating a radio-electric contrivance. But if we regard this picture as a pantomime, it has good moments: the songs are charming, the Technicolor no more dreadful than the illustrations to most children's books, and the sepia prologue on the Kansas plains, when the child runs away from home to save her dog from a spinster neighbour, and the tornado comes twisting across the horizon, is very fine indeed. Miss Judy Garland, with her delectable long-legged stride, would have won one's heart for a whole winter season twenty years ago, and Miss Margaret Hamilton as the spinster-witch, with her bicycle and her broomstick and her incredible razor-edged face, can compete successfully with a Disney drawing. The whole picture is incredibly lavish, and there's a lot of pleasure to be got these days from watching money spent on other things than war. Incidentally, the British Board of Film Censors have given this picture a certificate for adults only. Surely it is time that this absurd committee of elderly men and spinsters who feared, too, that *Snow White* was unsuitable for those under sixteen, was laughed out of existence? As it is, in many places, parents will be forbidden by the by-laws to take their own children to *The Wizard of Oz*.

Dust Be My Destiny is a faint echo of Muni's great chain-gang film, with John Garfield as a young man wanted for murder chased around with his sweetheart. Of course, he's only technically guilty, and he's acquitted in the end. One grim unhappy sequence is worthy of a less sentimental film. When the young penniless lovers are persuaded by a publicity agent who offers them money to be married on the local stage in stiff borrowed clothes, with a real parson and an audience shouting to them to speak louder and kiss more.

Fifth Avenue Girl has Ginger Rogers in it, and Walter Connolly, so it's worth seeing. It's a curious and sometimes witty variant on the old theme of 'pity the poor rich'. Ginger Rogers is picked up in the park by a lonely millionaire, and hired to make his wife jealous and his son work. There's a nasty jab at the Left in the shape of a Marxist prig of a chauffeur, and there are plenty of jabs at the Right – which accounts perhaps for a sort of lost feeling. The appearance of a Fifth Avenue mansion, all statues, stairways and majolica, is magnificent. It is the first time I have heard laughter in the cinema at the sight of a set.

African Skyways, a documentary made by Strand Films, is for the most part routine travelogue, shots of flying-boats, mail, passengers, beauty-spots, but when we reach Durban something happens: the camera swings from the subject of the Imperial Airways to record a horrifying vision of the Rand, the awful squalor of the mining compounds of Johannesburg, the hollow-chested queues for the daily ration of food (including one-sixth of an ounce of coffee per head), the heart-breaking mine-dances, with spears and shields that look as though they had come out of a pawn-shop, the sense of a hopeless exile, and a dying memory of tribal dignity.

The Spectator (9 February 1940)

The Wizard of Oz (USA, MGM, 1939) Dir.: Victor Fleming. Cast: Judy Garland, Bert Lahr, Ray Bolger, Jack Haley Jr., Margaret Hamilton, Billie Burke, Frank Morgan.
Dust Be My Destiny (USA, Warners, 1939) Dir.: Lewis Seiler. Cast: John Garfield, Priscilla Lane, Alan Hale, Frank McHugh, John Litel, Charles Grapewin, Billy Halop, Stanley Ridges.
Fifth Avenue Girl (USA, RKO, 1939) Dir.: Gregory La Cava. Cast: Ginger Rogers, Walter Connolly, Verree Teasdale, Tim Holt, James Ellison, Franklin Pangborn, Kathryn Adams, Louis Calhern.
African Skyways (GB, Strand Films, 1940) Dir.: Donald Taylor.

Dark Rapture · Destry Rides Again · The Hunchback of Notre-Dame

Dark Rapture is a film shot by an American expedition to the Belgian Congo – it ends abruptly in a bush fire which destroyed wagons, cameras, everything but these priceless reels of exposed celluloid: the word 'priceless' is used with intention. There has never been a film of Africa to equal this: it should be seen by all those who have watched *African Skyways* with its picture of the Rand compounds, the heartless industrialization and the dingy despair, for this is as near as we can get to what Africa was before the white man came: the wide rapid river, the dense tangled forest and the volcanic mountains that set the cameras trembling have preserved something for the tribesmen here. One carries away from the cinema a sense of innocence, of human dignity reduced to its essentials, no robes or decorations, just the skin and bone and hank of hair. The birdlike, whistling, attenuated voices of the pygmies go wandering deeper and deeper into the heart of darkness; they camp for a night in their makeshift huts of twigs and leaves and then go on, without possessions except their tiny childish bows, until a river stops them. They cannot swim or use canoes: every time they reach water they must accomplish an engineering feat equal to that of the designers of the Sydney Bridge – a man is catapulted on a long vine cable a hundred and fifty feet through the air to the opposite trees and then his fellow workers scramble over: the bridge finished they abandon it and go on, without purpose except the pursuit of food, wandering in a kind of theological Limbo like unbaptized children. Remember that these are the people whom Stanley with his Maxim gun and his Remingtons called 'vicious dwarfs'. With another tribe we watch the initiation of the boys (how was permission obtained to photograph this ceremony?): the little naked boys squat in a scared row while the old men grimly watch to see that everything is as it always was, that no child escapes the fear and pain they suffered, like parents at a commemoration: we see the set small desperate face during the circumcision standing out like something human among the peering masks. Then we cross the hot vibrating mountains and come down into the territory of giants, huge lobelias and heather forty feet high and men of seven feet – an aristocratic race which came centuries ago from Egypt; with fine thin Nephertite features the King's wives hobble, each under twenty pounds of anklets; the Court Poet recites before the sacred cows with their enormous Viking horns two yards between the tips – the beginning of a civilization nipped by the frost from Europe before it had time to spread. Then we watch almost in close-up – an extraordinary sight this – the snaring of the elephants with ropes – sensitive papillon ears, a lightning defence with the trunk. It is impossible to exaggerate the beauty of this film; perhaps it is not a picture for anthropologists: the impressions it gives are rapid, general, uninstructed, aimed at the imagination rather than the intelligence, but anyone who sees it is likely to lose his palate for cinema fiction that week.

Destry Rides Again is the first sufferer: a rather tired Western with a rather tired Dietrich. They have tried to turn Time back and put her exactly where they found her, before the slinky dresses and the long cigarette holders, in the tough husky world of *The Blue Angel*. But time tells ungallantly in the muscles of the neck: there is no falling in love again, even if we wanted to. James Stewart acts magnificently as the Sheriff who won't use a gun, but the picture doesn't take itself quite seriously enough – as though these incongruous actors, and Mischa Auer, Una Merkel, Allen Jenkins, Charles Winninger, were playing Western just for fun. They don't belong to the same world as Brian Donlevy, who has run crooked gambling joints for as long as we can remember and must feel odd in any Eastern clothes.

The Hunchback will appeal strongly to amateurs of the Gothick school – in its shocking way it's really very fine. The racks and scourges and spiked cords are handled with love, and Laughton's make-up is more horrifying than Chaney's was seventeen years ago – we've toughened in the interval.

The Spectator (16 February 1940)

Dark Rapture (USA, Armand Denis Productions, 1939) Dir.: Armand Denis.

Destry Rides Again (USA, Universal, 1939) Dir.: George Marshall. Cast: Marlene Dietrich, James Stewart, Charles Winninger, Brian Donlevy, Una Merkel, Jack Carson, Samuel S. Hinds, Mischa Auer, Irene Harvey, Allen Jenkins, Billy Gilbert, Warren Hymer.

The Hunchback of Notre-Dame (USA, RKO, 1939) Dir.: William Dieterle. Cast: Charles Laughton, Maureen O'Hara, Edmond O'Brien, Cedric Hardwicke, Thomas Mitchell, Harry Davenport, Walter Hampden, Alan Marshall, George Zucco, Fritz Leiber, Rod La Rocque.

Ninotchka · On Your Toes · A Chump at Oxford · These Children Are Safe

Seeing Garbo has always seemed to me a little like reading Carlyle: good, oh very good, but work rather than play, and a new apprehension was added by the slogan 'Garbo laughs' (no slogan has been plugged so relentlessly since 'Chaplin talks'). One expected the laughter to creak a little with greatness; but this is not merely a Garbo film, it is a Lubitsch film, and the result is enchanting – from the first appearance of the three Russian stooges, all celluloid collar, Adam's apple and secretive boyishness, who arrive in Paris as a trade delegation to offer a Grand Duchess's jewels for sale. They are too innocent to survive in the sly capitalist Lubitsch world of nubile cigarette-sellers and unlimited champagne, and they soon find themselves corrupted and outwitted by the Grand Duchess's lover (Melvyn Douglas), so that a special envoy has to be sent from Moscow to supersede them. The envoy, of course, is Garbo, a veteran Sergeant of the Polish War, with a granite face and an unbecoming hat and an uncompromising suspicion. 'How are things in Russia?' the delegates winningly inquire, and the tombstone voice replies, 'There have been many successful mass-trials. There will be fewer and better Russians.' The story, of course, is of her seduction, too – by capitalist elegance and by Mr Douglas, whose glittering foxy-faced pursuit is a little luscious and long-drawn. The Grand Duchess is forced to steal the jewels and make a bargain – the jewels for Russia without a lawsuit in return for the envoy's prompt departure, and there is a fine little satirical scene when Mr Douglas tries in vain to get an Intourist visa to follow her. The sequence in Russia – Ninotchka's reunion party with the stooges in the shared room with the shared eggs and neighbours going through all the time to the shared lavatory – is hardly comedy at all: it would be the bleakest tragedy if there were not, of course, a happy ending.

On Your Toes has been changed without any loss from musical comedy to straight comedy. It is the story, many will remember, of a young American composer and ex-hoofer who gets mixed up with an impecunious Russian ballet company, and it ends with the production of his Slaughter on Tenth Avenue, in which he dances under a Russian name watched by a couple of comic assassins in the stage box, who have orders to shoot when he stops dancing (his namesake was a traitor to some Russian cause or other). The dialogue has wit: Zorina, who played the prima ballerina in London, acts well, looks lovely and dances beautifully, and the photography of the ballet sequence is really magnificent. We are left happily wondering why we don't have ballet specially written for the screen. The moving camera and the changing emphasis of the cut and the close-up can offer something new.

Laurel and Hardy are together again – this is better news than anything the papers print. *A Chump at Oxford* ranks with their best pictures – which to one heretic are more agreeable than Chaplin's; their clowning is purer; they aren't out to better an unbetterable world; they've never wanted to play Hamlet. Laurel here is given more opportunity than usual for straight acting; a blow on the head brings back a lost memory, and instead of an American hobo sent to Oxford by a benefactor, he becomes Lord Paddington, an all-round athlete, who disappeared years before.

These Children Are Safe, Alexander Shaw's film of the evacuation, deserves far more space than it can be given here. Admittedly, it dwells most on the favourable side – we see nothing of the slums to which the children sometimes went, and little of the dirt and disease they sometimes brought with them; it is more a lyrical than a documentary film. One remembers afterwards the superb choice of faces in close-up, worried LCC faces, unhealthy bored women's faces, and breaking through all the time the absurd and beautiful faces of children; a sense of happiness and release, and room to play in; the sound of voices singing: 'Do you know the muffin-man who lives in Glory Lane?' The sense of poetry is much rarer in film direction than the sense of humour, let us welcome it whole-heartedly when it is there.

The Spectator (23 February 1940)

Ninotchka (USA, MGM, 1939) Dir.: Ernst Lubitsch. Cast: Greta Garbo, Melvyn Douglas, Ina Claire, Bela Lugosi, Sig Ruman, Alexander Granach, Felix Bressart.

On Your Toes (USA, Warners, 1939) Dir.: Ray Enright. Cast: Vera Zorina, Eddie Albert, James Gleason, Alan Hale, Frank McHugh, Donald O'Connor, Gloria Dickson.

A Chump at Oxford (USA, Hal Roach, 1940) Dir.: Alfred Goulding. Cast: Stan Laurel, Oliver Hardy, James Finlayson, Forrester Harvey, Wilfrid Lucas, Peter Cushing.

These Children Are Safe (GB, Strand Productions, 1940) Dir.: Alexander Shaw.

The Roaring Twenties · Prisons de Femmes · Hotel for Women

'D'you want a diagram?' asks one of the characters who wants the obvious made plain. A diagram of *The Roaring Twenties* would be the familiar one of the good guy Eddie Bartlett (James Cagney), who can't get a job, slides into bootlegging, rises to being a Big Shot, but is finally ruined by the repeal of the Volstead Act and by the stock market crash of 1929. Two companions of his early struggles are unaffected: one is a young lawyer who married Jean, Eddie's girl, and left bootlegging at the right moment, the other is the ferocious Mr Humphrey Bogart. He leads a rival gang, and later threatens the life of the lawyer, who is collecting evidence against him. Ruined and stubbly, Eddie is still the man to rub out a heel, as Jean opportunely recollects, and in an extremely entertaining scene Eddie goes to his enemy's house and, yet it's Sydney Carton again. The diagram, however, doesn't do justice to Mr Carton, of the bull-calf brow, who is as always a superb and witty actor. The morality is confusing: we are explicitly told crime doesn't pay. (Mr Carton keeps a stout heart, asserting 'There'll always be guys trying to set up quick, and I'm one of them'; certainly Mr Bogart keeps his dinner jacket to the end of the film). But the children of light, Jean and the lawyer, are quick to recognise a falling market, and they get out with two large diamond rings of undistinguished design and a great deal of money. Jean (Miss Priscilla Lane) sang the songs of the period in the night club, but was otherwise supposedly beyond reproach. She did not sing 'All I have to offer is a happy disposition and a wild desire to please', which would have suited her talents. Mr Bogart was, of course, magnificent – always a pleasure to see Mr Bogart pumped full of lead.

Prisons de Femmes is not a major French film; indeed the story is amazingly banal – about an innocent girl who goes to prison, gets a job in a shop when she comes out, marries a rich man, and is overtaken by her past: you know how it goes – blackmail, an assignation in a dingy hotel, a jealous prostitute, revolver shots, and while she lies in hospital her story is told to the husband by a sympathetic friend, and all is forgiven. (Love, as so often in French films, is luxurious and pale mauve like the picture postcards.) The story is hardly improved by M. Francis Carco, who plays M. Francis Carco, who in France is called a criminologist. The story is supposed to have really happened to him; he *is* the sympathetic friend, smug, patronising and unbearably literary in a dressing-gown. No, it's not a major piece, but when M. Carco is safely off the screen scribbling his little books, we are excited again and again by the authenticity the French always put into their sets and characters. A shabby hotel on the French screen never looks studio built. Those stone stairs and stained walls have grown there for a century.

Hotel for Women is a sentimental echo of *The Women.* The story might have come out of *Peg's Paper* except for a few amusing slants on the professional life of a successful advertising model (I liked the agent's brisk reply to an inquiry, 'Her price is fifty now. She won't do underwear.') The private life, of course, is dinners, cabarets, invitations to yachts, attempted seductions, and – finally – revolver shots. An awful lot of love this week seems to end that way – with a bang and a whimper.

The Spectator (1 March 1940)

The Roaring Twenties (USA, Warners, 1939) Directors: Raoul Walsh, Anatole Litvak. Cast: James Cagney, Humphrey Bogart, Priscilla Lane, Jeffrey Lynn, Gladys George, Frank McHugh, Paul Kelly, Elizabeth Risdon.

Hotel for Women (USA, Twentieth-Century Fox, 1939) Dir.: Gregory Ratoff. Cast: Elsa Maxwell, Linda Darnell, Ann Sothern, James Ellison, John Halliday, Lynn Bari, Alan Dinehart.

Sherlock Holmes

It is a pleasure to meet a well-mannered criminal again; we have suffered so long from 'Siddown you', and 'I said, Siddown'; at the Regal we are in 1894, and people say 'Pray be seated' and 'Precisely, Holmes.' In an admirable opening scene Dr Moriarty stands in the dock awaiting with his usual composure the verdict; this, as he expects, is an acquittal, delivered by both judge and jury with undisguised regret, and with a peevish reverence to the laws of evidence. At this moment Sherlock Holmes bursts into the court with some last-minute evidence – inadmissible, of course, and Moriarty is turned loose again. This is a brisk and promising beginning to a story which is not only exciting, but, more important, atmospherically correct; one feels Conan Doyle might have collaborated when he was not quite in his best form (as when he was writing *The Lion's Mane*, for instance); we are projected straight away – as Holmes shares a hansom with Moriarty from the Old Bailey – into that London of cobbles, mud, fast cabs and gas-lamps; lost London, one was going to say, of Ford Madox Ford's remembrance – of dimmed crescents, dark crowded interiors, and far too many fogs. (We know a darkness now, but it is less terrifying perhaps than the alternate gas-jet and shadow of those streets.) This is the *atmosphere* conveyed, I should make clear, and not the effect of the photography, which is very beautiful.

Dr Moriarty is, one feels, the central figure in the film, in spite of its title; his attempt on the Crown Jewels has the right stable financial touch. Acted by George Zucco, he is viciously correct – a man in the stern suave tradition represented by Colonel Moran ('the second most dangerous man in London'), who, it will be remembered, tilted back his silk hat to take better aim at Holmes with his new compressed-air shotgun, and by Sir George Burnwell (who also made an attempt to steal a crown). He is, of course, savage to inferiors, but at least once he is contradicted, and he takes it good-humouredly: 'Alas, poor Higgins; there was nothing left of him but his boots.' '*One* boot, Sir.' This air of having only just missed the best clubs is enhanced by the cut of the beard; he seemed a lesser man when he shaved it off in order to disguise himself as a police sergeant. Basil Rathbone is physically made for the part of Holmes; one feels he was really drawn by Paget, but mentally he forgets that he belongs to the end of the century, and probably met Wilde at first nights; one can't imagine this Holmes, indolent, mystical, or untidy (there were tobacco-jars and not – shouldn't it have been? – a Turkish slipper on the chimney-piece). Nigel Bruce as Dr Watson almost thumps a tail, and Miss Ida Lupino acts well and looks exquisite as the usual frightened caller in Baker Street.

The Spectator (8 March 1940)

Sherlock Holmes (USA, Twentieth-Century Fox, 1940) Dir.: Alfred Werker. Cast: Basil Rathbone, Nigel Bruce, Ida Lupino, George Zucco, Alan Marshall, Terry Kilburn, E.E. Clive, Henry Stephenson, Mary Gordon. (US title: *The Adventures of Sherlock Holmes*)

The Proud Valley · Dead Man's Shoes

It is unfortunate for everybody concerned in *The Proud Valley* that *The Stars Look Down* preceded it: if that fine film had not set a standard this picture of a Welsh mining village would have seemed a worthy, if rather dim, little picture: one might have been tempted to overpraise it for the sake of a few authentic scenes with a GPO touch – the meeting, for example, of the miners' choir to prepare for the Eistedfodd. No picture of a mining district ever seems to be complete without a disaster (we have two in this picture): the warning siren is becoming as familiar as the pithead gear shot against the sky – and that has joined the Eiffel Tower and the Houses of Parliament among the great platitudes of the screen; and yet a far worse tragedy in a district like this must be just inaction. This, perhaps, is the theme of the picture – women pretending sickness when the rate-collector calls, credit petering out at the general store, but too many red herrings scent the story line beside the disasters: colour prejudice is dragged in for the sake of Mr Paul Robeson who plays the part of a big black Pollyanna, keeping everybody cheerful and dying nobly at the end (Mr Robeson's fat sentimental optimism seemed to me a little revolting); and the theme dies out altogether at the close with patriotic speeches and crisis posters and miners dying for England. The direction of the quiet documentary scenes is good, but Mr Pen Tennyson, who may have been handicapped by an undistinguished cast and a wobbly script, seems ill at ease with drama.

We are getting a lot of retakes these days from the English studios: films are bought from France – not the best ones (these have been forbidden in their own country since the war began), the long shots are cut to save expense and the script is faithfully copied with hybrid results – the furniture and the faces look wrong and the emotions seem a little odd. Last week *Alerte en Méditerranée* was shown as *Hell's Cargo*, and the theme – international comradeship – was a little altered to meet the political situation. A Russian officer, instead of a German, died nobly beside his English and French comrades of the sea, but history moves too quickly, and it might have been better to make him an Italian. Now *Carrefour* has been reshot as *Dead Man's Shoes*: it's about a criminal who lost his memory in the last war and became a great industrialist by mistake, remembering nothing of his past until a blackmailer bobs up to remind him. The English film is very nearly worth seeing for the sake of two fine players who are too seldom seen on the English screen: Mr Wilfred Lawson as the blackmailer with a commercial background, impudent and pockmarked and tough as hell, and Miss Nancy Price as the ex-criminal's mother, who in a scene of quite moving melodrama persuades him that he is not really her son.

The Spectator (15 March 1940)

The Proud Valley (GB, Capad, 1940) Dir.: Penrose Tennyson. Cast: Paul Robeson, Edward Chapman, Edward Rigby, Rachel Thomas, Simon Lack, Clifford Evans, Allan Jeayes.

Dead Man's Shoes (GB, Associated British, 1939) Dir.: Thomas Bentley. Cast: Leslie Banks, Joan Marion, Geoffrey Atkins, Wilfred Lawson, Judy Kelly, Nancy Price, Peter Bull, Walter Hudd, Ludwig Strossel.

2

Essays and Articles

The Average Film

We are most of us nowadays considerably over-sexed. We either go to Church and worship the Virgin Mary or to a public house and snigger over stories and limericks; and this exaggeration of the sex instinct has had a bad effect on art, on the cinematograph as well as on the stage.

In the Elizabethan age women were not allowed to act, and the result was that the first great period in the history of our drama was unruled by sex. It is true that most of the plays had a love interest, but in the majority of cases it played a very subordinate part. *Macbeth, Lear, Hamlet, The Duchess of Malfi* even, depend for their strength on neither sentimental gloss nor sensual titivation. *Anthony and Cleopatra* [sic] with the splendour of its lust is healthy in its absolute openness: sex is relegated to its proper place as simply one of the enjoyable things of life. Like drink, it is pleasant, and like drink, it is not hypocricised into sanctity or sentiment, nor made indecent by mystery. 'My serpent of the Nile,' says Anthony, as one would say, 'My old Burton'.

Our drama, therefore, went off, as the Americans say, with a kick, and it is only just beginning to fall to that point at which cinema, owing to the lateness of its birth, has been forced to start. Shaw in London is being gradually overwhelmed beneath a flood of revues and musical comedies, with dialogue and dresses fashioned respectively by the Editors of the *Sporting Times* and *La Vie Parisienne.* As Mr J.B. Priestley remarks to the producer of a Recent Light Musical Entertainment, who boasted of its cast:

'If you paid thirty thousand for the stuff.
Flesh must be dear, for dirt is cheap enough.'

I should be the last to condemn this new form of entertainment, however, for I am one who prefers 'Cairo' to Hampstead, and in certain moods a limerick is more satisfying than a lyric, and the 'young lady of Detroit' more stimulating than 'the dark lady of the Sonnets'. But I will at least admit that the one is a lower form of art, because the satisfaction it gives is more transient.

I should like to thank Mr Seymour, of the Super-Cinema, for giving over the first half of term to a series of average films. By the time this article has appeared, Oxford will also have had a chance of seeing that very beautiful work of art, *The Niebelungs*, and the comparison will be a perfect illustration of my theme.

Exaggerated sex is the hallmark of the average film, whether it originates in England or America. I do not think that I have ever seen one of those moral American productions, dealing with Duty and the North-West Mounted Police, that has not its attempted rape. In the time of Elizabeth the rape would, at any rate, have been successful, but only unsuccess can stir the jaded appetite of the modern public. Neither melodrama nor comedy nor sentiment can stand by itself. *Mdlle Midnight* was a most exciting film, brilliantly acted by Mae Murray and Monte Blue, *Circusmania*, with Max Linder in the principal part, was extraordinarily funny, and *Lilies of the Field* (unconnected with the play of that name) was sentimental enough for the most Barriesque taste, and Miss Corinne Griffith was altogether charming. Yet much of the appeal of all these films depended on a certain sensual stimulation. There is no third road between the intellect and the senses, and it is because of this that the two films *Cyrano de Bergerac* and *The Gay Corinthian*, shown at the Electra Palace, failed, where *Mlle. Midnight* succeeded. Do away with art from a story, and you must put something in its place. Therefore, it will be long before I forget the Beardsley drama of *Zaza* (Electra Palace) or the dancing of Miss Mae Murray as Renée de Quiros, but I shall forget. But I shall still remember Harold Lloyd in *Girl Shy*, and the poignancy of his acting in the scene of disillusionment at the publisher's office, where not his heart, but (far more bitter) his MS. is rejected, and I shall remember that scene in *The Call of the Wild*, where the distantly seen figures of the two dogs, Buck and Spitz, trot to meet each other across the snow for their final duel. For these were not average scenes on the films, for they appealed to a sense of beauty and not to a sense of sex.

The Oxford Outlook (February 1925)

The Snob (USA 1924) Dir.: Monta Bell. Cast: Mae Murray, Monte Blue.
Mademoiselle Midnight (USA, 1924) Dir.: Robert Z. Leonard.
Circusmania (Clowns aus Liebe) (Austria, 1924) Dir.: Edouard-Emile Violet.
Lilies of the Field (USA, 1924) Dir.: John Francis Dillon.
Cyrano de Bergerac (Italy, Extra Films, 1923) Dir.: Augusto Genina. Cast: Pierre Magnier, Linda Moglia, Angelo Ferrari, Alex Bernard, Gemma de Sanctis, Umberto Castellini.
The Gay Corinthian (GB, 1924) Dir.: Arthur Rooke.
Zaza (USA, Paramount, 1923) Dir.:Allan Dwan. Cast: Gloria Swanson, H.B. Warner, Ferdinand Gottschalk.
Shy Girl (USA, Harold Lloyd Productions, 1924) Dir.: Fred Newmeyer. Cast: Harold Lloyd, Jobyna Ralston, Richard Daniels, Carlton Griffin.
Call of the Wild (USA, Hal Roach Studios, 1923) Dir.: Fred Jackman. Cast: Buck, Jack Mulhall, Walter Long, Sidney d'Albrook, Laura Roessing, Frank Butler.

The Province of the Film: Past Mistakes and Future Hopes

The Cinematograph Films Act has given the British Film industry a chance of breaking finally the domination of America, but success will come neither through a slavish imitation of past 'best sellers' nor through an indiscriminating revolt against Hollywood tradition. Great Britain, as Germany has done in the past, must maintain a high and adventurous standard of quality, but the time has come to consider whether adventure need necessarily be as costly as U.F.A. found.

Apart from the inflated salaries of 'stars', expense arises from waste of time and material. A film which takes an hour to show may easily have taken months to act. Out of 50,000 feet of film made perhaps 8,000 will be preserved. In most films there is no consecutive method of production. The actors will move from a happy climax to play their parts in an unhappy beginning. Cinderella will not leave the palace at the stroke of 12, but will try on her shoe. Scenes which do not follow each other in the completed film are made to follow in the production, so that one 'set' only need be used at a time.

This economy in one direction is a waste in others. Because of the handicap to the actors, unnecessary lengths of film have to be 'shot' before a satisfactory result is attained. It is to rehearse before the camera's mouth. A German director, working for an

American company, had the initiative to break away from the tradition in *Hotel Imperial*. A complete hotel 'set' was built and the photographer followed the players from room to room to the action of the story.

This method obviously entails a certain unity of place. A company cannot move from Central Africa to London and back according to a scenario writer's whim, though the unity imposed by a large studio and the limits of fake photography is not a severe one. The comparative unity of *Hindle Wakes* and the complete unity of *Salome*, where the whole action took place in the hall of Herod's palace, were in any case more impressive than the rapid scene-changes of *Ben Hur*.

What, if not breadth of scene, is the true province of the film? Because the film has shown itself in such pictures as *Ben Hur* and *The Birth of a Nation* a fine medium for melodrama, the cinema has grown to be regarded as a sort of enlarged Adelphi, the primrose path of small ragged urchins. It is significant that the screen is wrongly compared with the stage, not only by unsympathetic critics, but tacitly by the majority of producers, who try to compete with the stage. Germany broke away from this tradition in the exquisitely beautiful *Niebelungen*, but substituted another blind alley, that of static design. The film is more truly comparable with the novel, the progress of which it has followed from action to thought. If the best that America has done be compared – though not necessarily likened – to the English novel at the stage of Defoe, *Warning Shadows*, with its strange removal of action to the second hand, its shades of thought, represents the novels of Henry James and Conrad.

Words, however, are a clumsy, unmalleable material. They follow the creator, and not the creator them. Of the loveliest sonnet only the outline was formed in rapture, the rest had to be carved with toil. In the theatre Mr Shaw explains and explains, and we take away not the long discussions, but a few vivid images. The thought, which takes pages to express, arises from one sharply focused picture in the mind. The object of the film should be the translation of thought back into images. America has made the mistake of translating it into action. A love scene, because the speeches of Romeo are too long for sub-titles, has meant to the American producer 'close-ups' and kisses – all the pseudo-realistic paraphernalia of passion. Eric [sic] Von Stroheim, in *Greed*, seized on one image and conveyed infinitely more passion. The scene was a rainy day at a seaside 'resort'. The lovers were shown only as two backs, receding down a long breakwater, on each side a leaden sea and a lashing rain, which failed to disturb their complete self-absorption.

And for an image of despair and fatalism let us go to one adventurous film produced in America, Mr Chaplin's *A Woman of Paris*. A girl, deserted by her lover, stands on a village platform at midnight waiting in vain. The Paris express, in which they were to have gone together, draws into the station, but we do not see the train. Only across her still face the shadows of the windows pass and then stay still. There are no tears, no sub-titles, and no movement save of shadows. The film made a comparatively moderate profit, and Mr Chaplin has, therefore, not attempted another serious picture.

The Times (9 April 1928)

Hotel Imperial (USA, Paramount, 1927) Dir.: Mauritz Stiller. Producer: Erich Pommer. Cast: Pola Negri, James Hall, George Siegmann.

Salome (USA, Nazimova, 1923) Dir.: Charles Bryant. Cast: Nazimova, Mitchell Lewis, Nigel de Brulier.

Hindle Wakes (GB, Gaumont-British Picture Corporation, 1927) Dir: Maurice Elvey. Cast: Estelle Brody, Norman McKinnel, Humberstone Wright, Marie Ault.

Ben Hur (USA, MGM, 1926) Dir.: Fred Niblo, Cast: Ramon Novarro, Francis X. Bushman, Carmel Myers, May McAvoy, Betty Bronson.

The Birth of a Nation (USA, Epoch, 1915) Dir.: D.W. Griffith. Cast: Henry B. Walthall, Mae Marsh, Miriam Cooper, Lillian Gish, Robert Harron, Wallace Reid, Donald Crisp, Joseph Henaberry, Raoul Walsh, Eugene Pallette, Walter Long.

The Neibelungen (Germany, Decla-Bioscop, 1924) Dir.: Fritz Lang. Cast: Paul Richter, Marguerite Schon, Theodor Loos, Hannah Ralph, Rudolph Klein-Rogge.

Warning Shadows (Germany, Pan Film/Dafu Film Verlieh, 1923) Dir.: Arthur Robison. Cast: Fritz Kortner, Ruth Weyher, Alexander Granach, Fritz Rasp, Gustav von Wangenheim.

Greed (USA, MGM, 1923) Dir.: Erich Von Stroheim. Cast: Gibson Gowland, Zasu Pitts, Jean Hersholt, Chester Conklin, Dale Fuller.
A Woman of Paris (USA, Charles Chaplin, 1923) Dir.: Charles Chaplin. Cast: Edna Purviance, Adolphe Menjou, Carl Miller, Lydia Knott.

A Film Technique: Rhythms of Space and Time

The film is still the limping Pegasus of the arts, handled with suspicion by the artist, with patronage by the dramatist. Art demands some clear-cut contrasts to aid the eternal search for perfection. But the average film is ugly, irregular, thoughtless, wearying eyes and brain with a muddled battle of impressions. Out of these close-ups, fisticuffs, exaggerated embraces and buffoonery how is the least shadow of some permanent form to emerge? From certain isolated oases in a desert, in Mr Chaplin's films, in the *Niebelung*, in *Berlin*, an answer can be found. There must be rhythm in films – rhythm of time and of space.

A crude example of time-rhythm can be found in Mr Harold Lloyd's farces. The film begins slowly and gradually increases in the speed of its episodes until the climax. The greater the risks run by the principal actor, the greater the speed at which they are taken. This plan is effective only for a farce, but can be adapted for every type of film. A producer should plan his picture in the form of a graph, the graph line ascending towards a maximum speed and descending towards a still photograph. He will then plan his picture as one wave, rising and falling according to the type of story and the mood, but never broken. Only thus in a tragic film can some idea of an irresistible fate be expressed through the tangle of episodes and thus only can be avoided the sharp rises and falls of rhythm, which in the film constitute bathos. Along the lines of the graph the producer will, as it were, write the episodes of the film and the action which is to accompany them.

One very common mistake will show the value of this mathematical foresight. Only too frequently on the screen the heroine is menaced by a villain, while the hero in a high-powered motor-car drives to the rescue. The scene changes from one to the other. The wheels of the car go faster and faster, the villain's embraces grow less and less restrained. The car enters the villain's grounds. The heroine, choosing death to dishonour, is poised on the edge of a balcony. The rhythm of the film grows yet more rapid as the hero climbs the ivy, saves the girl from falling, and closes with the villain. This episode on the graph might be represented as a line running diagonally upwards from the lower corner to an upper corner of the paper. The line is too long and straight. By the time the climax is reached the mind, inured for self-protection to the increasing rapidity of the rhythm, will be unable to appreciate the climax. There should be an interval, a breathing space, and the line should curve a little downwards before it moves upwards again. The opponents for a moment should be still, eyeing each other, before they leap into the fight.

This is an obvious example of the time-rhythm. What is space-rhythm? A scene upon the stage must be built within three narrow walls, and every object on the stage must be its natural size. But on the screen no scenery is impossible, since the audience can be made to regard it at any distance which the producer requires. They can have a face thrust close into theirs, or, like gods, they can look down from the upper air, as in *Faust*, upon a miniature town with spires which pierce upwards no higher than slender grass blades. As form must be discovered through a confusion of events, so also it must be discovered through a confusion of scenes. The scenes should expand or contract out of each other. There should be no frequent changes in the size of the audience's outlook. To continue with the imaginary example, if the hero's car is shown at a distance as a small object darting along thin ribbons of road, the scene must not change to life-size figures of heroine and villain struggling together. They must also be seen from a distance, though not necessarily from such a great distance.

The graph for space and rhythm will have for its lower boundary the close-up, for its upper boundary distant views with figures appearing only in the background, where they will appear as small dots. As in the time-graph, so also here the producer must avoid straight lines, as wearying with monotony both eye and brain, and equally he must avoid angles, as being too sudden for the mind to grasp. There must be curves of line and curves of space, and the two must coincide. Rapid time-rhythm is unsuitable for either boundary of the space-graph. If the top line of the space-graph be 100 and the bottom zero, then rapid action should not be allowed to take place before twenty-five or after seventy-five. Fifty is most suitable for the quickest action which will gradually slow down as it moves from the centre line. The wave of rhythm must be planned, as it was planned in *Berlin*, to afford variety without breaking the continuity. Variety has hitherto been sought in a multitude of plots. How small is the variety in treatment is only realized when the camera for a moment turns from the restless race of actions to poetry, perhaps, an empty room, sun-drenched, barred with cool shadows. There is the tip of the rhythmic wave, perhaps of photographic art, and it should break, not once when it is too late to revive the battered eyesight, but at regular intervals – like the recurrence of the great ninth wave, which leaves its spray the farthest up the shore.

The Times (12 June 1928)

A Film Principle: Sound and Silence

Certain ill-advised critics have for a long time lamented the silence of the films, and now disastrously they have been answered. The Movietone has removed the silence, and it is now possible to hear an animated photograph of Mr Bernard Shaw speaking with a rather toneless reproduction of Mr Shaw's voice. It is perhaps unfair to criticize that tonelessness. The Movietone is a yet at an early stage of development, and may with the passage of a few more months or years learn to roar as softly as any sucking-dove.

But there is a principle at stake. The film has reached a point where it must choose finally between developing as a cheap imitation of the stage or as a separate art. Silence is not its vice but its virtue. From silence springs its own peculiar technique of acting and productions in which beauty must emerge not from the roll of syllables but from visual images, not from spoken words but from suggested thought. Silence has given opportunity for a particular sublety of acting to which the stage offers no exact parallel. On the stage the actor's performance must be sufficiently emphatic to reach the back row of the gallery. In a cinema the whole audience can be regarded as being in the front row of the stalls. A gesture of the fingers, which would pass unnoticed in the theatre, can rivet the attention of every watcher in a cinema. A dramatic critic has said with unnecessary scorn, 'You cannot film *Hamlet*,' and it is true, for *Hamlet* depends on the poetry of words. But a producer may yet arise who will make a new *Hamlet* to fit the new medium.

The film has neither colour nor solidity of form, and yet its reality is not impaired. In place of colour it has a very wide range of tones, and in place of solidity a stereoscopic effect, arising not from any artifice but naturally from the movement of the images in relation to one another. This effect is all-important, and it is this that the Movietone destroys. When the images are given another human attribute, an appeal to the ear, the artificial convention on which their reality depends is broken down, another reality is superimposed, and they appear as the flat photographs they are.

The same argument applies to the 'effects' with which certain cinemas imagine they improve a film. If the actor's voice cannot be heard, how can a bell ring? Only in war films can sound 'effects' be justified, for there, it may be argued, the roar of shells drowns the human voice. What a film needs, if it needs extraneous aid at all, is not a corroboration of suggested sound, but a commentary in the form of music. In the future many films must have their special music, and the Movietone will find its use in co-ordinating music and films with an accuracy beyond the powers of a human orchestra.

How far, then, without voices is the film dependent on sub-titles? In Germany there has been a reaction against any interruption of the flow of the film by lettering. *The Last Laugh* had no sub-titles, yet the story could easily be followed. In *Warning Shadows* the characters were introduced before the story began, and the course of the film was not afterwards interrupted. But what those films gained in unity they lost in emotional range. They were a too extreme revolt against the abuse of sub-titling in America, where the story is constantly delayed by unnecessary, undramatic, and ridiculously worded sub-titles. In Hollywood lovers cannot kiss without a soft green light flooding the film, the Wurlitzer again mooing gently like an abandoned cow, and some such title as 'And under the silvery light of the all-healing moon love's dream came true.'

It is generally, but wrongly, assumed that the sub-title is a relic of an early and crude technique. The first films had no sub-titles. The passage of time, the Elizabethan technique of stage 'effects' forced the playwright to put a description of the hour and place into a character's mouth, often in as crude a manner as that of the early film maker. There is nothing intrinsically wrong with a sub-title, if it be short, understanding of the progress of events or for marking the peak of an emotion. The 'exceeding bitter agency' demanded the 'exceeding bitter cry.' A phrase can crystallize an emotion which the face is powerless to express. The sub-title must have some of the scorching imagination and brevity of poetry. 'Cover her face: mine eyes dazzle: she died young,' 'Pray you undo this button' – it is on such compressed and poignant outcries that the sub-title should be modelled.

The Times (10 July 1928)

Film Aesthetic: Its Distinction for Drama – The Province of the Screen

Cinematographs, which began as ingenious mechanical toys, developed suddenly into a means of popular entertainment. At one moment they were little more than glorified magic lanterns;

the next, they were crude storytellers of the Wild West; then, as if by some enchantment, they became a vast international industry. When the artists and critics of the world awoke to that truth that what was potentially a new art had been born among them, they were too late. The films had already entrenched themselves in error; a great barrier of financial success had been erected between them and genuine experimentalists; the history of the growth of every other art had, in this instance, been reversed; and there seemed to be no way of return to first principles.

Since then persistent attempts have been made to return, but they have all been harassed by the popularity of the screen as it is. The chief reforms have, in consequence, not been aesthetic, but mechanical. Photography, lighting, and arrangement have greatly improved. Films are more elaborate, fuller of ingenious tricks, in all respects smoother and more accomplished than they were; but, except here and there, the direction of their artistic purpose is unchanged; they still lag miserably at the heels of novelists and dramatists, attempting to do what they can never do so well as their seniors in fiction, instead of exploring the territory that is proper to themselves.

Epic Pictures

What is this territory? Its three principle provinces are epic, fantasy, and mental process. Of these, epic, though not the largest, is the most important. Films can show one heroic movement of masses of human beings as it can be shown in no other medium, and by their use of those masses and their easy control of space and time can project from the massed background figures of genuinely heroic proportion. Alternatively – and here they keep yet closer to the core of their own art – they can use the mass itself as their hero, as it was used in *Grass*, or as it might be used in a film of the Exodus or of the Ten Thousand. Romain Rolland, in *The Fourteenth of July*, of which the principal personage was not any individual but the revolutionary mob itself, was attempting on the stage a task that belongs to the screen. The measure of his failure was the extent of his invasion of the film's territory. It is the part of drama to suggest the general, the universal, through the individual. It is the part of the films, in their epic province, either to regard collective life – the life of a crowd – as an end in itself or to cause an individual of more than individual significance to emerge from the crowd. This causing of an individual to emerge from the crowd is not to be confused with that common blunder of film directors – the tacking of some mean love story on to an epic subject. The individual, if he emerge at all, must be a part of the epic perspective. The mass from which he comes must be his gigantic father and mother. The Moses of the Exodus must exist because Israel first existed, and not for the sake of Pharaoh's daughter or all Pharaoh's chariots.

The Realm of Fantasy

The fantastic uses of the film are more easily distinguished in their simplest form. Silhouette films and the famous series called *Felix the Cat* indicate what might be on the screen and can never be on the stage. Hitherto the cinematographic uses of pure fantasy have been for the most part humorous, though there have been serious and very brilliant excursions into fairyland. But the greater part of the fantastic world remains to be conquered. Unfettered by the written words of the Brothers Grimm or of Sir James Barrie, forgetful of the order and form of prose narrative and of the straining wires and creaking 'transformations' of the theatre, films might take to themselves such a fantastic freedom as storytellers and dramatists have never dreamed of. There, if anywhere, is an opportunity for British directors, if they can but discover a fantasist who will think in terms of the screen, to establish a supremacy of their own, for the Americans are now deeply committed to talking-pictures, which threaten the final extinction of the films as an independent art, and it is the national tendency of the Germans to concentrate – on the last of the three film-provinces – that of mental process, directly and pictorially indicated. It is plain enough that the films can establish one participant's view of a drama as the stage cannot and as the novel can only with great difficulty and sacrifice. They can, without preparation, take you inside a man's mind; their images can approximate more closely than any narrative to the speed, the fluidity, the flashing inconsequence of human thought. They offer, as the Germans have discovered, a less laborious and more mobile form of psychological impressionism than art has revealed.

Talking Films

But the films have become an industry: they are weighed down by the expectations of millions of people; they are chained by the popularity of their aesthetic errors – a popularity which springs from cheapness, comfort, availability, and conservatism, not primarily from delight in the possibilities of a new aesthetic medium. The screen is still to a great extent the stage distorted and made accessible. Film epic, film fantasy, and film analysis of the mind have as yet played but a minor part; yet the few pictures, such as *Grass, Cinderella, Warning Shadows, The Street,* and *Greed*, which are generally recognized as having been, either in purpose or achievement, of peculiar promise or distinction have belonged to one of these three categories. They were evidence that the industry was feeling its way back to its aesthetic basis. Now it seems that the movement may have to wait until talking films have done their worst. If they succeed commercially the infant art of the screen may as well be abandoned, unless, separating itself from their uproar, it starts life again in independence and poverty; if they fail commercially, then, the industry dying, the art – of epic, fantasy, and mental process – may be born again. But it is a hard and distant hope.

The Times (19 March 1929)

The Middlebrow Film

'One thing I will say for my country's cinema: we don't get Hollywood films. They are all English!'

Neither her opinion nor the fact came as a surprise to me, for I knew Y. well, a woman rather under middle-age of an intelligence which nowadays is known as middle-brow, that is to say, an intelligence which has grown up as little as her face, so that the books and art which once seemed to the very young woman so lively and cerebral still excite her. And as for the fact, I had learned its truth grimly in many walking tours: the English film has definitely conquered the English provinces – it is even invading America. We used to think that its shortcomings were due to lack of money, so that players and technicians went to Hollywood: now Hollywood is in the hands of the bankers, the tide has turned the other way, English producers have all the money, the stars and the camera-men they need, but somehow the films haven't altered much.

I said, 'I won't argue with you about America, though I'm tempted to give one prod in passing and ask you when we have produced in this country fictional films of the standard of the early gangster film, *City Nights*, of *The Front Page*, or *Crime Without Passion*, comedies as good as Capra's *It Happened One Night*, melodramas even equal to such routine stuff as *China Seas* or *G-Men*.'

'You aren't going to talk about Art and Beauty, I hope?'

'No, only about Entertainment, and then only in fictional films, for otherwise I'd have to admit that no country in the world, even Russia, has produced documentary films of such value as Basil Wright's *Song of Ceylon*. *Song of Ceylon* was made by John Grierson's production unit, and though, like that amusing satire on the B.B.C., *The Voice of Britain*, it's been shown at the ordinary cinemas, most of the G.P.O. films – I wish you could see *Coal Face*, for which W.H. Auden wrote a chorus – are not released in the ordinary way. Grierson has built up a public of several millions, in clubs, lecture halls, provincial film societies, quite independent of the cinema circuits. So he need not please the exhibitor, and it would be unfair to compare his work with that of the ordinary studios. In any case we can damn them without the comparison.'

'Well, then, I counter your American gangster films with Hitchcock's. Didn't you like *The Man Who Knew Too Much* and *The Thirty-Nine Steps*?'

'I wasn't bored; I enjoyed the last film quite a lot. But is there very much in Hitchcock? Like Anthony Asquith he's tricky, not imaginative. Some of his tricks are quite good tricks: you remember in his last film how the scream of the charwoman finding the murdered woman was cut to the shriek of the Flying Scotsman rushing north. There was a time when both Asquith and Hitchcock were quite prepared to give interviews on nothing more important than tricks of that kind, and Hitchcock's films – especially *The Man Who Knew Too Much* – are simply made up of tricks, in their plots as well as their direction. They give a momentary impression of great liveliness, that's all. Only compare that kind of cutting with the cutting in *Song of Ceylon*, when the sounding of the priest's bell on a mountain side startles a small bird from its branch, and the camera follows the flight of the bird and the notes of the bell across the island. Both cuts are visual metaphors; if you reduce them to their literary terms you can tell the difference in quality, for all Hitchcock is saying, with the added vividness and speed of photography, is that the charwoman's scream is like the whistle of the express coming out of a tunnel.'

'You're coming too close to judging Hitchcock aesthetically. Remember we agreed to talk about films only as entertainment.'

'I know, but a melodrama is meant to excite (*Crime Without Passion* was ranting melodrama almost of *The Bells* order, and how it excited!), and my complaint about Hitchcock is that he amuses, but he doesn't excite. I should like to see him take over Ben Travers' excellent farces. He hasn't enough imagination to excite; he doesn't convince. For one thing he's so careless. Think of the ease in *The Thirty-Nine Steps* with which his hunted hero managed to get down from Scotland to the London Palladium, although all the way up to Scotland, and while he was in Scotland, his pursuers were always close on his heels.'

'I agree, but one didn't notice it at the time. Dr Dover Wilson admits that as a good enough excuse for an inconsistency in *Hamlet*, so surely we can allow it to Hitchcock.'

'But I did notice it. I'm certain – do forgive me – that if your observation had not been dulled by seeing too many English films at your country cinema, you would have been as irritated by it as I was. For it was an amusing film and could so easily have been an exciting one. The whole business of melodrama on the screen is interesting. You notice how film critics are always hailing melodramas – *The Thirty-Nine Steps*, for example, and in the underworld of criticism Walter Forde's two pictures *The Tunnel* and *King of the Damned* – as *great* pictures. It would seem odd if Charles Morgan reviewed *The Perfect Alibi* and *The Two Mrs Carrolls* as *great* plays. But this can be said for the film critics: melodramatic material is usually good material for the screen, because in spite of such well-meant art-and-craft efforts as *Riders to the Sea*, a version of Synge's play which was privately shown some time ago, a film should move and move fast. Cinema is an art of movement; the theatre, because of its limitations in space, is an art of discussion, a fact which Dryden's plays illustrate just as well as Shaw's. Montage, a method which one seldom sees in this country outside Mr Grierson's units, is really only a method of balancing speed of movement with speed of thought and idea.

'But perhaps we ought not to talk of melodrama in this way. The term melodrama should only be used disparagingly for failure: for violence insufficiently explained. *Othello* uses melodramatic material, but it is not melodrama. Now the stage has to transform melodramatic material by depth of characterization or by placing the individual drama in its general setting. It is less the characterization of *The Duchess of Malfi* than the vividness of the corrupt Italian scene which "explains" the violent material. But we have almost given up hope of hearing on the contemporary stage words with a vivid enough imagery to convey the climate of the play. Only one such transformation on the modern stage comes to my mind: the opening scene with the two prostitutes in Eliot's *Sweeney Agonistes*. But it is easier to work in pictures than in words, and the film possesses the advantage over the stage when genius is absent. Take, for example, the French film of the Spanish Foreign Legion, *La Bandera*. On the stage this would have been only one more melodrama of African heat and brutality and death, but the camera, because it can note with more exactness and vividness than the prose of most living playwrights the atmosphere of mean streets and water-front cafés and cheap lodgings, gives the story its setting, its authenticity. The violence is explained and therefore ceases to be melodramatic.

'But can we say that Hitchcock explains? Do you believe in his London streets and music halls? They always have a slight air of caricature about them. You can say it even less of Walter Forde. What both these directors need, if they are ever to transform their melodramatic material, is the documentary eye. As it is, they invent and do not see. This isn't an aesthetic question alone: we can't be properly *entertained* by their stories unless we are excited, and we can't be excited unless we are convinced. Take the case of Forde. He was a director of promise. His *Rome Express* was at least as good as Hitchcock's melodramas. The battle scenes in *For Ever England* were excellent (the period scenes were caricature and quite out of keeping), but one imagines that some of their quality may have been due to his technical adviser; it may have been a triumph for the Admiralty as much as for the director. Now he has been given a spectacle to direct, and in *King of the Damned* you see the weakness of his observation. A director can be judged to some extent by the casting of the smaller parts: it is on these that the setting chiefly depends, but Forde allows the reality of his tropical penal settlement to be broken by an O.U.D.S. accent among his convicts. As for *The Tunnel*, it was one of the very few films I have been unable to sit through.'

'You've forgotten Korda.'

'He's a great publicist, of course, the Victor Gollancz of the screen. Only a great publicist could have put over so many undistinguished and positively bad films as if they were a succession of masterpieces. *The Private Life of Henry VIII*: it wasn't a film at all, but a succession of stage tableaux, sometimes entertaining, sometimes amazingly cheap. *Catherine the Great* and *The Scarlet Pimpernel*: the first was a badly-directed film saved by Bergner's acting, the other a miscast and mildly entertaining film, such as Hollywood can turn out by the hundred. *Sanders of the River*: I grant you that Zoltan Korda brought back from Nigeria some really lovely pictures of native life, that some of the direction was exciting, especially the sequence when the false news of Sanders' death was carried into the interior by native drumming, but it was a supreme vulgarity to add to the African players with their natural voices the stagy, trained accents of Paul Robeson and Nina Mae McKinney and to set Arthur Wimperis to write lyrics for the adapted native tunes. And what astonishingly inept lyrics they were with their little classical allusions! 'The river sings, A real Orion', so went one song, which Robeson has to troll out as he paddled half-naked up a West African river. No, I can't believe that Alexander Korda's talent is for the films.'

'Well, you haven't said a word about comedies. At least English comedies haven't the vulgarity of the American.'

'Is *It Happened One Night* vulgar? or *Arms and the Girl*? But there really are no English film comedies. I've spent six months seeing films four times a week, and the only laughs which the English film industry has managed to raise from me have been with Tom Walls' excellent farces. But a picture like his *Foreign Affaires* is just a photograph of a stage play. It has gained nothing by being photographed, and I imagine it has lost a good deal. As for the pictures which feature Jack Hulbert and Cicely Courtneidge, I feel too strongly about them to write with detachment. Our stage comedians, with the honourable exception of Sydney Howard, have not learned the elementary fact that the audience in a cinema are all in the stalls. They still fling their grimaces at a gallery with distressing effect. And as for our comic scenario writers, I'm afraid they lack a sense of humour. Do you remember how that dreadful picture *Me and Marlborough* ended with a giant close-up of Cicely Courtneidge's face and the British troops marching to victory? That was a film by a veteran English director, Victor Saville. I had forgotten one ray of hope – the film comedies which J. B. Priestley has begun to write for Gracie Fields. They have a genuine provincial feel about them. They are directed though by Basil Dean, who's rather tied to stage methods.'

'*The Ghost Goes West*? You'll grant me that, won't you?'

'Is it an English film? The producer is Hungarian, the director French, the scenario writer and two of the three stars American. Only the original story, so typically *Punch*, is English.'

'Well, anyway, if you talk all night, I shall still hate the American accent.'

'There, I give in. It's not arguable. It's a matter of sex appeal.'

The Fortnightly Review (March 1936)

The Genius of Peter Lorre

It was in Fritz Lang's *M* that Peter Lorre first captured attention, captured it with terrifying vividness as a child murderer. Nobody who saw that film could fail to realise that he might be watching a great actor; might be, because the filmgoer learns caution, because he needs more than one film to tell him how much credit is due to the director, because he has been deceived often by a lucky part into believing that a Scarlett Empress is a Blue Angel.

But we were right when we thought there was more than a brilliant melodramatic director behind Lorre. There was nothing of the bogey, the lighted turnip, the Karloff about his performance; I still remember the expression of despairing tenderness he turned on his small victim, the hapless struggle in his face against a habit he could not break.

He exhibited the same sympathetic grasp of a psychological 'ease' in his third film, the rather inferior melodrama of Karl Freund's *The Hands of Orlac*. He acted the part of the depraved surgeon Gogol who grafts the hands of a guillotined murderer onto the stumps of his rival. A part you would have said of cheap Grand Guignol horror, something to frighten children, and a reading of the script would not have altered your view. It was to Lorre alone we owed the goodness, the tenderness of the vicious man. Those marble pupils in the pasty spherical head are like the eye-pieces of a microscope through which you can watch the tangled mind laid flat on the slide: love and lust, nobility and perversity, hatred of itself and despair jumping out at you from the jelly. His very features are metaphysical.

Lorre has run the usual course, from Germany to America and then to England, but in his case it is not the chart of a rising and then falling reputation. He has never failed, although he has never appeared in a good film since *M*. His nearest approach to failure was in Hitchcock's *The Man Who Knew Too Much*. He was given a perfunctory Peter the Painter part, but the director was too proud of his little melodramatic tricks to be interested in character.

Lorre – perhaps it is a misfortune – can do almost anything. He is a genius who sometimes gets the finest effects independently of his director (as I have said there is nothing in the script to explain his Gogol, the seriousness he introduced into the trivial film), but he is also a thoroughly reliable repertory actor, and so in his last film, Hitchcock's deplorable *Secret Agent*, he made a great success of a humorous 'character' part. There was no doubt here about his humour and the gusto with which he acted, and Hitchcock deserves some credit for developing the hint of comic powers observable in Sternberg's glossy popular *Crime and Punishment*, when as Raskolnikov he baited his sister's pompous suitor. It was a cheap little piece of comic relief, but Lorre got from it every possible laugh.

But that is not the Lorre one most wants to see: better Gogol a thousand times, and I have a horrible fear that film directors will find it easier to follow in Hitchcock's steps and provide Lorre with humorous character parts than discover stories to suit his powerful genius, his overpowering sense of spiritual corruption. He is an actor of great profundity in a superficial art. It will always be his fate to be cramped, not only by the shortcomings of directors but by the Board of Film Censors. The financiers are not interested in psychological truth, and the Board does not recognise morality.

World Film News (July 1936)

Is It Criticism?

Film criticism, more than any other form of criticism, except perhaps that of the novel, is a compromise. The critic, as much as the film, is supposed to entertain, and the great public is not interested in technicalities. The reader expects a series of dogmatic statements: he is satisfied, like any member of the Book Society, with being told what is good and what is bad. If he finds himself often enough in agreement with the critic, he is content. It never occurs to him to ask why the critic thought this film good and that film bad, any more than it occurs to him to question his own taste. The fictional film is more or less stabilised at the level of middle-class taste.

One need not deny to either books or films of popular middle-class entertainment a useful social service, as long as it is recognised that social service has nothing to do with the art of cinema or the art of fiction. What I object to is the idea that it is the *critic*'s business to assist films to fulfil a social function. The critic's business should be confined to the art.

Catching the eye

It is this which presents serious difficulties, for a critic concerned with an art needs at least two things: material for his analysis, for comparison and instruction, and a mind which, however sympathetic, is not prone to quick enthusiasms. But, to take the first difficulty, what in the cinema is the critic to write about? He is lucky if two or three films in the year can be treated with respect, and if week after week he produces an analysis of the latest popular film, showing how the script-writer, the director and the camera man have failed, he will soon lose his readers and afterwards his job. He has got to entertain, and most film critics find the easiest way to entertain is 'to write big'. One leading reviewer adopts a very masculine, plain man manner, which is as uncritical and has the same effect as the fulsomeness of more hack reviewers; it catches the eye easily. *Their* praise is usually unequalled by the official publicity writers. Indeed I once knew a daily journalist who never troubled to write his own copy, but handed in the publicity man's 'blurb' with a few adjectives knocked out. The public eye accustomed to the weekly 'masterpiece' and the daily 'tragedy', demands from these journalists Poignant Dramas and Tragedies of Frustrated Love rather than unenthusiastic and accurate estimates. A Hungarian producer at Denham, turning out a number of commercial films of rather low technical value, becomes – in a recent magazine – a Man of Destiny.

Reviewing of this kind contributes nothing to the cinema. The reviewer is simply adding to the atmosphere of graft, vague rhetoric, paid publicity, the general air of Big unscrupulous Business. He is not regarded by his employers as a critic so much as a reporter. One day he is required to write a fulsome interview with a visiting film star at the Savoy, the next to criticise a film in which she appears. The double role is too much for the reviewer, and his criticism reads like an extended interview, gossiping little paragraphs about the stars, an inaccurate sketch of the story, no mention of the director unless he is, like Capra or Clair, world-famous, and no mention at all of the film as a film, that is to say, sequences of photographs arranged in a certain way to get a certain effect.

For some months I, too, recieved from a patient American company about two telegrams a week addressed to my home inviting me at great length (they usually ran to forty words) to be present next day at the Savoy or the Carlton when a film personality, sometimes of remarkable obscurity, would 'hold court'. This was the invariable phrase. There would be, the telegrams usually added, refreshments.

Refreshing the critics

Refreshments: it is a key word to the murky business, to the world in which a new critic finds himself. Even publishers, with their cocktail parties, have not developed the racket to this pitch. It is still possible to review books, among books, in quiet, and I believe dramatic critics are not yet given free drinks at the bar between acts or offered, before the curtain rises, a glass of sherry and a cigarette (one film company even goes as far as champagne). It is assumed that the film critic is invariably thirsty and alcoholic even at the oddest hours. Nowhere else, except on the West Coast of Africa, have I been expected to start drinking by 10.30 in the morning, when the taste of the morning marmalade is still on the tongue. Sometimes the dubious hospitality extends to a lunch at the Carlton.

The film companies, of course, are not bribing the critics. No one is going to be bribed with a glass of sherry and a cigarette. The motive is less obvious and more kindly. The daily press is to a great extent controlled by advertisers. The film critics are not free to damn a bad film. Almost the only papers where you can find uncontrolled criticism are the periodicals: *The New Statesman, The Spectator, The London Mercury*, and *The Listener*. The glasses of sherry, so I believe, are charitably intended to make it easier for the so-called critic to tap out his fore-ordained notice: it would be a grim business otherwise.

The same motive perhaps lies behind the Gala performances: a Gala performance is usually allotted to an expensive but bad film: *Moscow Nights, The Dark Angel*, the two worst films of 1935, both had this curious setting of blue lights, squealing peeresses, policemen to keep back a crowd which wouldn't have assembled without the policemen, a strained attempt to make a bad film, if it can't be entertainment, at any rate something, a Show, a social occasion. It is in this atmosphere that, if ever there is a Shakespeare of the films, he will have to get a hearing. His films will not be damned, they will be praised, praised as highly and in the same terms as *The Dark Angel*. And it is in this atmosphere, too, that a Coleridge of the films would have to work. Indeed, when once his little vice became widely known, his kindly host would see that he was served with his individual opium pill instead of the glass of sherry.

Popular art and the middle classes

It is not that one wishes the cinema to be precious, eclectic, unpopular. The novel has long ceased to make any effort at being a really popular art: the novels of Mr Priestley or Mr Brett Young represent the people about as much as do the prosperous suburbs of Balham and Streatham. I doubt if we have had any popular art in England since the Shakespearean theatre, and I welcome the chance the cinema offers. Millions go to the cinema, but do they really get what *they* want or do they get what the middle-class public wants? – the cinema of escape. The thousands who come down to Wembley in charabancs from the north with favours in their caps don't want to escape. They want something as simple and exciting as a cup-tie, just as the Elizabethan public wanted something as brutal and exciting as what went on in the bear-pit. *The Texas Rangers* is nearer to popular art than *Anna Karenina*. I admire a film like *Song of Ceylon* more perhaps than anything else I have yet seen on the screen, but I would rather see the public shouting and hissing in the sixpenny seats. Instead – I look at my paper this week: *The Great Ziegfeld, Sins of Man, Follow Your Heart, East Meets West, The Singing Kid.*

Criticism by satire

What, to return to my earlier question, is the critic to write about? Almost the only approach possible at the present stage for a critic who is writing for readers uninterested in technical detail is the satirical. This is to make a flank attack upon the reader, to persuade him to laugh at personalities, stories, ideas, methods, he has previously taken for granted. We need to be rude, rude even to our fellow reviewers, but not in the plain downright way, which may help to kill a particular picture, but leaves its kind untouched. The cinema needs to be purged with laughter, and the critics, too (critics who can write: 'By sheer diligence and enthusiasm the cinema, which 25 years ago was producing such morsels as *What Drink Did* has now arrived at the point when the Queen, the Prince of Wales, and the President of the United States, are all prepared to patronise its shows within a fortnight'). Indeed, I am not sure whether our fellow critics are not more important subjects for our satire than the cinema itself, for they are doing as much as any Korda or Sam Goldwyn to maintain the popular middle-class Book Society *status quo*.

Sight and Sound (Autumn 1936)

Subjects and Stories

There is no need to regard cinema as a completely new art; in its fictional form it has the same purpose as the novel, just as the novel has the same purpose as the drama. Tchehov, writing of his fellow novelists, remarked: 'The best of them are realistic and paint life as it is, but because every line is permeated, as with a juice, by an awareness of a purpose, you feel, beside life as it is, also life as it ought to be, and this captivates you.' This description of an artist's theme has never, I think, been bettered: we need not even confine it to the fictional form: it applies equally to the documentary film, to pictures in the class of Mr Rotha's *Shipyard* (one remembers the last sequence of the launching: the workers who have made the ship watching from the banks and the roofs the little social gathering, the ribbons and the champagne) or Mr Wright's *Song of Ceylon*: only in films to which Tchehov's description applies shall we find the poetic cinema. And the poetic cinema – it is the only form worth considering.

Life as it is and life as it ought to be: let us take that as the only true subject for a film, and consider to what extent the cinema is fulfilling its proper function. The stage, of course, has long ceased to fulfil it at all. Mr St John Irvine, Miss Dodie Smith, these are the popular playwrights of the moment: they have no sense of life as it is lived, far less even than Mr Noël Coward, and if they have some dim idea of a better life, this is expressed only in terms of sexual or financial happiness. As for the popular novel, Mr Walpole, Mr Brett Young, Mr Priestley, we are aware of rather crude minds representing no more of contemporary life than is to be got in a holiday snapshot: Mr Walpole the house and garden, Mr Brett Young the village street, the old alms-houses and the vicar, Mr Priestley the inn, the forge, the oldest inhabitant.

I think one may say that *Dodsworth* represents about the highest level to which this type of writer can attain on the screen. *Dodsworth* as a book was far less readable than as a picture it was seeable. The dimmest social drama can be given a certain gloss and glitter by a good director and a good cameraman. No one, I think, could have been actively bored by *Dodsworth*. It had the great virtues of natural acting and natural speech; it did in its way, its too personal and private way, fulfil one of the functions we have named; it at least presented life as it presumably appears to an American millionaire, unhappily married to a wife who is determined to climb socially: perhaps one is rash in making even that claim, for the number of people who can judge its truth must needs be strictly limited. But as for life as it ought to be, the nearest *Dodsworth* comes to that is a quaint Italian villa on the bay of Naples and the company of a gentle, refined and flower-like widow. It is alas! still true of the theatre what Mr Ford Madox Ford wrote in 1911, in an essay on the functions of the arts in the republic, 'that, in this proud, wealthy and materially polished civilisation, there was visible no trace, no scintilla, no shadow of a trace of the desire to have any kind of thought awakened.' In those days before the great four years' deluge Mr Ford found that 'it is to the music-halls we must go nowadays for any form of pulse stirring,' the popular entertainment of that day. The cinema has to a large extent killed the music-hall, but has it absorbed its virtues or 'the sinister forms of morality' Mr Ford found in the theatre?

Writing this in the third week of February, 1937, I turn to the list of films now to be seen in London (perhaps it may amuse a few readers when this book appears to try to recall these films, and if a few do still stick obstinately in the memory, to try to recall their subjects, a few sequences): *Ernte, Maid of Salem, Magnificent Obsession, Mazurka, This'll Make You Whistle, The Great Barrier, Devil Takes the Count, The Texas Rangers, Beloved Enemy, Dreaming Lips, O.H.M.S., Aren't Men Beasts, Ramona, The Plainsman, Girls' Dormitory, His Lordship, Accused, La Kermesse Héroïque, Good Morning Boys*. It is not on the whole such an unfavourable week. I think three of those films may be remembered in a year's time. But how many of them show any inkling of the only subject-matter for art, life as it is and life as it ought to be, how many even fulfil what Mr Ford defines as the functions of merely inventive literature, of diverting, delighting, tickling, of promoting appetites? Only, I think the three I have mentioned: *La Kermesse Héroïque, The Texas Rangers, The Plainsman.* The first had at least an adult theme, that the sexual appetite is a great deal stronger than patriotism: it did present life – in fancy dress for safety – as it is; it had the characteristic personal exaggeration that Mr Ford demands of the imaginative writer: it was a Feyder film. The other two had good, if less interesting and more obvious themes: that when you have settled a new country, you must make it safe for the unarmed and the weak, themes which do contain of their very nature the two halves of Tchehov's definition.

But I am afraid in the plots of the others you will get the more representative film. *Mazurka*: fallen woman shoots her seducer to save her child from a similar fate; *Magnificent Obsession*: a woman loses her eyesight when a drunken young plutocrat smashes his car, the drunken young plutocrat turns over a new leaf, studies medicine, become the greatest eye surgeon of his day in time to cure and marry the girl while both are young; *Dreaming Lips*: a young wife falls passionately in love with a musical genius; unable to choose between the genius and the boy husband, she kills herself; *Girls' Dormitory*: an innocent and dewy schoolgirl falls in love with her headmaster, writes an imaginary love letter which is discovered by a prying mistress, is expelled for immorality, runs away in the rain pursued by the headmaster who then discovers the truth.

It is difficult to see what critical purpose is served by subjects like these. (I say *critical* purpose because the sense of life as it should be must always be a critical one. An element of satire enters into all dramatic art.) Is it possible that the glittering prizes the cinema offers defeat their purpose? The artist is not as a rule a man who takes kindly to life, but can his critical faculty help being a little blunted on two hundred pounds a week? A trivial point perhaps, but one reason why we do not look first to Hollywood or Denham for films of artistic value, for the poetic cinema.

I use the word poetic in its widest sense. Only of quite recent years has the term poet been narrowed down to those who write according to some kind of metrical or rhythmical scheme. In

Dryden's day any creative writer was called a poet, and it would be difficult to justify any definition which excluded James or Conrad, Tchehov or Turgenev from the rank of poets. Mr Ford Madox Ford has given us the most useful definition for the quality which these prose writers have in common with Shakespeare and Dryden: 'not the power melodiously to arrange words but the power to suggest human values.'

So we need not consider, I think, the various screen adaptations of Shakespeare. It isn't that kind of poetry we are seeking (the poetry made tautological by the realistic settings), nor will we find it in the smart neat *Dodsworths* and *Dreaming Lips* the power to suggest human values. We come nearer to what we seek perhaps in a picture like *Hortobagy*, the film of the Hungarian plains acted by peasants and shepherds. The photography was very beautiful, the cutting often superb, but photography by itself cannot make poetic cinema. By itself it can only make arty cinema. *Man of Aran* was a glaring example of this: how affected and wearisome were those figures against the skyline, how meaningless that magnificent photography of storm after storm. *Man of Aran* did not even attempt to describe truthfully a way of life. The inhabitants had to be taught shark-hunting in order to supply Mr Flaherty with a dramatic sequence. *Hortobagy* did at least attempt to show life truthfully: those wild herds tossing across the enormous plain, against the flat sky, the shepherds in their huge heavy traditional cloaks galloping like tartar cavalry between the whitewashed huts, the leaping of the stallions, the foaling of the mares shown with meticulous candour, did leave the impression that we were seeing, as far as humanly possible, life as it is. It was documentary in the finest sense: on the documentary side it has been unsurpassed: but Mr Basil Wright's *Song of Ceylon*, faulty in continuity as it was, contained more of what we are looking for, criticism implicit in the images, life as it is containing the indications of life as it should be, the personal lyric utterance.

It was divided, it may be remembered into four parts, and opened with a forest sequence, huge revolving fans of palm filling the screen. We then watched a file of pilgrims climb a mountain-side to the stone effigies of the gods, and here, as a priest struck a bell, Mr Wright used one of the loveliest visual metaphors I have seen on the screen. The sounding of the bell startled a small bird from its branch, and the camera followed the bird's flight and the bell notes across the island, down from the mountain side, over forest and plain and sea, the vibration of the tiny wings, the fading sound. Then, in a rather scrappy and unsatisfactory movement, we saw the everyday life of the natives, until in the third movement we were made aware of the personal criticism implied in the whole film. As the natives followed the old ways of farming, climbing palm trees with a fibre loop, guiding their elephants against the trees to be felled, voices dictated bills of lading, closed deals, announced through loud-speakers the latest market prices. And lest the contrast between two ways of life should be left too indecisively balanced, the director's sympathy was plainly shown in the last movement: back on the mountain-side with the stone faces, the gaudy gilded dancers, the solitary peasant laying his offering at Buddha's feet, and when he closed the film with the revolving leaves, it was as if he was sealing away from us devotion and dance and the gentle communal life of harvest, leaving us outside with the bills of lading and the loud-speakers.

Here, of course, with the director who acts as his own cameraman and supervises his own script, with the reduction of credits to a minimum, and the subsidised film, we are getting far from the commercial picture. The *Song of Ceylon* will always stand outside the ordinary cinema. We are getting closer to the poetic and yet commercially possible cinema with a picture like *The Song of Freedom*, an inexpensive picture made by a small British company, full of muddled thought and bad writing: the story of a black dockhand who becomes a famous singer and goes back to his ancestral home to try to save his people from the witch-doctors. Full of muddled thought and absurdities of speech, it is true, yet this film had something which the *Dodsworths* lacked. A sense stays in the memory of an unsophisticated mind fumbling on the edge of simple and popular poetry. The best scenes were the dockland scenes, the men returning from work free from any colour bar, the public-house interiors, dark faces pausing at tenement windows to listen to the black man's singing, a sense of nostalgia, of what Mann calls 'the gnawing surreptitious hankering for the bliss of the commonplace.'

The commonplace, that is the point. The poetic drama ceased to be of value when it ceased to be as popular as bear-baiting. The decline from Webster to Tennyson is not a mere decline in poetic merit – 'Queen Mary' has passages of great beauty – but a decline in popularity. The cinema has got to appeal to millions; we have got to accept its popularity as a virtue, not turn away from it as a vice.

Only the conviction that a public art should be as popular and unsubtle as a dance tune enables one to sit with patient hope through pictures certainly unsubtle, but not, in any real sense, popular. What a chance there is for the creative artist, one persists in believing, to produce for an audience incomparably greater than that of all the 'popular' novelists combined, from Mr Walpole to Mr Brett Young, a genuinely vulgar art. Any other is impossible. The novelist may write for a few thousand readers, but the film artist *must* work for millions. It should be his distinction and pride that he has a public whose needs have never been met since the closing of the theatres by Cromwell. But where is the vulgarity of this art? Alas! the refinement of the 'popular' novel has touched the films; it is the twopenny libraries they reflect rather than the Blackfriars Ring, the Wembley final, the pin saloons, the coursing.

'I'm not the type that I seem to be,
Happy-go-lucky and gay,'

Bing Crosby mournfully croons in one of his latest pictures. That is the common idea of popular entertainment, a mild self-pity, something soothing, something gently amusing. The film executive still thinks in terms of the 'popular' play and the 'popular' novel, of a limited middle-class audience, of the tired business man and the feminine reader. The public which rattles down from the North to Wembley with curious hats and favours, tipsy in charabancs, doesn't, apparently, ask to be soothed: it asks to be excited. It was for these that the Elizabethan stage provided action which could arouse as communal a response as bear-baiting. For a popular response is not the sum of private excitements, but mass feeling, mass excitement, the Wembley roar; and it is the weakness of the Goldwyn Girls that they are as private an enjoyment as the Art Photos a business man may turn over in the secrecy of his study, the weakness of Bing Crosby's sentiment, the romantic nostalgia of 'Empty saddles in the old corral,' that it is by its nature a private emotion.

There are very few examples of what I mean by the proper popular use of the film, and most of those are farces: *Duck Soup*, the early Chaplins, a few 'shorts' by Laurel and Hardy. These do convey the sense that the picture has been made by its spectators and not merely shown to them, that it has sprung, as much as their sports, from *their* level. Serious films of the kind are even rarer: perhaps *Fury, The Birth of a Nation, Men and Jobs*, they could be numbered on the fingers of one hand. Because, they are so rare one is ready to accept, with exaggerated gratitude, such refined, elegant, dead pieces as *Louis Pasteur*: the Galsworthy entertainments of the screen: or intelligently adapted plays like *These Three*.

'People want to be taken out of themselves,' the film executive retorts under the mistaken impression that the critic is demanding a kind of Zola-esque realism – as if Webster's plays were realistic. Of course he is right. People are taken out of themselves at Wembley. But I very much doubt if Bing Crosby does so much. 'They don't want to be depressed,' but an excited audience is never depressed; if you excite your audience first, you can put over what you will of horror, suffering, truth. But there is one question which needs an answer. How dare we excite an audience, a producer may well ask, when Lord Tyrrell, the President of the Board of Censors, forbids us to show any controversial subject on the screen?

The cinema has always developed by means of a certain low cunning. The old-clothes merchants who came in on a good thing in the early days and ended as presidents of immense industries had plenty of cunning. It is for the artist to show his cunning now. You may say with some confidence that at the present stage of English culture, a great many serious subjects cannot be treated at all. We cannot treat human Justice truthfully as America treated it in *I am a Fugitive from the Chain Gang*. No film which held the aged provincial J.P.s up to criticism or which described the conditions in the punishment cells at Maidstone would be allowed. Nor is it possible to treat seriously a religious or a political subject.

But that is not all to the bad. We are saved from the merely topical by our absurd censorship. We shall not have to sit through the cinematic equivalents of Mrs Mitchison's emotional novels. We are driven back to the 'blood', the thriller. There never has been a school of popular English bloods. We have been damned from the start by middle-class virtues, by gentlemen cracksmen and stolen plans and Mr Wus. We have to go farther back than this, dive below the polite level, to something nearer to the common life. And isn't it better to have as your subject 'life nasty, brutish, and short' than the more pompous themes the censor denies us? He won't allow us a proletarian political drama, and I cannot help being a little relieved that we lose the lifeless malice of Pudovkin's capitalist automatons, that dreadful shadow of Victorian progress and inevitable victory. Our excitements have got to have a more universal subject, we have the chance of being better realists than the Russians, we are saved from the tract in return for what we lose.

And when we have attained to a more popular drama, even if it is in the simplest terms of blood on a garage floor ('There lay Duncan laced in his golden blood'), the scream of cars in flight, all the old excitements at their simplest and most sure-fire, then we can begin – secretly, with low cunning – to develop our poetic drama ('the power to suggest human values'). Our characters can develop from the level of *The Spanish Tragedy* towards a subtler, more thoughtful level.

Some such development we can see at work in Fritz Lang: *The Spy* was his simplest, purest thriller. It has no human values at all, only a brilliant eye for the surface of life and the power of physical excitement; in *Fury* the eye was no less sure, but the poetry had crept in. Here in the lynching was the great thriller situation superbly handled; but not a shot but owed part of its effect to the earlier sequences, the lovers sheltering under the elevated from the drenching rain, good-bye at the railway station with faces and hands pressed to wet fogging windows, the ordinary recognisable agony, life as one knows it is lived, the human, the poetic value. And how was this introduced? Not in words – that is the stage way. I can think of no better example of the use of poetic imagery that in *We from Kronstadt.* At one level this was a magnificent picture of schoolboy heroics, of last charges and fights to the death, heroic sacrifices and narrow escapes, all superbly directed. But what made the picture remarkable was the poetry, critical as poetry must always be (life as it is: life as it ought to be). We were aware all the time that *We from Kronstadt* had been written and directed by the fellow countrymen of Tchehov and Turgenev, and curiously enough among the gunshots, the flag waving, the last stands, the poetry was of the same gentle and reflective and melancholy kind as theirs.

Indeed there was a scene in this picture of humorous and pathetic irony which might have been drawn directly from one of the great classic novelists. The hall and stairs of a one-time palace on the Baltic shore are packed nearly to suffocation with soldiers and marines; they lie massed together like swine: at dawn a door opens at the stair-head and a little knot of children, lodged for safety in the palace, emerges, climbs softly down, ready to start like mice at any movement. They finger the revolvers, the rifles, the machine-guns, climb quickly away when a man moves, percolate down again among the sleepers persistently, to finger a butt, a holster, the barrel of a Lewis gun.

There were many other examples in this picture of the poetic use of imagery and incident: the gulls sweeping and coursing above the cliffs where the Red prisoners are lined up for their death by drowning, the camera moving from the heavy rocks around their necks to the movement of the light, white wings; one sooty tree drooping on the huge rocky Kronstadt walls above a bench where a sailor and a woman embrace, against the dark tide; the riding-lights of the battleships, the shape of the great guns, the singing of a band of sailors going home in the dark to their iron home. Life as it is; life as it ought to be: every poetic image chosen for its contrasting value, to represent peace and normal human values under the heroics and the wartime patriotism.

The poetic cinema, it is worth remembering, can be built up on a few very simple ideas, as simple as the ideas behind the poetic fictions of Conrad: the love of peace, of country, a feeling for fidelity: it doesn't require a great mind to conceive them, but it does require an imaginative mind to feel them with sufficient passion. Griffith was a man of this quality, though to a sophisticated audience he sometimes seems to have chosen incidents of extraordinary *naïveté* to illustrate his theme. Simple, sensuous and passionate, that definition would not serve the cinema badly: it would enable us at any rate to distinguish between the values say of *Way Down East* and *Louis Pasteur*, and beside that distinction all other discussion of subject-matter seems a little idle.

from *Footnotes to the Film*, edited by Charles Davy (1937)

Film Lunch

'If ever there was a Christ-like man in human form it was Marcus Loew.'

Under the huge Union Jack, the Stars and Stripes, the massed chandeliers of the Savoy, the little level voice softly intones. It is Mr Louis B. Mayer, head of Metro-Goldwyn-Mayer, and the lunch is being held to celebrate the American Company's decision to produce films in this country. Money, one can't help seeing it written on the literary faces, money for jam; but Mr

Mayer's words fall on the mercenary gathering with apostolic seriousness.

At the high table Sir Hugh Walpole leans back, a great bald forehead, a rather softened and popular Henry James, like a bishop before the laying-on of hands – but oddly with a long cigar. Miss Maureen O'Sullivan waits under her halo hat . . . and Mr Robert Taylor – is there, one wonders, a woman underneath the table? Certainly there are few sitting anywhere else; not many, at any rate, whom you would recognize as women among the tough massed faces of the film-reviewers. As the voice drones remorsely on, these escape at intervals to catch early editions, bulging with shorthand (Mr Mayer's voice lifts: 'I must be honest to myself if I'm to be honest to you . . . a 200,000,000-dollar corporation like the Rock of Gibraltar . . . untimely death . . . tragedy'); they stoop low, slipping between the tables, like soldiers making their way down the communication trenches to the rest-billets in the rear, while a voice mourns for Thalberg, untimely slain. The bright Very lights of Mr Mayer's eloquence soar up: 'Thank God, I say to you, that it's the greatest year of net results and that's because I have men like Eddy Sankatz (can that have been the name? It sounded like it after the Chablis Supérieur, 1929, the Château Pontet Canet Pauillac, 1933, G.H. Mumm, Cordon Rouge, 1928, and the Gautier Frères Fine Champagne 20 *ans*).

'No one falls in the service of M.G.M. but I hope and pray that someone else will take his place and carry on the battle. Man proposes and God in his time disposes . . . ' All the speakers have been confined to five minutes – Mr Alexander Korda, Lord Sempill, Lord Lee of Fareham, and the rest, but of course that doesn't apply to the big shot. The rather small eyes of Mr Frank Swinnerton seem to be watching something on his beard, Mr Ivor Novello has his hand laid across his stomach – or is it his heart?

One can't help missing things, and when the mind comes back to the small dapper man under the massed banners Mr Mayer is talking about his family, and God again. 'I've got another daughter and I hope to God . . . ' But the hope fumes out of sight in the car smoke of the key-man. 'She thought she'd like a poet or a painter, but I held on until I landed Selznick. "No, Ireen," I'd say, "I'm watching and waiting." So David Selznick, he's performing independent now.'

The waiters stand at attention by the great glass doors. The air is full of aphorisms. 'I love to give flowers to the living before they pass on . . . We must have entertainment like flowers need sunshine . . . A Boston bulldog hangs on till death. Like Jimmy Squires (Jimmy Squires means something to these tough men. They applaud wildly. The magic name is repeated – 'Jimmy Squires'.) 'I understand Britishers,' Mr Mayer continues, 'I understand what's required of a man they respect and get under their hearts.'

There is more than a religious element in this odd, smoky, and spirituous gathering; at moments it is rather like a boxing match. 'Miss O'Sullivan bobs up to her feet and down again: a brown hat: a flower: one misses the rest. 'Robert Taylor' – and the world's darling is on his feet, and not far from Sir Hugh Walpole, beyond the brandy glasses and Ivor Novello, a black triangle of hair, a modest smile.

'He comes of a lovely family,' Mr Mayer says. 'If ever there was an American young man who could logically by culture and breeding be called a Britisher it's Robert Taylor.'

But already we are off and away, Robert Taylor abandoned to the flashlight men. It's exactly 3.30 and Mr Mayer is working up for his peroration: 'It's midday. It's getting late. I shall pray silently that I shall be guided in the right channels . . . I want to say what's in my heart . . . In all these years of production, callous of adulation and praise . . . I hope the Lord will be kind to you. We are sending over a lovely cast.'

He has spoken for forty minutes: for forty minutes we have listened with fascination to the voice of American capital itself: a touch of religion, a touch of the family, the mixture goes smoothly down. Let the literary men sneer . . . the whip cracks . . . past the glass doors and the sentries, past the ashen-blonde sitting in the lounge out of earshot (only the word 'God' reached her ears three times), the great muted chromium studios wait . . . the novelist's Irish sweep: money for no thought, for the banal situation and the inhuman romance: money for forgetting how people live: money for 'Siddown, won't yer' and 'I love, I love, I love' endlessly repeated. Inside the voice goes on – 'God . . . I pray . . . ' and the writers, a little stuffed and a little boozed, lean back and dream of the hundred pounds a week – and all that's asked in return the dried imagination and the dead pen.

Written in 1937; included in *Collected Essays* (1969)

Ideas in the Cinema

Not even the newspapers can claim so large a public as the films: they make the circulation figures of the *Daily Express* look insignificant. The voice of Mr Paul Muni has been heard by more people than the radio voices of the dictators, and the words he speaks are usually a little more memorable. The words of dictators do not dwell in the brain – one speech is very like another: we retain a confused impression of olive branches, bayonets and the New Deal. How easy it would be to draw an optimistic picture of the film industry, the perfect method of communicating simply and vividly to the greatest number the ideas of the artist, the reformer, the moralist. *Zola* after all preaches Truth; whatever we may think of its aesthetic falseness, the moral is impeccable. The moral indeed is always impeccable; whether we are present at a gangster picture or a news film there is always the villain and the hero. In *The March of Time* the bombs fall on the babies of Madrid and not on the babies of Granada: the Japanese imperialists wage ruthless war on whom? The Chinese warlord whose methods were described with such convincing horror in *La*

Condition Humaine, whose officers according to M. Malraux – burned their Communist prisoners alive in the boilers of locomotives? No, Time Marches On and the warlord is oddly transformed. It isn't altogether an ideological purpose which dictates these simplifications: the huge public has been trained to expect a villain and a hero, and if you think you're going to reach the biggest possible public, it's no good thinking of drama as the conflict of ideas; its the conflict – in terms of sub-machine guns – between the plainest Good and the plainest Evil.

But does reaching the public necessarily mean reaching the biggest, most amorphous public possible? Isn't it equally possible to reach a selected public with films of aesthetic interest? The artist needs an audience to whom it isn't necessary to preach, in whom he can assume a few common ideas, born of a common environment. I don't mean a small intellectual *avant-garde* public, but a national public, the kind of trench kinship which isn't a matter of class or education, but of living and dying together in the same hole. The cinema, of course, should be a popular art, but need that popularity be worldwide? What common ideas can be assumed between the middle-western farmer and the Cockney clerk, between the New York stockbroker and the unemployed man in a Welsh village? Few, I'm afraid, less vague and sentimental than the ideas of *Lost Horizon*. And yet the other day at a private discussion I heard one of the best English commercial directors (English by birth, a rare thing) state that he wasn't interested in making English films: he wanted to make international films. Was it a commercial boast or was it a confused relic of the political ideal we most of us shared till it was routed in the African mountains? Probably it was a little of both – the idealist dreaming of an art dimly connected with Geneva and the great dead Palace of the Nations, and the merchant trying to muscle in on the American market, and perhaps too the wise man making the best of his limitations. For art has never really left the cave where it began, and you cannot live, as an English ace producer does, between Denham and Hollywood, with a break in New York for business conferences, and betweenwhiles make a picture which is the product of saturation in a particular environment. What can you do in those circumstances – your territory the office, the liner, the aeroplane, the studio – but make an international picture? That is to say a picture without atmosphere or theme, of which the literary equivalent, I suppose, is something like *La Madonne des Sleepings*.

I daresay the producer (an intelligent man) would have admitted, if he had been pressed, that there's no such thing as international art, but art was not a word which came up at that discussion. England, it was assumed, was too small for a self-supporting industry. English films couldn't be made. A curious and disengenuous notion when you consider how much money English producers have lost with their international pictures. If the financial consideration was the only one, it would surely occur to them that nationality might *pay*. For if the expression is fine enough the world will listen, but the fineness of the expression demands on the integrity of the source – Shakespeare is English first, and only after that the world's. And to compare small things with great, *Mr Deeds* was an American and not an international picture. Mightn't it be the sensible, the economic thing to aim at the English markets alone and leave the world's to fate? Possibly, but that is to leave out of account human megalomania. Film magnates have this affinity to newspaper barons – they are really less concerned with money than with themselves, their own publicity. Better to make a picture for £200,000 and lose half your money than make a picture for £20,000 and clear a paltry profit. There's a kind of wild impracticability about these men – they don't really want money, they want noise. (I have myself played a modest part in the construction of a 'cheap' film which was shot hurriedly without a finished script and scrapped uncompleted at a cost of £45,000 – the total cost of the French spectacular film, *Mayerling*.) You can't, these men will tell you, make a film pay in this country alone. The French can, and the Swedes can, but apparently, with our much greater population, it remains for us an impossibility. Of course all they mean is that their production would be too small for glory, and to justify themselves they compute merit in terms of pounds. I have heard one of the leading men in the industry state confidently that a picture which costs £100,000 *must* be a better picture than one which cost £50,000 . . . and yet we all know that the 50,000 extra pounds may all have gone on a single star, on bad organisation so that the script was not finished when the star arrived from Hollywood. The sense of glory is the main thing that stands beween the artist and his public.

There's another. The artist belongs to the cave: he is national: and the men through whom he must transmit his idea, in whose company he must retain the integrity of his conception, are – very frequently – foreign. In what can with technical accuracy be termed an English company you may have a Hungarian producer assisted by a Hungarian art director and a Hungarian scenario editor. Among its directors there may be Frenchmen, Hungarians, Germans and Americans. The language is strange to them, the ideas are strange: little wonder that the characters are slowly smoothed out of existence, the English corners rubbed away. The public – you may say – has been reached by something, and they'll be reached again next week and the week after by so many thousand feet of celluloid; they haven't been reached by an idea: that has died on the way, somewhere in the central-heated office, at a conference among the foreign accents.

The Spectator (19 November 1937)

Movie Parade, 1937

From a lofty eerie GRAHAM GREENE surveys the passing pageant of the year:

It doesn't matter if we are late . . . There'll be another next year, and you won't be able to tell any difference, watching the parade from the top of the Odeon tower. It's not like literature: in 1915 when Henry James died, you knew it was the end of something important, but when Thalberg died last year – or was it in 1936? – everything remained just the same as before. No, the really interesting thing about 1937 was not the pictures themselves, they are the hideous occasional glimpse of the film mind. Louis B. Mayer saying at lunch, 'If ever there was a Christ-like man in human form, it was my friend Marcus Loew'; Jean Harlow corresponding with a fan she hadn't met – 'Dear Old Safety Valve, Stan, dear: If a girl ever relied on friendship, I do, and I have relied on yours . . . It's nine o'clock and the old blonde hair must be put in pins and the body put to rest . . . Best love to the grandest friend a girl ever had. (Signed) Me.' And, of course, we mustn't forget the leopard skin seats at the Odeon.

It's no good though – we've got to have the parade, and anyway in the Odeon tower we're a nice long way from what Miss Lejeune calls the old troopers: they won't be able to tell whether we are applauding or not. What's the statue in the middle of the square? With the little beard and the finger on the forehead? Oh, that's the man who wrote *The Christian* and *The Deemster*.

One feels up here like characters in the first act of *Troilus and Cressida* (scenery by Reinhardt), high on the Trojan battlements watching the heroes return from the Plain of Troy. Oh for the speech of Pandarus to distinguish them – 'asses, fools, dolts, chaff and bran, chaff and bran!' There goes the year's technihorror, *The Trail of the Lonesome Pine*. No it's not; it's *God's Country and the Woman*. The *Lonesome Pine* was 1936, but it doesn't make any difference; next year it will be *Only God Can Make a Tree* (a successful shot of a falling pine and some lake scenery). Any advance in colour? None that you'd notice. The films, like the Spanish War, just go on – they don't get any better. We clapped as much as we are going to clap at *Becky Sharp* in 1935.

There goes the worst film of the year – *The Last Train from*

Madrid. Give it a hand; it was funnier than most of the comics; and – an astonishing thing – none of the critics praised it. There are some other next-to-worst films just behind – Sidney Carroll is tossing his hat in the air and even Lejeune is showing enthusiasm: the Denham spy film, *The Dark Journey*, with its hopelessly involved script, *Thunder in the City* (special effects by Ned Mann), Jessie Matthews' *Head Over Heels*, and tieing with our English worsts an American and a couple of Continentals, *The Road Back, Der Ammenkoenig* – that heavy Teuton sportiness, those Goering rompers – and *Stradivarius*. Two more pictures from Denham I seem to see down there in the third-rate class: *Fire Over England* (in spite of Pommer) and *Elephant Boy* (in spite of Flaherty). Queen Elizabeth as headmistress of Cheltenham Ladies' College wins the devotion of all the junior mistresses and even some of the governors – though there's some dirty work with model ships in the swimming baths: as for *Elephant Boy*, whatever you feel about Flaherty's documentary camera, this was meant to be fiction, and as fiction it was incompetent. No extra elephants and rubber models could retrieve what Flaherty lost in India – a story line.

If you look hard enough you may be able to detect some really good English films. Nobody's taking any notice; everybody's looking at *Victoria the Great*, the most overrated film of the year with a sequence of technihorror. It is said that we can break into the American market with the right films, but it shows too, that you don't need to be an American to be ignorant of English history and English atmosphere. The best English films of the year to my mind are *For Valour*, with Tom Walls and Ralph Lynn, and *Oh, Mr Porter*, with Will Hay. I don't mean just technically English – with the producer and director foreign by birth, otherwise Feyder's valiant *Knight Without Armour* would need mention, but genuinely English – the music hall as nearly at its best as the censor will allow.

That? Oh, that's *Lost Horizon* (it has got out of its right place, which is with the third-rate films of the year), the typical middlebrow novel with its pretensions to poetry and thought for once presented on the screen in all its dreariness, unmitigated by revolver shots. There'll be another in next year's show because the long film has come to stay and you can't fill up two hours without padding. Let us pray the next Capra's not called *Sparkenbroke*.

What's the good of staying up here and enumerating pictures of which we can probably only remember they made an hour or two pass easily. 1937 had its good comedies like any other year: *Woman Chases Man, Easy Living, Saratoga* (Jean Harlow's last), *Theodora Goes Wild, Angel* (not up to Lubitsch standard); best of all, I think, *True Confession* (with John Barrymore starting pluckily over again as a buffoon with waggling hips and a signature tune) and *Amphityron* (a French version of the old Greek cuckolding story Dryden played about with, light, effervescent, deliciously unimportant, with charmingly transient music). 1937, too, had its good gangster dramas – *His Affair* (where they wore Edwardian boaters and parked Edwardian hats); *Winterset* (in which Eduardo Ciannelli, the most damned thing about the damned, made his fine screen début in a setting of doubtful poetry); *Dead End* (a magnificent picture of the environment which breeds the gangster but the credit belongs really to the stage). 1937 had its Western – *The Plainsman*, De Mille handling his crowds as superbly as he always does, but for once with a good story and fine actors – Gary Cooper and Jean Arthur. There were biographies – not as good as *Pasteur*, but in the same rather pompous Galsworthian tradition: *The Life of Emile Zola*, an incurably American picture of a French writer, and *Parnell*, less pompous but more fake. There were Garbos – *Camille*, Hollywood's version of *La Dame aux Camélias*, the story which Henry James described as having been 'blown about the world at a fearful rate . . . all champagne and tears' (Garbo can do the tears to perfection, but her gawky tragic body cannot manage champagne), and *Marie Walewska*, fine acting in an unfortunate script. There was a Marx Brothers – *A Day at the Races*, a little too glossy and expensive and reasonable, so that we missed the shaky sets of the primitive camera, and there was a fair average batch of social dramas, ranging from *Craig's Wife* (the most sophisticated) to *Make Way for Tomorrow* (the most sentimental and yet the most moving of all). There was an 'epic' – *The Good Earth*, and there was one of those 'Sports' which seem to get past the Hollywood executioners by accident; this year it was the ridiculous picture of political justice, *They Won't Forget*. I don't suppose 1936 could show a better lot than that: the trouble is, I don't suppose 1938 will either. Then, of course, there was the year's discovery – Deanna Durbin – Oh, God, Oh, Montreal; let's go down and sit in the dark on leopard skins and talk about the few pictures which still interest us now that the celluloid has stopped revolving.

There was Dickinson's first film, *The High Command*; not a very good story, uncertain dialogue, but moments of the finest cinematic sense – that time, for example, when the West African band played God Save the King and everyone stood stockstill in the clubhouse, while the Hamatan blew the potted plants over and banged the windows and not a servant dared to stir for three verses: a film important, too, because, though a unit was sent to West Africa, it yet cost only a third of an average Denham production, an example of the economy which is surely our only chance of establishing a national industry.

Then one remembers another brilliant and economical English picture, Edmond Greville's *Brief Ecstasy*, with its adult sexuality and brilliant camera sense. And last and best Duvivier comes to mind, and *Pépé le Moko* and *Un Carnet du Bal*, sense of violence and a sense of poetry: not in camera movement, like that last doomed symphonic walk of Pépé in his pointed polished gamin shoes down from the security of the Old Town of Algiers to the harbour and the tourist quarter where the police waited; or again that slanting floor in the abortionist's surgery in *Un Carnet de Bal*, which seemed to represent the seedy doctor's whole hopeless dream of escape from the habit of a lifetime, the grim climb up to the door, the easy slope to the surgical couch and the spirit flame 'Why, this is hell, nor am I out of it.'

Listen to the cheers. That must be one of the super-productions going by – or the last Grace Moore (I've already forgotten its name). Perhaps I was wrong when I said that a death didn't make any difference to the screen. Perhaps with Duvivier something might die we can't find elsewhere – a poetic realism, a sense of moral values. And perhaps he's dead now while I write and 1938 will see the tombstone laid, for he's left France for Hollywood. Cheers again. It must be *Love from a Stranger* or *Dreaming Lips* or *Storm in a Teacup*. 'Ne'er look, ne'er look,' as Pandarus said, when Troilus had passed. 'The eagles are gone: crows and daws, crows and daws.'

Sight and Sound (Winter 1937/1938)

PREFACE TO *THE THIRD MAN*

My film story, *The Third Man*, was never written to be read but only to be seen. The story, like many love affairs, started at a dinner table and continued with headaches in many places: Vienna, Venice, Ravello, London, Santa Monica.

Most novelists, I suppose, carry round in their heads or in their notebooks the first idea for stories that have never come to be written. Sometimes one may turn them over after many years and think regretfully they would have been good once, in a time now dead. So it was that long before, on the flap of an envelope, I had written an opening paragraph: 'I had paid my last farewell to Harry a week ago, when his coffin was lowered into the frozen February ground, so that it was with incredulity that I saw him pass by, without a sign of recognition, among the host of strangers in the Strand.' I, like my hero, had not the least inkling of an explanation, so when Alexander Korda over dinner asked me to write a film for Carol Reed – to follow our *Fallen Idol* which I had adapted from my short story 'The Basement Room' a year before – I had nothing more to offer him except this paragraph, though what Korda really wanted was a film about the Four-Power occupation of Vienna. In 1948 Vienna was still divided into American, Russian, French and British zones, while the Inner City was administered by each

Power in turn for a month and patrolled day and night by groups of four soldiers drawn from the Four Powers. It was this complex situation which Korda wanted to put on film, but he was prepared all the same to let me pursue the tracks of Harry. So to Vienna I went.

For me it is impossible to write a film play without first writing a story. A film depends on more than plot; it depends on a certain measure of characterization, on mood and atmosphere, and these seem impossible to capture for the first time in the dull shorthand of a conventional treatment. I must have the sense of more material than I need to draw on (though the full-length novel contains too much). *The Third Man*, therefore, though never intended for publication, had to start as a story, rather than as a treatment before I began working on what seemed the interminable transformations from one screenplay to another.

On the continuity and the story-line Carol Reed and I worked closely together when I came back with him to Vienna to write the screenplay, covering miles of carpet a day, acting scences at each other. (It's a curious fact that you cannot work out a continuity at a desk – you have to move with your characters.) No third ever joined our conferences, not even Korda himself; so much value lies in the cut and thrust of argument between two people. To the novelist, of course, his novel is the best he can do with a particular subject; he cannot help resenting many of the changes necessary for turning it into a film play; but *The Third Man* was never intended to be more than the raw material for a picture. The reader will notice many differences between the story and the film, and he should not imagine that these changes were forced on an unwilling author: as likely as not they were suggested by the author. The film in fact is better than the story because it is in this case the finished state of the story.

Some of these changes have obvious superficial reasons. The choice of an American instead of an English star involved a number of alterations – the most important, Harry had to become an American too. Joseph Cotten quite reasonably objected to my choice of name, Rollo in the story, which to his American ear apparently involved homosexuality. I wanted the name none the less to be an absurd one, and the name Holly occurred to me when I remembered that figure of fun, the nineteenth-century American poet Thomas Holley Chivers. An American, too, could hardly have been mistaken for the great English writer Dexter, whose literary character bore certain echoes of the gentle genius of Mr E.M. Forster. The confusion of identities would have been impossible, even if Carol Reed had not rightly objected to a rather far-fetched situation involving a great deal of explanation that increased the length of a film already far too long. Another minor point: in deference to American opinion a Rumanian was substituted for Cooler, since Mr Orson Welles' engagement had aleady supplied us with one American villain. (Incidentally, the popular line of dialogue concerning Swiss cuckoo clocks was written into the script by Mr Welles himself.)

One of the few major disputes between Carol Reed and myself concerned the ending, and he was proved triumphantly right. I held the view that an entertainment of this kind was too light an affair to carry the weight of an unhappy ending – indeterminate as it was, with no words spoken, Holly joining the girl in silence and walking away with her from the cemetery where her lover Harry was buried – would strike the audience who had just seen Harry's death and burial as unpleasantly cynical. I was only half convinced: I was afraid few people would wait in their seats during the girl's long walk from the graveside towards Holly, and the others would leave the cinema under the impression that the ending was still going to be as conventional as my suggested ending of boy joining girl. I had not given enough credit to the mastery of Reed's direction, and at that stage, of course, we neither of us anticipated Reed's discovery of Anton Karas, the zither player. All I had indicated in my treatment was a kind of signature tune connected with Lime.

The episode in the treatment of the Russians kidnapping Anna (a perfectly plausible incident in Vienna in those days) was eliminated at a fairly late stage. It was not satisfactorily tied into the screenplay, and it threatened to turn the film into a propagandist picture. We had no desire to move people's political emotions; we wanted to entertain them, to frighten them a little, even to make them laugh.

Reality in fact was only the background to a fairy tale, though the story of the penicillin racket was based on a truth, all the more grim because so many of the traffickers were innocent, unlike Lime. A surgeon I knew took two friends to see the film. He was surprised to find them subdued and depressed by the picture which he had enjoyed. They told him that at the end of the war, when they were in the Royal Air Force in Vienna, they had both sold penicillin. The consequences of their petty larceny had never occurred to them† till they saw the film and the scene in the children's hospital where watered penicillin had been used.

When Carol Reed came with me to Vienna to see the scenes which I described in the treatment I was embarrassed to find that between winter and spring Vienna had completely changed. The blackmarket restaurants, where in February one was lucky to find a few bones described as oxtail, were now serving legal if frugal meals. The ruins had been cleared away from in front of the Café Mozart which I had christened 'Old Vienna'. Over and over again I found myself saying to Carol Reed, 'But I assure you Vienna was really like that – three months ago.'

It had proved difficult to find my story – Harry's phoney funeral was the only scrap of plot I had to cling to. All that came as the days too rapidly passed were bits of photogenic background; the shabby Orienal nightclub, the officers' bar at Sacher's (somehow Korda had managed to fix me a room in the hotel, which was reserved for officers), the little dressing-rooms which formed a kind of interior village in the old Josefstadt Theatre (Anna was eventually to work there), the enormous cemetery where electric drills were needed to pierce the ground that February. I had allowed myself not more than two weeks in Vienna before meeting a friend in Italy where I intended to write the story, but what story? There were three days left and I had no story, not even the storyteller, Colonel Calloway, whom I see now always in my mind with the features of Trevor Howard.

On the penultimate day I had the good fortune to lunch with a young British Intelligence officer (the future Duke of St Albans) – my wartime connection with the SIS used to bring me useful dividends in those days. He described how when he first took over in Vienna he demanded from the Austrian authorities a list of the Viennese police. A section of the list was marked 'Underground Police'.

'Get rid of these men,' he ordered, 'things have changed now,' but a month later he found the 'underground' police were still on the list. He repeated the order with anger, and it was then explained to him that the 'undergound police' were not secret police, but police who literally worked underground along the enormous system of sewers. There were no Allied zones in the sewers, the entrances were dotted throughout the city disguised as advertisement kiosks, and for some inexplicable reason the Russians refused to allow them to be locked. Agents could pass uncontrolled from any zone to another. After lunch we dressed in heavy boots and macintoshes and took a walk below the city. The main sewer was like a great tidal river, and as sweet smelling. At lunch the officer had told me of the penicillin racket, and now, along the sewers, the whole story took shape. The researches I had made into the functioning of the Four-Power occupation, my visit to an old servant of my mother's in the Russian zone, the long evenings of solitary drinking in the Oriental, none of them was wasted. I had my film.

My last evening I gave dinner to my friend, Elizabeth Bowen, who had come to Vienna to lecture at the British Institute, as a guest of the British Council. I took her afterwards to the Oriental. I don't think she had ever been in so seedy a nightclub before. I said, 'They will be raiding this place at midnight.'

'How do you know?'

'I have my contacts.'

Exactly at the stroke of twelve, as I had asked my friend to arrange, a British sergeant came clattering down the stairs, followed by a Russian, a French and an American military policeman. The place was in half-darkness, but without hesitation

(I had described her with care) he strode across the cellar and demanded to see Elizabeth's passport. She looked at me with respect – the British Council had not given her so dramatic an evening. Next day I was on my way to Italy. It was all over except the writing . . .

. . . In Italy I wrote the treatment of *The Third Man*, but more important for the future I found the small house in Anacapri where all my later books were to be at least in part written. (I am proud now to be an honorary citizen of that little town of five thousand inhabitants.)

Writing a novel does not become easier with practice. The slow discovery by a novelist of his individual method can be exciting, but a moment comes in middle age when he feels he no longer controls his method; he has become its prisoner. Then a long period of ennui sets in: it seems to him he has done everything before. He is more afraid to read his favourable critics than his unfavourable, for with terrible patience they unroll before his eyes the unchanging pattern of the carpet. If he has depended a great deal on his unconscious, on his ability to forget even his own books when they are once on the public shelves, the critics remind him – this theme originated ten years ago, that simile which came so unthinkingly to his pen a few weeks back was used nearly twenty years ago in a passage where . . .

I had tried to escape from my prison by writing for the films, but *The Third Man* only beckoned me into another and more luxurious prison.[3]

[Part of this section of *Ways of Escape* had served as the Preface to the 1950 edition of *The Third Man/The Fallen Idol*. That Preface ended at the point marked † above.]

Preface to *The Fallen Idol*

The Fallen Idol unlike *The Third Man* was not written for the films. That is only one of many reasons why I prefer it. It was only published as *The Basement Room* in 1935 and conceived on the cargo steamer on the way home from Liberia to relieve the tedium of the voyage. *The Fallen Idol* is, of course, a meaningless title for the original story printed here, and even for the film it always reminded me of the problem paintings of John Collier. It was chosen by the distributors.

I was surprised when Carol Reed suggested that I should collaborate with him on a film of *The Basement Room* because it seemed to me that the subject was unfilmable – a murder committed by the most sympathetic character and an unhappy ending which would certainly have imperilled the £250,000 that films nowadays cost.

However, we went ahead, and in the conferences that ensued the story was quietly changed, so that the subject no longer concerned a small boy who unwittingly betrayed his best friend to the police, but dealt instead with a small boy who believed that his friend was a murderer and nearly procured his arrest by telling lies in his defence. I think this, especially with Reed's handling, was a good subject, but the reader must not be surprised by not finding it the subject of the original story.

Why was the scene changed to an Embassy? This was Reed's idea since we both felt that the large Belgravia house was already in these post-war years a period piece, and we did not want to make an historical film. I fought the solution for a while and then wholeheartedly concurred.

It is always difficult to remember which of us made which change in the original story except in certain details. For example the cross-examination of the girl beside the bed that she used with Baines was mine: the witty interruption of the man who came to wind the clock was Reed's. The snake was mine (I have always liked snakes), and for a short while it met with Reed's sympathetic opposition.

Of one thing about both these films I have complete certainty, that their success is due to Carol Reed, the only director I know with that particular warmth of human sympathy, the extraordinary feeling for the right face for the right part, the exactitude of cutting, and not least important the power of sympathizing with an author's worries and an ability to guide him.

Preface to *The Fallen Idol* (1950) – published jointly with *The Third Man*.

The Return of Charlie Chaplin: an Open Letter

Dear Mr Chaplin

I hope you will forgive an open letter: otherwise I would have added to that great pyramid of friendly letters that must be awaiting you in London. This is a letter of welcome not only to the screen's finest artist (the only man who writes, directs and acts in his own pictures and even composes their music), but to one of the greatest liberals of our day. Your films have always been compassionate towards the weak and the under-privileged; they have always punctured the bully. To our pain and astonishment you paid the United States the highest compliment in your power by settling within her borders, and now we feel pain but not astonishment at the response – not from the American people in general, one is sure, but from those authorities who seem to take their orders from such men as McCarthy. When Russia was invaded you spoke out in her defence at a public meeting in San Francisco at the request of your President; it was not the occasion for saving clauses and double meanings, and your words were as plain as Churchill's or Roosevelt's. You even had the impudence, they say, to call your audience comrades. That is their main accusation against you. I wonder what McCarthy was doing in those days?

Remembering the days of Titus Oates and the Terror in England, I would like to think that the Catholics of the United States, a powerful body, would give you their sympathy and support. Certainly one Catholic weekly in America is unlikely to be silent – I mean the *Commonweal*. But Cardinal Spellman? And the Hierarchy? I cannot help remembering an American flag that leant against the pulpit in an American Catholic church not far from your home, and I remember too that McCarthy is a Catholic. Have Catholics in the United States not yet suffered enough to stand firmly against this campaign of uncharity?

When you welcomed me the other day in your home, I suggested that Charlie should make one more appearance on the screen. In this would-be story Charlie lies neglected and forgotten in a New York attic. Suddenly he is summoned from obscurity to answer for his past before the Un-American Activities Committee at Washington – for that dubious occasion in a boxing ring, on the ice-skating ring, for mistaking that Senator's bald head for an ice pudding, for all the hidden significance of the dance with the bread rolls. Solemnly the members of the Committee watch Charlie's early pictures and take their damaging notes.

You laughed the suggestion away, and indeed I had thought of no climax. The Attorney-General of the United States has supplied that. For at the close of the hearing Charlie could surely admit to being in truth un-American and produce the passport of another country, a country which, lying rather closer to danger, is free from the ugly manifestations of fear.

The other day a set of Hollywood figures, some of them rather out-moded (Mr Louis B. Mayer and Mr Adolf [*sic*] Menjou were among the names) set up a fund to support McCarthy's fight in Wisconsin – a form of Danegeld. Now Hollywood uses English stories and English actors, and I would like to see my fellow-countrymen refusing to sell a story or to appear in a film sponsored by any organisation that includes these friends of the witch-hunter. Our action would be an expression of opinion only; it would not condemn them to the unemployment and slow starvation to which McCarthy has condemned some of their colleagues. They will say it is no business of ours. But the disgrace of an ally is our disgrace, and in attacking you the witch-hunters have emphasised that this is no national matter. Intolerance in any country wounds freedom throughout the world.

The New Statesman (27 September 1952)

London Diary

'L'Affaire Charlot' continues to amuse Europe and to mystify the United States. Last week echoes of it reached me even from a Swedish taxi driver. Violent language on one side: honours on the other. Pär Lagerkvist, Sweden's leading man of letters, proposed Chaplin for the Nobel Prize. President Auriol has promoted him in the Legion of Honour. And still in America there are those who do not know what all the fuss is about.

'Chaplin can get by Uncle Sam's investigations as regards health. He won't have difficulties proving he has a sound mind, although his productions have been flops since he deserted comics in favour of "thought" pieces. When we come to the "good morals" requirement, we had better draw a curtain over details [sic]. We shall simply state that Chaplin has few rivals in the race for top honours in giving Hollywood the reputation for being a moral cesspool.' Who is the author of this attack? Crude and illiterate, loose in thought and indentable in expression one might easily attribute it to the arch witch-hunter himself. Unfortunately, the words were written by a more responsible Catholic, a Catholic priest in an American Catholic magazine called *The Sign*.

★

The moral atmosphere created by McCarthy and exemplified by my quotation makes it difficult for some Americans to understand the motive of a foreigner who criticises the actions of their authorities. They assume that there must be some personal reason which is undisclosed. It is not for them sufficient to believe, with Tom Paine that 'we must guard even our enemies against injustice'. An editorial note to a correspondent in the American *Catholic World* suggests that a recent letter of mine in this journal, addressed to Mr Chaplin, was an outbreak of personal pique. 'The heart of the matter is that the State Department held up his visa for a time because he had been a Communist in his youth.' The facts are rather different. Because I wished to place myself under the ban imposed by the McCarran Act on all who at any age had been members of a totalitarian party, I deliberately disclosed to a *Time* correspondent that I had been a probationary member of the Communist party for four weeks at the age of 19. Many innocent people, refugees from Central Europe, are excluded by this Act and are unable in their anonymity and poverty to bring their case before the Attorney-General, who is the only one able to exempt them from the provisions of the McCarran Act. I applied for a visa because I was in a position to secure a measure of publicity against McCarthy and McCarran, not because I had any immediate need to visit America. For the same reason, the day I wrote my letter to Mr Chaplin I again applied for a six-month visa (the usual form of visa before the new Act). Because of my dangerous 19-year-old past, this entails a personal letter to the Attorney-General and answers to a long questionnaire. After four weeks I have been told that I can have an eight-week visa and pay more than £6 in cable charges (incurred in the course of the lightning decision). If I do not land in the United States before December 24, I am told, the whole business will have to be started again. I have refused both visa and payment.

The New Statesman (22 November 1952)

A Tribute to Korda

For a writer, with the death of Korda, fun has gone out of the film industry – yes, one begins to think of it again as just an industry. So long as he was alive the unexpected might always happen – a chance word at the dinner table and a week later it was quite possible that one might wake up in Hong Kong. He was always generous in trust. *The Third Man* began in much that way. Korda over the dinner table wanted a story written with the background of an occupied city. Berlin? Vienna? Vienna would be a more agreeable city to live in – he recommended Vienna and Sacher's cakes. I remember I reconstructed on the back of an envelope the opening sentences of an 'entertainment' I had long abandoned. The scene was the Strand – it could equally well be Vienna since there was no plot, no subject. Oh well, he said, perhaps a subject would turn up on the spot. The opening situation was all he required now to draw his contract. But I wanted peace to write in. London was impossible. Italy? I could settle down there for a couple of months away from interruption. After several weeks in Venice I had still not found my story, but Korda was unworried and never once during the two months in Italy did he ask for a report on progress.

The fun has really gone. He has no successor, no one with whom it is possible *not* to talk about films, the matter in hand, but about painting, poetry, music, anything in the world rather than that 'industry' which always seemed on the point of quietly, out of neglect, becoming an 'art' while he was away reading Baudelaire somewhere among the islands of Greece.

Sight and Sound (Spring 1956)

Ballade for a Wedding

Moments exist for you and me
Of solitude that's not for those
Within the fringe of monarchy:
They have the thorns and we the rose.
We could abide perhaps the prose
Of pressmen and the trumpets' blare,
The flashlights and the public pose,
But Father Tucker will be there.

Deep diving in the Middle Sea,
Where friendly lansoustes wave and doze
And cuttle-fish suck tenderly
Points of a prince's rubber toes,
In that green world where no tide flows,
Far from the *plein* and the *impaire*,
Dreams he of love? for nothing shows

That Father Tucker will be there.

Now at the Hôtel de Paris
The open friends and secret foes,
By that stone cavalier where we
Used to discuss our winning throws,
Gather for gossip: Hopper knows
Why Garbo's missing and the fair
Jane and Marlene, but all suppose
That Father Tucker will be there.

Envoi
Prince, you may draw your curtains close
And set your sentries on the stair,
Then lie down by the bride you chose,
But Father Tucker will be there.

Punch (18 August 1956). Lines written on the wedding of Grace Kelly and Prince Rainier of Monaco.

The Novelist and the Cinema – A Personal Experience

A memorial article should be free from bitterness, and now that the day of the film-story is over and, if the cinema should happen to survive, it is likely to be as a kind of circus-show presenting such enormous wide-screen features as *Around the World in 80 Days* or *War and Peace*, we can remember that once there were prizes for the writers, not so glittering as the popular journalists like to make out, but prizes none the less that helped many writers to survive through the lean sad years of the 'thirties – for working men the years of the dole and for the writer the years of the gramophone which could not be paid for, the life-insurance that had to be surrendered, of sleepless anxious nights.

How lean those years were the young writer may not realise who was launched by his publisher during the book-boom of the 'forties when every novel sold and it was only a question of how much paper should be allotted to this writer or to that. The position was not realised even at the time by the unreliable chroniclers of the popular press, and some of us found it ironic in 1939 to be regarded by journalists as best-sellers and to know what in fact our publisher's accounts showed. I can only take my own case and record that after eleven years and eleven books the numbers of my first edition had increased by 500 – from 2,500 printed of my first book to 3,000 printed of my eleventh. In those years neither the BBC nor the Central Office of Information had become the patrons of a young author or, in my age-group, of the not-so-young. His chance of surviving a little above the lean standard of the weekly reviewer (with all *that* entailed of deadening reading – so many books a week that were clearly food for worms) lay in the cinema – the small chance of winning a kind of Irish Sweep, of receiving money for the outright sale of work already done, or a little later the less desirable prize for employment for six weeks at £50 a week as a script-writer (and how difficult it was to realise that the £50 would cease and leave one committed to this expense or that at one's normal income of £12 a week). I won my first Irish Sweep in 1932, when my American agent sold a novel *Stamboul Train* to 20th Century-Fox. It was my fourth novel, I was down to £30 in the bank, a child was on the way, I had been refused the job of sub-editor on *The Catholic Herald* because my qualifications were held to be 'too good', and I had no prospects. The amount was not high by the standards of the publicity agent – I think £1,500 – but it enabled me to go on writing without seeking other employment until a second prize came my way in 1934, when Paramount bought *A Gun for Sale* for, I think, £2,500. It wasn't – in spite of the figures the journalists gave – possible to make a fortune by films, but they enabled one to live, and I feel glad to have been able to survive by such outright sales as these of work done for another purpose, rather than by taking employment in a Government department or a broadcasting corporation as would be the case now.

So my first feeling towards the films is one of gratitude. I suspect there are better writers than myself who have the same cause for gratitude, William Faulkner, Ernest Hemingway . . .

Now when you sell a book to Hollywood you sell it overnight. The long Hollywood contracts – sheet after closely printed sheet as long as the first treatment of the novel which is for sale –ensure that you have no 'author's rights'. The film producer can alter anything. He can turn your tragedy of East End Jewry into a musical comedy at Palm Springs if he wishes. He need not even retain your title, though that is usually almost the only thing he wishes to retain. *The Power and the Glory*, a story I wrote in 1938 of a drunken Mexican priest with an illegitimate child who he carries on his vocation stumblingly, sometimes with cowardice, during the religious persecutions of the early thirties, became *The Fugitive*, the story of a pious and heroic priest: the drunkenness had been drained away and the illegitimate child (I believe this is so, for I never saw Mr John Ford's film) became the bastard of the police officer who pursued the priest. One gets used to these things (like the strange intrusion of a girl conjuror into *This Gun for Hire*) and it is a waste of time to resent them. You rake the money, you go on writing for another year or two, you have no just ground for complaint. And the smile in the long run will be on your face. For the book has the longer life.

The most extreme changes I have seen in any book of mine were in *The Quiet American*; one could almost believe that the film was made deliberately to attack the book and the author, but the book was based on a closer knowledge of the Indo-China war than the American director possessed and I am vain enough to believe that the book will survive a few years longer than Mr Mankiewicz's incoherent picture. Again, why should one complain? He has enabled me to go on writing.

I repeat that I am grateful to the cinema. It made twenty years of life easier and now, if the inferior medium of television kills it, I wonder whether television will do as much for the author. At least the cinema, like a psychiatrist, has enabled one to do without it.

But the last sentence which slipped unthinkingly off the pen has a certain sadness. Am I the same character who in the 1920s read *Close Up* and the latest book on montage by Pudovkin with so much enthusiasm, who felt in *Mother, The Gold Rush,* in *Rien que les heures, Souvenirs d'Autonne, Warning Shadows*, even in such popular Hollywood films as *Hotel Imperial* and *Foolish Wives*, the possibility of a new kind of art? Of a picture as formal in design as a painting, but a temporary one. Quite quickly – even in so early a film as *The Perfect Alibi*, they too began to show here and there, in isolated scenes more often than in complete films, a selectivity of sound which promised to become as formal as the warning shadow – and they had a special interest to the writer. He was no longer merely the spectator or the critic of the screen. Suddenly the cinema needed him: pictures required words as well as images.

Thus another prize was offered to the writer in those lean thirties – employment. This was more dangerous to him, for a writer should not be employed by anyone but himself. If you are using words in one craft, it is impossible not to corrupt them by employing them in another medium under direction. (Proust even found conversation dangerous – the more intelligent, the more dangerous, 'since it falsifies the life of the mind by getting mixed up in it'.) This is the side of my association with the films that I most regret and would like most to avoid in future if taxation allows me to.

I thought that myself, and I do retain this happy memory of one unsuccessful film, *The Stranger's Hand*: days in Venice drinking grappa with Mario Soldati, running races down the Guidecca with Trevor Howard, the friendliness of the Italian unit. It encouraged me to go further along this road in a film which shall be nameless. To be a co-producer is no job for a writer. One becomes involved with the producer's monetary troubles: one has to accept actors who are miscast because another man's money is involved. As a writer one hasn't the blind optimism of the film-maker who believes against all evidence that somehow the wrong actors, the wrong director, the wrong cameraman, the wrong art director, the wrong colour-process, will all come together and produce a lucky accident.

It isn't the way books are made. We have to learn our craft more painfully, more meticulously, than those actors, directors, and cameramen who are paid, and paid handsomely, whatever the result. They can always put the blame for a disaster elsewhere which no novelist can. So the author – turned co-producer – shrugs his shoulders and gives up while the game is only half through. He knows what the result will be. Why go through the unpopular motions of fighting every battle lost at the start. He knows that even if a script be followed word by word there are those gaps of silence which can be filled by the banal embrace, irony can be turned into sentiment by some romantic boob of an actor . . . No, it is better to sell outright and not to connive any further than you have to at a massacre. Selling outright you have at least saved yourself that ambiguous toil of using words for a cause you don't believe in – words should be respected, for they are your livelihood, perhaps they are even your main motive for living at all.

International Film Annual No. 2

Memories of a Film Critic

Four and a half years of watching films several times a week . . . I can hardly believe in that life of the distant thirties now, a way of life which I adopted quite voluntarily from a sense of fun. More than four hundred films – and I suppose there would have been many, many more if I had not suffered during the same period from other obsessions – four novels had to be written, not to speak of a travel book which took me away for months to Mexico, far from the Pleasure Dome – all those Empires and Odeons of a luxury and an extravagance which we shall never see again. How, I find myself wondering, could I possibly have written all those film reviews? And yet I remember opening the envelopes, which contained the gilded cards of invitation for the morning press performances (mornings when I should have been struggling with other work), with a sense of curiosity and anticipation. Those films were an escape – escape from that hellish problem of construction in Chapter Six, from the secondary character who obstinately refused to come alive, escape for an hour and a half from the melancholy which falls inexorably round the novelist when he has lived for too many months on end in his private world.

The idea of reviewing films came to me at a cocktail party after the dangerous third martini. I was talking to Derek Verschoyle, the Literary Editor of the *Spectator*. The *Spectator* had hitherto neglected films and I suggested to him I should fill the gap – I thought in the unlikely event of his accepting my offer it might be fun for two or three weeks. I never imagined it would remain fun for four and a half years and only end in a different world, a world at war. Until I came to reread the notices the other day I thought they abruptly ended with my review of *Young Mr Lincoln*. If there is something a little absentminded about that review, it is because, just as I began to write it on the morning of 3 September 1939, the first air-raid siren of the war sounded and I laid the review aside so as to make notes from my high Hampstead lodging on the destruction of London below. 'Woman passes with dog on lead', I noted, 'and pauses by lamp-post.' Then the all-clear sounded and I returned to Henry Fonda.

My first script – about 1937 – was a terrible affair and typical in one way of the cinema world. I had to adapt a story of John Galsworthy – a traditional tale of a murderer who killed himself and an innocent man who was hanged for the suicide's crime. If the story had any force in it at all it lay in its extreme sensationalism, but as the sensation was impossible under the British Board of Film Censors, who forbade suicide and forbade a failure of English justice, there was little of Galsworthy's plot left when I had finished. This unfortunate first effort was suffered with good-humoured nonchalance by Laurence Olivier and Vivien Leigh. I decided after that never to adapt another man's work and I have only broken that rule once in the case of *Saint Joan* – the critics will say another deplorable adaptation, though I myself would defend the script for retaining, however rearranged, Shaw's epilogue and for keeping a sense of responsibility to another while reducing a play of three-and-a-half hours to a film of less than two.

I have a more deplorable confession – a film story directed by Mr William Cameron Menzies called *The Green Cockatoo* starring Mr John Mills – perhaps it preceded the Galsworthy (the Freudian Censor is at work here). The script of *Brighton Rock* I am ready to defend. There were good scenes, but the Boulting Brothers were too generous in giving an apprentice his rope, and the film-censor as usual was absurd – the script was slashed to pieces by the Mr Watkyn of his day. There followed two halcyon years with Carol Reed, and I began to believe that I was learning the craft with *The Fallen Idol* and *The Third Man*, but it was an illusion. No craft had been learnt, there had only been the luck of working with a fine director who could control his actors and his production.

If you sell a novel outright you accept no responsibility; but write your own script and you will observe what can happen on the floor to your words, your continuity, your idea, the extra dialogue inserted during production (for which you bear the critics' blame), the influence of an actor who is only concerned with the appearance he wants to create before his fans . . . Perhaps you will come to think, there may be a solution if the author takes his hand in its production.

Those were not the first film reviews I wrote. At Oxford I had appointed myself film critic of the *Oxford Outlook*, a literary magazine which appeared once a term and which I edited. *Warning Shadows, Brumes d'Automne, The Student of Prague* – these are the silent films of the twenties of which I can remember whole scenes still. I was a passionate reader of *Close-Up* which was edited by Kenneth Macpherson and Bryher and published from a *chateau* in Switzerland. Marc Allégret was the Paris Correspondent and Pudovkin contributed articles on montage. I was horrified by the arrival of 'talkies' (it seemed the end of film as an art form), just as later I regarded colour with justifiable suspicion. 'Technicolor,' I wrote in 1935, 'plays havoc with the women's faces; they all, young and old, have the same healthy weather-beaten skins.' Curiously enough it was a detective story with Chester Morris which converted me to the talkies – for the first time in that picture I was aware of *selected* sounds; until then every shoe had squeaked and every door handle had creaked. I notice that the forgotten film *Becky Sharp* gave me even a certain hope for colour.

Re-reading those reviews of more than forty years ago I find many prejudices which are modified now only by the sense of nostalgia. I had distinct reservations about Greta Garbo whom I compared to a beautiful Arab mare, and Hitchcock's 'inadequate sense of reality' irritated me and still does – how inexcusibly he spoilt *The Thirty-Nine Steps*. I still believe I was right (whatever Monsieur Truffaut may say) when I wrote: 'His films consist of a series of small "amusing" melodramatic situations: the murderer's button dropped on the baccarat board; the strangled organist's hands prolonging the notes in the empty church . . . very perfunctorily he builds up to these tricky situations (paying no attention on the way to inconsistencies, loose ends, psychological absurdities) and then drops them: they mean nothing: they lead to nothing.'

The thirties too were a period of 'respectable' film biographies – Rhodes, Zola, Pasteur, Parnell and the like – and of historical romances which only came to a certain comic life in the hands of Cecil B. de Mille (Richard Coeur de Lion was married to Berengaria according to the rites of the Anglican Church). I preferred the Westerns, the crime films, the farces, the frankly commercial, and I am glad to see that in reviewing one of these forgotten commercial films I gave a warm welcome to a new star, Ingrid Bergman – 'What star before has made her first appearance on the international screen with a highlight gleaming on her nose-tip?'

There were dangers, I was to discover, in film-reviewing. On one occasion I opened a letter to find a piece of shit enclosed. I have always – though probably incorrectly – believed that it was a piece of aristocratic shit, for I had made cruel fun a little while before of a certain French marquis who had made a documentary film in which he played a rather heroic role. Thirty years later in Paris at a dinner of the *haute bourgeoisie* I sat opposite him and was charmed by his conversation. I longed to ask him the truth, but I was daunted by the furniture. Then, of course, there was the Shirley Temple libel action. The review of *Wee Willie Winkie* which set Twentieth-Century Fox alight cannot be found here for obvious reasons. I kept on my bathroom wall, until a bomb removed the wall, the statement of claim – that I had accused Twentieth-Century Fox of 'procuring' Miss Temple for 'immoral purposes' (I had suggested that she had a certain adroit coquetry which appealed to middle-aged men). Lord Hewart, the Lord Chief Justice, sent the papers in the case to the Director of Public Prosecutions, so that ever since that time I have been traceable on the files of Scotland Yard.† The case appeared before the King's Bench on 22 March 1938, with myself *in absentia*, and on 23 May 1938, the following account of the hearing appeared among the Law Reports of *The Times*. I was at the time in Mexico on a writing assignment. It is perhaps worth mentioning in connection with the 'beastly publication' that *Night and Day* boasted Elizabeth Bowen as theatre critic, Evelyn Waugh as chief book reviewer, Osbert Lancaster as art critic, and Hugh Casson as architectural critic, not to speak of such regular contributors as Herbert Read, Hugh Kingsmill and Malcolm Muggeridge.

The case appeared as follows in *The Times* Law Reports:

HIGH COURT OF JUSTICE
King's Bench Division
Libel on Miss Shirley Temple: 'A Gross Outrage'
Temple and Others v. Night and Day Magazine, Limited, and Others
Before the Lord Chief Justice

A settlement was announced of this libel action which was brought by Miss Shirley Jane Temple, the child actress (by Mr Roy Simmonds, her next friend), Twentieth-Century Fox Film Corporation, of New York, and Twentieth-Century Fox Film Company Limited, of Berners Street, W., against Night and Day Magazines, Limited, and Mr Graham Greene, of St Martin's Lane, W.C., and Messrs Chatto and Windus, publishers, of Chandos Street, W.C., in respect of an article written by Mr Greene and published in the issue of the magazine *Night and Day* dated October 28, 1937.

Sir Patrick Hastings, KC, and Mr G.O. Slade appeared for the plaintiffs; Mr Valentine Holmes for all the defendants except Hazell, Watson, and Viney, Limited, who were represented by Mr Theobald Mathew.

Sir Patrick Hastings, in announcing the settlement, by which it was agreed that Miss Shirley Temple was to receive £2,000, the film corporation £1,000 and the film company £500, stated that the first defendants were the proprietors of the magazine *Night and Day*, which was published in London. It was only right to say that the two last defendants, the printers and publishers, were firms of the utmost respectability and highest reputation, and were innocently responsible in the matter.

The plaintiff, Miss Shirley Temple, a child of nine years, has a world-wide reputation as an artist in films. The two plaintiff companies produced her in a film called *Wee Willie Winkie*, based on Rudyard Kipling's story.

On October 28 last year Night and Day Magazines, Limited, published an article written by Mr Graham Greene. In his (counsel's) view it was one of the most horrible libels that one could well imagine. Obviously he would not read it all – it was better that he should not – but a glance at the statement of claim, where a poster was set out, was quite sufficient to show the nature of the libel written about this child.

This beastly publication, said counsel, was written, and it was right to say that every respectable distributor in London refused to be a party to selling it. Notwithstanding that, the magazine company, with the object no doubt of increasing the sale, proceeded to advertise the fact that it had been banned.

Shirley Temple was an American and lived in America. If she had been in England and the publication in America it would have been right for the American Courts to have taken notice of it. It was equally right that, the position being reversed, her friends in America should know that the Courts here took notice of such a publication.

SHOULD NOT BE TREATED LIGHTLY

Money was no object in this case. The child had a very large income and the two film companies were wealthy concerns. It was realised, however, that the matter should not be treated lightly. The defendants had paid the film companies £1,000 and £500 respectively, and that money would be disposed of in a charitable way. With regard to the child, she would be paid £2,000. There would also be an order for the taxation of costs.

In any view, said counsel, it was such a beastly libel to have written that if it had been a question of money it would have been difficult to say what would be an appropriate amount to arrive at.

Miss Shirley Temple probably knew nothing of the article, and it was undesirable that she should be brought to England to fight the action. In his (counsel's) opinion the settlement was a proper one in the circumstances.

Mr Valentine Holmes informed his Lordship that the magazine *Night and Day* had ceased publication. He desired, on behalf of his clients, to express the deepest apology to Miss Temple for the pain which certainly would have been caused to her by the article if she had read it. He also apologized to the two film companies for the suggestion that they would produce and distribute a film of the character indicated by the article. There was no justification for the criticism of the film, which, his clients instructed him, was one which anybody could take their children to see. He also apologized on behalf of Mr Graham Greene. So far as the publishers of the magazine were concerned, they did not see the article before publication.

His Lordship – Who is the author of this article?

Mr Holmes – Mr Graham Greene.

His Lordship – Is he within the jurisdiction?

Mr Holmes – I am afraid I do not know, my Lord.

Mr Theobald Mathew, on behalf of the printers, said that they recognized that the article was one which ought never to have been published. The fact that the film had already been licensed for universal exhibition refuted the charges which had been made in the article. The printers welcomed the opportunity of making any amends in their power.

His Lordship – Can you tell me where Mr Greene is?

Mr Mathew – I have no information on the subject.

His Lordship – This libel is simply a gross outrage, and I will take care to see that suitable attention is directed to it. In the meantime I assent to the settlement on the terms which have been disclosed, and the record will be withdrawn.†

From film-reviewing it was only a small step to scriptwriting. That also was a danger, but a necessary one as I now had a wife and two children to support and I remained in debt to my publishers until the war came. I had persistently attacked the films made by Mr Alexander Korda and perhaps he became curious to meet his enemy. He asked my agent to bring me to Denham Film Studios and when we were alone he asked if I had any film story in mind. I had none, so I began to improvise a thriller – early morning on Platform 1 at Paddington, the platform empty, except for one man who is waiting for the last train from Wales. From below his raincoat a trickle of blood forms a pool on the platform.

'Yes? And then?'

'It would take too long to tell you the whole plot – and the idea needs a lot more working out.'

I left Denham half an hour later to work for eight weeks on what seemed an extravagant salary, and the worst and least successful of Korda's productions thus began (all I can remember is the title, *The Green Cockatoo*). So too began our friendship which endured and deepened till his death, in spite of my reviews which remained unfavourable. There was never a man who bore less malice, and I think of him with affection – even love – as the only film producer I have ever known with whom I could spend days and nights of conversation without so much as mentioning the cinema. Years later, after the war was over, I wrote two screenplays for Korda and Carol Reed, *The Fallen Idol* and *The Third Man*, and I hope they atoned a little for the prentice scripts.

If I had remained a film critic, the brief comic experience which I had then of Hollywood might have been of lasting value to me, for I learned at first hand what a director may have to endure at the hands of a producer. (One of the difficult tasks of a critic is to assign his praise or blame to the right corner.)

David Selznick, famous for having produced one of the world's top-grossing films, *Gone with the Wind*, held the American rights in *The Third Man* and, by the terms of the contract with Korda, the director was bound to consult him about the script sixty days before shooting began. So Carol Reed, who was directing the film, and I journeyed west. Our first meeting with Selznick at La Jolla in California promised badly, and the dialogue remains as fresh in my mind as the day when it was spoken. After a brief greeting he got down to serious discussion. He said, 'I don't like the title.'

'No? We thought . . . '

'Listen, boys, who the hell is going to a film called *The Third Man*?'

'Well,' I said, 'it's a simple title. It's easily remembered.'

Selznick shook his head reproachfully. 'You can do better than that, Graham,' he said, using my Christian name with a readiness I was not prepared for. 'You are a writer. A good writer. I'm no writer, but you are. Now what we want – it's not right, mind you, of course, it's not right, I'm not saying it's right, but then I'm no writer and you are, what we want is something like *Night in Vienna*, a title which will bring them in.'

'Graham and I will think about it,' Carol Reed interrupted with haste. It was a phrase I was to hear Reed frequently repeat, for the Korda contract had omitted to state that the director was under any obligation to accept Selznick's advice. Reed during the days that followed, like an admirable stonewaller, blocked every ball.

We passed on to Selznick's view of the story.

'It won't do boys,' he said, 'it won't do. It's sheer buggery.'

'Buggery?'

'It's what you learn in your English schools.'

'I don't understand.'

'This guy comes to Vienna looking for his friend. He finds his friend's dead. Right? Why doesn't he go home then?'

After all the months of writing, his destructive view of the whole venture left me speechless. He shook his grey head at me. 'It's just buggery, boys.'

I began weakly to argue. I said, 'But this character – he has a motive of revenge. He has been beaten up by a military policeman.' I played a last card. 'Within twenty-four hours he's in love with Harry Lime's girl.'

Selznick shook his head sadly. 'Why didn't he go home before that?'

That, I think, was the end of the first day's conference. Selznick removed to Hollywood and we followed him – to a luxurious suite in Santa Monica, once the home of Hearst's film-star mistress. During the conference which followed I remember there were times when there seemed to be a kind of grim reason in Selznick's criticisms – surely here perhaps there *was* a fault in 'continuity', I hadn't properly 'established' this or that. (I would forget momentarily the lesson which I had learned as a film critic – that to 'establish' something is almost invariably wrong and that 'continuity' is often the enemy of life. Jean Cocteau has even argued that the mistakes of continuity belong to the unconscious poetry of a film.) A secretary sat by Selznick's side with her pencil poised. When I was on the point of agreement Carol Reed would quickly interrupt – 'Graham and I will think about it.'

There was one conference which I remember in particular because it was the last before we were due to return to England. The secretary had made forty pages of notes by this time, but she had been unable to record one definite concession on our side. The conference began as usual about 10.30 p.m. and finished after 4 a.m. Always by the time we reached Santa Monica dawn would be touching the Pacific.

'There's something I don't understand in this script, Graham. Why the hell does Harry Lime . . . ?' He described some extraordinary action on Lime's part.

'But he doesn't,' I said.

Selznick looked at me for a moment in silent amazement.

'Christ, boys,' he said, 'I'm thinking of a different script.'

He lay down on his sofa and crunched a benzedrine. In ten minutes he was as fresh as ever, unlike ourselves.

I look back on David Selznick now with affection. The forty pages of notes remained unopened in Reed's files, and since the film has proved a success, I suspect Selznick forgot that the criticisms had ever been made. Indeed, when next I was in New York he invited me to lunch to discuss a project. He said, 'Graham, I've got a great idea for a film. It's just made for you.'

I had been careful on this occasion not to take a third martini.

'The life of St Mary Magdalene,' he said.

'I'm sorry,' I said, 'no. It's not really in my line.'

He didn't try to argue. 'I have another idea,' he said. 'It will appeal to you as a Catholic. You know how next year they have what's called the Holy Year in Rome. Well, I want to make a picture called *The Unholy Year*. It will show all the commercial rackets that go on, the crooks . . . '

'An interesting notion,' I said.

'We'll shoot it in the Vatican.'

'I doubt if they will give you permission for that.'

'Oh sure they will,' he said. 'You see, we'll write in one Good Character.'

(I am reminded by this story of another memorable lunch in a suite at the Dorchester when Sam Zimbalist asked me if I would revise the last part of a script which had been prepared for a remake of *Ben Hur*. 'You see,' he said, 'we find a kind of anti-climax after the Crucifixion.')

Those indeed were the days. I little knew that the reign of Kubla Khan was nearly over and that the Pleasure Dome would soon be converted into an enormous bingo hall, which would provide other dreams to housewives than had the Odeons and the Empires. I had regretted the silent films when the talkies moved in and I had regretted black and white when Technicolor washed across the screen. So today, watching the latest soft-porn film, I sometimes long for those dead thirties, for Cecil B. de Mille and his Crusaders, for the days when almost anything was likely to happen.

International Film Annual (1958)

[Shorn of the passage between the two †, this piece served as the Introduction to *The Pleasure Dome* (1972), and, fully restored, was later incorporated into *Ways of Escape* (1980). It was also published as an extract called 'Mornings in the Dark' in *The Times* (4 October 1980).]

Preface to *Three Plays*

When a novelist has a play produced for the first time in middle-age, it is natural to assume that he has come rather late to the theatre. I feel sure that I would regard with suspicion the publication of Mr Rattigan's first novel. To put up with the disappointments and the difficulties, the false starts and false curtains, the stubborn intransigence of a method which depends for communication on dialogue alone, an apprentice needs to have a passion for his work, but can we believe in a passion that has only declared itself at the eleventh hour?

So this is an apology for a late-comer to the theatre – I am a late-comer, I want to explain, only to actual production. My life as a writer is littered with discarded plays, as it is littered with discarded novels. The first novel of mine to be published was the third completed (how thankful I am that the other two never saw the light of day), but I cannot count the number of plays which preceded *The Living Room*. I do know, however, that the first to be accepted was written when I was sixteen.

I was then very much under the influence of Lord Dunsany –

If with Henry Ainley was my favourite contemporary play, and I had myself played the Poet in his *Lost Silk Hat*, with royalty too in the audience. All I remember of this play, which had been preceded by many highly dramatic curtain-raisers inspired by such unlikely models as Rupert Brooke's *Lusitania* and Maurice Hewlett's medieval novels, is that it celebrated the poetry which I, somehow, considered inherent in the ceremony of afternoon tea, moving lavishly from scene to scene, London to Samarkand, trying to hold the whole gorgeous East in fee. I sent it to one of the many play-producing societies which existed in the early twenties and was astonished to receive a letter signed by a lady accepting it for production.

So I went up to London one morning to meet my first management. The address, so unlike Mr Albery's or Mr Beaumont's, was somewhere in St John's Wood, a district which in those days still retained the glamour of illicit love-nests. I cannot have made an appointment, for it was obvious that I was not expected. There was a long delay after I sounded the bell, and when at last it was answered, it was by a rather overblown rosy woman holding a dressing-gown together, who was watched from the end of the passage by a naked man in a double-bed. She stared in astonishment at my blue cap with a school crest as I explained that I had come about my play. I think she gave me a cup of rather weak Mazawattee tea (very different from the tea which I had been celebrating) and she became carefully vague, as she scrutinised me, about casting and date of production. I don't remember that I ever heard from her again, and the society, I am sure, soon ceased to exist. Perhaps my play was the last piece of wreckage at which she clutched, and down with it went all dreams of some rich sucker who would put up the expenses, incidental and accidental, of his play (including the quarter's rent and the milk-bill and all that went with the double-bed at the end of the passage).

Two years after that I found myself trapped into life-imprisonment by the novel – for some years with just as little success in the way of production, so that twice I tried to make a get-away, first into the British-American Tobacco Company and then into *The Times*.

Not for nearly twenty years did I seriously attempt a play again.

My first attempt, a comedy based on one of the frequent kidnapping incidents which took place in Japanese-occupied Manchuria before the last war, never reached the second act. I was pleased enough with the first: the scene a draughty railway station on the Manchurian border: the characters a Japanese officer always busy at his typewriter, a correspondent of the *Daily Mail*, a paper which had embarrassed the authorities by offering a large reward for the return of the kidnapped (there were no currency problems in those happy old-world days), the British Consul, a Chinese go-between, the anxious husband, and last the kidnapped couple – the wife and a young employee who had been taken by the bandits while riding at the local race-club. The husband's anxiety was less for his wife's safety than for his own marital security, since the couple, according to the Press, had been bound together by the wrists for the last fortnight, day and night. I liked my first act. There seemed to me a freshness and an authenticity in the setting, the action marched, but alas! when I came to it, the first act only lasted for eighteen minutes and a half. It was to be a play in two acts, and the second act was to be a little shorter than the first . . . I abandoned the play with reluctance.

Length has always bedevilled me. My novels as a rule fall below those seventy-five thousand words which publishers always used to consider a minimum length. Just before we were to start rehearsing *The Living Room* (a play written off-and-on over three years which I had sent to Mr Donald Albery under the mistaken impression that he was a theatrical management – however he became one in time to produce the play), we received an authoritative timing of one hour and a quarter. There was general despondency – for it was impossible to enlarge the play. However my own timing of an hour and three-quarters after all proved to be correct and by raising the curtain a little late, by imperceptibly (to those in the bar) increasing the interval beyond a quarter of an hour, it was possible to pass the minimum two hours which to a theatrical management remain as necessary as seventy-five thousand words once were to a publisher.

Thanks to Miss Tutin and Mr Portman *The Living Room* was a success, but to me it was more than a success. I needed a rest from novels. I disliked the drudgery of film-writing, I had discovered what was in effect a new drink just at that period when life seemed to have been going on for far too many years.

At the end of this first experience of the theatre I found myself writing with an excitement which I still feel:

> The novelist works alone: he is lucky if there is one other human being with whom he can discuss a problem or try out a difficult passage. Even the screen-writer in my fortunate experience works with only one other man, the director, but so soon as the shooting script is completed he is excluded from the act of creation. Unless a crisis arises in the studio and the director needs his presence to rewrite a scene, the author is a forgotten man who emerges again, a bewildered figure watching the rough cut, clearing his throat nervously at new lines that are not his, feeling a sense of guilt because he is the only spectator who remembers what happened once – like a man who has witnessed a crime and is afraid to speak, an accomplice after the fact. There had been, of course, moments of great interest in learning the new craft of film-writing, but so often the excitement of creation was confined to the preliminary idea, sketched at a dinner table, and lost again in the many rewritings, the first, second and third treatment, the first, second and third script. The screen is not there – like the page of foolscap – on which to test an idea; nor is there a stage from which the author can hear his lines brought to life or exhibited in their deadness. When the lines are at last spoken on the studio-floor the author is not there to criticise and alter. Another hand (earning, I suppose, a smaller salary and perhaps more easily controlled by the director) plays with his work. My own experience of screen-writing has been fortunate and happy, and yet with what relief I have gone back afterwards to that one-man business, to the privacy of a room in which I bear the full responsibility for failure.

But – the fact remains – one must try every drink once. I had imagined that to write a play and to write a film would be very similar: the author, even though he could not be excluded from rehearsals, would be an unwelcome stranger lurking ashamed in the stalls. A film studio – when you are allowed to penetrate it – has the callow comradeship of a great factory: signs, lights, clappers, cranes, and behind all the façade of Christian names (the union must be kept happy), the hierarchy of canvas chairs. I had not anticipated the warmth, the amusement, and comradeship of the theatre. Above all I had not realised that the act of creation, as with the novel, would continue for long after the first draft of the play was completed, that it would extend through rehearsals and through the opening weeks of tour. It is for the act of creation that one lives, and after the author has returned from tour, how empty the hours are, the telephone rings seldom – couldn't we have delayed the launching a little longer for the sake of the fun? I suppose that every author feels this, and that is why he writes another play.

There had been the excitement of acceptance, the excitement and frustrations of casting, the grim interest of auditions when every line became more leaden, the first reading with the complete cast, the conferences and changes over coffee, the delight of working with players interested not only in their own parts, but in the play as a whole (a film-actor is hardly aware of what happens when he is not on the set), nearly a dozen lively or informed, who have not worked on the play morning, afternoon and evening for many weeks, who don't yet know what the play is about and whose response is therefore conditioned by the momentary effect and not by the mood of the last curtain. Then one uncovers the unexpected laughs in the wrong places, the laughs legitimate but over strong, the coughs that indicate a failure in tension. For a night the writer may be discouraged, but how fascinating it is, when he has cut out this line here or altered that action there, to return the next night to the theatre and see – as with the novel he can never see – the effect of his changes, the laugh killed, the laugh modified, the apparent improvement in the epidemic of colds.

One newcomer at any rate was very happy in the theatre, in the deserted stalls at rehearsals, at the note-takings on the stage after performances, in the corridors and bars and dressing-rooms: the theatre even brought certain bizarre experiences which the cinema has never offered: a struggle on an Edinburgh hotel-floor at two in the morning with a breeder of prize bulls, a long session with a stranger whose gratifying response to the play, one found too late, had been conditioned by his stay in four different lunatic asylums – these, I suppose, are the everyday experiences of going on tour.

I had tried a new drink: I had liked the flavour. How I wished my glass were not empty and that it was not time to go.

So one approached the bar again to order another drink. Too soon perhaps after the first. No play was pressing on me from the unconscious. I deliberately took one of my abandoned novels (I had written a few thousand words of it in 1946) and fabricated *The Potting Shed*. I am fond of the first act – that is about all I can say. The material proved intractable. I was to make a better attempt, in my own opinion, to draw a 'hollow man' in *A Burnt-Out Case*. The intractability of the last act showed itself during the production in America where I rewrote the last scene unsatisfactorily against time, at rehearsals; then with the London production I went back with equal disatisfaction to the original. I think my main objection to the play was the old Aristotelian lack of unity – five scenes and three sets. I have met many a director who has told me: 'Write what you like, in as many scenes as you like. Treat a play as loosely as a film. It is my job to find a way of putting it upon the stage.' But I don't want a producer's play – I want an author's play, and anyway there is a fascination in unity, in trying to work in what Wordsworth called 'The sonnet's narrow room.'

My critics have so far, I think, failed to disinter the manic-depressive side of any talent I possess (in the future I feel sure that I will regret disclosing it to them). The strain of writing a novel, which keeps the author confined for a period of years with his depressive self, is extreme, and I have always sought relief in 'entertainments' – for melodrama as much as farce is an expression of a manic mood. So with my third play I sought my usual escape – only to find as I reached the final curtain that the depressive mood had contributed almost as much as the manic to the piece. Perhaps that was why I had so full a sense of enjoyment in the writing. I have never worked with less feeling of conflict between two moods, and perhaps I can be forgiven for defending the play, out of gratitude. It arrived suddenly one spring day in the country at the turn of a road and it moved with dreamlike quickness – four months at most – towards birth. Now that the fourth is struggling with all the accustomed difficulties to be born I regret the twilight sleep of that spring and summer.

Preface to *Three Plays* (1961)

Film Fragments

The following extracts are from *Ways of Escape* (1980), with the exception of Greene's account of seeing *Orient Express* in Tenerife, which is taken from *Journey Without Maps* (1936).

The Man Within had the temporary success that a first novel sometimes has through the charity of reviewers, and twenty years later a certain Mr Sydney Box made a highly coloured film of it. I had not sold him the rights – I had given them for a token payment to a documentary film director with whom I had once worked on a propaganda film for what was then called Imperial Airways. He told me that with this book he had the chance of making his first feature film. Well, at least he made a profit from the resale to Mr Box, and Mr Box made his film with an extraordinary script which showed torture with branding irons as part of the nineteenth-century legal system. The film unlike the book did not suffer from youth or naïveté, and I received a letter from Istanbul written by a Turk who praised the picture for its daring homosexuality. Had I, he asked, devoted any other novels to this interesting subject? After the experience I added a clause to every film contract forbidding a resale to Mr Box. In every way I was hurt by this treachery to my first-born more than by the later treachery of Mr Joseph Mankiewicz when he made a film of *The Quiet American*. I was confident that this later book would survive the film, but *The Man Within* was a more feeble growth. If I had been a publisher's reader, which I became many years afterwards, I would have turned it down unhesitatingly.

★

That year, 1931, for the first and last time in my life I deliberately set out to write a book to please, one which with luck might be made into a film. The devil looks after his own and in *Stamboul Train* I succeeded in both aims, though the film rights seemed at this time an unlikely dream, for before I had completed the book, Marlene Dietrich had appeared in *Shanghai Express*, the English had made *Rome Express*, and even the Russians had produced their railway film, *Turksib*. The film manufactured from my book by Twentieth-Century Fox came last and was far and away the worst, though not so bad as a later television production by the BBC.

★

I was still not earning enough with my books to make a living for my family (after the success of my first novel and the spurious temporary sale of *Stamboul Train* each novel added a small quota to the debt I owed my publisher), but reviewing films regularly for the *Spectator* and novels once a fortnight, I could make ends meet. I had recently had two strokes of good fortune, and these enabled me to see a little way ahead – I had received a contract from Korda to write my second filmscript (and a terrible one it was, based on Galsworthy's short story *The First and Last* – Laurence Olivier and Vivien Leigh, who had much to forgive me, suffered together in the leading parts, and for six months I acted as joint editor with John Marks of the weekly *Night and Day*.

★

Would they [the Brighton authorities] have resented the novel even more deeply if they had known that for me to describe Brighton was really a labour of love, not hate? No city before the war, not London, Paris or Oxford, had such a hold on my affections. I knew it first as a child of six when I was sent with an aunt to convalesce after some illness – jaundice, I think. It was then I saw my first film, a silent one of course, and the story captured me for ever: *Sophie of Kravonia*, Anthony Hope's tale of a kitchenmaid who became a queen. When the kitchenmaid rode with her army through the mountains to attack the rebel general who had tried to wrest the throne from her dying husband, her march was accompanied by one old lady on a piano, but the tock-tock-tock of the untuned wires stayed in my memory when other melodies faded, and so has the grey riding habit of the young queen. The Balkans since then have always been to me Kravonia – the area of infinite possibility – and it was through the mountains of Kravonia that I drove many years later and not through the Carpathians of my atlas. That was the kind of book I always wanted to write: the high romantic tale, capturing us in youth with hopes to prove illusions to which we return again in age in order to escape the sad reality. *Brighton Rock* was a very poor substitute for Kravonia, like all my books, and yet it is one of the best I ever wrote.

*

The title *The Ministry of Fear* I took from a poem by Wordsworth (Arnold's edition of his poems was one of the volumes I had brought with me from England), and the novel was bought unseen by an American film company on the strength of Wordsworth's title. Then came the problem of sending the manuscript home. In Freetown it was impossible to forget the menace of submarines – it was part of our everyday life; the reason why so many wives stayed throughout their husbands' tours, the reason why I had no refrigerator – it had been lost on the way out. So, having finished the book, I began the weary task of typing it out with one finger after dinner, and I was lucky to finish it before the scurry of the North African landings affected even my remote coast with cables at all hours.

I have written little here about the novel itself though it is my favourite among what I called then my 'entertainments' to distinguish them from more serious novels. I wish now that the espionage element had been less fantastically handled, though I think Mr Prentice of the Special Branch is real enough – I knew him under another name in my own organization when I was his pupil. The scenes in the mental clinic are to my mind the best in the novel, and it was surprising to me that Fritz Lang, the old director of *M* and *The Spy*, omitted them altogether from his film version of the book, thus making the whole story meaningless.

⋆

For the first time – and I think the last – I drew a principal character from the life. Dreuther, the business tycoon in *Loser Takes All*, is undeniably Alexander Korda, and the story remains important to me because it is soaked in memories of Alex, a man whom I loved. I have even used scraps of his dialogue. I can still remember him saying to me, in that hesitant Hungarian accent, which lent a sense of considered wisdom to his lightest words, what Dreuther said in my book to Bertram, the accountant who is going to marry and whom he promises a honeymoon on his yacht in Monte Carlo, 'My dear boy, it is not easy to lose a good woman. If one must marry, it is better to marry a bad woman.'

He even provided me with the plot of *Loser Takes All*. I was on holiday in Anacapri with a very dear friend when we received a telegram inviting us both to join him in Athens for a cruise in his yacht, the *Elsewhere*. The *Elsewhere*, so romantically named, was his way of escape, from film scripts and directors and the Prudential Insurance Company. At first she had been a rather incomplete escape – the *Elsewhere* was kept in the old port of Antibes, which I can see now from my window as I write; she was on a sort of tether there that allowed him to go ashore daily to telephone his office – from Monte Carlo, from Portofino, from Calvi, but as the years passed she was allowed to wander loose – in one small Greek island where we were weather-bound on the way to Istanbul (which we never reached) there was not even a post office. He could talk about pictures, the poetry of Baudelaire, the theatre – anything but films. We had an unspoken pact to change the subject quickly if anybody on board spoke of films.

This trip in Greek waters to which we had been invited was the first time, I think, when he let the *Elsewhere* loose. The rendezvous was the Hôtel Grande Bretagne, but when we arrived there was no *Elsewhere* and no Korda and no message. The hotel knew nothing of his coming.

Those were still the days of strict currency regulations and we had very little money with us and the Grande Bretagne was a very expensive hotel. The first day we were alone we were extravagant but waking a second morning with no news of the boat, we had to be careful . . . which meant being more extravagant: all our meals in the hotel rather than a cheap café; in place of a taxi an expensive hotel car which could be put on the bill. I still remember the severe price for a picnic lunch provided by the hotel – we ate it over the Corinth Canal in hope of seeing the *Elsewhere* below us making her way to Athens.

Well, Alex like Dreuther did eventually turn up in time to pay our 'honeymoon' bill, and the story of *Loser Takes All* had been born over the retsina wine of the anxious picnic lunch. I even sold the film rights, and the film proved a disaster of miscasting, with a middle-aged actress as the twenty-year-old heroine, a romantic Italian star as the unromantic English accountant, and Robert Morley playing Robert Morley. Over the casting Alex had his little revenge (he must certainly have recognized himself as Dreuther) by refusing permission for Alec Guinness, who was under contract to him, to play the part. All the same I don't think he was offended by the portrait, which was drawn with some of the deep affection I felt for him.

In spite of the Hungarian accent it mustn't be thought that Alex was monotonously wise. He had strange and endearing lapses. Only a foreigner could have plunged so deeply in that disastrous costume drama – was it even shown? – *Bonnie Prince Charlie*. It was often better not to take his advice when it came to films. I remember the only script conference Carol Reed and I had with him before starting work on our film, *The Fallen Idol*, the adaptation of my short story about a child and a butler called 'The Basement Room'. Alex wanted me to change the butler into a chauffeur 'because children are so interested in mechanics, Graham. And then, you see, you open the film at London airport and the parents are going away by plane and the little boy is very interested in the engine of the car . . . ' I objected. 'How many films begin with a plane leaving an airport or arriving at one?' He wasn't convinced, but he let us have our way.

His human wisdom was always greater than his film wisdom. The fifties were for me a period of great happiness and great torment – manic depression reached its heights in that decade, and I remember there was one more than usually suicidal suggestion – I forget what – which I had put up to a Sunday newspaper. He spoke to me on the telephone. 'My dear boy, this is so foolish what you plan. Co with me to Antibes. You are bored. All right. We will go on the *Elsewhere*.' How he penetrated my life. It was he who had taken me for the first time to Monte Carlo, and so it was that my character Brown in *The Comedians* was born in that city. I knew Antibes first with him, and now it seems possible that I shall end my days there.

Was it on that voyage in the *Elsewhere*, with two American couples as a fine cover, that he confided to me how he had obtained for both of us a currency allowance of some size from British Intelligence because we were going to photograph the length of the Yugoslav coastline? He was back playing with lenses as he hadn't played for years not since *The Six Wives of Henry VIII* [*sic*] and *Rembrandt*. He had helped the Secret Service during the war and he had a childlike delight now in spying all down the Adriatic coast without the knowledge of his American guests who, I think, would not have been prepared for that kind of holiday.

This was his mischievous side. Like Dreuther in the Hôtel de Paris, he liked to play an old sailor in a T-shirt and a battered yachting cap with a white stubble on his chin. One night in Naples, in a waterfront bar frequented by GIs, he persuaded the barman and the American soldiers standing around that Coca-Cola rendered men impotent – my word would have carried no weight with them, nor a film producer's, but from this old seadog who had learnt his wisdom 'on the seven seas' . . .

A sad wisdom it was too: I remember him saying to me, 'When my friends and I were young in Hungary, we all dreamed of being poets. And what did we become? We became politicians and advertisement men and film producers.'

★

All the same the faults the reviewers found in it [*Carving a Statue*] were curiously different from the faults I find, which are harder faults to defend, and I may be forgiven perhaps for not pointing them out. I was accused of overloading the play with symbols, but I have never cared greatly for the symbolic and I can detect no symbols in this play; sometimes there is an association of ideas which perhaps the reviewers mistook for the symbolic – the accurate use of words is difficult, as I knew from my own experience of a theatre reviewer, when one writes against time.

I remember that when my film *The Third Man* had its little hour of success a rather learned reviewer expounded its symbolism with even less excuse in a monthly paper. The surname of Harry Lime he connected with a passage about the lime tree in Sir James Frazer's *The Golden Bough*. The 'Christian' name of the principal character – Holly – was obviously, he wrote, closely connected with Christ's – paganism and Christianity were thus joined in a symbolic dance. The truth of the matter is, I wanted for my 'villain' a name natural and yet disagreeable, and to me 'Lime' represented the quick-lime in which murderers were said to be buried. An association of ideas, not, as the reviewer claimed, a symbol. As for Holly, it was because my choice of name, Rollo, had not met with the approval of Joseph Cotten. So much for symbols.

★

Soon after the war ended, my friend Alberto Cavalcanti, the Brazilian film director, asked me to write a film for him. I thought I would write a Secret Service comedy based on what I had learned from my work in 1943–4 of German Abwehr activity in Portugal. I had returned from Freetown – and my futile efforts to run agents into the Vichy colonies – and had been appointed to Kim Philby's sub-section of our Secret Service, which dealt with counter-espionage in the Iberian peninsula. My responsibility was Portugal. There those Abwehr officers who had not been suborned already by our own service spent much of their time sending home completely erroneous reports based on information received from imaginary agents. It was a paying game, especially when expenses and bonuses were added to the cypher's salary, and a safe one. The fortunes of the German Government were now in decline, and it is wonderful how the conception of honour alters in the atmosphere of defeat.

I had sometimes thought, in dealing with Portugal, of how easily in West Africa I could have played a similar game, if I had not been content with my modest salary. I had learned that nothing pleased the services at home more than the addition of a card to their intelligence files. For example there was a report on a Vichy airfield in French Guinea – the agent was illiterate and could not count over ten (the number of his fingers and thumbs); nor did he know any of the points of the compass except the east (he was Mohammedan). A building on the airfield which he said housed an army tank was, I believed from other evidence, a store for old boots. I had emphasized the agent's disqualifications, so that I was surprised when I earned a rating for his report of 'most valuable'. There was no rival organization in the field, except SOE, with whose reports of mine could be compared, and I had no more belief in SOE reports than in my own – they probably came from the same source. Somebody in an office in London had been enabled to add a line or two to an otherwise blank card – that seemed the only explanation.

So it was that my experiences in my little shack in Freetown recalled in a more comfortable room off St James's gave me the idea of what twelve years later in 1958 became *Our Man in Havana*.

The first version written in the forties was an outline on a single sheet of paper. The story was laid in 1938 in Taillinn, the capital of

Estonia, a reasonable enough setting for espionage. The English agent had nothing at this stage in the story to do with vacuum cleaners, and it was the extravagance of his wife and not his daughter which led him to cheat his service. He was a more besotted character than Wormold in *Our Man in Havana* and less innocent. As the 1939 war approached, his enemies, like Wormold's, began to treat him seriously – the local police too. The incident of the misused micro-photographs was already in this draft. Cavalcanti, before we started work, thought it necessary to get clearance from the censor, and he was told that no certificate could be issued to a film that made fun of the Secret Service. At least that was the story he told me. Perhaps he invented an excuse because he was not enamoured of the subject.

⋆

It was not until the middle fifties that I saw the cruel Evelyn [Waugh] in action. We were dining at Carol Reed's house and our fellow guests were Alexander Korda and the young girl he was later to marry. Suddenly Evelyn leaned across the table and launched an attack on Korda of shocking intensity, killing all the conversation around. Korda bore it with exemplary patience and courtesy. Next day Evelyn and I were sharing a taxi and I demanded an explanation, for I was very fond of Alex.

'What on earth induced you to behave like that?'

'Korda,' he said, 'had no business to bring his mistress to Carol and Pempe's house.'

'But I was there with my mistress,' I said.

'That's quite different,' he replied, 'she's married.'

Fornication more serious than adultery? It was not the orthodox Catholic view. I gave the problem up, and we were driven on in silence.

⋆

Ballyhoo

The cinema in Tenerife was showing a film which had been

adapted from one of my own novels. It had been an instructive and rather painful experience to see it shown. The direction was incompetent, the photography undistinguished, the story sentimental. If there was any truth in the original it had been carefully altered, if anything was left unchanged it was because it was untrue. By what was unchanged I could judge and condemn my own novel: I could see clearly what was cheap and banal enough to fit the cheap banal film.

There remained a connection between it and me. One had never taken the book seriously; it had been written hurriedly because of the desperate need one had for the money. But even into a book of that kind had gone a certain amount of experience, nine months of one's life, it was tied up in the mind with a particular countryside, particular anxieties; one couldn't disconnect oneself entirely, and it was curious, rather pleasing, to find it there in the hot bright flowery town. There are places where one is ready to welcome any kind of acquaintance with memories in common: he may be cheap but he knew Annette; he may be dishonest but he once lodged with George; even if the acquaintance is very dim indeed and takes a lot of recognizing.

Two Youthful Hearts in the Grip of Intrigue. Fleeing from Life. Cheated? Crashing Across Europe. Wheels of Fate.

Never before had I seen American ballyhoo at work on something I intimately knew. It was magnificent in its disregard for the article for which it had paid. Its psychological insight was either cynically wrong or devastatingly right.

> The real Orient Express runs across Europe from Belgium to Constantinople. Therefore, you will go wrong if you interpret the word 'Orient' to indicate sonething of a Chinese or Japanese nature. There is enough material of other kinds to arrange a lively colourful ballyhoo, as you will see as soon as you turn to the exploitation pages in this press book.
>
> *Date Tie-Up.* In the exhibitor's set of stills available at the exchange are three stills which show Norman Foster explaining the sex life of a date to Heather Angel, passing dates to Heather

Angel and Heather Angel buying dates from the car window. The dialogue is quite enlightening on the date subject at one point in the picture. Every city has high-class food shops which feature fancy packages of dates. Tie-in with one of these for window displays, and for a lobby display, using adequate copy and the three stills.

Another angle would be to have a demonstration of date products, the many uses of dates, etc. This would be quite possible in the much larger cities. And in cases where working with large concerns, patrons may be permitted to taste samples. These tie-ups must be worked out locally despite the fact that we are contacting importers of important brands.

Don't underestimate the value of a real smart window fixed with date products, baskets of delicious fruits and dates, and the three stills shown here with adequate copy for your picture. 'Buy a package of delicious dates, and take "The Orient Express" for Constantinople, a most thrilling and satisfying evening's entertainment at the Rialto Theatre.'

Do You Know That: Heather Angel's pet kitten Penang had to have its claws clipped because it insisted on sharpening them on the legs of the expensive tables;

That the pet economy of Heather Angel is buying washable gloves and laundering them herself;

That Una O'Connor permits only a very few of her intimate friends to call her Tiny?

The blast of ballyhoo had not sold the film; to my relief, because by contract my name had to appear on every poster, it had kept to the smaller shabbier cinemas, until now it was washed up in Tenerife, in a shaded side street behind an old carved door like a monastery's. This was what made it an agreeable acquaintance; it hadn't the shamelessness of success; it might be vulgar, but it wasn't successfully vulgar. There was something quite un-Hollywood in its failure.

The Canaries were half-way to Africa; the Fox film and the pale cactus spears stuck in the hillside, a Victorian Gothic hotel smothered in bougainvillaea, parrots and a monkey on a string, innumerable themes were stated like the false starts and indecisions of a lifetime: the Chinese job from which one had resigned, the appointment in Bangkok never taken up, the newspaper in Nottingham. I can remember now only the gaudy poster, the taste of the sweet yellow wine, flat roofs and flowers and an arbour full of empty bottles, and in the small dark cathedral a Christmas crib (castles and little villages and women with baskets of carrots, a donkey and a motor car and a comic man in a top-hat, little caves where hermits or gipsies sat asleep on moss-covered rocks, a man on an old-fashioned bicycle, and somewhere right up in a corner, dwarfed by the world, the flesh, those bright spring carrots, and the devil, the man in a top-hat, sat the Mother of God with an old-young child, wrinkled and careworn and cross-eyed, while Herod leant over a wall with his crown tilted).

My Worst Film

In January 1940, in my last months as a film critic of the *Spectator*, I wrote of a film which had caused me some disappointment, but a good deal of amusement in retrospect: 'Perhaps I may be forgiven for noticing a picture in which I had some hand, for I have no good word to say of it. The brilliant acting of Mr Hay Petrie as a decayed and outcast curate cannot conquer the overpowering flavour of cooked ham. Galsworthy's story, *The First and the Last*, was peculiarly unsuited for film adaptation, as its whole point lay in a double suicide (forbidden by the censor), a burned confession and an innocent man's conviction for murder (forbidden by the great public). For the rather dubious merits of the original the adaptors have substituted incredible coincidences and banal situations. Slow, wordy, unbearably sentimental, the picture reels awkwardly towards the only suicide the censorship allowed – and that, I find with some astonishment, has been cut out. I wish I could tell the extraordinary story that lies behind this shelved and resurrected picture, a story involving a theme song, and a bottle of whiskey, and camels in Wales . . . Meanwhile, let one guilty man, at any rate, stand in the dock, swearing never, never to do it again . . . '

I'm afraid, when the war was over, I broke my oath by writing two screenplays, *The Fallen Idol* and *The Third Man*, which were made, like the deplorable *21 Days*, for my friend Alexander Korda.

The mysterious mention of camels, whiskey and a theme song in my criticism puzzled some readers. Now when most of the protagonists are dead, the reference can be safely explained – as well as the incident of the coffee sugar which I might have included.

The director of *21 Days* was Basil Dean,[4] not one of the easiest men for whom to work; he was inclined like Preminger to bully his actors, and he was a stickler over trifles. I worked on the script with a man older and more experienced than myself and I can remember vividly one unhappy day during the shooting at Denham Studios. I had added to Galsworthy's short story a scene, during the course of the innocent man's trial, in which the Lord Chief Justice gave a bachelor dinner. All seemed to be going well (there had been two or three takes – crane shots from above the round dinner table) when Dean let out a cry of anguish. The dinner had reached the coffee stage and Dean pointed out with horror at the sugar bowl. 'That's not coffee sugar,' he cried. No coffee sugar was available at the Denham Film Studios, so a car had to be sent to London to Fortnum's and the shooting of the film was suspended at I don't know what cost until it returned with the coffee sugar.

This scene may have been an unfortunate side-effect caused by the loss of our assistant producer who had suddenly been removed by Korda. Korda needed him to accompany a train of camels to Wales where a far better film was about to be shot based on one of Kipling's stories.[5] So much for the camels.

There remains to be explained the business of the whiskey bottle and the theme song.

It was the last night of writing. My collaborator[6] and I were engaged against time in finishing the script. Basil Dean before going out to dinner had made us promise to deliver it next morning to Lajos Biro, Korda's fellow Hungarian, for final approval. We had no time to eat, but at least we had a bottle of whiskey. There was only one sequence left to write – we had laid it in the fun-fair at Southend where Laurence Olivier, tormented in his conscience, for it was he and not the man on trial who was guilty of murder, tries to forget things with Vivien Leigh on a switchback. Unfortunately their real-life love affair at that time had reached a climax and in spite of Basil Dean's efforts their carefree laughter on the screen was a little out of place.

It was that scene we were finishing and also the whiskey bottle. I said, 'At this point we ought to have a theme song.' (I was just as carefree as Olivier but with less excuse – not love of a beautiful woman but the whiskey bottle.) My friend agreed, and we wrote alternate lines of the theme song, which I cannot remember now. Off the script went to Lajos Biro and we to bed. I must admit that the next day we were a little surprised to learn that our script had been approved without comment or criticism.

The weeks passed and Basil Dean asked me to accompany him and his camera man to Southend to plan the shooting. We took a river-boat from Westminster, travelling second-class because Dean wanted to see how 'the other half' lived. We then began to walk around the fun-fair. Suddenly the moment which I had long feared arrived. Dean said, 'I didn't quite understand, Graham, about the song . . . ' but before he could finish or I could reply the camera man called to him from beside the switchback, 'Mr Dean, please come over here. I think I've found an angle . . .' and when Dean returned he had forgotten all about the song.

But when I saw the film on the screen I was not surprised, though a little disappointed, that the song had disappeared. I have always wondered whether before Dean abandoned it they had reached the point of setting it to music.

Written in 1987. Published in *Reflections* (1990), selected and introduced by Judith Anderson.

Screen Dreams

A strange experience remains printed on my brain like a newspaper headline – 'The Suicide of Charlie Chaplin'. It began with a rumour of my friend's death. I was in a great crowded cinema and I expected that at any moment an announcement would be made. I was even a little afraid of a panic among the audience at the news. However, later, the rumour was denied. A ring came at my flat door and when I opened it Charlie was assisted in. He really looked a dying man. Apparently he had taken poison but presumably not enough, and he made a gesture to indicate how much as he lay down. The poison had come from a tin. I asked his companion to give me the tin – 'It might prove useful for me one day.' It was an ordeal to watch Charlie slowly dying, as I believed, but the situation suddenly changed – he recovered and was able to leave without assistance.

★

In 1965 I was engaged in making a film with Peter Glenville, from an original story set in Mexico in the nineteenth century. Peter wanted to go riding with me and he had found a small black horse for me, but I don't care for riding and I let him practise alone, riding in circles.

We arrived at the point in the script where an innocent hero, Drew, in company of a man called Houghton, is being pursued by sheriffs after a bank robbery. They rest their horses for a moment by one of those branching cacti known as a 'candelabra'. Peter thought this presented an unnecessary difficulty, but I assured him that making a film about Mexico without showing a cactus was like filming Paris without the Eiffel Tower. He would only have to go a few miles south of Mexico City before finding such cacti.

The character Drew would see the candelabra and quote a nursery rhyme to Houghton, 'Here comes a candle to light you to bed, and here comes a chopper to chop off your head,' and at that moment the sheriffs' posse would appear on the horizon.

★

I was taking a walk in the West End with Randolph Churchill when he suggested that I help him to write a film script about his father.

The danger, I told him, was banality. I had an idea for an original treatment of the subject, with the title *A Great Man*. The story would be about minor fictitious characters showing how their lives were changed by certain emotional points in Churchill's life – VE Day, for example, and his last sickness. He liked the idea and told me he would try to get the Queen's co-operation.

★

I was commissioned to direct a film of one of Ibsen's plays, and I had done no homework. I had thought of no camera angles, cuts, etc. Ralph Richardson was to star in it, and someone had warned me that he intended to get me sacked and humiliated on the first day.

It was Richardson who introduced me to the *équipe* – about having twenty men sitting at long tables, having refreshments. I made the mistake of apologizing for my inexperience and they shouted back their mocking agreement. If only I could get through the first day's shooting, I thought, I'd be able to study the play at night.

A remark of Ralph's gave me a clue. 'I want to begin,' I said, 'with an exterior shot of your monocle lying on a doorstep. We pan up and see you cursing from a window above – whatever curses you are in the habit of using.'

But after that promising beginning we began to quarrel. He talked of appealing to his agent. 'Are you threatening me?' I said.

'Yes. I am.'

'I shan't appeal to anyone.' I told him. 'I shall cut your face open with a riding whip.'

from *A World of My Own* (1992)

3

Book Reviews

Pigs Be British

The pig in our literature has always been credited with qualities peculiarly British. Honest, a little stupid, commercially-minded perhaps, but with a trace of idealism in his love affairs, the pig's best nature is shown in domestic surroundings at a period of peace and material comfort. 'They led prosperous uneventful lives, and their end was bacon', Miss Potter has written of Miss Dorcas and Miss Porcas, but the sentence might stand as the epitaph of the whole race. In the latest variant on the tale of the *Three Little Pigs*, published by the Walt Disney Studios, one notices that same serenity in the portraits of the older generation hanging in the house of the provident pig: 'Mother', an old-fashioned parent drawn tenderly in the act of suckling eight children; 'Uncle Otto', changed to a Rugby football, but a football at rest, unprofaned, as yet by the clamorous, vulgar game; 'Father', uncarved, sporting his paper frill with the heavy dignity of a Victorian parent in a Gladstone collar. It is impossible to doubt this strong affection when we find it noticed by an earlier and less sympathetic observer than Miss Potter. The Rev. W. Bingley, using the very terms in which foreign historians have so often described Englishmen, wrote, 'Selfish, indocile and rapacious, as many think him, no animal has greater sympathy for those of his own kind than the hog.'

But perhaps the British quality of the pig has never been more thoroughly expressed than in the early poem: 'This little pig went to market (one remembers the pride with which Englishmen have always repeated Napoleon's jeer); This little pig stayed at home ('O sweet content! O sweet, O sweet content!'; 'Sweet Stay-at-Home, sweet Well-Content'; 'I love thee for a heart that's kind – Not for the knowledge in thy mind' – it is sometimes hard to remember that Dekker and Mr Davies are writing of men and not of pigs); This little pig had roast beef (no need to emphasize this parallel); This little pig had none; This little pig cried wee wee wee all the way home.' Perhaps no pig was more British than this last;

a literary pig, for the mother-fixation, the longing for the womb has been the peculiar peril of our minor poets. 'O mother quiet, breasts of peace': Rupert Brooke is the obvious modern example, but all through the Georgian period one is aware of the patter of little hoofs along the dark road that leads back to the country sty, the roses round the door, the Mothering Sunday that goes on and on.

Sexual references, it will be noticed, are quite absent from this early poem, as they are from the rather cruel, politically-conscious story of the *Three Little Pigs*. It really seems that at this period of pig literature the bigger the litter the greater the inhibition, a situation closely paralleled in Victorian England. Miss Potter, I think, was the first to throw any real light on the Love Life of the Pig, and this she did with a delicacy and a psychological insight that recall Miss Austen. She drew for the first time in literature the feminine pig. Hitherto a pig had been just a pig; one usually assumed the sex to be masculine. But in Pig-Wig, whom Pigling Bland, it will be remembered rescued from the cottage of the fatal Mr Peter Thomas Piperson, the female pig was revealed to be as completely British as the male: inquisitive, unromantic, demanding to be amused, fond of confectionery and admirably unselfconscious:

> She asked so many questions that it became embarrassing to Pigling Bland.
>
> He was obliged to shut his eyes and pretend to sleep. She became quiet, and there was a smell of peppermint.
>
> 'I thought you had eaten them?' said Pigling, waking suddenly.
>
> 'Only the corners,' replied Pig-Wig, studying the sentiments (they were conversation peppermints) by the firelight.
>
> 'I wish you wouldn't; he might smell them through the ceiling,' said the alarmed Pigling.
>
> Pig-Wig put back the sticky peppermints into her pocket. 'Sing something,' she demanded.
>
> 'I am sorry . . . I have toothache,' said Pigling much

dismayed.

'Then I will sing,' replied Pig-Wig. 'You will not mind if I say iddy tiddity? I have forgotten some of the words.'

It is impossible to deny that this is a peculiarly English love scene; no other nation, except perhaps the Russian, would have behaved or written quite like this, and the sentiment of the ending, the luxurious indulgence in wistfulness and idealism: 'They ran, and they ran, and they ran down the hill, and across a short cut on level green turf at the bottom, between pebble beds and rushes. They came to the river, they came to the bridge – they crossed it hand in hand' would be inconceivable to a race of pigs whose prosperity had been more precarious, to whom the struggle for existence had been more crudely presented. American pigs, for example, who meet their end, like so many other Americans, abruptly in Chicago, would have been at the same time more brutal and more soft-hearted.

Both these rather contradictory qualities appear in the Walt Disney Studios' brilliant adaptation of *Three Little Pigs* (and I should like, before I forget in the fascination of the story, warmly to congratulate all those concerned in the production of this film: the chief electrician, the cameraman, the fashion designer, the art editor, the scenario writer, the director and assistant director, the producer, the author and the composer of the theme song). These pigs are no longer quite so British, which is to say that they are no longer quite so priggish. The curled tails, the improvident flutings, the house of straw and the house of twigs and the house of brick have never been more tenderly portrayed, but the wolf never more brutally. This is the wolf of experience, not of dream; Wall Street smashes, financiers' suicides, the machine guns of the gangster are behind this wolf. Watch him outside the house of twigs, sitting in a basket, a sheepskin falling on either side of his ferocious muzzle like the wig of a Jeffreys: this is Justice conniving at unjust executions and letting the gangster free. And watch him again outside the house of bricks in a rusty hat, in an overcoat, in a false yellow beard: 'I'm the Kleen-e-ze Brush man, I'm giving away free samples': he is every share pusher personified, the man who knows of a new gold mine, a swell oil field.

But just because the whole story is more realistic than the English version, the American mind shrinks from the ruthless logical *dénouement*. The two improvident pigs are not swallowed by the wolf, they escape and take refuge with their brother in the brick house, and even the wolf escapes with a scalding. The wolf's escape, indeed, is the most American aspect of this transplanted tale. How often one has watched the methods of justice satirized upon the screen with a realism that would be impossible in England; yet nothing is done about it, the wolf escapes. The English story is the better one, to sacrifice two pigs that the third may live safely, to sacrifice the improvident pigs that the provident pig may be remembered forever in his famous aphorism: 'The price of liberty is eternal vigilance.'

The Spectator (23 March 1934); included in *Collected Essays* as *Pigs Be British*.

A Grammar of the Film by Raymond Spottiswoode

Mr Spottiswoode has written a very valuable book. It has been his aim, in his own words, 'to make as precise as possible the language and grammar which the film, as a prospective art-form has to acquire.' Note the phrase 'prospective art-form'; his study takes a very sane middle line; he is no canting enthusiast (a category in which one must regretfully include Eisenstein and Pudovkin) who believes that the film is already the most important of the arts. He is so cautious, an admirable quality in a grammarian whose business it is to give us 'the doctrine of the enclitic *De*' and settle *Hoti*'s business, that he pays altogether too much attention to ignorant detraction. Mr St John Ervine's views are not really worth so much attention.

The chief test of Mr Spottiswoode's definitions is the word montage, a word describing a method so vaguely apprehended that its very existence has been denied and its particular meaning has been swallowed up in the meaningless general term, 'constructive cutting.' Here Mr Spottiswoode, I think, succeeds admirably in detaching the special significance, even if his definition lacks neatness: 'the production of a concept or sensation through the mutual impact of other conceptions or sensations; in its structural aspect, the juxtaposition of shots, series and sequences in such a way as to produce this impact.' (Elsewhere he simplifies this definition: 'The essence of montage is its irruption of natural continuity,' and he might have given *The Waste Land* as a literary example of the method.) He then goes on to divide montage into primary, simultaneous, rhythmical, implicational and ideological montage. To him montage is the only true filmic method; he is as dogmatic on this point as James on 'the point of view' in the novel; it makes him condemn the use of the moving camera – so effective in *Jazz Comedy* reviewed on another page – because it makes montage impossible. But the film, just as much as the novel, needs dogma. If it is to prove an art, it needs a narrow conception of technique, so that directors may at least be aware of the rules they are breaking and know why they are breaking them. The effect of Mr Spottiswoode's dogmas is clarifying; it gives one a reason for one's dislike of the 'wipe', one's distrust of the 'dissolve' and of colour:

> Colour . . . would slow down the construction of the film. The complexities of a multiple colour-scale cannot be apprehended nearly so quickly as can monochrome. Hence, in order to allow for a full appreciation of each shot, it will have to be continued for a further length of time, and the exceptionally short shots, which contribute so much to the variation of tempo, and the building of specific effects upon which most of the excellence of the film depends, must be sacrificed.

The belief in montage as the only method is the strength of Mr Spottiswoode's criticism. It is the chief factor in his sane view of the cinema. How can he be an enthusiast for the present cinema when only in English documentaries and in Russian films can he find more than the barest indication that their directors have so much as heard of montage? There can be no doubt at all that if the use of montage became universal, the standard of film production would instantly rise. It would abolish altogether the potted play which, though it may, when it is as ably acted as *The Barretts of Wimpole Street*, have great entertainment value, must always be inferior to the same play on the stage. But the effect, after a while, would be very tiring, as tiring as to see a number of Mr Grierson's documentaties one after the other. Mr Spottiswoode in his puritanical objection to the moving camera writes (the italics are my own): 'The majority of non-Russian directors seem to think that if their story is slow and lifeless, it can be made to move merely by moving the camera; in fact, however, this results in a purposeless irritation, *the proper procedure being to cut from each point of vital attention to the next.*' That is my objection to the universal use of montage: the mind is kept at too high a tension: if the film is to deal faithfully with life, it must allow for the non-vital moments. Montage is often very close to melodrama: the objection to many of the very intelligent films of the GPO Film Unit is that they substitute a sense of the dramatic for the sense of the ordinary routine occupations they describe. The stage *has* to dramatise; the film has proved itself capable of greater fidelity.

The Spectator (27 September 1935)

Wings Over Wardour Street

Dallas Bower, *Plan for Cinema* and Paul Rotha, *Documentary Film*

In a few months now it will be possible for us to sit in our own homes and watch a film by television. Neither sound nor the improved colour in *Becky Sharp* represented so revolutionary a change, for they left film production in the same hands, the hands of large-scale financiers able to spend hundreds of thousands of pounds on a single film, but forced for the same reason to get their money back from the public the easiest and quickest way, to take no risks. That is one aspect of the star system: a comparatively inexpensive insurance against fallible directors, fallible story-writers: the quality of the films may vary so long as the public taste is stabilised on the star.

But what is going to be the effect of television on these huge financial organisations? Their position on the face of it looks desperate. Mr Dallas Bower, who speaks with technical authority, for he has been a sound recordist, a film editor and a director, foresees the necessity of handing over to television all that at present we mean by Cinema and inventing a new style, even a new type of theatre, with which television cannot compete. This is the very interesting subject of his book, though we have to reach it by way of some cheap and ingenuous social digressions. His post-television theatre is in the shape of an arena, with the screen, a cylindrical screen in the centre, played on by four overlapping projectors. The screen is translucent; when the theatre is in darkness we shall see no screen, but solid figures moving in the round. The idea of 'solid cinema' seems less fantastic than the idea that the great companies will be prepared to scrap their present theatres and begin to build anew. That must depend, of course, on the success of television as a creative, and not a merely reproductive medium.

The film companies, at any rate in this country, may not be in immediate danger; they have the stars, and television will have to appeal on other than star terms. Nor has the BBC in the past (we only have to remember the broadcast play) developed at all the creative side of broadcasting. The first cinemas to suffer will be the news cinemas, though even they may be allowed a breathing space, if the BBC fails to realise that *direct* television of *any* kind is impracticable. (Even Mr Bower speaks of direct television for news events, political speeches, talks by distinguished people, &c. But you cannot televise news directly and get results which for clarity, excitement or even apparent authenticity can compete with a news film where half a dozen cameras have been employed, the best shots chosen and the film edited; and even if you wish to televise a talk with no more than the features of the speaker, the close-up should surely be arranged as carefully as were the close-ups in the BBC film made by Mr Grierson's unit, and that, too, means film and film cutting.)

Mr John Grierson in a preface to Mr Rotha's *Documentary Film* states the case against the BBC:

> The BBC has been conservative till now in the use of its instruments. Its producers have used the microphone very much as the early film makers used their camera. They have accepted it as an essentially immovable object to which all action or comment must be brought . . . A few simple deviations there have been in the so-called 'actuality' programmes (in this borrowing from our documentary example), but they have been so tentative and ill-equipped, that for all its years of work and national fields of opportunity the BBC has created no art of microphonic sound, and in its own technique, not a single artist.

The BBC, of course, can reply that it is a department of public relations. From the broadcasting of a village fire-brigade to the Empire broadcast on Christmas Day its most important object is to teach one man how another man lives. We are not, the BBC may argue, primarily concerned with art any more than with entertainment in the sense of dance orchestras and plays. But I think Mr Grierson and Mr Rotha, who, as producers of documentary films, are equally concerned with public relations, with 'making things known that need to be known,' would be justified in retorting that nothing equals the persuasiveness of art and that as makers of documentaries they have developed an art unattained in any other branch of cinema, that under the direction of Mr Cavalcanti the GPO Film Unit is the first to realise the enormous possibilities in the editing and the invention of sound. Mr Grierson sees in television an even wider field for the documentary method, and surely one is not 'kill-joy' in believing that the main feature of television must lie, with story films occupying no more important a part in the programmes than plays do now. (I say story films because there is obviously no future for the direct television of plays.) We cannot yet speak of the 'art' of broadcasting; if television enables one documentary film to be made of the quality of *Song of Ceylon*, of *Coal Face*, of, even with all its faults of simplification and sentimentality, Mr Rotha's *The Face of Britain*, it will have introduced into broadcasting a creative element which at present it entirely lacks. There is the real threat to Wardour Street, the gradual realisation by the public of the finer excitement to be got in their own homes with documentary than in the super-cinema with the stars. There will always be an audience for the spectacular story film, but a very big audience is needed to carry the costs.

Mr Rotha is rather afraid of the word Art in relation to documentary films. Good photography, a pretty picture, skyline poses in the Flaherty manner, certainly do not make a good documentary film; but neither, as he points out, does bare realism. The news-reel is the closest the cinema comes to realism, but a news-reel is certainly not documentary, for the object of documentary is more than mere communication of fact; it is interpretation, persuasion, and the creative element, the *art* of documentary, lies there. The first part of Mr Rotha's book, so admirable when it reaches the actual making of documentaries, is rather tiresomely Marxist. He uses the word propaganda rather than persuasion because no object is so important to him as the political. But in that sense documentary has obviously little future in television under the present system. We fear our own vices, and it is interesting that Mr Rotha, whose films are seldom free from a certain prettiness and self-consciousness, should be so afraid of the word art which Mr Grierson, a producer almost aggressively free from style for style's sake, uses with admirable boldness. If propaganda, Mr Grierson writes, takes on its more political meaning, the sooner documentary is done with it the better. 'Art is wider than political doctrine and platform solution . . . It may, like politics, realise the social ills, but it must also sympathise more widely.' To sympathise more widely . . . I can think of no better distinction between art and propaganda, and with that object in view art may surely be allowed to find its way even into Broadcasting House. If it does, then indeed the wings are over Wardour Street.

The Spectator (24 January 1936)

Films and the Theatre

Allardyce Nicoll, *Films and the Theatre*

Professor Nicoll's book is not easy to read. His English is inclined to be inexact and his intentions sometimes cannot be disentangled from a curious jargon, in which technical terms are not always used correctly (the meaning of 'montage' has escaped Professor Nicoll) and nouns as often as not are employed as adjectives. 'Illusionistic', 'linkage', 'resultant audience reactions', such words and phrases do not suggest clear thought. But it would be a pity if readers were repelled by the style or by the rather elementary nature of Professor Nicoll's technical analysis, for he makes some valuable points.

Not the least valuable is his general attitude. 'If you wish to be a dramatist you must be prepared to write for the established theatres of your day: and if you esteem the cinema and believe it to be an art you must be prepared to discover that art among the commercial films of Elstree and Hollywood, calculated to appeal to the public at large.' And again, speaking of the usual criticism that most films are 'trivial in theme and often vulgar in expression,' he writes: 'Exactly in this way did Sidney speak a few years before Shakespeare entered into the service of the Lord Chamberlain's players.' That is well put. That the cinema is popular entertainment *ought* to encourage any artist who rejects the ivory tower, who wants his art to be part of the vulgar natural life – if only the parallel with the Elizabethan stage were more complete. But the audience has lost its vulgarity; it is refined and partly educated, and the artist will no longer be heartened by the direct applause, or criticized by the direct disapproval of the common people, the whispers of women with shopping baskets, the secret movements of courting couples.

Nevertheless Professor Nicoll's attitude remains essentially right. If there is to be an art of the cinema, it must be one which shakes the common people out of their indifference. Unfortunately Professor Nicoll's idea of good commercial films is: *The Private Life of Henry VIII, The House of Rothschild, David Copperfield, Man of Aran, The Barretts of Wimpole Street.* D.W. Griffith's work, even now, would be more to the point: these films show the 'literary', the refined professional bent, the 'artistic' compromise. Indeed his examination of cinema method is rather as if Henry James had illustrated the craft of the novel with quotations from Ouida: the tricks are good tricks, but in such contexts valueless. Nor does the examination go very deep. His first object is to defend the popular nature of the film, his second to describe its essential technique, but most of his analysis is so elementary that it would have been safe to assume that amount of knowledge among his readers before he began to write. He notes for example the dissolve, the cut, the fade-in and out, the wipe, but he makes no attempt to discuss their use to show why the wipe is – almost invariably – a mistake, how the functions of the cut, the dissolve, the fade should be, but seldom are, distinguished.

Nevertheless he leads, by unsatisfactory stages, to a valuable conclusion, that while the stage, with its living actors, should deal only with types, the film, by its very two-dimensional form, can deal far more adequately with characters.

> When living person is set before living person – actor before spectator – a certain deliberate conventionalizing is demanded of the former if the aesthetic impression is not to be lost, whereas in the film, in which immediately a measure of distance is imposed between image and spectator, greater approaches to real forms may be permitted.'

The Fortnightly Review (September 1936)

Movie Memories

Paul Rotha, *Movie Parade*

This is a record in pictures of more than thirty 'movie' years. Mr Rotha has chosen stills to illustrate 600 odd films from *The Great Train Robbery* of 1903 to the latest picture of the Marx Brothers. It is a delightful album for the sentimentalist: it will help anyone under the age of forty to recall his first film passion, whether he dates back to the War years, to the grand gestures of renunciation, the padded figures, the fateful flashing eyes for ever turned on the audience, the intoxicating hair in the Theda Bara style, the days when Lubitsch was making historical spectacles in German with Pola Negri as his star, or whether, like myself, he came to film consciousness in the romantic early twenties, when the German cinema broke into Otranto fantasy, the days of *Caligari, Warning Shadows* and the rest. This was when Greta Garbo (the picture is here) was posing in front of a little camera on a hand tripod and a couple of arc lamps in a Swedish lane, a matronly figure with a lot of drapery and no waist, and masses, masses of hair. Mr Aldous Huxley wrote of our fathers' passion: 'How the heart beat as the loosened bun uncoiled its component tresses!' but it is quite a shock in this book to discover how recent is the appeal of the big bust and the enormous *toupet*.

Alas, less than two hundred of the films survive for me at all vividly. My film memory does not really date back much earlier than 1919, a Thames-side scene with Lillian Gish, dimpled and smudged with tears (but the picture here is too small to record that) brooding over the barges. That film of D.W. Griffith's *Broken Blossoms*, heavy, simple, honest and sentimental, with a kind of rough poetry (he put the same folk quality into even so crude a melodrama as *Way Down East*, unfortunately not represented here by the great scene on the floating ice), takes all the sorrow out of the more cunning, better lit, 'artistic' still of the same story made in 1936. I miss here the *Sophy of Kravonia* of 1917 which contained my first film passion. I retain no more than an enchanting vision of a heavily booted flapping riding habit, an imperious switch, mountains, rebel guns rumbling across the keys of a simple Brighton piano up the pass, but the face of the actress is missing. I suppose she would have been hairy, too, and the film may not have been so important as I thought it at the age of twelve.

I am less sure that this album provides much more than sentimental memories with a useful reminder of directors' pasts, even with Mr Rotha's careful divisions and sub-divisions and his prefaces (a little heavily Left-Wing), for a still cannot give much indication of a moving picture technque (there are exceptions, of course, the glassy lady in black silk who, in a 1915 still, lies on a sofa facing the audience, while in a cloud above her head a gentleman in evening dress protects her from a smooth silk-hatted man twisting wax moustaches[7]). The art designer rather than the director is in evidence, though perhaps in Fritz Lang's case one should attribute to the director the incomparable vividness and realism of the settings: the barricaded door in *The Last Will of Dr Mabuse* with the striped mattress, the bullet-riddled ironing board bolted across, the flowery umbrella stand. A great many of the pictures are far too small (a film as admirable as *City Nights* is inadequately represented by a minute dark interior), and there are a few slips which should be corrected in later editions: *Bordertown* is printed in one place for *Borderland*, and Ruby Keeler not Ginger Rogers was the star of *Forty-Second Street*. It is easy to criticise an anthology for its omissions: I miss *The Robber Symphony, Dood Water, The Old and the Young King*, but no one can be other than grateful for the immense industry which has gone into this entertaining picture-book.

The Spectator (11 December 1936)

THE EXTRAORDINARY PROFESSION

Bardèche & Brasillach, *A History of the Film* (trs Iris Barry)

Did you know that talkies were exhibited at the Paris Exposition of 1900; that American movie producers opened their studios in

California only so as to escape process-servers and be able to disappear over the Mexican border at a moment's notice; that Charlie Chaplin began by wearing a forked beard and Harold Lloyd was first known as Lonesome Luke; that *The Italian Straw Hat* was Clair's *sixth* film; that in the uncensored version of *Shoulder Arms* the allies gave Charlie Chaplin a banquet after his capture of the Kaiser 'and the King of England creeps up and sneaks a button off his uniform as a souvenir'; did you know . . . ? One could go on a long while recounting the information, astonishing and bizarre, contained in this history book.

But their account of what the authors rightly call an 'extraordinary profession' has higher merits – rare quality in books on the film – it is well and wittily written: the authors don't take their subject too seriously, and no one before them has evoked so delicately and delightfully the world of the early film before the industry had developed along monstrous lines. We read of *Bathing Beach* in 1895 (a critic wrote of 'the marvellous realism of an unmistakably genuine ocean') and of little pictures of M. Lumière's home life. 'Beside a pool in the garden, Mme Lumière, in a tussure dress with a polka-dot bodice and a sailor hat tilted over her forehead, fishes for goldfish with a roguish air, under an arbour at the end of the garden, August Lumière and his friend Mr Trewey play piquet and drink beer.' Who could have foreseen from these honest beginnings the epics of Mr de Mille and the publicised malapropisms of Mr Goldwyn? The fair dealers and old clothes men had not yet taken over; the camera was still in the hands of its inventors – cultivated men with quiet domestic imaginations.

As a history of the film, the book contains many errors – the editor corrects some of them in footnotes. A distortion is due to the date (1935) when it was written, before the resurrection of the French film, but most mistakes can be put down to a lack of English (a handicap when writing of talkies) and to the quota limits of the authors' knowledge. The English cinema is completely ignored; the name of the pioneer Friese-Greene seems unknown to patriots who dwell lovingly on Lumière, and the work of Grierson, Balcon, Victor Saville, Hitchcock, receives no notice. Granted that we rank a long way after America, France, Germany and Russia, could not room have been found for us with Norway, Holland and Denmark? As criticism we may sometimes quarrel with the authors' predilection for the artistic and the literary, which makes them value Lang's *Nibelungen* over his *M* (though I hardly think it is the duty of their editor to 'put them right' in dogmatic footnotes), but as a record of the French cinema – and of the *silent* film generally – the book is admirable. Their quick surrealist-trained eye picks out the vivid detail, their comparisons – like that of Abel Gance with Victor Hugo – are illuminating, and they write with candour and *panache* (take their verdict on de Mille's huge cliché-crowned talent – 'He shares with the Italian film-producers the responsibility of having been the spiritual ally of the financiers.')

In some ways it is a sad book – a record of wasted opportunities: of debauched talents; of fine hopes dwindled down to a million dollars, and many readers will feel sympathy for the authors' lament at the end of the classic silent age:

> Even today it is questionable whether it is possible to love the film sincerely unless one knew it in the silent days, in those lost years which are inseperable from the days of one's youth. The Germans, the Russians, the French, the Americans and the Swedes had etched in unforgettable shadows on the screen . . . The faces of men and women had learnt to be expressive in those mute dramas by the aid of no more than an eyelid, the flicker of a glance . . . We demanded emotions and dreams, passion and suffering, and felt no need for words. There were quite ordinary films in which the extinguishing of a lamp at some window, a figure emerging from the pale mist and formless as a drowned body, the bend of a river revealing a road between two rows of trees, furnished us with that unique sensation of shock which a glimpse of the unknown world provides. Those actors, so well adapted to express subtleties, those plots which were of necessity so clear and so brief, may all be forgotten

in the future. But we who witnessed the birth of an art may possibly also have seen it die.

The Spectator (21 October 1938)

4

Film Scripts

The man on the horse takes three days and three nights to cover a hundred miles. A hundred miles is less than one hour's flight by air. The aeroplane flies in a straight line place to place. To the men in the machine, even the great natural barriers look no bigger than toys. But toys which have defeated and killed men since the beginning of civilization.

Flying for great distances over the perils of the earth, and the perils of the sea, with course set and engines running smooth, the pilot moves in security. Below are dangers unknown to the flier – the desert with its mirages and sudden sandstorms: the sea with its unexpected typhoons. From above, the draughtsboard of fields reveals man's cultivation of the earth.

As the aeroplane has conquered natural barriers, so radio has conquered weather. When the airliner leaves port, the pilot knows what the weather will be like several hundred miles away. He sets his course for it, he can fly across the world without ever losing touch with his fellow men. He sees the edge of the sea on the shore of the continent. The air has no boundaries. The aeroplane has won for men the freedom of the air.

Behind the triumph of this achievement is the brain of the scientist and the skill of the engineer.

In this tunnel is created a variety of wind streams which an aeroplane may have to meet in flight. A wing is being tested for drag and lift. On the result of these experiments depends the construction of a new machine.

This is an affair of pencil and paper, and set square: of design and draughtsmanship. New machines are no longer a matter of trial and error. There is no need to wait until one is built before experiment becomes fact.

Three thousand men are building these new flying boats. All over the workshops many thousands of pieces, each designed to give strength without weight, are being put together. Six thousand working joints lie behind this affair of arch and girder, tube and t-piece. Every known principle of mechanics is employed to give rigidity with minimum of bulk.

Four engines of 740 horse power each one fitted with variable pitch air screws so that eighteen tons of metal and load may reach a top speed of two hundred miles an hour through space. From wing tip to wing tip, each boat stretches 114 feet. A London bus could easily pass beneath the wings.

Section by section the great all-metal, double-deck structure takes form.

We have heard of the Wright Brothers in *Kittyhawk* in 1903: of Blériot, first to cross the Channel in 1909: of Allcock and Brown over the Atlantic in 1919: of those who came after: of Scott and Amy Johnson, and Hinkler, of Cobham, Lindbergh, of the Schneider Trophy men and the Russians who crossed the Pole.

In the early morning on the Solent at Southampton, this flying boat is waiting – waiting for thousands of letters which it will carry across the world. Letters from great office buildings, from country villages, from the depressed areas. Letters to brothers and cousins and sons and the man you met at the Coronation. Letters posted as if they were just going next door. Letters to the far ends of the earth.

Twenty-four passengers go on board: professors on their way to Egypt; merchants from Malaya; farmers back to Australia; wives to join husbands; army men going back to India after leave; people going home; people leaving home.

Equipped with the most scientific devices for navigation, with instruments for direction finding and automatic control, the product of the engineer, scientist, and mechanic lies ready.

In the control room, one of the men who will fly this machine through space and time prepares to start up the engines. The petrol cocks are turned. The throttles are opened. One by one the starters are pressed.

As regularly, as casually as the 6.15 carries home the office worker, the flying boat leaves the pontoon and taxis across Southampton Water. Dinner will be served in Rome.

Swiftly across the Channel, the shadow of the airliner sliding across the fields of France, past Paris, heading for the valley of the Rhône. Southward bound, the passengers lunch.

Across the Mediterranean, the ancient centre of the world, where each new form of transport – the elephants of Carthage, the slave-driven boats of Rome – brought invaders and differing civilizations. From the Italy of Caesar to Greece which fought for democracy two thousand and more years ago, the latest invader of all circles down over the roofs of Athens to refuel and pick up passengers in the calm bay of Salamis.

Off again over the Grecian islands. Next stop Egypt, the radio operator keeping in touch with the next port of call.

Towards Alexandria where the air route splits – one line going south to the Cape, the other East to Australia.

Here in Cleopatra's city, the passengers change to airliners and the flying-boat is beached. In the land of the most ancient faith of which we have full record, the oldest hymns we know echoed from the walls in this gigantic temple of Ra, hymns to flight three thousands years ago. In the *Book of the Dead* is written:

> 'Thou comest forth each day over heaven and earth. Thou passest through the heights of heaven. Thy heart hath decreed a day of happiness in thy name of traveller.'

The writer goes on to say:

> 'Thou dost travel over unknown spaces needing millions of years to pass over. Thou passest through them in an instant and thou steerest thy way across the watery abyss to the place which thou lovest. This thou doest in one little moment of time. Thou passest over the sky and every face watcheth thee through thy course. And then thou dost sink down and dost make an end of the hours.'

In the desert, across the sands, fast and skilful riders – the nomads, dwellers in tents – here about to see the new, peaceful invader.

Flying from one dead civilization to another, from Africa to Asia, the airliner carries letters from maiden aunts and homesick children, over the delta of the Nile, the fields of cotton, maize and wheat irrigated by the once sacred river every year. Over Palestine and across the places of the Bible, to the near East to Baghdad – the city of the Forty Thieves, where Haroun-al-Raschid walked with the people at night.

In the heat and glare of the Persian Gulf, some of that splendour remains. The Mohammedan faith retains its stern asceticism on the fishing island of Bahrain, which one hundred years ago was known only to slavers and gun-runners. Even here they await the new machine. As old Abdullah hoists the wind-stocking to give the approaching airliner the direction of the wind, so the pearl fishers hoist the sails of their boats. Often they stay out for two months at a time in the same sea which so often shipwrecked Sinbad.

Used to the strange, deep waters of the Gulf, that rapt face has seen visions stranger than any aeroplane. But the future, dropping out of the sky, hardly disturbs these islanders' routine.

Shoes from Bond Street tread the desert sand, shiny suitcases from Piccadilly reflect the glare of an Arabian sun. Refreshment for the travellers. Time to talk with strangers and have tea. To exchange news and to leave behind the paper only three days old. For the captain, news of the weather, of the westbound service. For the machine, oil and petrol. A small army of mechanics – some white, some dark – test engines, adjust small matters, a bolt here, a nut there.

The petrol tanks are filled. Four hundred-odd gallons checked by the agent's clerk. New mail is loaded. The flight clerk has his papers. The crew is refreshed.

Only the fisherman is left behind, with Allah and his Prophet and the seven peaks that guard the desert.

Eastward bound towards the Gulf of Oman. Like the shadow beneath, the radio operator keeps in constant touch with the earth telling them at the next night stop how many beds are needed, what special dishes might be needed in flight, sending a message to a friend.

In the airliner, the passengers play games, plot their course on maps, write letters home, while beneath them passes the coast of Baluchistan.

Over the globe, where India itself is ahead over the turn of the turning earth. They are carried across desert and sea to the land of 352 million workers, with their eight separate religions and 118 ruling princes.

To the land of the Lake Palace, where feudal rulers and Congress politicians govern side by side.

Letters to Indian civil servants; letters to the government in New Delhi; letters to the merchant in his open-fronted shop; letters to the contractor who uses the cheapest power there is, a power which is cheaper than the truck, cheaper than the tip, cheaper than the pulley, cheaper than the crane; letters to the rajah from his son at Oxford. Carried right across India, weather reports coming in from Karachi and then from Delhi.

Over the sacred places of the Ganges. Across a strip of the Bay of Bengal to Burma. Above the jungles of the Iriwadi and Rangoon. Over the gold-plated patella called Shwe Dagan.

Letters to the men cutting teak in the jungle on the borders of Siam and Burma. On over the unseen animals of jungle and swamp.

To Bangkok, city of gorgeous palaces and temples dedicated to Buddha, guarded by strange, fierce images. A place for palace retreats where the Asian and European lived side by side. A long history of sudden fortune, and then treachery and torture.

Here is the airport, with mechanics and all the paraphernalia of flying, schedules, timetables, tickets.

From Bangkok came the men who sacked an older, more magnificent city – Angkor – the great stone capital of the Khmers, hidden for centuries in the jungle. The jungle is still there, its roots twisting and gripping the carved stone temples. The trees have conquered, as the Siamese conquered the Khmers.

Only the stone effigies of the gods remain, staring out across the jungle, sentinels of a dead civilization, smiling as man's newest triumph passes across the sky.

Follow the shadow along the Malay Peninsula. Over Penang, where the branch Imperial Line flies out to Hong Kong.

The 'Atalanta' coming in at dusk to Singapore.

Letters to Chinese scouts; letters to people in rickshaws; letters to a centre of modern commerce in the middle of history, where ships came in by every trade route across the sea; letters of commerce to men trading in the products of the East – pineapples, tin, rubber, rice.

Singapore, where again passengers change to other machines. Away over Sumatra and the Java Sea to the Dutch East Indies . . .

The Future's in the Air (GB, Strand Films, 1937) Produced by Paul Rotha. Dir: Alexander Shaw. Commentary: Graham Greene. Photography: George Noble. Music: William Alwyn and Raymond Bennell. Spoken: Ivan Scott. [The British Film Institute holds what appears to be the only known extant copy of this film and this, sadly, is incomplete. The above text is, therefore, that of the first three reels only. Even with the kind assistance of staff at the BFI Archive, numerous air and postal museums, and Paul Rotha's estate, I have been unable to unearth a manuscript of the commentary.]

The New Britain

November 1918 – the end of the 1914–18 war. Three hundred and sixty-three thousand German prisoners, 6,400 captured German guns. Amongst the demobilised German soldiers was a corporal – his name was Hitler. Then Britain turned to build a new world. Over our one million dead we raised this colossal monument: a new architecture for our people: new university buildings and new seats of Government: new shops of glass and steel: new factories and power stations of brick and stone: we thought we had raised a monument more lasting than brass.

In the mountains of Scotland and Wales, valleys were flooded: lakes were made over night: water for electricity, water for the huge grid of pylons, to light lamps in the furthest corners of Britain.

We built new highways linking country to city, and the city to the sea. We built faster and faster trains, new streamlined expresses travelling at 80 miles-an-hour. Coming out of the long tunnel of war we thought the way was clear. Nature couldn't stop us – we drove a road under the Mersey, two and a half miles long.

We were the bridge builders from Menai to Sydney: we built the longest bridge in Britain over the Tyne at Newcastle. Across the Menai Straits, Thomas Telford's graceful bridge was strengthened for today's traffic. Across the Tees, we built the largest lift bridge in the world. Under the great central span the ships went by, busy with peace.

We built new docks and harbours. We guarded the sea for others as well as ourselves. Above the seven seas we showed our wings across the world in peace.

There were more achievements than we can remember now, linking man with man: telephones brought news, change, progress to the remotest villages.

There was airmail to the Empire for three-halfpence: letters to Africa and India costing no more than a letter to a man in the next street. There was a radio to Australia girdling the earth in six seconds. The perforated slip passing from the typewriter through the transmitter, direct across the world to Sydney. So small the world, we thought we had to live in peace.

London calling. We gave entertainment to millions for a few pence per week. This land of such dear souls, this dear, dear land. Dear for her reputation through the world.

We led the world in television – we picked faces out of the air to show on a screen.

It was for ordinary people that all these things were done – for you and I and the Smith family next door. Their happiness was the prize. We were building for a free people.

Maybe Mr Smith was a foreman in one of the new factories. There was light and cleanliness. His factory was only one of the thousands where the new employer and the new employee worked together for the common good. Perhaps his daughter worked there too as a stenographer, in the large airy office.

There were so many thousands of families like this – with life ahead for all of them and a future that was to be happier day by day.

When Mrs Smith went shopping, all the world served her with its foods. Fruit from South Africa, fish from the North Sea, meat from New Zealand, eggs and butter from Scandinavia. These were not the rich: they were just any family, living perhaps on one of the new housing estates. We built four million of these houses after the last war. Electricity lightened their work. At the touch of a switch they had heat, they had light, they had music, they had news of all the world.

This morning President von Hindenberg received Herr Hitler, leader of the National Socialist German Workers' Party and appointed him Chancellor of the Reich.

Life was ahead. We had a peaceful revolution here. We each of us paid our share for the new social services which looked after our people from birth to old age. There were infant welfare centres and day nurseries where the children were taught nothing but how to be happy. The finest doctors looked after their health; we gave our money ungrudgingly for stethoscopes not guns. We were building inhabitants for the brave new world.

The sky was the limit and life was ahead. In the council school and the technical college our children were prepared for peace: their only war was to be against the germ, the jerry-built building and the unjust law. Lack of money was no longer going to be a bar to any talent. For we had had our revolution, so quietly that we hardly noticed it.

It was not all work. We could laugh in Britain, sport was still a game. Our spare time was our own; we could play what we liked in our peoples' clubs.

And for our children we planned a better world yet; a world of laughter, peace, security. We read a new world in the untroubled breath, and on the contented mouth: no nightmare rode their sleep.

We will not let their future be ruined. The spirit of England will fight their battle, the spirit bred behind the long coastline and among quiet fields, simple, unboastful and unbreakable.

The New Britain (GB, 1941, Strand Films) Produced by Alexander Shaw for the Ministry of Information. Dir: Ralph Keene. Scenario: Reg Groves. Running commentary: Graham Greene. Commentator: Neal Ardan. Music: William Alwyn. Musical Director: Muir Mathieson. Camera: Charles Marlborough.

5

Interviews & Lectures

The Cinema

I have just seen two films – *Saratoga* and *The Son of the Sheikh*. One really begins to feel that the cinema has got a history when it's so full of ghosts. Miss Jean Harlow walking and speaking after death, and in the other film Rudolph Valentino with his sensitive dago face trying to express the pulsating passions, the enormous emotional drama, of fifteen years ago.

Here in the Valentino picture we have but a painting they would call a Primitive – made oddly enough by Mr Ernst Lubitsch. You go to laugh, as perhaps the cultured worldly wise Italian of the Renaissance may have smiled a little at his own Primitives when taste turned another way – but there isn't really so very much to laugh at. Over Valentino's acting now, of course, you feel the shadow of that grotesque funeral, the lying in state and the hysterical mob and the mysterious woman in a black veil kneeling at the tomb. It is like a dream from Mr Dunne's *Experiment with Time*. Past and future are hopelessly intermingled. The man is moving on the screen and at the same time he is dead and magnificently and absurdly entombed. No acting can quite survive the presence of that awful and simultaneous future.

The lustrous eyes narrow to slits, the too gentle mouth yearns and nuzzles over this blonde dancing girl, the world's darling hangs by the wrists for the torturers. 'My young lion,' the villain sneers in a caption, 'your people would gladly pay ten thousand francs to look at your face again.' Why they paid more than a million dollars and still pay in small and draughty picture-houses: I paid myself and found it well worth while.

It may be sentiment – because all this terrific drama in the desert, superhuman punishments and magnificent hatreds, happened a long time ago – but this Primitive seemed to me to have virtues I couldn't find in the more chic, the glossier, up-to-the-minute products, *Saratoga, For You Alone, A Castle in Flanders*, not such a bad crop, too, of average films. There is a kind of balletic quality in this old silent picture: a story of the barest simplicity, emotions which have only a poetic relationship to what we feel ourselves, and the whole of the film is movement. There was a time when many of us thought the talkies were going to be the end of true cinema. It may seem silly now, but if you see this film you will realise why we felt that. There is an inexpressible charm in the silence: the characters fighting, loving, hating, move to music only, the music probably of one rather out of tune piano: their gestures are ritualised. It is all a kind of dance. I am told that some women dancers in India can hold you with the play of their eyelashes alone: they sit in stillness except for their enamelled lashes moving to the music. There is a little of that quality in Valentino: his face is infinitely more expressive than the modern hero's – Mr Clark Gable's or Mr Robert Taylor's. There is a love scene in this picture, the man and woman sitting among some ruins in the desert, which goes on for several minutes without, of course, a word spoken: a few captions, that's all. It's a long time on the screen – Mr Gable and Miss Harlow wouldn't try to hold us, even with speech, that long. But Valentino has to, dancing like the Indian woman with his eyes alone.

I suppose the Left Book Club would dismiss this film as escapist: but that is its merit. Nobody can pretend for a moment that it bears any relation whatever to life. Popular and vulgar though it may be, it is art or nothing. The trouble with most films now is that they pay lip service to life. People talk, you see, and that's like life: soon they will be coloured and that's a bit more like life: and then they will be stereoscopic. But somehow life as we know it seeps away – and what's left is neither fish nor fowl. We look in vain for pictures with a real appeal to the huge audiences of the cinema, for a Dickens of the screen.

Those films – *Saratoga, For You Alone* and *A Castle in Flanders*, a German film, are meant to be, and for all I know are, popular films. But they aren't popular in the sense that Dickens was popular. They don't emerge out of life. Dickens' account of the blacking factory came out of ordinary life like some huge hippopotamus out of a primeval river, dripping and matted with the rank water and the weeds as well as the flowers, Little Nell as well as Mr Micawber sticking to his flank, smelling of his environment. People didn't in those days say: 'We know all that in our own lives. We want to be taken out of ourselves.' They enjoyed submerging with him in the common life.

Saratoga has a little of that quality, rough and common and exciting – it is about bookies and yearling sales and stud farms and racing specials, full of good interesting documentary detail – and within limits it's a very good film. It's a tough and funny: people behave up to a point – I'll come to that point later – like human beings, unscrupulously: Mr Edward G. Robinson's a good bookie; Miss Harlow gives one of her best blonde bombshell performances, and if you doubt whether that's acting remember she was a Vassar girl which is I believe America's equivalent of Cheltenham Ladies' College.

For You Alone too, has a not unpromising subject: the foreign singer whose permit to stay in America has expired and who has to marry a man – she buys him in a Mexican lock-up – to get back. What an interesting seedy course the story might have taken. Oh what an agreeably crazy course, into such wild fantasies the story might have developed. How we might have graduated in the technique of blackmail.

Indeed it *is* supposed to be a crazy comedy, but they won't let us do without the tenderest love even in a crazy comedy, though the trouble may be Miss Moore herself. Miss Moore is a fine singer, but as a personality, even when they dress her in long trousers and make her sing 'Minnie the Moocher' she is devastatingly sensible. All the same – if you aren't seeking either life or an ivory tower – this will amuse you – if it doesn't annoy you. It was written – though you'd never guess this – by the same man as *Mr Deeds*.

A Castle in Flanders begins with British officers in a camp near Ypres listening to a record of a woman singing and one, under the nervous discipline, ascesticism and strain of war, pledging his devotion. The German director is remarkably successful in conveying our pipe-smoking romanticism, though as with all these films life escapes after a reel or two and the studio love story takes its place.

A Castle in Flanders has some good moments in a dark wet post-war Ypres when another great singer – Miss Marta Eggerth this time – arrives for a concert and finds the only good hotel is mysteriously booked. The atmosphere here is excellent: rain and darkness and the small strange town: the awful hotel dining hall, the leering porter, one listens for what to the solitary person is the most sinister of continental sounds – the gurgle in the water pipes. The porter directs her to a neighbouring castle where guests are sometimes taken – so he says – and there by the huge fireplace in an old British uniform is the officer (reportedly missing) we last saw at zero hour, an ambitious and freezing presence. Now I can believe in ghosts: I can believe that there must be hauntings after horrors: and that a man dead in those violent days might retain in the spirit the crazy desire for a voice he'd heard in wax just before death. This part of the film is chilling and impressive, but then the studio version of life breaks in. This is no ghost, but just another great lover: a mysterious disgrace: 'Oh no, we never mentioned him' making good in Australia and all the rest of it. In all these pictures, as I have said, life escapes after a reel or two; and the love story takes its place: the bookie in *Saratoga* is after all only cheating for love: Miss Harlow cheats too, but it's for love, and the great singer, who married to get into America, falls with hideous inevitability in love with her husband.

You have the sense that the writers and directors have for years ceased to have contact with ordinary life. They can remember no blacking factory in their childhood as Dickens could.

For life you must go to the documentary movement, to Mr Paul Rotha's *Today We Live*, for example, a picture of unemployment and the work of the National Council for Social Service: or to Mr Cavalcanti's *We Live in Two Worlds*, a film about Switzerland, about international communications in a country hemmed in by frontiers, a picture beautifully shot and excitingly cut, though a little spoilt by Mr J.B. Priestley's vague commentary and the fact that Mr Priestley's face is plugged as insistently as a film star's without the same excuse.

Mr Rotha's picture: of tenements worming out to the edge of

slag heaps, of the hoarded cigarette ends, the group at the street corner, the little hopeless gatherings in cafés – is deeply impressive. The Wall Street Crash, beggars selling matches, city men in top hats, all contribute to the imagery of this film. The Welsh miners go singing down the kerb and their voices are laid over deserted streets and silent pits, the great abandoned furnaces, the slopes where unemployed men scrabble for surface coal. The actors are the men themselves, miners from the Rhondda Valley, officials of the National Council of Social Service.

But what I want to leave in your mind is the idea that here in the small documentary companies are directors still living the common life, getting imaginative material in the street and the house next door: not shut away with so many hundred pounds a week in huge muted chromium offices, trying to remember how people lived in the days when they lived too, trying to remember the gas burner and the coffee essence and the week's notice, with the memory fading out as the secretary pads across the pile so that they fall back with a sigh – on just eternal love.

Broadcast on the BBC National Service (29 August 1937)

The Spanish Talks

[Extracts from the talks given by Graham Greene for the BBC Spanish Service in 1941.]

Bernard Shaw, at the age of 84, has just made a film of his *Major Barbara*. There is however a difference that we note in wartime that we did not feel in peacetime. Only someone who believes in God can blaspheme; only a man who, like Cervantes, believes in chivalry can laugh at Don Quixote, and we perceive sadly that Shaw doesn't believe in anything. So the cinema where *Major Barbara* is showing is almost always empty, and the theatre where we laugh at the new Home Guard, at colonels, at policemen, at mischevious child evacuees and women in uniform – is always full.

At any rate *Major Barbara* shows that the British war film industry can produce interesting works, war or no war. And enjoyable works, too, like *Quiet Wedding* by Anthony Asquith, in which we also laugh at ourselves – at the seriousness of life in the country, at parish curates, at charity tombolas and at village cricket matches. There is a new detective comedy *Inspector Hornleigh Goes To It* in which our incomparable comic actor Gordon Harker (without equal in the portrayal of low life characters in the seedier parts of London), joins the army to search out and capture supposed traitors. We wouldn't be able to laugh so noisily and so heartily if we were really a people that would produce the Quisling type.

There is no doubt that the most important film which is being shown is an American film, *The Ramparts We Watch* (The Battle of the Atlantic does not deprive us from receiving a rounded assortment of the latest films from Hollywood, such that in the West End one can see the same films as on Broadway). *The Ramparts We Watch* is a historical account of the last war made from newsreels of that time with certain dramatized scenes. It traces the change of opinion in the United States between 1914 and 1917: the gradual change from the policy that was being followed (the policy of isolation), to the mobilization of industry and men, to the anger brought about by the German submarine campaign, and finally to involvement in the war with torrents of men and machines.

Throughout the film the American commentator underlines the parallel between that time and the present – the victories that led nowhere and the high sounding German communiqués, 'Our forces have advanced all along the front'. But perhaps the greatest attraction of the film is that it revives before our eyes images of the dead and the disappeared – images that time had given a romantic tinge as it does to ruins. There is the Kaiser, among his generals still believing that they are going to win the war, and walking with those peculiar short steps of the early film. There is old Franz Josef, Emperor of Austria, laboriously climbing into his car amongst feathers and medals, he is linked inseperably to the disaster, just like the Duce today. One man arrests our attention, with his broad, curved shoulders, and the teasing smile of the undismayed realist who knows what's really happening. He is the First Lord of the Admiralty, Mr Winston Churchill.

26 April 1941

Major Barbara (GB, Gabriel Pascal, 1941) Directors: Gabriel Pascal, Harold French, David Lean. Cast: Wendy Hiller, Rex Harrison, Robert Morley, Robert Newton, Marie Lohr, Emlyn Williams, Sybil Thorndike, Deborah Kerr, David Tree, Felix Aylmer, Penelope Dudley Ward, Walter Hudd, Donald Calthrop.

Quiet Wedding (GB, Paramount/Conqueror, 1940) Dir.: Anthony Asquith. Cast: Margaret Lockwood, Derek Farr, A.E. Matthews, Marjorie Fielding, Athene Seyler, Peggy Ashcroft, Margaretta Scott, Frank Cellier, Roland Culver, Jean Cadell, David Tomlinson, Bernard Miles.

Inspector Hornleigh Goes To It (GB, Twentieth-Century Fox, 1940) Dir.: Walter Forde. Cast: Gordon Harker, Alastair Sim, Phyllis Calvert, Edward Chapman, Charles Oliver, Raymond Huntley, Percy Walsh, David Horne, Peter Gawthorne.

The Ramparts We Watch (USA, RKO, 1940) Dir.: Louis de Rochemont.

★

The best North American film – seeing that the latest one of the Marx Brothers didn't have the success which was expected – is *The Lady Eve* – an excellent comedy in which the son of a millionaire falls in love with the daughter of a professional card player. The plot has nothing to do with the war, but I believe that a German in the auditorium would note with surprise that the public laughed deafeningly at the scene where a waiter picked up a clothes brush from the floor, put it to his upper lip, lifted up his arm and began to shriek hysterically. He would probably not be surprised that the North Americans would believe that his Führer is a comic character, but the fact that Londoners also believe this is something that a German who feels great respect for a policy of terror and material successes, would not be able to understand. The Spanish, having seen the triumph and fall of a Napoleon would understand it perfectly.

There is a poem in the new poetry book that has just been published by the Irish writer Lord Dunsany, in which is expressed very well the English point of view; he tells of the German victories one by one, but each verse finishes with the same refrain: 'The Kaiser needs a footman; each day Hitler gets closer to Doorn'.

Apart from *The Lady Eve*, lately the best films have been English. Apparently the war has helped our studios by stopping directors wasting money on complicated sets and costly North American stars. In London the most successful of all is the film based on the novel of H.G. Wells entitled *Kipps*.

28 May 1941

The Big Store (USA, MGM, 1941) Dir.: Charles Reisner. Cast: The Marx Brothers, Margaret Dumont, Douglass Dumbrille, Tony Martin, Virginia Grey, Virginia O'Brien, Henry Armetta.

The Lady Eve, (USA, Paramount, 1941) Dir.: Preston Sturges. Cast: Henry Fonda, Barbara Stanwyck, Charles Coburn, Eugene Pallette, William Demarest, Eric Blore, Melville Cooper, Martha O'Driscoll, Janet Beecher, Robert Greig, Jimmy Conlin, Luis Alberni.

Kipps (GB, Twentieth-Century Fox, 1941) Dir.: Carol Reed. Cast: Michael Redgrave, Phyllis Calvert, Diana Wynyard, Arthur Riscoe, Max Adrian, Helen Haye, Michael Wilding, Lloyd Pearson, Edward Rigby, Hermione Baddeley, Frank Pettingwell, Beatrice Varley, Kathleen Harrison, Felix Aylmer.

★

Another of the films that we have seen in London is about the sinking of the *Bismarck*. The battle photographs were taken by an official on one of the ships that were following her; in them we can see the shells of the *Bismarck*, missing their targets as the ship sailed imperiously towards its end. We see the ships that surround it and their crews tell the camera of their experiences; the impassive black cat of the aircraft carrier *Victorious* did not lose any of its seven lives. The aviator who fired the first torpedo, the lookout who spied the enemy first, the captain of the *Norfolk* who stalked the *Bismarck* throughout its voyage, without losing it from view, all tell us their stories.

All British warships carry on their forecastle plaques with the names of the battles in which they have fought, and on the *Rodney* we see them placing a plaque with the name of the *Bismarck*. A little above it there is written another glorious memory: *Sebastopol* 1854.

18 June 1941

★

Marlene Dietrich, Deanna Durbin, Vivien Leigh, Mickey Mouse, Joan Crawford and other less well-known artists have appeared recently on the screens in London, but the standard of their films has not been on the whole very high. Deanna Durbin has been filmed in her first love scene, Joan Crawford has appeared supposedly as a criminal with her face disfigured, Mickey Mouse has been incorporated into the Philadelphia Orchestra, and Marlene Dietrich has acted for the first time under the orders of director René Clair. Less extraordinary perhaps is the performance of Vivien Leigh and Laurence Olivier in their respective roles of Lady Hamilton and Nelson.

We English have a soft spot for Nelson, it even extends to liking his monstrous statue in Trafalgar Square, but his love life interests us less than it does the movie-makers. In this film one learns nothing about Nelson as the great seaman who defeated the strongest power in Europe, and let us not forget that although ten years passed before Napoleon was eliminated from the face of Europe, his fate was written long before the last cannonball of the Battle of Waterloo was fired. The English people have not forgotten this, but apparently the movie-makers have.

Marlene Dietrich has appeared in a new film *The Flame of New Orleans*, a film that will be presented to the Spanish-speaking public under the title of *La Mujer Manda* (*The Woman Commands*). If one leaves out the fact that the staging and costumes have been planned more cleverly than before, one would scarcely know that she has changed director; with gently swaying figure and husky voice, she plays the temptress and another is tempted, the ingredients are the same as always. Marlene looks as young as when she brought to life *The Blue Angel*, in those days when Germany made real films, and not simply pieces of propaganda.

Another expatriate, Herr Fritz Lang, is making films in Hollywood, and recently we have had the chance to see his *Western Union*, entitled *Espiritu De Conquista* (*Spirit of Conquest*) in Spanish. It is a good film on an old theme, with the traditional Red Indians and cavalry galloping through expansive prairies firing their rifles from horseback etc. Now we are waiting impatiently for what America considers to be his best film. It is called *Man Hunt*, and in it an Englishman who is a great hunter tries to capture the Führer with the same tenacity and exhilaration with which he used to hunt lions.

Of course it is a fantasy film, but the American newspapers have seen a symbolic value in it, now that such a large number of young Englishmen fly over Germany every night following, so to speak, the scent of the Führer. There is also another film on this subject called *Target for Tonight*, but before I talk about it, I have to tell you something rather sad about Walt Disney.

Disney, who for years has been a true artist without knowing it, has consciously become intellectual in his latest film, *Fantasia*. This film, which lasts almost two hours, comprises of visual accompaniment to musical compositions such as the *Toccata and Fugue in D Minor* by Bach, Stravinsky's *Rite of Spring* and Beethoven's *Pastoral Symphony* amongst others. It has earned as much criticism as approval. To illustrate Beethoven with a romantic ballet of centaurs and a comic Pegasus, is almost aesthetic blasphemy. The film has scenes of great beauty – if one manages to forget the music that has been joined to the dainty and capricious fantasies of Disney. The world of Disney is a world of children's storybooks, in which flowers comb their coloured petals, and pale nymphs contemplate their languidness reflected in translucent fountains, and scenes of horror are no more than childish dreams. It was without doubt a mistake to want to connect such a world with the mature imaginations of Bach and Beethoven.

One of the curious experiences of war-time London is to contrast the fantasy of Disney with the most notable success of the year, the film *Target for Tonight* – a documentary on the activities of bombers of the Royal Air Force, from the moment when a reconnaissance plane drops a parcel of photographs by parachute on to the base until the last bomber lands safely on the runway after leaving the petrol storage facility at Freihausen in flames. Dreadful as it may seem, this and not the world of Disney, is the world that is more familiar to us nowadays, in spite of the fact that a few years ago such a world would have seemed as fantastic to us as Disney's enormous whales and fantasy sharks. Disney's standard of nightmare has disappeared to be changed into a nightmare that is the most natural thing in the world, as these men from the base commander down to the lowest technician carry out their difficult and dangerous job in daily routine like shop or office workers. In the film we watch their daily life as it is, with nothing fictitious to adorn or disfigure it.

The reconnaissance photos are developed in an underground room, and examined in detail by experts: 'This is really interesting' is the only comment. While the raid is being planned ground crew see to the preparation of the aircraft and make wagers on what tonight's target will be. Meteorological reports are received and all the required navigational information is prepared. Kiel is the main target, but the destruction of the new petrol stores at Freihausen is the task assigned to the squadron that we will follow.

The crews are briefed on every detail that can help them with their work and are given final instructions. 'A delayed action bomb should be included in every bomb load,' it is ordered. We go with the pilots and hear their conversations as they equip themselves, we follow them in the trucks that take them to the runway. This is everyday routine that has been repeated hundreds of times now. Everything is natural, there is none of the bombastic language, the bragging, and the threats that characterize the German film *Baptism of Fire*. What we see is no more than a technical exercise, just as the destruction of the *Graf Spee* was for its pursuers, and one realizes that the values of our naval tradition are embodied in the new service too, there is no sign of excitation, nor of conceited boastfulness. The only menace that is heard is in the humorous exclamation of one of the pilots on take-off, 'Freihausen, here we come.' In this plane we fly above the scattered Arctic clouds, we descend breaking through them over the target, and while flak comes towards us with the phosphorescent froth of a great wave, we release the bombs and contemplate the rising flames of the burning petrol stores. This film has had an enormous success and its release has coincided with the notable change in the air war, with our growing supremacy extending day and night further and further across the Channel.

14 August 1941

Nice Girl? (USA, Universal, 1941) Dir.: William A. Seiter. Cast: Deanna Durbin, Franchot Tone, Robert Stack, Walter Brennan, Robert Benchley, Helen Broderick, Ann Gillis.

A Woman's Face (USA, MGM, 1941) Dir.: George Cukor. Cast: Joan Crawford, Melvyn Douglas, Conrad Veidt, Osa Massen, Reginald Owen, Albert Bassermann, Marjorie Main, Donald Meek, Connie Gilchrist.

Lady Hamilton (GB, London Films, 1941) Dir.: Alexander Korda. Cast: Laurence Olivier, Vivien Leigh, Gladys Cooper, Alan Mowbray, Sara Allgood, Henry Wilcoxon, Halliwell Hobbes. (US title: *That Hamilton Woman*)

The Flame of New Orleans (USA, Universal, 1941) Dir.: René Clair. Cast: Marlene Dietrich, Roland Young, Bruce Cabot, Mischa Auer, Andy Devine, Frank Jenks, Eddie Quinlan, Laura Hope Crews, Franklin Pangborn.

Western Union (USA, Twentieth-Century Fox, 1941) Dir.: Fritz Lang. Cast: Randolph Scott, Robert Young, Dean Jagger, Virginia Gilmore, Slim Summerville, John Carradine, Chill Wills, Barton MacLane.

Man Hunt (USA, Twentieth-Gentury Fox, 1941) Dir.: Fritz Lang. Cast: Walter Pidgeon, Joan Bennett, George Sanders, John Carradine, Roddy McDowall, Ludwig Stossel, Heather Thatcher, Frederick Worlock.

Target for Tonight (GB, Crown Film Unit, 1941) Dir.: Harry Watt.

Fantasia (USA, Walt Disney, 1941) Supervising director: Ben Sharpsteen. Cast: Leopold Stokowski, the Philadelphia Orchestra, Deems Taylor.

THE SCREENWRITER

Q. *Do you prefer to work from original material, or from adaptations of either your own work or that of other writers?*

A. Apart from my disastrous first script of a John Galsworthy short story, and a later script of Shaw's *St Joan* (filmed in 1957, directed by Otto Preminger), my screenwriting has been with either original material or adaptations of my own novels or stories. I certainly prefer to work, as with *The Third Man* (1949, directed by Sir Carol Reed), from original material, or from a short story. Condensation is always dangerous, while expansion is a form of creation.

Q. *How full a script do you prepare?*

A. I begin with a treatment containing a good deal of the dialogue. In fact the published version of *The Third Man* was the treatment for the film. The treatment to my mind has to create the characters and not simply recount the story. I have only once had to write a full shooting script, for *Brighton Rock* (1947, directed by John Boulting). My work finishes with the completed screenplay. This may very well contain suggestions for camera angles, etc., but to my mind for the author to attempt a full shooting script is a waste of time. This is the job of the director.

Q. *Do you work closely with the director in the early stages?*

A. I work closely with the director from the very beginning. After the first period of discussion I usually go away to work by myself on certain sections and then bring them back for further discussion. How often the consultations with the director take place is a matter of geography. When I worked with Carol Reed on *Our Man in Havana* we occupied two bedrooms in the same hotel in Brighton with a sitting-room in between for the secretary, and I passed my material through the secretary to Carol and we discussed matters at lunchtime. This degree of closeness is not always possible.

Q. *Do you spend much time on the set during shooting?*

A. It varies a great deal. With *Our Man in Havana* I spent about ten days at the beginning, but this was less for the sake of the script than to help with the political situation, as Castro's government had only been in power for four months. Of course, I had already done a reconnaissance with Carol Reed to Havana to discuss possible settings. In the case of *The Comedians* (1967, directed by Peter Glenville) I spent two weeks in Dahomey and I visited the studios occasionally in Nice and Paris, but this was mainly if not entirely for my own satisfaction. We had made the script, as we believed, sufficiently watertight to require no changes, but a screenwriter learns a great deal from watching the actual shooting.

Q. *Do you know who is to play the leading parts before you start work, and does this affect your treatment of a story – in the case of an adaptation, for instance?*

A. In almost all cases I have known who was to play the lead, but I don't think I have ever altered the emphasis of a film to fit the star. It usually happens the other way round; one chooses the star to fit the film.

Q. *How long, on a rough average, does it take you to prepare a script?*

A. It's difficult to say. I once did a rough job – *St Joan* – in six weeks, but I would say that four to six months were required after the preliminary discussions and after the general line has been agreed.

from *The Making of Feature Films: A Guide* by Ivan Butler (Pelican, 1971)

Graham Greene: On the Screen

Q. *When did you become interested in the cinema?*

A. At Oxford, in the days of silent films. There was a review, long since defunct, called *Close Up* which dealt with all the major directors of the time. [He showed me a bound volume.] Besides writing film criticism in the 1930s, I did two film scripts around 1937. One of them, *The Green Cockatoo*, was terrible.

Q. *In 1936 you contributed an article to a collection of essays called* Footnotes to the Film, *in which you said: 'The cinema has got to appeal to millions; we have got to accept its popularity as a virtue, not turn away from it as a vice. The novelist may write for a few thousand readers, but the film artist must work for millions.' You added in 1939 in your column in* The Spectator: *'A film with a severely limited appeal must be – to that extent – a bad film.'*

A. I think I should stand by that. By limited appeal, I mean a flop. A good film is seldom a complete flop. Whereas a book can be very good and still be a flop.

Q. *Do you agree with those of your critics who feel that your narrative style has been affected by your script writing for the screen?*

A. I don't think my style as a writer has been influenced by my work for the cinema. *It's a Battlefield* was intentionally based on film technique, and it was written before I did any film scripts. It is my only deliberate attempt to tell a story in cinematic terms, and it is one of the few which I have written that has ever been filmed.

Q. *In your preface to* Three Plays by Graham Greene *you describe the scriptwriter as a 'forgotten man' once a film goes into production: 'When the lines are at last spoken on the studio-floor' the scriptwriter 'is not there to criticize or alter . . . My own experience with scriptwriting has been fortunate and happy, and yet with what relief I have gone back to the privacy of a room in which I bear the full responsibility for failure.'*

A. Film is not mainly dialogue as is a stage play. It is impossible for the screenwriter to have the technical knowledge to control the filming of his script. This is a fact, not a complaint. I have been fortunate in my work for the screen. My scripts have not often been altered. I haven't suffered much in that way.

Q. *You have written the script for five of your own stories:* Brighton Rock (*1947*), The Fallen Idol (*1948*), The Third Man (*1949*), Our Man in Havana (*1959*), and The Comedians (*1967*). *How did you proceed in making adaptations of these works for the screen?*

A. My approach is to write a treatment of the story which is then turned into a script. I cannot write the kind of treatment that is in the historical present. I write the treatment like a novel. What today is known as the novel of *The Third Man* was really the treatment I did before writing the script. That is why I say in the preface to the published version that it was not written to be read, but only to be seen.

Q. *What is your favourite among the scripts which you have done?*

A. *The Fallen Idol* is my favourite screen work because it is more a writer's film than a director's. *The Third Man*, though it was more popular because of the song, 'The Third Man Theme', is mostly action with only sketched characters. It was fun doing, but there is more of the writer in *The Fallen Idol*.

Q. *In some of the screen versions of your fiction, the ending of the story has been significantly altered. For example,* Brighton Rock *(which was called* Young Scarface *in the* US*): after the death of the gangster Pinkie, Rose goes home to play the record which he made for her at the amusement park. She thinks that it will be a declaration of his love for her but the reader knows that it is a declaration of hatred. In the film the needle of the gramophone sticks and the camera pans up to a crucifix. Did your collaborator on the screenplay, Terence Rattigan, provide this ending?*

A. Terence Rattigan wrote a treatment of a few pages with quite a different ending which was not used: the script was not really a collaboration. I like the ending of the film and I am completely guilty. I have complete justification for the needle sticking on the gramophone record: I knew the distributors would not accept the ghastly ending of the book. I also knew that thinking people would realize that one day Rose would move the needle beyond the crack and thus get to the shock with which the book ends. The ghastly outcome was only delayed. It was the director's idea to pan up to the crucifix on the wall. This gave the impression that the needle stuck miraculously. Earlier in the film Pinkie had tried to destroy the record but was interrupted by Rose. This explains the crack in the record: there is nothing miraculous about it.

Q. *Do you retain much of your original dialogue when you adapt your own fiction to the screen?*

A. I use actual dialogue from the novel when it seems to fit. Often in the first version of the script a great deal of the original dialogue is kept. But it is slowly whittled away, in order to reduce the dialogue as much as possible. What has the right rhythm in the book because of the surrounding paragraphs may seem unreal on the screen and must be modified. Dialogue in fiction must have the appearance of reality, without having to be real, while on the screen the camera emphasizes the reality of the situation: you have to be closer in a film to real-life conversation in order that the dialogue will match the realistic settings.

Q. *TV critic Jack Gould wrote of the 1967 Laurence Olivier version of* The Power and the Glory *(which was released in Europe as a commercial film) that the 'omission of the climax of Mr Greene's novel*

– the arrival of the new priest to replace the cleric who had just perished before the firing squad – was especially unfortunate.' Although John Ford's 1947 film of the same novel, called The Fugitive, *departed greatly from the book, that film did at least have the shadow of the new priest falling across the doorway.*

A. More than the shadow of the priest should be there. It is important to have the dialogue of the new priest with the child to show the change of mind in the child towards the dead priest, whom he did not respect until his death, and also to indicate that the Church goes on.

Q. *Father John Burke, the technical adviser for the film of* The Heart of the Matter *(1953) has told me that against his advice the suicide of the policeman Major Scobie was greatly obscured in the film's ending because the film makers thought Catholics would object to a Catholic taking his own life. Instead Scobie is killed trying to break up a street brawl.*

A. I tried to persuade the company to leave it in. Trevor Howard, who played Scobie, and who is an intelligent actor, said he would do a re-take of the ending without charge. I even figured out a way of doing it without Trevor Howard: I wanted to show Scobie writing a suicide note with the gun at hand, thus making it clear that he intended to take his own life. At that moment he would be called away to the police action and be killed, apparently with the intention of suicide in his mind. I disclaim the ending of the film as it is. At any rate, I do not like the novel, and have never re-read it.

Q. *I have often wondered why films like* The Heart of the Matter, *which include peculiarly Catholic concepts like the sacreligious reception of Holy Communion, appeal to the large non-Catholic audience.*

A. For the same reason that they seem to buy the books on which the films are based. Any author writing strictly for a Catholic audience would not reach a large public. It goes back to what I said in the *Footnotes to the Film* essay which you mentioned earlier: if you excite your audience first, you can put over what you will of horror, suffering, truth. This is still true and applies to the novel as well as to the film. By exciting the audience I mean getting them involved in the story. Once they are involved they will accept the thing as you present it.

Q. *You once were quoted as saying, with reference to the controversy over the meaning of* The Heart of the Matter*: 'I wrote a book about a man who goes to hell* - Brighton Rock – *another about a man who goes to heaven* - The Power and the Glory. *Now I have simply written one about a man who goes to purgatory. I don't know what all the fuss is about.'*

A. What I really meant was that, for example, *Brighton Rock* is written in such a way that people could plausibly imagine that Pinkie went to hell, and then I cast doubt upon it in the ending. The real theme of the three novels is embodied in the priest's phrase at the end of *Brighton Rock*: 'You can't conceive, my child, nor can anyone else, the . . . appalling strangeness of the mercy of God.'

Q. *Would you say that the period of your Catholic novels is over?*

A. For one period I did write on Catholic subjects: from *Brighton Rock* to *A Burnt-Out Case.* But the majority of my novels do not deal with Catholic themes. One only began with a Catholic subject because one found it a great interest of the moment. *The Comedians*, for example, is not a Catholic novel. Brown happens to be a Catholic; it was this formation that made him the type of person he was. But Brown, as I said in the preface, is not Greene. *The Comedians* is essentially a political novel. My period of Catholic novels was preceded and followed by political novels. *It's a Battlefield* and *England Made Me* were political novels. I was finding my way. Even the early thrillers were political: *The Confidential Agent* deals with the Spanish Civil War. *The Quiet American* and *The Comedians* are political novels. One has come full circle in a way. I am not taking back anything from my Catholic novels. The fact that Brown seems to continue in disbelief at the end of *The Comedians* should not be thought to mean that.

Q. *Didn't* A Burnt-Out Case *explore both belief and unbelief? Incidentally, that is one of the few novels which you have written that was never filmed.*

A. Plans to film that novel were abandoned when we could not get the director and the cast that we wanted. In *A Burnt-Out Case*

I wanted to show various grades of belief and disbelief. The hero's faith was lost temporarily and came back. There was a fanatical believer in the novel; a good believer, the superior of the mission, who was too busy to concern himself with doubt; and the doctor, who had a real belief in his atheism.

Q. *To get back to* The Comedians, *how did you conceive that the screenplay should be written?*

A. For the purposes of the screen I had to leave out Brown's whole past. Beginning with the present, without the past, he would not have any character. But slowly, bit by bit, I brought out different sides of his character and developed them in the dialogue. My big problem when adapting one of my novels for the screen is that the kind of book I write, from the single point of view of one character, cannot be done in the same way on the screen. You cannot look through the eyes of one character in a film. The novel was told from Brown's point of view. Brown remains the character who is on the screen more than any of the others. His comments on the others are often there. But we still do not see others completely from his point of view as we do in the novel. For example, Martha's husband is despised by Brown in the book, but on the screen he is seen by others as a noble character.

Q. *Once again, the ending of the film differs from that of the book.*

A. Brown is a beachcomber-type character. He had been washed up on the beach in Haiti. He is a person who could not be better than he is, although he would like to. At the end of the novel, which is black comedy, he becomes an undertaker: he is just washed up on another shore. In the film the ending is different but the point is the same. Brown is forced to join the guerrillas in the hills because he cannot return to Port-au-Prince. He does not want to go and he has no experience in guerrilla warfare, but he made the best of the situation. I would not know what the future of Brown or of any my characters would be at the end of one of my stories, however.

Q. *Since the title of your most recent volume of short stories,* May We Borrow Your Husband? *is being filmed, I am reminded of a review of the book in which a British critic raised once again the old charge of*

Jansenism in your work, referring to what he called your habit of damning or exulting characters 'in either case for capricious, Jansenist reasons.'

A. People who think they are getting at Jansenism in my novels usually do not know what Jansenism really means. They probably mean Manichaeism. This is because in the Catholic novels I seem to believe in a supernatural evil. One gets so tired of people saying that my novels are about the opposition of Good and Evil. They are not about Good and Evil, but about human beings. After Hitler and Vietnam, one would have thought good and evil in people was more understandable. Still, I do not wish to judge any of my characters. I would hope it was common to most of us to have sympathy for the unfortunate part of the ordinary human character. As I once told another interviewer, I'm not a religious man, though it interests me. Religion is important, as atomic science is.

Q. *Even though your fiction has turned more toward pollitics than religion, will religion continue to be an important element in your work?*

A. Space hasn't influenced my views of religion. I don't look for God up there, do you? He's not up there. He's down around here.

Interview with Gene D. Phillips, S.J.

The Catholic World (USA, August 1969), and also *The Month* (GB, June 1970)

The John Player Film Lecture

[Unfortunately, the National Film Theatre's archive recording of Greene's interview with Philip Oakes is incomplete. However, judging from Oakes's article in that week's *Sunday Times*, the lecture began with mention of Greene's earliest film recollection (*Sophy of Kravonia*, seen when aged twelve in Brighton), which he doubted had exercised much influence on his subsequent film-writing career. At a later point he revealed that 'films influenced me a good deal more before I started reviewing them than afterwards', before recounting the story of his involvement with *The Third Man*, complete with the Selznick anecdotes and views on collaborating with Carol Reed, to which he returned in the *Guardian* Film Lecture, given in full later in this section.

By the time the recording begins, the discussion has moved on to *Brighton Rock*]:

Philip Oakes: *Were there any censorship problems on that film?*

Graham Greene: I don't remember any, no.

PO: *I think the censor . . . I mean this was, what 1949, wasn't it?*

GG: Something like that, yes, or even earlier. '48, '47.

PO: *Most untypically and anachronistically liberal I'd have thought for that time. I was looking at a list of films that you'd picked out as some of your favourites when you were film critic of* The Spectator. *They include, it's a very mixed batch: Pudovkin's* Mother, Ten Days That Shook the World, *and* Things to Come, *actually which you said you'd detested. They're all rather big pictures and yet . . .*

GG: *Things to Come* I could swear I'd given a very bad review to.

PO: *Well, you know, there it is on the page. But they're all rather big pictures, and yet in your own film work you seem to have concentrated on what you'd probably describe as 'entertainments'. Have you ever been tempted to tackle, you know, a big subject?*

GG: No, certainly not.

PO: *What puts you off it?*

GG: I don't like big books either. I think unless one is, well I would say as a novelist, unless one is a Tolstoy, one does not want to try and write a *War and Peace*. I think I'm only happy with compression.

PO: *And expanding from something which is compressed, as you said.*

GG: Yes.

PO: *Are there any questions?*

Audience: *In the clips we saw from* The Third Man, *the last clip, the best effect for me was the dialogue. Do you find the demands different from dialogue in a novel and dialogue in a film, especially with regards to timing?*

GG: Yes, very different. Often in a first film draft one uses a lot of dialogue from the novel to help tell the story and to feel one's way into the dialogue for the film. But practically one has to alter nearly everything in a dialogue, I think. It may be only altering – cutting it, altering a phrase, making something a little bit more colloquial. But the whole timing, as you say, is different.

And also the film is a much more realistic thing than the novel, I think. A novel, like the stage, is a more artificial medium than the cinema.

Aud: *Mr Greene, there is a rumour that I've heard that Orson Welles wrote his own part in* The Third Man, *or a good deal of it . . .*

GG: He wrote the best line – the only thing – but it was the best line in the film. He wrote the piece about the cuckoo clock.

PO: *My God, that's generous.*

Aud: *Would you like to say something about* England Made Me, *Mr Greene. It happens to be my favourite novel of yours.*

GG: Thank you, I like it myself. It's one of the less popular, but I like it. A film hasn't been made. An option has been sold for a film. I don't know if a film will eventually be made. I had a curious experience of once reading a very highly intellectual article on my earlier novels, where the critic, who was, as I say, highly intellectual, disinterred the motif of incest. He complained that the author didn't really know what he was writing about. That the dialogue between the brother and sister always seemed to avoid the issue, break off at the relevant moment, as if the author was afraid of his own subject. It hadn't occurred to him that one was writing from the point of view of the characters, who were afraid of recognizing their incest.

Aud: *What is the basic philosophy of life that you want to put over in your novels, because I find them utterly depressing.*

GG: There is a great deal of difference between an English public and a French public. The French public find my books optimistic.

Aud: *How do you find them?*

GG: I have no basic philosophy, but if one was seeking for a common feature in, we'll say, three or four of the books, I'd have to say they were, speaking in religious terms, about the mercy of God, which is a very optimistic subject.

Aud: *Mr Greene, did you intend to write a real theological treatise on priesthood in* The Power and the Glory?

GG: No, I don't think I had any intention of writing a treatise at all, but a story. I'd been in Mexico during a persecution and one had heard the story of the drunken priest who'd fled into the mountains and who had an illegitimate child and people occasionally brought him their children for baptism and he was often too drunk to get the names right. And one wished to explain that character to a non-Catholic country. Because I'd often, even in the days before I was a Catholic, I'd often been irritated by elderly relatives who came back from Spain and complained that the priest in the village they'd visited was living with his housekeeper. It always seemed to me to be a singularly unimportant part of a priest's life.

Aud: *Do you think, Mr Greene, that we can defend the Whisky Priest? Did he die in innocence without committing a real mortal sin?*

GG: Well, I've never really believed in mortal sin.

Aud: *Well, what we used to call mortal sin. Because, Mr Greene, there are two mortal sins we could say the priest committed – drunkenness and lust.*

GG: I have no theories, Father, on this. I feel that is really more your domain than mine.

PO: *Without disrespect, are there any more earthbound questions?*

Aud: *Mr Greene, when you sell your books to a film company or producer, which has the greatest influence on you – the monetary consideration or the person you're selling it to? I mean one thinks back to your comments on some of the directors that handled your work and apparently there were some rather unhappy experiences, and so one might have thought that you'd be more concerned about who was going to direct the film than anything else.*

GG: If one sells to an American company, I'm afraid, it's for the money, which in the old days was not so very much, you know. I mean one would receive perhaps £2,000 for film rights and one needed the money. It was no use saying 'I don't want this director or that director'. The only way to have any control whatever over a film, and then it's only a limited control, is if you do the script yourself, the screenplay yourself, with a director with whom you can work in an amicable way.

Aud: *So what . . .*

GG: Money.

Aud: *Mr Greene, following on from that if somebody gave you a script to write, to make a film yourself, with total control, i.e. yourself behind the camera in, say, the position of director, would you do it?*

GG: No, because I wouldn't feel competent. I think that unless I knew enough about camera work and so on, I wouldn't do it because I would be in the hands of my cameraman, and he would be, to all intents and purposes, the director of the film. All I could do would be to help the actors a little, but with interpretation. But I would not be capable of doing the camerawork.

PO: *I've never yet met a writer who didn't think he could direct. Are there any more questions?*

Aud: *You seem to talk about films, Mr Greene, as though they were entertainments, equivalents of what you call 'entertainments' in writing. You seem to imply that the medium's out of control and we don't know what to do with it. And you suggest* Once Upon a Time in the West *as one of the best films of the last decade. Do you not think . . .*

PO: *No, he didn't quite say that, it was a film Mr Greene enjoyed, one of the two he enjoyed most in the last twelve months.*

Aud: *Do you not really take film as seriously as you did once?*

GG: I take it absolutely seriously and I take *Once Upon a Time in the West* seriously, and also the other film I mentioned in the same breath, Bergman's *The Silence*. I don't think anything I've said means that I don't take the cinema seriously. I don't take the bad films that have been made out of my books seriously, or the bad films that I've made myself seriously.

PO: *Could I just interpose? Mr Greene saw it in France, which I think was a completely different version from the one we saw here. We saw a much shortened version, anyway the question stands.*

GG: Yes, what irritated me when I saw the film, what irritated me about the criticisms I'd read in England, in the English press, about it, was that it was criticized the whole time for being so slow. And I don't see why a film shouldn't be slow. I think you can have wonderful films which are very quick in action, quick in photography, quick in cuts, whatever you like. But it seems to me equally valid that one could have a very slow and admirable film and I love the kind of almost ballet quality in *Once Upon a Time in the West*, especially in the opening quarter of an hour or so.

Aud: *Can I ask a rather dotty question, Mr Greene? When you go abroad on your travels, do you find that some people whom you meet in the way of entertainment are fairly obviously hoping that you may put them in a book or do they take pains to introduce you to other people that they know and describe them in an interesting way hoping that you'll put them in a book as their friends?*

GG: I haven't noticed it, no.

PO: *That's a very devious plot you're suggesting. I'll use it if I may.*

Aud: *What do you think of M. Bresson's films?*

GG: M. Bresson? I've only seen, which one was it that I saw . . . *Journal d'un Curé*. I think that was M. Bresson, wasn't it? I think that's the only one I've seen.

Aud: *What did you think of it?*

GG: I liked it. I liked it, but I was not an enthusiast. But I wasn't an enthusiast, either, for the book.

PO: *Any other questions?*

Aud: *When you start with an idea, do you know whether you're going to end up with a novel or a short story or a play or a film? Do you have the idea and then think 'Aha! This is going to be a short story' or as you go on writing it might turn into a full-length novel or even a play or a film?*

GG: No, I know from the word go. I know from the word go that if it's completed it will be a short story of such and such a length or a novel of 70,000 words or 100,000 words. And it generally turns out to be, even the length, to be fairly accurate.

Aud: *Mr Greene, you said 'if it is completed'. Is there a lot of uncompleted work?*

GG: Oh, an enormous number. I should think about six novels.

PO: *What about films?*

GG: Films, no.

PO: *Because they are always done on commission?*

GG: Yes.

Aud: *Is there any hope of your reprinting your film criticism?*

GG: No. If somebody would publish it I would. No, it's a little bit *vieux jeu* now.

PO: *There's period value in the films. You said in one interview, I think it was with Tom Wiseman in the* Evening Standard*: 'When people read my stories they think they would make good films. Then, when they come to do them, they realise they won't, so that they are obliged to change them.' Do you anticipate the changes that people are going to make?*

GG: No. Sometimes one's taken completely by surprise. Like in the case of *The Quiet American*, where the story was completely reversed. Instead of being a story with Communist sympathies, it became the story of an Englishman who is a dupe of the Communists and the girl at the end of the story goes off nobly in a kind of Girl Guide fashion to fight for President Diem. America at that time not having decided to have President Diem assassinated.

PO: *Do you think there's a place for political cinema?*

GG: Very much so, I think.

PO: *For example? In the commercial cinema?*

GG: There's a gaping space for it, which hasn't yet been filled. Although we did have political cinema at the end of the silent days with the great Russian films. I suppose you could say that *If . . .* was a political film.

PO: Yes, I think you can. The director's here, actually.

Aud: *What did you think of* If . . . ?

GG: I liked it enormously, but I saw it in France and I found that the French took it with very deadly seriousness as a realistic portrait of English public school life.

Aud: *Mr Greene, you mentioned returning to Conrad after twenty years of not reading him. Are there any films that you avoided seeing and came upon later?*

GG: I can't remember any, no. I mean there are certain directors one wouldn't go to films because they were directing. I mean one goes to a Bergman film because he's directing. To a Lindsay Anderson film because he's directing. But I wouldn't, for instance, have gone to a Basil Dean film because he was directing.

Aud: *What do you think of Hitchcock's films?*

GG: I'm not a one hundred per cent enthusiast. I mean one has happy memories of his earlier English films and yet I always found enormous gaps in the logic of a story. You know, you enjoyed them at the time, you came out and thought, 'Yes, but why did so and so do that?' and 'Why didn't he go to the police at that point?' I think he's brilliant, but erratic in his logic.

Aud: *Why didn't Hale go to the police in* Brighton Rock?

GG: He was dead before he had a chance. He had no evidence. What would he have complained of? That he'd seen a man in a pub who had passed rather ambiguous remarks to him? He'd also, if you remember, been mixed up in the former race gang of a man called Kite.

Aud: *Would you say that Carol Reed has been your most successful collaborator on the screen?*

GG: Yes, I think so.

Aud: *Although you said working with Peter Glenville is more amusing?*

GG: Yes, I enjoy working with him more.

PO: *What was the difference? There must have been two different kinds of collaboration. Can you distinguish between them?*

GG: Well, I think Carol Reed is one hundred per cent professional and his interests are one hundred per cent film, while with Peter Glenville I've many, many other interests in common and one can get away from the film very easily.

Aud: *What other than your experiences in making* The Quiet American *coloured your feelings about America and American films?*

GG: I think my anti-Americanism can be traced right back into the thirties, you know. A long, long time.

PO: *Mr Greene can't tell it, but I can. It was when he was the film critic of a magazine called* Night and Day, *and he ventured a criticism of a Shirley Temple film called* Wee Willie Winkie, *and he ventured some remarks about who fancied Shirley Temple, and the judge at the time called it 'the grossest, the most outrageous', I can't remember the exact words, but shortly afterwards Mr Greene went to America and holed up in Mexico for a while, and his alleged anti-Americanism is supposed to date from that time.*

GG: No, that's just the malicious truth. I think my strong

anti-Americanism dated from the years that I visited Indo-China during the French war. I went there every winter for about five years and one saw the beginnings of American policy there. They were not in control at that time.

Aud: *What influence did Orson Welles have on* The Third Man, *because in the clip we saw both the script, the over-lapping dialogue and certainly the camera angles – it really looks like a Welles film, as if he'd actually written and directed it.*

GG: Yes, I think he was very astute. I think he realised that the part was a very small one, but which would steal the film and, in fact, it did.

PO: *Two more questions.*

Aud: *When you think about writing a novel, have you had the experience of saying, 'What I want to say can only be expressed visually on the screen', even though you're seeing it as a novel?*

GG: No, never. Never.

Aud: *Can you tell me why you've lost faith in Catholicism?*

GG: I haven't lost faith in Catholicism. If I may quote a recent novel of mine about a woman called Aunt Augusta. She remarks: 'I am a Catholic because I don't believe all they believe.' That is a little bit, that has always been my attitude.

PO: *One more question. Well, can I ask a final question which is, we've witnessed the total collapse of film censorship, it seems, certainly it's collapsed in America, and it seems to be grinding to an end here. As a film writer, do you find this encouraging and in a kind of permissive state of cinema are there any subjects which you would like to tackle as a writer?*

GG: No, I don't feel so. My feeling about film is, I think, the same as with the novel. Now you can write about anything in the novel and use any scenes of physical description. My only criticism of that is that I don't want it. I think a personal censorship is required instead of a public censorship, because it becomes too easy. To describe two people making love – after all we all have to do it – becomes awfully boring when it's done in detail, I think, which is now permissible. You know, Wordsworth talked about 'the sonnet's narrow room' and I think that every writer, and probably this applies also to films, needs a sense of a narrow room in which he has to exercise his skill to convey something without full liberty.

PO: *The sort of corset that keeps you in trim?*

GG: Yes.

PO: *Can I say thank you on your behalf to our guest this afternoon, Mr Graham Greene.*

GG: Thank you very much.

GUARDIAN FILM LECTURE

Quentin Falk: *We've just seen a clip from* The Fallen Idol *and it brings back many memories and, of course, looking at it now and seeing the clockmaker coming through – that I gathered brought back a slight memory to you about it.*

Graham Greene: I can't praise myself for that. That was an idea of Carol Reed. It came perfectly to make a pause in the interrogation.

QF: *This brings up the whole point of your relationship with Carol Reed, and the collaboration you had. It must have been quite remarkable.*

GG: Yes, he was the only director, really, that I've enjoyed working with. We worked very closely. We generally stayed in the same hotel. He would sleep in the morning and I would work, and then we would discuss what I had done over lunch. There was always a moment when one thought, 'this is hopeless'. It was always I who thought it was hopeless, and I would say, 'Let's give it up. This isn't working. It doesn't work.' And that was the critical moment. After that everything went well.

QF: *In the case of* The Fallen Idol, *how much did things change between your short story, which was published some time before, more than ten years before, and the screen because Alexander Korda was involved?*

GG: Yes, but Korda didn't interfere at all with us. He was very good in that way. The only suggestion he made was that the character played by Richardson should be a chauffeur and not a butler, because, he said, children were so interested in motor cars, and that the film might begin at an airport with the parents flying away and then the chauffeur showing the child the inside of the car and so on. But my only reply was 'But dear Alex, how many films have started at an airport?' He didn't insist.

QF: *Of course you changed the character of the boy, or at least the nationality of the boy and made it a slightly different sort of household as well. Was that you, or a combination of you and Reed?*

GG: That was agreed between us, because the story was written in the thirties and we were now in the forties, post-war, and people didn't have butlers. Ordinary people no longer had butlers, so it was a good idea to make it an embassy.

QF: *Let's jump back a bit and talk about your first involvements with the film industry. You were a film critic and you were writing rather unpleasant things about Alexander Korda, who at that stage was our great British film mogul.*

GG: Yes.

QF: *You were particularly unkind about him. Why did you feel so strongly about him at that time?*

GG: I didn't like his films, it was as simple as that. But I never knew that I'd become a very fond friend of his. He invited me to go and see him at Denham and I went down. He asked me whether I had an idea for a film, and I invented one on the spur of the moment, the beginning of a film. Because I was very short of money, I found myself being employed for, I don't know, eight weeks at £250 a week, which was a lot of money.

QF: *This was* The Green Cockatoo, *of course.*

GG: Yes, I can remember nothing about that at all. I can only remember the opening which I described to Korda. I can't remember anything else about it, I can't even remember writing it.

QF: *You continued the relationship. You did a second film with Korda. You have greater memories, I think, of this?*

GG: That was the worst film I ever made, I think. That I helped in making. That was called *Twenty-One Days*, and it was after a story of John Galsworthy. Well, it didn't go right. It didn't go at all well and it was put in cold storage for a time and was presented in 1940. I wrote a review of it in *The Spectator*. Perhaps I could read you my review of it?

QF: *I think we'd love to hear it. A very curious position to be in to actually review a film that you actually wrote yourself. Do you have any thoughts about doing that?*

GG: Well I felt so strongly about the badness of this film, which starred Laurence Olivier and Vivien Leigh. I think it was their first film together and one of the problems was, of course, that they decided to quit their spouses during the course of the film and became quite haywire for a time, so that most of the gloomy scenes were interspersed with giggles and laughter. But the review I wrote, I think, was a very fair one: 'Perhaps I may be forgiven for noticing a picture in which I had some hand, for I have no good word to say of it. The brilliant acting of Mr Hay Petrie as a decayed and outcast curate cannot conquer the overpowering flavour of cooked ham. Galsworthy's story, *The First and the Last*, was peculiarly unsuited for film adaptation, as its whole point lay in a double suicide (forbidden by the censor), a burned confession, and an innocent man's conviction for murder (forbidden by the great public). For the rather dubious merits of the original the adaptors have substituted incredible coincidences and banal situations. Slow, wordy, unbearably sentimental, the picture reels awkwardly towards the only suicide the censorship allowed – and that, I find with some astonishment, has been cut out. I wish I could tell the extraordinary story that lies behind this shelved and resurrected picture, a story involving a theme-song, and a bottle of whisky, and camels in Wales . . . Meanwhile, let one guilty man, at any rate, stand in the dock, swearing never, never to do it again . . . ' I broke my promise seven years later with *Brighton Rock*.

QF: *Can I be the first, before everybody puts their hand up, to ask you about that extraordinary story. What was the extraordinary story or can you tell us some of the elements involving the camels, the theme song, the whisky . . .*

GG: Yes, also there was a story about sugar. I had written in a story about a dinner, a bachelor dinner with the Lord Chief Justice, because the background of the film was a trial. Basil Dean was the director and it was a big crane shot above a round table. The shooting began with several characters around the table when Basil Dean interrupted and said, 'You've got white sugar on the table, not coffee sugar.' So the scene was stopped and a car was sent into London from Denham to get coffee sugar at considerable cost.

The camels in Wales: the assistant producer was taken off the film without consulting the director to take camels to Wales for a film of one of Kipling's stories. The whisky bottle was the last night of doing the script. I was helped by someone of more experience – an elderly gentleman whose name I can't remember. Basil Dean had gone to the theatre and he told us that the script had to be finished by the time he got back from the theatre. And round about 11 o'clock at night, we had got through a bottle of whisky and we had got through the script. But as a result of the whisky I suggested that we wrote in a theme song, and the theme song was called 'Ship o'Dreams'. We each wrote an alternative line. The script was handed over and it was passed to Mr Lajos Biro, who was the Hungarian editor of scripts, and passed to production.

Basil Dean asked me to go down to Southend with him to look at locations, because there was a big scene where Laurence Olivier (who is guilty of the crime, although it was an accident, and knows an innocent man has been convicted of murder), goes down to Southend with his girl and roars with laughter on one of those dippers. The roaring with laughter was not in the script, but they were enjoying themselves. I was walking around with Basil Dean and Basil Dean said to me, 'Graham, what was the point of that song?' and at that moment a cameraman came up and said, 'Mr Dean, would you come over here. I think I've found a place for shooting,' and he never said another word. So when I came to see the film, I hoped in vain that the song was in. But it wasn't.

QF: *In fact, there was another occasion with a film in which you in fact weren't involved,* The Confidential Agent, *where you'd written a song in a nightclub sequence, where you actually rather hoped they might use that, too.*

GG: Yes, because that was one of the few, the only, American film which was faithful to one of my books. It was so faithful that I thought I was going to hear my song. But I didn't. They substituted another one.

QF: *I wonder if at this stage we could start to have some early questions.*

Audience: *It's often said, and it's said in the brochure, that Mr Greene doesn't like most of the adaptations of his books into films. Does he think that anyone likes the adaptions of their books into films?*

GG: Well, some people, like Tolstoy, are lucky and are dead. But I can't answer for the others. I have liked the adaptations that I've done myself. I quite liked the adaptation of *Brighton Rock*. I quite liked, it wasn't too bad, the adaptation of *Our Man in Havana*. I liked *The Fallen Idol*. But I can't speak for other writers. But what I do find is that the American adaptations have been outstandingly bad. And one of the curious things is that perhaps some of the worst films, which you will be showing in this ambiguous festival, some of the worst films have been done by great directors. Henry [*sic*] Ford who did an intolerable film of *The Power and the Glory*, under the title of *The Fugitive*, where he gives the illegitimate child to the chief of police instead of to the priest, which was the whole subject of the novel. Mankiewicz, who directed *The Quiet American*, made it into a propaganda film for America in Vietnam, when it had been an attack on the American influences in Vietnam. Now, who was the third I had in mind?

QF: *Cukor?*

GG: Cukor, *Travels with My Aunt*. I had smuggled to me from Spain while they were shooting, a copy of the script, and the script was intolerably bad. I haven't seen the film as a whole. They put it on the television once in France and I couldn't bear it. I turned it off after five minutes.

QF: *Fritz Lang, I think, was probably the other.*

GG: Fritz Lang, yes, whom I admire enormously, but he came up to me once in a bar in Los Angeles and apologized for what he had done with *The Ministry of Fear.* He said that he had signed the contract having read the book and then been presented with a ready-made script, which cut out the whole central part of the book, where most of the point of the book lies. He had refused to do it, but they pointed out that he had signed the contract and he couldn't get out of it. I think there is only one scene in the whole film which recalls a bit of the great director, Fritz Lang.

QF: *I think this comes back neatly to the point where you were a film critic yourself, because Lang, I think, regularly got rather good reviews from you – you obviously enjoyed his work. Did you as a writer yourself think particularly of writers when you were writing your reviews or did you just look at the adaptations of the films themselves or did it nag at you if a great work was being adapted by some other director? Did you try and isolate the problem?*

GG: I don't remember that problem at all. I mean one certainly didn't go out and read the book before I wrote the criticism of the film. It would have been intolerably long and so many good films have been made out of bad books.

QF: *Did it make you more sympathetic, perhaps, to the directors? I mean the two mediums were rather different. A film is a film is the old cliché, but a book is a book.*

GG: Yes. I think one thing is certain that a short story makes a much better film than a novel. A novel is too long. There is too much material. There have to be too many compromises. The cuts made may seem unimportant but you suddenly find that an unimportant cut has changed the whole character of a character. Short stories make far better films and I've been very happy with the Thames series of my short stories – there were only about four that I disliked out of eighteen – and three or four are among the best films that have been made out of my work. It's difficult to judge whether the film or the story came first.

QF: *You said that it was a little time before you worked again on a movie after your experiences on* Twenty-One Days.

GG: Seven years.

QF: *Yes, how did your experiences compare on* Brighton Rock, *because again you came in in a rather curious way on this, didn't you? Somebody else had already written a screenplay, I think?*

GG: No, no. Terence Rattigan had written a treatment. It was an organised film where everybody was going to get not much money and share out the profits. Terence Rattigan had been taken on, he had done a treatment which ended in a happy ending. I can't remember how happy it was. It was *very* happy. In fact I did the whole screenplay myself. He didn't contribute anything to the screenplay. The Boulting Brothers gave me too much rope and they asked a bit too much in a way. They asked for almost a shooting script and a writer is not really capable of doing a shooting script – it's a waste of time. He can put in an idea for a shot, but to do the complete set-up of long shots, travelling shots, everything else, is out of his range. And so it was rather a fatigue doing it and I saw very little of the Boulting Brothers, but simply sent my pages along to them. I think I didn't like Hermione Baddeley, who played Ida Arnold as if she was in a music hall, but otherwise I thought it was not a bad film. But it was heavily censored and the censor didn't feel that a murderer should be concerned in any religious sense at all. I'm afraid it was not the success which the Boultings deserved.

QF: *This was a form of pre-censorship, was it, rather than the finished product? I mean in terms of what you'd written? Did you have to de-theologize it yourself?*

GG: No, cuts were made. In the dialogue.

QF: *Of course the ending itself was slightly changed.*

GG: Yes, that's my fault. I didn't like the way in which it was done. It was my fault. I thought that the ending of the book, where she's going off to play a gramophone record saying, 'I hate you, you little bitch', or whatever it was, was a bit strong for an audience and so I thought one had had a scene in which he throws the record down on the floor and cracks it so that the needle sticks on the point where he says 'I love, I love, I love'. But I thought that most people would go home and think, 'Well next time she'll move the needle and get the message.' But those who wanted a happy ending would have had it. But I didn't expect

. . . I wrote in my script that it was an old wizened nun in a rather shabby hospital – there was no crucifix on the wall, there was no dove flying out of the window while this went on, and that was the Boultings' fault.

QF: *A touch of Hollywood was introduced do you think?*

GG: Well, not Hollywood so much as . . .

QF: *Welwyn Garden City Studios.*

GG: Yes.

QF: *Another question.*

Aud: *My question is, have you ever been tempted to rewrite someone else's work to make it better?*

QF: *In terms of a film script or in terms of a novel?*

Aud: *In terms of a novel which you were reading and which you thought you could do better yourself.*

GG: No. No, definitely no.

QF: Short answer. Another question please.

Aud: *Mr Greene you've mentioned the problems you had with the censor and you've written elsewhere that a film review once nearly landed you in prison. I'm thinking of the Shirley Temple film.*

GG: Well, not in prison.

Aud: *Were you exaggerating perhaps when you wrote it?*

GG: No, I never said I was in danger of prison. I said I suffered a very heavy fine.

Aud: *Well, my question was, have you found your dealings with English bureaucracy very frustrating?*

GG: More in the theatre, I think, than in the cinema. The theatre censor, in the days of the censorship of the theatre, was a very nice old colonel in the Guards. He was very nice to chat to, but it didn't help much and I had trouble with him with my first play, which was called *The Living Room*, because there was the sound of a lavatory flushing, and he didn't like that.

Aud: *Mr Greene have you seen the recent film of* Dr Fischer of Geneva, *and if you have, could you comment on it?*

GG: I haven't seen it yet. I'm going to see it tonight. I want to say here that any pleasure I have in seeing it is rather overcast by the death of James Mason. I watched some of the shooting of the bomb party in Switzerland last Christmas. It was in the open air between ten o'clock in the evening and two o'clock in the morning in bitter cold and I was amazed at the patience and good humour and the helpfulness for others shown by James Mason. Also, I was delighted to see him in the part of Dr Fischer. For me Dr Fischer in future will have the face of James Mason. His eyes conveyed simultaneously enormous pride and a profound sadness and that was what I wanted to convey. But I hope the film will be good, but I don't know.

QF: *You mentioned, just going back to the point about the Boultings wanting a shooting script, and you felt that a writer shouldn't be involved in that – it comes back, maybe, to one of the central points that critics have talked about your writing being cinematic and how you've been influenced by the moving image and so on – that presumably is a point you'd go along with.*

GG: Yes I'd go along with that because I began film criticism at the age of twenty at Oxford in the days of the silent cinema. Therefore, I've been mixed up with films for a very very long time, until the last ten years and I don't think I've seen twelve films in the last ten years. But it obviously influenced my writing, I think – just as the Victorian novel was a great deal influenced by painting – you have whole pages of Walter Scott which are like descriptions of a painting by Constable or somebody.

QF: *Presumably the theatre, too.*

GG: Yes. Henry James was very influenced by the theatre.

QF: *Do you think it's over-emphasized? Do you get fed up when every critic always mentions it, or writer, about you, you know, that it's so cinematic?*

GG: Well, actually I don't mind, but the answer is that very few good films have been made out of my books so they can't be all that cinematic.

Aud: *Could you mention something about the effect of the invention of the cinema on the technique of novel writing from the point of view of the modern novelist.*

GG: I can't speak for other people, but speaking for myself I think it means that, for instance, in a description one uses a moving camera instead of a stationary one. That description is part of the movement of a story and not a paragraph inserted as a stationary thing in a novel. That I think is where it's influenced me, but I can't speak about other people.

Aud: *Mr Greene, in your earlier books you were very concerned about religious matters. You don't seem quite so concerned now. Are you not?*

GG: Well, some of my characters were concerned. You must remember that I've been a Catholic since 1927. My first novel was published in 1929 and nobody knew that I was a Catholic until a review appeared in *The Tablet* of *Brighton Rock* in 1938. So it wasn't very obvious, apparently. And as for it having dropped out, I'm afraid you haven't read my last novel, *Monsignor Quixote.*

Aud: *Mr Greene, you made a point about Henry James having been influenced by the theatre – nevertheless he never succeeded himself as a playwright. Do you seen any contradiction in that?*

GG: No, none at all. He was very depressed by his lack of success and he tried over and over again until *Guy Domville* was such a disaster that he gave up. But his novels, like *The Awkward Age*, are very much based on the theatre. It's almost entirely in dialogue.

Aud: *Mr Greene, is there a particular reason why* A Burnt-Out Case *has never been filmed? Is it due to the fact you said earlier that it might well be badly made or that the cast would be very important, such as a younger Trevor Howard or a younger James Mason? I wondered why that has never been filmed.*

GG: Well, thank God for that. Mr Otto Preminger bought two options on it at intervals but having seen *The Human Factor* I'm very glad he never made *A Burnt-Out Case.*

Aud: *Would you like it to be made into a good film?*

GG: Yes, but I know that the author can't ensure that it will be made into a good film and I would much rather it was never made at all.

QF: *A number of film-makers have come to you and you've been very helpful, when you've adapted your work. Either the film has been made or has not as the case may be – would you . . .*

GG: That's not quite true, you know. I've never received any suggestion to be helpful to any of the American directors.

QF: *Not the Americans, but I'm just thinking in general. I mean* The Honorary Consul, *for instance, in its early stages you were helpful to its original director.*

GG: Yes, when I thought that Peter Duffel was going to make it and he did a very good first script, but alas it passed out of his hands.

QF: *You make the point about Americans versus British – is it something uniquely American that they tend too muck your work up – is that your feeling what Americans do?*

GG: Well, it may be a coincidence. Let me see, I would say that in this season which you are having, you're celebrating with what I consider eight very bad films, and . . .

QF: *Could you say why they're bad as well.*

GG: Not one of those very bad films was made by an English director, and one, I think, good film, which you won't agree with me, was made by an American – *The Confidential Agent.*

QF: *Tell us the ones that you think are particularly bad. You've mentioned them* en route, *but a little bit of the reasons why you think that.*

GG: Well, I've mentioned *The Ministry of Fear.*

QF: The Quiet American *you've mentioned,* The Power and the Glory, *of course.*

GG: *The Man Within* is an English one and is, I think, shockingly bad. Just at the beginning of the War I did a little work for a documentary director in the Grierson group and he told me that after the War he had a chance of breaking into feature films and he wanted to make a film of *The Man Within* and I sold it to him for a song. But he resold it to Sydney Box and after that I put into all my contracts that on no account was a film to be resold to Sydney Box. The story, was set, it's not a very good book, the story was set around the 1820s in England and Sydney Box made torture part of the English legal system of that period. It also had a strong note of homosexuality and I received a letter from a gentleman in Istanbul, a Turk, asking me whether I'd written any other book on this interesting subject.

Well, the other bad ones . . . *Short Cut to Hell* is very bad. *Travels with My Aunt*, I think is very bad.

QF: *You must admit you haven't seen very much of* Travels with My Aunt, *have you?*

GG: No, but I read the script. *The Honorary Consul*, I haven't seen, so I mustn't say anything about it. I didn't care for *This Gun for Hire*, which introduced a female conjuror into the story. Well, there you are.

QF: *Well, two of the films in your hate filmography,* The Man Within *and* The Human Factor, *of course, are not in this season, actually.*

GG: *The Human Factor*'s down.

QF: *They're not showing it.*

GG: They aren't?

QF: *No.*

GG: Oh no, it's not.

QF: *Of course, you've mentioned Preminger. I think you worked very hard for him not to make it – or you hoped he wouldn't. Why was that particularly?*

GG: I didn't feel it was a suitable subject for him and I was proved right, in spite of having a script by Tom Stoppard, whose plays I admire very much. He wasn't strong enough to withstand Otto.

QF: *But, of course, they had problems with money, too, didn't they?*

GG: They had terrible problems with money.

QF: *Like no money at all.*

GG: Yes.

QF: *Another question.*

Aud: *Have you seen any good results come from writing the book,* J'Accuse?

GG: Well, there are results. I've got three actions for defamation coming on in November. We have one in the Court de Concession in Paris and in the Appeal Court of Nîmes over the custody of the child, but the child is not yet in the hands of the mother. And this is a very critical ten days or so at the moment, which is why I'm hurrying back to France.

Aud: *Mr Greene mentioned that some of the best film adaptations of his work have been made for television. Is that anything to do, do you think, with the medium itself or the book?*

GG: I wouldn't like to answer that really. I think that even in the cinema the short story makes a better film than the novel, as I've said, because there are too many compromises in cutting a novel. For instance, *The Fallen Idol* was a long short story. *The Third Man* was a long short story. And they were much truer to the original than you get with a novel. I think I was very lucky with the Thames series, apart from three or four which I didn't like, but out of eighteen. *Under the Garden, Two Gentle People, The Dream of the Strange Land*, I think of at once as being extremely good films.

QF: *Of course, American television has been involved with your work, hasn't it? They actually remade* The Power and the Glory, *didn't they?*

GG: They remade it not much better than Ford. Well, a bit better. I remember Laurence Olivier being very bad as the priest and George Scott being very good as the policeman.

Aud: *Have you ever wished to direct a film yourself?*

GG: No, it's too difficult. You need to be in control of your cameraman as well as in control of your actors, and you have to make your shooting script. All this is too difficult, I think, for me. I found working on films, even a screenplay, very exhausting. You generally had three versions of a screenplay before the final one, and one was too tired to do any other work for a year afterwards.

QF: *You did work as a producer, or co-producer, on a couple of occasions, didn't you? So you were involved with more the nuts and bolts of things.*

GG: Yes, that was, I think, a little film, not a bad little film called, *The Stranger's Hand*, which we made in Venice. I was co-producer. It was based on a paragraph which had won a second prize in a *New Statesman* competition.

QF: *You'd written?*

GG: Yes, it was a parody of myself.

QF: *And you only came second?*

GG: I came second. But that was my experience of co-production. Things have changed since those days. It was soon after the War. An Italian and English co-production. We had a great deal of difficulty with the English. We were shooting on a small raft in the middle of the Grand Canal – the only Englishmen actively working were the producer, the assistant director and the clapper boy. At four o'clock in the afternoon, with the Italian electricians working in this tiny set, putting lights between people legs and what not, suddenly the clapper boy would clap – it was a tea-break. The Italians had never heard of a tea-break. But if we hadn't had a tea-break the rest of the English electricians, who were sailing boats off the Lido or having ices in the piazza, would have been able to charge overtime. They also complained bitterly, they all were lodged in hotels on the Grand Canal, and they complained bitterly that they couldn't get eggs and bacon. It was soon after the War. I gathered things have changed very much now because I've never seen a happier lot of technicians than those who were working under very difficult conditions on *Dr Fischer*.

QF: *Didn't you also do some editing on* The Stranger's Hand?

GG: I did a little bit on that machine, what do you call it?

QF: *A moviola.*

GG: Yes. A little bit of cutting in England.

QF: *And you made the first of your two guest appearances in movies in* The Stranger's Hand, *I think?*

GG: No, only my hand. Undoing a rope.

QF: *Another question.*

Aud: *You spoke about your style being very cinematic. It seems to me that one of the most cinematic in its construction is* It's a Battlefield. *Were you thinking of the cinema when you wrote it and why do you think it's never been made into a film?*

GG: I think partly perhaps for political reasons. It was the one book which I definitely modelled myself on a film in writing. And there was a time when Simone Signoret wanted to make a film with it. But nothing ever came of that. I think probably it was politically unpopular at that period.

QF: *When you said, 'it was modelled on', did you model on a specific film?*

GG: No, no! On the technique.

Aud: *When you were adapting* The Comedians*, why did you decide to drop the structure of flashbacks and make it into a chronological narrative?*

GG: Did I? Well, I think flashbacks can be overdone, but I'm not very happy with *The Comedians*. I'm unhappy because I don't think the script was as good as it should have been. I don't think the direction was as good as it should have been. I think it should have been made in black-and-white and not in colour and Elizabeth Taylor was a disaster. I can't remember what flashbacks there are in *The Comedians*. I'm afraid it's a long time since I read the book.

QF: *You've explained, I think, in your volumes of autobiography about the character of Brown, played by Richard Burton in the film, and how, in fact, there is a fair amount of flashback about his past life, that you used in conversation rather than in flashback.*

GG: Ah, yes.

QF: *You explained parts of his past presumably to simplify. As one knows the novel is set in Haiti during Papa Doc's reign. Of course, you couldn't film in Haiti.*

GG: No. Papa Doc had issued a brochure against me called *Graham Greene Demasqué – Finally Exposed* – in which he accused me of being a necrophobe, a drug addict, a shame to proud and noble England, a spy of a foreign power, and what has always puzzled me, a torturer.[8] A torturer from Papa Doc was a curious compliment. I wouldn't have liked to have gone back to Haiti, but what was rather a shock to me, I went out with the camera unit to Dahomey where we were shooting and coming out of the airport at Dahomey I suddenly saw sketched out in big letters across the road in Porto Novo – *Bienvenu Haiti* – and for an awful moment I thought, 'My God, have we come down in Haiti?'

Aud: *Why do your books seem to get shorter and shorter?*

GG: Because I get older and older.

Aud: *Do you have any more books in prospect?*

GG: Well, I've got a non-fiction book coming out at the end of September about my friend Omar Torrijos Herrera of Panama, who was killed in an aeroplane crash two years ago, perhaps by the CIA. It's called *Getting to Know the General*, and it's about Central America and the situation in Nicaragua, and what not. I also have begun a novel which I temporarily abandoned, but I might get back to it. One never knows.

Aud: *What's it about?*

GG: Oh, I can't tell you what it's about because it's as if I've written the book and then I'd never write it.

Aud: *Was the Shirley Temple action the sole cause of the demise of* Night and Day?

QF: Night and Day *was a magazine for which Mr Greene wrote in the* 1930s.

GG; And part-edited.

QF: *And the Shirley Temple libel, I'm not sure if you're supposed to repeat a libel..,The Shirley Temple libel case, was it totally responsible for closing the magazine down?*

GG: No, the magazine was in difficulties. It was a rather extravagant magazine in the sense that we had different coloured covers each week by different artists and the advertising was not really paying. The advertising was not paying for the production and Chatto, who were the publishers, were losing money. So the libel action was just the last straw.[9]

QF: *Are you allowed to actually explain why this libel case arose?*

GG: Well, Twentieth-Century Fox were unhappy about some other reviews I'd done of Shirley Temple and other films of theirs and I think they thought this was a way of silencing me. They even wrote to *The Spectator*, with whom I had previously been doing reviews, more or less menacing them if they took me on again, but *The Spectator* paid no attention and took me back.

Aud: *It's generally agreed, I think, that most of the films of Mr Greene's religious novels have not been entirely satisfactory. Could you say which you think was the most nearly satisfactory?*

GG: I suppose the least unsatisfactory was *The End of the Affair.* Deborah Kerr gave an extremely good performance in that. The scenes in the blitz were not badly done. It was spoiled by the casting of a young actor named Van Johnson to play the middle-aged writer. I don't know how Deborah Kerr fancied her scenes with him. I went one day to the shooting and they were doing an embrace standing up, they were embracing each other. The camera was first of all doing it from Deborah Kerr's point-of-view, and then Van Johnson's on Deborah Kerr. When the camera was on Deborah Kerr, Van Johnson put some chewing gum in his mouth while embracing her and chewed. When the camera turned the other way he took the chewing gum out and parked it. It didn't seem to me that it would have inspired very good acting from Deborah Kerr.

QF: *I suppose we must mention* The Heart of the Matter. *I really like* The Heart of the Matter. *I think it's a marvellous film, but obviously you don't.*

GG: Not the last version.

QF: *No, not the co-produced version. No, I mean the Trevor Howard version.*

GG: No, I think that Trevor Howard was extremely good. No, I don't think it was a bad film at all. But then I don't like the book much.

QF: *I suppose it's one of the most popular of your books in terms of sales and so on. Why don't you like it?*

GG: I think it was exaggerated and the religious point-of-view was exaggerated in it. I like bits of it. I think that Freetown is well described, but the dilemma of Scobie seems to me an exaggerated one. I think that's mainly why I dislike it.

QF: *Because the compromise they came up with in the film seemed in a sense true to the book.*

GG: Yes, there again this business of suicide. It was still the censor in those days.[10]

QF: *Were you consulted about trying to provide an end?*

GG: Well, I suggested a change in the end which would make it a little more obviously a suicide interrupted by a real death, and Trevor Howard was willing to work for nothing to make the change, but the director didn't want it.

Aud: *Mr Greene, what did you think of the Graham Greene parody that knocked you into second place?*

QF: *This was the parody of the* New Statesman *piece that won.*

GG: *The Stranger's Hand.* I can't remember who won it and I can't remember what the winner was. But I then enlarged the paragraph or whatever it was to one piece of notepaper and somebody else – Guy Elmes – did the script. I worked on the script a bit with him, as a co-producer, and my friend Mario Soldati shot it. Dilys Powell paid the compliment . . . It came on at the Dominion, which was not regarded as the West End and Dilys Powell did a very nice review of it, saying it was better than any of the films in the West End.

Aud: *You mentioned* The Third Man, *like* The Fallen Idol, *was a long short story. There seemed to be so many conflicting versions of how* The Third Man *came to be, in the first place, who wrote what at various points?*

GG: The screenplay was entirely mine, except for the passage about the cuckoo clocks, which was written by Orson Welles. Orson Welles, I believe, has claimed that he wrote a lot of the script, but in actual fact, that was the only passage that he wrote. The thing came about at a dinner with Alex Korda and Carol Reed. Korda wanted to have a film made about the three-power, or four-power was it, occupation of Vienna and so I went to Vienna to try and find a story. After about a fortnight I hadn't found anything and then luckily, I had lunch with a young intelligence officer in the British Army, who is now the Duke of St Albans, and he took me down the sewers and told me the curious story of how the Russians refused to have the exits of sewers closed, and that there were special sewer police. And he also told me about the penicillin racket. So that these two things came together and I went to Italy to work on the treatment for four weeks and the treatment is the published version of *The Third Man.* I hadn't meant it to be published, but after the film was made, they wanted to have a paperback, and so on, of the story. But in actual fact, what is printed is the treatment and that's all my own, and so is the screenplay with the exception of that one passage.

Aud: *Did you alter the treatment for publication?*

GG: No, I didn't alter the treatment for publication, but I altered the screenplay a good deal from the treatment. For example, the scene at the British Council was at one time going to be acted by two leading comic actors whose names I've forgotten. In the end, it was acted by one man, Hyde-White.

QF: *Basil Radford and Naunton Wayne.*

GG: That's right, yes. But there were various changes and I had a dispute with Carol Reed over the end, because I thought that people would be getting up for that long walk, you know, at the end, people would be getting up, taking their macintoshes from under their seats and going out knowing that there'd be a happy ending, or believing that it was going to be a conventional happy ending. But Carol Reed was right. He made a magnificent ending with the help of the music of the zither.

QF: *So it was a question, really, of a very close collaboration and accepting some of his ideas and presumably resisting David Selznick's ideas as well, because he tried to interfere very much, didn't he?*

GG: Oh yes. We didn't accept any of his ideas. The trouble was that in the terms of his contract with Korda he was to supply Alida Valli and Joseph Cotten and he had the right of discussion within six weeks before shooting. So Carol Reed and I had to go out to Hollywood and meet every night with Selznick. The first meeting didn't go very well, because he began by saying, 'Graham, look. You're a writer, you know. You can get a better title than *The Third Man*. Who's going to want to go and see a film called *The Third Man*? What you want, I'm not a writer, you're a writer, but something like . . . *Night in Vienna*.'

And he went on to say, 'And what's all this buggery, boys? What's all this buggery?' I said, 'Buggery?' He said, 'Look. Chap goes out to find his friend. Doesn't find him. He's apparently dead. Why doesn't he go home?' I said, 'Well, look . . . he's got a motive of revenge. He's been assaulted by the British military police. He's fallen in love with a girl.' 'Yes, but that's after twenty-four hours.

Why didn't he go home before that?' Our collaboration went on rather in those terms and one terrible night towards the end, it was getting on for midnight and we had to go back to our hotel outside Hollywood, and he said, 'I can't understand, Graham, why you made Harry Lime do something or other.' And I said, 'But he doesn't.' He'd been chewing benzadrine to keep himself awake. He said, 'Christ, boys, that was another film.' He complained afterwards. He sent pages of criticisms and notes to Korda, but Korda put them in a drawer and told Carol not to mind.

QF: *The two films that are most fondly recalled are perhaps* The Fallen Idol *and* The Third Man, *but you perhaps tend to differentiate between the two. I mean, you have a fondness for one more than the other, don't you?*

GG: In a way I was more fond of *The Fallen Idol* because it was more, I felt, a writer's film, and *The Third Man* more a director's film.

Aud: *I often get the impression from your novels that the central point is not necessarily conveyed by the narrator. Do you think that is why your novels haven't always translated successfully into films?*

GG: Oh, I think that's very true, yes.

QF: *Do you want to enlarge on that at all?*

GG: No, I don't think I do.

Aud: *Can you tell us about the rediscovery of* The Tenth Man?

GG: It's a very curious story. First of all I received a letter from a stranger in America saying that Metro-Goldwyn-Mayer were putting on sale a story of mine called *The Tenth Man*, which awoke a vague memory. I thought it was an idea. I'd been under contract to Metro-Goldwyn-Mayer when I came out of government service at the end of the war, because I was uncertain of being able to support my family with books. I remembered having done an idea for a story, which I remembered as being, you know, two sheets of notepaper, and I didn't see how anybody could sell that. But then I heard that an English publisher, Anthony Blond, had bought it for quite a large sum of money. He allowed me to see it and to my astonishment, it was rather longer than *The Third Man*, and what disconcerted me was that I thought it was rather good and that the royalties, of course, belonged to Metro-Goldwyn-Mayer. But it's being published in February next year.

QF: *Of course, there's also a rather tantalizing titbit of the same time that there was another film that was actually made which was based on one of your synopses. And a well-known film, but they didn't actually say what it was.*

GG: Oh, that was my first version of *Our Man in Havana.*

QF: *For which, I think, Alfred Hitchcock, originally had bid for rights, didn't he?*

GG: Yes, I refused. I refused to let him have it.

QF: *Why was that?*

GG: Well, I haven't got all that admiration for Hitchcock, that we'll say M. Truffaut has.

QF: *Can you say why?*

GG: And he was offering a rather derisory sum, and announced that he had bought it – so I said no.

Aud: *Mr Greene, you were here twelve years ago and you said that your two favourite films at that time were:* The Silence, *Bergman's film, and* Once Upon a Time in the West. *If you've seen a few since then, have you changed your mind?*

GG: Which were the two?

Aud: The Silence *by Bergman and* Once Upon a Time in the West.

GG: What was the first one?

Aud: The Silence *by Bergman.*

GG: Ah, yes. I've seen some I liked. The film which I've liked more than anything else in recent years, I think, is the Australian one . . . *Buster* . . .

QF: *Breaker Morant.*

GG: Which I thought was a magnificent film.

QF: *Why did you particularly like that?*

GG: I thought it was most moving.

QF: *There must be in ten years. I mean, have you caught up?*

GG: Well, as I say, I think I've only seen twelve films probably in the last ten years. I find films are no longer part of my life.

QF: *So tonight will be a rather rare moment for you to watch a movie up on screen.*

GG: Yes.

Aud: *Mr Greene, in* The Honorary Consul *there's a very passing reference to what you describe as 'yet another Falklands crisis'.*

GG: In *The Honorary Consul?*

Aud: *In* The Honorary Consul, *it comes up on the telex, I believe.*

GG: I'd forgotten that.

Aud: *I wonder if you could say, with that in mind, whether you are dismayed or impressed by recent British foreign policy.*

GG: I'd like to tell you a story about the Falkland Islands, and that is that just before our troops landed, they were on the point of landing, or they may have just landed, I received a letter from a woman journalist in Buenos Aires asking for my impressions of the War. And I wrote back and said that the difference between our two countries was that you won't be able to publish my letter, but I'm sure that I'll be able to publish your opinion. And I said after that I think this is a silly war. The first fault was that of the British government in their long drawn out negotiations over the years. The second fault was Argentina's in invading South Georgia which has never been Spanish or Argentinian and that the only good that would come out of this stupid war was the fall of the military junta. I received a clipping from *Clarion*, the principal Buenos Aires newspaper, containing my letter completely uncut, including the reference to the fall of the military junta, which was astonishing, I thought.

QF: *Just a couple more questions.*

Aud: *Of your plays, which have given you the most pleasure in doing and the most satisfaction in writing?*

GG: I think, perhaps *The Return of Raffles*. After that *The Complaisant Lover*, which was the most successful.

QF: *They were planning to make a film, in fact you were heavily involved in,* The Living Room, *and one stage.*

GG: We never got the money, no.

Aud: *I think without exception, Mr Greene, all your titles have a command upon the reading public. There are two parts to my question. One: where does the title come from? Is it the beginning or the end? And secondly, is it to the title that Hollywood film-makers are so often attracted and then find it very difficult to put into effect that which you have written?*

GG: That's true of *The Ministry of Fear.* The Americans bought that during the War in view of the title alone before the book had been published. But actually the title came out of Wordsworth, you may be surprised to hear. I wrote it in West Africa, in Sierra Leone, and I had Matthew Arnold's selection of Wordsworth with me. I'd never been able to read Wordsworth before and I became an admirer in Sierra Leone and found the phrase 'the ministry of fear' in one of his poems. Generally, in fact, I think, always I think I've got the title before I start writing.

QF: *In a sense the title acted against you, of course, with* The Honorary Consul *because the Americans, in their great wisdom, changed the title to* Beyond the Limit.

GG; Yes they did. Why, because there must be honorary consuls in every city of the United States.

QF: *We're showing a clip at the very end now from* The Third Man, *and it's going to be the scene where there's something of a misunderstanding when Holly Martins is seized, and he thinks he's being kidnapped, and, of course, he's attending a British Council meeting. Do you recall anything about writing this sequence or about the sequence itself?*

GG: I remember it very well and I remember it in both the treatment and in the screenplay of the film.

QF: *Were you poking fun at writers particularly?*

GG: No, I was poking fun at the British Council.

QF: *Well, on behalf of us all, can I thank Graham Greene for coming tonight.*

GG: Thank you.

Guardian Lecture at the National Film Theatre (3 September 1984)

6

Letters

Greene reviewed *Tudor Rose* in the *Spectator* on 8 May 1936. On 22 May, the film's director, Robert Stevenson, responded angrily that if Greene did not like his history, 'I do not like his'. 'His preposterous assertion that Jane Grey was "the nearest approach to a saint the Anglican Church has produced," sounds to me more like the language of a cinema poster than that of a responsible critic'. Questioning whether Greene's claim that Jane was 'a scholar of the finest promise' was based on Victorian lithographs or Harrison Ainsworth, he goes on to cite the work of a number of thirties' historians who considered that Ascham exaggerated his pupil's ability – 'her four Latin letters which are extant read to me like good fifth form work'. Anticipating that Greene might counter with the glowing reports of Jane's learning contained in Ulmer's correspondence with Bullinger, Stevenson dismissed such unreliable writers as 'needy divines seeking patronage from Jane's father and in every case extreme Protestants anxious to extol the learning of a white hope of Protestantism'. In response to criticism of the incident in which Edward VI 'wants to go out in the garden and play with a gun', he suggests Greene consult Soranzo's account of the training the king received from Northumberland included in the *Venetian Calendar*. The letter concludes: 'It is odd for a film critic and a film director to be arguing about history, but it was Mr Greene who started it: and if he accuses me of taking refuge in a *tu quoque* argument, I would plead that I have dramatic licence to mangle history, whereas he, as a scholarly critic, has no excuse at all.'

On 29 May, a Mr Walter Crick of Eastbourne wrote to admonish Stevenson for querying Greene's use of 'saint' with regard to Jane Grey. He explained that Greene had not applied the word in a Roman Catholic but in an Anglican sense, and that having lived a holy life in accordance with Christ's example, Jane could rightly be considered a saint.

Mr Greene writes: I am unrepentant, though it is chivalrous of Mr Stevenson to defend the scenario of *Tudor Rose*, a film in which his part as director was so adequately performed. I do take seriously Ascham's evidence. There is no reason (Mr Stevenson's flat disbelief is unreasonable) to doubt the truth of the conversation Ascham recalls with 'that worthy and noble lady'. She was not *his* pupil and the dead could not reward him. The whole passage in which Lady Jane Grey describes to him the harsh discipline her parents impose on her when she is dancing or playing, so that when she is called from her gentle teacher 'I fall a weeping, because whatsoever I do els but learning is ful of grief, trouble, feare and whole mislikeing unto me', reads like the grim truth to anyone who has suffered the tyranny of English recreation. As for my own opinion of her character, it is at any rate shared by Professor

Pollard, who couples her name with that of St Thomas More.

The Spectator (22 May 1936)

During the summer months, the BBC had been in the habit of discontinuing its regular film review broadcasts. However, in 1937 the Corporation decided to ask 'different critics to come to the microphone each fortnight and talk about the films of the preceding two weeks'. On 22 June 1937, one N.G. Luker wrote to Greene asking if he would like to broadcast on Sunday 29 August. A further letter from Luker was required before Greene agreed. The script of that talk is included in this volume on page 511.

Dear Luker,

Many thanks for your letter of August 5th. I will await the instructions of your colleague. Perhaps he would give me too a few hints – do you mention the names of the cinemas in which films are being shown? Can I deal with interesting pictures, such as some of the documentaries, which are not to be seen at the immediate date of the talk?

(6 August 1937)

Basil Wright had preceded Greene as film critic of the *Spectator*, and along with Stuart Legg and Christopher Shawe, he frequently stood in for him during his travels and the lifetime of *Night and Day*. Indeed, on the opening page of his autobiography Wright acclaims Greene as 'a child of the film age'. For his part, Greene cites Wright's film *Song of Ceylon* as one of the great pieces of 'poetic cinema' in his 1936 article 'Subjects and Stories'. This makes their dispute over Robert Flaherty's contribution to *Elephant Boy* all the more interesting.

Wright began: 'Mr Graham Greene enjoys a wide reputation as the most acute and reliable film critic in this country. It was, therefore, something of a shock to read his review of Flaherty's *Elephant Boy*, in which he does less than justice to one of the most important figures in the Cinema today.' He next accused Greene of being incapable of distinguishing between the function of the producer and the director. Though shifting the responsibility for the film's shortcomings onto Alexander Korda, Wright proceeded to justify Korda's decision to add the sequences Zoltan Korda filmed at Denham to Flaherty's location work in the interests of box office receipts. Doubting that the sum total of Flaherty's Indian shoot was 'a scene of elephants washed in a river, a few shots of markets and idols and forest', Wright concluded by inviting Greene to see the additional footage and perhaps 'rewrite his review with a little more respect for Flaherty's unique feeling for cinema, his depth of human understanding, and, let me emphatically add, his intense personal sincerity'.

Sir

– In spite of Mr Basil Wright's generous championship of Mr Robert Flaherty I am unrepentant. Mr Flaherty was sent to India to direct a fictional film. A director several thousand miles from his studios and his producer must undertake some of the responsibilities of production as well as of direction, and nothing Mr Wright mentions alters the fact that Mr Flaherty has not delivered the goods – the right setting for a particular story. Mr Wright exhibits what I can only call a religious faith in something he admits he hasn't seen – the unused Mysore material. A critic must depend on the evidence of the eyes, and my memory of the bogus shark's hunt in Mr Flaherty's last picture does not incline me to believe in 'his depth of human understanding', any more than the melodramatic plotting of *Man of Aran* convinced me of Mr Flaherty's 'unique feeling for cinema'.

The Spectator (30 April 1937)

Greene might have had little regard for the majority of adaptations of his novels, but whenever blame (or credit) was wrongly apportioned, he was quick to straighten the record, (*viz* the case of the opera of *Our Man in Havana*, included below). This letter concerning *Brighton Rock* was printed beneath the headline: 'Razor-Slasher Film is Defended by the Man who Wrote the Book'.

Sir

– I have read the somewhat violent attack by your critic with bewilderment. If he had said that the book was 'false, cheap, nasty sensationalism', it would have been, to me, a quite possible personal point of view, but to praise the author of the book at the expense of the directors of the film is surely unbalanced.

As it happens, I am also the author of the film play, and I can assure your critic that John Boulting (the director, while his twin brother Roy was producer) worked quite as hard as myself to retain the religious theme. And modifications of that theme are the responsibility of the British Film Censor, who objected to various passages in the dialogue of a specifically religious nature. Apparently one is allowed a certain latitude in using the name of

God as an expletive, but any serious quotation from the Bible is not permissible on the English screen.

But in spite of this handicap I should have said that what your critic describes, almost too kindly, as 'the subtle religious theme' was as present in the film as in the book. Mr Whitley remarks that 'Hollywood has banned the production of gangster films because they give a false impression of life in America', but in fact Hollywood has not banned the production of gangster films but only the production of films that hold the gangster up to the sympathy of the audience. Obviously this has not been done in the case of Pinkie Brown, and your critic's disgust is an indication that one purpose of the film – the presentation of a character possessed by evil – has been successfully achieved.

Naturally, parents will not want their children to see it (must all films be made for the juvenile market?) nor would they be allowed to take their children to it without breaking the rules of the cinema, since the picture has been granted only an adult certificate.

Daily Mirror (9 January 1948)[11]

One or two bibliographies of Graham Greene's work list a BBC radio broadcast with Charlie Chaplin. These letters to Harman Grisewood, Director of the Spoken Word, and his assistant Anna Kallin, show that Greene soon regretted his decision to appear in the programme, which was scrapped.

Dear Harman,

Many thanks for your letter. Naturally I am much honoured by your suggestion that I should have a discussion with Charlie Chaplin, though I think it would be very difficult indeed for anyone to stand up to him before the microphone. I hate broadcasting, but if a really amusing and interesting subject could be agreed I certainly would not turn it down offhand! Perhaps we could meet next week sometime and have a talk.

(1 December 1952)

Dear Miss Kallin,

I am afraid on second thoughts I find that I have too much work to do in the course of the next few months over my play and a novel I am writing to be able to do the broadcast you want. The temptation in Mr Grisewood's letter was too great and I did not consider the matter carefully enough. Do forgive me for troubling you by my indecision, but I do realise now that the whole thing is impossible.

(5 December 1952)

In his 1958 article 'The Novelist and the Cinema: A Personal Experience', Greene echoed the sentiments he first expressed to Alan Brien in an *Evening Standard* interview on 25 January 1957: 'when you sell a book to Hollywood you sell it outright. The long Hollywood contracts – sheet after closely printed sheet as long as the first treatment of the novel which is for sale – ensure that you have no "author's rights". The film producer can alter anything. He can turn your tragedy of East End Jewry into a musical comedy at Palm Springs if he wishes. He need not even retain your title, though that is usually almost the only thing he wishes to retain.'

On 24 August 1956, shortly before principal shooting began, Greene told Thomas Wiseman in another *Evening Standard* interview, that he already suspected that writer/director Joseph L. Mankiewicz had every intention of misrepresenting *The Quiet American*: 'I don't suppose they can film it in the way that it is written. They'll probably make it so that it looks as if the American was being bamboozled all the time by the Communists or somebody.'

On 9 January 1957, *The Times* carried a report from Saigon revealing that Mankiewicz had indeed betrayed Greene's novel. However, not every voice was raised in protest: 'some commentators here are mildly shocked that Mr Greene should permit this travesty of his work, others are saying "it serves him right for writing such an anti-American book"'. Ironically, Greene was staying at the Hotel Algonquin in New York, when the story reached him.

Despite an intense dislike of Fritz Lang's *The Ministry of Fear* and John Ford's *The Fugitive*, Greene eventually reconciled himself to even the shoddiest adaptations of his work – with the notable exception of Muriel and Sydney Box following their 1947 version of *The Man Within*. As he told Ronald Harwood during a 1975 discussion on the BBC radio arts programme, *Kaleidoscope* (this time reiterating the 'Novelist and Cinema' article): 'I was never miserable about the kind of film made, even when, as in the case of *The Quiet American*, the whole story was twisted politically. One always felt that if a book was of any value it would survive a few years longer than the film.'

Sir – Your report of 9 January from Saigon has only just

overtaken me. It is certainly true that if a story is sold to Hollywood the author retains no control over the adaptation. But perhaps a Machiavellian policy is justified – one can trust Hollywood to overbid its hand. If such changes as your Correspondent describes have been made in the film of *The Quiet American* they will make only the more obvious the discrepancy between what the State Department would like the world to believe and what in fact happened in Vietnam. In that case, I can imagine some happy evenings of laughter not only in Paris but in the cinemas of Saigon.

The Times (29 January 1957)

Sir

– Why do American moviemen require pith helmets, salt tablets, quinine pills to visit the Cao Dai capital, Tayninh. The climate is somewhat similar to a Washington summer. Perhaps the inhabitants were mystified by their strange attire and eccentric diet.

Time (18 March 1957)

Graham Greene would perhaps not have been everyone's first choice to adapt George Bernard Shaw's *St Joan* for the screen. He confessed to Thomas Wiseman during their 1956 *Evening Standard* interview that he was not an admirer of Shaw, although *St Joan* was one of the few plays with which he had much sympathy. His task was made no easier by the fact that director Otto Preminger gave him only six weeks to complete the script.

When the film was released the *New Statesman*'s film critic, William Whitebait, had nothing remarkable to say about it, but in a review of Raymond Rouleau's *The Witches of Salem*, he castigated the screenwriter, Jean-Paul Sartre, for giving a Marxist slant to events in 1692 Massachsetts. He continued: 'This is, I'm afraid, typical of the parasitic film-monger. Graham Greene was brought in to de-Protestantize Shaw's *St Joan*; Sartre is brought in to add the Party line to Arthur Miller. The point is that in each case two dissimilar talents are wasted where one might have succeeded. *St Joan* was a respectable flop. *The Witches of Salem* isn't that; indeed, it is so good, up to a point, that it is a pity the major chance should have been thrown away.'

Henry Adler's letter of 21 September labelled the film 'a vulgar travesty of Shaw's intention' and while blaming Preminger and his star, Jean Seberg, for their part in the proceedings, he considered Greene the primary culprit for omitting the

Gentleman from Rome and the epilogue and for depicting Joan as 'the crudest kind of miracle worker'. He concluded by asking whether 'Shaw's remarks on the attitude of the Church and people to saints proved embarrassingly to strike near home?'

Greene's replies in each case were as follows:

Sir

– Your film critic writes that I was brought in to de-Protestantize Shaw's *St Joan* – a rather offensive suggestion. Such a role was never proposed to me nor would I have accepted it. I suspect that your reviewer remembers little of Shaw's play and knows less about Catholic doctrine. There is nothing in Shaw's play offensive to Catholics, although there are a number of historical inaccuracies. The play of course had to be cut for film purposes, but these cuts were mainly drawn from the long discussions on the growth of nationality and the decay of feudalism which would hardly have been understood by film audiences. No line was altered for the purpose of watering down Shaw's Protestantism or instilling a Catholic tone. Even the 'miracle' which your film critic in his notice attributed to my influence he could have found in the original play if he had been familiar with it. Perhaps the most intelligent appreciation of Shaw's play and the best defence of Shaw against ignorant Catholic criticism was written in the *Month* by Father Thurston, the distinguished Jesuit, at the time the play was produced.

New Statesman (14 September 1957)

Sir

– Really Mr Adler should stick to the point. I was not defending the film version of *Saint Joan*, or even my part in it, I was replying to the offensive statement that I had been brought into the film in order to Catholicize it. However, if Mr Adler will look again at Shaw's play he will find the incident of the hens laying is left unchanged in the film – except for the exclamation 'Christ in Heaven!' which no censor would pass. What, of course, happened is that in place of a curtain, which gives the audience time to laugh happily at Baudricourt's reaction, there is a 'fade': a curtain lasts ten minutes, a 'fade' as many seconds: a film has to go on. This kills the laugh and I don't see how the killing could have been avoided without recourse to a drastic rewriting of Shaw's text.

Personally I have always found the incident of the wind changing in Shaw's play sentimental and unconvincing and it remains sentimental and unconvincing in the film. Personally I would have liked to omit the scene altogether, but then what would Shaw admirers have said? None of the three so-called miracles in Shaw's *Saint Joan* has been omitted, but then none of them has been made to look any more authentic than in the original play. The criticism of the third 'miracle' is left, as Shaw wrote it, in the mouth of the archbishop. I have a haunting impression that it is a long time since your correspondent read Shaw's play.

Certainly there were cuts in the epilogue, but rather less cuts perhaps than in the rest of the play. I doubt whether Mr Adler's reverence for Shaw would have stood up to a film of three and a half hours. There is a very simple reason why the Gentleman from Rome was cut. When the play was first produced the canonization of Saint Joan was still a recent event and the dialogue of the Gentleman from Rome had a lively contemporary flavour. Now to the vast majority of any film audience Saint Joan's canonization has faded into past history; it is no longer an issue, and surely they would have been mystified by the sudden appearance of a gentleman in a top hat, announcing something which they had known all their lives, in a costume they could not easily identify.

Mr Hobbs makes a great song-and-dance about what Mr

Christopher Hollis once wrote about Shaw's play. With all due respect to Mr Hollis I can hardly accept him as the voice of the Church. The best critical appreciation of Shaw's *Saint Joan*, as I wrote before, is that by Father Herbert Thurston, SJ, which appeared at the time of the first production in the pages of *The Month*. Of course Shaw was critical of many things Catholics believe, but does Mr Hobbs really expect Catholics to find criticism offensive? What a strange angry young life he must live if he finds any opposition to his ideas 'repugnant' and 'offensive'.

New Statesman (28 September 1957)

In 1962 *Our Man in Havana* was turned into an opera by Malcolm Williamson, an Australian composer resident in England. Greene was originally approached to write the libretto, but as he told the *Sunday Times* on 9 June 1963, he had refused as 'writing for me is a cold act. I write against the grain. It's a cold war, not a hot one. I couldn't feel the passion.' Into the breach stepped Sidney Gilliat, who had co-written (and often co-produced) with Frank Launder such British film classics as *The Lady Vanishes, Night Train to Munich, Waterloo Road, The Rake's Progress* and *Green for Danger*.

Premièred at Sadler's Wells, the opera drew cool reviews, including an anonymous notice in *The Times* that pronounced that it was 'a poor opera, in certain respects a bad one, and as a representation of a great novel it is a travesty'. The libretto was similarly decried: 'One had not dared to hope that the depths and distances of Greene's novel would be retained, but one had expected some shape and consistency which does not show itself in this version.'

Greene responded:

Sir,

As I had no hand in the opera of *Our Man in Havana* may I be allowed without vanity to disagree with your Critic? To me the opera was in no way a travesty of the novel and I admired the great skill with which the libretto had compressed the action and yet brought out every political point. Surely it is a little odd to write of 'the weak characterization of the head of the Secret Service', for he is a very minor character in the novel. Perhaps your Critic had in mind Sir Ralph Richardson's brilliant performance in the film. As the author of the film script may

I say that I infinitely preferred Mr Gilliat's libretto?

I haven't spoken of the music only because it would be impertinent on my part to disagree with your Music Critic on his own ground. All the same to me it was very satisfactory and added a new dimension to the story.

The Times (4 July 1963)

In the course of the John Player Lecture at the National Film Theatre in 1970, Greene confessed to having seen as few as a dozen films in the previous decade. The discovery of the cartoon accompanying *The Americanization of Emily* was thus a happy chance. I suspect the 'cat-and-mouse' cartoon in question is a 1964 Tom and Jerry short called *Much Ado About Mousing*, in which Jerry befriends a vicious bulldog who tells him to 'just whistle' whenever Tom attacks. However, Tom turns the tables with a pair of ear-plugs and the protector is (for a brief spell) rendered powerless. This would perhaps explain Greene's reference to the cartoon's satirical view of US involvement in Vietnam, although there is a 1965 Tom and Jerry short, called *The Cat's Me-Ouch*, in which Jerry hires a miniature dog to counter Tom's threat who proves every bit as invincible as a bigger breed, his teeth remaining embedded into Tom's paw even as he's laid up in hospital. However, this seems to have been released later in the year.

Directed by Arthur Hiller, the main feature was adapted from William Bradford Huie's novel by Paddy Chayevsky and starred Julie Andrews, James Garner, Melvyn Douglas, James Coburn, Liz Fraser, Joyce Grenfell and Keenan Wynn. It earned cinematographer Philip Lathrop an Oscar nomination. Otherwise it was an amiable, if forgettable, Second World War story about an English war widow who volunteers as an army driver and inspires her cowardly passenger to bravery through her love.

Sir

Film cartoons are very seldom noticed by film reviewers, and for that reason I would like to draw attention to the brilliant cartoon shown, perhaps significantly with *The Americanization of Emily*, at the Empire Theatre.

Metro-Goldwyn-Mayer have had the courage, in the disguise of what some may regard as a conventional cat-and-mouse cartoon film, to make a scathing attack on the American policy in Vietnam, and the inability of the Pentagon to understand the nature of guerilla warfare.

The satire in *The Americanization of Emily* is gentle compared with the savage cartoon.

Daily Telegraph (24 April 1965)

John Coleman reviewed *The Comedians* in the *New Statesman* on 19 January 1968. Puzzled why one of Greene's weakest novels should have 'turned up again as such a negligible film', Coleman proceeded to offer his condolences to a cast that had struggled with a script that had proved itself a 'real opponent'. The 'small sorties into local colour' that had succeeded in the book he considered 'nasty or picturesque or both' and the transformation of Brown into a heroic opponent of the Tontons Macoute was denounced as a 'saccharine sop to the box office'. 'Did Mr Greene settle for this? And if he didn't, why is his name on the credits as sole writer?'

In response to the last line of Greene's letter – 'obviously Mr Coleman and I do not smile at the same things' – Coleman wrote: 'Obviously not.'

Sir

– In defence of my friend and director Peter Glenville, I would like to take full responsibility for the script of *The Comedians*. To my mind Brown's closing scene is comic and not in the least heroic. A sense of humour however is personal and not universal, and obviously Mr Coleman and I do not smile at the same things.

New Statesman (26 January 1968)

On 13 February 1976, the books section in the *New Statesman* included two reviews with which Greene found fault: George Melly on Robert Windeler's biography of Shirley Temple and Eric Rhode on Karol Kulik's *Alexander Korda*.

Sir

– Will you allow me to correct 'for the record' two points made by your reviewers (*New Statesman* 13 February)?

(1) Mr George Melly writes that my criticism of Shirley Temple 'helped curtail the career, as a film critic, of Mr Graham Greene'. The libel case to which he refers came to court in March 1938 and I ceased to review films two years later in March 1940 owing to rather more serious events than a libel action by Miss Temple or the strictures of the Lord Chief Justice.

(2) Mr Rhode asks whether Harry Lime's charm in *The Third Man* 'derives from Korda'. All to Korda's honour the answer is 'no'. One of Korda's great qualities was to leave alone a director whom he trusted. I think Carol Reed will agree that Korda never interfered, even to the extent of a single script conference, in the two films we made for him together.

New Statesman (27 February 1976)

Greene's intense dislike of most Hollywood versions of his novels was well-known, but he remained too informed and discriminating a critic to disregard genuine moments of quality. In his 1936 *Sight and Sound* article, 'Is It Criticism', he likewise demonstrated a bitter antipathy to the London journalists whose attendance at studio-sponsored preview shows and gala receptions somehow entitled them to the title 'film critic'. As the following letter proves, he apparently retained this view also.

Sir

– Mr Philip Purser writes that Lauren Bacall was 'insanely miscast in her third picture *The Confidential Agent* and having given – as she admits – a lousy performance, she nevertheless bitterly resented the cool notices that came her way'. I also as the author of the book resented those cool notices. This remains the only good film ever made from one of my books by an American director and Miss Bacall gave an admirable performance and so did Charles Boyer. For some reason the English critics thought that a young American actress should not have played an English 'Honourable'. However the Honourable in my book was only removed by one generation from a coal miner and to me there seemed to be an extraordinary chauvinism and snobbism in their criticisms. Her performance was admirable.

Sunday Telegraph (28 January 1979)

Entitled 'Pale Shades of Greene', Philip French's *Observer* review of 3 February 1980 showed the film version of *The Human Factor* little mercy. While commending Tom Stoppard's 'respectful job of dramatizing the story', he lambasted the insensitive casting, ill-lit sets, and sloppy and lacksidaisical direction. 'I do not think Graham Greene would have much objection to the pallid celluloid artifact drawn from his last novel being called Otto Preminger's *The Human Factor*.' Few would guess, he continued, that this film was based on a 'sombre, comic, ironic fable set in the author's own version of contemporary Britain, which is really an extension of that old Greeneland he mapped out in the 1930s. The cinema may have closed in Berkhamsted, but people there still have buttons on their flies.'

Greene's response dwells on this latter point because, for some reason, it had also been a preoccupation of fiction reviewers when the novel was originally published in 1978.

French signed off: 'If I owned a veil I would happily give it to Preminger to draw over this film.'

Sir

– I entirely agree with every word of Philip French's criticisms of the film *The Human Factor*, but what is all this fuss about buttons on flies?

All my suits have buttons as they are all around fifteen or sixteen years old. I don't suppose the man in the inn yard at Berkhamsted had a newer suit than I have.

Observer (10 February 1980)

Sir

– Constantine FitzGibbon in a charitable spirit has much exaggerated the help I gave to Norman Douglas towards the end of his life. I was certainly not in a financial position to give money to my friend Mario Soldati 'to buy the film rights to *South Wind*'. What happened was this: we both wanted to find some 'pocket money' for Norman and we hatched a plot together. Together we went to Mr Carlo Ponti, the film producer, and we persuaded him that if he bought a film option on *South Wind* I would write the script of the film and Mario Soldati would direct. All that I and Mario contributed were a few weeks of unpaid work in Capri trying to produce a treatment which would be acceptable to Mr Ponti and not a betrayal of the book. Unfortunately no script emerged, but Norman has his pocket money and Mr Ponti very generously never asked us to refund what he had paid for the option. Norman knew all about our little plot and appreciated the joke.

Times Literary Supplement (30 May 1980)

The fullest account of the *Wee Willie Winkie* libel case can be found in Greene's article 'Memories of a Film Critic'. 'Atticus' here is Stephen Pile, compiler of the *Heroic Failures* books. The *London Magazine* suit Greene refers to was brought by American author Donald Windham following Dotson Rader's article on his collection of Tennessee Williams's letters.

Sir

– A petty reason perhaps why novelists more and more try to keep a distance from journalists is that the novelists are trying to write the truth and journalists are trying to write fiction. Atticus writes that *Night and Day* of which I was joint editor was closed because of a review written by me of a film *Wee Willie Winkie* which 'was so defamatory that Lord Stewart adjudged it a gross outrage. The damages were £2,000 and the magazine closed'. I have never even heard of a Lord Stewart – Atticus is perhaps referring to Lord Hewart – a notorious judge in the 30s, but then why did he not check the facts? The damages were not £2,000 and the paper closed many months *after* the libel action from high costs and lack of advertising support. It was nearing the rocks long before the libel action. I sincerely hope that Atticus is equally inaccurate when he writes of the difficulties of the admirable *London Magazine*.

Sunday Times (18 January 1981)

7

Film Stories & Treatments

No Man's Land – A Film Treatment

Chapter One

(I)

I had noticed him for days in the Club Restaurant sitting there in the same spot, always alone with a book propped in front of him: a man in the early forties with an expression of tired patience as though his life were spent waiting around in just such unrewarding spots as the leave-centre of Braunlage. He was surrounded by the angular discontented faces of the occupying wives who would come in on a few days' leave, sometimes with their husbands and sometimes in small hen parties with no other object than inspecting a NAAFI shop – Nylon stockings, a few scarves, some Molineux scent, gloves, a selection of bad children's books. It wasn't the skiing season, so they came and went rapidly, while he stayed on, a civilian with a book. I wondered sometimes whether he was waiting for a girl to join him, but surely then there would have been some signs of impatience, and of that I could never have accused him.

Once I met him walking in the forest alone. Even then he had his book with him stuck in his pocket. We were a couple of kilometers east of Braunlage and I thought it just as well to have a word with him, so I said 'Good afternoon', and fell into step. He was perfectly polite: nobody could ever have said that he resented his solitude being broken – even the army wives had nothing to complain of, he was just neutral that was all.

I said 'The paths here are a bit tricky. Have you a compass?'

'Oh,' he said, 'I don't go far enough to need a compass.'

'My name's Redburn of the Boundary Inspection.'

'My name's Brown,' he said, 'Richard Brown' – even his name was neutral.

'Control Commission?'

'No. Just a holiday. Spending my fifty pounds.'

'All alone?'

'I'm expecting a friend any day'

'You want to be careful if you walk much.'

'Careful?'

'Not to lose your way. We are only a kilometre from the Russian Zone.'

He gave me back an annoying smile. 'Ah, the famous Iron Curtain.'

'It's a stupid phrase,' I said, 'even if the Great Man did invent it. There'd be no difficulty if the curtain were really iron, but it's like any other curtain – you can push your way through, only it has so many folds and you can easily get lost in the folds.'

'Yes,' he said, 'they can hardly patrol these hills properly.' The trees stretched all round us as regular as pillars, a vast hall of pillars – one could see no doorway anywhere. 'I suppose I'd better go along down,' he said. 'That way?'

'No, that way.'

I didn't see Brown for a good many days after that. We were having a certain amount of trouble on the Boundary Inspection Service because of a vision – yes, a vision, it was as simple and as absurd as that. The vision had taken place – taken root would be the fitter phrase – during one of the dark days of the war. The Hartz is staunchly Protestant, but in a village called Ilsenhof there were enough Catholics to maintain a church. Protestants don't go in for visions, though of course in the old days in these parts they went in for witches and in the shops at Goslar you can buy little old ladies in spectacles and poke bonnets mounted on broomsticks. But this wasn't a witch, it was the Virgin herself who appeared to a couple of children at the entrance to a natural cave outside Ilsenhof. It was winter – the first snow had fallen, and she gave the children a rose. That was the one inexplicable part of the story – and so personally I disbelieve it. I am a busy man in a position of some authority and I have no room in my life for the inexplicable, but oh what a nuisance it can be. Within a few months Ilsenhof was a centre of pilgrimage. People would walk from as far as Catholic Bavaria; they would come from the other side of the Wesser; even Czechoslovakia sent its pilgrims; and when the war was over it became an allied problem. The village was first of all in the British Zone, but in readjusting the zones and eliminating an enclave, the village became several kilometres inside Russian territory. The Catholics were indignant, though I should have thought if they had faith in this vision they would have been glad to see it planted in the enemy soil, but one can hardly alter geography all over again for the sake of what two children said they had seen nearly ten years ago. The local Russian command, of course, we assumed would simply demolish it. The sound of an explosion in the hills started a rumour that the cave had been dynamited, but you always have to treat most anti-Russian stories with reserve, for six months later the pilgrimages were on again. If the Russian commander had really objected, he had been overruled by someone.

It was a tricky position for the Russians. New uranium deposits had been found around Eisleben in the Hartz area, and there was an obvious clash between the requirements of propaganda and security. For the sake of propaganda and for the sake too of a contented population (for even the Protestants had developed a local pride in the Virgin of Ilsenhof) the Russians would have liked to leave the pilgrimage intact, all the more so perhaps because of the dark rumours that centred round the Czech uranium mines. Forced labour after all is not in the long run as good as free labour – or shall we say controlled labour?

Propaganda apparently won for the time being, but the pilgrimage, I should imagine, must have suffered a good deal in commercial value; you would have to be very religious indeed or very ignorant before you entered the Russian zone for the sake of somebody else's vision. Certain roads were allotted to the pilgrims and special passes given them and this gave my office a good deal of work. I sometimes wished we could close the pilgrimage from our side, but the democracies could hardly show themselves less tolerant than the Russians. Their tolerance caused an immense amount of friction – some people holding proper passes would be turned back, some would be admitted without passes at all, and there were always rumours of people who never returned.

At one time the story was spread that a whole pilgrimage had been sent to the uranium mines – there wasn't a word of truth in it, of course.

Then one afternoon I got word from the German Frontier patrol that one of my countrymen was down by the block on the Nordhausen road with no apparent object, I drove there to look at him. Beyond Braunlage the frontier of the Russian zone approaches nearer and nearer to the highway. By the time you reach the village of Hohengeisse, the frontier is just across a few yards of ground spotted with the sawn trunks of trees like a battleground. Beyond the village, on the road to Nordhausen, where they used to make the best Schnaps in Germany until the town disappeared into the mysterious regions of 'over there', the left hand ditch is Russian, the right British. I never feel quite at my ease on those three kilometres (one of our officers was shot there last year 'accidentally'), with the thick woods on either side, where the East and the West patrols work through the shadows, looking for smugglers or deserters. A frontier sign, a notice announcing the road block and then the block itself, just a few tree trunks, a tangle of brown twigs, the rusty radiator of an old car, twenty yards of no-man's land, and then the other boundary post and a crossroads lying wide open and the sense of an unfathomable emptiness that the propagandists of two worlds have imposed on our minds.

Brown stood there looking across the block to the little group of East German police in their blue uniforms and a single Russian soldier in green khaki who for some reason had his arms full of grass. A frontier patrol with his rifle unslung watched Brown from our side of the road and the East German police waved to him and called out to him that the road was open on their side and invited him to climb across the barrier. An old car drew up beside them and the driver watched too, and the empty road behind them ran on towards Nordhausen and Asia.

'Good afternoon, Brown,' I said, 'want anything?'

'No, oh no, nothing.'

'You look as if you had an appointment.'

He smiled. 'Oh no, just curiosity.'

'I wouldn't trust them too far.'

'There is something strange and sad, isn't there, about a no-man's land – even when there's only twenty yards of it. A place on this earth where nobody can ever build or sleep.' He looked at the trees on the Russian side. 'Is that No-Man's Land too?'

'No, that's Russian. I'm not sure whether they claim the ditch you're standing in.'

He said, 'They don't put up any wire.'

'No. I told you it's not an iron curtain.'

'Well, I'd better be getting back.'

'Have you got a car somewhere?'

'No, I've walked. Began to feel the need of exercise, you know, sitting around.'

'Your friend hasn't turned up?'

'No.'

'Overdue?' I don't know what made me use a term more applicable to a lost ship than a lost appointment. He hesitated and said, 'I expect him any day,' and his voice, like a wireless operator forced against his will by a revolver in his back, sent out an involuntary signal of anxiety and distress.

(II)

Why should a civilian called Brown have so weighed on my mind? God knows, I had plenty to do. There was, for example, the question of the Polish refugees. We had agreed to accept twenty-five thousand of them in the British zone and now the Russians were rumoured to be sending a quarter of a million. They began to arrive by trains and we couldn't shunt them back, walking cases, stretcher cases without stretchers and the bodies – there were quite a number of bodies. And there was the murder near Walkenreid, a shocking murder however used one had got to shocks in the last four years. Three smugglers had agreed to convoy a German over the demarkation line. He had a family in the Russian zone and he was carrying two suitcases when in the railway station at Walkenreid the smugglers spotted him. They told him of the trouble he would have at the frontier and he agreed to set out with them in the darkness over the mountain. No Walpurgisnacht on the Brocken can have contained quite so much horror as that scene when they halted and beat him on the head. He wouldn't stop screaming so they bludgeoned him again. But he was still able to get on his knees and pray for mercy and the leader crammed his victim's scarf into his mouth and thrust it further and further down his throat with a walking stick until he died – there is a photograph on the police files, of the dead face and the dribble of scarf out of the mouth. We know what happened because one of the men gave himself up.

I only mention these things because such incidents are the background to a frontier life. Who was it who said 'The world has been abandoned into the hands of men'? It certainly seemed true in that year on that particular border. Occasionally I found myself envying those who could believe in a winter Virgin carrying a rose. Brown was waiting for I don't know whom and I was waiting for I don't know what. So was a whole occupying army, and with what absurdities we tried to occupy ourselves while we waited. That too is part of the background.

The Combined Forces and the Control Commission were holding their annual Drama Festival at Bad Hartzburg. Every night three one act plays were staged before a suave patronising judge fetched out from the Academy of Dramatic Art in London and an audience filled with a kind of stifling good will. It took one back to the old days of school where any serious criticism in the magazine would have seemed like a breach of tact because it would have discouraged the boys. At the end of the evening the judge came forward and commented on the individual productions. 'Now the Herford Club – that was a really good production, excellent characterisation, and the way the door kept on blowing open – that really did admirably convey the effect of storm. Then the Goslar Club – really good characterisation here, excellent production. You really felt the producer knew what he was after.

The visitors from Frankfurt – very intelligent choice of play. Admirable characterisation. I'd like to congratulate the producer on that little bit of business with the cigarette lighter . . . '

In the interval between the first and second play, as though inevitably now, I picked out from all those rows of officers and wives the face of Brown, sitting there, talking to nobody, though one of his military or official neighbours, I suppose, must have invited him or he could hardly have got in. I had noticed him first because he was always in the same place at the same time, for that reason he gave an effect of patience: now that he was as it were continually cropping up he conveyed the sense of restlessness, as though he had come to an end of his patience and was roaming a room, from wall to wall and back again. I felt that he would ultimately open a door and walk out, and that was exactly what he did.

The second play was an extraordinary piece of 'ham' found in God knows what paper-covered collection of plays suited to amateurs. It was called *The Lordship of the Sea*, and it was about a family of fishermen called the Combers who would come striding in to hang up oilskins, swallow some tea, make trenchant remarks about 'there's always been a Comber in the lifeboat' and dash out again to drown one by one, while the mother and sisters watched with dour approval and sweethearts tried to lure the Combers to infant graves. Clouds rushed across the backcloth, clouds clunked like iron, and the Combers shouted passionately and fraternally 'As long as there's a Comber alive, that old devil the sea . . .' I heard a slight disturbance behind me and looking back saw Brown making for the exit. R.A.S.C. officers in mess kit stared rigidly at the stage, but their wives were obviously disturbed by Brown's breach of taste: even the actors noticed his persistent and long drawn out exit down the row and fumbled their lines.

I felt great smpathy with Brown, but I hadn't his courage – or was it as one of the wives suggested later, just ignorance? A great deal that happened was due to his ignorance. Though it was a long time before I heard and put together the details of what happened to him when the night took him out of earshot of the last Combers. I suppose the third play of the evening – a bonhomous piece of optimism and good will by Priestley had just started and we had put Brown right out of mind about the time he entered the Russian zone. What followed is reasonably accurate. Unhappy people confide even in strangers.

Chapter Two
(I)

Bad Hartzburg is a rather ugly spa town that straggles from the valley up the slopes of the foothills. The Teutonic houses try unsuccessfully to recall the fancifulness of Swiss architecture, but yellow beams turn liverish and scarlet gardens and the fir trees that come down the hills towards the houses are like fellow actors who have also not mastered the atmosphere, an atmosphere that depends after all on more than a century of peace. There are no zones in Switzerland. There is no need to indicate on tree stumps the approach of a border. Brown had only three kilometres to go.

If he had known his way about he couldn't have chosen a better point to cross. Smugglers operate further from British centres and the German patrols are less dense here than in the area around Braunlage. Smugglers are human too and they prefer the less mountainous routes. Brown had some stiff climbing to do in the dark before he reached the frontier.

There were no incidents at all. Once he lost his footing on a tree trunk bridging a little rapid mountain stream and went in up to his knees: once he thought he saw a border patrol standing with unslung rifle awaiting his approach, and after a long pause he went forward in an attitude of surrender, hands above his head, to greet a tree split by some last year's lightning flash. He went forward from one zone into the next unchallenged. The curtain opened at a touch to receive him into its folds.

When he was certain that he had left the British zone right behind, he lay down in some underbrush and slept, slept as he hadn't slept for a week. He told somebody later. 'You see I was at peace. I was doing something. I wasn't waiting any more.' When he woke it was broad daylight and from the edge of the trees he looked down at a waste of almost empty fields (one man was burning leaves a long way off) and the roofs of a village. There was nothing to tell him except the sun that he was looking east and not west: there was nothing sinister any longer now that the road block had been crossed. It was like the peace that follows an interrogation.

In the village he made a bad mistake. He went into a shop to buy some bread and offered his Western marks in exchange. The woman held them in her hand and looked at them and at once he remembered the difference in currency. There was nothing to do except wait patiently for the next move.

She said, 'Sie kommen aus dem Westen?'

'Ja.'

The notes lay in the palm of her hand like an exhibit in court. She said nothing. She was looking over his shoulder at the street behind. He turned and looked too. A car had drawn up. There was something wrong about the car and it was a moment before he realized what was wrong – it was a good car, that was all, an expensive car, a well-groomed car, in fact a Mercedes. He turned back to the woman of the bakery and held out his hand – whether to take the notes back or to appeal to her, he could not have said. The car lay like a watchdog across the doorway. He watched the worn eyes of the shopwoman shift this way and that and he thought 'finis, it's finis'. Then suddenly her fist closed on the notes and put them out of sight, and a woman's voice asked for bread.

He described it later – and my informant told me that for some reason we neither of us then understood that he spoke with asperity or perhaps bitterness – 'I was tired, you see, and scared and there she stood quite humbly, waiting for her bread. It was only a small village – I didn't even know its name and she was beautiful, she even had a good suit on that might have come from Dior. You don't expect a beautiful woman in a small village, do you, and she was more beautiful than you would expect in a whole world of women. I tell you I was tired and scared: perhaps at an Embassy cocktail party, talking about the opera or the books she had been reading lately, it wouldn't have had any effect on me, but as it was, I loved her. It was as simple as that. Perhaps its the middle-aged. We haven't time to lose. And the baker woman thrust the goods across to her as if she were mud and she took time and went back to her Mercedes and drove away.'

'Yes, and then?' my informant asked.

Brown told him with a kind of disgust, 'Oh then, all the worry began. You see then I wanted to finish, to get out, to live.'

(II)

When the car had driven away, the baker's wife opened her hand. Brown wanted to ask her who the woman was, but what was the good? In a car like that the roads were open as far as Moscow: there were no road blocks to the East. She had most of Europe to be lost in.

The woman said, 'Come inside,' and he followed her.

'Have you any more of this?' she asked him. He emptied his pockets of notes; they were no longer any good to him. He kept a few BAFS for luck: British army currency was no good to him here, it might be a danger, but one had to assume that one day he would be going back. He watched her take the money, put it in a drawer and lock it. Then she counted out the equivalent number of Eastern marks. He was impressed and grateful: only later did it occur to him that she had made a very good deal for herself, since every Western mark was worth at least seven Eastern.

'It is good of you,' he said and was about to leave the shop when she reminded him that he hadn't paid for the bread. Again he was on the point of leaving when it occurred to him that there was no reason not to trust her a little further. He took out of his wallet the photograph of a man some ten years younger than himself: an amused tough face with a scar from the corner of the left eye running towards the mouth. He asked her, 'Have you seen anyone like that around here?' She shook her head, wasting no words on him, as though she compromised herself less that way.

He said, 'Which is the road to Ilsenhof?'

'Turn right. There is a sign post.'

'Is it far?'

'No.'

She might have told him how many kilometres, he thought, but I suppose she had no breath to waste, since the big yellow sign soon told him that. Four kilometres – one only had to walk down the road. There was nobody at all in sight, and he felt expected, under observation, walking down the long straight way, pale with dust. He wondered whether the Mercedes car had driven that road ahead of him. It was odd, disturbing, rather sad being interested in an unknown woman again – almost antique, pre-war.

As he approached Ilsenhof the road became less deserted. Small knots of dark-clothed elderly people came out onto it from the side roads, a crowded bus went hooting by – he was reminded of the approach to a not very important fairground. But there were still no police. He had not seen a single frontier patrol since he crossed the border. Man is difficult to satisfy. He had heard so much of a thing called the police state that he was worried by their absence: he was reminded of those men who had waved to him from the other side of the road block, smiling, encouraging . . .

There must have been about fifty people on the road ahead of him now, and he could see below in the valley the red sloping roofs of Ilsenhof. He stopped and tore a piece of bread off his loaf: he noticed that his hand trembled when it went to his mouth. He wondered what plays they would be doing at the drama festival that night: was it possible that he could still do what he had to do and be back by curtain rise?

On the right twenty yards ahead a path ran up into the forest. In a miniature penthouse at the foot of the path Christ dangled upon a cross. All the way, up the path, small noticeboards (he couldn't see the writing on them) hung from the trees, like notices to trespassers. But if that was what they were, there were plenty of trespassers – all but one of the people ahead of him turned up the path. Brown went on down the road to Ilsenhof.

It would have been like any other village he had seen in the

Western zone (except that the shops were nearly empty and outside what might have been once the Rathaus a large board proclaimed the headquarters of the local Communist party) if it hadn't been for a strange ribbon development along the way east of the town. A row of ugly villas looked as though they had been run up almost overnight by people who had not intended to stay – it was like a boom town in a mining area, but the boom had passed on. A window full of holy junk caught Brown's eye – bad plaster images of a Virgin carrying a rose, always the same Virgin and the same attitude, turned out by the hundreds in a factory, at Dresden probably; cheap rosaries, boxes full of holy medals, picture postcards of the grotto taken in a bad light, some imaginary scenes in the worst possible taste of two children kneeling in the snow before this vision with a rose. Over all the contents of the shop was a feeling difficult to define in dust and unchangeableness: you felt that everything had come from the factory a long time ago. Brown entered.

A very old woman emerged from the parlour behind and stared at him with hostility and suspicion: Brown wondered whether he carried his scepticism on his clothes like a badge. He chose a holy medal and paid for it, a sense of guilt growing under her unwinning gaze. He said in German, 'Have you by any chance . . . ?' but whatever question he was going to ask wilted before her suspicion. She put her hand under the counter and pulled out a pair of steelrimmed spectacles and put them on to see him better: then she thrust out at him a second box of medals identical with the last.

He was daunted by her and against his own will he ran his fingers through the junk – one would believe if one could, in visions and eternal love, but he wasn't there for that. There were not only medals in the box: there were hideous paper knives bearing the pious painted image; knives with liturgical inscriptions; even a cigarette case with a picture of the grotto on the lid; buttons in the shape of the miraculous rose, but again he felt that nobody had looked at these objects for a very long while. Perhaps he ought to buy one more medal in order to get away, but did Catholics carry two medals? It was the kind of fact he should have known and checked like a military flash. He lifted up the cigarette case and saw there, half hidden among the medals, a knife . . . He found his heart pounding and his hand was unsteady again as it reached in the box. He thought: it's not possible, not possible that on the other side of the knife I shall find my own initials, R.B. He would have liked to walk straight out, back to the woods, back to the stream, the shattered tree, the ugly houses on the other side before despair struck. He picked the knife out of the tray and there the initials were, almost obliterated, etched awkwardly in by a boy thirty years ago with the help of a chemical outfit, and the woods and the stream and the tree seemed out of reach for ever.

(II)

He couldn't understand the singing any more than he had understood the holy medals and the statues, and the postcard booth at the first halt on the path where the stations of the cross began. They too were in the worst possible taste – the fervour of the old women jabbering their prayers and moving on in their high black boots was ugly to him. At the second halt a cripple was selling candles, and though Brown pretended to be engaged in prayer, this didn't prevent the man from pestering him until simply for the sake of peace he bought and carried his candle with all the others up the steep path to the grotto from which the singing came. He thought how can a faith survive this?

'Or this,' he thought, kneeling with a hundred others at the mouth of the cave, where the same hideous image magnified six times held out the rose towards them, and the priest moving from this side to the other of the altar said his mass. The walls of the cave were hung with cheap replicas of hearts and legs and even human kidneys, and he remembered how with more dignity in Horace's Ode the fishermen had hung out their nets at the shrine of Venus. How right the Russians were to leave this – thing, these rites, an exhibition of the absurdities of faith. While the others prayed he put his face in his hands and thought. A couple of women who formed the only choir chanted their Gloria in Excelsis, and he thought, 'if he got as far as this, why isn't he here by now? It took me a few hours across the hills and an hour in the valley: if he got as far as this . . . ', and the knife in his pocket hopelessly answered 'He was here and he ended here'.

He realised suddenly that all those around him were on their feet and he alone was kneeling. There were no seats and there was a continual coming and going in the mouth of the grotto; the old woman who had been standing next to him when he first came had moved away; an old man succeeded her, a woman . . . He stood up and heard the priest reciting the Credo: 'I believe, I believe . . . ' and his mind answered firmly, 'Yes, I believe, I believe in the geigercounters that at this moment men are carrying over the hills, searching for the new veins of uranium; I believe in the mines at Eisleben, the concentration points beyond Halle.'

'Et in unum Dominun Jesum Christum.'

'I believe in the crushing mills, the daily input and output, the railway trucks moving east.'

'Who for us men and for our salvation.'

'I believe that somewhere he died to save the world. Do these old women think they can save it this way?'

'Descendit de coelum.'

A voice in English said, 'Kneel, kneel quickly,' and he saw that all around him people were on their knees. When he rose again he looked at the woman beside him, but as he said later he knew at once without seeing her who had spoken. He was so certain that this voice could only belong to that face, he was in no hurry to prove his guess true. As he knelt he looked everywhere but at her and for the first time noticed the hard observant gaze of a man who knelt round the edge of the altar, so that three-quarters of the congregation was in his view. A shaven head, fat neck, absurd green shorts. Men of the same profession, though to a different branch. Brown was not a murderer but nor was this man a detective – like Brown he belonged to the underground, he was stamped with the seal of a police agent, even in the silly green shorts.

It was only then, when he rose, that he bothered to confirm his belief. One look was all he allowed himself: there would never in life, he thought, be time to look enough: one had to deal with the world and the world was the police agent, the necessity to stay alive. For a moment he tried to catch her gaze, but she looked only at the altar – it was as if she had put in his hand the only help she could. Presently with others she went to the altar rails to take her communion. Suddenly there were no kneeling figures any more between the police agent and himself – while the priest moved round the rail of the altar they looked at each other across the cave mouth. This was something Brown could understand. If only, he thought, it was a gun I had in my pocket instead of two holy medals: the world is controlled by uranium, not by God. He rose slowly to his feet and turning his back on the altar moved away: there was nothing wrong in moving: people came and went all the time. It was only when he was twenty yards away he remembered, 'I should have genuflected'. The desire to look behind him was almost irresistible.

As he walked down the hill past the women moving up he prepared himself in advance for an interrogation. He took the photograph out of his wallet and chewed it until it was a meaningless pulp that he spat out beside the path. Lies too easily give out; one must be ready, as far as possible, with the truth. I am Richard Brown, an English writer, I am writing a book about the Hartz, its people, its superstitions. I came over here from Bad Hartzburg to see this place of pilgrimage. I know I have no business to be here. I know you have every right to arrest me and investigate me, but that's the truth, the sole truth, will you please get in touch with the British Resident at Goslar? After he had gone a hundred yards, he looked round: high up the track a small figure with fat exposed knees came trotting down, past the stations of the cross. The end already?

If one is to keep one's nerve, one must not run away. Brown sat down under a fir tree by the path and taking out his knife prepared to cut himself a piece of bread. The figure came slowly on down the hill, a very bourgeois figure now that it had placed a respectable green Homburg hat with a kind of shaving brush in it over the pink head. It never occurred to Brown that he might be mistaken: that wide flat pasty teutonic face, blank and anonymous, reminded him of a prison wall. You would have had to excavate to find the eyes. Brown opened his knife and cut himself a slice. The man stopped a few yards away and looked at him.

'Guten Morgen,' Brown said and to save speaking further words put the bread into his mouth. The man said nothing, watching him eat. Suddenly Brown thought: why did she speak to me in English? What is so English about me? The man's silence disconcerted him. It was as though somewhere poking out of his pocket he carried his country's flag. He cut himself another slice of bread and to conceal his uneasiness he began to play with the knife. So many times when he was a boy he had opened that crooked blade, which he was always told was used for taking stones from horses' hoofs; the only use he had ever made of it was to dig up tough weeds in the garden at Shepperton.

The man in the Homburg turned momentarily away from him and raised his hand. On the road at the foot of the hill two policemen jumped off their bicycles. So I don't see the curtain rise, Brown thought, tugging at the stiff blade and reciting in his own mind that nearly true story: 'I am Richard Brown, an English writer. I am writing a book about the Hartz.' The policemen were climbing the hill; they had unslung their rifles. Two old people muttering their prayers before the station of the cross did not even look up at them. Well, if we were fighting for survival there was this to be said for the old people; they had survived a long time, longer than he was likely to do.

The tool opened. It had become stuck because wedged in the fork was a tiny scrap of paper on which numerals were written. So that the man in the Homburg should not see what he was doing, Brown rose to his feet and began to walk down the hill. As he walked he made a bread pellet and screwed the paper inside it. Then, with the motion of a man who is troubled by wax, he pushed the pellet into his ear. It occurred to him that if they beat him about the head the pellet would probably fall out, but it was the best he could do under the circumstances.

The policemen stopped and waited for him – or was it only, a wild hope struck him, for the man in the Homburg? Were his nerves inventing a danger that wasn't there? Would they let him pass?

'Guten Morgen,' he said to the policemen and all his hopes died when the man behind him spoke quietly in English, 'Perhaps you would not mind coming with us to the police station?'

Chapter Three

(I)

On the desk when he turned round from the wall he could see the contents of his pockets spread out – the knife was there, his cigarette case, his passport, his money – East German marks and BAFS, two holy medals, a novel of Turgenev's that he had not quite had time to finish, and a candle he had forgotten to light. Then his knees gave way, and the clock that had been at eye level soared up out of sight towards the ceiling. He saw only the well polished boots of the two policemen and the fat knees of the man in the Homburg hat. He said, 'My name is Richard Hartz. I was an English author. I am writing a book about the . . . I mean, my name is Richard Brown.'

'You have told us all that,' the man in the Homburg said. 'Now you have rested, Mr Brown, please stand up again facing the wall. No, as before please. You may support yourself with your fingers – no, the same two fingers, Mr Brown.'

They were like little shapeless lumps of red putty but they had not lost the feeling of flesh.

'I am telling them to send out for some beer and cigarettes, Mr Brown. Soon you will like to sit down and relax and have a good drink. What made you cross into this zone, Mr Brown?'

'Superstitions of the Hartz.'

'What is your rank?'

'English Author.'

'To what organisation do you belong?'

'Writing a book.'

The door opened and closed behind him. He prayed to somebody he didn't believe in: don't let them pour the beer into a glass so that I can hear. A clock struck five and he thought: six hours. In the war they had always been given a time limit before a mission – after so many hours you can tell everything, but on this occasion he was quite alone – there was no limit, just as there was no war. He longed for someone to strike him – that would be the beginning of the end.

'For whom are you writing your report?'

With a dying humour he said, 'William Heinemann.'

'How do you spell the name? Is he a West German?'

There was an eager note in the Homburg's voice.

Another voice that he had not heard before said, 'Mr Brown is joking. It is the name of an English publisher, see – the name is on this book. Come and sit down, Mr Brown.'

He turned; he wondered whether the worst was about to begin. The newcomer was in a green uniform with officer's badges, a man of much his own age and much his own build. From his face you might have said, of much the same experience.

'Captain Starhov,' he announced.

'Starhov,' Brown said, 'Starhov.'

He sat heavily down and winced when his two fingers touched the desk. 'Starhov,' he said, 'there was a character . . . which book . . . '

'A comic character, Mr Brown. An elderly libertine. Do you read Russian?'

'No. There is a good translation . . . '

'No translations can convey the style . . . '

Brown suddenly began to laugh. He put his head in his hands and laughed. When he looked up the Russian was watching him with sad unsmiling patience. 'I am sorry,' Brown said, 'it sounded like a conversation at home. We should go on to agree that poetry is really untranslatable.'

'I know very little about poetry,' the Russian said. He said to the Homburg hat, 'Pour Mr Brown a drink.'

'And suddenly,' Brown told my informant, 'I began to cry. I don't know why, except that always when you are tired, any kindness . . . I knew this was the most dangerous moment of all up till now. I was capable of sobbing out the truth; I wanted desperately to ask him one question. I had such a strong conviction that he would tell me the truth. And then suddenly before I had time to recover he asked me exactly that.'

'Have you ever heard of a man calling himself Kramer? Paul Kramer?' Captain Starhov asked.

Brown shut his eyes to try to hold his tears in.

'Kramer? Paul Kramer?'

'No,' Brown said, 'No, I've never heard of him.'

'A younger man than you, with a scar running from the left eye . . . ?'

Brown shook his head.

'He too was interested in this grotto of ours.'

'I tell you,' Brown said simply, 'I don't know the man.'

'Drink your beer, Mr Brown. These fools had no business to question you the way they did.'

The glass of beer stood there like a temptation. It is foolish to resist a temptation too long. Brown drank.

'You are not a Catholic, Mr Brown?'

'No.'

'Why did you buy these holy medals?'

'I have two children who are.'

'Your wife is a Catholic?'

'She's dead.'

'I'm sorry, Mr Brown.'

'It's no concern of yours.'

The sad tempting eyes watched him. 'Of course you think this is part of my performance. You are wrong. One may know what it is to lose someone one loves – or to fear . . . '

Captain Starhov never moved his eyes.

'I know also that one can use one's own experience quite

cold-bloodedly to trap another person. You are right to distrust me as I am right to distrust you.'

'You speak English very well.'

'We have good schools in Russia, whatever your propaganda may say.'

'Are you going to release me?'

'Of course, in time. But you must expect us to check your story.'

'Will that take long?'

'So much depends, Mr Brown.'

'Where will you keep me?'

Captain Starhov spoke sharply in German to the man in the Homburg, but Brown missed what was said. He felt hopelessly tired, beaten . . . Captain Starhov said, 'They have only two cells in the station here.'

'I am not a criminal,' Brown said.

'I could take you to my house, but it is not a very easy house to guard. I would have to ask for your parole.'

What an odd, old-fashioned word it sounded, Brown thought: I must not show myself too eager. He said, 'I will give it to you for a week.'

(II)

They drove into what seemed in the dusk a vast courtyard. An 18th-century stone house faced a long line of stables: one side of the great square was formed by the houses of the workers – a whole village seemed to be enclosed there. Even a church stood like a mere barn in a corner of the courtyard, part of the farm. The farm carts were driving in – long low vans with two horses apiece, beating up in the dust like chaff. Captain Starhov said, 'The house will be pulled down, of course, in the end. The farm has been collectivised.'

'Who lived here?'

'The owner. I have let the owner stay for the time being. It is convenient as long as I am here.'

A soldier opened the door of the car and Captain Starhov stood for a moment, watching the low shadows of the buildings: a horse whinnied in the stables, and the carts drove slowly in. He said, 'I have read of such places in books, but never before . . . '

'Do you expect to go?'

'We always move on,' Starhov said gloomily.

'It's very beautiful here.'

Starhov turned his back abruptly on the courtyard and led the way into the house. The hall was almost bare: an old stove, a wooden chair, and the 18th-century curved staircase had lost part of its balustrade. Grandeur had died a long while ago. Starhov said, 'The soldier will show you your room. You will want to rest. At dinner we can talk again.' As Brown turned away, he added, with a note of surliness, 'Will you leave me your book until then?'

Brown said, 'They have already examined it for marks at the police station.'

Starhov said stiffly, 'If you would do me the favour . . . '

The room was almost as bare as the hall and almost as large: a narrow iron bedstead, a stove that didn't work, a wash-hand stand, one chair and one light in the centre of the ceiling. It was better than a cell and easier to escape from. As soon as he was alone he took the pellet of bread from his ear. He disinterred the scrap of paper, but the writing was so small he had to climb on the chair and hold it nearer the light to read the little rows of figures which only he could decypher – as soon as he could safely work out his square. He memorised them and then because they had removed his matches, he screwed the paper back into the bread pellet and swallowed both. There had been one chance in a thousand he would find the knife, that the message would ever be read: life certainly at times taught one to hope for the impossible. After all even now he might be of use.

He looked out of the window; the dark was nearly here. He had memorised the direction they had taken from Ilsenhof as well as he was able. As for his parole, that might be of importance to a soldier to whom sanctions applied, but he was no soldier. When once he had decyphered the message he would decide how to act. From the stables a woman crossed the great shadowy square. It was so nearly dark that he could not believe the evidence of his eyes.

He left the room and waiting on the balcony of the hall he watched the handle move. Once he had seen her, twice, and now the third time she came into his life and looked up at him, this time not as a stranger but as a face he had remembered all through the hours of interrogation, and he grinned stupidly back at her because in that moment he was happy. He didn't care that there was no welcome, only resentment in her look. To feel oneself, however, momentarily, part of a design is like peace. It was the nearest he had ever come to belief. He was relieved of responsibility. He was in the hands of a god.

She said, 'Who are you?' not moving from the door.

'Richard Brown,' he said. 'I have seen you twice before – you came into a shop to buy bread.'

'Does Nicolai . . . ?'

'Captain Starhov has invited me to stay. You see, there wasn't enough room at the police station.'

'You'd have been better off there.'

'I doubt it,' he said and held out his raw and swollen fingers.

She flinched and looked quickly away. 'I'll try and find some oil if you let me by.'

'Let you by? But I am up here and you are down there. I'm not blocking the stairs.'

She said with bewilderment, 'Of course, I don't know what I meant. It was a foolish thing to say.'

She walked quickly to the stairs and climbed them with head bent. She said, 'I'll send somebody with bandages to your room,' moving away from him.

He said, 'I don't want to let you by,' and she stopped and looked back at him.

'What do you mean?'

He said slowly, as though he were reciting a mathematical equation, 'Any passage, any path, any doorway you have to pass, I'd like to be there blocking the way.'

She replied immediately with an honesty that confused him as though she were announcing the second half of the equation, 'You have been – all today.' She went on with what seemed to be anger, 'You won't be satisfied till I say it, will you? Alright, I have said it. I have spoken two words to you today. This morning. And now I have said that to you. You have got your triumph. Now, for God's sake let me alone.'

'But why? I don't understand.'

'It can happen to a woman, can't it, just as much as to a man? You stood there like a fool while we knelt . . . '

'Three words, not two. Kneel, you said, kneel quickly.'

'I'd never see you again because you'd be safe.'

'I'm glad I don't believe in prayer.'

'Is Nicolai here?'

'Do you mean Starhov, yes?'

'He can probably hear every word we are saying.'

'Does it matter?'

'Yes, I love him.'

It was like a douche of cold water in the face.

'And me,' he said wearily. 'I am sorry. I'm tired. Confused. I didn't understand. I thought you said . . . '

'It's an obsession. We can get rid of an obsession, can't we? In one way or another. I'll come to your room if you want me to when Nicolai is asleep.' She opened the door and there Starhov was asleep at his desk with a book open before him. It occurred as a new fact to Brown that Russians, too, were human.

(III)

Starhov stirred his coffee. He said, 'I am a reasonable man like you. I had a good scientific education at Stalingrad. I have no sympathy at all with these supertitious pilgrims, but to suppress them at the present moment would do more harm than good. The General at Erfurt had given orders to destroy the grotto. I countermanded them.'

'Countermanded a general's orders, Captain Starhov?'

'A captain in the M.K.V.D. does not take instructions from a general. I told him there were two reasons why the pilgrimages should continue. It is good propaganda in the West and it keeps people contented. This is not a Catholic population but pilgrims have always come from Czechoslovakia. He was anxious about the security at Eisleben.'

'Eisleben?'

He realised at once that he had made a mistake: he realised too that his interrogation had not finished: at the police station it had only begun. Clara watched him with anxiety.

'Mr Brown, surely you won't pretend that you know nothing of the uranium mines at Eisleben? It has been in the papers. There is no secret. Why do you pretend?'

'Of course, I know about the uranium, but Eisleben – I'd forgotten the name.'

'I suppose it is a more important name to us. I took a big risk when I countermanded the general's orders. If anything should go wrong, it will be my responsibility. I have to watch my step very carefully. My orderly reports on me. My second in command would like me to go. The military . . . In my position one trusts nobody. Nobody at all.' Was it coincidence, Brown wondered, that he looked across the table at Clara?

'Give Mr Brown another cup of coffee.'

As Brown took the cup from Clara, Starhov said, 'A week ago we caught an agent here.'

Brown saw that Starhov was not watching his face but his hand that held the coffee cup. He stiffened the muscles of his hand to resist, but he heard the cup chink chink in its saucer. He tried rapidly to cover himself. He said with much irritation, 'I wish you'd drop this idea that I am a spy. It's too melodramatic. Surely spies are little men on a salary who watch railway crossings and steal blotting paper . . . or so I have read.' He worked himself up into irritation to explain the shaking of his hands. 'Did you find any markings in my book?'

Starhov said, 'A book code does not require marks. Do you really read Turgenev, Mr Brown?'

'Yes . . . '

'Do you remember Insarov?'

'The Bulgarian whose country was oppressed by foreigners?'

'Yes . . . '

'And Harlov?'

'The Lear of the Steppes. Yes. And do you remember, Captain Starhov, *A Month in the Country*?'

He had passed that examination.

'Always the early autumn,' Starhov said, 'and love just beginning . . . not ending, petering out, no quarreling except as young people quarrel. Summer lightning.'

'Sometimes it rains even in Turgenev.'

'And the puddles are full of autumn leaves.'

'It was a very different Russia.'

'You have to lose something,' Starhov said, 'when you make something. A carpenter's floor is covered with sawdust, isn't it, scraps of wood?' He said moodily, 'I wasn't only looking for marks in your book, Mr Brown. That was my first purpose. But afterwards I fell asleep reading. It was odd reading Turgenev in English. Passages I knew by heart in Russian came to me as though they were by a strange writer. There is one that goes . . .' and Starhov began to speak in Russian – a few sentences only.

'I would like to learn Russian,' Brown said, 'for the sake of Turgenev. Not for Dostoevsky, not even Tolstoy. They are too great and important and stormy.'

'Read me that passage in English, Mr Brown.'

'You would have to find it for me.'

'Of course, I forgot. One always thinks other people speak one's own language.'

But had he thought that, Brown wondered, or had he laid another inconspicuous trap, had he some reason to suppose that indeed he did know Russian?

Lights passed across the great farm yard: a soldier with an electric torch, a woman carrying a lighted ember. In the stable a stallion neighed and kicked his stall. Clara rose to draw the curtains.

'Let them be,' Starhov said, 'there is nothing to conceal here. Not at this moment. Three people together in a quiet house in the country, and one reading a book. In a house like this, that must have been a common sight. Before the war, before your husband was killed, it must have happened many times, Clara.'

'I suppose so. I wouldn't remember a thing like that.'

'And yet it has never happened before to me. Here is the passage, Mr Brown.'

Brown read: 'It was an exquisite day. I fancy there are no days like that in September anywhere but in Russia. The stillness was such that one could hear, a hundred paces off, the squirrel hopping over the dry leaves, and the broken twig just feebly catching at the other branches and falling at last on the soft grass – to lie there for ever, not to stir again till it rotted away. The air, neither warm nor chill but only fragrant, and as it were keen, was faintly, deliciously stinging in my eyes and on my cheeks.'

Brown looked across at Starhov. He sat with bent head, and his trigger finger twitched and twitched on his knee. Brown read on: 'A long spider web, delicate as a silver thread, with a white ball in the middle, floated smoothly in the air and sticking to the butt-end of my gun, stretched straight out in the air – a sign of settled and warm weather. The sun shone with a brightness as soft as moonlight.'

'Thank you, Mr Brown.' He repeated the last phrase in Russian. He lifted his hand from his knee. 'This week two men have been shot. I had to give the *coup de grace* myself.' Again he looked quickly up at Brown: it was almost as though he was imploring him to put an end to all this quiet together in the lamp-lit room with the big yard all around them and the gentle movements in the stove, to make life normal again. The agent. The informer. The long interrogation. The ordinary understandable world. Confess, he seemed to implore, but the only confession was his own. 'The sun shone with a brightness as soft as moonlight, that's Russian too.'

(IV)

Brown lay awake listening for a sound he did not expect and when at last at two in the morning it came, he felt disappointment. When you are in love only then all the pains and longings are small, almost pleasurable like sensation coming back to a dead limb, but after possession too often one loves, and love is hard and cruel and jealous, love is selfish, 'I want, I want' becomes the burden of the mind. But when she was quiet again by his side, there was no room between their bodies for regret, there was only joy and peace. He felt for that moment that he would never be in love again. They didn't even speak until she said, 'I have to go. If I fall asleep now, I feel I shall never wake up again.'

'The obsession – have you got rid of it?'

'No. Now you have driven it in too deep.'

Chapter Four
(I)

He had trained his memory so well that it never occurred to him that he could forget a short cypher, but the next morning he struggled in vain with that last message. The only word that emerged from the mutilations was 'wax' and that might itself be a mutilation. He thought, 'what a failure I am'. There was nothing to do now but get back across the border and report the loss of a better agent than himself.

A soldier brought him coffee in his room and later in the morning he saw Starhov drive out of the courtyard. He felt an odd relationship with him, a kindliness, because they loved the same woman. For the first time he regretted the need to break his parole. It might very well mean death to Starhov. And all for the sake of a very meaningless word 'wax'.

He had left the door open, so that he could see Clara go by and he called to her immediately she passed. She came and stood in the doorway and he thought, 'I have never loved a beautiful woman before'. It worried him. He felt hopelessly insecure because the whole world must want her.

'Yes?'

'Come in,' and it astonished him that she obeyed him.

'Close the door.' He thought, if there was a mirror I would look at myself, I must be different to what I thought I was – I must be worthwhile. He said, 'Starhov's gone, I saw him go.'

He turned her towards the window and put his hands on her breasts and the back of her head was against his neck and he could feel on his body the division of her thighs, like an impress on sand.

'There'll be tonight,' she said.

'One never knows.'

'His orderly is in the next room.'

'Lock the door.'

'There's no key.' Suddenly she took his hands off her and walked over to the bed. 'It doesn't matter,' she said, 'it doesn't matter.'

When they were quiet again, for the first time they talked. He had the sense that life would not be long enough to contain all the talking they had to do.

'How old are you?' he asked.

'Thirty. You?'

'Forty-eight. A big difference.'

'Not so great. When I am forty-five, you will only be sixty-three. It's a good age, sixty-three. Are you a writer – or is that a story?'

'I have written a few books. Why were you at the grotto?'

'It was Sunday. It's the only place left for Mass.'

'Was it? I didn't know. Are you a Catholic then?'

'Yes.'

'And you believe all that – the vision – the rose?'

'I think it may be true. Why were you there?'

'They asked me that at the police station for six hours. I told them I was writing a book about the Hartz mountains and its superstitions.'

'Are you?'

'No.'

'What are you doing?'

He looked at her. It was the stock situation of all melodramas; you were trapped by a woman. But was it possible to love and not to trust – most of the time, in most things? He said cautiously, 'I was looking for somebody.'

'A man called Kramer?'

A man was whistling his way across the yard. He remembered three people in a room reading a book. Why couldn't the world be like that?

'Yes,' he said.

'Who was he?'

'My brother – my half-brother.'

She began to cry. He said, 'My dear, my dear, I've guessed he's dead. I knew it really before I came over here. These things happen.'

'Did you love him?'

'Yes.' She turned her head on the pillow as though she could stop tears as you stop blood, with the pressure of a bandage. He said, 'We had the same mother, she left my father. I don't blame her. She loved somebody else. It happens, doesn't it? I didn't meet my brother until five years ago. She married a German, you see. He was very like her except for his scar.'

She whispered something he could not hear.

'Yes?'

'Your mother?'

'Oh,' he said with false lightness, 'we killed her. For all I know I killed her myself. You see, I was in the R.A.F.'

'And I killed your brother.'

He tried to brush it aside, 'Oh, the Russians did that. Or the East Germans.'

'No,' she said, 'I mean it. I killed him myself.'

'What's troubling you?' he asked and tried to touch her hair, but she moved his hand away and lay with her back to him.

'I killed him,' she said. 'I gave him away. I saw him there in the grotto just as I saw you. He wasn't a Catholic either and he made the same mistakes. Afterwards I sent a message to Nicolai and I followed him. He had gone into a shop that sells . . . oh statues and things. They arrested him there. He was turning over a tray of medals. I don't know why.'

He said bitterly, 'And they stood him against a wall propped on two fingers for hours on end. Why did you do it? You aren't a Russian?'

'I love Nicolai.' she said. 'Where would I be if it wasn't for him? Without a home. In a labour camp. Then I saw that man. I thought this is the end of Nicolai. He allowed the pilgrimages. He guaranteed the security. He protected us.'

'For the sake of propaganda.'

'How do you know? How do I know? He is a man. He can do stupid things for love, like the rest of us.'

She got off the bed and made for the door keeping her face away from him. She said, 'We should never have talked. Just made love till we got tired of it. Not talked.'

As she felt for the handle, he asked , 'Why did you tell me to kneel? Why didn't you send for Nicolai again?'

She answered him bitterly between the opening and the closing of the door, 'Because I fell in love. At first sight. Like a schoolgirl.'

When she had gone he looked at his two fingers. 'Paul,' he said, 'Paul.' Then furiously he began to tear at the cool comforting white bandages that soothed his hurt.

(II)

Starhov said, 'So far the reports are favourable. You seem undoubtedly to be Mr Brown who writes books. The British Resident at Goslar is making inquiries. He has asked for our assistance.'

Brown lit a cigarette. 'What did you reply?'

'That we had no trace of you at present, but that we were making inquiries. Where is Clara?'

'I haven't seen her since this morning.'

Starhov got restlessly up. 'She is nearly always here when I come back from town. Perhaps she is about the farm. They do not like her there because of me.' He led the way out of the house and across the courtyard. He said, 'I gave them everything and yet they hate her because she gave me – a little.'

They searched for her in vain, in the stables, the dairy. Men spoke to Starhov subserviently, and he barked out his questions at them like an owner. Brown said, 'What will happen to her when you move on?' and got no reply. He said, rubbing the sore spot on his mind, 'She is very fond of you.'

'I cannot tell that,' Starhov said. The twilight was coming down: it was the hour for intimacies that later one regrets. He said, 'I had read about women like her. I had never met one. Now I still feel as though I had – read about her.' He added with longing, 'If only I had no protection to give her.'

'I don't understand.'

'She needs us all too much. How can we feel trust? Perhaps she loves me. Perhaps she loves her house. There are so many refugees anywhere needing foodcards, needing passports. How does a man learn to trust when he has no authority?'

'And yet you trusted my parole?'

Starhov grinned at him with unhappy humour. 'I expected you to break it last night. You wouldn't have got two miles from here. Every path is guarded.' He added, 'It was a point in your favour that you did not try.'

Brown thought: this man is to be pitied. This man who killed my brother. He said, 'I think you are wrong about her.'

'I was twelve years old when the revolution came. We have watched over and over again how people are trusted – engineers, writers, generals – we have seen them betray us. The man who taught us everything when we were young. Our heroes. They betrayed us.'

They came into the great barn and there they found her lying in the straw, asleep, with an appearance of complete exhaustion. Starhov stood and watched her. He said, 'You see I cannot even trust myself. If she said to me, come across over there, live with me for ever . . . '

'Would you do it?'

'No. Perhaps a year ago . . . but people do not live together for ever. There is no such thing as "Forever". And yet you can want what you read in books, even though you know that it's always only propaganda, propaganda.'

'Even Turgenev?' Brown asked with malice.

'He makes us want the past, doesn't he? They don't exist any longer in my world or yours, the women of Turgenev.'

As they watched her she woke. She woke with an expression of happiness that immediately faded. She said, 'I have slept a long time. It's nealy dark.'

'You were dreaming,' Brown said.

'Yes.'

'You are beautiful asleep,' Starhov said sadly and Brown turned away thinking of the daily joy of waking and seeing her as she had been then, and he thought angrily how quickly when I watch her I can forget my brother.

That night it was a little past midnight when she came to him. They had dined almost in silence. Even the hidden interrogation had stopped. She said, 'I am not going to stay. Only a moment. Even if you won't speak to me. But this morning I had no time, I was shocked. I had no chance. I wanted to defend myself, but I don't know how.'

He touched her face and said with a kind of despair, 'This is your defence.'

'I wanted you to know – he didn't suffer. He was shot at once trying to escape.'

'I wonder if my mother suffered? My dear, my dear,' he said, 'we all have so much guilt it cancels out.'

'I wanted – before you went home. You'll be going home soon?'

'If he doesn't find out . . . '

'Is there so much to find out? No, don't tell me.'

'You had no reason to tell me what you had done. You could have kept quiet. I may as well be honest too. If we don't trust each other any more than *they* do, it's a bad world.'

'Please tell me nothing, nothing.'

'Paul was bringing back a report – on the Czech mines and the mines at Eisleben. The daily input and output. The number of trucks going eastwards. The position of the laboratories, perhaps even the destination in Russia. He was a good agent. That's why I sent him.'

'You sent him?'

'He was my best agent.'

'They will kill you if they find out.'

'Yes.'

'Then why did you tell me? I can betray you to Nicolai. I can talk in my sleep like other people. I can make a mistake, can't I?'

'It wouldn't matter to me much,' he said. 'I have nothing – not even the report.'

'And if you had got your precious report – would it have made any difference?'

'The authorities would have had something to put on their card indexes. They might be able – I don't know – to calculate the chance of war next year, the year after . . . '

'Is that useful?'

He shrugged his shoulders. 'Not very. We'll all be dead anyway by then. But this is a profession like any other. We give the best answers we can – the questions may be futile, but that's not our responsibility.

'What are you going to do?'

'I thought I would simply break by parole, but he is not as careless as all that. The place is guarded as well as it can be. And there is no hurry now.'

But every day you are here, they are investigating . . . ,' she said. 'If only you had something to report, you would go. You'd escape somehow. Then it would be your damned duty to save your life.'

'Paul left a message, but I can only work out one word. He was cyphering against time perhaps.'

'What word?'

'Wax. If he guessed he was followed – he must have guessed that, then he would have tried to hide the report and have left some clue.'

She said, 'He knelt when other people stood, and stood when they knelt. He crossed himself wrong, like you. He went up and took communion – I hated him for that.'

He asked with wonder, 'You really believe?'

'Yes.'

'You pray at night? You really think that God answers prayers?'

'Yes.'

'And still wars come. And still the atom bomb goes off.'

'We don't all pray for what matters.'

'Don't we pray for peace in all the churches?'

'And what sort of peace do we mean – the Council of Europe, the powers of UNO? They are toys, aren't they? And twenty years ago we prayed for the League of Nations.'

'What do you pray for?'

'Oh, I pray for stupid things, contradictory things – that Nicolai will somehow survive. That you will be alive next week. Sometimes I remember to pray that I shall love God. If we loved God do you think all this would exist?'

He said, 'I can't get further than loving a woman.'

'My dear,' she said, 'my dear. Some people can't even do that. Nicolai . . . '

'Doesn't he love you?'

'He doesn't believe in me. He doesn't trust me. I gave him your brother's life, but he doesn't trust me.'

'You can give him mine now.'

She said sadly, 'No. I am going to give you his. You are going to have everything – even your precious report.'

'I'd almost forgotten the report.'

'When your brother knelt, after he had seen his mistake, there was a bracket for candles. Candles are made of wax, aren't they?'

'I don't understand.'

'There is always a deposit of old candle wax in the socket. If the report was small enough . . . '

'He would have used microfilm.'

'He could have gouged out a hole for it and lit another candle on top. And I don't suppose anyone ever clears the wax away.'

'Can I get to the grotto?'

'We can try. You couldn't get away yourself, but I think I know where Nicolai stations his men.' She added with bitterness, 'Two children thought they saw the Mother of God and she gave them a rose. Candles have always burnt there ever since, and now one of them is a spy's report on the output of uranium.'

'I'm sorry,' he said.

'And so is she. But she's sorry for the whole world, not Western Union.'

(III)

They met again on the balcony at the head of the stairs.

'Asleep?'

She whispered back, 'He sleeps like the dead always. Poor Nicolai.'

He started to go down, but she put her head on his arm. 'Wait. He has a sentry the front of the house. You can see his shadow when he passes the window.'

'And I really believed him when he asked for my parole.'

'There.' she said. 'Now count until he returns.'

It took the sentry three minutes to the left and then three and a half minutes to the right. 'When he next goes to the right, we have one and three-quarter minutes to get clear,' Brown said. 'Are the grounds lighted?'

'No. Aim a little to the left, the corner of the stables.'

They went down into the hall and stood with the backs of their hands touching by the cold stove. She shivered.

'You should have brought a coat.'

'No,' she said, 'if we don't get clear it's not so incriminating.'

The shadow passed to the left. She said, 'You can buy me a coat in England.' It was the first time she had admitted in so many words that she was going with him – the whole way. Suddenly he felt fear. She so belonged to this place, he couldn't conceive it possible that a time would come when they could wake daily in a peaceful world – peaceful until the bomb fell.

He said, 'I have two children . . . '

'I would like you to have a third.'

The shadow passed going to the right. He said, 'Pray. I can't. . .' She opened the door and led the way on to the steps and suddenly she was lit up. She stood braced and still against the blinding light. Her whisper hardly reached him. 'Get back upstairs. Into your room,' and as he went the sound of a car driving in through the gates of the farm reached him; the scramble on the path as the sentry came back. He thought, thank God we were not half across the yard, that she was not wearing her coat.

At the window of his room he looked straight down on the car. A stout man wearing a green Homburg hat held the door for the General to descend: the shaving brush in his hat pointed like a pistol upwards to Brown's face. He heard Clara's voice saying in German, 'A late hour, General,' and as the General entered the house the man looked up, the sunken eyes seemed to screw up in an attempt to penetrate the darkness between them, and in his two fingers Brown felt the nerve of pain beating again.

Through his open door he heard Starhov going downstairs. A harsh angry voice could be heard at intervals; he could not hear Starhov's answers: then the voice moved out of hearing and a few minutes later an orderly summoned him below.

Both men were on their feet, Starhov in his dressing gown, the general booted and medalled, a younger man than Starhov, with a blunted Mongol face. Starhov said, 'The General wanted to take a look at you. You are dressed?'

'I could not sleep,' Brown said. 'I was going to take a walk in the yard.'

'You had better tell me first another time, so that the sentry can be warned.'

The General asked angrily in Russian what they were discussing and Starhov replied curtly that they were talking of insomnia. Brown's Russian was not adequate to understand the argument that boomed and growled like a storm over his head. Starhov turned suddenly and said, 'You can go now. I must apologise for the stupidity of this man.' For a moment he thought the General would bar the way, but he contented himself with spitting on Starhov's polished floor.

Clara stood on the balcony above the hall. He looked up at her and said, 'We were lucky,' then turned and saw where the man in the Homburg stood quietly watching them from beside the stove.

(IV)

Starhov said, 'It's quiet now that he has gone.' He had come into Brown's room and lay back on Brown's bed with an effect of intimacy, assumed or not Brown was uncertain.

'What did he want?'

'He had only just heard of your presence. He thought I should have told him and that you should have been kept at the police station. He also considered I was wrong in interrupting your interrogation. I told him that it had not been interrupted but had been continued in another form. He warned me again about the pilgrimage. I told him he needn't worry. It is my responsibility just as you are.'

'Can a captain talk like that to a general?'

'Generals are two a penny. An M.K.V.D officer does not take orders from a general.'

'And if you are mistaken about me?'

'He will have a chance of revenge.' He turned his head sideways on Brown's pillow and looked at the book beside the bed. 'Not finished the story yet?'

'I have begun it again.'

'If I stayed in one place for a year, perhaps, I would have some books too.' His eyes were heavy with sleep.

'Do you in the West ever feel trust?'

'Sometimes.'

'Insarov trusted Dersenyev. He trusted Elena. A strange dead world where men were friends and women were faithful. Where's Clara?'

'She went to her room.'

'That man disturbed me.' He shut his eyes. 'Do you remember who it was in Turgenev who said, "one wants to do nothing, one wants to see no one, one looks forward to nothing, one is too lazy for thought"?'

'No.'

'Nor do I. But the words stick. In that world they had happy memories, sad memories, not memories that disgust. Sometimes I think we've killed enough men.'

'Starhov, I want to walk for a little while in the yard.'

'Yes.'

'I will be coming back.'

'I trust you. Why? Trust. That's an odd thing to say. I have fallen in trust.' He lay with his eyes shut. He said, 'The pass word for the sentries is . . . ' His voice fell so low that Brown had to stoop to catch the word.

'Sleep here for a while. I'll be back in half an hour.'

'Put the book beside me in case I wake,' but before Brown had reached the door Starhov was already asleep, like the dead, like the effigy on his own tomb, Brown thought, except that there would be no effigy on the tomb of one who had committed the crime of trust. Had it been a temptation all his life, to which now, at last from near exhaustion, he had succumbed? But why now? Why me? Because I had read Turgenev, Brown wondered.

(V)

When they were in the comparative security of the forest she took a gun from her coat pocket and gave it to him. She said, 'It's the first time he ever left it out. Always he locks it up – when it is not at his side it's under his pillow.'

'You are wearing your coat.'

'It's too late to bother about evidence now.'

When they were still a quarter of a mile from the grotto they could detect it by the flicker of the candles the pilgrims had lit. They reached the path a hundred yards below the grotto and walked up together past the hideous Stations. There was no point now in concealment. He said, 'We have to reach the boundary before daylight,' but he had no belief that he would ever find himself again in the world of officers' wives and British clubs and NAAFI shops. He wasn't even certain that he desired to.

'What are you thinking?' she asked.

'I was wondering whether we should end here where we began.'

The Mother of God held out her absurd pink rose and he stood while Clara knelt. There was no need any longer to do the right thing. One old woman knelt by a rack of candles telling her rosary. When Clara rose he asked her, 'On which side did Paul . . . ' She indicated the old woman, and he stood beside her waiting for her to move. Steadily the old woman worked through her beads. The process was endless. He looked at his watch and saw how far the night had advanced. Only one candle that presumably the old woman had lit was burning in the bracket.

Cautiously he scraped at the first candle holder with his finger – there were six of them. He found nothing there. The second had too little wax left in it to conceal anything larger than a pea. The chances were a hundred to one, he thought, that the film – if the report had been filmed – had been found. The woman muttered her prayers.

Where had she come from at this hour of the night? Where could she possibly find a lodging? What was the passion that drove these people?

Brown felt a tide of sympathy for Starhov. Uranium against uranium. The mines in the Hartz against the mines in the Congo. In a way they were allies, doing the same job of destruction. He looked at her, but she would not look at him though she knelt at his side – the third, the fourth, the fifth holder contained nothing, there remained only one holder where the candle was burning. The old woman reached the end of her beads and started all over again. Brown put out his hand and snatched the candle and the flame flickered and went out. 'No,' Clara said, 'no.' The old woman looked up from her beads. She looked at him with astonishment and grief. She said in German, 'It is for my son'. He dug his finger into the soft wax, and felt, to his own surprise, a little tight roll. While the woman watched him put the candle back and felt for a match. He had no match.

'Come away,' he said to Clara, but she had taken the candle and crossed the grotto to relight it at another flame. He waited with impatience and saw at the entrance to the cave the man with the Homburg hat.

(VI)

Brown said, 'He must have followed us all the way through the forest. He had obviously stayed behind when the General left. He had gone over, I suppose, to the General's side, feeling fairly certain that Starhov would lose in the end. Of course, he couldn't have guessed that I would be armed.

'He could not see me very clearly, all the light was on the other side of the grotto where Clara was lighting the old woman's candle. It was my duty to shoot and my pleasure to shoot. It was my duty to go back across the border with that roll, and it was my pleasure to revenge the two damaged fingers – and Paul. I suppose it was the damaged finger on the right hand that made my shot miss: it crashed into the grotto wall among the offerings and the tin hearts and legs. I wonder if he would have hung a piece of himself up there if he had survived?

'I called to Clara, "Put out the candles," just as he fired again. His bullet scraped my left hand, so that I dropped the roll and the bullet went on to bury itself in the Virgin's image: I could hear the plaster crack. Then the candles went out and he was standing clearly in the moonlight. He peered and I came cautiously forward. I wasn't going to let my damaged finger interfere this time. I shot again when I was quite certain. The hat rolled a little way down the path.

'I went back into the grotto to find the film and Clara. There was no light to see by, but I found the roll quite soon. I could tell at once from the feel that it was quite useless – the bullet had ripped it into wastepaper. I put it in my pocket as a souvenir of a hopeless mission. Clara was kneeling by the dead man. I said, "There is nothing you can do for him."

'She said, "You are so damned certain of everything, aren't you? I can pray, can't I?" She looked down at that ugly face as though he were her brother.'

I said to Brown, 'And then?'

'That's all,' he said, 'there wasn't any time to lose. The Ilsenhof police would have heard the firing. We made good time to the border, and there a patrol stopped us. I thought it was an Eastern patrol, so I threw away my gun and what was left of Paul's report. The only one who brought anything away was Clara.'

'What did she bring?'

'Three-quarters of a plaster rose.'

I told him, 'That's all that's left of the grotto. The pilgrim passes have been stopped and this time I think the place has really been dynamited. We heard rumours that a new M.K.V.D. officer had arrived in the district.'

'Poor Starhov,' Brown said. 'It was bad luck, wasn't it, that he started trusting just when I came on the scene.'

'It's bound to happen sometimes.'

'Is it?' Brown said. I couldn't understand his look of misery.

'And Clara?'

'Oh,' he said, 'We are getting married. Of course she will be a British citizen then, with a British passport.'

'Good luck to both of you.'

He looked at his two fingers – they were nearly healed now. He said, 'Redburn, I don't know you from Adam. We've only met two or three times, but,' he broke out, 'there was something Starhov said that I can't get out of my mind. "She needs us all too much, how can we feel trust?"'

And it was then that Clara came into my office to find him, I hadn't seen her before and I felt like shaking Brown and telling him what a fool he was. You see she was not only beautiful, she was so perfectly – convincing. I wished that I could stake a lifetime on her.

I saw them again. It was the last night of the week's drama festival and they sat together four rows behind me. The platitudinous judge in the dinner jacket finished his discourse on 'Excellent characterisation' and 'clever production' and the cup was handed over by the C.I.C. I could hardly believe it but the prize for acting went to those lifeboat Combers of the first night and one of them came up in his oilskins to receive it. He must have been tipped off or brought them with him on the chance. We clapped like anything and looking round I saw the future Browns. I gained from the glance no sense of happiness at all and I thought is distrust as infectious as all that? Does it stop at no boundaries?

As we went out I caught them up. I had what I thought was a last word to say to them. 'Brown,' I said, 'it's been confirmed. Starhov's gone.'

'Where?' he asked rather stupidly.

'We shall never know that.'

Clara turned and walked out of the theatre and stood in the darkness. She didn't want Brown to see her tears. He was in a mood to misunderstand her. I said, 'And that damned grotto . . . '

'Yes?'

'The thing's happening on our side now. Two labourers instead of two children. The picture dealers and the manufacturers of statues and the photographers are all bothering for concessions and the Russians, of course, would like to issue passes for pilgrims over here.'

'Clara believes in the rubbish,' Brown said, 'or says she does – I wish I did. I wish I believed in anything.' He went on watching Clara where she stood on the steps as the officers went by.

'You are very lucky.' I said. I suppose there was too much warmth in my voice because he turned and looked at me with suspicion. But in my case he was right not to trust. If I here described Brown's story in detail it's because I've heard it from two people, because I swore that night that one thing in life was worth fighting for – after all in the long run Brown had to discover that you can't love and not trust.

The Stranger's Hand

In May 1949, Walter Allen set *New Statesman* Weekend Competition No.999, which offered a prize of one guinea for the best imitation or parody of the opening lines of a novel by any writer named Green or Greene. The competition was won by one D.R. Cook. Second place was awarded to N. Wilkinson with the following entry:

The Stranger's Hand
An Entertainment

> The child had an air of taking everything in and giving nothing away. At the Rome airport he was led across the tarmac by his aunt, but he seemed to hear nothing of her advice to himself or of the information she produced for the air hostess. He was too busy with his eyes: the hangars had his attention, every plane on the field except his own – that could wait.
>
> 'My nephew,' she said, 'yes, that's him on the list. Roger Court. You *will* look after him, won't you? He's never been quite on his own before,' but when she made that statement the child's eyes moved back plane by plane with what looked like contempt, back to the large breasts and the fat legs and the over-responsible mouth: how *could* she have known, he might have been thinking, how often I am alone?

N. Wilkinson was none other than Graham Greene. A visitor to Greene's home in Anacapri had drawn his attention to the competition, and Greene had entered out of that notorious 'sense of fun'. However, Italian director Mario Soldati was convinced that these two paragraphs had the makings of a worthwhile film story. He had recently returned from Trieste, where he had learned of the spate of kidnappings perpetrated by Yugoslav agents using drugs to sedate victims before smuggling them aboard merchant ships. At his behest, Greene began to work on a treatment. Only fitfully inspired by the theme of his 'joke', Greene abandoned the manuscript after just thirty handwritten pages.

Undeterred, Soldati brought the story to the attention of Captain Peter Moore, Alexander Korda's man in Italy, who set the ball rolling back in London. Korda assigned the project to John Stafford, who sent screenwriter Guy Elmes to Anacapri to consult with Greene. Elmes persuaded Greene to turn the waiter, Roberto, into Roberta, a hotel secretary, and to drop Roger Court's rather clichéd fascination with the underworld of Mr Hogan. Elmes also felt that the narrative was over-dependent on outrageous coincidences – characters seeming to bump into each other as if in a small *pension* not a labyrinthine city. Having discussed the ending of the story, Greene cheerfully took a back seat, agreeing to act as associate producer once shooting began. Guy Elmes left for Venice to verify locations, and there devised two pieces of business which were to relieve the strain on the audience's credibility.

Troubled by the ease with which Greene allowed Roger fall in with Vivaldi,

Elmes introduced the device of the doctor playing with a cat's cradle, which intrigues the child sufficiently to drop his guard and accept the stranger's kindness. This in turn led to the idea of the string rings, which Vivaldi makes from the cat's cradle and one of which he gives the boy to ward off loneliness.

The second film gimmick concerned Roger's inability to recognize his father in the tenement room. Sitting in a Venetian café, Elmes had watched a small child drawing beards onto pictures in a newspaper and noticed how the ink seeped through the paper and altered the appearance of a photograph on the preceding page. A similar ploy was thus used to prevent Roger identifying Major Court.

The finished script is almost exclusively the work of Guy Elmes, although in order to satisfy Italian quota rules, Moore was obliged to hire and credit Giorgio Bassani for his advice on the authentic Venetian expressions, used, chiefly, by Eduardo Cianelli's Commissioner.

Elmes had no sooner finished the script than the cast and English crew arrived in Venice. Moore had secured the services of Alida Valli to play Roberta, Trevor Howard (Greene's preferred leading man) had agreed to play the Major, and Richard Basehart, in no hurry to leave Italy after his marriage to Valentina Cortesa, took the part of Hamstringer.

Greene himself tells of the problems that confronted the unit in 'The Novelist and the Cinema'. Guy Elmes also recalls the fact that John Stafford spent much of the shoot raising funds in Britain, that Valli was preoccupied with the infamous Montese murder case, in which her boyfriend was involved, and that the lack of English-speaking extras meant that the nanny hired to look after the children of the cast and crew found herself impersonating an air hostess, John Stafford's wife doubled as Roger's aunt, and Guy Elmes played the captain of the Yugoslav ship. Even Graham Greene's hand made an appearance untying one of the fire brigade gondolas.[12]

The following is the text of Greene's unfinished manuscript. A brief précis of the story's conclusion is appended.

The Stranger's Hand
(Previously unpublished film treatment)

Part One: Chapter One
(I)

The child had an air of taking everything in and giving nothing away. At Rome airport he was led across the tarmac by his aunt, but he seemed to hear nothing of her advice to himself or of the information she produced for the air hostess: he was too busy with his eyes: the hangars had his attention, every plane on the field except his own – that could wait.

'My nephew,' she was saying. 'Yes – that's him on the list. Roger Court. You *will* look after him, won't you? He's never been quite on his own before,' but when she made that statement the child's eyes moved back plane by plane with what looked like contempt, back to the large breasts and the fat legs and the over-responsible mouth: how *could* she have known, he might have been thinking, when I'm alone, how often I'm alone?

His aunt was quite capable of holding up the plane with her garrulity: 'If you'll just see him to the Europa,' she said, 'when you get to Venice – it is a good hotel, isn't it? He's no trouble, no trouble at all. I've had him on my hands – goodness, long enough to know that. His father's coming home tonight from Trieste.' And she would undoubtedly have gone on to give a testimonial to her brother too if the air hostess had not managed, with a certain brutality, to interrupt her.

'You'll have to say goodbye now,' she said, as the last of the child's fellow passengers climbed the companion way.

His aunt said emotionally, 'O Roger, my dear, Roger,' and made a grab at him, but he evaded her and turning solemnly half way up the companion he made his dry reply, 'Goodbye, Aunt Rose.'

'In a fortnight, dear . . . ' but she was already addressing a back.

It seemed like a deliberate action to avoid her waving hand when he chose his seat on the opposite side of the plane even though that entailed the danger of some curious stranger sitting down beside him. A child's privacy is never quite secure: nobody even hesitates to intrude: privacy has to be guarded behind a locked door ('how often have I told you not to turn the key?') or in the centre of a hedge ('we looked for you everywhere'). As soon as the plane was in the air he opened his small attaché case, not forgetting an automatic glance around him, and pulled from between the folds of his pyjamas the copy of a children's paper – a bright gaudy common paper, that he had no business, according to his aunt, to waste his time on. He was a little shortsighted and held his head bent over the paper, like a scholar, while he read how a cruel smile of triumph crossed the features of Mr Hogan. He didn't trouble to undo his safety belt, though the warning light had long gone out, for Mr Hogan had by this time locked the barn door and taking out his lighter was about to set fire to the thatch. Roger Court sighed and looked away. It was the end of *that* instalment and it was most unlikely that anywhere in Italy he would find the succeeding number. His brain must provide the sequel. The author – who was called Captain Peter Day – would have undoubtedly seen a way of escape from that barn, though the door was locked and there were no windows, but authors always contrived happy endings, and even at eight years old one knew that all endings were not happy.

'Have you been in an aeroplane before?' The air hostess had sat down beside him, but she received as icy a reception as his aunt.

'Yes,' he said: at that moment the barn was in flames and Major Ronnie Dunne was struggling in the smoke to find a way out, but it was no friendly author now who watched his struggle, ready to point out a convenient trap door: a realist was in charge.

'Was that your mother you were with?'

'No.'

'Is she in Venice?'

'No.'

'In England?'

'No.'

'She's not dead is she?' The air hostess's voice prepared the sympathetic note, but the savagery of his reply silenced her. 'She doesn't live with us any more.'

'Oh,' she said, 'I see,' but to judge from her bewilderment she was as much too young to see as the child was old enough. He could remember the long absences, the strain of nerves that led to sudden punishments and sudden treats, the arrival of his aunt and the strong words that floated up the stairway to the nursery landing, phrases like 'selfish', 'not even for the child', 'let his father do his share', 'love nobody but yourself'- that last was the most often repeated. It lodged in the child's mind in the very tones it was first uttered in, so that sometimes during the two years in Rome when his aunt appealed in vain for some sign of love – 'after all I've done' – he expected it again to be repeated, expected it with a sense of guilt, for certainly there was no one he was aware of loving. His father wrote to him regularly once a week (it was not his father's fault that he could obtain no leave from Trieste), and his aunt, regularly, every Saturday afternoon, thought of a treat for him. But we do not love people for what they do for us. Love happens to us; it isn't created.

He said reluctantly because he couldn't help realizing that in her own way she intended well: 'My father's a policeman.'

'I thought he worked in Trieste.'

'He does.'

'Oh.' It was the colloquial English phrase she was most adept in. 'You'll be glad to see him, I expect?' but that sentence, he obviously considered required no answer and she left him alone after that, until their arrival. One sign of approval he did give, when he saw that the bus to take him from the airport was a motor-launch: an indrawn sigh of satisfaction.

At the Europa he was handed over to the reception clerk, and his feet slid on the long floors that glistened like water. He had been handed a letter from his father and he held it screwed and unopened in his hand while he followed the clerk. He was not deceived by the clerk's patronage that took the whimsical form of behaving to him as though he were an adult. The clerk opened a door on the first floor. 'I hope this will suit you, sir,' and he stepped into an enormous room. It seemed to be all floor and light. The jetty on the Grand Canal outside strained and creaked.

'Major Court asked us for a double room, sir. I think you will be comfortable here.'

'Yes,' the child said. He went to the window and stared across the water to the stone steps and the great dome of Santa Maria. A dirty crowded waterbus pushed its way up the Canal, setting the rank of gondolas outside the hotel bumping on its wave. The clerk lingered a moment: he wasn't certain of himself, confronted with a back more concentrated and self-contained than a millionaire's. 'If you want lunch, sir, I can show you the restaurant.'

'Must I?' the child said.

'But aren't you hungry?'

'No.'

'Major Court won't be arriving till the eight o'clock train. He asked us to look after you.'

The child turned rather as a prisoner might turn towards a warder. 'All right,' he said, and followed the clerk back the opposite way, flowers and his own face flashing at him in the continual mirrors as though he were standing like a diver among the underwater plants. The head waiter, taking over from the clerk, put him at a table by the window, so that he could see the traffic to and fro on the Canal: suitcases were being loaded into a gondola at the hotel jetty and the manager had come out into the sun to speed a passing guest. The gleam and wetness dazzled the boy's eyes and he turned away towards the almost empty restaurant (it was too early for visitors). Somebody was wheeling towards him a whole table of hors d'oeuvres. Passively he allowed his plate to be heaped; he would explain to nobody the nausea in his nerves.

When he took up his fork he remembered the letter crumpled in his right hand. He was forbidden to read at meals, and the hour of open rebellion would not strike for two years or more, so he laid it by his plate and tried to eat. He managed a few beans, a little potato, but the anchovy burnt his tongue with salt and he gave up. He looked secretively this way and that: he longed to make a run for it to the shelter of his room, but a head waiter blocked the doorway. Then a voice spoke beside him: 'Lonesome?'

Yet another grown-up had assumed the right to intrude, and nothing could possibly daunt this one – certainly not the child's monosyllable. Flushed with her wine at lunch, boisterous with the bonhomie of the New World, she adored children and knew all about children. Hadn't she five kids of her own back in Philadelphia? There wasn't a thing anybody could tell her about children – and certainly a child couldn't, and she had discovered all the unimportant details about this one from the head porter before she accosted him.

'Too much oil? I felt like that myself the first week. Couldn't eat more than two courses a meal. And *you* wouldn't be used to butter. Now don't you fast any longer, but come with us and see the sights. We're catching the five o'clock train, but there's time for a run around first. You'll have a wonderful appetite for your supper.'

She was at any rate powerful and ruthless enough in her assurance to dredge out of him the longest sentence he had formed since sitting down in the Venice plane. 'I've got to wait here for my father – he's coming here.' Even after two years the words 'my father' lay heavily on his tongue. That was what his aunt always called him – with a slight note of disapproval. Once, in very early days, he had challenged her. 'Has Daddy done something wrong?' and her reply left behind a vague impression that all was not as it should be. 'Your father's a good man. Of course he's done nothing *wrong*,' but once he overheard from the stairs the phrase 'a man ought to be able to keep a woman', which, equated with another of his aunt's expressions, 'we can't afford to keep a dog with meat the price it is', gave him the idea that his father had been unable to afford either his mother or himself. Poverty, like the beggars on the Spanish Steps, was shameful, and soon the formal phrase that seemed to remove him further from his father became usual on his tongue.

'But you don't have to stay till he comes,' the American woman said, and at that moment her husband joined her and the bonhomie and the boisterousness were increased by exactly one hundred per cent. The restaurant that had seemed empty was full of the two of them. The boy's eyes moved from the man's round soft unlined face that looked that looked as though it had come straight from the kneading fingers of a masseuse to the astonishing handpainted silk tie, all reds and exotic flowers and a nymph strangled in the knot.

'You're young Roger Court, aren't you? We're going to give you a runaround.'

It was no good fighting against *this* fate: he was bundled up and tied like a rucksack and flung across the shoulders by their appalling kindness: they sat over him at Florian's until he had finished every bit of a large chocolate ice cream: they ran him through St Mark's as though they were on a steeple-chase, giving nicknames to the bearded Byzantine saints: they got him back to the square in time to see the pigeons fed at two: pushed him into a gondola and out again to sit in the glare of a furnace and watch glass blown out like balloons: back into another gondola with a glass dog clutched, like his father's letter, in his hand. They had the firm conviction that he was lonely and they talked and bantered so steadily to keep his spirits up that they never noticed his silence. They bought him half a pound of sugar almonds (he couldn't attract their attention long enough to tell them he didn't like almonds), they hauled him onto the jetty to say goodbye and watch them depart by motor-boat for the station and Mrs Loftheim (that was what he made her name out to be) thrust his own handkerchief into his hand to wave with. For a long time he heard their voices come back over the water as they told each other what a cute kid he was, and silence when it returned at last was as resonating as a noise. He turned and went back into the hotel and climbed the stairs to his room (he was too shy to take the lift) and sat down in a corner of the huge room by one of the beds. The glass dog had lost its tail, snapped cleanly off in Mrs Loftheim's last embrace, but the letter was still there unopened.

It was nearly dark: the late sunlight lay on the canal like the guilding of an eighteenth-century couch: he turned on the bedside light to read his letter.

'Dear Roger' (the phrase had the same distance as 'my father': they seemed to be signalling to each other tentatively over the No-Man's-Land of two years, a waste filled with the wreckage of other lives than their own), 'I shall be arriving at Venice by the eight o'clock train from Trieste. I'll come straight to the hotel and we'll have dinner together. It won't hurt you, will it, to stay up late one night? I shall be hungry because there's no food on the train, and we don't eat so much here as you do in Italy. It will be fun to see St Mark's with you and the glass blowing and have rides in gondolas.' Have I got to do all that again, the child wondered: Mrs Loftheim has shown it all to me already. Surely there must be something else in Venice? But when he read on his father only wrote: 'You won't have had an ice yet in Florian's?' He dropped the letter on the bed: there was nothing left except the conventional gestures, the 'love froms' and the crosses which had been the nearest to a touch they had had during these years. Obediently he would repeat them back in his own letters, but he had forgotten what they meant: they were like hieroglyphs of an extinct tribe. The boy lay back and thought of Mr Hogan, and thinking of Mr Hogan he fell asleep.

The telephone woke him and for a short time he couldn't think where he was: he thought it was somebody ringing the bell of his aunt's flat in Rome. It was quite dark in his room and when he put out his fingers for the light he couldn't find it. Everything had moved around: even the window and the bed. Then he remembered that he was in Venice and this was – who?

He didn't recognize the voice, but more than a quarter of his life had passed since he last heard it. The voice said, 'Roger. Is that Roger?'

'Yes.'

'This is Daddy – your father.'

'Yes.'

'I've just got off the train. Are you awake, dear?'

'Yes.'

'Glad to see me?'

'Yes.'

'I shan't be very long now, but these gondolas charge too much. They want a thousand lira to the hotel. I'll catch the waterbus.'

'Yes.'

'We have to go all round the canal, so I'll be about half an hour. Starving?'

'No.'

'It'll be good to see you, old chap. I'll be off now.'

'Goodbye.' the child said politely and rang off. His watch said eight-fifteen and curling his feet under him again, he occupied his mind for a while with Mr Hogan. At eight-forty he heard the whistle of a waterbus and went to the window: the lamplit panes under their belt of black smoke went by: strangers stared out onto the canal and some looked up at the windows of the hotel where he stood – one of the strangers, he imagined, was his father. Fifty yards away at the San Marco jetty, the bus drew up, but by five to nine his father had not yet come. He had missed that bus, but there would be one (the air hostess had told him) every ten minutes, and for the next hour the boy stood there watching them go by – the same sounds and lights and faces and the same silence afterwards. Soon he began to cry with the sense of mystery rather than with the sense of fear or loneliness or bewilderment, but after a time he remembered that his nurse in the old days of a home had told him that a watched pot never boiled, so he lay down on his bed with his back to the window and the canal and counted the *vapori* as they passed with his ears only, until, his face thrust down into the damp pillow, at last he fell asleep. While he slept the lights in the hotel one by one went out in all the rooms, leaving only the gloomy light of passages and presumably the last *vapore* went emptily by to its anchorage at two in the morning.

(II)

Major Court hung up the receiver with a dim feeling of disappointment. He had travelled from Trieste with mounting excitement. It was nearly three years since he had seen his son, and now that his wife had left him, the boy represented to him the whole of family life – that vaguely desired condition which he had never really enjoyed, that the war had broken for ever. (He never blamed his wife for what had happened: the war had broader shoulders on which to lay the blame for everything.) He hadn't been able to wait till he reached the hotel, but talking to his son on the telephone was like giving an unwanted present to somebody without the tact to pretend pleasure. He thought: Oh well, there are ten days – ten days, he meant, in which to tie the two of them together, to re-establish a family. He was, he knew it himself, an incurable optimist.

The *vapore* lurched towards the pier, belching its smoke, unwashed and rusty. It was nearly low tide, and there was no grandeur in the green weedy foundations of the houses: they were for the connoisseurs of decay. This was something for which Major Court felt no appreciation. The peeling palaces, the rotted gondola posts, unused and wearing away between the level of the tides, the sense of a city sinking – he held these impressions obstinately at bay, standing in the bows in his too-new civilian suit. Once he saw a rat scramble from the canal into a drain that the low tide had exposed and he turned abruptly away and set up his position on the other side. Then he gazed out again seeing only what he was determined to see – a fine cast iron lantern, a roof garden in the last sun, a beautiful Moorish façade. He stood there, looking one way, like an unbalanced expression of belief.

Perhaps he would have stayed there, staring out in safety at what he wanted to see all the way to San Marco if he hadn't turned at the sound of an American voice referring to Lord Byron's palazzo. He didn't think again about Lord Byron because beyond the American he saw a back he felt certain he knew: hadn't he had the case of that particular narrow back and bent shoulders for quite a while in Trieste? He wondered what Peskovitch, if it really was Peskovitch, was doing in Venice. His men had seen to it that he was passed safely through to Rome and there surely he should have stayed.

Major Court moved round until he could see the face . . . Yes – it was Peskovitch unquestionably. The momentary hesitation had been due, well to the extraordinarily tired face, the look of surprise, and perhaps to the fact that for once he was without those steel rimmed elderly spectacles. He had been in better condition after a prison camp and a journey without food for forty-eight hours across the mountains that he seemed to be in now. Major Court called across the deck to him, 'M. Peskovitch' (even in two days he had taken a fancy to the man) and saw Peskovitch's eyes blink short-sightedly back at him.

Major Court began to make his way beween the passengers. He said, 'How nice to see you again. You remember me – Court of the Venezia-Giulia police?' A voice said, 'There is some mistake. This is my great-uncle, Mario Varezi.'

For the first time Major Court noticed that Peskovitch – he could have sworn that it was Peskovitch – was accompanied. Two men were with him – the young man who spoke now and an elderly man with a weary grey moustache. They stood one on each side of – whoever it was and Major Court was suddenly reminded of his first meeting with Peskovitch, who was brought into his office in Trieste between two policemen. 'He says his name is Peskovitch,' one of them had reported. Court asked with astonishment, 'Not *the* Peskovitch,' and heard the stranger reply in English, 'I suppose I was – last year.' 'He was reported dead.' 'I am the late Peskovitch,' the stranger had replied with humour and pride.

The other man said, 'It is not the first time this mistake has been made. M. Peskovitch seems to have a number of friends.'

'A great many,' Court said, watching the eyes of Varezi – if he was Varezi. The *vapore* swung in towards the Ca d'Oro stop, and passengers pushed between them towards the side. Certainly in those tired dulled eyes there was nothing that could be taken for recognition. Again they were under way, lurching across to the next stop on the other side of the canal. Major Court said, 'I'm sorry. It is a startling likeness', and moved away.

But he was worried: he tried to believe in Mario Varezi. He looked at his watch: half an hour had passed since he called his son, and he thought with unimaginative tenderness and anxiety: he'll be needing his dinner even if he isn't glad to see me. The Rialto bridge arched over them and again there was a crush of passengers to the side. Only three more stops, he thought, and then family life began again: he would be a father and not an unwanted police officer working with strangers and he started to plan the excursions they would do together, and presently, presently he would learn how to talk to a child. Three men moved together towards the gang plank.

Major Court told himself that this was none of his business: his business came to an end at the edge of the international zone. A man called Mario Varezi was no concern of his, and at the moment of the thought Varezi looked back, peered back shortsightedly, not with any trace of recognition or appeal, but with a puzzled air, as though Major Court did perhaps remind him of a face he had once seen a long time ago, in another life. Another life. This is the age of reincarnations. His elderly companion said something to Varezi, gently, leaning close to his ear, as though he did not want to draw the attention of the young man, who was pushing a way for them. Major Court quite suddenly decided that after all he was concerned. As the three men mounted the slope of the Rialto bridge and descended towards the fish market, Major Court followed fifty yards behind.

(III)

The shine of the jetty and the slap of the water marked the turning of the tide. In the clock tower by St Mark's the iron man beat out the hour of four, the east wind off the Adriatic carried the sound of his strokes down the first rank of the Grand Canal, just as it set the gondolas rocking on their rank outside the Europa Hotel. The noises entered the boy's dream and became the traffic of a railway station where he waited interminably for his father, while the trains went in and went out. A man in a Christmas mask took his hand and said, 'You're young Roger, aren't you? I'm going to give you a run around.' 'Oh no, no,' he implored him. 'I must wait for my father,' but the man paid no attention, dragging him away from the platform towards a little dark doorway. 'You don't need to be scared of me,' he said, 'I've got a kid just like you. I'm Mr Hogan', and the boy woke, sweating with his fear and found that in the great glossy hotel room with the twin beds and the big mirrors there was only himself and all the shadows of the early hours.

Chapter Two

(I)

Roger Court watched the police launch move in against the

Europa jetty. The manager stood there ready to greet the police official who uncurled long weary legs from the cabin: a uniformed officer aided him ashore with a lift under the elbow. The manager put out a hand to take his brief case but with a sudden hop skip and jump that reminded Roger Court of a grasshopper, the official was ashore. The boy went back into his room and sat on the unused bed and waited for the telephone to summon him. It was nearly midday: the police seemed as slow to arrive as a doctor when the layman considers a case serious.

The boy had finally woken at half-past seven and had lain in bed wondering what to do until eight. Then he had dressed and gone downstairs. At the reception desk he said, 'My father has not come.'

The clerk said, 'Oh, he'll be on the morning train, I expect.'

'No. He came last night. He telephoned to me from the station. I think he had been murdered.'

The clerk laughed. The boy said 'Why didn't he come then?' and the clerk suddenly lost his laugh, leaving the smile baselessly in mid-air – 'Well,' he began, and then fled into the room behind to find the manager. The manager told him not to worry: they would see about everything: he was just to go on into the restaurant and have his breakfast. It was half-past eight. By nine o'clock the manager had decided unwillingly to telephone to the police.

But a man is not like a banknote. If a banknote is lost there is every reason to hurry on the search. If a man has been murdered he is safely out of circulation; sooner or later his body will turn up, in the canal or the lagoon; the earlier one begins to search, the earlier the undesirable publicity will start. And if – the more probable solution – he is alive, has only missed his train or spent his night in a brothel, the greater the delay, the more chance of keeping the whole affair from the newspapers for everybody's sake, even for the sake of the Press who never seem to realize that they are slowly strangling with their stories of violence, this aged goose that for so many years had been laying its golden eggs.

The telephone rang and the boy lifted the receiver gingerly: he was not yet confident about which end was which and he tried at first to speak through the earpiece. The manager said impatiently, 'Are you there, Mr Court?'

The boy got the receiver straight and said, 'But he hasn't turned up.'

'I mean you. Please come down to my office.'

The man in uniform opened the door for him. The long thin man drooped in an easy chair and the manager sat very upright at his desk. He said 'The Commissioner wants to ask you a few questions.'

'Do you speak Italian?' The boy shook his head.

'I can translate for you.' the manager said.

'It is not necessary. I was a prisoner in England for four years.'

The boy said, 'Where's my father?'

The Commissioner said, 'Don't worry. Nobody can disappear in Venice – if he is in Venice.'

'But he is.'

'That has to be investigated.' He began to clean his nails with a toothpick. 'I have telephoned to Trieste. I have no evidence that he was ever on the train.'

'But I heard him, he spoke to me.'

'When did you last see him?'

'Three years ago.'

'How do you know it was he who spoke to you?'

'But it was. Of course it was. He said, "Is that you, Roger?" He asked if I'd had dinner. He said he would be with me in half an hour.'

'Did you recognize his voice?'

'His voice . . . ' The boy began to cry: he had no idea what all this was about: why should anyone pretend to be his father? That suggestion was more terrifying than his father's disappearance: it belonged to the world of Mr Hogan.

'It might have been anybody,' the Commissioner said. 'He may never have reached Venice.'

'But why? Why?'

The telephone rang. 'For you, Commissioner.'

The Commissioner said wearily, 'Yes. Yes. Oh well . . . there might easily have been some mistake.' He rang off and asked the boy, 'Have you a photograph of your father?'

'No. But my aunt has.'

'Where is your aunt?'

'I don't know. She wrote her address down. She's gone to France on a holiday.' He began to feel in his pockets. Several scraps of paper came out – the newspaper photograph of an elephant, a recipe for making pistol caps at home, a code on which he had been working in private. He said dismally, 'I don't seem to have it.'

'She'll have to be told,' the manager said, 'if Major Court doesn't turn up today.'

'I suppose so,' the Commissioner said gloomily.

'She is in charge of the boy.'

'Is your mother dead?' the Commissioner asked.

'No.'

'Where is she?'

'I don't know.'

'You'd better turn out all your pockets.'

The collection on the desk grew: a lot of mottoes out of Perugina chocolates: a knife with a broken blade: the works of an old watch: a Boy Scouts Diary for 1939.

'Did you write it in there?' the Commissioner asked.

'No. It's on a bit of paper.'

But the bit of paper was nowhere. The last pocket produced only a wisp of tissue paper wrapped round a grey pebble the size of a pea.

'What's that?' the Commissioner asked with interest, as though he would like to change the whole course of the investigation to a more appealing subject.

'Something for making gunpowder.'

'What's it called?'

'Nobody knows. I call it ingredient X2.'

The manager impatiently interrupted them. 'But there must be some way of getting in touch with your aunt.'

'I don't know.'

'Didn't she tell you where she was going?'

'Something beginning with Sainte . . . '

'Well, run along now.' the Commissioner told him with a slight sigh as though really they two could have got along better by themselves without the other policeman and the manager, certainly without the case that lay so heavily on all their hands. He began to help the boy shovel the objects back into his pockets. When he reached the diary he paused. 'This seems a little out of date.'

'The tables aren't.'

'You mean weights and measures?'

'International Morse,' the boy said.

'Yes, of course. That's useful. I wish I had learnt it myself.'

'You don't know morse?'

'No.'

The boy said reluctantly, 'I might be able to lend it to you for a few days.'

'I will borrow it when I have time.'

Standing in the doorway the boy appealed to all of them. 'But my father . . . ?'

The Commissioner said, 'Oh, he will turn up. You may be sure. If not today tomorrow. You will hear from him. There is nothing to worry about. Nothing.' He held out a hundred lira note. 'Buy yourself some sweets.'

'I have enough, thank you.' The boy shut the door behind him. He was an adept at detecting false comfort.

The light from the water danced in the mirrors and the pale furniture of the lounges glowed like honey in the sun. He walked through room after empty room, his rubber soles squeaking on the parquet, and for the first time he missed the loud friendly voices of the Americans who had such a capacity for just filling space. Now space stretched all round him with nothing to fill it but himself and the loneliness and the fears loped on his track, like unknown beasts who were waiting till nightfall to approach. It would not be long before a whole day had passed since his father had said down the telephone, 'Half an hour.' That was a fact not even a policeman could avoid: there was no safe or happy explanation that he could find. A waiter in a white coat went by him from the bar carrying drinks towards the manager's office.

The boy came out on the jetty. The police launch had gone off on some other errand. He heard voices and recognized them and realised that he was close to the window of the manager's office; they spoke in Italian and he could only understand a few words here and there. Once he heard 'no evidence' and once 'we shall try the hospitals'. He could hear the sound of glasses laid down on the desk and the sound made him feel as though he and his father were completely forgotten.

(II)

Although it was the hottest hour of the afternoon a candle burning in a bottle gave the only light inside the little cavernous wine shop. The boy peered in and moved off down the street. He had crossed the Rialto bridge for no reason that he knew and making his way past the stalls into the Ruga Vecchia San Giovanni had stared up one of the dark narrow side streets where the sun never came. The houses on either side leaned for support on the arches above his head. He walked as though in sleep with no rational aim: two fingers of his left hand were crossed for luck and every thirteen paces he changed step and at every seventh doorway he paused and looked within. He used every charm he knew and invented others: by this means he had a faint hope that he might see his father.

He tried to remember what his father looked like. His aunt's photograph had been taken more than twenty years ago, when his father was a very young man and it bore no resemblance to the middle-aged stranger who had bid goodbye to him two and a half years ago. He had been five and a few months then – a child, and he was a little embarrassed to think of the way his father would have remembered him – sitting in that green toy motor car on the gravel path of the Laurels. His father had shaken hands with him and said, 'So long, old chap, so long,' and suddenly bending down and blowing the smell of beer and cigarette smoke into his face before kissing him roughly and quickly and shamefacedly on the forehead. Then his father had moved off down the path to the gate, limping a little from his bad left leg: he had sounded his horn and his father had turned and waved, and he had released his brake and got his feet ready on the pedals with the intention of a quick rush towards his father – one of his record-breaking Brooklands rushes just to show his father the daring of which he was capable, but he had become aware of his mother watching from a window and he took his feet from the pedals and ran indoors. So now he could remember nothing but a limp and a clean-shaven face.

Through every seventh doorway he peered for a clean-shaven man with a limp: he listened for any English words: his ears read into the creak of timber or the cry of a child a call for help. When he reached the Rio delle Beccarie he peered into the water expecting to see a clean-shaven face washing by with the old tins and the garbage. He felt no grief at the idea of his father's death, but he was aware of his own loneliness and fear in this city of strangers and he was sorry for his father because he was in the same case. It seemed to him that this was a situation that his mother should have shared and he blamed her for not being there.

One, two, three, four, five, six, seven – a courtyard of tall, dirty tenements and the washing hanging right across from every floor like flags that have been left out too long after a triumphal parade. Two men were talking in the yard – an elderly man with a drooping moustache shook his head and said in Italian, 'sick, very sick', and the other commiserated with him on the illness of his wife? His son? His friend? 'It is fortunate you are a doctor', the boy could understand that much. The doctor saw him watching and came towards him with an air of gentle kindliness. He was very thin, so thin, that his trousers hung in ungainly folds around his legs and his wrists were as slight as a woman's. Once Mr Hogan had prepared a bath of lime for Major Ronnie Dunne; 'in a few hours', he had said, 'you will be a skeleton.' It was as if the bath in the doctor's case had been interrupted.

He took in the boy's foreign clothes and asked him if he were lost and suddenly at the sound of the word 'lost' – the boy realized that in fact he had no idea of how to regain the Rialto bridge. The word haunted him, the gentle sympathetic face in this word of Mr Hogan's moved him, so that the tears became heavy behind the eyes. He nodded his head.

'You are American?'

'English,' he said.

'Where do you want to go?'

'To the Rialto.'

'But where are you staying?'

The boy became suddenly secret and said, 'I can get the waterbus there.'

'Where is your mother?' and for no particular reason at all except perhaps that he was tired of answering that particular question with the confession that he did not know – he said, 'At the hotel.'

'Which hotel?'

He lied again with the first name that came into his head. 'The Grand.'

The doctor put out his hand and said, 'I will show you the way,' and he felt the doctor's fingers placed like a bundle of pencils in his palm. They walked in silence and the boy no longer counted or changed his step: he was aware of the depressing truth that adults carried round with them – there was no such thing as magic. The doctor said suddenly, 'Do you like ice-cream?'

'Yes.'

'There is a café near here: a clean café – one has to be careful in this place because of the water.' The boy swam a little in his wake like a dinghy: he had no longer any will of his own. The last hope of finding his father himself had vanished with the magic: loneliness lay like ballast in his stomach. 'You must tell your mother to be careful – not to drink water out of taps.' He sat the boy down at a table and called 'Luigi. A chocolate ice.' He explained to the boy, 'Chocolate is more healthy. Vanilla is all right, but it is not so nourishing as food, and the fruit ices are all chemical.'

The boy pursued his own train of thought: he recognized

kindliness sitting there on a little iron chair with an empty plate watching him eat. 'You could manage another?'

He drew a deep breath and said, 'I told you a lie.'

'A lie.'

'I am not staying at the Grand Hotel. I am staying at the Europa.'

'You are a strange boy,' the doctor said. Though he had led him by the hand to this place, he talked to him like a grown man. He said, 'I have never been married and I have no children. You see my health was not good enough. One must not pass on one's sickness. Why did you lie?'

'You asked too many questions.'

'Yes, yes. I see. That is what it is to be a doctor. One gets used to asking. "Is the pain here or there?" I live with sickness and we ask the sick questions.'

'Do you work in a hospital?'

'You see – you ask questions too. No, I have private patients. I worked in a hospital once when I was a young man. That was a long time ago.'

The boy scraped round and round his glass. He said, 'Do your patients die?'

'Sometimes.'

'Have you any dying now?'

'I don't know. I have two bad cases of typhoid – the water again. Perhaps they will recover. Perhaps not. Please have another ice.'

The boy said, 'I told two lies. My mother isn't here.'

'Ah. It's your father who is looking after you?'

'My aunt sent me here to meet him.'

'You have no mother?'

'She has gone away.'

The doctor said quickly, 'And you love your father? There you see how it is, asking questions again. Always asking questions.'

Sucking his spoon, the boy looked up at him, a careful scrutiny. 'I don't mind,' he said. He took another suck and another look. 'I don't know where he is.'

'You have lost each other,' the doctor said. 'Venice is difficult for strangers. You should go back to your hotel. He will be anxious. You will find him there.' It was like a promise.

'Yes.' the boy said and rose.

(III)

But the promise was not fulfilled. His father had not come. The clerk at the desk said, 'We have had to move your room. We will give you a big room again when your father comes.' He showed the boy into the lift and as they rose he tried to encourage him. 'The police are trying to trace your aunt. They have telegraphed to the Surêté in Paris.' But surely it was his father they should be trying to trace.

His new room was very small with heavy old-fashioned furniture. Workmen swung on a platform outside his window preparing the façade of the hotel for the season. He was out of sight of the canal and there were no passing *vapore* now to remind him that his father was not on board. For a while he stood and watched the workmen – there was nothing else to do, except to look again at the paper he had already read more than once. When he searched for it in the attaché case which somebody had packed for him, he found that he hadn't even that to fall back upon – the paper was missing. He amused himself for a while opening the cupboard doors and testing the walls for secret hiding places where somebody might at sometime have left a message or even a piece of stolen jewellery, but he was unsuccessful. A bell by the bed was marked with some pictures of the people who would come at a call: a man dragging a trunk, a maid with a broom, a waiter with a tray, and his hand hovered for a moment over the three buttons. Then he went into the bathroom, filled the bath and tried to construct with the help of a loose piece of wood from the cupboard a waterfall down which a man might shoot in a barrel or a tooth glass. It was very unconvincing and when the floor was uncomfortably awash, he stopped. He hadn't really wanted to play that game. It was as if all the time he was keeping something at bay.

Back in the bedroom it occurred to him that he might organize a race between the maid, the porter and the waiter. He counted his money and finding that he had exactly five hundred lira, he betted himself five to one that the waiter would win. He put his stake – a hundred lira note – under the ashtray and with scrupulous justice used the palm of his hand to press all three buttons simulataneously.

He was out of luck, the maid and the porter arrived simultaneously. He could tell from their attitude that they would not appreciate his motive, so he told them that he had rung by mistake. The porter left at once with an air of not liking children: the maid lingered sypathetically until a thin trickle of water emerged from under the bathroom door. He had forgotten to turn off the tap. Luckily she could speak no English, but the clatter she made in mopping up the water expressed her feelings, and he felt it wisest not to ask her (as he had intended) to find his magazine and some notepaper. He would have been at a complete loss if he had not found at the back of a drawer, so cunningly concealed in the bureau that one might almost have classed it as a secret one, a small stub of white chalk. With this he was able to construct on the floor the materials for a game of cricket. A large circle enclosed a lot of numbers and penalties. He only had to choose two teams and then by throwing the chalk into the circle find the score. He captained one team putting himself in to bat third man and thus providing backbone to his side – very luckily as a boy called Droopy was LBW first ball. His team made 110.

When it came to choosing the second team, he put his head against the side of the bed and began to cry: loneliness and fear had returned in his attempt to write down his father's name as captain. Some day the police would trace his aunt and she would arrive and fetch him – a woman's world would enclose him again. He knew for the first time that he had wanted to see his father. He didn't hear the two knocks on the door and he only became aware that he was not alone by seeing two feet standing on the cricket scores. 'Allo,' a voice said. The boy raised his head and saw the waiter as though he was coming down a long road towards him through a blur of rain: an ugly, cheerful, savage face with a big crooked nose and the appearance of a sailor rather than a servant.

'Allo,' he said again. 'You're the kiddo,' (he used some extraordinary words). The boy said nothing, letting the tears run, there was no point now in trying to hide them.

'Well, say something.' the waiter said in a tone that could easily have been mistaken for fury. 'You rang, didn't you? I came hoity presto. What do you want, eh?'

It was as though in his misery he had slipped back two years. He whimpered at the waiter, 'My father.'

'And can I find him for you?' the waiter demanded. 'You have to leave that to the police. No? What?'

'They'll never find him,' the boy said.

The waiter squatted down on his haunches beside the boy and raising the bed cover peeped under the bed. 'Are we alone?'

'I think so.'

'Have you searched the cupboard?'

'Yes.' the boy said and suddenly grinned.

'Fine, fine,' the waiter said, 'leave everything to me. What is that game you are playing?'

'Cricket.'

'But where is the bat and the ball and the stakes?'

'Stumps.'

'Stumps, then.'

The boy began to explain and the waiter threw the chalk. It landed on a six and he clapped his hands with pleasure. 'I was the best batter in the camp.'

'Were you a prisoner?'

'Yes.'

'So was the Commissioner of Police.'

'Ah, but not like me. I fought to the last round. I killed dozens. Even the enemy cheered me when I was carried in full of bullets.'

'Have you got a lot of scars?'

'No. Now the surgeons are very clever. They sew you up

without any scars.' He threw the chalk again, and it landed on the letter C. 'What does that mean?'

'Caught.'

The waiter threw the chalk impatiently away. 'This is not real cricket. In real cricket I was never catched. I would smote the ball over the border,'

'Boundary.' The boy had forgotten to cry. He was no longer alone. He felt an enormous sense of trust – here was someone who would give him a straight answer. 'Will the police find my father?'

The waiter said, 'They will be ringing for me. I have been up and down to this floor all day. I call it the thirsty floor.' His eyes seemed to beseech the boy not to repeat his question. He said, 'I must be going,' and at the same time he sat down on the edge of the bed and touched the boy's hair. 'What's your name?'

'Roger.'

'Mine is Roberto Salvini.'

'Will they find my father?'

The waiter said, 'There is always hope.' – it was the most hopeless thing he could say. He went on 'You have got to know these things and there is no one here who will tell you. A man – a foreigner – disappeared from Rome nearly a week ago. He was recognized on the Venezia train, but the police here have not found him yet. It did not matter so much – he was a refugee from Yugoslavia. Now your father has disappeared. It looks bad. They wish it not happened at all. They would like to prove that it not happened here.'

'I don't understand.'

'They say he must have disappeared from the train. I listen to them, you know, when I carry in the drinks.'

'But he *spoke* to me.'

'They say *somebody* spoke to you.'

He rose from the bed and said, 'They will be ringing and ringing. Listen. We will meet at six. I have the evening off. We will have a drink together. Things are not so bad if you have a friend.'

'Please,' the boy said, 'will you find my father, Roberto?'

The waiter pulled the lobe of the boy's ear, once, twice, three times. 'Why not?' he said. 'Why not? A little thing like that.'

Chapter Three
(I)

Roberto ordered himself another vermouth, and a second ice-cream for the boy. He said, 'It would be more easy if you had a photograph.' The evening crowd filled the narrow street off the piazza, and the boy stared through the windows of the café at the swim of faces that moved as slowly as fish in a tank; sometimes they hung suspended for a while outside staring back.

'We have to make sure, you see, that he did arrive.'

'I know that. He spoke to me. I told you so.'

'But, kiddo, you see we must make the police admit it is true. Then they will have to search properly. Now they say it was not him who spoke.'

'Can't you find him without them?'

'Well, maybe, yes. Roberto can do the hell of a lot of things. One day I tell you some of them, but today, kiddo, I would rather the police helped. Now you just describe your father to me. Make believe he is sitting here just beside you. Would he have a moustache?'

'I don't know.'

'Is he tall?'

'Yes. No.'

'But kiddo, he can't be both.'

The child's eyes filled with tears as though a mere hint of impatience was a threat of dissention. 'He's taller than you.'

'Now we're getting somewhere. He must be a fine big man if he's bigger than Roberto.'

The child said with nodding solemnity, 'There he is.'

Roberto swung quickly round. 'Where?'

The child said, 'He went by the window.'

'You're joking.' but the child's face answered for him that he hardly knew the word. 'Quick,' Roberto said, 'we must to catch him.' He called out something to the waiter in Italian and dragged the boy through the door. 'Which way?'

'Right.' but when Roberto began to pull him that way the child hung back.

'No, the other.'

'One day somebody's got to teach you a lot, kiddo,' Roberto said. They pushed their way together through the evening crowd. Outside each café they paused and peered within. 'You were not just imagining things, were you?' Roberto asked.

'I saw him.' the boy said with confidence.

'How did you know him? Did you see his face plain?'

'I didn't see his face. There,' the child said, 'there, there he goes.' but in spite of his words he had to be dragged by Roberto in the wake of the limping man, as though already he realised that all men who limped were not his father; he had not really needed the explosion of excited Italian when Roberto seized the man by the shoulder to learn that.

'Now what made you say that to me?' Roberto complained, watching the indignant municipal councillor limp away.

'It was the way he walked.'

Roberto raised his hands indignantly. 'Of all the stupid things I have done, to pick a kiddo like you,' but suddenly, seizing the boy in a friendly painful way by the ear, he said, 'You mean your father – he had a limp like that?'

'Yes.'

'And why do you keep so many secrets from your friend Roberto? Maybe your father he has a long white beard and no teeth: maybe he is a very fat man: maybe he has a stammer. Maybe he is a giant or a dwarf, like Luza.'

The boy shook his head.

'Well,' Roberto said, 'that is fine to get along with. We know something now – we can look for a man. He has a limp. Now does he limp this way or that way?' and Roberto, finding a few feet of freedom in the crowded street, imitated a limp first with the right, then with the left foot.

'That way – I think.' the boy said, trying to make out the way his father walked out of his life down the gravel path.

'Was he wounded in the war?'

'I don't know.'

'You not know where your mother is, you not know what your father looks like – you lead a strange life, kiddo,' but he could never have convinced the boy of that: there is no strangeness where there is no companion. This was his only life and he led it the only way he could. He said, 'Have *you* got a father?'

'Oh, a mighty fine one. When he was young he could knock down a bullock – so.'

'And a mother?'

'Bellissima. She had ten children before she was lucky and had me.'

They had reached the café and sitting at the table they had left was the smallest man the child had ever seen – he was an inch shorter than himself and he had little beady belligerent eyes. He was drinking a glass of wine, but he gave an impression of holding it in his palm – so – only the better to fling it in an enemy's face. The grudge he had against the world was as old as his birth. He said to Roberto in Italian, 'You are late. I have many appointments.' He wore a peaked cap like a soldier, and he glared at the child as though he would gladly have put him to the sword: it was as if he had measured his height and took the extra inch for an insult.

'This is the kiddo.' The two men talked for a long while in Italian and the boy picked up only a word here and there – especially the word 'police' repeated often with venom. Presently Roberto said to the boy, 'This is Giorgio Luza. He take the tickets for the waterbus. I have asked him whether he remembers a lame man buying a ticket after the train came in from Trieste.'

'Does he remember?'

'He says he is too busy to remember things like that.'

'It isn't any use then?'

'Ah, but you see he has a great hatred for the Commissioner. That is why I asked him to come. He is prepared to tell the Commissioner that he saw your father. The Commissioner will not be pleased. He will have to do things now. He will have to search the city. There will be a lot of publicity and if he does not find your father it will be very bad for him.'

It was too complicated for the child. He only said: 'I wish he had really seen my father.'

They walked back in silence towards the hotel. It was dark and the pigeons had left the square: it was long past bedtime. The little venomous dwarf moved in the boy's imagination – in the stories he had read the hero never had such allies. Why couldn't it have been the Commissioner who helped him – that tall, lazy man who had spoken to him quite so kindly? Under the little humped bridge which they had to cross a gondolier slid rapidly by, his long boat gleaming into the lamplight and out again like a water serpent. Roberto said, 'One moment, kiddo.'

He led the boy into the shadowiness of a great empty church. Two old women prayed by a side altar and one ragged figure stood in front of the crucifix on the high altar, giving the bowed figure a long straight stare back like an equal. Roberto said softly, 'One has only a small small belief, but it does no harm to try everything.' He crossed the church and stood before the statue of St Anthony, the meaningless figure with the child in his arms, the utility saint so useful for lost keys and lost sweethearts. 'Go on,' Roberto said, 'pray to him. Ask him to find your father.'

'I'm not a Roman Catholic,' the boy said. He was scared of the shadows, the suggestion of magic, the obscure doings of the old women with candles.

'That is not important.' Roberto said with a kind of contempt. 'He finds things for everybody, even Germans. Go on. Tell him you will make an offering.' The boy had no idea what an offering was, and he knew he was not good at making things, but he had to obey, if Roberto considered that it might work. He whispered, 'Please Saint Anthony, find my father and I will make an offering.' When he turned Roberto for a moment was not in his sight, and the fear of desertion came over him again, and he put his fingers to his mouth in a gesture he hadn't used for four years.

Then he saw Roberto turning away from a statue of God's

Mother. Roberto held his hand as they left the church. The boy asked him, 'Did you pray too?'

Roberto said, 'One never knows,' in a tone of sombre hope.

'Did you pray that we'd find my father?'

Roberto looked down at the boy and pressed his hand more tightly. Children belonged to the world: they could not be hidden from it. He said, 'I prayed that we might find him alive, kiddo.'

Part Two – Chapter One

'One must take things as they are, Major Court.' the doctor said, moving his thin arm with the rolled up sleeve as though he would indicate how things were: the damp and airless room, the kitchen chairs, the occasional table with the remains of marquetry that had known better days. The basin of water, the towel, the syringe, the torn mattresses – you could hardly distinguish the human form on one of them from the grey army blankets. Major Court stood at the locked window and watched far below a gondola pass by, laden with ash cans. It was early morning and the hour for sewage. The empty tins bobbed in the dark water like fishes. It was preferable to the sight of the small crowded room and the two men dozing against the wall with their guns in their laps.

'I don't believe in the inevitable.' Major Court said. It occurred to him that it was a strange hour and place for philosophical argument, for the kind of opening gambit that he might have played as a young don in the senior common room after a good dinner in the days before the second war. One of the two men coughed without waking: he had done it all through the night.

'Like Pascal,' the doctor said, 'I put my trust in the greatest probability.'

'Will he die?' Major Court asked, nodding at the grey blanket.

'Almost certainly.' Major Court tried to detect the breathing under the blankets, but there seemed no more life there than a rag doll has.

'Oh, not of this,' the doctor said, making a little movement of his hand as though it still held a syringe, 'or here, but there, you know, over there.'

Major Court stared down into the canal. There was nothing to see outside that he hadn't made a note of long ago – how long ago? For some reason of their own they had taken away his watch and it was difficult to keep count of time. He supposed they were calculating on that: to be without the measurement of time was an effective minor torture: it made the days interminable. 'You may be miscalculating the probabilities.' he said.

'Of course. Like Pascal. But the stake on one side is so much greater. One can count on the mercy of – the other side.'

'I doubt it now. We've learned a good deal and we've picked up a lot of – bad manners. Remember Nuremburg.'

'Oh well . . . ' The doctor sighed. Certainly, Major Court thought, his choice of probability had not made him happy – it hadn't even made him prosperous or fat. 'Would you mind rolling up your sleeve, Major Court?'

'You agreed there was no harm in waiting till morning.'

'It's half past five.'

'I wouldn't have known. I haven't got a watch.'

'We'll wait another half hour if you like. I know you have an idea that the police will find you – oh, they'll probably begin searching in a day or two, but we'll have moved by then.'

'You think it will work on me as effectively . . . '

'A rather larger dose perhaps.'

'He was a good man.' Major Court said, looking at the bed. 'Won't you feel rather bad when he's disposed of?'

'Of course, but I shall persuade myself that if it hadn't been me who helped them, it would have been another. For your people have not left us a livelihood. There are always unemployed – technicians – like myself to be used.'

'Your belief in the inevitable again. History's against you. Even recent history.'

'The inevitable is somtimes postponed. It was postponed in 1815, 1918 and 1945. The process goes on. Do you know Venice, Major Court?

'Not well.'

'Look out of the window. You see how high the water rises on the steps. Venice is sinking an inch into the lagoon every hundred years. Already once a year at the highest tide you can take a gondola into the square of St Mark's. In six hundred years the water will be all over the floor of the cathedral. It will be abandoned. Presently we shall float over it in our boats and see the dome like a great barnacle below the keel.' It was the doctor's favourite theme. He never tired of that particular simile – it sounded to him like literature. The thin fingers made gestures of seaweed indicating the end of everything lovely. Major Court remembered the rat he had seen climb out of the canal and disappear into a drain. The smell of decay blew up from the canal. 'That is what I mean by the inevitable,' the doctor said.

'One can never tell. Major Court replied. 'Some engineer might invent something . . . ' It sounded a weak argument even to his own ears.

'And just so.' the doctor concluded. 'Your world. My world is sinking.'

'One can only do what one can.'

'I respect you, Major Court. I wish you had never seen us with Peskovitch on the waterbus. Or if only you had not followed. Now I can do nothing but obey orders. I am trying to persuade them to leave you here when they take him away. You can't cause any trouble after this.' He began to wash his syringe in the basin.

'I am not quite convinced that I ought not to make a fight.'

'What's the good? We should have to shoot.'

'The shot might be heard.' The doctor didn't even bother to answer him: they had been over that point so many times. It was really a kind of mercy they were showing him. If the authorities on the other side wanted him shipped across for interrogation (for some reason they seemed convinced that just because he knew Peskovitch, that he belonged to some brand of intelligence) he could be moved the more easily and comfortably. If he had to be eliminated, he would never know the moment of death, and, of course, there was always hope. It was only those who believed in the inevitable that who were not handcuffed sooner by that theological virtue.

'How quickly does it work?' Major Court asked.

'A matter of seconds. At first you will just sleep . . . '

'Does the brain ever recover?' It was strange standing there doing nothing, watching the drug prepared that would turn him presumably into such an automaton as Peskovitch had become, so that he had not even recognized his name when he had addressed him, standing between two strangers on the waterbus.

'Of course, of course,' the doctor said reassuringly, as though he were talking to a patient. A terrible langour fell over Major Court's spirits. He said, 'In a way I shall be glad to sleep. He isn't the worst worry. There's my boy . . . '

'No harm can come to him.'

'I know that. But I don't like the idea of his loneliness . . . I suppose he's back with his aunt by now. I would have liked seeing him again.'

'You mustn't despair, Major Court.'

The doctor was washing his hands now. Usually before an operation, one had the comforting sense of benevolence: one submitted to the anaesthetist with confidence that all was for the best, even though the worst might happen. In this dirty room, four floors up over the dingy branch canal, where the dozing man coughed and coughed over his old army revolver, there was no confidence in anything at all.

'Do you mind pulling up your sleeve, Major Court?' As the doctor advanced with his syringe Major Court thought – is this really the inevitable, is this the shabby future for us all?

Chapter Two

The boy didn't know why he was there, for nobody seemed to require him. He had been fetched by the consulate motor-boat and now sat in the Commissioner's office listening to the veiled insolences that went back and forth between the grown-up men.

The British Consul – a short man with a breezy commercial manner and astute brown eyes – said, 'Of course, Commissioner, I realize you know your business best, but a British subject has been missing for three days now . . . I don't want a Peskovitch case involving one of us, though what possible motive . . . '

'You know as well as I do, Mr Harrington, that one must begin a case at the beginning. I had no evidence that Major Court was even in Venice . . . '

'He had promised to meet his son that night and he telephoned from the station.'

'Somebody telephoned. I have been trying to trace the Major's movements from the Trieste end. I have had very little co-operation. Naturally, at the same time, I have been trying to pick up traces of him in the city. We have our sources.'

'Again I realize you have greater experience than I have in these matters, Commissioner, but I should have thought a house to house search, at least in the more dubious areas, the docks, behind the fish market.'

'It's not a thing one undertakes lightly. Until we had this evidence of the limping man, I wasn't prepared . . . '

'But I take it now you are going ahead with your habitual energy?'

'We are starting behind the docks and sealing off the canals round every block. We shall need the child with us – that's why I asked you to bring him. There's nobody else who can identify Major Court. Tomorrow we shall take another area.'

The Consul lowered his voice, and the boy, knowing that secrets were being spoken, leant back in his corner, with his eyes shut, intently listening. 'Careful nothing unpleasant,' were the words he caught.

'I have children of my own, Mr Harrington.'

'Yes,' the Consul said. He turned dubiously to the boy and said, 'Roger.' The boy opened his eyes. 'The police want you to help them. You won't be afraid to go with them in one of their boats, will you?'

'No.'

'They are very fine boats – speed boats. Latest type. You will be interested in the engines.'

'Yes.'

'When you come back, I want you to come and stay with us at the Consulate. I have a boy not much older than you. You'll get on well together.' he added dubiously. 'It will be better than the hotel until we can find your aunt.'

The boy began to cry silently in his corner, the tears swelling like blisters in the corner of his eyes and bursting between the lids.

'I expect you are lonely at the hotel,' the Consul said. The boy shook his head.

'You aren't scared of us, are you?' the Consul asked with timidity. He wished this hadn't happened in front of the Commissioner, who watched the scene like an outsider who could have done better. The boy said obscurely through his tears, 'But Roberto . . . '

'What's that?'

But what was the good. the child thought, of using that name here. None of them knew Roberto. Nobody knew that only Roberto had the wit and courage to find his father. Nobody in this room of strangers knew that loneliness only now beginning.

Chapter Three
(I)

The first day the police searched the area of the docks without result. At ten thirty in the morning of the second day they closed the Rialto bridge – unwillingly: that was something you couldn't keep out of the papers. A routine search in dockland was of little interest but there are no editors in the world who couldn't find room for a paragraph that contained the name Rialto. A whole quarter behind the Rialto was sealed off: on two sides the Grand Canal and on the other two those narrow waterways, the Rio delle Beccarie and the Rio dei Meloni. In that dark sunless network of streets, the people seethed like disturbed flies round a pile of ordure. Shoppers who had come from outside to the fish market found themselves forbidden to recross the bridges, and men of dubious profession who were always uncertain of police motives retired discreetly into their kitchens and became helpful to their wives. The *vapore* did not call that morning at the Rialto pier, and the police patrols pressed steadily inwards between the canals, checking papers.

The boy sat in the police launch by the Rialto pier. The men who yesterday were amused and interested by his presence were today rather bored and irritated. They had worked off all their vicarious paternal feelings and now were aware only of the impediment he represented. They could not tell how much Italian he understood and they were prevented from joking freely. A tired constraint hung over the launch and its shadow crept over the boy. He fidgeted unable to sit still. That awful sense of loving nobody – the dark night of maturity – touched him prematurely. Did it matter, he wondered, whether they found his father? Who was his father, a man with a limp?

A policeman signalled from the bridge and one of the men said sharply to the boy, 'They want you over there.'

'What for?'

'Perhaps they've found your father.'

He half-recognized the streets they led him down – he thought perhaps that on that first day of fear and action he had been there before. That was when he still felt love. Now he shuffled in the policeman's wake, a small and loveless figure who was tired and wanted to go home and forget the whole thing.

In the gateway of a tenement block a police officer waited. 'Come along,' he said. 'I want you with me.' He explained. 'Upstairs there are two sick men who arrived the night your father disappeared. I want you to have a look at them.'

A group of them moved up the stairs together: a long steep climb. On the second floor a man opened a door, saw them and closed it hurriedly: they paid him no attention, moving up. 'Stay here,' the officer told the boy, just before they topped the last landing, and when he did not immediately obey, the officer stamped his foot and said furiously, 'I said stay.' The boy stopped.

He heard the officer knock at the door, but he couldn't see him because of the top step. The officer had to knock twice. Then he heard the door open and a muddle of Italian voices, the shuffle of feet and silence. He sat down on the stairs and put his head in his hands and felt tired and very old. He thought, to encourage himself, 'There's Roberto. Later I will see Roberto,' but on this grey damp Venetian morning he felt no love even for Roberto. He was empty. A voice called to him, 'Come.'

He came through the door. He saw that the officer's holster was undone, but the gun had not been drawn. The doctor stared at him with astonishment. 'Why, little one . . . '

'Do you know each other?' the officer asked the boy. All the men seemed perturbed by the unexpected. The boy nodded.

'Where did you meet?'

'He gave me an ice-cream.'

'What were you doing?'

'He had lost his way,' the doctor explained, 'and was frightened.'

'I was looking for my father,' the boy said.

'Why him?' the officer asked.

'I was just looking.'

'Look again then,' the officer said. He was suspicious now that there was something he did not understand. He went across to the mattresses. 'Look at these men. Is one of them your father?' The doctor moved his hand nervously. He was leaning against the table and now he put his hand on the book he had been reading, Spengler's *Decline of the West*, as though to draw from the very feel of the book confidence in the inevitable.

The boy looked down at a man under a blanket: the thin elderly features of a stranger. He said, 'That's not my father.'

'And this one?' the officer asked.

'They are very sick,' the doctor said. 'I would pray you not to disturb them.'

'Is this your father?' the officer asked.

The boy looked down a second stranger: a man with a coarse three days growth of beard dressed in an old striped shirt open at the neck. This was like yesterday – they showed him all the wrong people. 'No,' he said. The doctor looked at the floor which shifted and then moved firmly back into place.

But with something the officer was not satisfied – perhaps it was only a quality in the doctor's silence: perhaps he had protested too much, or not enough. The officer laid his hand on the shirt and tried to shake the stranger awake.

The doctor said, 'You have no right . . . You have seen their papers. You hear what the boy says.' The officer shook the man again and the eyes opened.

'Look again,' the officer commanded and the boy looked with revulsion at the unwashed face and the three days' dirt. The stranger's eyes were trying to focus on him like a drunkard's. 'Of course he's not my father,' the boy said, and the stranger's hand moved at the sound of the English words.

'Please,' the doctor implored, but the officer paid him no attention, turning with vexation sharply to the door.

The doctor watched the man's eyes trying to focus. The lips were moving and as the door closed the doctor thought he could make out the first syllable of a boy's name before the hand fell hopelessly back and the lids shut again on whatever vague vision the brain had registered of his small son moving away.

(II)

The waiter said uneasily, 'But kiddo, you shouldn't have come.' The boy sat very upright in a recess of the great smart lounge and Roberto stood over him, tray in hand.

'I wanted to see you.' the boy said sullenly.

'But how did you manage it?'

'They gave me money for sweets,' he said. 'I got on the *vapore*.'

'You are better off at the Consulate.'

'No.'

'They are kind to you, aren't they?'

'Yes. I hate Morgan.'

'Who's Morgan?'

'The boy there. He thinks he can order me around. He's jealous because I went out on the police boat. He says I'm soft.' This was the longest statement the boy had made since he came to Venice: it was as if something inside him were breaking up with pain and letting the words out. 'Cameriere, cameriere.' somebody called and Roberto went off with the tray. The boy watched patiently the door through which he had disappeared. He didn't move an inch, not even his eyes, till Roberto came back.

Roberto put a glass of orange juice before the boy and stared. 'You mustn't mind him, kiddo.'

'Roberto,' the boy said, 'can't we find my father without all of them?'

'They are trying to help.' Roberto said.

'They are so stupid – the people they showed me. None of them was like my father. And tomorrow it will happen all over again.'

'There is sense in it, kiddo. You can't hide a man in Venice. If he has been kidnapped, they will find him.'

The wail of a siren rose over the canals and bridges and descended behind the domes. 'Come quickly,' Roberto said, 'and you will see a sight, kiddo.' He pulled him out onto the jetty and with a roar and an insolent rush they came, a troop of six scarlet speed boats, setting the gondolas flapping on their moorings, rocking the jetty with the wave of their passing, a gleam of nozzles and helmets. Boatmen rowed wildly to clear a path and a man in the first speedboat waved his hand and called something out to the boy, but it was lost in the roar and the wash of their passage.

'Fire practice.' Roberto said.

The boy's lips were wet with longing. He said 'Morgan says they are the best boats on the canal – better than the police boats.'

'Yes.'

'Morgan went on a practice once. His father fixed it.'

'When we've found your father,' Roberto said, 'he will fix anything for you.'

'I want to stay here, Roberto.'

'But you can't, kiddo. It's past your dinner time. They will be anxious. If they find you here talking to me. Oh mercy sakes,' Roberto said, 'what an imbroglio.'

'I want to be here.'

'The Consul is a good man.'

'I ought to be here. My father might telephone to me here.'

'He will know where to find you. They will tell him.'

'Has the Consul got a telephone?'

'Of course he has.'

'But Roberto, if they don't find him we must do it.'

'Listen, kiddo. I'm going to ask the manager for permission to take you home.'

'It isn't home.'

'Be good, kiddo and we will stop off on the way and meet a friend of mine. Roberto has not been idle. Roberto has found out a few things.'

'Not that little man?'

'No. Somebody else.'

'He scares me. He's wicked.'

'We will not have to see him again. He has done what we wanted. This friend is a good friend. He is a sailor, an American sailor and he knows what goes on in ports. Roberto has a hunch.'

'What's a hunch.?'

(III)

They landed from the *vapore* at the Porta St Elena where the big ships lay and cut through the public gardens. There seemed to be women on every seat, behind every tree, they had bright acquisitive eyes and the air of marksmen alert for the moving targets, and men with an air of authority and swagger moved among them, keeping an eye on them like sergeants. Roberto quickened his pace.

The boy asked, 'Are they waiting to go on board?'

'They are waiting for friends.' Roberto said.

In a café near the Campo del Grappa a sailor sat over a glass of beer. He wore a double-breasted jacket and a peaked cap – he was an ordinary seaman, the boy could tell that, and he wondered whether he was a mate. The word 'mate' had always stuck in his head since the first sea story he had read.

'This is the young shoofa.' Roberto said.

'I can't stay long.'

Roberto said to the boy. 'We have a small small business to discuss first. You just go off and get yourself a drink. And order a strega for me.'

When the boy came back the sailor was saying: 'Two thousand Camels,' and the boy momentarily had a vision of a vast desert, a little square of redcoats led by an officer with a lame leg, assaulted by savage tribesmen, and over the sand dunes the long line of the Camel Corps lurching to the rescue. He dug his own heels firmly into the flank of the leading camel (he was the only one who had known the route to lead them) and saw his father's face with sudden clarity looming ahead of him, a smear of mud like a two days' beard over the chin and cheeks. It was the face he had seen turning at the garden gate: it was a face that reminded him of he couldn't remember what.

'Same price. Same place.' Roberto said and his father looked up at him with astonishment and joy and his lips moved, but he was still too far away to hear the words.

'This jeezer,' Roberto said, 'is a yank off the *U.S. Grant.*'

The boy turned his eyes unwillingly from the beleaguered square to the round pink shaven face under the peaked cap. 'He is the steward,' Roberto said, 'if you know what that means.'

'Any news of the kid's father?'

'Nothing.'

'You know I'm fond of kids,' the steward said with an air of injured innocence, 'you know I'd help if I could, but I'm damned if I can see . . . I'm no flatfoot.'

'This is what I have been thinking.' Roberto said. 'His father arrived on Wednesday night. This is Saturday. If they have killed him – listen, kiddo, you mustn't mind me saying that: you and I know he is not dead, for why? Nobody bothers to hide a body. You remember that Englishman who was found shot in a gondola in the lagoon – he was not missing twelve hours. You do not have to hide bodies in Venice – you set them afloat.'

The boy listened without distress. The conversation had no reality – or rather it had the reality of a strip cartoon, of things that happened to other people.

'There's such a thing as lead,' the steward commented, glinting at the boy, and silence fell for a moment in their café, as though the argument itself had been tied carefully up and dropped over the side. The boy was back with the thousand camels charging down.

Roberto said: 'Well, we have to believe . . . '

'What can we do that the flatfoots can't?'

'If you wanted to hide a man in Venezia . . . '

'Why should you want to hide a man anywhere?'

'You're a fine jeezer,' Roberto said, 'but you have no imagination. If you had committed a murder and I knew about it, you might want to put me out of the way while you escaped.'

'I'd bump you off right away,' the steward said. 'I'd liquidate you.'

'Liquidate?' Roberto brooded. 'This boy's father was a policeman in Trieste. There is an awful lot of politics in Trieste.'

'It don't get us anywhere.'

Roberto took a look at the boy, but he was absorbed in something, leaning forward in his chair, bumping gently on his seat. Roberto said: 'If it is a body, it'll bob up somewhere. That is what the police hope. Fell into the canal. Death by natural causes. We just have to believe . . . '

'I'm ready to believe any dammed thing you tell me if it'll help.'

'Venezia is easy to search when once you begin. You would not want to keep a live man in Venezia long. Why that chap, the Yugoslavs picked up in Rome. They didn't even keep him in Rome long. The police traced him as far as Padova.'

'You bet he is in Yugoslavia by now.'

'Then he had to go by boat, or by plane. What boats are in now, Hamstringer, or just gone?'

'There haven't been any out in the last three days, except your coasters. There's my ship – you don't suspect that, do you? There's an English ship from Malta. There's that new Italian ship on the Egyptian run – tourist. There's one of our War Transport ships (Marshall Aid). A French freighter. A Yugoslav . . .' He fell suddenly silent staring into his beer glass.

Just before he reached his father a spear slid under his father's guard and he went down with the blade in his shoulder. Then the whole square broke into cheers and the Mahdi's followers were scattered and fleeing over the plain, while he knelt by his father's body, looking down at the face . . . looking down at him thus, he would hardly have known him.

The steward said, 'I went on board there last night. They should have sailed twenty-four hours before.'

'Which?'

'The Yugoslav. The steward's a friend of mine. He said there'd been some trouble about stores.'

[Although the following events are based on the action of the film, Roger Court's chief ally remains a waiter called Roberto.]

Joe Hamstringer uses his contact with the Yugoslav steward to discover that the 'trouble about stores' is merely a delaying tactic to allow Peskovitch and Major Court to be transferred to the ship, which will carry them behind the Iron Curtain for interrogation. Despite this further evidence, the Venetian authorities are still reluctant to concede that Major Court is in peril, and the ship has already left port before they are finally convinced. The pursuit is made in one of the gleaming red speed boats of the Venice fire brigade, and the ship is successfully boarded. However, the enemy agents refuse to surrender their prisoners without a fight and a gun battle ensues, during which the doctor sacrifices himself to protect Major Court.

Peskovitch and the major are brought ashore, and Roger is reunited with his father on the jetty. As befits a boy wrapped up in the world of Mr Hogan, Roger overcomes his shyness to demand for details of the dramatic rescue. He asks if anyone was killed during the shootout, and his father replies, 'Nobody, just a stranger,' unaware that his son is probably closer to the dead man than to himself. The film version of the story ends with a close-up of the 'stranger's hand' and the ring of string on his finger.

Introduction to *The Tenth Man*

In 1948 when I was working on *The Third Man* I seem to have completely forgotten a story called *The Tenth Man* which was ticking away like a time-bomb somewhere in the archives of Metro-Goldwyn-Mayer in America.

In 1983 a stranger wrote to me from the United States telling me that a story of mine called *The Tenth Man* was being offered for sale by MGM to an American publisher. I didn't take the matter seriously. I thought that I remembered – incorrectly, as it proved – an outline which I had written towards the end of the war under a contract with my friend Ben Goetz, the representative of MGM in London. Perhaps the outline had covered two pages of typescript – there seemed, therefore, no danger of publication, especially as the story had never been filmed.

The reason I had signed the contract was that I feared when the war came to an end and I left government service that my family would be in danger from the precarious nature of my finances. I had not before the war been able to support them from writing novels alone. I had indeed been in debt to my publishers until 1938, when *Brighton Rock* sold eight thousand copies and squared our accounts temporarily. *The Power and the Glory*, appearing more or less at the same time as the invasion of the West in an edition of about three thousand five hundred copies, hardly improved the situation. I had no confidence in my future as a novelist and I welcomed in 1944 what proved to be an almost slave contract with MGM which at least assured us all enough to live on for a couple of years in return for the idea of *The Tenth Man.*

Then recently came the astonishing and disquieting news that Mr Anthony Blond had bought all the book and serial rights on the mysterious story for a quite large sum, the author's royalties of course to be paid to MGM. He courteously sent me the typescript for any revision I might wish to make and it proved to be not two pages of outline but a complete short novel of about thirty thousand words. What surprised me and aggravated me most of all was that I found this forgotten story very readable – indeed I prefer it in many ways to *The Third Man*, so that I had no longer any personal excuse for opposing publication even if I had the legal power, which was highly doubtful. All the same Mr Blond very generously agreed to publish the story jointly with my regular publishers, The Bodley Head.

After this had been amicably arranged mystery was added to mystery. I found by accident in a cupboard in Paris an old cardboard box containing two manuscripts, one being a diary and commonplace-book which I had apparently kept during 1937 and 1938. Under the date 26 December 1937 I came on this passage: 'Discussed film with Menzies [an American film director]. Two notions for future films. One: a political situation like that in Spain. A decimation order. Ten men in prison draw lots with matches. A rich man draws the longest match. Offers all his money to anyone who will take his place. One, for the sake of his family, agrees. Later, when he is released, the former rich man visits anonymously the family who possess his money, he himself now with nothing but his life . . . .'

The bare bones of a story indeed. The four dots with which the entry closes seem now to represent the years of war which followed during which all memory of the slender idea was lost in the unconscious. When in 1944 I picked up the tale of Chavel and Janvier I must have thought it an idea which had just come to my mind, and yet I can only now suppose that those two characters had been working away far down in the dark cave of the unconscious while the world burnt.

The unexpected return of *The Tenth Man* from the archives of MGM led also to a search in my own archives where I discovered copies of two more ideas for films, and these may amuse readers of this book. The first idea (not a bad one it seems to me now, though nothing came of it) was called 'Jim Braddon and the War Criminal'.

Here is how the outline went – a not untimely story, even today, with Barbie awaiting trial.

Jim Braddon and the War Criminal

There is an old legend that somewhere in the world every man has his double. This is the strange story of Jim Braddon.

Jim Braddon was a high-grade salesman employed by a breakfast cereal company in Philadelphia: a placid honest man who would never have injured anything larger than a fly. He had a wife and two children whom he spoilt. The 1941 war had affected him little for he was over forty and his employers claimed that he was indispensable. But he took up German – he had a German grandmother – because he thought that one day this might prove useful, and that was the only new thing that happened to him between 1941 and 1945. Sometimes he saw in the paper the picture of Schreiber, the Nazi Inspector-General of the concentration camps, but except that one of his children pretended to see a likeness to this Nazi, nobody else ever commented on the fact.

In the autumn of 1945 a captured U-boat commander confessed that he had landed Schreiber on the coast of Mexico, and the film opens on a Mexican beach with a rubber dinghy upturned by the breakers and Schreiber's body visible through the thin rim of water. The tide recedes and the land crabs come out of their holes. But the hunt for Schreiber is on, for the crabs will soon eliminate all evidence of his death.

The push for post-war trade is also on, and Braddon is despatched by his firm for a tour of Central and South America. In the plane he looks at *Life*, which carries the story of the hunt for Schreiber. His neighbour, a small, earnest, bespectacled man full of pseudo-scientific theories, points out the likeness to him. 'You don't see it,' he says. 'I doubt whether one person in ten thousand would see it because what we mean by likeness as a rule is not the shape of the face and skull but the veil a man's experience and character throw over his features. You are like Schreiber, but no one would notice it because you have led a very different life. That can't alter the shape of the ears, but it's the expression of the eyes people look at.' Apart from the joking child he is the only person who has noticed the likeness – the stranger leaves the plane at the next halt. Half-way to Mexico City the plane crashes and all lives but Braddon's are lost.

Braddon has been flung clear. His left arm is broken, he is cut about the face, and he has lost his memory from the concussion. The accident has happened at night and he has cautiously – for he is a very careful man – emptied his pockets and locked his papers in his brief-case which of course is lost. When he comes to, he has no identity but his features, and those he shares with a dead man. He searches his pockets for a clue, but finds them empty of anything that will help him: only some small change, and in each pocket of the jacket a book. One is a paper-covered Heine: the other an American paperback. He finds that he can read both languages. Searching his jacket more carefully, he discovers a wad of ten-dollar notes, clean ones, sewn into the lining.

It is unnecessary in this short summary to work out his next adventures in detail: somehow he makes his way to a railroad and gets a train to Mexico City. His idea is to find a hospital as quickly as he can, but in the wash room at the station he sees hanging by the mirror a photograph of Schreiber and a police description in Spanish and English. Perhaps the experiences of the last few days have hardened his expression, for now he can recognize the likeness. He believes he has found his name. His face takes on another expresssion now – that of the hunted man.

He does not know where to go or what to do: he is afraid of every policeman: he attracts attention by his furtiveness, and soon the papers hear the news that Schreiber has been seen in Mexico City. He lets his beard grow, and with the growth of the beard he loses his last likeness to the old Jim Braddon.

He is temporarily saved by Schreiber's friends, a group of Fascists to whom Schreiber had borne introductions and who are expecting him. Among these are a brother and sister – a little, sadistic, pop-eyed Mexican whom we will call Peter for his likeness to Peter Lorre and his shifty, beautiful sister whom we will call Laureen for obvious reasons of casting. Laureen sets herself the task of restoring Jim's memory – the memory which she considers Schreiber *should* possess. They fall in love: in her case without reserve, believing that she knows the worst about this man: in his with a reserve which he doesn't himself understand.

Peter, however, is incurably careless. His love of pain and violence gets in the way of caution, and as a result of some incident yet to be worked out, Jim is caught by the Mexican police, while the others escape.

Schreiber could hardly have complained of rough treatment. Nor does Jim complain. He has no memory of his crimes, but he accepts the fact that he has committed them. The police force him to sit through a film of Buchenwald, and he watches with horror and shame the lean naked victims of Schreiber. He has no longer any wish to escape. He is content to die.

He is sent north to the American authorities, and the preliminary proceedings against him start. The new bearded Schreiber face becomes a feature of the Press. His family among others see the picture, but never for a moment does it occur to any of them that this is Jim.

Among the spectators at the trial, however, is the little spectacled pseudo-psychologist who was on the plane with Jim. He doesn't recognize Jim, but he is puzzled by Schreiber (Schreiber is not acting true to character), and he remembers what he said to the man in the plane, that likeness is not a matter of skull measurements but of expression. The expression of horror and remorse is not one he would have expected to see in Schreiber's eyes. This man claims to have lost his memory, and yet he denies nothing. Suppose after all they have got a man who is simply similar in bone structure . . .

Meanwhile Peter and Laureen, who escaped from the police trap which had closed on Jim, travel north. They plan a rescue. What their plan is I don't know myself yet. Violent and desperate, it offers one chance in a hundred. But it comes off. Jim is whipped away from the court itself, and the hunt is on again. But this is not

Mexico, and the hunt is a very short one. They are trapped in a suburban villa.

But Peter has taken hostages: a woman and her child who were in the house when they broke in. Jim has been obeying his companions like an automaton: there hasn't even been time to take off his handcuffs, but at this last example of Fascist mentality his mind seems to wake. He knocks out Peter with the handcuffs and gets his gun. The woman too has a gun. They face each other across the length of the room like duellists. She says, 'My dear, you won't shoot me.' But he shoots and her shot comes a second after his, but it isn't aimed at him: it hits her brother who has regained his feet and is on the point of attacking. Her last words are, 'You aren't Schreiber. You can't be. You're decent. Who the hell are you?'

Braddon gives himself up, and the truth of the psychologist's theory is glaringly exhibited. The likeness to Schreiber has proved to be physical only. I imagine the little man remembers at this point the man he talked to on the plane, he gives evidence, produces Braddon's family. The happy ending needs to be worked out, but the strange case of Jim Braddon really comes to an end with the shots in the suburban villa. After that there's just the reaching for coats under the seats. Anyone in the stalls could tell you what happens now.

Nobody to Blame

The sketch for a film, entitled *Nobody to Blame*, was written about the same time for my friend Cavalcanti. He liked the idea, but our work on it never began, for when he submitted it to the Board of Film Censors, he was told that they could not grant a certificate to a film making fun of the Secret Service. So this story too joined the others for a while in the unconscious, to emerge some ten years later as a novel – simplified, but not, I think, necessarily improved – called *Our Man in Havana*.

There is no censorship for novels, but I learnt later that MI5 suggested to MI6 that they should bring an action against the book for a breach of official secrets. What secret had I betrayed? Was it the possibility of using bird shit as secret ink? But luckily C, the head of MI6, had a better sense of humour than his colleague in MI5, and he discouraged him from taking action.

(I)

Richard Tripp is the agent of Singer Sewing Machines in some Baltic capital similar to Tallinn. He is a small inoffensive man of a rather timid disposition with a passionate love for postage stamps, Gilbert and Sullivan's music and his wife, and a passionate loyalty to Singer Sewing Machines. Unofficially he is Agent B.720 of the British Secret Service. The year is 1938/39.

Mrs Tripp – Gloria – is much younger than Tripp and it is to give her a good life that he has allowed himself to be enlisted in the Secret Service. He feels he must spend more money on her than Singer provides to keep her, although she has a genuine fondness for her dim husband. She knows nothing, of course, of his activities.

At HQ in London Tripp is regarded as one of their soundest agents – unimaginative, accurate, not easily ruffled. He is believed to have a network of sub-agents throughout Germany and he keeps in touch with HQ through the medium of his business reports written to his firm. What HQ does not know is that in fact Tripp has no agents at all. He invents all his reports and when London expresses dissatisfaction with an agent he simply dismisses one notional source and engages another equally notional. Naturally he draws salaries and expenses for all the imaginary agents.

His active imagination, from which he has drawn the details of a large underground factory near Leipzig for the construction of a secret explosive, does on one occasion lead to a little trouble with the local police. From an independent source London learns that B.720 is being shadowed, and they send him an urgent warning, but the warning arrives too late.

At the end of a programme of Gilbert and Sullivan opera by the Anglo-Latesthian Society in which Tripp takes a leading part the Chief of Police, who is sitting in the front row, hands up a bouquet with a card attached and the request that he may have a drink with Tripp immediately in his dressing-room. There he tells Tripp that the German Embassy have complained of his activities. Tripp confesses to his deception.

The Chief of Police is amused and pleased that Tripp's presence will keep out any serious agents, and he accepts the gift of a sewing machine for his wife. He will ensure that Tripp's messages go safely out of the country – and to keep the German Embassy quiet, he decides, they can have a look at them on the way. London's warning comes on the heels of the interview, and Tripp sends back a message announcing that he has appointed the Chief of Police himself as one of his agents, enclosing that officer's first report on the chief political characters of Latesthia and requesting that as first payment and bonus the Chief, who he says is an ardent stamp collector, should receive a rare Triangular Cape, and when the stamp arrives of course he sticks it in his own album. This gives him an idea, and soon the Chief of the Secret Service is commenting to the HQ officer in charge of Tripp's station, 'What a lot of stamp collectors he has among his agents.'

'It might have been worse. Do you remember old Stott's agents? They all wanted art photos from Paris.'

'Stott's at a loose end, isn't he?'

'Yes.'

'Send him over to take a look at Tripp's station. He may be able to give Tripp some advice. I always believe in letting two sound men get together.'

(II)

Stott is a much older man than Tripp. He is bottle-nosed and mottled with a little round stomach and a roving eye. Tripp is naturally apprehensive of his visit and expects to be unmasked at any moment, but to his relief he finds that Stott is much more interested in the foods and wines of Latesthia, and in the night life, than in the details of Tripp's organization. There are even fleeting moments when Tripp wonders whether it could possibly be that Stott also had run his station on notional lines, but such a thought of course can hardly be held for long.

The first evening together Stott remarks, 'Now, the brothels, old man. You've got good contacts there, I suppose?'

Tripp has never been in a brothel in his life. He has to own that he has overlooked brothels.

'Most important, old man. Every visiting businessman goes to the brothels. Got to have them covered.'

He has a night round the town with Stott and gets into trouble with his wife for returning at two in the morning. Stott moves on to Berlin, but he has sown seeds in Tripp's mind. His notional agents in future follow a Stott line. London is asked to approve in rapid succession the madame of a high class 'house', a café singer, and, his most imaginative effort to date, a well-known Latesthian cinema actress who is described as Agent B.720's (ie Tripp's) mistress. Of course he had never spoken to her in his life, and he has no idea that she is in fact a German agent.

(III)

A second crisis – needing more delicate handling than Stott's – blows up. The threat of European war is deepening and London considers that Tripp's position in Latesthia is a key one. He must have a proper staff: Singer Sewing Machines are persuaded in the interests of the nation to build up their agency in Latesthia and they inform Tripp that they are sending out to him a secretary-typist and a clerk. Tripp is innocently delighted that his work for Singer has borne such fruit and that sewing machines are booming. He is less pleased, however, when the clerk and typist arrive and prove to be members of the Secret Service sent to assit him in handling his now complicated network of agents.

The clerk is a young man with a penetrating cockney accent and an enormous capacity for hero-worship – and heroine-worship. His devotion is equally aroused by what he considers the experience and daring of Tripp and by the legs and breasts of

Tripp's wife. His name is Cobb, and he has an annoying habit of asking questions. He says himself, 'You don't have to bother to explain things, Chief. Just let me dig in and ask questions, and I'll get the hang of things for myself.'

The typist – Miss Juxon – is a withered spinster of forty-four who regards everyone and everything with suspicion. She believes that even the most innocent labourer is in the pay of the secret police, and she is shocked by the inadequacy of the security arrangements in the office. She insists on all blotting paper being locked in the safe and all typewriting ribbons being removed at night. This is highly inconvenient as no one is very good at fixing typewriter ribbons. Once she finds a used ribbon thrown in the wastepaper basket instead of being burnt in the incinerator and she begins to demonstrate the danger of the practice by deciphering the impress on the ribbon. All she can make out is 'Red lips were ne'er so red nor eyes so pure', which turns out to be a line of a sonnet written by Cobb – obviously with Mrs Tripp in mind.

'He's really rather sweet,' Mrs Tripp says.

The chief problem that Tripp has to solve is how to disguise the fact that he has no sources for his reports. He finds this unexpectedly easy. He goes shopping and returns with envelopes that have been handed to him, he says, from under the counter: he makes a great show of testing perfectly innocent letters about sewing machines for secret ink: he takes Cobb for a round of the town and then in the restaurants points out his agents.

'A very discreet man. You'll see he won't show the least flicker of recognition.'

The monthly payments to agents present a difficulty: Miss Juxon objects strongly to the payments being made by himself.

'It's irregular, insecure: HQ would never countenance it.'

By this time, for the sake of his assistants, he has drawn up an impressive chart of his sources: with the immediate head agents who control each gang. Miss Juxon insists that from now on he shall cut off his personal contacts with all but his head agents (of whom the cinema actress is one) and that he should meet them on every occasion in a different disguise.

Disguises become the bane of Tripp's life. What makes it worse, of course, is that his wife knows nothing. Miss Juxon shows a horrible ingenuity: Tripp's make-up box for the operatic productions of the Anglo-Latesthian Society is requisitioned. He finds himself being forced to slip out of back doors in red wigs and return by front doors in black wigs. She makes him carry at least two soft hats of varying colours in his overcoat pockets, so that he can change hats. Spectacles, horn-rimmed and steel-rimmed, bulge his breast pockets.

The strain tells. He becomes irritable and Mrs Tripp is reduced to tears. Cobb is torn between hero-worship and heroine-worship.

(IV)

Next crisis: the enemy begins to take Tripp seriously. He becomes aware that he is followed everywhere – even to the Anglo-Latesthian musical *soirée* – 'an evening with Edward German and Vaughan Williams'. Miss Juxon's security arrangements have been a little too good and the Germans are no longer able to keep an eye on the reports he sends.

She has objected to the use of the Chief of Police as transmitter and has evolved an elaborate method of sending secret ink messages on postage stamps. (There is a moment when Miss Juxon skirts shyly round the possibility of bird shit as secret ink.) Unfortunately the ink never develops properly – single words will appear and disappear with disconcerting rapidity.

Tripp, in order to be able to fake his expenses sheet and show the expenditure of huge sums for entertainment, is forced to dine out at least three times a week. He hates restaurant meals – and in any case it would be fatal if one of his assistants saw him dining alone. He therefore rents a room in the suburbs and retires there for a quiet read (his favourite authors are Charles Lamb and Newbolt) or the writing of a bogus report, taking a little food out of the larder with him. (In his account book this appears as 'Dinner for three (political sources) with wines, cigars, etc., £5.10s.0d'.) This constant dining out had never been necessary in the old days before his assistants came, and Mrs Tripp resents it.

The domestic crisis reaches its culmination when on pay day Tripp has to pretend to visit the home of the cinema actress with pay for her sub-sources. Cobb keeps guard in the street outside and Tripp, wearing a false moustache, proceeds up to the actress's flat, rings the bell and enquires for an imaginary person. He turns away from the closing door just as Mrs Tripp comes down from visiting a friend in the flat above. His excuse that he was trying to sell a sewing machine seems weak to Mrs Tripp in view of his false moustache.

Domestic harmony is further shattered when Cobb, anxious to make peace between his hero and his heroine, tells Mrs Tripp everything – or what he thinks is everything. 'It's for his country, Mrs Tripp,' he says.

Mrs Tripp decides that she too will go in for patriotism. She begins to dine out too, and Tripp, not unduly disturbed, takes the opportunity of appointing her as an agent with a notional lover in the Foreign Ministry.

'That fellow Tripp,' they say in London, 'deserves a decoration. The Service comes even before his wife. Good show.'

His notional mistress and his wife's notional lover are among his most interesting sources. Unfortunately, of course, his wife does not believe that his mistress is notional and her dinner companion, unlike the notional member of the Foreign Ministry, is a very real young man attached to Agriculture and Fisheries.

Mrs Tripp gets news of Tripp's hide-out and decides to track him down. She is certain she will find him in the company of the actress and that he will not be engaged in work of national importance.

The enemy are aware of his hide-out.

(V)

Tripp has got his legs up on the stove, some sausage rolls in his pocket, and he is reading his favourite poet Newbolt aloud, in a kind of sub-human drone which is his method with poetry. 'Play up, play up and play the game . . . the dons on the dais serene . . .' He is surprised by a knock at the door. He opens it and is still more surprised by the sight of his notional sub-agent, the cinema actress. Her car has broken down outside: can she have his help? Outside in the car two thugs crouch ready to knock Tripp on the head. A third – a tall stupid sentimental-looking German of immense physique – keeps watch at the end of the street. Tripp says he knows nothing about cars: now if it had been a sewing-machine . . .

Mrs Tripp is coming up the road. She has obviously lost her way. Tripp by this time is demonstrating the special points of the Singer sewing machine . . . Mrs Tripp is cold and miserable. She leans against a fence and cries. A little further down the road the sentimental German watches her. He is torn between pity and duty. He edges nearer.

Mr Tripp is talking about poetry to the cinema actress . . .

Mrs Tripp weeps on the German's shoulder and tells him how her husband is betraying her at this moment, but she can't remember the number of the house . . .

The Germans in the car are getting very cold. They get out and begin to walk up and down . . . Tripp is reading Newbolt to the actress . . . 'His captain's hand on his shoulder smote . . . ' Mrs Tripp and the German peer in at the window. He hasn't realized that this treacherous husband has anything to do with him. Mrs Tripp moans, 'Take me away,' and he obeys at once – in his comrades' car. Somebody – he is too sentimentally wrought up to care who – tries to stop him and he knocks him down. He deposits Mrs Tripp at her own door.

Tripp is still reading poetry when there is another knock at the door. One German pulls in the other German who is still unconscious. There is a babble of German explanations. 'He was trying to mend the car,' the actress explains, 'and it ran away from him.'

'I'll ring up the garage,' Tripp says. He goes in an alcove, where nobody has seen the telephone.

They prepare to knock him out. 'Wrong number,' he says furiously. 'It's the police.'

When he puts down the receiver again they knock him out.

(VI)

Mr Tripp has not returned home for some days. Cobb and Miss Juxon are worried. Mrs Tripp is furious but finds consolation.

Tripp comes to himself inside the German Embassy. Enormous pressure is put on him to betray his organization, but he has no organization to betray. The threat forcibly resolves itself into this: either he will remain a prisoner in the Embassy until war starts, when he will be handed over to the Gestapo as a spy, or he will send a message for them – containing false information carefully devised to discredit him – to London and then in due course he will be released. They show him films of concentration camps, they keep him from sleeping: he is shut up in a cell with the sentimental German, now disgraced, who wakes him whenever he tries to sleep and reproves him for betraying his wife.

The German Ambassador, in collaboration with the Military Attaché, plans out the message for him to send. On one sheet the Military Attaché notes the facts to be concealed: the date of invasion; number of divisions etc. On the other they note the lies to be revealed. A breeze from the open window whips the papers around. The wrong notes (that is to say the true notes) are handed to Tripp to write in secret ink. Tripp gives way. To send one more message of false information seems a small price to pay.

To make all secure and ensure that no Tripp message will ever be believed again, the Germans instruct the Chief of Police to go to the British Ambassador and expose Tripp's dealings with him – the invented messages which he used to show to the Germans before transmitting them. He gives the impression that Tripp knew that the Germans saw them.

Tripp is arrested by the police immediately he leaves the German Embassy. He is escorted home where he is allowed to pack a bag. Mrs Tripp is not there. Cobb shows him a decoded cable from London: 'Dismiss Agent X.Y.27 [his wife]. Intercepted correspondence to school friend shows she is carrying intrigue with . . . of Agriculture and Fisheries Ministry instead of . . . of Foreign Ministry. Unreliable.'

Tripp says goodbye to his home, to Cobb and Miss Juxon, to his make-up box, presented to him by the Anglo-Latesthian Society, to his collected works of Gilbert and Sullivan. He empties his pockets of the false moustache, soft hats, spectacles. 'These were the trouble,' he says sadly to Miss Juxon.

He is put on board a plane to England.

An official enquiry awaits him at HQ. His Ambassador's report has been received, but opinion among his judges before he comes is divided. The trouble is that his reports have been welcomed by the armed forces. The whole Secret Service will look foolish if they have to recall hundreds of reports over the last two years – ones which have been acclaimed as 'most valuable'. The head of the enquiry points out that it will discredit the whole Service. Any of their agents could have done the same. None of them will be believed in future.

A message arrives that Tripp is in the outer office, and the youngest member of the enquiry – a dapper, earnest FO type – goes out to see him. He whispers to him urgently, 'Everything will be all right. Deny everything.'

'If only,' the chairman is saying, 'he hadn't sent that last message. All his other messages are matters of opinion. You remember the underground works at Leipzig. After all, they are underground – we can't be *sure* he invented them. General Hays particularly liked that report. He said it was a model report. We've used it in our training courses. But this one – it gives a time and date for zero hour, and the source claimed – the German Military Attaché himself – you can't get round that. Such and such divisons will cross the frontiers at ten o'clock today. If we hadn't been warned by the Ambassador we'd have had the whole Army, Navy and Air Force ringing us up to know who the devil had sent such nonsense. Come in, Tripp. Sit down. This is a very serious matter. You know the charges against you.'

'I admit everything.'

The dapper young man whispers excitedly, 'No, no, I said deny.'

'You can't possibly admit everything,' the chairman interrupts with equal excitement, 'it's for us to tell you what you admit and what you don't admit. Of course this last message – ' The telephone rings: he raises the receiver: 'Yes, yes. Good God!'

He puts the receiver down and addresses the enquiry board. 'The Germans crossed the Polish frontier this morning. Under the circumstances, gentlemen, I think we should congratulate Mr Tripp on his last message from Latesthia. It is unfortunate that bungling in the British Embassy resulted in no use being made of it – but those after all are the chances of the Service. We can say with confidence among ourselves that the Secret Service was informed of the date and the time of war breaking out.'

Tripp is given the O.B.E. He is also appointed chief lecturer at the course for recruits to the Secret Service. We see him last as he comes forward to the blackboard, cue in hand, after being introduced to the recruits as 'one of our oldest and soundest officers – the man who obtained advance news of the exact date and even the hour of the German attack – Richard Tripp will lecture on "How to Run a Station Abroad".'

The Blue Film [13]

'Other people enjoy themselves,' Mrs Carter said.

'Well,' her husband replied, 'we've seen . . . '

'The reclining Buddha, the emerald Buddha, the floating markets,' Mrs Carter said. 'We have dinner and then go home to bed.'

'Last night we went to Chez Eve . . . '

'If you weren't with *me*' Mrs Carter said, 'you'd find . . . you know what I mean, Spots.'

It was true, Carter thought, eyeing his wife over the coffee cups: her slave bangles chinked in time with her coffee-spoon: she had reached an age when the satisfied woman is at her more beautiful, but the lines of discontent had formed. When he looked at her neck he was reminded of how difficult it was to unstring a turkey. Is it my fault, he wondered, or hers – or was it the fault of her birth, some glandular deficiency, some inherited characteristic? It was sad how when one was young, one so often took the signs of frigidity for a kind of distinction.

'You promised we'd smoke opium,' Mrs Carter said.

'Not here, darling. In Saigon. Here it's "not done" to smoke.'

'How conventional you are.'

'There'd only be the dirtiest of coolie places. You'd be conspicuous. They'd stare at you.' He played his winning card. 'There'd be cockroaches.'

'I should be taken to plenty of Spots if I wasn't with a husband.'

He tried hopefully. 'The Japanese strip-teasers . . . ' but she had heard all about them. 'Ugly women in bras,' she said. His irritation rose. He thought of the money he had spent to take his wife with him and to ease his conscience – he had been away too often without her, but there is no company more cheerless than that of a woman who is not desired. He tried to drink his coffee calmly: he wanted to bite the edge of the cup.

'You've spilt your coffee.' Mrs Carter said.

'I'm sorry.' He got up abruptly and said, 'All right. I'll fix something. Stay here.' He leant across the table. 'You'd better not be shocked,' he said, 'You've asked for it.'

'I don't think I'm usually the one who is shocked,' Mrs Carter said with a thin smile.

Carter left the hotel and walked up towards the New Road. A boy hung at his side and said, 'Young girl?'

'I've got a woman of my own,' Carter said gloomily.

'Boy?'

'No thanks.'

'French films?'

Carter paused. 'How much?'

They stood and haggled a while at the corner of the drab street. What with the taxi, the guide, the films, it was going to cost the best part of eight pounds, but it was worth it, Carter thought, if it closed her mouth for ever from demanding 'Spots'. He went back to fetch Mrs Carter.

They drove a long way and came to a halt by a bridge over the canal, a dingy lane overcast with indeterminate smells. The guide said, 'Follow me.'

Mrs Carter put a hand on Carter's arm. 'Is it safe?' she asked.

'How would I know?' he replied, stiffening under her hand.

They walked about fifty unlighted yards and halted by a bamboo fence. The guide knocked several times. When they were admitted it was to a tiny earthed-floored yard and a wooden hut. Something – presumably human – was humped in the dark under a mosquito-net. The owner showed them into a tiny stuffy room with two chairs and a portrait of the King. The screen was about the size of a folio volume.

The first film was peculiarly unattractive and showed the rejuvenation of an old man at the hands of two blonde masseuses. From the style of the women's hairdressing the film must have been made in the late twenties. Carter and his wife sat in mutual embarrassment as the film whirled and clicked to a stop.

'Not a very good one,' Carter said, as though he were a connoisseur.

'So that's what they call a blue film,' Mrs Carter said. 'Ugly and not exciting.'

A second film started.

There was very little story in this. A young man – one couldn't see his face because of the period soft hat – picked up a girl in the street (her cloche hat extinguished her like a meat-cover) and accompanied her to her room. The actors were young: there was some charm and excitement in the picture. Carter thought, when the girl took off her hat, I know that face, and a memory which had been buried for more than a quarter of a century moved. A doll over a telephone, a pin-up girl of the period over the double bed. The girl undressed, folding her clothes very neatly: she leant over to adjust the bed, exposing herself to the camera's eye and to the young man: he kept his head turned from the camera.

Afterwards, she helped him in turn to take off his clothes. It was only then he remembered – that particular playfulness confirmed by the birthmark on the man's shoulder.

Mrs Carter shifted on her chair. 'I wonder how they find the actors,' she said hoarsely.

'A prostitute,' he said. 'It's a bit raw, isn't it? Wouldn't you like to leave?' he urged her, waiting for the man to turn his head. The girl knelt on the bed and held the youth around the waist – she couldn't have been more than twenty. No, he made a calculation, twenty-one.

'We'll stay,' Mrs Carter said, 'we've paid.' She laid a dry hand on his knee.

'I'm sure we could find a better place than this.'

'No.'

The young man lay on his back and the girl for a moment left him. Briefly, as though by accident, he looked at the camera. Mrs Carter's hand shook on his knee. 'Good God,' she said, 'it's you.'

'It *was* me,' Carter said, 'thirty years ago.' The girl was climbing back on to the bed.

'It's revolting,' Mrs Carter replied.

'I don't remember it as revolting,' Carter replied.

'I suppose you went and gloated, both of you.'

'No, I never saw it.'

'Why did you do it? I can't look at you. It's shameful.'

'I asked you to come away.'

'Did they pay you?'

'They paid her. Fifty pounds. She needed the money badly.'

'And you had your fun for nothing?'

'Yes.'

'I'd never have married you of I'd known. Never.'

'That was a long time afterwards.'

'You still haven't said why. Haven't you any excuse?' She stopped. He knew she was watching, leaning forward, caught up in the heat of that climax more than a quarter of a century old.

Carter said, 'It was the only way I could help her. She'd never acted in one before. She wanted a friend.'

'A friend,' Mrs Carter said.

'I loved her.'

'You couldn't love a tart.'

'Oh yes, you can. Make no mistake about that.'

'You queued for her, I suppose.'

'You put it too crudely,' Carter said.

'What happened to her?'

'She disappeared. They always disappear.'

The girl leant over the young man's body and put on the light. It was the end of the film. 'I have new ones coming next week,' the Siamese said, bowing deeply. They followed their guide back down the dark lane to the taxi.

In the taxi Mrs Carter said, 'What was her name?'

'I don't remember.' A lie was easiest.

As they turned into the New Road she broke her bitter silence again. 'How could you have brought yourself . . . ? It's so degrading. Suppose someone you knew – in business – recognised you?'

'People don't talk about seeing things like that. Anyway, I wasn't in business in those days.'

'Did it never worry you?'

'I don't believe I have thought of it once in thirty years.'

'How long did you know her?'

'Twelve months perhaps.'

'She must look pretty awful by now if she's alive. After all she was common even then.'

'I thought she looked lovely,' Carter said.

They went upstairs in silence. He went straight to the bathroom and locked the door. The mosquitoes gathered around the lamp and the great jar of water. As he undressed he caught glimpses of himself in the small mirror: thirty years had not been kind: he felt his thickness and his middle age. He thought I hope to God she's dead. Please, God, he said, let her be dead. When I go back in there, the insults will start again.

But when he returned Mrs Carter was standing by the mirror. She had partly undressed. Her bare thin legs reminded him of a heron waiting for fish. She came and put her arms round him: a slave bangle joggled against his shoulder. She said, 'I'd forgotten how nice you looked.'

'I'm sorry. One changes.'

'I didn't mean that. I like you as you are.'

She was dry and hot and implacable in her desire. 'Go on,' she said, 'go on,' and then she screamed like an angry and hurt bird. Afterwards she said, 'It's years since that happened,' and continued to talk for what seemed a long half hour excitedly at his side. Carter lay in the dark silent, with a feeling of loneliness and guilt. It seemed to him that he had betrayed that night the only woman he loved.

Originally written in 1954. Collected in *Twenty-One Stories* (1954).

All But Empty

It is not often that one finds an empty cinema, but this one I used to frequent in the early 1930s because of its almost invariable, almost total emptiness. I speak only of the afternoons, the heavy grey afternoons of late winter; in the evenings, when the lights went up in the Edgware Road and the naphtha flares, and the peep-shows were crowded, this cinema may have known prosperity. But I doubt it.

It had so little to offer. There was no talkie apparatus, and the silent films it showed did not appeal to the crowd by their excitement or to the connoisseur by their unconscious humour. They were merely banal, drawing-room drama of 1925.

I suspect that the cinema kept open only because the owner could not sell or let the building and he could not afford to close it. I went to it because it was silent, because it was all but empty, and because the girl who sold the tickets had a bright, common, venal prettiness.

One passed out of the Edgware Road and found it in a side street. It was built of boards like a saloon in an American western, and there were no posters. Probably no posters existed of the kind of films it showed. One paid one's money to the girl of whom I spoke, taking an unnecessarily expensive seat in the drab emptiness on the other side of the red velvet curtains, and she would smile, charming and venal, and address one by a name of her own; it was not difficult for her to remember her patrons. She may be there still, but I haven't visited the cinema for a long time now.

I remember I went in one afternoon and found myself quite alone. There was not even a pianist; blurred metallic music was relayed from a gramophone in the pay-box. I hoped the girl would soon leave her job and come in. I sat almost at the end of a row with one seat free as an indication that I felt like company, but she never came. An elderly man got entangled in the curtain and billowed his way through it and lost himself in the dark. He tried to get past me, though he had the whole cinema to choose from, and brushed my face with a damp beard. Then he sat down in the seat I had left, and there we were, close together in the wide dusty darkness.

The flat figures passed and repassed, their six-year-old gestures as antique as designs on a Greek coin. They were emotional in great white flickering letters, but their emotions were not comic nor to me moving. I was surprised when I heard the old man next to me crying to himself – so much to himself and not to me, not a trace of histrionics in those slow, carefully stifled sobs that I felt sorry for him and did not grudge him the seat. I said:

'Can I do anything?'

He may not have heard me, but he spoke: 'I can't hear what they are saying.'

The loneliness of the old man was extreme; no one had warned him that he would find only silent pictures here. I tried to explain, but he did not listen, whispering gently, 'I can't see them.'

I thought that he was blind and asked him where he lived, and when he gave an address in Seymour Terrace, I felt such pity for him that I offered to show him the way to another cinema and then to take him home. It was because we shared a desolation, sitting in the dark and stale air, when all around us people were lighting lamps and making tea and gas fires flowed. But no! He wouldn't move. He said that he always came to this cinema of an evening, and when I said that it was only afternoon, he remarked that afternoon and evening were now to him 'much of a muchness'. I still didn't realize what he was enduring, what worse thing than blindness and age he might be keeping to himself.

Only a hint of it came to me a moment after, when he turned suddenly towards me, brushing my lips with his damp beard, and whispered.

'No one could expect me to see, not after I've seen what I've seen,' and then in a lower voice, talking to himself, 'From ear to ear.'

That startled me because there were only two things he could mean, and I did not believe that he referred to a smile.

'Leave them to it,' he said, 'at the bottom of the stairs. The black-beetles always came out of that crack. Oh, the anger,' and his voice had a long weary *frisson*.

It was extraordinary how he seemed to read my thoughts, because I had already begun to comfort myself with the fact of his age and that he must be recalling something very far away, when he spoke again: 'Not a minute later than this morning. The clock had just struck two and I came down the stairs, and there he was. Oh, I was angry. He was smiling.'

'From ear to ear,' I said lightly, with relief.

'That was later,' he corrected me, and then he startled me by reading out suddenly from the screen the words, 'I love you. I will not let you go.' He laughed and said, 'I can see a little now. But it fades, it fades.'

I was quite sure then that the man was mad, but I did not go. For one thing, I thought that at any moment the girl might come and two people could deal with him more easily than one; for another, stillness seemed safest. So I sat very quietly, staring at the screen and knew that he was weeping again beside me, shivering and weeping and shivering. Among all the obscurities one thing was certain, something had upset him early that morning.

After a while he spoke again so low that his words were lost in the tin blare of the relayed record, but I caught the words 'serpent's tooth' and guessed that he must have been quoting scripture. He did not leave me much longer in doubt, however, of what had happened at the bottom of the stairs, for he said quite casually, his tears forgotten in curiosity:

'I never thought the knife was so sharp. I had forgotten I had had it reground.'

Then he went on speaking, his voice gaining strength and calmness: 'I had just put down the borax for the black-beetles that morning. How could I have guessed? I must have been very angry coming downstairs. The clock struck two, and there he was, smiling at me. I must have sent it to be reground when I had the joint of pork for Sunday dinner. Oh, I was angry when he laughed: the knife trembled. And there the poor body lay with the throat cut from ear to ear,' and hunching up his shoulders and dropping his bearded chin towards his hands, the old man began again to cry.

Then I saw my duty quite plainly. He might be mad and to be pitied, but he was dangerous.

It needed courage to stand up and press by him into the gangway, and then turn back and be lost in the blind velvet folds of the curtains which would not part, knowing that he might have the knife still with him. I got out into the grey afternoon light at last, and startled the girl in the box with my white face. I opened the door of the kiosk and shut it again behind me with immeasurable relief. He couldn't get at me now.

'The police station,' I called softly into the telephone, afraid that he might hear me where he sat alone in the cinema, and when a voice answered, I said hurriedly, 'That murder in Seymour Terrace, this morning.'

The voice at the other end became brisk and interested, telling me to hold the line, and then the seconds drummed away.

All the while I held the receiver I watched the curtain, and presently it began to shake and billow, as if somebody was fumbling for the way out. 'Hurry, hurry,' I called down the telephone, and then as the voice spoke I saw the old man wavering in the gap of the curtain. 'Hurry. The murderer's here,' I called, stumbling over the name of the cinema and so intent on the message I had to convey that I could not take in for a moment the puzzled and puzzling reply: 'We've got the murderer. It's the body that's disappeared.'

First published in *Strand Magazine* (March 1947), then in *Ellery Queen's Mystery Magazine* (December 1949).

Appendices

I The Films of Graham Greene

Orient Express
USA, 1934, Twentieth-Century Fox (Paul Martin)
d Paul Martin *w* Paul Martin, Carl Hovey, Oscar Levant, William Conselman (from the novel *Stamboul Train*)
Heather Angel, Norman Foster, Ralph Morgan, Dorothy Burgess, Herbert Mudin, Una O'Connor, Irene Ware, Roy D'Arcy, Lisa Gova, William Irving

The Green Cockatoo (aka: *Four Dark Hours* or *Race Gang*)
GB, 1937 (released 1940), Twentieth-Century Fox/New World Pictures (William K. Howard/Robert T. Kane)
d William Cameron Menzies *w* Edward O. Berkman, Arthur Wimperis (after Greene's story and scenario)
John Mills, Rene Ray, Robert Newton, Allen Jeayes, Bruce Seton, Charles Oliver, Julian Vedey, Frank Atkinson

The Future's in the Air
GB, 1937, Strand Film Company (Paul Rotha)
d Alex Shaw *w* Graham Greene (see p. xxx)

Twenty-One Days (aka: *The First and the Last*); (US title: *Twenty-One Days Together*)
GB, 1937 (released 1940), London Films/Columbia (Alexander Korda)
d Basil Dean *w* Graham Greene, Angus MacPhail, Basil Dean and divers hands (from 'The First and the Last' by John Galsworthy)
Laurence Olivier, Vivien Leigh, Leslie Banks, Hay Petrie, Robert Newton, Esme Percy, Francis L. Sullivan, Victor Rietti, Morris Harvey

The New Britain

GB, 1941, Ministry of Information (Alexander Shaw)
d Ralph Keane *w* Graham Greene (after scenario by Reg Groves) (see p. xxx)

This Gun for Hire

USA, 1942, Paramount (Richard M. Blumenthal)
d Frank Tuttle *w* Albert Maltz, W.R. Burnett (from the novel *A Gun for Sale*)
Veronica Lake, Alan Ladd, Robert Preston, Laird Cregar, Tully Marshall, Roger Imhof, Marc Lawrence, Mikhail Rasumny, Harry Shannon

Went the Day Well? (US title: *Forty-Eight Hours*)

GB, 1942, Ealing Studios (Michael Balcon)
d Alberto Cavalcanti *w* John Dighton, Diana Morgan, Angus MacPhail (from the story 'The Lieutenant Died Last')
Leslie Banks, Elizabeth Allan, Frank Lawton, Basil Sydney, Valerie Taylor, Mervyn Johns, Edward Rigby, Marie Lohr, David Farrar, Thora Hird, Harry Fowler

The Ministry of Fear

USA, 1943, Paramount (Seton I. Miller)
d Fritz Lang *w* Seton I. Miller
Ray Milland, Marjorie Reynolds, Carl Esmond, Dan Duryea, Hilary Brooke, Erskine Sanford, Thomas Louden, Percy Waram, Alan Napier, Helena Grant

The Confidential Agent

USA, 1945, Warner Brothers (Robert Buckner)
d Herman Shumlin *w* Robert Buckner
Charles Boyer, Lauren Bacall, Katina Paxinou, Peter Lorre, Victor Francen, George Coulouris, Wanda Hendrix, John Warburton, Dan Seymour, George Zucco, Miles Mander, Holmes Herbert

The Man Within (US title: *The Smugglers*)

GB, 1947, General Film Distributors/Production Film Service (Sydney and Muriel Box)

d Bernard Knowles *w* Muriel and Sydney Box
Richard Attenborough, Joan Greenwood, Michael Redgrave, Basil Sydney, Jean Kent, Francis L. Sullivan, Felix Aylmer, Ronald Shiner, Ernest Thesiger, Maurice Denham, David Horne

The Fugitive
USA, 1947, RKO (John Ford and Merian C. Cooper)
d John Ford *w* Dudley Nichols (from the novel *The Power and the Glory*)
Henry Fonda, Dolores del Rio, Pedro Armendariz, Leo Carillo, Ward Bond, J. Carroll Naish, Robert Armstrong, John Qualen

Brighton Rock (US title: *Young Scarface*)
GB, 1947, Associated British Pictures (John and Roy Boulting)
d John Boulting *w* Graham Greene
Richard Attenborough, Carol Marsh, Hermione Baddeley, Harcourt Williams, William Hartnoll, Wylie Watson, Nigel Stock, Alan Wheatley, George Carney, Charles Goldner

The Fallen Idol
GB, 1948, British Lion/London Films (Alexander Korda/Carol Reed)
d Carol Reed *w* Graham Greene, with Lesley Storm, William Templeton (from the story 'The Basement Room')
Ralph Richardson, Michèle Morgan, Sonia Dresdel, Bobby Henrey, Denis O'Dea, Jack Hawkins, Walter Fitzgerald, Bernard Lee, Geoffrey Keen, Dora Bryan, George Woodbridge, Dandy Nichols

The Third Man
GB, 1949, London Films (Alexander Korda)
d Carol Reed *w* Graham Greene
Joseph Cotten, Orson Welles, Alida Valli, Trevor Howard, Bernard Lee, Siegfried Breuer, Paul Hoerbiger, Ernst Deutsch, Erich Pontu, Wilfred Hyde-White

The Heart of the Matter
GB, 1953, London Films/Associated Artists (Alexander Korda)

d George More O'Ferrall *w* Ian Dalrymple (after scenario by Lesley Storm)

Trevor Howard, Elizabeth Allan, Maria Schell, Peter Finch, Denholm Elliott, George Coulouris, Gerald Oury, Earl Cameron, Michael Hordern

The Stranger's Hand

GB/Italy, 1954, British Lion/DCA (John Stafford, Peter Moore)
d Mario Soldati *w* Guy Elmes (based on a treatment by Graham Greene)
Trevor Howard, Richard O'Sullivan, Alida Valli, Eduardo Ciannelli, Richard Basehart, Stephen Murray

The End of the Affair

GB, 1955, Columbia/Coronado (David Lewis)
d Edward Dmytryk *w* Leonore Coffee
Deborah Kerr, Peter Cushing, Van Johnson, John Mills, Michael Goodliffe, Stephen Murray, Nora Swinburne, Joyce Carey, Charles Godner, Frederick Lister

Loser Takes All

GB, 1956, British Lion (John Stafford)
d Ken Annakin *w* Graham Greene
Robert Morley, Rossano Brazzi, Glynis Johns, Tony Britton, Felix Aylmer, Albert Lieven, A.E. Matthews, Walter Hudd

Saint Joan

GB, 1957, United Artists (Otto Preminger)
d Otto Preminger *w* Graham Greene (from the play by George Bernard Shaw)
Jean Seberg, Richard Widmark, Richard Todd, Felix Aylmer, Finlay Currie, John Gielgud, Anton Walbrook, Harry Andrews, Barry Jones, Bernard Miles

Across the Bridge

GB, 1957, Rank/IPF (John Stafford)
d Ken Annakin *w* Guy Elmes, Denis Freeman (from the story by Graham Greene)

Rod Steiger, Bill Nagy, Bernard Lee, Noel William, David Knight, Marla Landi, Eric Pohlmann, Faith Brook

Short Cut to Hell
USA, 1957, Paramount (A.C. Lyles)
d James Cagney *w* Ted Berkeman, Raphael Blau, W.R. Burnett (from the novel *A Gun for Sale*)
Robert Ivers, Georgeann Johnson, William Bishop, Jacques Aubuchon, Peter Baldwin, Yvette Vickers, Richard Hale

The Quiet American
USA, 1957, United Artists/Figaro (Joseph L. Mankiewicz)
d Joseph L. Mankiewicz *w* Joseph L. Mankiewicz
Audie Murphy, Michael Redgrave, Claude Dauphin, Georgia Moll, Bruce Cabot, Kerina, Fred Sadoff

Our Man in Havana
GB, 1959, Columbia/Kingsmead (Carol Reed)
d Carol Reed *w* Graham Greene
Alec Guinness, Jo Morrow, Noël Coward, Ralph Richardson, Maureen O'Hara, Ernie Kovacs, Burl Ives, Paul Rogers, Gregoire Aslan, Jose Prieto

The Comedians
USA/Bermuda/France, 1967, MGM/Maximilian (Peter Glenville)
d Peter Glenville *w* Graham Greene
Richard Burton, Elizabeth Taylor, Peter Ustinov, Alec Guinness, Paul Ford, Lillian Gish, James Earl Jones, Raymond St Jacques, Cicely Tyson, George Stanford Brown, Roscoe Lee Browne, Douta Deck

Travels With My Aunt
USA, 1972, MGM (Robert Fryer, James Cresson)
d George Cukor *w* Jay Presson Allen, Hugh Wheeler
Maggie Smith, Alec McCowan, Lou Gossett, Robert Stephens, Cindy Williams, Robert Flemyng, Jose Luis Lope Vasquez, Valerie White, Corinne Marchand, Raymond Gerome

England Made Me
GB, 1972, Hemadale/Atlantic (Jack Levin)
d Peter Duffell *w* Desmond Cory, Peter Duffell
Peter Finch, Michael York, Hildegard Neil, Michael Hordern, Joss Ackland, Tessa Wyatt, Michael Sheard

La Nuit Américaine (US title: *Day for Night*)
France/Italy, 1973, Films Du Carosse/PECF/PIC (Marcel Bébert)
d François Truffaut *w* François Truffaut, Jean-Louis Richard, Suzanne Schiffman
François Truffaut, Jacqueline Bisset, Jean-Pierre Aumont, Valentina Cortesa, Jean-Pierre Léaud, Dani, Alexandra Stewart, Jean Champion, David Markham, Graham Greene (as Henry Graham)

The Human Factor
GB, 1979, Rank/Sigma/United Artists (Otto Preminger)
d Otto Preminger *w* Tom Stoppard
Nicol Williamson, Iman, Ann Todd, Derek Jacobi, Robert Morley, Richard Attenborough, John Gielgud, Tony Vogel, Martin Benson, Paul Curran, Fiona Fullerton, Cyd Hayman, Joop Doderer, Richard Vernon

A Shocking Accident
GB, 1982, Flamingo/Virgin/National Film Finance Corporation (Christine Oestreicher)
d James Scott *w* James Scott, Ernie Eban
Rupert Everett, Jenny Seagrove, Barbara Hicks, Benjamin Whitrow, Tim Seely, Sophie Ward, Oliver Blackburn, Robert Popper

The Honorary Consul (US title: *Beyond the Limit*)
USA, 1983, Twentieth-Century Fox (Norma Heyman)
d John Mackenzie *w* Christopher Hampton
Richard Gere, Michael Caine, Elpidia Carrillo, Bob Hoskins, Joaquim de Almeida, A. Martinez, Leonard Maguire, Geoffrey Palmer

Loser Takes All (US title: *Strike It Rich*)

USA, 1990, Enterprise/Miramax (Christine Oestreicher, Graham Easton)
d James Scott *w* James Scott
Robert Lindsay, Molly Ringwald, John Gielgud, Frances de la Tour, Max Wall, Simon de la Brosse, Margi Clarke

TV Movies

The Power and the Glory
USA, 1961, CBS Television (David Susskind)
d Marc Daniels *w* Dale Wasserman
Laurence Olivier, George C. Scott, Julie Harris, Mildred Natwick, Martin Gabel, Cyril Cusack

Stamboul Train
GB, 1962, BBC Television (Prudence Fitzgerald)
w Christopher Williams
Susan Burnet, Peter Birrel, Richard Warner, Anna Burden, Ivor Salter

Il Treno per Istambul
Italy, 1979, Rai-Radiotelevisione/Magyar Radio es Televisione
d Gianfranco Mingozzi *w* Gianfranco Mingozzi, Giacomo Battiato, Gyorgy G. Kardos
Mimsy Farmer, William Berger, Lea Padovani, Stefano Satta Flores, Joseph Madaras, Alfredo Pea, Mirella D'Angelo

The Heart of the Matter
Germany, 1983, Telemunchen (Peter Weissenborn)
d Marco Leto *w* Gerald Savory
Jack Hedley, Erica Rogers, Manfred Seipold, Wolfgang Kieling, Silvio Anselmo, Tim Kwebulane

Dr Fischer of Geneva
GB, 1984, Consolidated Productions/BBC Television (Richard Broke)
d Michael Lindsay-Hogg *w* Richard Broke
James Mason, Alan Bates, Greta Scacchi, Clarissa Kaye, Barry

Humphries, Cyril Cusack, Hugh Burden, David de Keyser, Jacques Herlin

Monsignor Quixote
GB, 1985, Euston Films/Thames Television (Christopher Neame)
d Rodney Bennett *w* Christopher Neame
Alec Guinness, Leo McKern, Ian Richardson, Graham Crowden, Maurice Denham

May We Borrow Your Husband
GB, 1986, Yorkshire Television (Keith Richardson)
d Bob Mahoney *w* Dirk Bogarde
Dirk Bogarde, Charlotte Attenborough, Francis Matthews, David Yelland, Simon Shepherd

The Tenth Man
USA, 1988, CBS/Norman Rosemont-William Self (David A. Rosemont, William Hill)
d Jack Gold *w* Lee Langley
Anthony Hopkins, Kristin Scott-Thomas, Derek Jacobi, Cyril Cusack, Brenda Bruce, Timothy Watson

TV Series: *Shades of Greene*
GB, 1976, Thames Television (Alan Cooke)

The Case for the Defence (*d* Peter Hammond *w* John Mortimer – Kathleen Harrison, Brian Glover, Michael Gough)

When Greek Meets Greek (*d* Alan Cooke *w* Clive Exton – Paul Scofield, Roy Kinnear)

The Blue Film (*d* Philip Savile *w* John Mortimer – Betsy Blair, Brian Cox, Koo Stark)

The Destructors (*d* Michael Apted *w* John Mortimer – Nicholas Drake, George Hillsdon, Phil Daniels)

A Little Place Off the Edgware Road (*d* Philip Savile *w* John Mortimer – Tony Calvin)

Alas, Poor Maling (*d* Graham Evans *w* Graham Greene – John Bird)

A Chance for Mr Lever (*d* Peter Hammond *w* Clive Exton

– Freddie Jones, Christopher Benjamin, Shane Briant, James Cossins)

A Drive in the Country (*d* Alan Cooke *w* Philip Mackie – John Hurt, Lesley Dunlop, Ronald Lacey)

Special Duties (*d* Alastair Reid *w* John Mortimer – John Gielgud)

The Root of All Evil (*d* Alastair Reed *w* Clive Eaton – Donald Pleasence, John Le Mesurier, Bill Fraser)

Cheap in August (*d* Alvin Rakoff *w* Philip Mackie – Virginia McKenna, Leo McKern)

Two Gentle People (*d* Herbert Wise *w* William Trevor – Harry Andrews, Elaine Stritch, Elizabeth Sellars, John Carson)

The Overnight Bag (*d* Peter Hammond *w* Clive Eaton – Tim Brooke-Taylor, Joyce Carey, Eleanor Summerfield, Dudley Sutton)

Mortmain (*d* Graham Evans *w* John Mortimer – Ronald Hines, Susan Penhaligon, Eleanor Bron)

Chagrin in Three Parts (*d* Peter Hammond *w* John Mortimer – Genevieve Page, Zou-Zou, Anthony Bate)

The Invisible Japanese Gentleman (*d* Alastair Reid *w* John Mortimer – Denholm Elliott, Celia Bannerman, Royce Mills)

Dream of a Strange Land (*d* Peter Hammond *w* Robin Chapman – Ian Hendry, Niall MacGinnis, Graham Crowden)

Under the Garden (*d* Alan Cooke *w* Robin Chapman – Denholm Elliott, Arthur Lowe, Vivien Pickles, Bruce Purchase)

II Unseen Greene

Anthony Sant, Fanatic Arabia, Lucius, The Rear Column, The Horror Comic, The Clever Twist, The Ceremony of Afternoon Tea, Damien . . .

Most Greene bibliographies list the wealth of novels, plays, stories, biographies, and articles that still remain unpublished or incomplete. These surveys also mention numerous film projects with which Greene was involved at various stages of production. Many failed to materialize at all; some were completed by journeymen screenwriters in Hollywood or elsewhere; a few were set aside to emerge later (with fresh settings and reinvented characters) as novels, and others still were abandoned all together.

The Tenth Man, Jim Braddon and the War Criminal, and *Nobody to Blame* were all written during Greene's short sojourn in Hollywood in the mid-forties. The fact that they remained forgotten in a studio vault for over thirty years and that Greene's only memory of them was as two-page outlines scribbled on notepaper suggests the difficulties facing the compiler of an 'unmade' filmography. One can but speculate on the likelihood of additional material still languishing in the MGM archive. The problem is further compounded by the fact that Greene only had vague recollections of many of his involvements, and in a number of cases (such as the scripts written for the Ministry of Information) accurate identification is prevented by the destruction of pertinent documents.

For the reasons stated above, any list of unfulfilled film projects can not claim to be exhaustive: in all probability there are other 'unmades' awaiting discovery. This checklist, however, is more comprehensive than any published to date.

Unnamed film 1937

In early 1936 Greene was approached by John Grierson to try his hand at producing a film. By May he was producing *Calendar of the Year* for the GPO Film Unit. Directed by Evelyn Spice, this documentary short celebrated the part played by the Post Office in a variety of seasonal activities. Neither the film's credits nor the review in *Sight and Sound* mention Greene, and it is doubtful whether he had any hand in the script.

A letter to his brother Hugh later in the month mentions this film and the possibility of adapting Galsworthy's 'The First and the Last' for Basil Dean. It also refers to a proposed collaboration with Alberto Cavalcanti, but nothing more seems to have come of the enterprise.

In 1937 he scripted *The Future's in the Air* for Paul Rotha. Later in the year, in his *Spectator* article 'Ideas in the Cinema', he confesses that: 'I have myself played a modest part in the construction of a cheap "film" which was shot hurriedly without a finished script and scrapped uncompleted at a cost of £45,000 – the total cost of the French spectacular film *Mayerling*.' This film remains unidentified.

Spanish Civil War Film

The January 1965 issue of the *London Magazine* contained a letter from Graham Greene correcting a number of factual errors in Julian Maclaren-Ross's article 'Excursion in Greene Land'. One of the things that went unchallenged was the recollection of a visit Maclaren-Ross paid to Greene's house on Clapham Common in 1938. In response to a question about forthcoming 'entertainments' Greene confided he was working on a story 'based on an original idea I started to work on for Korda, only his outfit thought it would be too dangerous to film. About a Spanish Government agent who comes to London on a mission during the Civil War and finds that the war has followed him here.'

This story evolved into the novel *The Confidential Agent*, which was published in 1939. It was eventually filmed by Herman Shumlin for Warners in 1945 with Charles Boyer and Lauren Bacall. The casting was attacked by Philip Purser in the *Sunday Telegraph* in January 1979, prompting the letter from Greene to be found on page 576.

The Book Film

Towards the end of his life, Greene recalled a commission he received in the late 1930s to write a documentary on books for Paul Rotha. The only film on this topic made by Strand Films during this period was known throughout its production as *Preface to Life*. Directed by Alexander Shaw and sponsored by the National Book Council, it included interviews with A.P.

Herbert, Richard Blaker, Somerset Maugham, Julian Huxley, Rebecca West, Sapper and T.S. Eliot. Released in September 1936 as *Cover to Cover*, it closed with a verse sequence written by Winifred Holmes. A second version directed by Stanley Hawes, called *Chapter and Verse*, was issued shortly afterwards. With an exclusively prose commentary, it was intended for non-theatrical use only. *The Story of a Book*, a silent version of *Cover to Cover*, produced for use in schools, appeared in 1942.

Cover to Cover enjoyed the distinction of being the first film other than newsreel to be broadcast by BBC Television. It was favourably reviewed by Greene in the *Spectator* on 11 September 1936, but no mention was made of his possible involvement. Paul Rotha sheds no light on the subject in his *Documentary Diary*.

There is an off-chance that Greene may have misremembered his dates, for Rotha produced another film on the subject of books in 1941. Made for the Ministry of Information while Greene was employed there. *The Battle of the Books* was an attack on Nazi censorship and depicted scenes of mass book-burnings in the Reich. The film gives no writing credit and as few MOI documents have survived, there is little likelihood of authenticating Greene's authorship.

The News in English

The short story 'The News in English' was completed in the summer of 1940 while Greene was working for the Ministry of Information. Drawing on an aspect of his courtship of Vivien Dayrell-Browning, it told of an Englishman who is captured and pressganged into broadcasting for the Nazis. He is considered a traitor until his wife realizes that he is now using the code that they had employed during their courtship to pass endearments to convey vital information.

A film treatment was written sometime in the same year, although I have been unable to discover who planned to produce the picture. The treatment's whereabouts are unknown.

Fame is the Spur

In 1943 producer Paul Soskin approached Greene to produce a treatment with dialogue of Howard Spring's *roman á clef* of Ramsay MacDonald. Greene was too busy and the task was finally undertaken in 1946–7 by Nigel Balchin.

Selznick Films

Paramount had bought *A Gun for Sale* and *The Ministry of Fear* almost on publication. Considering him a hot property, Myron Selznick invited Greene to Hollywood in December 1943. The offer was declined, but offers continued to come in from that quarter.

When Greene met Myron's brother David in New York shortly after their uneasy collaboration on *The Third Man*, (see pages 543 and 557), he was asked to consider scripting a life of Mary Magdalene. Undaunted by polite refusal he continued. 'I have another idea. It will appeal to you as a Catholic. You know how next year they have what is called a Holy Year in Rome. Well, I want to make a picture called *Unholy Year*. It will show all the commercial rackets that go on, the crooks . . . ' When Greene doubted permission would be granted to shoot in the Vatican, Selznick enthused, 'Oh sure they will. You see, we'll write in one Good Character.' Neither film was ever made.

Obviously regarded in Hollywood as a leading authority on most matters religious, Greene was even approached by Sam Zimbalist to revise the final part of an early draft of the script of *Ben Hur*, because they had 'a kind of anticlimax after the crucifixion'.

The Iliad

In 'The Middlebrow Film', Greene wrote about Alexander Korda: 'He's a great publicist, of course, the Victor Gollancz of the screen. Only a great publicist could have put over so many undistinguished and positively bad films as if they were a succession of masterpieces.'

He freely admitted, however, that he had been at least partly responsible for two of them – *The Green Cockatoo* and *Twenty-One Days*. The latter film had figured in Korda's grand design to make a huge international star of Vivien Leigh. In his *Spectator* review of 10 July 1936, Greene wrote of Ida Lupino: 'Miss Lupino as yet is a dummy, but she is one of the more agreeable screen dummies to whom things are made to happen, and I feel some remorse when I think of the shootings and strangulations she will have to endure next year in a story of my own.' Was she originally intended to play Leigh's part, or was this another film altogether? Another 'unmade'?

However, eager to exploit Leigh's romance with Laurence Olivier, Korda announced that the couple would headline in a Greene-scripted version of Homer, with Vivien in the role of Helen of Troy. It should come as no surprise that nothing more was ever heard of the scheme. Here was the 'great publicist' in action, keeping his protégé in the media eye in the company of the most fashionable names.

Jim Braddon and the War Criminal

The full story of this particular 'unmade' is given by Greene himself in the preamble to his précis of the plot (see page 666).

Nobody to Blame

Two versions of the genesis of 'Nobody to Blame' can be found in this volume. The first (on page 468) was contained in *Ways of Escape* in 1980. The second forms the brief preface to the story outline (page 671), originally published in *The Tenth Man* in 1985. Yet another variation on the theme was confided to Marie-Françoise Allain in *Conversations with Graham Greene*: 'In the introduction to the book I wrote that originally, just after the war, I had a film in mind. My friend, Alberto Cavalcanti, asked me for a screenplay, and I wrote the outline of a story making fun of the Secret Service. The story was to be set in Estonia before the war and concerned the recruitment of a somewhat unorthodox agent by the English. The film never saw the light of day because the censors did not appreciate the notion of poking fun at the Secret

Service. I realized subsequently that it wasn't easy to make a joke out of a person like my hero, who had perhaps indirectly helped Hitler. So when I came to write the novel I moved the scene from Estonia to Cuba, which I had known well enough in Batista's day.'

Brideshead Revisited

Evelyn Waugh had travelled to Hollywood in 1946 to attempt his own adaptation of *Brideshead* for MGM. Little came of the trip other than the inspiration for *The Loved One*.

Following the success of *Brighton Rock, The Fallen Idol* and *The Third Man* Greene's stock was high with the film community, and in 1950 he was approached to adapt the novel, much to Waugh's delight. He wrote to Greene on 27 July 1950: 'Please don't try to get out of *Brideshead*. I'm sure you can make a fine film of it.' If Greene did produce a treatment, there is now no trace of it. In the event funds were soon exhausted and the project folded. John Mortimer's adaptation, directed by Charles Sturridge, was produced by Granada Television in 1981.

South Wind

The only information available on the proposed adaptation of Norman Douglas's novel is contained in Greene's letter to *The Times* of 30 May 1980. As Douglas died in 1952, one can only surmise that Greene and Mario Soldati approached Carlo Ponti in either 1950 or 1951.

Ballet Film

On 27 July 1953, Greene participated, with Basil Taylor and Therese Denny, in a discussion on the BBC 'Stage, Screen and Studio' programme, introduced by Princess Indira. Towards the end of the broadcast, Denny jokingly asked if Greene had any plans to move into the field of the musical: 'It's about the only one left to you.'

Probably to her genuine astonishment, Greene replied that he had 'plans for a ballet film with Margot Fonteyn . . . But whether that will ever come off . . . It was to be a ballet in which the principal dancers are silent, but in which the corps de ballet spoke, with stylized dialogue. But I mean to describe it would be to describe the whole story and there isn't time for that.' The interview concluded with Greene assuring Denny that the 'whole work would be done by the choreographer and the dancers', he would simply provide the story on which the ballet was based.

Nothing else appears to be known about this production – choreographer, composer, or, more to the point, Greene's storyline.

A Mystery Solved

Despite problems with the English technicians on *The Stranger's Hand*, Greene appears to have enjoyed his first taste of feature film production. In 'The Novelist and the Cinema' (1958), he fondly recalled 'days at Venice drinking grappa with Mario Soldati, running races down the Giudecca with Trevor Howard, the friendliness of the Italian unit'. He continued, 'it encouraged me to go further along this road in a film which shall be nameless.'

Although *The End of the Affair* was the next Greene novel to be brought to the screen and he did spend time on the set, he was certainly not involved in the picture's production. It is, therefore, more likely that the 'nameless' film is *Loser Takes All* (1956), which was produced by John Stafford, one of Greene's co-producers on *The Stranger's Hand*. One suspects the experience was less happy. In the same 1958 article, he pronounced 'to be a producer is no job for a writer'.

The Living Room

Greene's first produced play opened in London in 1953. Directed by Peter Glenville (who would later direct *The Comedians*), it starred Eric Portman and Dorothy Tutin. In 1960, John Sutro, Greene's friend from Oxford days and the co-founder of the spoof Anglo-Texan and John Gordon societies proposed a film version to star English actress Samantha Eggar. As Greene told Quentin Falk in *Travels in Greeneland*: 'We wanted a new face, just as Dorothy Tutin had been and John had a feeling that this girl was worth something; she'd been to drama school and she seemed right for the part. As we hadn't set up the film yet, we decided to pay her a small sum every month to be available for a year.' The *Daily Mail* printed an article that appeared to suggest that Eggar was Greene's kept woman and he sued successfully for £2,000. The project promptly folded.

In 1964, it was reported that Greene had agreed to adapt the play for West German director Helmut Kautner. The same year Greene, along with Anthony Quayle as director and Alec Guinness as star, formed a Swiss-based company to finance a shoot in Madrid. Nothing more was heard. Finally, this most enticing yet elusive property was subject to a bid by Michael Powell in 1969. ABPC announced a cast list that included Richard Attenborough, Athene Seyler and Nigel Davenport. It went the way of its predecessors.

A Burnt-Out Case

Asked during the *Guardian* lecture in 1980 why *A Burnt-Out Case* had never been filmed, Greene answered: 'Well, thank God for that. Mr Otto Preminger bought two options on it at intervals, but having seen *The Human Factor* I'm very glad he never made *A Burnt-Out Case.*'

The first option was taken in 1961, just four years after Greene's unhappy collaboration with Preminger on *St Joan*. In view of his distate for the Austrian's style, one is tempted to ask why he did not insist on clauses similar to those preventing Sydney Box taking up further options following his less than distinguished adaptation of *The Man Within*? The apparent strength of this antipathy makes Preminger's successful bid for *The Human Factor* (even with a Stoppard script and Richard Attenborough in the cast) all the more puzzling.

According to Fr Gene D. Phillips in *Graham Greene: The Films of His Fiction*, Ken Russell considered a version of the novel in the early 1970s. Although undoubtedly tempted to enhance the reputation he earned as a skilled adaptor of modern fiction with his version of D. H. Lawrence's *Women in Love*, Russell was never to make the film.

The Shipwrecked

Greene's association with Sweden dated back to 1935, when he modelled the character of Erik Krogh in *England Made Me* on the Swedish Match King, Evar Kreugar. Twenty years later, he revisited the country on his way to Poland. Dining with Michael Meyer, he was introduced to Anita Böjrk, the widow of the novelist and playwright Stig Dagerman and star of Alf Sjöberg's acclaimed 1950 film version of Strindberg's *Miss Julie*. Greene's affair with her was to last four years.

It was during this time (1959) that he first came across *The Shipwrecked* and considered the possibility of bringing it to the screen. The Board of Film Censors had already forced Greene to bowdlerize Galsworthy's 'The First and the Last' in scripting *Twenty-One Days*. Unwilling to compromise in this case, he appears to have bowed to the inevitable before commencing on a treatment.

A decade later, when Lars Magnus Lindgren (best known for his 1964 film, *Dear John*) began work on an adaptation for Partus Films, Greene extended his best wishes.

Our Man in Havana

As a critic, Graham Greene rarely had a good word for the films of Alfred Hitchcock. *The Thirty-Nine Steps, The Secret Agent, Jamaica Inn* and *Sabotage* were all dismissed as 'amusing' or 'tricky' movies packed with 'inconsistencies, loose ends, psychological absurdities' that 'mean nothing' and 'lead to nothing'.

Consequently, when Hitchcock put in a pre-publication bid of £50,000 for *Our Man in Havana* the odds were already heavily stacked against him. During the *Guardian* lecture at the NFT in 1980, Greene remained unrepentent in defending his refusal: 'I haven't got all that admiration for Hitchcock, that we'll say M. Truffaut has . . . and he was offering a rather derisory sum, and announced that he had bought it – so I said no.'

Produced for Columbia Pictures in 1960, Carol Reed's film was to be his last collaboration with Greene.

May We Borrow Your Husband?

In *Graham Greene: The Films of His Fiction*, Fr Gene Phillips refers to Dmitri Tiomkin's purchase of the options to this short story in 1969. By all accounts Tiomkin, one of Hollywood's leading composers and an Academy Award winner for his scores for *High Noon. The High and the Mighty* and *The Old Man and the Sea* intended to produce, but his ambitions remained unfulfilled at his death a decade later. The rights were sold to commercials director Bob Mahoney in the mid-1980s. Made for Yorkshire Television, his film starred Dirk Bogarde, Charlotte Attenborough and Francis Matthews.

The Honorary Consul

Fred Zinnemann was the first film-maker to express an interest in adaptating this 1973 novel. However, Greene had been quietly impressed with Peter Duffel's version of *England Made Me*, and was more than willing to assist him in his attempt to bring the ordeal of Charley Fortnum to the screen, even going so far as to suggest locations. Duffel, however, was confronted with obstacles at every turn. On the casting front Robert Redford and Al Pacino shunned the opportunity to play Plarr and after five years' labour he was finally forced to abandon hope of ever getting financial backing.

In 1977, after Orson Welles had failed to pay for his one-month option, Zinnemann (again) and then Louis Malle were linked with the film, while Richard Burton (who was keen to play Fortnum) was busy urging Norma Heyman to buy the rights. These she secured, with Duffel as intermediary. Ultimately, even his script was abandoned in favour of one by Christopher Hampton and John MacKenzie ended up directing Michael Caine and Richard Gere in the roles of the chief protagonists.

Brief Mentions

a) In a letter to Vivien Dayrell-Browning of 21 March 1927, in which he announces that he is going to the opening night of Lang's *Metropolis* in London, Greene refers to an appointment with 'Maxwell, managing director of British National Pictures'. Nothing seems to have accrued from this visit, but it remains of interest as one of Greene's earliest attempts to break into the film industry.

b) Rights to *Travels with My Aunt* were bought by MGM in 1972. Greene almost immediately suggested Katharine Hepburn for the part of Aunt Augusta, especially as the film's director was to be George Cukor, who had guided her through such classics as *Little Women, The Philadelphia Story, Keeper of the Flame* and *Adam's Rib*. The freedom given Hepburn to order rewrites of Jay Presson Allen and Hugh Wheeler's script cost her the part, which fell to Maggie Smith.

c) Jack Levin had began to assemble a production of *England Made Me* in the late 1960s. The original script had been adapted by Wolf Mankiewicz (a British novelist and screenwriter, and no relation of the Mankiewicz who had betrayed *The Quiet American*). His first choice as director was the same Lars Magnus Lindgren who had made *The Shipwrecked*, and when he withdrew American and Yugolav co-productions were contemplated before Peter Duffel assumed artistic control. He abandoned Mankiewicz's script in favour of one by himself and Desmond Cory. Richard Attenborough can also recall a time when he was going to attempt the film.

d) Critics (Greene among them) have always been divided on the merits of the thirty-four big screen and TV-movie adaptations of Graham Greene's fiction, and ever since James Scott's 1990 version of *Loser Takes All* rumours have been rife about any number of remakes and updates. *The Quiet American* and *The Ministry of Fear* are among those most frequently mentioned, and there was even a ludicrous report that a new *Third Man* was under consideration. At the time of writing, there have been no further developments.

III Other Film Books

The Pleasure Dome

Edited by John Russell Taylor, with an Introduction by Greene himself, *The Pleasure Dome* was published by Secker & Warburg in 1972. Oxford University Press issued a paperback edition in 1980.

Notwithstanding its subtitle 'The Collected Film Criticism 1935–1940', the book is, in fact, an incomplete record of Greene's film reviews for the *Spectator* and *Night and Day*. The following is a list of the material restored in this volume.

1935
5 July *Wings in the Dark* and *Car 99*
26 July *Private Worlds, Living on Velvet* and *Rome Express*
2 August *Shanghai*
9 August *Devil Dogs of the Air*
16 August *False Faces* and *All the King's Horses*
6 September *The Barretts of Wimpole Street*
20 September *Gentlemen of the Navy*
4 October *Musik im Blut* and *The Dark Angel*
22 November *The Tunnel* and *The New Babylon*
29 November *The Irish In Us*
6 December *Woman Tamer*
13 December *Page Miss Glory, A Fire Has Been Arranged, Here's to Romance* and *The Port of Five Seas*
20 December *Thanks a Million*
27 December *Foreign Affaires*

1936
10 January *King of the Damned*
24 January *Koenigsmark, The Three Musketeers* and *I Give My Heart*
31 January *The Amateur Gentleman*

8 May *La Belle au Bois Dormant*
15 May *A History of the Film*
12 June *The Ex-Mrs Bradford* and *Thirteen Hours by Air*
19 June *Letzte Rose*
25 December *Confetti* and Walt Disney Season

1937
9 April *After the Thin Man*

1938
10 June *Orage*
12 August *Gold Is Where You Find It* and *Liszt Rhapsody*
19 August *The Battle of Broadway*
4 November *Any Old Iron*
11 November *There Goes My Heart*
25 November *Stranded in Paris*

1939
14 April *The Three Musketeers*
12 May *Tail Spin*
19 May *J'Etais une Aventurière* and *The Londoners*
16 June *You Can't Cheat an Honest Man* and *The Good Old Days*
7 July *Boy Slaves* and *Captain Fury*
14 July *Man of Conquest*
21 July *Undercover Doctor, The Modern Miracle* and *Man About Town*
18 August *There Ain't No Justice*
25 August *Young Man's Fancy* and *The Golden Gloves*
1 September *Dodge City* and *Five Came Back*
22 September *I Was a Captive of Nazi Germany*
6 October *L'Homme du Jour*
13 October *The Story of Vernon and Irene Castle* and *Dark Victory*
10 November *The First Day*
24 November *Rulers of the Sea*
1 December *Where's the Fire?*

8 December *In Name Only*
15 December Paramount News
22 December *Ducks and Drakes* and *Espionage Agent*
29 December *The Rains Came* and *Remontons les Champs-Elysées*

1940
5 January *Each Dawn I Die*
9 February *Dust Be My Destiny* and *Fifth Avenue Girl*
1 March *The Roaring Twenties, Prisons des Femmes* and *Hotel for Women*
15 March *Dead Man's Shoes*

Norma Countryman Stine's thesis, *As it is and as it ought to be: Graham Greene on the Cinema*, presented to the University of Nebraska in 1969, contained all the *Spectator* and *Night and Day* reviews, as well as the following articles: The Middlebrow Film; Subjects and Stories; Ideas in the Cinema; Film Lunch; Charlie Chaplin; An Open Letter; The Novelist and the Cinema: A Personal Memoir.

Garbo and the Nightwatchmen

Edited by Alistair Cooke, this 1937 anthology of British and American film writing was 'possibly the first book about the movies by writers who are so busy seeing them that they have no time to write books'. In his Introduction, Cooke echoed the concern first voiced by Greene in 'Is It Criticism' that too much was expected of the film reviewer writing in the popular press: 'The critic in his time becomes tipster, narrator, propagandist, father-confessor, and when he is left alone, a fan.' The 'fans' whose work was included in this selection were Robert Herring (of the *Guardian), Don Herold (Scribner's*), John Marks (*Granta, New Statesman, Spectator, Sight and Sound, Observer, World Review*), Meyer Levin (*Esquire*), Cooke himself (BBC), Robert Forsythe (*New Masses*), Otis Ferguson (*New Republic*) and Cecilia Ager (*Variety, Harper's, Vogue*). The following reviews were selected from Greene's *Spectator* columns:

Abyssinia, St Petersburg, Song of Ceylon, The Case of the Lucky Legs, Rose of the Rancho, If You Could Only Cook, Kliou the Tiger, The Petrified Forest, Rhythm on the Range, Mr Deeds Goes to Town, Nutrition, Romeo and Juliet, The New Gulliver, The Garden of Allah, The Plainsman and *Modern Times.*

Greene wrote his own brief introduction to his chapter.

'Born Oct. 2 1904. Educated Berkhamsted and Balliol (Exhibitioner in Modern History). Jobs: Ten days in the British-American Tobacco Coy., three months on the *Nottingham Journal*, four years on *The Times*, which he left in 1930. Literary Editor, *Night and Day*, 1937. Film Critic of *The Spectator*, 1935–37, and since then of *Night and Day*. Married, one son, one daughter. Religion, Catholic.

Author of *The Man Within, It's A Battlefield, England Made Me, Stamboul Train, A Gun for Sale, Brighton Rock* (in preparation), *Journey Without Maps, The Basement Room.*

Stamboul Train was filmed by Fox – an awful picture called *Orient Express. A Gun for Sale* is being produced by Paramount in America.'

Other reviews are contained in anthologies of both *The Spectator* and *Night and Day*.

Notes

For convenience, when quoting or referring to material contained in this book, I have given the relevant page reference after the abbreviation *MITD* for *Mornings in the Dark*. Dates and sources of their original publication can be found at the end of each particular item.

Introduction

1 *A Sort of Life* (Penguin, 1971) p.11

2 Martin Shuttleworth & Simon Raven, *Paris Review* (No.3, Autumn 1953)

3 John Player Film Lecture, *MITD*, p.559

4 Basil Wright, *The Long View* (Paladin, 1974) p.94

5 'Movie Memories', *MITD*, p.492

6 Norman Sherry, *The Life of Graham Greene: Volume One 1904–1939* (Penguin, 1990) p.107

7 'Graham Greene: On the Screen', *MITD*, p.524

8 'The Average Film', *MITD*, p.385

9 'At the Super-Cinema', *MITD*, p.3

10 *The Oxford Outlook* (October, 1924)

11 'The Average Film', *MITD*, p.385

12 Letter (6 March 1925)

13 Letter (26 June 1925)

14 Sherry, p.181

15 Letter (26 July 1925)

16 Letter (18 November 1925)

17 Letter (4 November 1925)

18 Letter (24 February 1926)

19 Sherry, p.243

20 Interview with Quentin Falk, *Travels in Greeneland* (Quartet, 1990) p.161

21 Interview with David Lewin, *Daily Mail* (26 May 1975)

22 Letter (17 February 1927)

23 Letter (21 March 1927)

24 Letter (February 1928)

25 Letter (12 April 1928)

26 Letter (27 September 1928)

27 Letter (14 January 1929)

28 Letter (31 May 1928)

29 'Save Me Only from Dullness', *Evening News* (23 January 1930)

30 Sherry, p.410

31 Letter (25 October 1932)

32 Marie-Françoise Allain, *Conversations with Graham Greene* (Penguin, 1991) p.146

33 *MITD*, p.446

34 'Graham Greene at 75' (*Listener*, 4 October 1979)

35 'The Marriage of Corbal', *MITD*, p.109

36 'Private Worlds', *MITD*, p.12

37 'Subjects and Stories', *MITD*, p.414

38 *ibid*, *MITD*, p.414

39 *ibid*, *MITD*, p.414

40 *ibid*, *MITD*, p.415

41 *ibid*, *MITD*, p.415

42 *ibid*, *MITD*, p.412

43 Judy Adamson, 'Graham Greene as Film Critic' *Sight and Sound*, Spring 1972)

44 'We from Kronstadt', *MITD*, p.179

45 'Subjects and Stories', *MITD*, p.118

46 John Atkins, 'The Curse of the Film' in E. Robert Evans (ed), *Graham Greene: Some Critical Observations* (University of Kentucky Press, 1963)

47 Adamson, *as* 43

48 Sherry, p.588

49 Neville Braybrooke, 'Graham Greene as Critic' (*Commonweal*, 6 July 1951)

50 Atkins, *as* 46

51 'Laburnum Grove', *MITD*, p.125

52 'Top Hat', *MITD*, p.40
53 'They Won't Forget', *MITD*, p.235
54 'The Road Back', *MITD*, p.227
55 'Captain January', *MITD*, p.128
56 Atkins, *as* 46
57 'Klondyke Annie', *MITD*, p.103
58 'Knight without Armour', *MITD*, p.225
59 'Saratoga', *MITD*, p.216
60 'For You Alone', *MITD*, p.219
61 'If You Could Only Cook', *MITD*, p.92
62 'Der Herrscher', *MITD*, p.201
63 'The Middlebrow Film', *MITD*, p.399
64 'One Way Ticket', *MITD*, p.92
65 'The Middlebrow Film', *as* 63
66 'Memories of a Film Critic', *MITD*, p.448
67 Grahame Smith, *The Achievement of Graham Greene* (Harvester Press, 1986), p.211–12
68 'The Hands of Orlac', *MITD*, p.16
69 'Ideas in the Cinema', *MITD*, p.424
70 'The Marriage of Corbal', *as* 35
71 'Dark Journey', *MITD*, p.188
72 'The Middlebrow Film', *as p*63
73 'The Marriage of Corbal', *as* 35
74 'A Tribute to Korda', *MITD*, p.440
75 'Memories of a Film Critic', *as* 66
76 'Graham Greene at 77', an interview with Mort Rosenblum (*St Louis Post Dispatch*, 12 September 1982)
77 Morton Dauwen Zabel in *Graham Greene: A Collection of Critical Essays*, edited by S.L. Hynes
78 Allain, *as* 32, p.146
79 *ibid*, p.132
80 'Graham Greene at 75', *as* 34
81 Allain, *as* 32, p.133
82 *The Month* (July, 1951)
83 Atkins, *as* 46
84 Smith, *as* 67

85 *ibid*
86 'Memories of a Film Critic', *as* 66
87 Letter 29 February 1936
88 'Memories of a Film Critic', *as* 66
89 *ibid*, *as* 66
90 Letter 11 November 1936
91 Letter 26 December 1936
92 *Paris Review*, *as* 2
93 'The Novelist and the Cinema – A Personal Experience', *MITD*, p.445
94 *ibid*
95 Allain, *as* 32, p.132
96 'Memories of a Film Critic', *as* 66

Reviews

1 The review of *Marked Woman*, with its allusions to the *Anglo-Saxon Chronicle* and the reign of Stephen, was based entirely on a half-heard line of dialogue. The American voice actually said 'it's futile' *not* 'it's feudal'. The truth was revealed by Julian Maclaren-Ross in 'Excursion in Greeneland', his contribution to Alan Ross's 1965 collection, *Memories of the Forties*. Greene refuted a number of his recollections in a letter to the *London Magazine*, but this particular revelation was allowed to pass unchallenged.

2 The *Nurse Edith Cavell* review was reprinted in full in the John Player Lecture programme notes.

Articles

'Preface to *The Third Man*'

3 *The Third Man* won the Grand Prix at Cannes in 1949. In the days when the British Academy awarded two Best Feature prizes (one for a British film and one for a picture from anywhere else in the world), *The Third Man* followed *The Fallen Idol* as Best British Film. It completed a hat-trick of wins for Carol Reed, who had directed the 1948 choice, *An Outcast of the Islands*. *The Third Man* was also the only 'Greene' feature to scoop an Academy Award,

Robert Krasker taking the Oscar for Best Cinematography. James Scott's *A Shocking Accident* also won an Oscar, when it was voted Best Live-action Short in 1982. Maggie Smith (Best Actress) and Douglas Slocombe (Best Cinematography) were both nominated, but unsuccessful, in 1972 for *Travels with My Aunt.*

A more trivial note concerns cats. The anecdote telling how Harry Lime's cat refused to brush against Orson Welles' until his trouser legs had been daubed with sardines is now well known. What is less-often mentioned is the fact that three separate cats were used during the shooting in Vienna and at Denham – each one being of a different size and with quite individual markings.

'My Worst Film'

4 Basil Dean had directed Galsworthy's original play, *The First and the Last,* at the Aldwych in the 1920s.

5 In fact, the animals being transported to North Wales were not camels but elephants, for Korda's production of *Elephant Boy*.

6 The scriptwriter whose name eluded Greene was Walter Meade.

Book Reviews

7 The film Greene liked was *Blue Pearls* (1915), directed by Daniel Frohman

Lectures

8 Duvalier took out an injunction in the French courts in an attempt to prevent the film being shown. When this failed, he sued Greene for libel damages of £1,800,000. He won his case, but was awarded only 1 franc.

9 The editors were quick to exploit the storm once it broke and a special pink poster was produced for newstands, with the headline:

NIGHT AND DAY
SEX & SHIRLEY TEMPLE
SIXPENCE EVERY THURSDAY

In addition to repeating the article, the poster also carried the following statement of claim:

> By the said words the Defendants meant and intended and were understood to mean that the infant Plaintiff was a depraved and degraded child, that the said film was of a lewd and unhealthy type designed to appeal to the baser instincts; that the American Company had exploited the childhood of the infant Plaintiff for its own gain and had trained her in habits of sexual suggestiveness; that the American Company had caused and procured the infant Plaintiff to play the leading part in the said film for which she had accordingly become well-fitted by virtue of her sexual precocity; that the said film was one which should be shunned and avoided by all decent-minded people but that the English Company had nevertheless caused it to be exhibited and had thereby deliberately exploited its disgusting character.

In his 1957 book, *Graham Greene: A Biographical and Literary Study*, John Atkins claimed that Hollywood was so unnerved by Greene's review that the studios attempted to prevent him resuming his reviewing career. The introduction to Norma Stine's thesis included a letter of 21 April 1969 written on Greene's behalf by his secretary, Josephine Reid, which would suggest that he did not deem himself the victim of a conspiracy:

> With reference to your letter of April 5 Mr Graham Greene has asked me to say that there is very little which is accurate in John Atkins' book and he is completely wrong in saying that there was any ganging up against him. However, it is true that 20th Century Fox went beyond the limits for an ordinary action for libel by writing to an editor and trying to get his criticisms stopped in (sic) future. He considers that if he waged a vendetta at all it was only against the worst aspects of Hollywood and he can remember praising very highly some of Hollywood's products.

10 *The Heart of the Matter* was banned in Hong Kong, Singapore and Malaya. The Irish authorities only gave it a certificate after heavy cutting.

Letters

11 Reg Whitely's review and Greene's letter were reprinted in the programme notes when *Brighton Rock* was screened at the NFT.

Film Stories

'The Stranger's Hand'

12 Greene's only subsequent venture before a movie camera came in October 1972. His long-time friend Michael Meyer had been invited to Nice during the shooting of François Truffaut's *La Nuit Américaine*. One day on the set, he was approached by Truffaut's assistant, Suzanne Schiffmann, to audition for the minor part of an English insurance agent in a preview theatre scene. Rejected for looking 'too intellectual', Meyer decided to chance Truffaut's notorious antipathy to practical jokes, and arranged for Greene to meet the director that night at one of the picture's regular drinks parties. Greene's reluctance to appear on television meant that few recognized him readily, and posing as retired businessman, Henry Graham, he was awarded the part.

Despite an early morning bout of stage fright (which he always denied) and his insistence that the line 'three-quarters of an hour' was changed to 'half an hour' to skirt his pronunciation problems, Greene completed the scene. On-set boredom between takes affected his concentration and several retakes were required. Sensing himself the victim of a ruse, yet still unable to place the face, Truffaut eventually demanded the truth. Quaking into laughter he considered it all 'a wonderful joke' and the two former critics spent the evening happily disputing the merits and demerits of Hitchcock.

Truffaut was not alone in failing to recognize Greene. When the film was released, Pauline Kael of *The New Yorker* was the only reviewer to suspect his presence. However, the absence of his name from the credits raised doubts which were only assuaged by a series of frantic phone calls. The name on the cast list was, in fact, Henry Graham's.

'The Blue Film'

13 Greene was apparently no stranger to 'blue films' himself. In *Ways of Escape*, he recalls 'the Shanghai Theatre where for one dollar twenty-five cents one could see nude cabaret of extreme obscenity with the bluest of blue films in the intervals', while in *Not Prince Hamlet* (Oxford Paperbacks, 1990), Michael Meyer describes an evening in Paris in March 1957: 'After dinner, Graham and I visited the Crazy Horse strip club, where he was clearly well known. Much to my disappointment, he suggested in the interval that we should forgo the second half of the show and move on to a brothel, where, Selton, Mortre, they could arrange a better exhibition. We paid to see two girls put on an unconvincing lesbian performance.'

Similarly, Guy Elmes recalls the party given to celebrate the completion of 'The Stranger's Hand', during which Greene took a hand in helping dress John Stafford's wife as a man to satisfy her curiosity to see the inside of a brothel.

Index of Names

Index of Films

APPLAUSE
NEW YORK • LONDON

APPLAUSE
NEW YORK • LONDON